THE MONASTIC WORLD

THE MONASTIC WORLD

A 1,200-YEAR HISTORY

Andrew Jotischky

YALE UNIVERSITY PRESS
NEW HAVEN AND LONDON

Copyright © 2024 Andrew Jotischky

All rights reserved. This book may not be reproduced in whole or in part, in any form (beyond that copying permitted by Sections 107 and 108 of the U.S. Copyright Law and except by reviewers for the public press) without written permission from the publishers.

All reasonable efforts have been made to provide accurate sources for all images that appear in this book. Any discrepancies or omissions will be rectified in future editions.

For information about this and other Yale University Press publications, please contact:
U.S. Office: sales.press@yale.edu   yalebooks.com
Europe Office: sales@yaleup.co.uk   yalebooks.co.uk

Set in Van Dijck MT by IDSUK (DataConnection) Ltd
Printed in Great Britain by Clays Ltd, Elcograf S.p.A

Library of Congress Control Number: 2024945272

ISBN 978-0-300-20856-6

A catalogue record for this book is available from the British Library.

10 9 8 7 6 5 4 3 2 1

For Caroline, as always

Contents

	List of Plates	x
	Acknowledgements	xi
	Introduction	1
One	**The Emerging Tradition**	13
	Origins	13
	Egypt and the Construction of Monastic Ideals	20
	Wider Monastic Trends: Palestine, Syria, Asia Minor	38
	The Western Empire	54
Two	**A School for God's Service: Early Medieval Monasticism in the West**	69
	The *Rule of Benedict*	70
	Monasticism in the Frankish Lands after Benedict	78
	Early Monasticism in England	85
	Early Irish Monasticism	94
	The Carolingian Reform	101
Three	**Parallel Paths: Monasticism in the Ninth and Tenth Centuries**	117
	The Studite Reform in Constantinople	117
	Mount Athos	126

CONTENTS

	Asceticism and Eremitism, *c*. 800–1000	131
	External Threats to Monasticism	149
	'Profession of a Sublime Resolve': Cluny in the Tenth Century	156
	Giving to Cluny	163
	Reform in the 'Age of Iron'	166
Four	**'There Are Angels Everywhere': Reform in the Eleventh and Twelfth Centuries**	**176**
	Cenobitic Monasticism in the Eleventh Century: A Snapshot	176
	Byzantine Cenobitic Reform	186
	Reform in the West	190
	The Cistercians and Reform	206
	Bernard of Clairvaux	215
	The Augustinians	223
	How Significant was 'Reform'?	228
Five	**The Mill and the Grindstone: Monasteries and the World, *c*. 1100–1300**	**236**
	In the Houses of Princes: Monasteries and Rulers	239
	Monks and the Laity	249
	Economy and Land Management	259
	Bishops and Monasteries	269
	Abbots and the Governance of Monasteries	278
	Violence, Rebellion and Strife	288
	Monks, Pilgrims and Crusaders	293
Six	**Fruit in Its Season: Late Medieval Monasticism**	**302**
	Monastic Organisation after the Fourth Lateran Council: Provincial Chapters	304
	Learning and Scholarship in Late Medieval Monasteries	313
	Later Byzantine Monasticism	319
	Hesychasm	325

CONTENTS

Reform Movements in the Late Middle Ages	327
Dissolution	336
Epilogue	343
Glossary of Terms	348
Notes	350
Select Bibliography	396
Index	405

Plates

Photographs are by the author unless otherwise stated.

1. The Holy Lavra of St Sabbas. Волошин Алекс / CC BY-SA 3.0.
2. The monastery of Mount Quarantana (Jebel Quruntul). Alexey Goral / CC BY-SA 3.0.
3. The monastery of Our Lady of Saidnaya.
4. The monastery of Vatopedi.
5. San Vittore alle Chiuse di Genga. Massimo Roselli / CC BY-SA 2.5.
6. The monastery of Clonmacnoise.
7. The convent of Sant Joan de les Abadesses.
8. Rievaulx Abbey.
9. Dormitory of Cistercian monastery at Alcobaça. Michal Sikorski / Alamy.
10. Cloister of St Peter, Moissac. Benh LIEU SONG / CC BY-SA 4.0.
11. Decorative stone relief in the chapter house at the Cluniac priory at Much Wenlock.
12. Monks at work splitting a felled log, from Gregory the Great's *Moralia in Job*. Bibliothèque Municipale MS 170, f.59r. Bridgeman Images.
13. The 'fish house' at Meare Abbey. NotFromUtrecht / CC BY-SA 3.0.
14. Clay jars excavated at Melrose Abbey. © Crown Copyright HES.
15. A bishop accepts the vow of a Benedictine nun, Pontifical de Senlis, MS 148, f. 80, Bibliothèque Sainte-Geneviève. Public domain.
16. Tomb effigy of Rowland Leschman.

Acknowledgements

WRITING THIS BOOK HAS taken about five years, but it has occupied me for many years longer than that; in a sense, for my whole academic career. Naturally, I have benefited from the help, advice and support of a huge number of colleagues and friends. My first academic debt is to the many students with whom I have had the pleasure of exploring medieval monasticism at Lancaster University and subsequently at Royal Holloway University of London. Their curiosity and instinct for asking the right questions have shaped the way this book has developed. Many libraries and collections have made the research possible, but I am especially thankful to have been able to work at the Warburg Library and the Institute of Historical Research in London: in different ways, both incomparable treasure houses for medievalists. I am grateful to the staff at both institutions for their efficiency and kindnesses. I would also like to thank my editor, Heather McCallum, and Rachael Lonsdale and Katie Urquhart, also at Yale University Press, for helping to make this a better book than it would otherwise have been. A list of all the scholars who have offered advice and support would be impossible to compile, but over the years I have benefited from conversations about monasteries and their inhabitants with Frances Andrews, Janet Burton, Scott Bruce, Kate Cooper, Cecilia Gaposchkin, David Gwynn, Jonathan Harris, Paul Hayward, Peregrine Horden, Anne Lester, Stella Moss,

ACKNOWLEDGEMENTS

Jonathan Phillips, William Purkis, Keith Stringer, Edmund Wareham, Patrick Zutshi and many others. For the invincible ignorance that doubtless remains despite their best efforts, I claim the credit myself. My greatest debt, of course, is to Caroline: constant companion, friend and support.

Feast of St Dymphna, 2024

Introduction

A DEMON ONCE APPEARED to a monk just as the bell was ringing to summon the community to Matins. 'Why do you monks work so hard, leaving your bed so early in the morning to chant psalms, and enduring fasts?' he taunted the monk. 'Is it worth it? Don't you think that secular priests will get the same reward in the end?'[1] This story, told by the eleventh-century monk of Cluny Ralph Glaber, reflects concern on the part of a monk to promote the merits of an enclosed and regular religious life. But it also speaks of anxieties about commitment to such a life. Most monks and nuns took vows to live for the rest of their lives in an enclosed community following a routine of liturgical worship, without possessions of their own, eating in common, and giving up the rights to basic privacy. Was it necessary for men and women to sacrifice so much in order to be saved?

One way of rephrasing the question posed by the demon would be to ask why men and women in the Middle Ages became monks and nuns in such large numbers. This is a question that will be addressed, albeit obliquely, in this book, since it is far too open-ended to be resolved. Reasons for taking monastic vows might involve family circumstances, upbringing, societal expectations and other conditions that are susceptible to historical analysis, but ultimately, where a choice was made, this is only rarely something that can be recovered by the historian. A more fruitful way of posing the question would be to ask why monasteries existed. Who were they for? What kind of people founded and built them, and how were they maintained? What exactly went on inside them? And, most fundamental perhaps, how did monasticism change over the thousand years or so of the Middle Ages? These are the questions I have tried to address in this book.

Monasteries were the engine rooms of medieval society. At the height of their activities and influence (*c.* 800–1300), monasteries provided intellectual leadership for the institutions of Church and civil governments, innovation in religious thought and practice, pastoral care, medical provision, education, visual culture and agricultural development. They did all this while apparently observing self-imposed isolation from the wider community. For monasteries were intended to function as places set apart from the world, in which monks and nuns devoted their lives to a permanent rhythm of liturgical observance, prayer and study. Liturgical prayer and praise lay at the heart of monasticism. Both those following this life and those outside believed that monastic lives were led for the benefit of wider society, and that the sacrifices made by monks and nuns in separating themselves from 'normal' human contact functioned as penances on behalf of the community as well as for their own salvation. Monks and nuns were regarded as leading parallel lives that had the power to save themselves and others.

Monasteries, though other-worldly, also had to function in the world. The earliest monasteries had been largely self-sufficient, in the sense that they tried to sustain themselves with minimal reliance on external society. This could be accomplished either through monks' direct farming of the land – which cut into the time available for spiritual obligations – or through their acceptance of gifts of landed property and the labour to farm it. Because the services they carried out for society were considered so important to the spiritual health of the wider community, it was accepted as normal for patrons and benefactors to provide for monasteries through such donations and subsidies. This meant that by *c.* AD 1000, monasteries all over Europe were, effectively, part of the property-owning elite.

As such, monasteries were complex institutions. The demands of property ownership included systems for collection and receipt of rents,

INTRODUCTION

and thus methods of accountancy and management of finances and human resources. But even the fulfilment of their spiritual functions of communal worship required internal systems and management. The correct performance of the liturgy required training in chant and sacramental theology. It also required service books and specific sacred objects for celebration of the eucharist. In order to fulfil the expectation of constant prayer and praise, the liturgical offices were spread across day and night, which in turn meant that light – from candles or oil, depending on the region – was needed for several hours. All of these items had to be produced or procured. Monasteries thus needed supplies ranging from bread and wine to wax and parchment, and the technical know-how to process these. Moreover, the schools that monasteries developed to train their own monks also provided opportunities for a largely non-literate society to educate their young.

Monasteries can sometimes be seen as fixed, static nodes of knowledge passed on from one generation to the next; as centres of self-perpetuating local experiences. But we should also understand them as dynamic and fluid populations defined as much by knowledge transfer and exchange as by stability and continuity. Practices and ideas were exchanged through the transfer and copying of texts, but such exchanges could only take place in a framework of human mobility and interaction. Almost all monasteries received visitors and gave hospitality to guests: people on official business; pilgrims; merchants; prominent neighbours; even royalty. Monasteries operated as market places of knowledge, where new and old knowledge could be tested, exchanged and applied.

Monasteries were complete and complex social organisms. They operated within frameworks of internal governance that created hierarchical systems of management and accountability. Typically, they followed a written Rule, and in most cases a set of bespoke constitutions in addition. The earliest Rules were composed in the fourth century, but these were intended to provide a general blueprint for monastic life rather than to regulate for every eventuality of administration. Moreover, once the conditions of the original composition no longer applied, modifications became necessary, so over time (largely between the tenth and twelfth centuries) monasteries developed their own detailed constitutions and protocols. In the Greek Orthodox world, where no generic Rule prevailed, every monastery had its own specific set of regulations.

Yet systems of regulation are always subject to the human element of implementation. Both Rules and constitutional modifications present ideal pictures of regulation, hierarchy and order, but the realities presented by contemporary evidence reveal human interactions in which disorder, conflict and emotion acted as disruptive and creative elements. Monastic Rules were complex documents in which regulations were underpinned by spiritual meanings. Monks and nuns had to develop relationships with each other that involved negotiating the spirituality of obedience and service as part of the observance of regulatory frameworks. There is abundant evidence from a variety of contemporary monastic sources that friction often resulted from the relationship between the hard realities of running an institution and the demands of fulfilling the spiritual expectations of monastic life. Although monastic Rules were designed to subordinate the individual desires and will of monks and nuns to the community, and thereby to enable practitioners to attain a state of true humility before God, the successful running of any institution inevitably demands and stimulates competition and the play of personal ambition. It goes without saying, of course, that we should hardly expect monks and nuns as a body of people to have behaved better or worse than other members of society. Expectations of a higher standard of morality might have been greater than for those not living in such a community, but it would be unrealistic to expect that holiness was more readily acquired within the walls of the monastery.

Whichever Rule or regulatory framework they followed, the main functions of monasteries derived from spiritual imperatives. At the same time, however, they performed a wide range of functions for the wider community, connected for example with education, charity, medical care or economic proprietorship. Some of these functions derived from spiritual imperatives, whereas others were contingent on their continued economic sustainability. Performance of these functions raised questions that monastic communities still have to confront today, and which should be borne in mind when considering the historical problems of monastic functionality addressed in this book. How did monasteries decide who to deploy in such roles, and on what factors were these decisions based? How easy was it for monks or nuns engaged in such functions to switch modes, and did they develop strategies to cope with the competing demands of engagement and withdrawal?

Inhabitants of monasteries and convents in the Middle Ages had not always made a personal choice to become monks or nuns in the way that we might at first imagine. Men and women who enter the religious life today have in the first place discerned a vocation to be 'professional' religious; then, an order or way of life. I was once gently reminded by a monk at the Vatopedi monastery, whom I had asked how he had chosen that celebrated monastery rather than any other of the twenty foundations on Mount Athos, that God, rather than he, chose the place for him to exercise his vocation. Nevertheless, the exercise of the will is a prerequisite for a religious life in our own day: one has to be receptive to the call. In the Middle Ages, in both East and West, monasticism was 'an occupation as much as a calling, to be weighted and measured for what it offered lay society and how well it was carried out'.[2] It is in no way to diminish or doubt the genuineness of the profession of medieval monks and nuns to acknowledge that in a society in which monasticism was a normative and ever-present form of living, and in which monasteries as institutions dominated landscapes, local economies and social relations, personal choice did not play the same role as it has come to do in the western post-Enlightenment world. The investment of local families in the material health of a monastery gave them ties to the community that operated at both a social and a spiritual level, but that could also bring immediate material benefits and influence to the donor families. The older and more venerable the monastery, the greater the reflected renown on associated families. Having members of a family become a part of a monastic community conferred respectability and demonstrated to local society the commitment of a family to the monastery, the saint-patron of the community and thereby also to the wider region that looked to the saint for protection.

A crucial element of communal living according to monastic rules was the denial of individualism. Despite this, the role played by individual emotional response in the internal governance of monastic communities must have been considerable. Monks and nuns were enjoined to subsume their wills, desires and choices into the community through service and obedience. Yet it is clear from a variety of monastic writings that this demand placed sometimes unmanageable pressures on individuals. Equally obvious is that expectations of harmonious communal living were often frustrated as monks and nuns competed for favour, position or privilege. Monks and nuns may have chosen a life in community, but they did not choose the fellow members of the community. What could monastic leaders do to obviate the disruptions caused by ordinary human likes and dislikes, and how successful were they in negotiating the needs for emotional expression within tight-knit communities of people who had not chosen each other's company in the first place?

Medieval monasteries may seem at first sight to be very remote from the normal experience of most people who might read this book. Yet some of the questions posed above will have resonance for anyone who has experience of working in a large institutional setting. Although spiritual underpinnings no longer play a role in most institutional settings, organisations nevertheless seek to represent themselves through ideological mission statements or codes of conduct – not to mention legal frameworks – that make claims to principles of equity, fair treatment and accepted social norms of behaviour. Employers recognise both social and legal obligations to employees and clients, and develop policies designed to promote well-being in the workplace and the smooth running of public-facing operations. Like contemporary industries, monasticism was based on internal institutional management. This included complex operations such as feeding, housing and clothing monks or nuns; the maintenance of the building estate and its fabric; ensuring smooth relations within the community among the fraternity or sorority; and enabling a system of well-being for them. But monasteries were also underpinned by external public-facing operations, which included the provision of alms for the poor, hospitality for travellers, education for the children of local people, the management of income-deriving property, and fundraising from potential benefactors. Many of the issues of governance that produce friction between regulation, social obligation and individual personality are as normative today as they were in medieval monasteries. Understanding the institutional workplace is, therefore, one route towards understanding the functioning of a medieval monastery.[3]

INTRODUCTION

Although the research for this book has taken place over a number of years, I started to write it in the aftermath of the Covid-19 pandemic. During the course of thinking through the implications of monastic withdrawal and isolation for communities and individuals, it struck me that the societal conditions of the pandemic lockdowns presented situations that were at least dimly analogous in some respects. There has, perhaps, never been a more appropriate time to understand how medieval monasteries operated. Studies of how businesses, families and individuals have adapted, or struggled to adapt, have focused on issues of isolation, the sameness of routine and lack of interaction with the outside world as factors leading to changes in patterns of mental health. Monasticism – without in any way reproducing the conditions of life in time of pandemic – offers us a paradigm of structured routine – what Foucault called 'the regulation of cycles of repetition'.[4] Monasteries designed strategies for dealing with lockdown as a regular framework for life, paying particular attention to the need to maintain the mental health of monks and nuns.

As 'technicians' of regulated lives, medieval monasteries offer valuable perspectives on how to live under constrained conditions. Monks and nuns pursued lives of relentless routine that most people in modern developed societies would find burdensome, tedious and lacking in opportunities for self-expression. Yet those who still choose such a life today often speak of the freedoms provided by an apparently restricted life.[5] Medieval monastic thinkers were fascinated by the paradox that deliberate restrictions on freedom of action could at the same time lead to contentment, and that the rhythms of unvarying routine can provide a framework for mental well-being in a world of random events, fears and dangers. Equally, there is plentiful evidence in contemporary sources that seclusion and routine endangered the mental health of some monks, and that this was understood as a generic problem of monastic life.

I hope that these reflections offer some indications of why a book on medieval monasticism may be of interest beyond a traditional academic readership. There are also compelling reasons within more traditional academic parameters for attempting a general book of this nature. Most general studies of medieval monasticism have drawn the reader's attention at the start to the eastern Mediterranean, where the practice of

Christian monasticism is acknowledged to have begun, before moving the centre of enquiry to western Europe, and retaining it there for the duration of the story. In this way, the historiography of medieval monasticism has privileged western European models of monastic practice by seeing them as developments from an original eastern set of circumstances. In particular, a narrative arc has emerged in which 'normative' Benedictine monasticism, grounded in the western reception of foregoing eastern practices in the sixth century through the emergence of the *Rule of Benedict*, underwent profound reform from within *c.* 1050–*c.* 1150, which in turn led to the creation of multiple monastic Orders and identities. In this later medieval proliferation of identities, 'traditional' enclosed monasticism lost its purpose and became ripe for reform, or even abolition, in the Reformation.

Two implications follow from this narrative arc. First, the East has been left out of the picture after the 'golden age' of early monasticism, the last throes of which are generally typified as the years preceding the Persian and Arab conquests of the seventh century. By implication, the role of the eastern Mediterranean is over once the generative force in monastic development has passed to Italy and thence further west. In this way, the history of monasticism mirrors the *translatio imperii* trope of medieval political thought. Most western monastic historians see monasticism after the seventh century in exclusively western terms – as though nothing happened, or changed, in monastic practices in the eastern Mediterranean after this period. In fact, Byzantine monasticism itself underwent analogous cycles of reform, dynamic change and retrenchment to be found in the West, but just as western monastic specialists have focused their attentions on a European story, so Byzantinists have largely been content to understand monasticism within the linguistic and doctrinal world of Orthodoxy. There has been very little examination of parallel developments in eastern and western monastic practices or ideals. Nor has it been acknowledged that Greek and Latin religious were tackling questions about poverty, independence of lay control of monastic property, manual labour and so on at more or less the same period.

A second implication is that the history of monasticism was driven by cycles of reform emanating from a western European 'core', more or

INTRODUCTION

less to be identified geographically as corresponding to eastern and northern France, southern England and western Germany. The main principles underlying reform are generally held to have been a drive to rediscover the principles of the *Rule of Benedict*. Although recent historiography has nuanced the picture, this basic paradigm remains at the heart of most studies of medieval monasticism. While this narrative has remained powerful in large part because it is compellingly 'true', it is not without problems. One such is that it is based on, and perpetuates, narratives constructed by medieval authors who identified themselves as 'reforming', and in contrast other monastic practitioners as 'unreformed'. In other words, it is a narrative largely fed by the story that some elite monastic leaders wished to tell. Another is that it tends to downplay, or even ignore, other forms of monastic practice that did not privilege the *Rule of Benedict* or its strict interpretation. In many parts of western Europe — such as Ireland, Italy south of Rome, the Iberian peninsula and eastern Europe — the *Rule of Benedict* was only one of a number of possible ways of living a regulated and enclosed monastic life. While this book does not offer an alternative geography of monasticism, it draws attention to diversity of experience and form as well as to the dominance of Benedictinism in the West.

Diversity of another kind is also fundamental to the way this book has been conceived. Women as well as men were founders of monasticism as a form of life from the fourth century onwards. In both East and West, they became an increasingly important presence in monasticism from the late eleventh century onwards. Foundations of monasteries and convents for women increased in number across Europe between *c.* 1050 and *c.* 1200. Women's convents differed in character and functionality from men's, since even wealthy and powerful convents required the agency of male priests to provide the sacraments. Moreover, the functions that could be performed by female convents were constrained by their enclosure, which reflected sexual identity construction in the period. Women's monasteries did not run schools or serve parishes, and abbesses were less able to deploy the political significance of their office than were abbots. For these reasons, women's monastic experiences are less obviously present in much of the source material. This is not helped by the fact that most of the chroniclers of monastic life were men, some of them hostile or indifferent to women, whether as religious or lay. As far as possible, I have tried in this book to include examples of women's experiences in the cloister as well as men's, by way of showing either parallels to or contrasts between male and female monasticism.

A book that attempts a general history of medieval monasticism from its origins to the sixteenth century inevitably follows in well-established tracks. Debts to previous single-volume studies will doubtless be obvious, particularly to English-language readers. C.H. Lawrence's *Medieval Monasticism* has been a staple introduction to students at various levels for a generation; its longevity through several editions since 1984 is a testament to its enduring value. English medieval monasticism has been particularly well served by the monumental work of David Knowles, whose *The Monastic Order in England* remains the gold standard of writing on the subject. Janet Burton's *Monastic and Religious Orders in Britain, 1000–1300* is a fundamental and comprehensive text that serves in many ways as a role model for anyone attempting to build on Knowles's foundations. Profound debts will also be evident to perhaps the most important historian of monasticism writing in English since Knowles, and my own 'academic grandfather', Giles Constable. Less obvious but equally important are those to Gert Melville and Jean Leclercq, both of whose works run like hidden streams beneath the surface of this book. Byzantinists will see the influence of *Byzantine Monastic Foundation Documents*, an indispensable compilation of texts and scholarship edited by Angela Hero and John P. Thomas, covering regulation of monastic life in the Byzantine world from the fourth to fifteenth centuries. Other guides to Byzantine monasticism, such as Rosemary Morris, Alice-Mary Talbot and Nicholas Oikonomides, have also been fundamental to the present work. In certain areas, geographically and chronologically, I have been guided by the work of specialists in those areas too numerous to list here, but I pay particular tribute to a few whose work has been particularly valuable in shaping my thinking or overcoming my own areas of ignorance: Lisa Bitel, Scott Bruce, James Clark, Marilyn Dunn, Vera von Falkenhausen, Susan Ashbrook Harvey, Graham Loud, Tore Nyberg, Annick Peters-Custot, Richard Price, Steven Vanderputten and Bruce Venarde. The influence of the recent comprehensive *Cambridge History of Medieval Monasticism* is also pervasive.

INTRODUCTION

Naturally, difficult choices have had to be made with regard to coverage. At an early stage of thinking about the book I decided to focus on monasticism in its narrowest sense of enclosed and regulated communities. This is both in order to keep the material to manageable proportions and to preserve as far as possible the parallel glance from East to West and back again. This means that, unlike some other general histories of monasticism, I have omitted the mendicants altogether, as representatives of a new development from western monasticism. This is, of course, only one gap in my coverage. Every such choice necessarily sacrifices other ways of approaching the subject. Throughout the book, I have kept the focus on how monastic communities developed and functioned. Although eremitical communities, and some solitaries, are discussed in early chapters, I have largely left anchorites and anchoritism as a way of life after the twelfth century out of the book. Another obvious gap in coverage is the wealth of monastic literary culture. Except where it has a bearing on the direction of historical development, I have not dwelt on this aspect of medieval monasticism, on the grounds that it is impossible to do justice to the subject in what would, of necessity, be a superficial manner.

With the exception of Chapter Five, the book is conceived chronologically, as a narrative from 'beginning' to 'end'; or, at least, to the end of the medieval period. As such, the principal analytical tool of enquiry is the study of change over the course of centuries. Chapter One, 'The Emerging Tradition', explores the origins of monastic practices and ideals from the first appearances of the term 'monk' and the spread of these practices to most parts of the Roman world. In the second chapter, 'A School for God's Service', the development of distinctively Roman and western forms of monastic institution and regulation is examined, through the creation of Rules and constitutions, and the role played by monasticism in an emerging post-Roman society. Chapter Three, 'Parallel Paths', explores the parallel developments in institutional monasticism in the period of the separation of eastern and western Christian worlds in the early Middle Ages. The subject of Chapter Four, 'There Are Angels Everywhere', is the series of reforms of cenobitic monasticism in Orthodox and Latin traditions that occurred in the eleventh and twelfth centuries, and the ways in which they transformed the landscape. In Chapter Five, 'The Mill and the Grindstone', a different approach is adopted in order to convey something of the normal modes of interaction between monasticism and lay society. Finally, Chapter Six, 'Fruit in Its Season', shows how monasteries developed as instittions in the period from *c.* 1200 to the mid-sixteenth century, when they experienced profound disruption across the Christian world. This is, I hope, the most meaningful and coherent way of explaining medieval monastic history to those who are coming to it from a position of inexpert or incomplete knowledge. If this results in what may look to established scholars rather like an impressionistic patchwork of anecdotes, I hope that at least my selection of such stories may be taken as representative of currents more profoundly and artfully followed in existing scholarship.

CHAPTER ONE

The Emerging Tradition

ORIGINS

IN AD 339, ATHANASIUS, bishop of Alexandria, having been forced out of the seat of his bishopric by one of the frequent twists in the ecclesiastical politics of the fourth century, made a dramatic appearance in Rome. According to the testimony of Jerome, writing a couple of generations later, Athanasius was accompanied by a group of black-clad, austere-looking figures the like of whom had never been seen before in the imperial capital.[1] These were monks from the Egyptian desert and, if Jerome is correct, they may have been the first monks ever to have set foot in the western Roman Empire. In fact, Jerome was probably telescoping different times and events for rhetorical effect, and certainly by the time he was writing, monks from Egypt and other parts of the eastern Empire were a much more familiar presence. But Jerome's Letter 127, in which the striking image of Athanasius's monastic companions occurs, provides a fitting moment with which to begin this study of the emergence of monasticism, because the origins of the phenomenon are so difficult to separate from the literary production of the period. Much of what we know – or think we know – about early monastic ideals and practices, and about the monks and nuns themselves, comes from literary texts that are rhetorical in nature. This makes it difficult to separate the question of who the first monks and nuns really were, and how they lived, from the contemporary accounts in which their frequently extraordinary lives are memorialised.

Monks and nuns became a feature of a Christian landscape that was in a state of rapid change. When Athanasius was born, in *c.* 298, Christians accounted for perhaps 10 per cent of the population of the Roman Empire. Their spread throughout the Empire, however, was far from even. The Christian Church had strong roots in cities, and it was the eastern half of the Empire – roughly east of an imaginary line in the Adriatic Sea – that was more densely urbanised than the west. Some cities, moreover, had longer-established Christian traditions than others. Large parts of the countryside, especially in the West, had little or no Christian clerical presence at all. Estimating the depth and extent of Christianity in the Empire is, of course, fraught with the problem of identifying what it meant to be Christian. Historians cannot easily measure adherence to beliefs, even if data on membership of the Church were available, which of course it is not. But we can track the increased reach and power of the Church in the fourth century in two other ways. First, as a consequence of the momentous decision of Emperor Constantine (r. 307–37) to adopt Christianity publicly as his preferred religious affiliation in 312, the period of persecution of Christians by the Roman State came to an end. And second, the imperial family's overt favour towards the Church enabled it to become, very quickly, a substantial propertied power in many cities. Inevitably, the obvious advantages of being Christian resulted in larger congregations and churches. Historians are right to be wary of terms such as 'conversion' in a context in which multiple religious allegiances had been quite normal, but it cannot be disputed that by the time of Athanasius's appearance in Rome, the Church had become politically and economically important in an astonishingly short space of time.

Power, wealth and influence tend to have disruptive effects, not least on the institutions that acquire them. Although Christianity was already a religious identity when Constantine made his public avowal in 312, and the Church an institution with an established hierarchy and liturgical expression, its theology and teachings were still in a state of formation. The fourth and fifth centuries were periods of often painful and disputed development in determining what Christians were right to believe. The process by which these teachings were accepted was a series of 'ecumenical' councils, in which delegates from across the Empire participated. But these councils were rarely free from the gravitational pull of imperial politics, and Constantine himself set a precedent for trying to shape theological agendas. Moreover, Christian communities across the Empire used different languages and had developed different traditions, responses to persecution and ideas about what the Scriptures really meant. Councils became arenas of competing regional interests and identities, as the powerful Church hierarchies of Egypt, Syria and Asia Minor, where the longest-established Christian communities were located, vied with each other for influence. Dominating the theological agenda was not just about determining a set of beliefs. Wrapped up in the ways in which teachings were expressed theologically was a whole set of practices, memories, visual, musical and literary culture that represented a regional identity. Given such stakes, it was not surprising that leadership in the Church was jealously guarded and fought over. For men such as Athanasius, being forced into exile, or faced with violent mobs, was an occupational hazard.[2]

The earliest appearances of the term 'monk' in the sources predates Athanasius's appearance in Rome with black-robed men dedicated to a religious life. Perhaps the first such mention occurs in a court case from the Egyptian countryside in 324, in which a villager of Karanis called Isidore, complaining about an assault by neighbours, attests that he was rescued by two men, one of whom was a monk by the name of Isaac.[3] As other historians have pointed out, the laconic mention in the evidence of a man whose profession is given as 'monk' suggests that this was a well-enough established label by this period to require no further explanation. It also suggests that no exact point of origin for monasticism as a profession is possible. Nobody thought to record 'the first monk' or the moment at which men and women began to live a monastic life, presumably because the practice did not seem so out of the ordinary when it started as to demand the need for anyone to write about it. Another legal record from a little later in the fourth century uses the term *aeiparthenos* ('perpetual virgin') to describe a woman named Thaesis who was involved in a property dispute with her co-heirs. This seems to have been a way in which the court feminised the term 'monk' by drawing attention to her sexual status as the characteristic of her withdrawal from normal society. It is even possible, as one historian of early monasticism has suggested, that the ascetic movement in Egypt began with women. According to this theory, a pattern in which unmarried women lived in seclusion in their parental home developed into dedicated communities of virgins living together, or sometimes even cohabiting with men sworn to ascetic lives.[4] Athanasius may have been crucial to the formal development of women's monasticism, owing to his scepticism about the value of ascetic cohabitation within lay society. Unmarried girls or widows who lived with ascetic men might come under their control financially or sexually in ways that undermined both the norms of Roman law and the authority of the local bishop.

Early monks and nuns cannot be defined as having been one particular type of religious figure, or to have lived in a specific manner. On the contrary, from the beginning monasticism encompassed a rich variety of forms and styles of living. Monks might live absolutely alone – the original derivation of the word is the Greek word for 'solitary' – or in small loosely arranged groups, or in highly organised communities. They might live in the desert or the fringes of settled areas of habitation, but they might equally be found in villages or towns, and women dedicated to the religious life might be considered nuns even when living in their family home. Some monks and nuns withdrew as far as possible from human relationships and contacts with the outside world, whereas others acted as intermediaries between communities, or dispensed advice and performed miracles on behalf of villagers and townspeople. Some monks worked and were economically active, while others appear to have devoted themselves to lives of pure contemplation, or to have limited their work to growing sufficient food for their own needs. Most monks and nuns, of course, remain completely unknown and unknowable figures. The very small minority of whom we know anything were those who either attracted the attention of observers or, in some cases cultivated such attention. Monks could be deeply paradoxical figures: opting for lives of withdrawal and rejection of societal values, they might at the same time proclaim their special qualities or manners of living from the tops of columns and, like Symeon the Stylite in fifth-century Syria, become international celebrities. The monastic life was one of abnegation, peace and the denial of competition, yet they could also be mobilised – as for example by Athanasius – as political forces, and influence the course of decision-making in the Church. Revered, feared, loved and despised, monks were at the same time on the margins and at the heart of late Roman society.

If we cannot be certain when the first monks and nuns appeared, can we say anything about why the late Roman east Mediterranean region gave rise to these forms of life? One of the terms found in papyrus records similar to that recording the case of Isidore of Karanis is *apotaktikoi*, a word that literally means 'renouncers'. What were such people renouncing? The scholar who brought to light the case of Isidore, Edwin Judge, suggested that the *apotaktikoi* were a wider and more amorphous group of people out of whom the first monks, such as Isaac, the rescuer of Isidore, came. According to Judge's theory, these people lived in small groups in villages and towns in Egypt in the early fourth century. Some of them were women, who were following a pattern recommended by Church leaders for a life of renunciation of sexual contact with men, perhaps after having been widowed. Others may have been married men who wanted to follow a way of life that was more defined as 'Christian' according to the teachings of the Church.[5] Such groups do not make an appearance in the early sources describing monks and nuns because they had neither made the radical break with society that set them apart as a distinct group, nor had they challenged the institutions of the Church or of Roman society. Only once some of the *apotaktikoi* followed the logic of their original renunciation and withdrew more completely, both physically and emotionally, from society, did monks such as those who accompanied Athanasius to Egypt, or about whom Athanasius was to write in his landmark *Life of Anthony*, become distinctive figures in the religious landscape. Not all historians have accepted this account of monastic origins.[6] Most would probably agree that the appearance of the first monks indicates how complex and rich the religious landscape was, without necessarily seeing the *apotaktikoi* as a 'missing link' between informal practices of renunciation and institutional monasticism.

Several theories have been suggested to explain the emergence of monasticism. One such theory, which Jerome himself helped to popularise, was that the first monks were Christians who fled to the desert in order to escape detection in the period when Christianity was persecuted by the Roman State.[7] After Emperor Constantine removed the prohibition on Christian worship in 312, and flight to the desert was no longer necessary, the ideal of voluntary withdrawal and sacrifice of normal life came to be a way of associating oneself with the martyrdom suffered by the early Christians. Monasticism, in other words, was a symbolic form of martyrdom for a time when martyrs were no longer being produced. The neatness of the theory masks problems, however. First, martyrdom was only rarely the outcome of State persecution, and in large areas of the Empire, there is little evidence to suggest that the State had much enthusiasm for systematic persecution unless Christians drew attention to their refusal to worship in traditional ways. The law did not prohibit beliefs, but rather public refusal to participate in worship. Another problem is that we cannot be so sure that asceticism was an imitation of martyrdom. In fact, in Syria, a province where monasticism was to become a powerful spiritual and social force, traditions of asceticism were stronger and older than those of martyrdom, which was fairly sporadic during the Persecution.

Another theory is that early monks were forced to flee settled habitation by a changing economic climate, especially by heavy demands for taxation.[8] There may indeed be some truth in the idea that entering a monastery or joining a group of monks provided welcome relief and a reliable source of food for villagers hard pressed by straitened circumstances. But this will not serve as an explanation for all regions where monasticism can be seen by *c.* 400 – not only Egypt but the provinces of Palestine, Syria and Asia Minor, as well as Gaul and Italy – because economic conditions were not the same everywhere. Moreover, as Richard Price has astutely remarked, even if Christians were being pushed towards de-socialised lives in deserted regions by economic hardship, this would hardly explain why such existence came to be seen as a spiritual ideal.[9]

Equally problematic is any idea that we can pinpoint a geographical origin of monasticism. It was once assumed that, because the first mention of monks occurs in texts from Egypt, we should look there for the origins of the phenomenon. Such an assumption appears at first sight to be borne out by the circumstances of composition of some of the widest-read texts; for example, it is now accepted by most historians that one of the foundational texts explicating early monastic ideals, the *Apophthegmata Patrum*, was written in Palestine by Egyptian monks who had settled there in the fifth century. The supposed 'Egyptian origin' of early Christian monasticism was bolstered by two further factors. First, the nature of textual survival. The earliest documents mentioning monks come from Egypt, because late Roman Egypt was a thoroughly governed society with a plethora of municipal and legal documentation written on papyrus, which survived particularly well in the dry climate. Syria, a frontier province in which important urban centres were changing hands between Romans and Persians, has a less full documentary record across all areas of activity, so it is not surprising that mentions of monks are not found at such an early period in, for example, tax records, as is the case in Egypt.

Second, and perhaps more telling, the Egyptian collections consciously promoted an idea of the pre-eminence of Egyptian monasticism. We shall examine this in more detail in the following section, but it is important here to be clear that although we have neither papyrus records nor a text such as Athanasius's *Life of Anthony* to show it, Syrian monasticism may indeed have been as old as Egyptian. If this is the case, then it did not derive from Egyptian exemplars but from adherence to different traditions and interpretations of Christian teaching, among them the Gospel of Matthew and a number of apocryphal texts in which ideals of personal asceticism are promoted.[10] In fact, the archaeological evidence shows that monasteries in parts of Syria, especially the north, followed a different model from the Egyptian and Palestinian tradition of enclosed communities. This may indicate parallel evolution rather than a developmental theory of influence.

If we cannot pinpoint either a starting point or a place of origin for monasticism, we can nevertheless offer some thoughts about why it became such a feature of religious life. The ideal of separating from society in order to pursue a path towards God is common to several religious traditions, although the reasons for such withdrawal are not necessarily similar. Christianity, as an outgrowth of Judaism, is a religion of personal salvation, and the contemplative life of withdrawal and rejection is a means towards that end rather than a search for enlightenment for its own sake. A precedent for this pursuit of salvation through communal asceticism can be found in the Essenes, groups of Jews who lived in the Judaean desert in the Second Temple period. Early Christians in the first generation or so after the Resurrection probably thought that they were living in the end times before the second coming of the Messiah and the end of the world as pictured in the Apocalypse. In such circumstances, living as perfect a life as possible according to the teaching of the Church was a matter of immediate concern.[11] This meant following strictly a moral code that demanded standards of behaviour that differentiated Christians from many, though not all, outside the Church. This was especially noticeable when it came to attitudes to violence, aspects of civil society and sexual conduct. Even after expectations of an imminent end of the world became less plausible, the precarious position of Christians in the Roman Empire demanded the formation of close community groups sustaining each other in living out their beliefs. But even at the time of the Great Persecution in the late third and early fourth centuries, Christians had become a well-established feature of most eastern Mediterranean towns, and the Church an effective agency of education and social care as well as spiritual life. As increasing numbers of people in the Empire accepted Christians as ordinary citizens and the Church as a normative part of the scene, it must have become more difficult for Christians to retain the idea of perfection that would lead to their salvation. Monasticism – as a way of life above and beyond the norm – provided such a route to salvation, through escape from everything in everyday life that appeared to threaten no longer the existence of Christianity but its capacity to lead people to perfection.

EGYPT AND THE CONSTRUCTION OF MONASTIC IDEALS

Accounts of the lives of monks and religious women began to circulate from the later fourth century onwards. Athanasius composed his *Life of Anthony* during a period of exile in the Egyptian wilderness in 356–8.[12] Written in Greek, it was translated into Latin by Rufinus, an Italian who had gone to Egypt in 374 and collected accounts of monks there, and it achieved a wide audience across the Christian world. The *Life of Anthony* is without doubt the most widely read 'biography' of a monk in the history of the Church. The Latin translation was read and copied throughout the Middle Ages, and had an incalculable influence on monastic ideals and practices throughout the period covered by this book, to the extent that Anthony was accepted as having been 'the first monk'. Athanasius did not invent Anthony as a historical figure. We know from the evidence of a group of letters that Anthony himself wrote, and from the independent testimony of a letter by Bishop Serapion of Thmuis written after Anthony's death in 356 to two of his disciples, and from versions of the *Lives* of Pachomius, that a historical character of that name seems to have begun a life of asceticism in Egypt in *c.* 271. Athanasius probably knew him, though he may only have met him once, when Anthony came to Alexandria in 338.[13] Nor did Athanasius try to make Anthony into the first monk, since in the narrative when Anthony begins to live as a monk he entrusts his sister, for whom he was responsible, to other monks in or near their village. Nevertheless, it is clear that Athanasius shaped the raw material of Anthony's life and career in such a way as to create something distinctive and full of literary artifice. Biographies of holy men were an established genre by the time that Athanasius was writing, and he drew on the literary portraits of pagans such as Plotinus and Apollonius of Tyana. But the overall impression of the *Life* is that it serves as a manifesto for how to live a solitary monastic life. Gregory of Nazianzen (329–89) characterised Athanasius's *Life* as a monastic Rule in the form of a narrative; alternatively, a recent modern historian has seen it as a 'social discourse' between Athanasius and his readers.[14]

Anthony's parents, who were Christians, died while he was still a young man, leaving him substantial agricultural property in the village where he had been brought up.[15] One day, in *c.* 271 when he was about twenty years old, he heard the Gospel passage in which Jesus advises a rich young man who has asked him how to be sure of getting to heaven to sell his possessions and give the money to the poor (Matthew 19.21). Touched in a personal way by the message, Anthony did exactly that, leaving only a portion to provide an income for his sister. Athanasius tells us that at that time there were few monasteries in Egypt, and that anyone who wanted to lead a monastic life did so by living in isolation near his own village. Anthony first attached himself to an older monk on the outskirts of the village from whom he could learn the discipline of monastic craft. This entailed practical work such as basket-weaving, which was a staple form of economic support for solitary monks, but also the routines of spiritual asceticism: night-time vigils of prayer, recitation of the psalms, living off an austere diet based on bread, vegetables and water. These ascetic practices were thought to enable the monk to build up discernment: the ability to deal with random thoughts, desires and memories in such a fashion that they did not distract him from his purpose. After fourteen years, Anthony was ready for a different kind of challenge. He went further away from the village into the desert, enclosing himself in a tomb in a necropolis. Here he suffered but survived physical and psychological attacks by demons disguised as wild beasts. Only after he had learned to cope with these assaults was he ready to move far away from settled habitation, and chose an abandoned Roman fort for his withdrawal, or, in the word used by Athanasius, his *anachoresis*. During the twenty years he spent in the fort, he was not quite out of sight or mind, since friends would stop by with supplies. The demons continued to trouble him, but when he emerged from this self-imposed isolation, it was as an expert in the ascetic life, an initiate in a mystery. Thirty-five years after having first determined on a monastic life, Anthony had reached a state of inner transformation. In *c.* 306, he began to train disciples in monasticism and, in Athanasius's famous phrase, 'the desert was made a city by monks'. At this point in the *Life*, the narrative is interrupted by a lengthy rhetorical passage, comprising about a quarter of the whole work, in which Anthony instructs his followers on how to recognise and deal with demons. After this, there follows a further spell in the desert, before the story shifts gear again as Anthony re-engages with the world, first to support Christians being persecuted by the State, then to draw attention to new powers he has gained. He performed miracles of healing and delivery from danger on behalf of villagers and other monks. But he also revealed a new dimension of his spiritual powers as a consultant on spiritual matters, a reputation gained through a remarkable intellectual performance in which he refuted the arguments of a group of Neoplatonic philosophers. From this point onwards, Anthony was recognised far and wide for wisdom as well as spiritual authority. Anthony finally died – according to Athanasius's chronology, at the age of 105 – as a famous and revered ascetic who had established two distinct groups of disciples and who had effectively 'invented' ascetic monasticism by showing monks how to live in the desert.

I have paraphrased the *Life of Anthony* at some length because although it is not the earliest account of monastic life, it is surely the most influential. Athanasius identifies and develops a set of themes that would come to dominate subsequent writing about the monastic life. By framing Anthony's career as a progression from apprenticeship to mastery, he established the idea of the monastic life as a craft composed of certain vital skills. As we shall see, this would become a standard metaphor for understanding the religious life throughout the Middle Ages. Nevertheless, Athanasius's *Life of Anthony* was also rooted in the realities of late Roman provincial life. If we are to understand the picture of the monk that Athanasius was drawing, we need first to appreciate some of these features.

Anthony's withdrawal to a monastic life was preceded by his adoption of the biblical injunction to renounce his wealth. Striking though this undoubtedly was as a gesture of a new spiritual direction, it also has a socio-economic dimension. Inheriting property in late third-century Egypt entailed a set of public financial obligations (known as 'liturgies'). Emperor Diocletian (r. 284– 305) enacted legislation to enforce the obligations of landowners to village communities, among which was responsibility for meeting tax demands. The term coined by Athanasius for Anthony's withdrawal from society – *anachoresis* – did not originally have specifically religious connotations, but could denote any form of escape from obligations, including flight from taxation. A mandate of 370/3 by Emperor Valentinian I orders that anyone who has entered monastic life in order to evade customary obligations should be removed from the desert and returned to their town.[16] Athanasius was presenting his ideal monk in terms that were understood by contemporaries. The features of Anthony's spiritual life that were to be most enduring for later centuries – his battle against demonic forces and his feats of abstinence – were also rooted in recognisable experiences and beliefs. The descriptions of the demons as physical beings are the parts of the *Life of Anthony* most likely to be understood figuratively by modern readers. Most of us are probably more comfortable seeing them as psychological torments, and the struggles of that period of his life in terms of mental issues – as we might say, 'dealing with his inner demons'. But to men and women of the late Roman period, demons were physical rather than psychic realities. The demonic theory that takes up so much of the *Life* was rooted in a set of beliefs about what we call the supernatural that was, to some degree, common to Christians, Jews and pagans. Demons were thought to inhabit the spaces between earth and the heavens, where they might block human access to the divine. Moreover, deserts – regions that were useless as well as dangerous – were thought to be the natural habitation of demons. By invading the desert – and Anthony's use of a Roman military fort is striking here – monks were taking the war to the Devil.[17]

In bringing monks into the desert, Athanasius was challenging the norms of pre-existing monastic life. He was aware, of course, that other forms of monasticism co-existed with Anthony. The *History of the Monks of Egypt*, written in *c.* 400, recounts a journey along the Nile in which the narrator visits monks in various locations. Many of these monks were located in towns: Oxyrhynchus was bursting with 10,000 monks and 20,000 nuns. The monastic leader Ammon had apparently gathered 3,000 monks and Serapion as many as 10,000. The range of habitation, and the sheer numbers of monks alluded to – even allowing for exaggeration – not only make for a startling contrast with Anthony's experience, but suggest that in telling the story of Anthony, Athanasius was conscious of composing not the history of the 'first monk' but of a new kind of monasticism. Texts such as the *History* have led historians to ask whether towns and settlements, rather than the desert, were in fact the normative habitations of monks and nuns. For James Goehring, the desert was more a literary construct than a numerical reality.[18]

Monks had already in the late third century begun to live in small self-perpetuating groups in which elders instructed disciples, but we only start to learn more about how these operated from the 330s. In *c.* 330, a group of monks including Macarius, Amoun and Ammonas founded a community at Skete, about 80 miles southeast of Alexandria in the wadi Natrun. This was one of the monastic centres described in the *History of the Monks of Egypt* seventy years later. It was located in a vast wilderness . . . and the way to it is not found or shown by any track or landmarks on the ground, but one journeys by the signs and courses of the stars. Water is hard to find, and when it is found has a bad smell, bituminous, yet inoffensive to the taste. Here men are made perfect in holiness, but none but those of austere resolution and supreme constancy can endure such a terrible spot.[19]

Skete was 40 miles from an earlier monastic settlement, Nitria, which had been founded by one of Anthony's disciples, Amoun, in *c.* 315 on a cliff formation that stands on the edge between the Nile Delta and the desert. Whereas Nitria has been described as 'a desert city with clerical leadership', Skete was run more like a community of anchorites living alongside each other. By *c.* 390, when Macarius died, Skete had four distinct groupings: the monastery of Macarius; the monastery of Anba Bishoi; the monastery of the Romans' and the monastery of John the Little. Although these were not yet architecturally separate units, each had its own church, groups of cells and bakehouse. A monastic council upheld discipline, and reported to the bishop of Alexandria. At Kellia, a development from Nitria, the monks' cells were spread out so that they would be unable to hear each other. Rufinus, the Latin translator of the Greek text of the *History of the Monks of Egypt*, characterised the effect of this as 'immense silence and great peacefulness'.[20] Archaeological excavations in 1964 revealed a site of some 49 square miles, divided into different groups of cells, each group clustered around an oratory. The cells were made of mud brick, sometimes decorated inside, often with painted crosses but sometimes with animals or decorative shapes.[21]

A strict schedule, later observed and described by a theorist of Egyptian monasticism, John Cassian, was followed at these anchoritic communities. Monks spent the week from Monday to Friday in their individual cells. They said the night offices – a recitation of twelve psalms with prayers – privately, then meditated until dawn, after which they began their regime of manual work. At weekends, the monks joined together for worship. The liturgy (*synaxis*) for Vespers and for the night office was identical, consisting of the solo chanting of psalms, followed by silent prayer with arms extended, then prostration, and prayer said aloud (the 'collect'). This pattern was repeated eleven times, then followed by the Alleluia, and doxology, and two readings from the New Testament. The eucharist was celebrated, probably at the third hour (9 a.m.) on Saturday and Sunday but not on weekdays. It was followed by the Agape, a communally taken meal. After this, the monks collected their food and the raw materials for their work for the coming week and returned to their cells. At Kellia, the monk Evagrius of Pontus, who abandoned a career in the imperial government in Constantinople to become a monk there in 382–3, used to teach monks on Saturdays and Sundays, and encouraged them to come to him with theological and doctrinal questions.

During daylight hours the monks were mostly engaged in manual work. Rope-making or basket-weaving were common, because these were occupations that made use of easily available local resources and also allowed for mental absorption. As Cassian expressed it, they practised manual labour 'in such a way that meditation on the psalms and the rest of the scriptures is never entirely omitted'.[22] Cassian cited the example of the Apostle Paul, who continued to practise his profession of tent-making during his ministry so as not to be a burden on the Christian community.[23] As he remarked, a working monk was likely to be troubled only by a single demon, whereas an idle one was vulnerable to a whole host of them.[24] Even a monk who did not need to work in order to feed himself because he had ample food to harvest near his cell chose to weave a fixed number of palm leaves every day as a mental discipline.[25] Some monks devoted themselves to growing food, either on their own plots or hiring themselves out as agricultural labourers.[26]

John Kolobos, a fourth-century Egyptian monk who appears in the collection known as the *Apophthegmata Patrum* (Sayings of the Fathers), is supposed to have defined monasticism by work: 'What is a monk? A monk is work. The monk works at everything he does.'[27] For John, the work was a necessary attribute of prayer, and he is reported in one anecdote to have woven together two baskets into one because he was so absorbed in prayer while working with his hands.[28] But this ideal was one that older monks would later recall as an example of the degeneration of monastic practices. After Skete had to be temporarily abandoned in 407 because of raids from hostile tribes, one of the older monks recalled that when he had been a monk there, 'the work of our soul was our real job, and our manual labour we regarded as a sideline. But now the work of the soul has become the sideline and the craftwork has become the real job.'[29] Similarly, in an early seventh-century collection of stories about Egyptian and Palestinian monks, the *Spiritual Meadow*, a monk recalls a story that had come down the generations from an elder at Skete of how the Devil once appeared to a group of monks, carrying a bundle of hoes and baskets telling them that he wanted to provide them with a distraction so that they would become careless in their real work.[30] Doubtless older generations are always prone to think that standards have slipped among the younger, but it is striking how Skete came to define the ideals of Egyptian monasticism from the fifth century onwards.

At almost the same time as Nitria was founded in the Nile Delta, hundreds of miles to the south a different vision of monastic living was being brought into being. Rather than attempting the feats of endurance necessary to survive in the desert, Pachomius (292–346) established communities of monks in the settled heart of Upper Egypt, in the strip of land irrigated by the Nile. For Pachomius, as for Anthony, the monastic life was an unending battle against the Devil, but one most effectively waged in numbers rather than alone. Pachomius founded his first monastery, Tabennesi, in 323, after he had spent a period learning the monastic craft with an anchorite who had gathered a few followers around him. Pachomian monasticism was a family affair: his brother was one of his earliest monks, and in 329 Pachomius founded a convent for his sister to live in after she had visited him in his community. The point of this kind of monasticism was not to populate the desert but to create an alternative kind of Christian community. As one historian has put it, Pachomius's monks and nuns were 'pioneers in the art of Christian living, called to resurrect the New Testament's most radical vision of human community'.[31] This was rejection of societal norms, but in a different way from either Anthony or the monks of the Delta.

Tabennesi was followed by other Pachomian foundations in the same area: Pbow, Seneset, Tbew, Tmousons, Phnoum and Tse, Tkashmin and Tsmine. Together these form what is known as the Pachomian *koinonia*, or commonwealth. They were connected geographically by the Nile itself, but conceptually by the operation of a Rule – the first-known monastic formula for living. In fact it is more correct to speak of the

Pachomian Rules, since there are four, in Greek and Coptic versions and in a Latin translation made in 404 by Jerome. Monastic life as revealed in the Rules was highly regulated. The monks – a few hundred in each monastery – were divided into 'houses' of about thirty to forty monks, and schedules were organised by house. There were two 'synaxes' (house liturgies) every day, one in the morning and one in the evening, consisting largely of structured prayer, gesture and recitation of psalms, with monks sitting or kneeling on mats on the floor of the church. Excavations of the church at Pbow in 1989 revealed a structure of 49 metres by 24 metres. Aside from the church, Pachomian monasteries and convents had a kitchen, a bakehouse, dining hall, assembly hall, guest house and the houses for the accommodation of the monks and nuns, which were subdivided into cells. The monasteries and convents were surrounded by walls and a gatehouse regulated comings and goings, which were strictly limited. The women's convent at Tabennesi lay across the river from the men's monastery. According to Palladius, who visited in the late fourth century, the manner of life for women was the same as for men in most particulars except clothing. At least in theory, monks might visit female relatives in the women's monasteries, but this does not seem to have worked the other way around. Palladius reported that nuns who died in the convent were brought across the river for burial to a men's monastery, implying that the convents did not have a consecrated cemetery of their own.[32] And of course, women's monastic communities always needed the liturgical services of ordained priests who could only be male.

Like the monks of Lower Egypt, Pachomian monks and nuns worked. Probably most of this labour was agricultural, since the hundreds of monks needed to be fed, and the monasteries cultivated fields of beans, onions, millet and other crops, and water buffalo and cattle were kept for dairy products. Baking bread for the monastery was in itself hugely labour intensive, since bread was part of the daily diet. Monks worked to knead the dough in huge troughs, under the supervision of the baker according to a rota. In addition, they wove baskets and mats, and made leather goods and metalwork in workshops. The overall impression of Pachomian monasteries is one of control and order imposed hierarchically. The scale of the operation demanded attention to practical detail but also strict management. Not surprisingly, this gave rise to disagreements, and eventually to the sidelining of Pachomius himself for a while. The temptation in reading Pachomian sources is to allow their institutional focus to mask the realities of the monastic profession. For Pachomius, the collective endeavour of worship and work was a means of recreating a Christian community that came as close as was possible on earth to living out the Gospel. Service to others is the theme that underscores all parts of the Pachomian Rule, and the ideal of asceticism as expressed in community life was no less powerful for being carried out in populated and settled areas rather than in the desert.

The Pachomian *koinonia* is well known to historians because the main texts concerning its operation and describing the monasteries were written in Greek.[33] By the 380s, however, other monasteries with little or no dependence on Pachomius, but following a broadly similar model of collective asceticism and worship had been established. In *c.* 385, a Coptic-speaking Egyptian from the Thebaid, Shenoute of Atripe (*c.* 348–*c.* 464), became abbot of a monastery near Sohag known as the 'White Monastery'. As at Pachomian monasteries, the monks – and nuns, since this was an institution for both sexes – could be numbered in the hundreds. Like the Pachomians, Shenoute's monks were organised according to teams of houses, and their schedule of public prayer, work and communal eating is also similar. There were differences in tone. The White Monastery seems to have been more ascetic, with only one meal per day and a tradition of corporal punishment. But the widest divergence from the Pachomian *koinonia* is probably the presence of women as well as men, which sometimes led to tensions and practical problems but probably also to an enhanced sense of spiritual community.[34]

Shenoute was also an activist, especially in the struggle against heretics and pagans in the Egyptian countryside, and he organised his monks as a posse of enforcers who went around stripping pagan temples of inscriptions and images and 'reclaiming' them for Christianity. Such traits have made Shenoute an unattractive figure to some historians.[35] But this is almost certainly not the reason why Shenoute and the traditions represented by the White Monastery were largely ignored in most western histories of monasticism until the 1980s. As William Harmless has remarked, Shenoute is a reminder of the limits of the 'classic' sources for the history of monasticism.[36] Because this history has been largely written from texts originally composed in Greek, many of which were subsequently translated into Latin, the monasticism they present is that articulated by the educated elites who used those languages. Indeed, it is this very process of composition and translation that has constructed a 'genealogical' history of monasticism as emanating from the Egyptian models of desert, hermitage and cenobitic monastery, and mediated via translators and compilers such as Jerome, Rufinus and John Cassian, to other parts of the Empire, and to posterity. Monastic history for the Middle Ages — and thus, the exemplars followed by the Middle Ages — was largely drawn from such translations from Greek. But this represents only what was available to and selected by the translators. It left a great deal of monastic history out: not only Shenoute's Coptic tradition but, as we shall see, a whole monastic landscape in Syria and Palestine. This point is worth making here as a reminder that we are limited not only by source survival but also by a process of source selection that started at the very time of the history we are examining. The Egyptian tradition as mediated by the *Life of Anthony*, the Pachomian Rules and the *Apophthegmata Patrum* became the monastic ideal.

The *Apophthegmata Patrum*, which was probably composed in Palestine in the middle of the fifth century, is centred on a group of ascetics, many of whom were disciples of Anthony, in the Nile Delta hermitages.[37] As a composite collection, it represents the need to recover and pass on the ideals of the 'hermitage' monks of Skete, Nitria and Kellia to the generations after those communities had dispersed in 407. Although one of these monks, Arsenius, returned and re-established the hermitage at Skete, it was the first generation in the fourth century that lay at the heart of the collection. The *Apophthegmata* is really two works that are presented together in many of the surviving manuscripts. The so-called 'Alphabetical Collection' is based on sayings of and stories about monks and nuns arranged alphabetically by name. The vast majority — 120 — are men, though the sayings of three women, Sarah, Theodora and Syncletica, are also included. Sarah seems to have lived in a cell near Pelusium in the Nile Delta. In the entry for Bessarion, we learn of another woman living as an ascetic, though her sex was only discovered after she had died. It is frustrating that we do not know as much about the circumstances in which these women lived as we do about the men, though there was – and is – a distinctive literature centred on 'desert mothers'.[38]

The Alphabetical Collection derives partly from earlier fifth-century texts by monks reminiscing about their experiences in the Egyptian hermitages, notably John Cassian's *Institutes* and *Conferences* and Palladius's *Lausiac History*, both written in the 420s, and the works of Evagrius of Pontus. Cassian, whose work we will turn to later, became a monk in Palestine in the 380s but then lived at Skete until *c.* 400; Palladius likewise moved in 388 from Palestine to Egypt, settling at Nitria in 391 and then Kellia a year later; and Evagrius lived at Kellia from 383 until 399. Their departure from the hermitages came about before the raids of 407 dispersed the monks, as a result of suspicion and hostility that had fallen on the practice of monasticism in the Delta from the patriarch of Alexandria, Theophilus. Thus, the monks whose sayings are quoted were already well known, but the enterprise of which they were part had fallen apart. In several manuscripts, the Alphabetical Collection is followed by a series of anonymous sayings arranged thematically, known as the 'Systematic Collection'. This survives in a number of different forms, including a Latin translation from the original Greek. There is still no standard edition of the *Apophthegmata*, because the manuscript tradition is fearsomely complex, and scholars do not yet know for certain whether the two parts of the overall collection were composed at the same time and by the same hands.[39]

For our purposes, what the compilers of the *Apophthegmata* were trying to accomplish is more important than who they were or how they worked. The first point to make is that it falls squarely within the Athanasian tradition of monasticism. Monks are shown living in solitude or in small groups. The *mise en scène* is the hermitage, and its locale on the edge of the desert. There is barely a hint that elsewhere in Egypt different forms of monastic community were being developed. The desert, whether seen as a real or metaphorical place, lies at the heart of the text. Second, the *Apophthegmata*'s spare, laconic prose is perfectly suited to the matter at hand. As Columba Stewart has remarked, the form of the *Apophthegmata* 'derives from and leads back to the desert', and the desert gives the monks 'a landscape which mirrored what they sought for their own hearts: an uncluttered view through clear air'.[40]

Of the several themes that we might pick out from the collections, one that emerges very clearly is the relationship between older and more experienced monks and younger disciples. This was, indeed, the structural framework of the hermitage that guaranteed the continuity of the practices and ideals being described. As we saw from the *Life of Anthony*, apprenticeship to an established monk was one of the earliest features of monastic practice. Teaching was multi-layered, involving not only moral and spiritual guidance but also the business of survival. The manual work undertaken by monks had to be learned from elders, and since it was this labour that might provide the means of a monk's survival, a degree of responsibility was implicit in the relationship. Teaching was also a means of imbuing monks with the ideal of obedience to authority from the start of their journey. Rousseau has spoken of the 'docile faith' shown by the monastic disciple in this practice, but rather than viewing this as passivity, we should see this kind of obedience, which was centred on the self-disclosure of the subject to a figure of authority, as a heroic activity directed towards the development of virtues.[41] It is true that elders sometimes come across as arbitrary and even cruel, as for example in the story of the elder who deliberately destroys a younger monk's vegetable plot with a stick as a test of how he will endure suffering and evil. But in this story the younger monk is able to reprimand his teacher gently by telling him that if he leaves the last cabbage intact, they can eat it together and neither will go hungry.[42] This suggests that the relationship went both ways, and might demand as much of the older as the younger monk. Elders sometimes appear to have been reluctant to engage in teaching, perhaps less because they regarded it as a distraction from their own pursuit of God than because it implied possession of an authority to which they were reluctant to admit. Isaac, a monk of Kellia, recalled that his teacher, an elder called Cronius, never gave him instructions to do anything, but performed all the tasks needed for them to live together himself. When taken to task by other elders for this, Cronius replied: 'Am I the ruler of a coenobium, that I should give him orders? If he wishes to learn what to do, it will be through watching my example.'[43] Given that humility was one of the lessons to be learned, the story of Abba Poemen declaring himself unable to contribute to a conversation with another anchorite about Scripture, but finding himself full of things to say when the subject turned to human passions, was in itself an instruction for younger monks.[44]

The monk Abba Moses is said to have remarked to a disciple: 'Go and sit in your cell, and your cell will teach you everything.'[45] If the desert was the wider backcloth against which the monk played out the journey towards perfection, the cell was the engine-room of the operation. Being able to endure the cell, said Arsenius, was what put a monk's thoughts in order. The cell was a place of combat, a place of compunction, a place of refuge, and the monk's workplace. As one of the Systematic sayings expressed it, 'Let your thought think what it likes, but do not let your body out of your cell.' Contemplation and private prayer were difficult to accomplish without giving in to boredom and idleness, but even to sit in the cell without giving way to temptation was a step in the monastic life. Yet it would be wrong to see the monasticism of the *Apophthegmata Patrum* as solitary. On the contrary, the sense of community dominates the text. For monks of Skete, Nitria and Kellia, the most dangerous fault was the sin of slander. This indicates intense concern lest personal relations between monks deteriorate to a degree that jeopardised their individual profession. These were small societies that relied on trust and mutual respect, and could fall apart as a result of harbouring grudges and letting jealousies fester. This is why so many of the sayings concern small acts of kindness: bringing fruit to a sick monk; letting a monk who has fallen asleep during the night office use one's knee as a pillow rather than waking him rudely; giving the benefit of the doubt to a monk suspected of theft.[46] This is also why many of the sayings in the *Apophthegmata* emphasise moderation in personal austerity. The 'royal road', as one elder put it, was to eat a little regularly rather than to indulge oneself in feats of fasting.

Broadly speaking, it is probably correct to think of the first two generations of monks in Egypt – roughly up to the time of Athanasius's *Life of Anthony* – as representing 'native' traditions and comparatively uneducated monks. From the 360s onwards, however, an influx of intellectuals from across the Empire started to visit Egyptian monasteries and to participate in the ascetic life of the Delta monasteries. This prompts the question of what kind of background most Egyptian monks came from. Famously, Evagrius of Pontus supposedly asked the elder

Arsenius, 'How is it that we, with all our education and our wide knowledge get nowhere, while these Egyptian peasants acquire so many virtues?'[47] It is easy to assume from this a readily observed demarcation between the uneducated and largely illiterate Coptic-speaking monks and the Greek-speaking leaders of the ascetic movement, who were well networked, mobile and in touch with what was happening in the Church more widely. As Steven Driver has argued, 'simplicity' of faith and lack of sophistication are important components in standard accounts of the 'story of monasticism'.[48] According to Driver, the notion of a sharp division between 'nativist' Coptic and 'foreign' Greek monks in Egypt is a misleading oversimplification. Coptic as a language developed organically in the mixed milieu of Egyptian and Greek, and the biographies of Delta monks present something of the complexity of this milieu. Macarius, one of the founders of Skete, was a camel driver and smuggler before he embarked on the monastic life. Anthony himself was from a prosperous farming family, but uneducated at least in a conventional sense. Arsenius, to whom Evagrius posed the question about education and the monastic life, had been a tutor in the imperial family. He himself was once asked how it was that he, a highly educated man, asked for guidance in spiritual matters of a Coptic-speaking monk from a peasant background. His reply was that knowledge of Latin and Greek did not enable him to understand the new vocabulary of asceticism that the Egyptian monks had discovered and developed.

Evagrius, the son of a *chorepiskopos* (rural bishop) in northern Asia Minor, was ordained as a lector by Basil of Caesarea, then went to Constantinople with Gregory of Nazianzen in the 370s, and served on his staff at Council of Constantinople in 381.[49] Soon afterwards he went to Jerusalem where he met Rufinus and Melania, and became a monk himself, and it was on Melania's recommendation that he went to Nitria. Evagrius spent a little over fifteen years as a monk at Kellia. He left a large and complex body of work about monasticism: complex partly because so much of it is gnomic and abstract rather than descriptive. Harmless has characterised his writings as 'an elegant polyphony, a fuguelike weave of motifs'.[50] A brief taste of his approach is encapsulated in a sentence in the introduction to his *Praktikos*, a collection of one hundred chapters about the practical acquisition of virtue: 'Christianity is the dogma of Christ our Saviour/It is composed of practice and physics and theology.'[51] In addition he wrote the *Gnostikos*, comprising advice for more advanced monks (*gnostikoi*) who were ready to teach younger ones; the *Kephalaia gnostika*, a dense explanation of his cosmological vision owing a great deal to the theology of the second-century Alexandrian teacher Origen; a work on the theory of prayer, the *De oratione*; a work that has been described as a 'scriptural battle manual',[52] the *Antirrhetikos*, which comprises 487 temptations, with suitable Scriptural texts for each to help the monk counter it; the *Scholia*, brief biblical commentaries on Proverbs, Ecclesiastes, Psalms; and a collection of sixty-four *Letters*, most of which survive only in Syriac. It was Evagrius who first theorised the 'seven deadly sins', as they would come to be known in Christian thinking. Evagrius saw himself as the mediator of a tradition of practical asceticism that he had learned as an inheritance from an earlier generation, and which he passed on to a future generation. Wisdom had been learned from the practice of those such as Macarius, who had taught him that 'the monk should always live as if he were to die tomorrow but at the same time should treat his body as if he were to live on with it for many years to come'.[53]

The gravitational pull of Egyptian monasticism undoubtedly owes a great deal to textual practices. Monastic intellectuals such as Evagrius, many of whom were not themselves Egyptian, described a particular form of monasticism drawn mostly from practices in the hermitages of the Nile Delta, and it was from such accounts that the ascetic practices and ideals that would shape much of subsequent medieval monasticism were drawn. In this kind of monasticism, asceticism was above all a personal transformation on the individual's route to God.

Pre-eminent among such accounts were the two books written in the 420s by John Cassian, the *Institutes* and *Conferences*.[54] Cassian probably became a monk at Bethlehem in the 380s, before leaving to find a more ascetic regime in Egypt.[55] In or soon after 399 he was in Constantinople, where he became a protégé of the bishop, John Chrysostom. He seems to have gone to the West for the first time in 404 when he was sent as Chrysostom's emissary to Rome. By *c.* 420 he was in Marseille, where he founded two monasteries, one each for men and women. He was then asked to write about his Egyptian monastic experiences by Castor, the bishop of Apt. The very fact that, as a recent émigré from the East, Cassian was seen to have particular authority in writing about monasticism indicates that Egyptian methods already enjoyed considerable prestige. This is particularly striking given that monasticism had already reached Gaul before the end of the fourth century, through the agency of Martin, bishop of Tours (d. 397). Evidently Castor was looking for something different from the type of monasticism to be found, for example, in Sulpicius Severus's account of Martin's life.

Recently, as a wider range of textual and archaeological evidence has become available, the assumptions that scholars used to hold about Cassian's representation of Egyptian monasticism have been challenged. J.-C. Guy, for example, has argued that a great deal of what Cassian claims to have heard and seen is in fact his own reconstruction or imagination at work.[56] And, as William Harmless has pointed out, one of Cassian's traits was to make unfavourable comparisons between the slackness of Gaulish monks and those of Egypt.[57] Cassian had experience of monastic life from both Palestine and the Nile Delta, and he was aware that it took many forms. The ideals and practices he represents, however, are those from Nitria, Kellia and Skete, and although he does not make his debt explicit, he was largely dependent on the teaching of Evagrius. Steven Driver has commented that the challenge to which Cassian was responding in undertaking Bishop Castor's commission was to make this form of monasticism not only comprehensible but accepted as the dominant form in Gaul. This was no simple matter, both because the Gaulish tradition privileged miracles and wonders over seclusion as signs of divinely channelled authority and because Evagrius and his followers had become highly suspect in the West after their condemnation for adherence to the teachings of Origen in 399.[58]

Cassian's introduction to Egyptian Delta monasticism for western readers takes a dual form. The *Institutes*, the earlier of the two books, presents the theory of asceticism through an anatomy of the Egyptian hermitage in institutional terms. Beginning with the clothing worn by the monks, he proceeds to describe the liturgical offices, and the rules for receiving new monks, before taking the reader through a discussion of the eight vices (gluttony, fornication, avarice, anger, sadness, *acedia* or listlessness, vainglory and pride). Even when dealing with apparently outward matters such as clothing, he not only describes but also explains the hidden meaning of the habit. This is deliberately not a narrative of monastic heroism; in fact, it might be said that his focus on the pitfalls and dangers lying on the path to monastic perfection is quite the opposite of a work such as the contemporary *Lausiac History* of Palladius, a more biographically directed 'map of holiness' in which virtue and charity are foregrounded.[59] The use of the term 'Institutes' deliberately evokes organisational life of a kind that is mostly absent from the biographical *Lausiac History* or the elliptical *Apophthegmata Patrum*. In the *Institutes*, Cassian was textually constructing rather than simply recording such levels of organisation. In the *Conferences*, however, he tries to do something rather different. This is a huge text, by far the longest work on early monasticism by anyone involved in it. The 'conferences' are twenty-four thematic treatments of topics grouped in three sets. The topics include some, such as the vices, already covered in the *Institutes*, but also chastity and desires of the flesh, grace and free will, Scriptural understanding, friendship, self-mortification and the meanings behind the different types of monk. Although Cassian frames these discussions as teachings by monastic elders – some of whose thoughts would also be recorded in the *Apophthegmata Patrum* – John's own sense of what it meant to succeed in the monastic profession underlies the *Conferences*. Nowhere is this more obvious than in the conference that was to prove highly influential in the medieval West, on different types of monks. Through the mouthpiece of Abba John of Diolcos, a monk who had experienced both anchoritic and cenobitic monasticism, Cassian explains the fundamental spiritual paths and goals of each. The cenobitic monk 'crucifies desires' through participating with the community in a relentlessly fixed routine in which each day resembles the last, thus removing the need to think about the next. In contrast, the anchorite aims to empty the mind of all earthly thoughts so that it can be united with Christ. As someone who had experienced both, John of Diolcos speaks like the survivor of a long drawn-out trauma. The 'unbroken silence of the desert', while empowering monks to develop earthly perfection, can also destroy them and make them unfit for human society. The solitary monk, with no recourse to others, is vulnerable to the sin of spiritual pride.[60] The contrast between the two types is, of course, highly stylised in the same way as Athanasius's *Life of Anthony*. The monasticism that Cassian experienced at Skete was not solitary, though monks might engage in spells of anchoritic living, and the yearning for the freedom of the desert evokes an idealised and imagined past. Yet there is method in Cassian's approach, even if we cannot take it as a literally accurate record of Delta monasticism. Steven Driver has suggested that Cassian was trying to reconfigure Egyptian monasticism textually, as an interaction between the reader and the text. In this fashion, reading the text prayerfully took the monk progressively along the path being described in the *Conferences*, just as if he were moving in real space from one elder to another in the hermitage at Skete.

WIDER MONASTIC TRENDS: PALESTINE, SYRIA, ASIA MINOR

By the end of the fourth century, monasticism was already becoming an international phenomenon. That is to say, not only were monasteries being established in Palestine, Syria and Asia Minor as well as in Egypt, but also monks from around the Roman world were visiting and trying out different kinds of monastic experiment. Jacob of Nisibis, the first recorded Christian ascetic in Syria, died in 338. In Pontus, in Asia Minor, Macrina, the sister of Basil of Caesarea and Gregory of Nyssa, embarked on an ascetic life on the family estates in the 340s. Chariton, founder of hermitages known as *lavrae* in Palestine, died in *c.* 350. Martin of Tours, the subject of the first Latin biography of a monk, died in Gaul in 397, having practised monasticism in Italy before becoming bishop of Tours.

The real significance of these parallel developments lies in the textual interplay between them mediated by individuals in search of the most suitable monastic life. We have already seen how Jerome used the figure of Athanasius to bring a literary monastic presence to Rome. In 373 Melania, a propertied Italian woman, founded associated male and female monastic communities on the Mount of Olives outside Jerusalem, while her one-time mentor Jerome established a monastery at Bethlehem.[61] Rufinus, a one-time friend of Jerome, went to Egypt to learn monasticism in 373, and on his return to Italy in 403 translated the *History of the Monks of Egypt* into Latin. Palladius, author of the *Lausiac History* (420s), was from Galatia in western Asia Minor but in the 380s lived in monasteries in the Holy Land before moving to Egypt and in 392 becoming a disciple of Evagrius of Pontus at Kellia.[62] Evagrius himself had been a career civil servant in Constantinople from the 370s before being drawn to Egypt to learn 'the alphabet' of Egyptian monasticism. In the Systematic Collection of the *Apophthegmata Patrum*, Evagrius makes an appearance as the interlocutor of the elder Arsenius in an exchange about the value of education in embarking on a monastic life. John Cassian, like Palladius, began as a monk in the Holy Land in *c.* 380, before settling at Skete from *c.* 385 to 399. Scholars disagree about his birthplace, but he seems to have been a native Latin speaker. Two of the most influential fifth-century monastic figures in Palestine, Euthymios (from 405) and Sabas (from 469), were natives of Asia Minor. John Moschus, author of the *Spiritual Meadow* (*c.* 600), was originally from Damascus but lived as a monk in *lavrae* in the Holy Land before visiting Egypt.

The contrast between desert and habitation, between community and solitude, was more marked in Egypt than any other part of the late Roman monastic landscape. This meant that monasticism was more external to society here than, for example, in Syria or Palestine. The pious and the curious among the laity might visit monks in their habitations, but it meant a demanding journey for an uncertain welcome. In contrast, the relationship between those leading an ascetic life and the laity was more nuanced, more subtle and more complex in other regions.

Monasticism developed in the Holy Land side by side with the unique attribute of sacred geography. In the 380s a western visitor, Egeria, who may have been a nun from Spain, described an itinerary she undertook in the Holy Land as part of a group. It is clear from her account that monastic communities were not only to be found at many of the places associated with the events of Scripture, but also that monks had responsibilities for maintaining the sites, for undertaking liturgical duties there, and for instructing pilgrims about the importance of the sites.[63] Monasticism in the Holy Land may have begun in the Gaza region in the third century, but it was the identification and public promotion of the holy places that gave impetus to its further development. Women were intensively involved in this process from the start. The impetus behind the promotion of the sites associated with Jesus's earthly life supposedly came from Emperor Constantine's mother Helena as early as the 320s. By the 350s, a group of aristocratic women from Roman families were publicly adopting ascetic and chaste lives: Marcellina, sister of Ambrose of Milan, in 352/3; Marcella, a Roman aristocrat, in 355; her friend Paula a little later; and Melania, a Spanish noblewoman, before 372. There may have been many more unmarried or widowed women with similar inclinations who were unable to make such decisions because of the refusal of their families to cooperate. Both Paula and Melania spent some time with monks in Egypt – at Nitria, in Melania's case – before settling in the Holy Land. Melania, together with Rufinus, founded monasteries for men and women on the Mount of Olives in 379–80. Marcella and Paula had both been introduced to the idea of asceticism as a way of life by Jerome, who in 385, after a short but controversial period in Rome, also settled in the Holy Land.[64]

Before these cenobitic monasteries had been established by wealthy Romans, communities closer in type to Egyptian Delta monasticism had already taken shape in fourth-century Palestine and Syria. The founder of Palestinian anchoritic monasticism was a monk from Asia Minor called Chariton, who had been drawn not to the sites of holiness at Jerusalem or Bethlehem but to the wilderness of the Judaean desert. In this region of rocky plains, wadis and gorges to the south and east of Jerusalem, Chariton found a landscape that provided the same kind of challenges that Anthony had found in the Egyptian desert. This was a hostile environment in which for much of the year it was difficult to find or grow food, and in which wild animals – including snakes, scorpions and lions – and potentially hostile nomadic people posed constant threats for the unwary. Precursors of Christian monks, the Essenes, had lived in communities near the Dead Sea in the first century, and early in the third century Narcissus, bishop of Jerusalem, retired to a retreat in the desert to escape the burden of office.[65] But the Judaean desert also had a feature that the Egyptian desert did not possess: it was where Jesus had been tempted by, and overcome, the Devil. His followers fully expected that they would attract the same attention. Just as in the Egyptian desert, demons might inhabit caves, wadis or cliffs. Chariton founded three communities, known as *lavrae*. These were Pharan, northeast of Jerusalem, Souka, near Tekoa in the desert south of Jerusalem, and

Douka, on a ridge overlooking Jericho, to the east of Jerusalem by the Jordan river.[66] The *lavra* was a local version of the Egyptian Skete type. Superficially, the way of life in the *lavra* corresponded to the Egyptian type. Monks spent most of the week in their cells but gathered in an oratory for communal worship and teaching at the end of the week. A bakehouse provided bread sufficient for each monk's needs for the week. Like the Egyptian monks, *lavra* monks worked at making baskets or rope in their cave cells, and these were traded by the community for food.[67] Excavations at some *lavrae*, notably that founded in the Kidron Valley by Sabas in the later fifth century, reveal the cultivation of a garden and orchard at the bottom of the wadi. Yet in some important ways the *lavra* was very different from the arrangements at Skete, Nitria or Kellia. Instead of mud-brick cells grouped around an oratory and bakehouse, the *lavra* was, literally, a path, often along a narrow ledge in a wadi, linking cells hollowed out of caves in the walls of the cliff face. Because the path often lay along the bottom of a wadi, the spatial layout of the *lavra* differed from the hermitages of the Nile Delta. Since accommodation was provided by natural phenomena – caves – the spatial relationship between the monks was random rather than constructed by the founder. Moreover, the geography of the wadis, many of which have steep-cliffed sides, meant that access to them was often difficult without a ladder.[68] The intense, sometimes paradoxical sociability that historians have found underlying the *Apophthegmata Patrum* is thus less obvious in the *lavrae* of the Holy Land.

Chariton died in *c*. 350, but fifty-five years later another monk from Asia Minor, Euthymios, settled at and revitalised Pharan, then with his companion Theoktistos founded two further communities, a cenobium in a remote wadi in the desert southeast of Jerusalem, and another *lavra*, which later became a cenobium with his name, at Khan al-Ahmar (now Ma'ale Adumim), just to the east of Jerusalem on the road to Jericho.[69] The placement of the latter recalled to later pilgrims the site of the Gospel parable of the Good Samaritan, who rescued a man from bandits on the road to Jericho. Euthymios was to become the mentor of Sabas, who in 469 started to live at the cenobium of Theoktistos and nine years later settled in the Kidron Valley and eventually founded the 'Great Lavra' that bears his name and which is still in existence, albeit as a cenobitic monastery. Most of what we know textually about Palestinian monasticism in the period between the fourth and sixth centuries comes from the writings of Cyril of Scythopolis (*c.* 525–*c.* 558), who was a monk at the Great Lavra. Cyril's account comprises biographical accounts of seven monks in Palestine in the century and a half between 405 and the mid-sixth century, but the bulk of the text of the *Lives of the Monks of Palestine* concerns Euthymios and Sabas.

The geography of the Holy Land determined the course of monasticism in the Judaean desert. To a much greater extent than in Egypt, cenobitic monasteries and *lavrae* were interdependent. They occupied the same landscape, and often shared personnel. Fluidity between cenobitic monasteries and *lavrae* was frequent, and cenobitic monks might adopt anchoritic styles of living for periods, sometimes for devotional purposes. Indeed, some cenobitic monasteries in the Holy Land seem to have begun as *lavrae*. Cyril of Scythopolis explains that the monasteries founded by Theoktistos and Euthymios had originally been founded as *lavrae*, and Sabas founded both coenobia (monasteries) and *lavrae*. When Euthymios and Theoktistos first settled in their cliff gorge at wadi Mukallik, they planned to make a *lavra* like Chariton's Pharan, which they had just left. But 'when they saw that no one could get to the church by night, because . . . the place was impassable, they gradually transformed it into a coenobium, with the cave for the church'.[70] The division between the two types was eventually recognised institutionally by the patriarch of Jerusalem, who appointed Sabas as archimandrite with responsibility for *lavra* monks while Theodosius the Coenobiarch, who presided over a monastery near Bethlehem, had responsibility for cenobites (that is, monks living together in communities). The original distinction, however, originated in the spiritual needs of monasticism. As Cyril recounts, Sabas, who had originally become a monk as a young man in Cappadocia, asked to join Euthymios's *lavra* after 'hearing from almost everyone about the ascetic contests . . . in the desert to the east of the holy city', but was advised by Euthymios to join the monastery of Theoktistos first. As Euthymios told him, 'I do not think it right for you as a youth to stay in a *lavra*, for neither does it benefit a *lavra* to have a youth nor is it suitable for a youth to live among anchorites.'[71] Sabas was later to give exactly the same ruling as founder of the Great Lavra, recounting not only that this was what Euthymios had advised him, but also that Euthymios had received this rule from 'the ancient fathers of Skete'.[72] The custom thus developed that young men who wanted to become monks would first of all learn the craft of monasticism in a cenobitic monastery and only when they had mastered the discipline might they be admitted to a *lavra*. This discipline entailed, first of all, learning the psalter and the correct way to sing the psalms; second, 'keeping a watch on their minds, purifying their thoughts from recollection of the things of the world'.[73]

Notwithstanding the clear undertones of the dangers of a sexual nature implicit in this practice, it also shows the adaptation of the same master–disciple relationship that we have seen as a central theme of Egyptian Delta monasticism. Such relationships might also be continued in less formalised ways that also demonstrate the centrality of landscape. One of the most striking features of the monasticism described by Cyril of Scythopolis is the custom of elder *lavra* monks taking younger disciples with them on their annual itineraries around the Dead Sea. Each year Euthymios, and after him Sabas, would spend the forty days of Lent making a circuit of the Dead Sea on foot, living off the plants that grew wild there. This was an opportunity to mentor one or two promising younger monks. Living in and off the wild was a way of teaching practical lessons about survival, and at the same time testing the character of novice monks.

The custom of spending Lent in this way in deserted regions emphasised the penitential character of monasticism. Although this was not unique to Palestinian monasticism – Macarius, the founder of Skete, had supposedly begun a monastic life as a penance after killing a man – it was a facet peculiarly suitable for a monastic landscape so inextricably linked to pilgrimage. Excavations at monasteries such as Euthymios's foundation near Jerusalem have revealed the existence of *xenodochia*, or guest houses for pilgrims.[74] To make a pilgrimage to the Holy Land was to re-live the Scriptures by treading the ground where the story of human salvation had taken place, and parts of this story, in both Old and New Testaments, took place in the desert. The Israelites wandered in the wilderness of Sinai before reaching the Promised Land; the prophet Elijah fled to the desert; Jesus withdrew to the desert to prepare himself spiritually for his ministry. In the Holy Land, the desert was a place of purging, refinement and preparation. It is hardly surprising that the desert's capacity to purge featured in monastic stories in which sinfulness precedes penance and eventual embrace of the monastic life. A classic version of the story is the *Life of Mary the Egyptian*. An Alexandrian sex worker, Mary goes to the Holy Land to ply her trade on the pilgrim boats. When she arrives in Jerusalem she tries to enter the Church of the Holy Sepulchre but is, miraculously, unable to cross the threshold. She goes to live in penance alone in the desert, and after many years she is discovered naked, so burned by the sun as to be scarcely recognisable as human, by another monk. Her death and burial, which follow quickly after her discovery, confirm that she has given satisfactory penance for her past sins.[75] This story, which is certainly an example of what Peter Brown has called 'the extensive rubbish heap of Near Eastern misogyny',[76] is also testimony to the power of the desert to transform and redeem.

Monasticism in the Judaean desert was uniquely accented by the presence of the holy city. Notwithstanding the remoteness and inaccessibility of the environment, few of the monasteries or *lavrae* were more than a day's walk from Jerusalem. The total area of the Judaean desert was small enough that monks could communicate not only with Jerusalem but also with each other, and archaeological fieldwork has revealed the existence of networks of paths linking them.[77] The importance of these connections, both with each other and with Jerusalem, can hardly be overestimated in thinking about the character of monasticism in the Holy Land. For one thing, it meant that it was easy for monks from the desert *lavrae* and monasteries to get to Jerusalem, and this in turn meant that they were from early on an important factor in the development of liturgical practices in the major shrine churches. Jerusalem's importance as a spiritual centre lay in the presence of the shrines – principally the Holy Sepulchre, the place of Christ's resurrection from the dead, Mount Zion, the site of the coming of the Holy Spirit at Pentecost, and therefore the birthplace of the Church, and the Mount of Olives, from where Christ had ascended to heaven. The shrines brought pilgrims, money and spiritual authority to Jerusalem, and the liturgical rites that developed to serve the shrines were the primary expression of this importance. Monastic association with Jerusalem gave both the monks and the patriarchate of Jerusalem unique and mutual sources of authority. Jerusalem is a constant presence in the pages of Cyril of Scythopolis, particularly in the career of Sabas. Positions in the Church at Jerusalem were often filled by monks, and Sabas was a frequent presence in the city. The relationship is portrayed as mutually beneficial and balanced. A sympathetic patriarch such as Sallustius (486–93) was prepared to invest financially in Sabas's building projects for monasteries; on the other hand, Sabas was required to account for his management of the monasteries over which he had authority, especially when monks complained about him.[78] The influence of Palestinian monasticism, however, went much further. For Cyril, monasticism in the Holy Land was an intrinsic part of a wider landscape of empire and its fortunes. Both Euthymios, who was present at the Council of Chalcedon (453) and Sabas in the early sixth century, are represented by Cyril as having influenced the direction of the Church's theological teaching and the governance of the Church. Sabas in particular enjoyed considerable influence over Emperor Anastasius.[79]

To a degree, monasticism had always, at least since Athanasius, been weaponised by those contending for authority in the Church. Athanasius himself saw monks as important components of Christian society – just because they had withdrawn from society, that did not exempt them from their obligations of leadership in Church. This is doubtless also why he was so active in intervening in disputes among monks over their practices – even to questions such as how much sleep was acceptable.[80] Athanasius would have recognised the attitude taken up by Sallustius in his deployment of Theodosius and Sabas as agents of episcopal authority. In the 320s and 330s he understood the need to walk a line in dealing with charismatic and powerful monastic leaders. Putting pressure on Pachomius to be ordained as a priest – something that the monastic founder initially resisted – was a way of bringing monasticism under episcopal authority. At the same time, however, it recognised a fait accompli, since Pachomius had already overstepped that authority through his founding of a parish church at Nitentori. By the time Sabas was active, the Council of Chalcedon (451) had enshrined in canon law the authority of bishops over monasteries in their diocese. This was to prove one of the most fraught and contentious elements of the framework within which monasticism operated throughout the Middle Ages.

Because there was no real dispute over the virtue of monastic ideals – although, of course, there might be 'bad monks' who failed to practise those ideals properly – political elites could show their own reflected virtue through association with monks. But the degree of political and theological involvement in Cyril's text also reflects the choices he made as an author in representing Palestinian monasticism. Cyril grew up in the ambience of the Church – his father was employed in the residence of the bishop of Scythopolis – and lived all his adult life as a monk at the monastery of Euthymios and then the Great Lavra. When he first arrived in Jerusalem in 543, however, monasticism in the Holy Land was riven with theological controversy. A group of monks sympathetic to the teachings of Origen had taken over Sabas's New Lavra, and mobilised public opinion against Sabas and his followers. This echoed the circumstances in which many monks had fled Skete in 399, after Evagrius and his followers were accused of Origenism. It is also a reminder of the degree to which, in a society governed by competing religious identities, monasticism was always susceptible to being politicised.

As Richard Price has pointed out, Cyril of Scythopolis was one of the very few writers about early monasticism to have been native to the way of life in the region about which he was writing, and to have been simply a monk rather than a member of the hierarchy of the Church or of government, or to have founded and led communities.[81] Although – rather simplistically – he understood monasticism as a practice originating in Egypt and passed on to the Holy Land from Skete, his interests did not really go far beyond the Holy Land. In contrast with Athanasius, Rufinus, Evagrius or John Cassian, Cyril's purpose in writing is rather elusive. He says that he was primarily interested in recording events and details accurately, for the good of posterity.[82] This is very different from the overtly ideological agenda behind Athanasius's construction of monastic solitude in the *Life of Anthony*, or the view of Egyptian monasticism so explicit in Cassian's work. Nor, unlike Evagrius, was he particularly interested in reflecting on the spiritual meaning of the monastic practices he describes in the careers of his monks. There is very little in the way of spiritual guidance in his *Lives*, other than the practical example provided by Euthymios, Sabas and John the Hesychast.

What takes the place of the abstract spirituality of the *Apophthegmata Patrum*, the discourses on demons in the *Life of Anthony*, or on vices and how to avoid them in Cassian's *Conferences*, is the miraculous. Price counts ninety-four miracles in the *Lives of the Monks of Palestine*, a huge number if we compare it to the dozen in Athanasius's *Life of Anthony*. The miracles are varied in type, effect and purpose. Some use dreams, visions or clairvoyance to show the receptiveness of the virtuous monk to God's power; others are miracles of healing. The largest category, however, concerns the natural world. We might take as an example the five occasions on which Sabas was apparently able to control lions. In the first, the Devil appeared to Sabas in the form of 'a most terrifying lion, advancing against him and bristling threateningly'. Sabas challenged the lion to attack if it had received authority against him, citing Psalms 91.13 ('You will tread on the asp and basilisk and trample on the lion and dragon'), in response to which the lion vanished. After this, says Cyril, God made every carnivorous and poisonous beast subject to him. On another occasion a lion tried to drag Sabas out of a cave where he was reciting the night office alone, and was reprimanded by Sabas for his interruption. On the final occasion, Sabas trained a lion to act as a guard over a grazing ass belonging to his disciple, having first tamed it by removing a thorn from its paw. The relationship ended suddenly one day when the disciple had sex with a woman and the lion, as if triggered by this breach of chastity, instantly ate the ass.[83]

The lions serve to remind the reader of the precariousness of life for *lavra* monks in the Judaean desert. But all of these lion stories, and others of the same type to be found in the works of later reporters on Palestinian and Syrian monasticism such as John Moschus and Leontios of Nablus, took place in situations when monks were outside the *lavra*. Even the cave where Sabas was disturbed by the lion was selected by him at random rather than being his regular habitation. This feature of the stories also draws attention to an apparent fluidity between settled and fixed states. Cyril's monks spend more time either on the move or outside the monastery or *lavra* than would be imaginable from the literature of the Egyptian desert. In this respect, the monasticism of the

Judaean desert has more in common with that of Syria than the Egyptian exemplar invoked by Cyril.

Syrian Christianity inherited from Judaism a religious tradition that stressed the importance of behaviour, and from early on developed a characteristic focus on renunciation of the world.[84] Susan Ashbrook Harvey has argued that in Syrian monasticism the symbolic value of action was emphasised over inner spirituality as a means of perfecting human nature. In the most characteristic texts about monks and monasticism in Syria, it is those traditions and passages in Scripture in which personal asceticism is held up as an ideal that are particularly prominent.[85] We have already made the point that, in contrast with Egypt and other parts of the Empire, martyrdom was comparatively rare in Syria. The greatest authority on Syrian monasticism, Arthur Vööbus, summarised the distinctive features of its asceticism as primitivism, a reliance on the natural world, and withdrawal from settled areas in favour of a vagrant form of eremitism.[86] One of the most striking themes in contemporary texts about Syrian monastic men and women is the idea that renouncing the settled world in order to live naked or wearing animal skins in the wilderness, exposure to the elements, consumption of only raw food gathered in the wild, and living among wild animals, is a kind of fulfilment of humanity. Living 'off the grid', in contemporary parlance, was a means of recovering an eschatological Paradise by returning to the imagined life in the Garden of Eden before the Fall.

If such a thing as a Syrian version of Palladius's *Historia Lausiaca* or Cyril of Scythopolis's *Lives of the Monks of Palestine* may be said to exist, it is the *History of the Monks of Syria* written in c. 440 by Theodoret, bishop of Cyrrhus. Theodoret's subject matter was 'the many and differing ladders for the ascent into heaven'. Some accomplished the ascent by living in tents, cells, caves or holes in the ground in which they chanted praise to God; others by 'giving their bodies to the naked air endure contrasts of temperature, sometimes frozen by unrelieved frost, sometimes burned by the fire of the sun's rays. Of these again the life is various: some stand all the time, others divide the day between sitting and standing; some, immured in enclosures, shun the company of the many; others, with no such covering, are exposed to all who wish to see them.'[87] In contrast with Cyril of Scythopolis, who characterised

Sabas embarking on the cenobitic life as preparing for combat, Theodoret continually employs the language of athletic endeavour.[88] Monks were athletes, and the monastery or hermitage was a wrestling ground or a racecourse. Monasticism was competitive rather than combative: holy men and women competed against their fallen nature in order to perfect bodies that were subject to decay.

To an even greater degree than is the case in the work of Cyril of Scythopolis, Theodoret presents us with a picture of monastic life in which the boundaries between solitary and communal monasticism, comparatively clear in Egypt, are fluid and porous. The two figures whom he deploys as founders of Syrian monastic asceticism, Jacob of Nisibis (d. 338) and Julian Saba (d. 366/7), lived and generated their awesome thaumaturgic powers as solitaries, but returned to society. Jacob became bishop of Nisibis, while Julian supervised the growth of an ascetic community around him.[89] Typically a holy man gathered disciples in a more passive and far less strategic fashion than in the cases of Euthymios or Sabas. Marcianus, who had retired from court life, occupied a cell too small for anyone else to cohabit, so he told those who attached themselves to him to follow his example to build themselves similar huts a little way away.[90] In Theodoret's most celebrated example, the narrative arc shows progression from cenobitic to solitary monasticism. But it also shows the extremes of ascetic behaviour that characterised Syrian monasticism.

Symeon the Stylite entered a monastery at Teleda, in northern Syria, having already spent two years as disciple to two ascetics. At the monastery, at which he spent ten years, he outdid other monks in feats of personal asceticism – constricting his breathing with bands of cord around his waist, abstaining from food for a week at a time. In Syrian tradition, ascetics were 'institutionalised', in the sense that within monasteries there was a place for them as monks pursuing a chosen course of practice. Typically, monks practised 'athletic' feats of asceticism at night, for instance by wedging themselves into niches where they had to stand all night. The sixth-century writer John of Ephesus describes a scene in a northern Syrian monastery in his day:

> [there were] others ranged in rows and standing on resting-posts, and others who had fastened their bodies to the walls all night

without standing-posts, and others who were tied to the ceiling of the room by ropes and vine branches, and were suspending themselves by them in a standing posture all night, having put them under their armpits, and others who were sitting on seats and never falling on their sides.[91]

Symeon, however, seems to have gone so far in his practices that his abbot became worried that younger and less able monks would do themselves serious harm by trying to imitate him. When asked to moderate his austerities, he refused and was expelled from the community. On his own, he first lived in a disused well, then had himself walled up in a cell before, in *c.* 412, hitting on the strategy that was to make him famous throughout the eastern Empire. He climbed to the top of a column from a disused pagan temple and simply made it his home. Over the years he added to the height, and contrived to support himself by means of a platform. A pulley system was rigged up to supply him with food and to remove his waste. The genius of Symeon's arrangement was that he was at the same time completely removed from human society, suspended as it were between heaven and earth, and also constantly visible. He was watched at prayer, performing the offices, in meditation.[92] Peter Brown has shown how holy men like Symeon were also suspended between human society and their own solitude. Symeon's form of monasticism was highly dependent on the cooperation and belief in him of the villagers on the border of whose territory the column stood. This was a symbiotic relationship in which the monk was, effectively, sponsored to be the community's holy man, performing services that included giving judgement and advice based on his clairvoyance, healing and spiritual teaching through example.[93] In sixth-century Amida, the Syrian town that forms the setting for John of Ephesus's *Lives of the Eastern Saints*, the political world was all too present. This was a frontier town, subject to devastation and sack by competing Persian and Roman armies at the beginning of the century, and famine and plague in mid-century. The physical dangers of the locale had the result of bunching ascetics in small spaces in or near the city; retreat into the wilderness was simply not an option.[94] John of Ephesus, moreover, was writing in a time of ecclesiastical turmoil after the formation of a Syriac-speaking Church that rejected the

Chalcedonian formula. John's ascetics were men and women at war with the establishment in Constantinople. They were, as Susan Ashbrook Harvey has remarked, people caught up in their times, who had 'no wondrous solutions for the hardships at hand' except the hard work they could offer for the local community.[95]

Syrian monks lived on the margins of society in order to critique it. In some ways they were closer to enacting the role of the Old Testament prophet than to the penitent. The Syriac version of Symeon the Stylite's biography emphasises his prophetic ministry by making comparisons between his behaviour and Isaiah walking about naked, Hosea marrying a harlot and Jeremiah wearing a yoke.[96] Like prophets, they might be quick to anger. They could be savage and unrelenting, or play the fool in order to expose social hypocrisies. Jacob of Nisibis cursed the village girls, whom he caught staring at him, so that their hair turned prematurely grey.[97] Symeon 'the holy fool', a seventh-century Syrian monk, went to the town of Emesa after leaving his monastery for a life of itinerant anchoritism. There, he deliberately flouted the townspeople's norms and values to draw attention to their emptiness: defecating openly in the marketplace; walking around naked with his clothing on his head like a turban – but also driving away demons and praying for the deliverance of the citizens from evil.[98] Similarly, John of Ephesus's *Lives of the Eastern Saints* includes a married couple from Amida who worked as mime artists in the market square by day, acting out the roles of harlot and pimp, but were secretly ascetics.[99] Tellingly, Symeon's biographer Leontios of Neapolis says of his subject that 'it was entirely as if Symeon had no body'.[100] Symeon's monastic aspirations began when he was told by his companion, John, that the monasteries they could see before them in the Jordan Valley as they descended the road to Jericho were the houses of angels. 'Can we see them?' Symeon asked. 'If we will become like them, yes.'[101] The purpose of the ascetic life was to lose one's bodily identity.

This might be attempted in different ways. One was through living not only with but like wild animals. Jacob of Nisibis did not eat 'that which is laboriously sown and reaped, but that which grows of its own accord. He gathered the spontaneous fruits of wild trees and herbs which looked like vegetables; of these he gave the body the necessities of life, renouncing the use of fire.'[102] Jacob was following a practice that would become recognisable among some Syrian monks. As the fifth-century historian Sozomen remarked, 'they were called *boschoi* [grazers] when they first embarked on the philosophic life, because they had no dwellings, ate no bread or meat, and drank no wine . . . When it was time for food, each one would take a sickle. They would then go up into the mountains and feed on what grew there, like animals out to pasture.'[103] A sixth-century Syrian, Simeon the Mountaineer, wandered in the territory of upper Euphrates, 'going about the mountains like the wild beasts . . . and had no intercourse except with God'.[104]

Another way was to lose one's sexual identity. We have already seen this at work in the story of Mary the Egyptian, who as an anchorite in the desert cut her hair short and exposed her body to the elements, and in the unnamed woman in the *Apophthegmata Patrum* known to Bessarion, who concealed her sex by the expedient of not speaking and remaining in her cell weaving baskets. Sarah, one of the three named women in the *Apophthegmata*, tells a group of monks who visit her that 'according to nature I am a woman, but not according to my thoughts'.[105] As Susanna Elm observes, 'For a perfect ascetic the question of male or female no longer exists, because he or she has risen above the limits determined by the body; asceticism means annihilation of sexual distinction.'[106] Gregory of Nyssa wrote about his sister Macrina, who lived as an ascetic on the family estate in the 340s: 'A woman is the starting point of our story, if indeed it is right to call her a woman, for I do not know whether it is appropriate to call someone a woman who was by nature a woman but who was in fact far above nature.'[107] The few women included by Theodoret in his exemplars of monastic virtue rose above perceived norms of female behaviour, typically as outstanding penitents. But they also bore witness to the ascetic fortitude and self-control of the male ascetics with whom they came into contact. They were there because they were notably 'unwomanly' and as such did not do what was usually expected of women – tempt men sexually. Cyril of Scythopolis simply ignored the women ascetics whom we know must have been active in the Holy Land in his day.

If, for women, ascetic virtue entailed becoming indistinguishable from men, for male monks celibacy was essential. In Syriac, the word for 'virgin' (*bthula*) was sometimes synonymous with 'Christian', because it was the feature of Christian conduct that set them apart from the rest of society. It is tempting, but misleading, to interpret ascetic self-denial, whether evidenced by sexual renunciation, torment of the body or extremes of fasting, as a perverse hatred of the body, or of a mind–body polarity. This does indeed seem at first sight to underlie some of the teachings of Egyptian monks, as developed by Evagrius and represented in the *Apophthegmata Patrum*, about the need to master bodily instincts and appetites. Withdrawing from village life, remaining in one's cell, exhausting the body through work, controlling consumption so as to cut out meat and other 'moist' foods, were all methods of submitting desires to the will. Of course, as Cassian explained, even experienced monks might be prey to sexual desires and to nocturnal emissions, and the monk's task was continually to wage war against them. Syrian ascetics, however, are more typically shown as *losing* their embodiment than in mastering it.

It is notable how many founders and initiators of monastic communities in the Holy Land were originally from Asia Minor. We know very little for certain about the beginnings of monastic practices in Asia Minor, but Basil of Caesarea began to live as an ascetic in 357 in the hermitage previously occupied by his brother Naukratios, at least ten years after their sister Macrina had taken vows of virginity. This was a wealthy landowning family, which could afford to put rural property to this kind of use and, equally important, could afford to maintain economically unproductive members in the ascetic life. Basil and his other brother Gregory of Nyssa, together with Gregory of Nazianzen, the so-called Cappadocian Fathers, were to become theological leaders in the Greek-speaking world. His importance for the history of monasticism, however, lies in his compilation of Rules, known as the Longer and Shorter Rules, which were to be highly influential in the development of cenobitic monasticism in the Greek-speaking world, and in other works such as the *Ascetic Treatises* attributed to him, and which were often copied in Greek monastic manuscripts.[108] Although it would be misleading to think of Orthodox monasticism as 'Basilian', Basil's ideas had a strong influence on later Byzantine monastic practice. Some of the characteristics of his Rules, such as his suspicion of solitary living, his insistence on manual labour, especially for postulants, his concern with diet and the care of sick monks, and with literacy and teaching, find their way into later Byzantine monastic practices of philanthropy and acts of charity. As we shall see, these features became particularly important in the cenobitic revival in Constantinople in the eleventh and twelfth centuries.

Basil had been inspired originally by Eustathius of Sebaste, who led what has been vividly described as 'a radical asceticism of a free-wheeling pre-monastic type', before he got into trouble with the authorities for contraventions of social norms.[109] One of the problems with the Eustathians, as far as contemporaries were concerned, was their apparent lack of discretion, both sexual – they included women and men – and social. They were accused of allowing women to live like men, of admitting escaped slaves to their communities, and of denouncing property ownership. In this way, they were not only rejecting the values of the world, but openly flouting them and denying their validity. Such a challenge to norms was also a challenge to authority – which, by the mid-fourth century, meant the authority of the Christian State. Basil's style of cenobitic monasticism owed something to radical Eustathian ideas, most notably his insistence on the renunciation of personal property and the pooling of all resources by the community. If this stipulation has the tint of privilege – since he clearly envisaged a group of monks or nuns with wealth to pool in order to sustain the community – in other ways Basil was alive to the direct precepts of the Gospel. Above all, he thought that a monastery was a community of charity. Like Augustine, who developed his precepts for the formation of a monastic community in the very late fourth or early fifth century, Basil was less interested in the self-transformation that is so indispensable a part of the Egyptian ascetic tradition as transmitted by Athanasius, the *Apophthegmata Patrum* and Cassian than in renunciation as the means of living out the Gospel. Basil's model for monastic community was to prove the most lasting and influential in the Greek-speaking world throughout the Middle Ages. Its outline, and indeed much of the detail, shaped the subsequent development of monasticism from Byzantine Syria to Sicily.

THE WESTERN EMPIRE

The first western monk is often identified as Martin of Tours, a soldier from Pannonia (modern Hungary) who, after wandering in the Balkans and northern Italy, settled as an ascetic on an island in the Ligurian Sea. In 371 he was made bishop of Tours by popular acclaim, largely for his supposed miraculous powers. On the banks of the Loire he established a group of hermit cells, ostensibly on the model of Skete or Nitria, though, according to Sulpicius Severus, encompassing the apostolic model of communal living in Acts 4.32–4. On the whole, this seems to have been a rather comfortable kind of monasticism, in which most of the monks were from privileged backgrounds. Notwithstanding Sulpicius's inclusion of some recognisable elements of Delta monasticism – steadfastness, patience, suffering – the Loire is hardly the Egyptian desert, and there is little in Sulpicius's account to suggest the progressive and painful self-transformation that marks the asceticism known to his contemporary Evagrius. It would doubtless be cruel, but perhaps not wholly misleading, to see Martin as presiding over a group of wealthy converts who were enthusiastic about a simple life in community, but who still relied on peasant labour to provide their food.

What did Latin speakers understand by monasticism in the fourth and fifth centuries? *Monasterion* was a Greek word, and when it appears in Latin writing for the first time, in *c.* 370, it is as a translation of the ideal promoted in Athanasius's *Life of Anthony*. Jerome, Ambrose, Augustine, Paulinus of Nola and Sulpicius Severus had all used the word before 400. In its first use, it referred to the habitation of a single monk, but Jerome used it to speak about a gathering of monks in his *Life of Malchus*, written in 390, and it probably always had a range of connotations in Latin as in Greek.[110] Language could scarcely keep up with the widening range of possible practices developing among ascetic Christians. Ambrose refers to monks living on islands off the Ligurian coast of Italy – as Martin of Tours had done – as men choosing to hide themselves from the world to avoid the pitfalls of life, and whose chanting of psalms complements the waves breaking on the shore.[111] Elsewhere he listed the necessary characteristics of the monastic life for men as common prayer with the singing of hymns, reading and handiwork to occupy the mind, fasting and separation from women.[112] Orosius, an early fifth-century Christian apologist, attempted a general definition of monastic life, calling monks 'Christians, who, having renounced the varied activities concerned with worldly things, confine themselves to the one work of faith.'[113] As Robert Markus has perceptively remarked, this left unexplained the question that many Christians of the time urgently needed to have answered for them: how much asceticism was needed for perfection to be achieved?[114] What was the qualitative difference between the different types of monastic life, and was that difference to be measured in social or spiritual terms? One classic definition of the monk, suggested in 1936 by Karl Heussi, is that the monk, regardless of gender, habitation or circumstance, is someone who inhabits a *sonderwelt*: a separate world.[115]

Such a conceptual separation is what Orosius's more famous contemporary, Augustine of Hippo, seemed to be getting at in his reflection of what monasticism meant. Augustine's conversion and reception into the Christian community at Milan brought him into contact with ascetic communities in Milan and, later, Rome.[116] Although he does not use the terms *monachi* or *monasterium* in describing them, he calls upon memory of these communities in listing what he saw as the four types of monk. First, there were monks who lived in eremitical solitude, like Anthony. Then there were eremitical communities such as those known to western visitors to Skete. Third, virgins who lived in communities, and finally, those who lived in cenobitic community. These last ate together once daily, but abstained from both meat and wine. The specificity of this detail suggests that Augustine knew of communities that called themselves monastic, but which did not adhere to such practices, but that he did not consider them to be genuine monks.[117] Augustine was interested in the apparent contradiction implicit in cenobitic monasticism. The communities with which he was familiar were urban, yet they led a style of life that was not only separate from but in opposition to civic ideas. They were conceptually rather than geographically removed from society. This suggests that a version of the Pachomian, Palestinian or Basilian monastery had not yet reached the West.

Augustine (354–430) came to asceticism when already bishop of Hippo. As suggested above, his vision of monastic life owes more to the communality of Acts than to an individual path to God through discipline. He probably had in mind a community of priests, and he may have written down his precepts as a practical guide for priests in his diocese to live a chaste life together. Certainly his Rule, probably composed in the 390s, envisions members of the community participating regularly in a public liturgy. The Rule is unusual in permitting considerable latitude on movement among the monks or nuns – for he also adapted the Rule for a community of women – even to the point of use of public laundries and baths. Perhaps idealistically, Augustine relied on the bonds of charity rather than internal discipline to moderate conduct. He took it as axiomatic that a community would moderate its practices so as to ensure that mutual respect and consideration, rather than adherence to outward regulation, became the guiding principle. To this end, he was more interested in underlying meaning rather than strict observance or show. Realism about behaviour informs much of the precepts. Thus, for example, it is recognised that when monks go out they are quite likely to see women as well as other men. There was no point, Augustine realised, in trying to enforce absolute separation to the point demanded by an enclosed Rule such as that of Pachomius. Rather than forbidding his monks to see women, therefore, he reminded them that they should not *want* to associate with them, or to seek out their company. Similarly, he advised monks not to draw attention to themselves by any extremes of behaviour when outside the monastery. The best monks were those who passed unnoticed. It was the flexibility of his Rule, as much as his hopefulness about collective human endeavour, that made it so important to the medieval West, when it was adopted for use not only by clerical communities such as cathedral canons but also by enclosed religious houses, hospitals and, in the thirteenth century, mendicant friars.

The career of a contemporary of Augustine, Paulinus of Nola, shows us how a particular type of monastic community might come into being. Paulinus was born a year later than Augustine, in 355, but whereas Augustine came from a middle-ranking provincial family in North Africa, Paulinus's family were among the wealthiest and most privileged and influential in the western Empire. Although they lived on substantial estates in Provence, one of the most Romanised parts of the Empire, they also owned property in Spain and Campania. Paulinus enjoyed the education common to the senatorial aristocracy, and in 381 was made governor of Campania. Although his family may already have been Christian, it was here that he encountered a new kind of veneration, in the festal celebration of St Felix at the town of Nola. After returning to Provence he lived quietly some years and married a woman from a similar background, Theresiana. It was his brother's unexpected death, possibly as a result of political vicissitudes, that led him on the path to asceticism. In 393 he began selling off his property in Gaul and Spain, was ordained priest and settled with Theresiana at Nola, where they adopted a life of married ascetics. At some point between 404 and 415 he was made bishop of Nola, and he died in 431.

Becoming an ascetic, for Paulinus, entailed neither total separation from his wife nor the abandonment of his literary life and friendships. He retained a wide correspondence with Christian aristocrats, including Melania. Yet he referred to himself as a monk. What, then, did his monasticism entail? We are fortunate to possess not only Paulinus's own descriptions in a series of vignettes in his letters and poems, but also the archaeological excavation of the monastery he founded at Nola. This comprised a group of three buildings around a central courtyard. Two of these were churches: the original church of St Felix that Paulinus renovated soon after he settled there, and a new one that he built next to it. The third building, double-storied and containing a large hall and several separate rooms, was probably the living accommodation for the community and visitors and pilgrims to the shrine. Both visitors and the monastic community were segregated by sex from each other, even if, like Paulinus and Theresiana, they were married.[118] Community life was centred on daily prayer and worship with psalms, held in the evening before the sole meal of the day. The food consisted of bread, pulses and vegetables: no meat, though wine was drunk in moderate quantities.[119] Paulinus's asceticism was defined in part by a rueful acknowledgement of what he had given up. He describes a foul-smelling stew cooked by the monk Victor of boiled millet and beans, which he said helped remind him of the need for humility.[120]

As some contemporaries pointed out to him, this was not a particularly hard regime. Apparently no manual labour was required of the monks and nuns, which suggests that labour and maintenance was imported – and, presumably, paid for. Paulinus may have sold most of his properties, but he clearly retained enough capital to be able to build, and the community must have lived off some income. Perhaps we should compare the monastery at Nola not so much with a Pachomian monastery in Egypt, or Martin's community at Tours, as with the life Paulinus had renounced. Ambrose, at any rate, would have recognised what went on at Nola as monasticism. The lack of any firm consensus about monasticism is evident from Paulinus's correspondence with Sulpicius Severus. When a courier from Sulpicius showed up at Nola claiming also to be a monk, Paulinus wrote to Sulpicius complaining that he certainly did not look like one, with his military cloak and sandals and his ruddy, weather-beaten face. A monk should look like a monk, wearing distinctive if generic poor clothing, with dishevelled and unbarbered hair.[121]

The idea that a monk should be recognisable from his clothing and demeanour as someone who led a particular kind of life probably indicates that there was some concern about people who claimed to be monks but could not sustain such claims. Jerome was scathing about 'false' monks (whom he called *remnuoth*), who lived in groups of two or three and supported themselves by craftwork which they sold at the highest price. Such people affected poor clothing and went about barefoot; they fasted publicly, but stuffed themselves on feast days; they visited virgins, and defamed the clergy.[122] Jerome seems to have been responding in part to a particular situation that had arisen in Rome in the 380s. But there were also challenges to monastic ideals such as fasting and chastity, for example from the former monk Jovinian, in the late fourth century. It was against this background that the notion of an approved form of monasticism developed, which as we have seen came to be represented in the West, through the works of Rufinus and Cassian, by the Egyptian desert.

Challenges and doubts also doubtless gave rise to the composition of monastic Rules. During the fifth century a number of Rules for monastic communities in the West were written for specific circumstances or foundations. A group known as the *Rules of the Fathers*, comprising five separate but similar texts, shows the continuing influence of some of the ideas of eastern monasticism – evident for example in the *Rule of Macarius*, or in the *Rule of the Four Fathers*, all of whom are identified as Egyptian monks of the Nile Delta. In fact there is very little Egyptian about these Rules. Rather, they show a superficial legacy of Cassian's project of 'Egyptianising' monasticism in Gaul. In so far as there is a particular theme to this collection, it is the hierarchy that is supposed to operate within a monastic community: all stress the importance of the role of *praepositus*, or superior, of the community. As Marilyn Dunn has remarked, the more weight is given to the role of the superior, the more is at stake in ensuring that the men chosen had the right ability and character.[123] From these Rules, it appears that fifth-century Gaulish monks followed a routine that would become familiar from the *Rule of Benedict* to medieval monks: liturgical offices characterised by psalmody and ritual prayer, reading and meditation, communal meals and, sometimes, manual labour, though this remains rather unspecified. Alongside these kinds of communities, in the fifth century a type of monastery with quite a different point of origin emerged. We have already seen the close link between monks and holy places or shrines that was distinctive in the monasteries of the Holy Land. In a similar way, some monastic communities in Italy and Gaul grew up around the shrines of martyrs. This seems to have been initially a Gaulish practice beginning at Tours, Paris and Agaune in Burgundy, but a monastery was also in place at the tomb of St Peter in Rome by 461. The purpose of these monasteries was liturgical, and the monks did not invariably live a strict communal life. Liturgical observances replaced manual labour, and these communities were dedicated to memorialising the virtuous dead so that their protection could be invoked for protection of the living. Such monasteries were supported by the income accruing to the shrine from alms, or from the diocese. They were institutional expressions of a bishop's spiritual power base, but also of a city or region's devotion to and identification with the memory of a given saint. In this respect they prefigured one of the main characteristics of the monastery typical of the western Middle Ages.

The emergence of the shrine-centred or 'basilical' monastery is probably connected to a further development mentioned briefly already: the Council of Chalcedon's ruling in 451 that monasteries should be under the ultimate authority of the diocesan bishop, and further that his permission was needed before any new monastery could be founded. While this did not in itself mean that only bishops might establish monasteries, it surely made it more difficult for monasteries to be created simply as the pious expression of an individual charismatic figure. By the later fifth century some bishops in Italy and Gaul were taking the initiative in founding monastic communities. An early proponent – perhaps, indeed, the first founder of a monastery in the West – was Bishop Eusebius of Vercelli (344–71). While in exile (355–63) Eusebius had spent some time in the Thebaid monasteries of Egypt, and on his return to his diocese he encouraged his urban clergy to live according to monastic principles. Ambrose, bishop of Milan (374–97), recommended that one of Eusebius's successors adopt an ascetic life when, in 396, he intervened in a dispute at Vercelli over the virtues of fasting and chastity.[124] And, as we have seen, Augustine developed his notion of monastic life for his clergy after becoming bishop of Hippo.

Given the emergence of 'episcopal monasticism', it is worth considering what kinds of men became bishop in the western Empire. Martin, a former soldier, stood out among bishops as having come from a humble background. Paulinus and Ambrose, both from aristocratic backgrounds, were more typical of the bishop of the later Roman Empire in the West. They were from the class of 'natural leaders', well educated and well networked in the society from which civic and military leadership came. They were chosen as bishops precisely because they brought with them knowledge of the levers of power and patronage, and the connections to make things work. Even – or especially – after the collapse of imperial government in the fifth century, the administration of both towns and their dependent regions continued to lie in the hands of aristocracy and bishop, working with a town council and magistrates who were responsible for tax collection, law and provision of public services. The wealth of aristocratic bishops was indispensable in restoring the fabric of towns, founding or renovating churches, shrines and monasteries. Bishops such as Hilarius in the deeply Romanised provinces of southern Gaul built up a Christian landscape as in a previous generation the rich villa aristocracy might have built an amphitheatre or circus for their town. Monastery and basilica were the 'Christian idiom of patronage'.[125]

The dynamics of episcopal monasticism are illustrated clearly in the career of Caesarius of Arles. Born into an aristocratic family at Chalons in *c.* 468, Caesarius joined the monastic community at Lérins in the 480s. This monastery had been founded on a small island 4 kilometres from the coast of southeastern France in the first decade of the century. When John Cassian was writing in the 420s it was already a sizeable community, and during the course of the century it became the preferred monastery of the Gallic aristocracy, developing a reputation as a centre of monastic spirituality. By the time Caesarius joined, the monks were probably following the *Rule of Macarius*, one of the group of the so-called *Rules of the Fathers*.[126] Around a core of what might be called 'Cassianic' monastic principles derived from his reconstruction of Egyptian Delta practices, this way of life added an Augustinian element of communal charity and renunciation based on Gospel ideals of service. Monks were housed in individual cells under a common roof; or, if they preferred, in cells dotted around the island. They followed a daily routine of communal worship, beginning at dawn, interspersed with private study and reading and manual labour, which was probably of a light housekeeping nature in the main, and took their single daily meal together in the afternoon.

Caesarius was obviously highly enough regarded to be appointed as the community's cellarer, but he became unpopular with some of the other monks for, apparently, withholding supplies of food from them. Reading between the lines, we might see here an idealistic young monk observing too high a standard, and using his position to enforce his own ideals of austerity on the community.[127] After being dismissed from this position, Caesarius, probably thinking he had nothing to lose, undertook a personal regime of fasting, eating only on Sundays and cutting bread out of his diet altogether. In doing so he was, as William Klingshirn has remarked, breaking Cassian's own dictum that fasting should be carried out in pursuit of perfect charity rather than for its own sake.[128] Not surprisingly he was unable to sustain this regime for long before his health broke down, and, probably between 495 and 499, he was sent to recover at Arles, an old Roman town that had good medical facilities. Caesarius happened to be related to the bishop and, young as he was, it can hardly have been a surprise when he succeeded him as bishop of Arles in 502. As bishop, Caesarius tried to adhere to the ideals promulgated over a century earlier by Eusebius and Ambrose, that bishops should themselves lead ascetic lives in common with their clergy. In Caesarius's case, this may have been a form of personal compensation for his failure as a monk at Lérins. Caesarius brought the clergy attached to the cathedral at Arles into his official residence to live in a community that excluded women, that ate in common and observed the night office together.[129]

Caesarius's most important contribution to the development of monasticism, however, was his foundation for women at Arles. In 508 he established a convent to be directed by his sister Caesaria; this was destroyed during the siege of Arles but rebuilt in 512. The 'Rule for virgins' that he composed for the convent is the first Rule written specifically for women. Not surprisingly, given Caesarius's own monastic heritage, the influence of Cassian's *Institutes* and the *Rule of the Four Fathers* is clear, but Caesarius also shows familiarity with Augustine's precepts for clergy.[130] To a modern reader, the most distinctive – and probably the most troubling – feature of the Rule is the insistence on the strict enclosure of the nuns, who were prohibited from leaving the convent on any account. Only after death, when their bodies were laid to rest in stone sarcophagi in the basilica, did they leave the confines of their enclosure. Moreover, everything was done to keep men away from the community: only the clergy who came to celebrate the eucharist, the steward, who was a man, and slaves brought in under supervision to maintain the fabric of the buildings were allowed entry.[131] In regulating so strictly in this regard, Caesarius was treating the convent as a substitute for the Roman family. The convent had to provide the kind of protection that unmarried women could otherwise have expected from their families. In this sense, Caesarius was, perhaps necessarily, taking a pessimistic view of the prevalence of male aggression in his society. He was particularly concerned about loss of reputation (*fama*), and the consequences for women of their own victimhood at the hands of predatory men.[132]

Caesarius's convent was a hierarchically run community. Obedience was demanded of the abbess and her deputy, the prioress. All nuns save the abbess and prioress were required to take turns in the daily work of the community, which included cooking the daily meal eaten in common, but also handicraft such as weaving. The pattern of life was determined by the daily offices in church, but the nuns were also expected to engage in spiritual reading. They slept in a dormitory rather than in the individual cells that were usual in male Rules at this date. Following

Augustine, Caesarius insisted that everything the nuns might need was to be distributed to them centrally, on the basis of their individual need.

This was a firmly episcopal foundation. In order to provide an income for the community, Caesarius not only sold off some diocesan property – an action for which he later had to defend himself – but acted in much the same way as a modern fundraiser, by soliciting an endowment and donations and the wealthy laity.[133] The practical implications and costs of establishing a monastic community determined to a large extent how that community matched the definitions and ideals espoused by monastic writers and thinkers. Many of the monastic experiments about which we know were made by wealthy people who put money or property at the disposal of the foundation. This was true for example of Basil in Cappadocia, of Melania in Jerusalem, Paulinus of Nola, and the foundation at Vivarium in southern Italy made by Cassiodorus in the 550s. Cassiodorus, a Christian aristocrat and public servant, was forced to retire from high office during the political crisis resulting from Emperor Justinian's invasion of Ostrogothic Italy. Vivarium, self-consciously a place of scholarship as well as a monastery, contained his library and a scriptorium for copying texts. Cassiodorus established a programme of reading and study rather than a Rule, but he expected the monks to live in community. The emphasis lay on the preservation of a Christian literary and spiritual heritage rather than in pursuit of asceticism for its own sake, but Cassiodorus conceived of his foundation in the same way as Basil or Paulinus. None of these would have been possible without substantial private means. The only viable alternatives were the kind of community that depended on manual labour to provide food, as we have seen in the Pachomian *koinonia* in Egypt, or hermitages where monks could grow their own produce and supplement this with seasonal 'grazing'. Even a community that attempted to be self-sufficient, such as Sabas's Great Lavra, needed bailing out from time to time with timely gifts of food from the city.[134] And an anchorite of the type of Symeon the Stylite expected to be supported by neighbouring villages. In essence, he was anticipating on a small and informal scale the kind of arrangement put in place by Caesarius, whereby material support of ascetics was expected as a regular obligation of the laity. Women were less able than men to support themselves wholly through manual labour, partly because most women's convents were founded in or near urban areas, and this meant that they were always more likely to have to follow the kind of monastic life that entailed economic dependence.

By the middle of the sixth century, monasticism had reached far beyond the Mediterranean lands of its origins. Evidence of monastic life is known from some Roman villas in Britain. Lullingstone (Kent) and Llandough (south Wales) may have been similar in type to Vivarium, though certainly much less fully equipped with books. But there were also monasteries that more closely corresponded to ascetic norms. Illtud, perhaps a Briton of Roman descent, founded a monastery in Glamorgan that had a school and was capable of attracting the powerful in society. One of those educated at Illtud's monastery in the last years of the fifth century, Samson, was a local aristocrat who would go on to found a monastery in Cornwall. In the early decades of the sixth century a number of ascetic communities burgeoned in Celtic-speaking areas of England and Gaul. It is difficult to know how much if anything such figures knew about the origins and history of monasticism in the East, but given that material objects from the eastern Mediterranean were present in the British Isles, codices containing texts such as the *Life of Anthony* may have penetrated as far as this.

Monasticism may have reached Ireland, where it was to flourish and develop in particularly fruitful ways, in the fifth century. This may be the earliest reach of monasticism beyond the borders of the Empire. Palladius, a deacon from Auxerre, was sent to Ireland in 431 to minister to Irish believers, and it is possible that he established monastic practices there. At some point in the fifth century, Patrick, a young man of noble British stock, was kidnapped and taken to the north of Ireland as a slave. Having escaped, he returned later to evangelise the Irish, and has the reputation of having established monastic life as part of his mission of conversion. We have already seen traces of this link between evangelism and the spread of monasticism at other frontier regions of the Empire, for example in the example of Symeon the Mountaineer. In the case of Patrick it is difficult to know what the 'monks' he refers to in his *Confessio* might have been, or how they might have lived.[135] There is no real evidence for anything like organised monasticism resulting from Patrick's mission, nor indeed in his writings. This is not to say that he was not infused with a sense of spiritual progression learned from reading of monastic history, but that must remain speculative. By the end of the sixth century some of the writing of Jerome and Cassian was certainly being read in Ireland. Clearer evidence is provided by the founding of monasteries in west and central Ireland in the 540s–50s, Clonmacnoise by Ciarán and Clonfert by Brendan. In the north, Comgall founded a monastery at Bangor that became what Theodoret would have called the 'training ground' of Columbanus, one of the most important figures in monasticism in the generations after Benedict. We will consider in due course the unique contribution of Columbanus to monasticism, but we may note for the present the strong contemplative strand that seems to have been a feature of Irish monasticism from the start. It is striking how practices such as periods of individual withdrawal in Irish and later northern English monasticism – to small islands, to huts, to seashores – echo very similar practices in monasticism on the eastern edges of the Empire at the same time. Cyril of Scythopolis, the witness to *lavra* monasticism, was after all a contemporary of Ciarán and Brendan.

Monasticism had, by the end of the sixth century, become an indispensable feature of Christian society. Protean and permeable from the start, monasticism now encompassed a bewildering variety of forms of religious life. The nature of a geographical survey such as this, following as it does a set chronology, is that it is easy to forget that things still continue to happen in places that the narrative has left behind. It is Egypt that provides us with the first evidence for the kinds of monastic life that by *c.* 600 we can see everywhere in the former Roman Empire. But because we know so much about very specific forms of monasticism in Egypt, it is also tempting to characterise Egyptian monasticism as being of that particular kind – the monasticism of the *Apophthegmata Patrum* and the writings of John Cassian – just as we characterise Palestinian monasticism as being exclusively that of the *lavra*, or Gaulish and Italian as being dominated by aristocratic landowners in retirement on their estates. In fact, all kinds of monks – and to a lesser degree, nuns – could be found in almost all places where monasticism was practised.

For this reason it is perhaps salutary to end this chapter by considering briefly a little-known monastery founded in Egypt in the late sixth or early seventh century. The monastery of Phoibammon the Martyr was established by Abraham, bishop of Hermonthis (*c.* 540s–610/20), in an abandoned temple in the region of Thebes. Abraham was a Coptic rather than a Greek speaker, so the community may have reflected traditions deriving from Shenoute's White Monastery; but in fact we know nothing about how the monastery was run, how many monks lived there, whether they followed an existing model of monastic living or a regime devised by Abraham himself. More or less everything we know comes from a single surviving document, the 'Testament', in which he lays out not how he wants the monastery to be run, but rather how he wants the monastery to be left after his death.[136] The monastery of Phoibammon was Abraham's property, and in the 'Testament' he specified that it should pass to his chosen successor, Victor, who in turn passed it on to his successor. The only stipulation made by Abraham as to its disposition was that the property 'down to a cinder' should be kept out of the hands of his own family. Victor had the right to 'possess, take care of, manage and improve the property, to dwell in it, build on it, enjoy [the revenues], rent it out, sell it, cede it, alienate it, give it as donation, grant it as a charitable gift or grant, and do everything concerning it as full owner without hindrance, and spend the revenues on the management of the aforementioned holy place and providing for the poor who come over'.[137] Beyond the wish that the revenues of the property should in some way be used to maintain it as a holy place, and that alms should be given, no restrictions were put on Victor's management of the property.

Such a conception of a monastery makes us confront the hard realities of institutional religious life. A single hermit, even a small group of monks, might be able to sustain life in deserted territory where they were not in anyone's way, or where nobody else had a claim to the cave, cell or ruin they were using. The monastic literature of the period – much of it hagiographical in tone – often deals with questions of a founding figure's succession and legacy, but this is usually couched in spiritual or pastoral terms. The 'deathbed speech' is a trope of such literature, but it rarely deals with the monastery as an institution that comprises buildings and moveable property. Since the mid-fifth century monasteries had been, at least in canon law, placed under the control of the bishop of the diocese where they had been founded. This was reinforced in the sixth century by Emperor Justinian's law that all religious foundations should be under ecclesiastical control.[138] Bishops were often property owners in their own right, or came from property-owning families, and the ownership of land and buildings was already in the fourth century one of the methods by which churchmen were able to grasp the levers of power.[139] Founding a monastery entailed forethought about how the monks or nuns were to be maintained – on a subsistence basis through their own labour on previously uncultivated land? Or from the labour of paid agricultural workers – in which case a surplus income beyond the food needed by the community was also required? Or from a donation of land that could be rented out to guarantee an income stream? Rich bishops who wanted to found a monastery could afford to alienate property for this purpose. But it was not only bishops who saw merit in founding a monastery, and lay founders – from the landed classes such as Paulinus of Nola to Frankish kings – might have their own ideas about how, and for whom, their foundations should be run. As the external pressures on the Empire began to tell, and central control became more difficult to impose; and as monasticism spread beyond the imperial remit to places that had never known bishops or Roman laws, local solutions to these questions had to be found. The following chapter will consider how monasticism developed in the early medieval worlds that emerged from the Roman Empire.

CHAPTER TWO

A School for God's Service
Early Medieval Monasticism in the West

We are founding a school for the service of God.

Prologue to the Rule of Benedict

A LITTLE MORE THAN a hundred years after Symeon the Stylite had sought the help of local villagers to enclose him in a stone hut on the first stage of his journey to perfection, a scene that he would have understood was being enacted on a remote island in the North Sea off the coast of Northumberland. Cuthbert, a northern English monk originally from Tynemouth, was building himself a stone hut with the help of some of his monks on the island of Farne. Cuthbert was prior of Lindisfarne, a community on the Northumbrian coast founded in 633 by Aidan, a monk at the Irish foundation of Iona, but in 676 he secured permission to live as a hermit on this uninhabited island a few miles south of the abbey. The island, like Anthony's fortress in the desert, was inhabited by demons, whom Cuthbert was able to disperse. Also like Anthony, Cuthbert had first withdrawn to a secluded place in the outer precinct of the monastery, in order to 'win victory over the invisible enemy by solitary prayer and fasting' – in other words, to learn gradually how to be a hermit. As Cuthbert's biographer, the Northumbrian monk Bede (673–735), explained, 'after a long and spotless life', he moved to 'the stillness of divine contemplation'.[1] On Farne, he built 'a city': an almost circular structure with high walls of rough stone and peat, initially windowless so that he could only see the sky over his head; an oratory; and a guest house for visitors. According to Bede, he found a life of solitude easier than monastic life: 'In that life everything is subject to the abbot: the times of prayer, fasting, vigils and work are governed by his will.' In an echo of Theodoret's account of Syrian monks, he described Cuthbert as 'Christ's athlete'.

Anyone who comes to Bede's biography with some knowledge of previous monastic history will immediately see in the religious world of northern England both striking parallels with and important departures from the deserts of the eastern Mediterranean and the 'country house monasticism' of the late Roman Empire. Bede was writing with a knowledge and appreciation of different traditions of monasticism. In writing about Cuthbert's solitude, he references both Benedict and Anthony. The construction of the guest house indicates that, like Symeon Stylite, he expected to be visited by others, though in his case mostly monks from his community at Lindisfarne. An heir to 'Roman' ecclesiastical traditions, Bede was also deeply invested in the Irish influence of the northern English monastic landscape of the seventh century. His writings exemplify the tensions between parallel, and sometimes competing, strands of religious life on the northern frontier of the former Roman world. Bede was born more than a hundred years after the *Rule of Benedict*, which was to be seen by later centuries as the foundational document of medieval monasticism in the West. Yet, although as a monk at Wearmouth and Jarrow he lived according to the Rule, which had been introduced into Northumbria about ten years before he was born by Wilfrid, he also idealised Cuthbert's Lindisfarne, which followed a different tradition. Bede thus encapsulates the complex overlapping varieties of monastic life that characterise the early Middle Ages. Before we consider some of these, we need first to consider the contribution made by Benedict and his Rule to the development of monasticism.

THE *RULE OF BENEDICT*

Benedict of Nursia is all but unknown as a historical figure, since other than his *Rule* itself most of our information about him comes from the semi-legendary *Dialogues* of Gregory the Great. According to this tradition, Benedict was born in *c.* 480 and educated in Rome, but abandoned his studies in liberal arts in order to become a solitary. He lived for some years in a cave at Subiaco, and had already developed a reputation as a hermit living in solitude in the caves of Campania, when he was approached by a group of monks who asked him to lead their community. Benedict's gruff warning that the monks would not like the experience went unheeded; he duly imposed a discipline they could not sustain, and only escaped being murdered when a miracle shattered the jar of poisoned wine they had prepared for him.[2]

The story is revealing in a number of ways, even if we regard it as a literary creation. In showing Benedict as an experienced elder to whom other monks gravitate for advice, Gregory inserts Benedict into the established tradition, familiar to readers of Cassian, the *History of the Monks of Egypt* and the *Apophthegmata Patrum*, of the anchorite who has perfected himself through solitude and ascesis. But there is no sense of a progression between monastic states. Benedict had not reached the state of perfection through first having been a cenobitic monk, in the same way that Sabas, in the *Lives of the Monks of Palestine*, was sent to Euthymios to the monastery of Theoktistos before being permitted to join the *lavra*. Yet at the same time there is an acknowledgement of the need for guidance from an experienced elder, and a nod therefore to the central theme of the master–disciple relationship that we have seen in previous monastic landscapes. We should also note the implication in the story – already seen in Cassian and further repeated in Benedict's Rule – that groups of unregulated monks were prone to lose their direction.

Central to the conception of monastic life in the *Dialogues* is the apparent autonomy of the solitary monk. Marilyn Dunn has drawn attention to the anomaly that Benedict – along with other figures in the *Dialogues* – is shown not only as a hermit but also as a preacher.[3] This is curious given that most of Italy had already been evangelised by this date, and that other monks who engaged in such activities were mostly on the frontiers of the Empire. But it helps us to place the Benedict that Gregory wished to portray within a context of dislocation and social and economic stagnation. By the time that Benedict composed the Rule, perhaps in the years 546–50, there were monastic communities of many types, as well as individual monks, throughout Italy. Probably many were in towns, since Italy was more urbanised than other parts of the western Empire. Some, notably in Rome, were of the basilical type, but a variety of Rules and traditions was known. Italy was undergoing the effects of long-lasting war from Emperor Justinian's attempt to reconquer the peninsula from the Goths and to restore the former extent of the Empire. The archaeological evidence shows that during the sixth century urban populations declined, and that the wars brought or exacerbated food shortages, serious outbreaks of disease and collapsing long-distance trade.[4] Armed forces were a dangerous and debilitating presence in Campania, where Benedict founded his monastery of Monte Cassino. It has been suggested that one factor behind the Rule was the danger posed to groups of monks living loosely in the countryside by the presence of rampaging soldiers.[5] An apparent decline in standards in the quality of life is not, of course, a necessary condition for monasticism. But it helps to explain the particular quality of the Rule that Benedict composed, in which the *sonderwelt* is more fully realised and plainly articulated than in any previous writing about how a monastic community might actually function.[6]

The Rule that would become one of the standard guides to monastic living for much of western Christendom is quite short.[7] At a little over thirteen thousand words divided into seventy-three chapters, it can be read comfortably in a couple of hours. The brevity and conciseness of expression is part of the genius of the work, for of course the words on the page are a gateway into an experience of living. It is all the more remarkable that within this brief document Benedict offers both spiritual guidance and specific instructions for the daily arrangement of living. One of the hallmarks of the text is its fluidity, and the way it shifts from specific detail to spiritual guidance of a more abstract kind. The Rule is structured carefully. After a prologue outlining what the monastic life means, and how the different kinds of monks are to be defined, Benedict discourses on the role of the abbot and the means by which the abbot is to govern and receive advice. There follows a chapter listing good works as the instruments of the spiritual craft, one on the virtue of moderation of speech, and then a discussion of the importance of humility. This comprises the first section of the Rule. In Chapters 8 to 19 Benedict switches to practical instruction on the celebration of the divine office in the monastery, the *opus Dei* ('work of God'), according to the seasons of the year. There is a chapter on silent prayer, then a series of regulations of aspects of daily life: the office of dean, the communal dormitory, discipline and punishments for breaches, other officials in the community, a prohibition on private property, regulation of the kitchen and care for the infirm, conduct of meals and quantities and types of food and drink, and minor infringements of the Rule. Benedict then explains the provision for manual labour, hospitality, communication with the outside world and the kind of clothing to be worn in the monastery. There are regulations for how the community is to admit new members, visitors and the working of the novitiate. Benedict then turns his attention to the election of the abbot and appointment of other officials. Finally there is a short series of exhortations on the functioning of the community through charity, and an epilogue in which Benedict acknowledges that the Rule he has provided is merely a starting point, and recommends supplementing its advice with Cassian's *Conferences* and *Institutes*, the *Rule of Basil* and the Lives of saints.

Benedict's entire conception of the monastic life is conveyed in the Prologue. The Rule is a means to salvation, because only in the kind of community outlined therein can the Gospel truly be followed. But by its very nature it is a 'school for God's service'. This is a crucial feature of Benedict's attitude not only to regulation but also to monastic life. For him, monasticism is a constant process rather than a completed fact. The monastery is an evolving organism because it consists of individuals who are growing in spirituality as they progress in the pursuit of God. Moreover, the pace and rate of growth is unequal, partly because monks and nuns die and are replaced by new recruits but also because human lives are susceptible to change, doubt and inconsistency. Monasticism, moreover, is a craft that must be learned through practice. As in any school, learners require instruction from those more experienced.[8] But the learning can only be absorbed fully if the principle of obedience is accepted. The relationship between the abbot and the community reproduces that between a father and his family, or between God and humanity. Obedience, however, is to be given not only to the abbot as a human, but also to the Rule and the principles of community that it articulates. Benedict's chapters on humility underscore this most effectively.

Humility does not mean self-abasement, but acceptance that the community is more important than the individual. Monks and nuns must allow themselves to be absorbed into this social organism even at the expense of their individuality. Everything turns on this logic, and Benedict underlines it in different ways throughout the Rule. It is implicit in the daily routine of the liturgy, in the regulation of common eating and sleeping, but also in – to take just two examples – the instruction that monks are not to receive private letters or gifts from outside the community without the abbot's permission, or that one monk should not defend another, even if they are related to each other.[9] At first sight this last provision seems to strike a false note in the context of the 'charity of brotherhood' alluded to in the penultimate chapter.[10] Yet in fact it is crucial in establishing the point that the monk, in entering the monastery, becomes a member of a new family in which there should be total equality. Preferences among monks within the community are dangerous, not only because they can lead to sexual scandal, but also because the formation of friendship groups undermines the balance of the relationship of the community to itself and to God as a whole. Instead, monks or nuns should see themselves as parts of a bigger whole, contributing to the generation of a communal energy.[11]

In practical terms, the underlying principles of the Rule were intended to result in a community that was a self-contained and self-supporting unit (Chapter 66).[12] This meant that it needed to be located in a place where agriculture was possible to the extent of feeding the community from the work of their hands, and providing all other resources for maintaining the material fabric of the monastery. Taken to a logical extreme, this would include livestock whose skins could provide leather, wool and even parchment for making the office books necessary for the liturgy – though in fact the full extent of self-sufficiency was never achieved universally by monasteries following the Rule. The day was ordered, as in previous Rules which Benedict must certainly have known, in order to strike a balance between liturgical offices, which probably took up an average of four hours per day, private meditative reading (another four hours) and work of some kind that might be manual or intellectual, perhaps taking up six hours. The remainder of any given twenty-four-hour period would include time for rest, sleep and eating. As the twentieth-century Benedictine Thomas Merton observed, time does not hang heavy on the hands of monks, because simply observing the Rule keeps them busy.[13]

One of the most famous passages in the Rule is the first chapter, 'On the different kinds of monks'. As we have already seen, opinions had already been voiced on this theme for a century and a half by the time Benedict articulated his definition. Like Cassian, Benedict distinguished between cenobites (monks living in a regulated community), anchorites living in solitude, and 'sarabaites', who lived in small groups but without any obedience or master–disciple relationship. These latter were, in Benedict's eyes, the worst kind of monk, 'untested, as gold is by fire, but soft as lead'.[14] So far, so Cassianic. But Benedict added a final category of monk, for which he coined the term 'gyrovague'. This word is untranslatable from Latin, but it connotes a person who literally wanders around from place to place in a kind of perpetual spin. Benedict was trying to evoke the image of aimlessness and lack of purpose, but the defining feature of the gyrovague was his instability. 'All their lives they wander in different countries staying in various monasteries . . . [T]hey are restless, servants to the seduction of their own will and appetites . . .' So distasteful is this type of monk to Benedict that in fact he declines to say anything further about them.[15] For Benedict, the critical point about monasticism was that it was not a way of life that could be taken up and set aside at will, nor lived without commitment to stability of place. Once a monk or nun had been received into the community and taken full vows, they were expected to remain there until death. The monastery was 'real life', the outside world a shadow world that, in theory, scarcely impinged on the reality of the ascent to God through regulated observance.

In rejecting the validity of 'sarabaites' and 'gyrovagues' and basing his definition of monasticism on the regulated community, Benedict was implicitly shifting the ground away from much of the way in which monasticism had developed since the late third century. Gone from his picture of acceptable monasticism were the *lavra* monks of Palestine who left the community to wander around the Dead Sea during Lent, foundational figures of Syrian monasticism such as James of Nisibis and Symeon the Stylite, and the urban monks and nuns of Lycopolis and other towns.

But it was also too narrow a picture to accommodate many western precedents such as Paulinus's at Nola, which provided for chaste married couples in the same community, or even Augustine's clerical community visiting the baths as part of their regime. This does not mean, of course, that central elements of such precedents were not absorbed by Benedict; naturally, much of his Rule is recognisable from previous practice. But Benedict could only work from what he knew, and how much he knew about eastern practices outside Cassian's, Jerome's and Rufinus's mediations of Egyptian monasticism is obscure.

Benedictine monks looking back from the vantage point of the twelfth and thirteenth centuries to the history of monastic life tended to see an unbroken chain of succession from Benedict to their own day. As the twelfth-century Norman monk Orderic Vitalis told the story, Benedict sent one of his monks, Maurus, to Gaul with a copy of the Rule, where with the help of the Merovingian king Theudebert (d. 547), he built a monastery at Glanfeuil and recruited 140 monks. Orderic was relying on a tradition that dates back to the ninth century and was recorded in the *Life of St Maur*, but which presented a misleading and simplified picture of the progress of Benedictine monasticism in the West.[16] Because, as far as he knew, Benedict's Rule was the standard tool for governing monasticism in the medieval West, it made sense for Orderic to assume that from the mid-sixth century most monasteries must have used it. But this is far from being the case. As we have seen, a variety of monastic experiences was being lived out across the Christian world, and continued to be well after the Rule had been adopted in parts of Italy. In fact we know very little about how the Rule came to a wider audience than the community that Benedict himself founded at Monte Cassino. According to an early tradition, Monte Cassino monks fleeing a subsequent wave of invasion in the 570s came to Rome and joined the monastery at the Lateran, thus bringing knowledge of the Rule to the attention of Pope Gregory the Great (r. 590–604). This is a neat genealogy, but it is now known that there is no evidence for knowledge of the *Rule of Benedict* in Roman monasteries as late as the seventh century.[17] Moreover, doubt has been cast on whether Gregory was even the author of the text known as his *Dialogues*, and thus whether he even knew of Benedict himself.[18] In fact, Gregory's understanding of the monastic ideal as articulated in some of his Homilies, with a focus of rigorous asceticism, seems to indicate a genealogy that owes more to the Desert Fathers.[19] Marilyn Dunn has argued that the route by which the *Rule of Benedict* came to be known more widely was via the anonymous *Rule of the Master*, a much longer and more rigorous text also written in the sixth century.[20] Most scholars see the relationship as being the other way around, and the *Rule of the Master* as predating Benedict's Rule, but this leaves unanswered the question of how Benedict's Rule was known. It was certainly known and used by Frankish monasteries in the seventh century, and the route of transmission may well have been Bobbio, a monastery in northeastern Italy founded by the Irish monk Columbanus.

The contempt with which Benedict dismissed forms of monasticism other than that practised by anchorites or enclosed monks and nuns provides a clue in itself as to the state of the religious life in a world that was enduring transformation. This is not the place to debate the question of when the Roman Empire became something more recognisably 'medieval', let alone whether 'decline' is an apt word for what seems to have happened in the fifth and sixth centuries. Two important points can be made, however. First, whether or not it is appropriate to think of this process in terms that might engender moral judgements about a society, we can say definitively that the material fabric of life in much of the Roman Empire changed – put simply, a world of marble and brick turned into one of wood.[21] The second point, however, is that this change did not happen everywhere at the same pace. In the parts of the Roman world where the deepest roots had sunk into the rocky Mediterranean soil – Italy, Spain and southern France – roads and buildings remained usable for centuries after the Empire had disappeared in political terms. In the eastern half of the Empire, which had always been more urban than the west, the Roman infrastructure never disappeared. Medieval crusaders marched into Asia Minor along a Roman road, and western visitors were amazed at the sheer size and extent of buildings in Constantinople, Antioch and other cities.[22] Variation in standards and quality of material life is important when we are thinking about why different forms of monasticism took hold in different regions. Conformity with a particular monastic tradition or ideology was only possible if those drawn to the monastic life were aware of a range of ways of 'being monastic'. And such awareness could only be possible in a world of assured communication. Jerome, Augustine, Evagrius, Cassian, Paulinus of Nola lived in such a world; Benedict and his contemporaries much less so. Many 'sarabaites' and 'gyrovagues' were probably unaware that there was any question mark against the integrity of their practices. The enduring force of monasticism has always been its capacity to reformulate and reshape practices designed to achieve ideals that are commonly understood.

MONASTICISM IN THE FRANKISH LANDS AFTER BENEDICT

By *c.* 600 there were probably about 220 monasteries and convents in formerly Roman Gaul; more than double that number a century later. Since the late fifth century Gaul had been settled by groups of Germanic peoples who took over the levers of power and funded their political control of institutions through tribute and taxation. The Franks turned out to be the most militarily powerful of these peoples, and in 509 their king, Clovis, was baptised. Partly because, unlike other Germanic peoples such as the Goths in Italy, the Franks adopted the most orthodox form of Christian teaching, Clovis and his successors were able to form close political alliances with the bishops, many of whom were in the sixth century still representatives of the former Roman landowning elites.

One of the 220 religious houses was the convent of Holy Cross founded in Poitiers by Radegund (*c.* 520–587), a Germanic princess married to the Frankish prince Clothar I, who had abandoned her marriage after bearing children and dedicated herself to a life of ascetic virginity. Three years after Radegund's death, forty nuns, led by Clothild and Basina, left the convent in a rebellion against the abbess. The episode became a cause célèbre in which the bishop and the king were involved, because both of the ringleaders were members of the Frankish royal house: Clothild was the daughter of King Charibert (r. 561–7), and Basina was (or claimed to be) the daughter of King Chilperic (r. 561–84). The rebel princesses gathered a group of followers who threatened the convent and caused damage to its property. They then brought accusations of misconduct against the abbess, and refused to return. The royal princesses seem to have been tapping into a seam of discontent in the community, though probably for more than one reason. A nun who had adopted the life of a recluse in her cell in the convent took advantage of the chaos to break down her door and escape to join Clothild. This was not the first time she had rebelled, having become a recluse some time before 587 as penance for having climbed over the wall of the convent to spread false accusations about Radegund's misconduct.[23]

The revolt at Holy Cross provides a useful – albeit atypical – snapshot into the institutional dynamics of monasticism as it developed in early medieval society. The picture, as provided by Gregory, bishop of Tours (530s–94), is scarcely objective. Gregory was devoted to the memory of Radegund, whom he regarded as truly saintly.[24] The convent of Holy Cross had been founded as a place of refuge from an unhappy marriage, but it seems to have become a useful repository in which the militarised aristocracy of Merovingian Gaul could place high-born women who either posed a political threat or who might be regarded as nuisances at court, but who had no real vocation for a monastic life. The custom of monasteries and convents being used as 'dumping grounds' for politically inconvenient royals had a long future. In 802, the English queen Eadburh fled to the Frankish court after poisoning her husband King Beorhtric of Wessex. According to the later biographer of King Alfred of Wessex, Asser, she was looking for the sanctuary of a new marriage to a Frankish royal, but Charlemagne installed her instead as abbess of 'a large convent of nuns' in order to keep her out of trouble. She was thrown out eventually – according to Asser after being caught breaking her vows of chastity – and took to a life of aimless wandering before dying in poverty in Pavia.[25] Clothild's revolt at Holy Cross turned out to be an attempt to seize control of the convent herself. Although she complained about the irregular regime of the abbess, this was somewhat undermined by her criticism of the poor quality of the food and the obligation on her to share sanitary arrangements in the convent. When Gregory tried to persuade her to return to the convent, she complained that, as a king's daughter, she was being treated as though she were the daughter of a low-born serving woman. Convents had always been filled with – and often founded by – aristocratic women, but the situation described by Gregory shows powerful families using monasteries to try to extend their power by ecclesiastical means. The advantages of monasteries to aristocratic families in accomplishing these aims are not difficult to see. Where land had been granted to a family or individual by the crown, ensuring leadership of a monastery founded on the land was a way of safeguarding the land in the family's hands. Land tended to pass out of a family's hands, either through being split after a landowner's death or as a daughter's marriage portion. But this could be obviated if a family member controlled the property. Thus, for example, the landowner Burgondofora, whose brother was a monk of Luxeuil, founded a monastery on patrimonial land, thus turning monasticism into a family concern, and in principle retaining control over estates down the generations. In theory, this should not have been possible because since the fifth century bishops were supposed to have oversight of monasteries, down to the use of their property and the Rule they followed. In practice, however, the case of Holy Cross shows how fragile this situation was, especially where a bishop's authority was weak or where he had little interest in monastic life.

Because early medieval western Europe was primarily an agricultural society, land was the currency of wealth and power. Land that provided a regular income was essential to support a monastic community, whether the monks or nuns worked the land themselves or lived off rents and sale of produce. This meant that the monasticism that developed in Gaul, as also in England, Ireland, German-speaking lands and indeed most of Europe, was primarily rural and based on estate-farming not dissimilar to the economy of the Roman villa. But from the crown's point of view, dispensing land in this way was also advantageous. Early medieval kings had neither the resources nor the infrastructure to exploit all of the land under their control themselves. Much of the land was, in any case, unsuitable for agriculture without considerable investment of labour: marshes needed to be drained, forests cut down, scrub cleared. Giving it to aristocratic followers was a means of ensuring efficient clearance and agricultural use. And monasteries, especially if led by enterprising and driven men and women, could be a singularly efficient work force. Monastic leaders realised that it was important to be able to deal with those who held the levers of power, and in this way monasteries became the enablers of the aristocratic exploitation of the countryside.[26]

We should not think of monastic growth simply in instrumental ways. The spiritual prestige of monasteries, especially where founded by a charismatic leader – a Columbanus or a Radegund, for instance – was alluring. The perceived sanctity of such men and women reflected back on the families that enabled and promoted their enterprises. Monasteries also aided in the commemoration of the dead: not only their own, who were buried in their precincts, but those of supportive families. Monasteries were sometimes built around the tombs of the especially virtuous dead, especially martyrs and founders. St Denis and St Martial in Gaul, St Albans and later Bury St Edmunds in England are examples of a monastic community dedicated to the memory of a martyr.

Radegund's convent was a private foundation, but in principle such establishments required episcopal confirmation. Gregory of Tours includes in his discussion of the revolt at Holy Cross the text of the letter apparently sent by the bishops of Gaul to Radegund confirming its legitimacy in their eyes. The letter alludes to Martin of Tours as the founder of monastic life in Gaul, but also indicates that Radegund was using the *Rule of Caesarius of Arles* as the formula for living in the convent.[27] The hard discipline of this Rule, especially the stipulation on strict enclosure, may indeed have been a major factor in the dissatisfaction of some of the nuns. Clearly, by the late sixth century the *Rule of Benedict* had not yet caught on in Frankish lands.

The writings of Gregory of Tours show how important the figure of the independent solitary 'holy man' was in Gaul as well as in the eastern Roman Empire. In his *Vitae patrum*, the hermit is a crucial figure in the conversion of the rural landscape. Independent solitaries may, indeed, have been more recognisable and representative as charismatic religious figures to many people than bishops. How did one know, however, whether they were authentic holy people? The *Life of Radegund* by Venantius Fortunatus shows her, while still a queen living a holy life in the world, taking personal charge of any itinerant religious figure seeking hospitality at court so that while washing their feet and making them welcome, she could also question them about their beliefs and teachings.[28] For a bishop such as Gregory of Tours, *viri Dei* ('men of God') were to be handled with care. Fundamentally, the authenticity of a holy man was linked to his willingness to accept Gregory's authority as bishop. The importance of episcopal authority as a guarantor of authenticity is expressed effectively in the touching story of the hermit Wulfilaicus. Unusually for a solitary in Gaul, Wulfilaicus lived on a column in imitation of Symeon the Stylite. Summoned to a meeting by his bishop, he left his column and set off, only to find on his return that the bishop had arranged for it to be dismantled in his absence.[29] Clearly the bishop regarded this kind of imitative behaviour as a potential challenge to his own spiritual leadership. This is not to say that Gregory, or other religious figures, would not tolerate independent religious: on the contrary, he was quite prepared to allow even apparently disreputable figures such as the runaway monk Minogundis to live in his diocese as hermits. It is striking how different some of Gregory's requirements for permitting a hermit to live in his diocese were from what we might expect by comparison with eastern traditions or even western forerunners. The prohibition on accumulating wealth and the expectation that the hermit should stay in a fixed location are understandable. Less so perhaps are the stipulation that hermits should have no contact with other holy men and not be part of a network of hermits; that they should not follow an ascetic Rule; have no involvement with theological questions; nor make any claim to a tradition linking them to the Desert Fathers. As we shall see in a later chapter, membership of a network of monks past and present, and demonstrable master–disciple relationships among monks, were precisely the determinants of authenticity in the Byzantine tradition of solitary monasticism. But Gregory's stipulations were clearly intended to ensure that solitary monks were wholly dependent on him as bishop, without being able to claim allegiance to or direction from any alternative authority; hence the otherwise surprising prohibition on following a Rule.

A mark of the variety and fluidity of the monastic landscape in the early medieval West is the impact of a charismatic monk who fulfilled none of Gregory's ideas of how a holy man should behave. Throughout the seventh century and into the eighth, a strong impetus for monastic life in northern Gaul and Germany came from the Irish tradition brought to the Continent by Columbanus. Informed by the monastic writings of Basil, Jerome and Cassian, Columbanus developed a distinctive form of monastic life which he brought to northeastern Gaul in the 590s. He founded monasteries in ruined Roman buildings – perhaps consciously echoing eastern models, although reusing existing building material also made practical sense – first at Annegray and then, more famously, at Luxeuil. Further satellite foundations followed – a practice that had Irish roots. Columbanus was skilled both at gaining favour with the Merovingians, which shielded him to some extent from episcopal jealousy, and at exploiting the rivalries in the Merovingian royal house to his advantage. As a 'peregrinus' – a charismatic monastic leader but one with a history of restlessness – he was suspect to bishops because he could bypass their authority by moving from one diocese to another. This was particularly attractive to lay founders, who were often reluctant to see property in which they had invested pass into the control of the bishop. Columbanus developed the policy of founding monasteries on the fringes of bishops' authority and relying on aristocratic and royal patronage to counterbalance episcopal power.[30] In the late seventh and eighth centuries some such monasteries came to be at the forefront of the mission field in Germany, where there were substantial non-Christian populations. But this does not necessarily mean that Columbanan monasticism was anti-episcopal; on the contrary, the Frankish episcopacy was also formed in part by his movement, since several aristocrats who had been monks at Luxeuil later became bishops. Nor was Columbanus the only Irish 'peregrinus' to found monasteries in Gaul. Fursey, an Irish monk given to visionary experience, established a monastery in East Anglia in 633, before settling in Gaul under the patronage of Clovis II and establishing another monastery.[31]

The Irish model of charismatic monastic leadership entailed pastoral work as well as enclosure. Columbanus seems to have administered penance, probably to large crowds. He may have preached in villages and scattered rural communities, as Cuthbert, also trained in the Irish model, did when at Melrose.[32] But he also understood the monastic life as a penance in itself. Jonas of Bobbio, his biographer, describes throngs of people wanting to join him 'for the remedy of penance'. Early in the seventh century Columbanus was forced out of Gaul and settled in northern Italy, where in 614 he founded a new monastery at Bobbio. In 628 Bobbio was exempted from episcopal authority by the pope – probably the first instance of what was to become a fraught and contested privilege over the centuries. By 640 Bobbio had a series of satellite dependent houses. This was a region where a number of influences and traditions, especially from Rome and Milan, played across each other, and the establishment of Bobbio created another such centre of gravity.[33]

Columbanus's monasteries followed a Rule that he wrote for them, which followed Irish liturgical practices. The liturgy was characterised by a full night office involving the chanting of thirty-six psalms at times of the year when the nights were longest in late autumn and winter, and double that number on Saturdays and Sundays. This differed from the practice still current in the eastern Mediterranean, where only twelve psalms were sung but in four stages during the night. These kinds of differences counted when it came to the lived experiences of monks. As Columbanus observed, on a winter night the office of psalmody at sunset, midnight, cockcrow and morning were spread out over a number of hours, but on summer short nights it meant constant waking for the office, and this was more tiring than simply observing an all-night vigil. To compensate for sleepless nights, however, Columbanus's monastic Rule allowed for fewer offices over any twenty-four-hour period.

Columbanus's Rule was less concerned with the institutional structure and regulation of his monasteries than with the conduct of his monks. It is shorter than Benedict's, comprising ten chapters that are mostly directed at the monks as individuals, enjoining them to follow personal austerity, avoid vice, maintain silence and be obedient. The influence of Cassian in regard to personal perfectibility is striking. The Rule has often been characterised as uncompromising in its demand for austerity of life. 'Let [a monk] not do as he wishes; let him eat what he is bidden, keep as much as he has received, complete the sum of his work, be subject to whom he does not like.' Benedict would not have disagreed. But in other ways Columbanus seems closer to the epithetical style of the *Apophthegmata Patrum*: 'let [a monk] come weary to bed and sleep on his feet, and let him be forced to rise when his sleep is not yet finished'. Nor does his Rule show the same quality of empathy as

Benedict's Rule. Disciplinary punishments were not only harsh but imposed for apparently trivial offences: for example, fifty strokes of the whip for coming to church too slowly, or with a head covered.[34]

Some Irish practices failed to make headway in continental Europe. In 600 Columbanus had to defend his usage of reckoning Easter according to Irish custom in a letter to Pope Gregory I. The Irish practice, although probably older than that used on the Continent, was out of step, and it meant that in his monasteries the most important feast in the Christian calendar was being celebrated on a different day. This might appear a matter of administrative detail, but it mattered in a Church in which unity of belief and practice was hard won. Celebrating Easter on a different day also meant alternative dates for feasts whose dates were derived from it, such as Ascension Day and Pentecost, and that the Lenten fast covered a different range of dates. Conformity to the same monastic rules, however, was not so critical in the seventh century. Luxeuil was still following Columbanus's Rule into the 620s, even after the *Rule of Benedict* had started to spread in Gaul. In some monasteries a mixed version of the *Rules of Benedict and Columbanus* seems to have been adopted. Marilyn Dunn has argued that such a mixed Rule at Bobbio resulted in the set of regulations known as the *Rule of the Master*, though most scholars would date this to before the *Rule of Benedict*. In any case, a mixed Rule seems to have been known at Lérins by the 660s. Rules were also written, as in earlier periods, specifically for women. Recently Albrecht Diem has argued that an anonymous seventh-century Rule for nuns, the *Regula cuiusdam ad virgines*, was written by Jonas of Bobbio, and thus that it might be seen as part of a putative Columbanian family of monastic regulation.[35]

EARLY MONASTICISM IN ENGLAND

Famously, Pope Gregory the Great established the mission to convert the English to Christianity under Augustine, later first archbishop of Canterbury, in 597. Augustine was prior of the monastery of St Andrew that Gregory had founded in Rome, and although scholars now no longer assume that this followed Benedict's Rule, it is surely significant that the pope chose a monk to head this mission – as indeed he also chose monks to lead missions elsewhere in Frankish and Italian territories.[36] Geography determined the way monasticism developed in the England of the Heptarchy. Augustine established a basilical monastery at Canterbury, and in the south of England during the seventh century Roman and Frankish influences prevailed in the foundation of monasteries and convents. Most of these were probably aristocratic or royal in origin.

Roman and continental influence was further strengthened by the appointment of Theodore of Tarsus, who brought with him scholars from the centre of the Christian world such as Hadrian Africanus. One of the most prominent English monks of the seventh century, Aldhelm, studied with Hadrian at the school he and Theodore established in Canterbury, probably sometime after 669. Aldhelm, born in the 640s, probably came from aristocratic origins in Wessex, and this may explain why he was able to become abbot of the newly founded Sherborne Abbey in Dorset (fd 675–80) at such a comparatively young age. We know little about his abbacy, except that at some point before his death in *c.* 709/10 he visited Rome, suggesting that continuing personal connections were an important means of sustaining early English monasticism. Something of the network of monks and nuns can be glimpsed in his voluminous writings, for example the treatise on virginity that he dedicated to Hildelith and her community of nuns at Barking in Essex. During the seventh century a number of other monasteries were founded in eastern England, according to Bede modelled on Frankish examples.[37] As we have seen, this in itself meant that a variety of overlapping types and customs were current.

The overlap of monastic customs is nowhere more evident than in the career of Biscop, a Northumbrian aristocrat who visited Rome for the first time in 653, and on a subsequent visit in the 660s spent some time en route at Lérins, where he professed as a monk. On this occasion he was commissioned to escort Theodore of Tarsus back to England to take up his appointment as the new archbishop of Canterbury. Biscop was thoroughly imbued with Roman monasticism, visiting four times in all. Similarly, Wilfrid of Hexham, a contemporary of Cuthbert, went to Rome to study and it was probably there that he decided to become a monk. At the end of his life Biscop told the monks of the monasteries he had founded at Monkwearmouth and Jarrow in Northumbria that he had visited seventeen monasteries during his life.[38] These were functional visits for the purpose of gathering information, making contacts and learning new methods. In 679–80 he brought back with him John, the cantor of St Peter's in Rome, to introduce the Roman order of chant to his monasteries. Among the practices he brought back was the *Rule of Benedict*, which he used as the foundational principle for his own monasteries. Roman monastic practices had already been introduced to Northumbria in the early years of the century by the Roman monk Paulinus, a member of Augustine's mission who accompanied Ethelberga of Kent to the north on her marriage to King Edwin. But it was not until Biscop and his contemporary, Wilfrid of Hexham, in the 660s, that the *Rule of Benedict* made headway.

As in Francia, royal patronage was crucial to the development of monasticism. Jarrow, founded in 682, was endowed directly from Northumbrian royal estates. Wilfrid of Hexham, while still a young and fairly inexperienced monk, was given the monastery of Ripon by the sub-king of Deira. Early medieval monasteries and convents, in both England and the Frankish territories, could have very large numbers of monks or nuns – the twin monasteries of Monkwearmouth and Jarrow probably housed 600 monks by 716 – and such numbers could only be supported by royal resources. The endowment of land to Monkwearmouth of seventy hides would have supported seventy families, or a sizeable rural community. Nor was it only land that was given. Biscop was able to import masons to build in stone, and even to glaze the windows of the church at Monkwearmouth, which as Bede pointed out was a craft unknown at the time in England.[39] It is also striking how instrumental the local aristocracy was in promoting monasticism. Both Biscop and Ceolfrith, abbot of Jarrow, were from the Northumbrian aristocracy. As in Francia, there were dynastic reasons for the nobility to found or endow monasteries. In English law it was difficult or impossible to alienate land that had been inherited from relatives, but 'bookland' (land given by the king) was not inalienable and could be disposed of in various ways. Kings retained the right to recover such land; for example, if the family proved untrustworthy or even on the death of the recipient, so founding a monastery on and to be supported from such land was a useful expedient to retain control over it. The success of such a tactic depended, of course, on the aristocracy's ability to appoint its own kin to abbacies, but the number of men and women from such families who entered monasteries originally founded by their kin suggests that the expectation of eventual control over property was high, even when they did not immediately take charge of the monastery. Churchmen like Bede could see what was happening, and might protest against the 'pretence of building monasteries', as he expressed it, but the idea that the laity could run monasteries, though challenged, was never dispelled.[40] Indeed, we shall see that this was a thorny point of contention in the reform of monastic life at various stages in both western and eastern Christendom.

What were these early English monasteries like? Notwithstanding the efforts of Biscop – who even took the name Benedict – and Wilfrid to centre Northumbrian monasticism on the *Rule of Benedict*, we cannot be certain how far they conformed to a model that Benedict might have recognised. David Knowles suggested that Monkwearmouth and Jarrow were probably as close to Monte Cassino as anything on the Continent. But it is difficult to know how far Benedict's stipulation on manual labour, for example, was followed. Even in a largely agricultural society this might be considered the exception rather than the rule, though writers such as Bede not only mention agricultural and building work but also single out an abbot such as Eosterwine at Monkwearmouth for his participation in such work. Yet in the deathbed speech to his monks that Bede put in his mouth, Biscop tells them to follow the rule of life that he gave them from his own experience.[41] Bede's portrait of Biscop shows deep concern for correct observance of worship and for sustained intellectual pursuits at his monasteries. The books he brought back from his visits to Rome were to be kept together as a collection in a library, of which Bede himself was a beneficiary. The Codex Amiatinus, now in the Biblioteca Laurenziana in Florence, and other Bible manuscripts show something of the artistic and literary productivity of the monks fostered under Biscop's Rule. Biscop also supplied 'everything necessary for the service of church and altar': vestments, the sacred vessels for celebration of the eucharist, and presumably service books. Much of this was imported from the Continent, which suggests that

Biscop was trying to reproduce what he saw as a 'correct' style of liturgical observance. Most telling, perhaps, Biscop's deathbed speech urges the monks to follow Benedict's Rule in one particular: they were to elect his successor themselves, giving consideration to morals and to 'soundness of doctrine' rather than rank or family influence.[42] This offers a clear indication of the prevailing situation of hereditary succession in which some monasteries found themselves.

The careers of Biscop and Wilfrid show how important connections to the Continent were for the development of English monasticism. Bede was the outstanding scholar of early medieval England, but besides Monkwearmouth and Jarrow, other monasteries evidently had the resources to produce works of learning. Hilda, abbess of Whitby, had a reputation for learning, and may have taught the six bishops who were apparently educated in her double house. Someone, either a monk or a nun of Whitby, wrote a Life of Gregory the Great at Whitby in the early eighth century. The texts available in England included, from the later seventh century, some eastern monastic literature: Theodore of Tarsus brought a copy of John Moschus's *Spiritual Meadow* to England. Likewise Barking Abbey, a convent founded in the seventh century by Erkenwald, bishop of London, was a noted centre of learning. Marilyn Dunn has made the interesting if provocative suggestion that the *Dialogues* attributed to Gregory the Great were in fact a product of a seventh-century Northumbrian monastery. Her argument rests on the connection between Northumbria and Rome maintained by Biscop; specifically, *Dialogues* contains elements of the theory of the purgation of the soul according to a series of tariffed penances, which derives from Irish practices, and which Gregory himself could not have known in Rome during his lifetime. Biscop, on the other hand, had opportunities to learn enough about Italian monasticism to have been able to weave together such ideas with the pastoral monasticism that is such a feature of the *Dialogues* into its distinctive landscape.[43] If this is correct, it is testimony to a profound understanding of monastic culture in seventh-century England.

Bede's reverence for Biscop as a monastic father is unmistakable, as is his own loyalty to the *Rule of Benedict*. Yet he also admired the parallel tradition of monasticism in Northumbria represented by the abbey of Lindisfarne, where one of his heroes, Cuthbert, became prior and then abbot. Lindisfarne had been founded in 635 by Aidan, a monk from the Irish monastic settlement on the island of Iona, after the collapse of the Roman mission to Northumbria and the revival under King Oswald. Alan Thacker has commented that for Bede Iona was like a 'mother church' for Northumbria.[44] This meant that he also saw Lindisfarne as an ideal community, but one that operated more like a mission. At Lindisfarne, as also at another Ionan foundation, Melrose, the ordained monks went out into the countryside to preach to the people. Aidan was both contemplative and pastoral, and this pattern was followed by Cuthbert from the 680s. Their monasticism comes across from Bede's account as zealous, simple and evangelical. But of course this is precisely the impression that Bede wanted to give. Preaching to rural communities can present a picture of windswept moors with heroic monks battling against the elements to persuade stoical peasants, but the reality was probably rather different. Lindisfarne and Melrose were nodes in a network of pastoral organisation in regions where parochial coverage was patchy or non-existent. Particularly in the case of a monastery established near a royal centre, such as Yeavering in Northumbria, the pastoral function was probably rather similar to the situation described by, for example, John of Ephesus in sixth-century Syria. And of course their intended audience was not always disposed to listen: Bede tells the story of peasants jeering at monks who were trying to save rafts carrying wood for building during a storm at the mouth of the Tyne.[45]

The introduction of the *Rule of Benedict*, and Roman practices more generally, proved divisive among the northern English in the seventh century. The story of the synod of Whitby (664) has been told often enough to preclude a retelling here, but it brought together proponents of 'Roman' and Irish practices, specifically to settle the dating of Easter. The Irish practice, already alluded to as causing problems in Gaul at the beginning of the seventh century, was prevalent along with other customs brought from Iona in some northern monasteries. The council had been summoned by King Oswiu, probably because of the difficulty of reconciling his own family's Ionan-learned practices with the Roman customs of his Kentish queen. Feelings ran high among some communities. In fact, it is misleading to speak of 'Irish' and 'Roman' in representing the two sides, since most of Ireland had already adopted the continental dating for Easter. In practice, what was at stake was the cultural identity of the Northumbrian monasteries that had been founded directly or indirectly from Iona. To the 'Romans', the nativist position seemed obscurantist. As Wilfrid remarked at the council, a handful of people in a corner of a remote island were claiming that they were correct and that the universal Church was wrong.[46] For Wilfrid this was the story of his personal journey. As a young man he had been a monk at Lindisfarne, before making the pilgrimage to Rome where he not only learned the Scriptures by heart but was also introduced to Roman styles of clerical dress and tonsuring. Wilfrid was prone to controversy. As bishop of Hexham he extended episcopal authority over Northumbrian monasteries. A curious line in Eddius Stephanus's *Life of Wilfrid* remarks that he arranged for almost all abbots and abbesses to make over their property to him by naming him as heir, in his capacity as bishop, in their wills. This led to an extended conflict with Archbishop Theodore, as a result of which Wilfrid had to defend himself before the pope and was later even imprisoned by King Aldfrith. Property seems to have been at the root of this dispute, if Eddius Stephanus is correct. On the point of signing a concord with the king, Wilfrid was warned against falling for a ruse the upshot of which would be that 'every single parcel of land you are known to possess in Northumbria, whether belonging to the diocese or the monasteries or coming to you in any other way, will be taken from you'.[47] Wilfrid was adept at persuading high-ranking people to dispose of land. After the wife of King Ecgfrith, Aetheldreda, had left the convent of Coldingham in 672 to found her own convent on her estates at Ely, she gave Wilfrid the land on which he was able to found his monastery at Hexham.

By the middle of the seventh century there were at least a dozen double houses of men and women in England. Some of these, such as Whitby, Wimborne and Barking, would be important for centuries, even after the double identity had been lost. As in Francia, a convent was seen as good way to retain family control of property, while permitting women in the royal house to exercise authority as abbess. Hilda, who presided over the synod of Whitby in 664, had previously considered going to the convent at Chelles in Francia where her sister, the mother of the king of East Anglia, had professed as a nun, but when

Aidan gave her a piece of land to try out living a monastic life with other women, she founded and ruled over a convent at Hartlepool before going on to found Whitby. The monks and nuns at the double house at Coldingham lived in separate spaces, but according to a twelfth-century writer the separation between men and women broke down and they fell into the habit of talking and feasting together, and perhaps even more. The nuns, 'despising the sanctity of their profession', spent their time sewing fine clothing for themselves.[48] For this writer, Symeon of Durham, the fire that eventually devastated the monastery was the inevitable judgement on such lapses from true monastic conduct. But Symeon was writing at a time (1104–8) when the idea of the double monastery – or of women ruling over a religious community that included men – was abhorrent to most men in monastic leadership. As we shall see, when double communities emerged again in the twelfth century, they provoked mixed reactions from contemporaries, and Symeon's account of Coldingham in the ninth century reflects the hostility and suspicion that attached to the concept in a later period.

Not all religious houses where women lived were double houses, of course. Minster, on the Isle of Sheppey, founded in the mid-seventh century by Seaxburgh, wife of King Eorcenberht of Kent, was still functioning at the end of the ninth century.[49] Alan Thacker has in any case warned against calling all religious houses presided over by abbesses 'double houses'.[50] But the notion of women acting as 'soldiers of Christ' alongside men was evidently a familiar one, as employed by Aldhelm in his treatise for Barking Abbey on virginity. It is perhaps worth emphasising that for early medieval people – as indeed for late Roman Christians throughout the Mediterranean world – a virgin was not necessarily a young woman without sexual experience, since the term referred to current sexual status and could therefore refer to widows or women no longer sexually active, such as Radegund or Aetheldreda after they had professed as nuns. As Sarah Foot has observed, in England the word *nunne* could simply be 'a title usually given to elderly persons'. Such women were active in religious communities and might even be considered 'the female counterpart to the secular priest or canon'.[51]

Unlike in Italy, and even parts of the Frankish lands, England's diocesan structure was of necessity rural rather urban. For much of the seventh and eighth centuries, bishops tended to minister from monasteries and, because of the large geographical areas of dioceses, to be peripatetic. Some parts of the country – for example, west of the Pennines – had no pastoral organisation at all. Relationships between monasteries and the episcopacy were often intertwined and overlapping. Following Irish practice, the abbot of Lindisfarne was also a bishop. 'Let no one be surprised', Bede advised, 'to hear that Lindisfarne, as well as being an episcopal see . . . is also the home of an abbot and community . . . [T]he episcopal residence and monastery are one and the same and all the clergy are monks.'[52] The abbot was elected by the bishop and monks, and governed the monastery, while the clergy lived a fully monastic life together with the bishop. As abbot, however, Cuthbert also carried on a pastoral role. When he was in turn elected bishop while living in solitude on Farne, he returned to the mainland to take up an active ministry. In a rather different way, Hilda's double house at Whitby, on the Yorkshire coast, also served as a pastoral centre. This was also clearly happening in parts of the Continent, where attempts to convert non-Christians were continuing into the eighth century. Fulda, a German monastery founded in 744, along with other 'missionary' monasteries, served as pastoral centres. Fulda had as many as 400 monks, many of whom were ordained priests.

The question of how far monasteries across the English kingdoms broadly speaking served as pastoral centres has been the subject of considerable debate for over a generation. In part this stems from the meaning of the term 'minster', and how far such institutions corresponded to monasteries of the kinds that we have encountered. The Latin word *monasterium* had fluid meanings, and could be used to describe either a cenobitic monastery or basilical type. The so-called 'minster thesis', as proposed by John Blair and others, argued that in the pre-Viking age (i.e. before the ninth century), all churches were served by communities of clergy in what might be called 'team ministries' run out of minsters (*monasteria*).[53] As a result of the Viking conquests in the ninth century, the territories served by minsters became fragmented. Some landowners built their own churches, while strong bishops started to create a parochial system. By the early eleventh century, legal definitions of types of churches can be seen, of which the monastery or house of canons was a distinctive type.[54] But before the middle of the eighth century this was unlikely to have been the case. This theory has the considerable merit of offering a cogent model to make sense of the lapidary statements and allusions in contemporary sources about the relationship between monasticism and pastoral work. It has not been universally accepted by historians, however.[55]

For our purposes, the important question is whether, even if pastoral work was undertaken by clergy working in teams, this necessarily means that such provision was driven by monks rather than by bishops. As usually happens with theories based on general models, wedges can be driven in at various points to undermine the whole. One such is that, where such results are available, as for example for the Test Valley in Hampshire, the archaeology indicates that concentrations of groups of smaller churches did exist.[56] Nevertheless, the more densely populated and fertile Wessex countryside cannot necessarily be used as an indicator of conditions throughout the English lands, especially in the period before the mid-eighth century where different traditions overlapped.

EARLY IRISH MONASTICISM

Irish monks have been mentioned so far at some length both in England and on the Continent. But it would be misleading to assume that the monasticism introduced by Columbanus into Gaul and the Ionans into northern Britain is entirely representative of monasteries and monastic life in Ireland. Here, monasticism developed in ways that suggest intriguing parallels with other parts of the Christian world, but that at the same time indicate a unique interpretation of religious life. An important starting point for understanding these differences is to reinforce an obvious point, that Ireland, uniquely among places where monasticism developed in this period, had never been part of the Roman Empire or under Roman influence. This meant, for one thing, that although Irish Christians may have seen Rome as the centre of their spiritual world, the *Rule of Benedict* was not imported. Although monastic traditions from the East were well known, the ideals they represented were interpreted by the Irish in their own ways.[57]

Writing about early Irish monasticism means engaging with an extensive hagiographic literature. Most of what we know about monasteries, monks and nuns in Ireland before the twelfth century comes from collections of saints' lives in three manuscript collections.[58] The saints' lives present three models of sacrificial behaviour: white martyrdom, which is renunciation of the secular world; green, which entails penance and mortification; and red, meaning death. Because there was no persecution of Christians in Ireland in the same way as in the Roman Empire, red martyrdom is absent from Irish monasticism. In so far as monks and nuns had power and influence, it derived from their guardianship of and access to saints. The most powerful tool wielded by monks and nuns was power in 'places where heaven met earth', in other words, where the saints were thought to dwell in the monasteries dedicated to them.[59]

Monastic settlements in Ireland were usually located on upland sites, partly for the better drainage properties they offered in a wet landscape. Woodland was also needed, for fuel, food and building materials, and the combination of these requirements meant that monks often re-used older sites such as Iron Age hill forts – a pattern also seen in other regions. Unlike in Francia, still less the Mediterranean, there were no Roman ruins, and probably very few buildings from which stone could be re-used. No importing of stone masons or glazers here, as in Biscop's Northumberland. Monastic architecture in early medieval Ireland was organised around displaying the saints' relics. A monastery such as Clonmacnoise still retains, despite later medieval additions, the distinctive shape of the Irish monastic system. A concentric series of walls protected the inner sanctum where the saint's shrine stood. These walls were often low and could easily have been climbed: unlike the walls around, say, St Sabas in the Judaean desert, they were not intended to ward off attack. Instead, they signalled wealth and social status. The more circles of walls, the more important the monastery.[60] Where possible, monasteries used a curvilinear enclosure, echoing the kingly hill forts of pre-Christian Ireland. Lisa Bitel has called this 'an attempt to create a place that existed simultaneously on this earthly plane and on the eternal plane'.[61] The architectural symbolism was further invoked by circular processions around the buildings in the enclosure: as, for example, when St Máedóc protected his client settlers from raiders by redrawing the boundaries of the monastic sanctuary around people and cattle.[62] Besides the encircling wall and a cemetery, the other feature common to all monasteries was the church or oratory. This was usually small, closed to the laity and designed for the exclusive ritual of the saint. The shape of the church was variable, but from the eighth century onwards it was usually stone-built. Around the church was the zone of sanctuary (*termonn*), inside which only the laws of the guardian saint applied. From the eighth century, monasteries were obliged in Irish synodal canons to create ritual divisions between enclosures in order to designate the innermost as the holy of holies, which laity and women were not permitted to enter.[63] The different zones in the monastery corresponded to different activities. Domestic buildings were probably furthest away from the oratory, and a single main building often functioned as refectory and scriptorium, where there was one. Most monasteries, unlike in the Benedictine Rule but in line with eastern Mediterranean traditions, probably had individual cells for sleeping. This feature alone distinguished monastic life from the rest of early Irish society, where families and groups usually slept in the same space. The abbot usually occupied a separate house, to indicate his prestige in the community. As can still be seen at Clonmacnoise, an open space between the church and the rest of the enclosure formed a transitional zone.

By the time that monasteries were being established in Ireland from the sixth century onwards, competition for suitable land was already intense. This meant that monastic founders, usually the charismatic individuals celebrated in the hagiographical literature as saints, had to persuade landowners to offer them prime land for settlement in exchange for something. Lisa Bitel has remarked that the exchange was usually the offer of ritual services or the threat to withhold such services, perhaps take them elsewhere.

One reason for distinguishing holy and profane space was the number of different kinds of people who came to a monastery – from alms seekers and travellers to kings. Many of these would be 'clients' of the monastery, usually dependent farmers who settled outside the enclosure walls. Ireland was an entirely rural society, and monasteries were part of the rural landscape. Some monasteries were enclosed within lands belonging to free farmers, who might agree to become clients of the saint, whereas other monasteries, especially if founded with an endowment from a major landowner, might have farmers granted as chattels as a part of endowment. The benefits of entering into a client relationship were both practical and spiritual. As a client of the saint, one was physically close to the relics, even without having direct access. This might be of comfort in the face of the physical dangers of rural life: weather, disease, freak accidents and so on. But Lisa Bitel has also drawn attention to the frequent access to the liturgy, and to the only opportunities that might be available to hear the Gospels and thus understand the basis of Christian teaching.[64] The hagiographical literature suggests that learned monks might also have preached to the laity gathered outside the church.[65] For monastic communities, client farmers were also essential. None of the Irish monastic customs appear to have regarded manual labour as an obligation for monks, in the way that the *Rule of Benedict* and some of its predecessors and contemporaries did. Where it is mentioned, it appears as a penance rather than a fundamental part of the monastic profession.[66] We might well ask whether monks or nuns could really have supported themselves adequately through manual labour in any case. Even if the numbers of religious were not large, all communities attracted dependants – the elderly, lepers, guests – who were unable to work but needed to be fed. This is a question we will consider in more depth later, since performance or non-performance of manual labour came to be a fraught issue in reform movements within monasticism. An obvious point to consider is how useful monks, especially those who had been in monasteries since youth, could really have been in heavy agricultural work in a demanding environment. For convents, the question of labour was more difficult still. Clearly, as very many societies have amply demonstrated, women are no less able than men to do agricultural work, but since most nuns were probably from high-status families, both in Ireland and elsewhere social expectations demanded hired manual labour for female communities.

Another category of dependant in Irish monasticism was the guest. Like early Egyptian monks, Irish monks were often on the move between monasteries, visiting each other to exchange gifts and receive hospitality. Most monasteries probably had separate guest houses within the monastic enclosure. Hospitality was a mutual benefit, obviously giving the traveller sustenance and shelter, but also providing the host with the opportunity to confer the sacred duty of charity. Certain rituals were observed: the guest's feet were washed and food served. As in many societies, the offer and acceptance of food was a process in which relationships of power were negotiated. The importance of hospitality is underscored by the list of prohibited food and drink in the Irish penitential handbooks. These included horseflesh, carrion, anything that had been touched by dogs and blood.[67] In principle monks and nuns only ate plant-based food and dairy products – and raw food was a sign of particular spiritual merit[68] – but archaeological evidence of an animal and fish diet suggests this was not strictly observed, at least in the guest house. Alcohol was permissible in certain circumstances. Monenna's nuns at Cell Sléibe were delighted when Derlasire turned the table water into beer in honour of the visit of their bishop, and both the nuns and their guest 'were rendered so merry that if the bishop had not stopped them almost all would have become drunk'.[69]

The hagiographical literature in which monastic life features presents at once a sharp dichotomy and a complex mutual interdependence between the monastery and the world outside. In a largely tribal and kin-based society, a monk or nun was taking a radical step in giving up an existing group for what was essentially a new family. This was true not only of Irish monasticism, of course, but of most early medieval religious life. For this reason, both Benedict's and Basil's Rules characterised the abbot as father to his monks, and in some medieval monastic literature abbots also feature as mothers. Nuns were in a different position, since they moved from the guardianship of their father to that of the Church. Moreover, not all women were able to choose monastic virginity. Since they might be useful economic assets for families, women who wished to remain unmarried often faced opposition.

But unlike Benedictines or those following Basilian Rules, Irish abbots had no written source of authority, no constitutional document on which to rely in guiding their community. In the absence of a written Rule, the abbot or abbess directed all aspects of life in the monastery, including discipline but extending also to the times at which their 'family' ate and went to bed. The autonomy exercised by a particular head made monasticism in the Irish tradition particularly personal, since the tone of life was set by him or her. One consequence of this was that monks could wander from one to another until they found a way of life they preferred. Undoubtedly this sense of choosing the right 'father' underlies the character of Irish monasticism as it spread to England and the Continent as well. But the lack of a codified set of regulations could give an arbitrary character to the governance of monasteries, especially when an abbot's authority might be challenged. Without a text to fall back on, there was no way to enforce stability in the community except through the reputation of the head of the house. Within the monastery, monks or nuns might be divided hierarchically into seniors and juniors. But, in contrast to the *Rule of Benedict*, Irish monasticism encouraged particular friendships to develop between an elder and a chosen junior. This might also be a confessorial relationship. This system seems to echo the characteristic feature of early Egyptian – and indeed later Byzantine – monasticism, as encountered in the *Apophthegmata Patrum*, of a master–disciple relationship. On the other hand, relations between monks of the same generation might be strained, and jealousy is a not uncommon feature of the hagiographical literature.[70]

The hagiographic canon suggests that nuns' lives differed significantly from monks' in the internal structure of their communities. One of the curious points about early Irish monasticism is the evidence for convents for women that seemed to disappear from the ninth century onwards. One theory to explain this is that women found it more difficult to sustain monastic foundations in a property-holding system skewed towards male interests. Since Irish women could only inherit land as a life interest, without the capacity to pass it on to heirs, their only opportunities to endow a foundation with land came from property that had been gifted to them. But by the eighth century, land was scarce for religious and lay communities alike.[71] Putative founders might of course try to persuade landowners to give away land to them for the purpose, but traditions of shared ownership by kin groups made this challenging. Bitel has surmised that many Irish nuns may have been settled on family lands in specifically female enclosures where land was not immediately needed by kin, and where, as she remarks, the family had 'more unmarried women than they could dispose of'.[72] In such cases the community probably dispersed at the founder's death and the land reverted to the family. This, she argues, is one reason for the transient nature of women's monastic communities. Moreover, women were seen by the hagiographers on whom we are dependent for our picture of the monastic landscape in early Ireland as, simply, less impressive as miracle workers. In contrast to a monastic saint who could move mountains and fight with demons, miracles of refilling butter jars were indicators that women were to be viewed as lesser spiritual beings.[73]

Early Irish monasteries emerged as critical players in a political landscape that was deeply fissured and endemically violent. Monastic communities, as guardians and representatives on earth of saints, claimed an intangible authority that bypassed normal channels of power. Where warring clans and kings were unable to end a cycle of violence, it was the saints, through their monks, who could bring a measure of security by mediating between them. The notion of an intangible otherworldly power channelled by monks owes a great deal to the model of personal holiness argued so persuasively by Peter Brown in a pioneering study of fifty years ago.[74] Lisa Bitel has remarked, perceptively, that the Irish monastic scene differed from the eastern Mediterranean examples that formed the backbone of Brown's analysis in one important way. Whereas the Syrian and Egyptian ascetics drew their chilling power from being outsiders, the Irish monks and nuns' influence derived from exactly the opposite: they were the consummate 'insiders', with intimate links to the feuding families, to kings and princesses.[75] It was the personal relationships that founding saints and their successors as abbots or abbesses were able to establish with the powerful that enabled them to wield the authority that protected their monasteries and communities. As late as the eleventh century, according to the *Annals of Clonmacnoise*, an ascetic could command authority over most of Ireland during a period without kingship.[76] Sometimes political treaties were agreed at monasteries, where both parties could sit down together under the eye of the saint. In a later example, it was monks of Lis Mór who persuaded Diarmuit ua Briain to accept his brother's rule and end his own struggle for the high kingship in 1093. But before they could come to an agreement, monks had to take their power visibly to the protagonists through prayer, cursing and persuasion. The monks of Clonmacnoise recorded in their Annals not only their ritual pleas to their patron saint but also his responses to their pleas as they played out in the course of conflict. Of course, monks might also take the initiative, working with kings they regarded as virtuous. As Francis Byrne has observed, the early medieval concept of kingship developed as much in monasteries as in courts.[77]

If it came down to a trial of strength between an abbot and a secular ruler, naturally the abbot had (as Stalin might have put it) no divisions. But as far as the hagiographical authors were concerned, the relationship was unequal in another way. Part of the attribute of the saint was being wiser than ordinary people, especially kings. At its most extreme, this was manifested in the trope of the 'kingly fool' Suibne Geilt, who insulted St Rónán and was cursed by him with the result that he grew feathers and flew around Ireland reciting poetry, until he eventually died on a dung heap.[78] The wider point to draw from this moral tale is that laity and religious were caricatured as opposites but were in fact riveted to each other in a system of mutual support. The laity validated the existence of monasticism: their foolishness, weakness, reliance on human agency and lack of understanding made the work of monks and nuns necessary.

THE CAROLINGIAN REFORM

In 829 a synod convened at Mainz to hear the complaint of a young monk called Gottschalk; namely, that he had been forced into the monastery of Fulda against his will and contrary to canonical norms. He now demanded to be allowed to leave the cloister. The bishops at the synod agreed, but Gottschalk's abbot at Fulda, Hrabanus Maur, furiously protested and demanded his return. Hrabanus even wrote a treatise, the *Liber de oblatione puerorum* (Book on the Oblation of Boys), which in a deliberate act of escalation of the dispute he sent to the emperor, Louis the Pious.

The case became a cause célèbre of its day.[79] Fulda was a famous abbey, founded in 744 in what was then a mission field by the English monk Boniface of Crediton, who was martyred ten years later. By the time Gottschalk entered the monastery, probably in around 814, it was a royal abbey with close connections to the Carolingian imperial family.

Moreover, Gottschalk was not simply a rebellious young monk but the son of a Saxon count with important political associations and, at the time of his entry, a large property in his own right. And Hrabanus Maur was a famous scholar who had been a linchpin of the court of Louis's father Charlemagne. All the ingredients were in place for a drama at the top of Carolingian society. As it turned out, it ended unsatisfactorily, in a way even tragically. But the case was important not only for the personal element, but also for what it tells us about the nature of Benedictine monasticism in the early ninth century.

Gottschalk entered Fulda as an oblate – in other words, as a gift from his family to the monastery. The *Rule of Benedict* recognised that prominent families would sometimes wish to 'offer a son to God's service', and specified how this was to be done where the child was under age. Parents were obliged to write a petition to the monastery, to wrap the altarcloth in the abbey church around the boy's hands, and place the document and whatever other gift was being made to the community on the altar.[80] Boys – and girls – offered to a monastery in this way were brought up in the community until they came of age, when they either took vows as novices or left the monastery. Oblates were supervised at all times by older monks under the eye of the novice master or schoolmaster, and participated in a community life of their own that echoed that of the adult monks. Gottschalk stood out as a boy for his intellect, and Hrabanus, who was at that time novice master, regarded him as a highly promising theologian in the making. He was evidently tonsured as a monk at Fulda soon after 822, which would probably place him in his early twenties when he took his case for release from his vow to the synod at Mainz. Most of what we know about the case comes from the treatise by Hrabanus Maur, who responds to his arguments.[81] But of course this means that we only know those elements of Gottschalk's case that Hrabanus considered weak enough to be countered. One such was that the witnesses to the original oblation had been Franks, rather than Saxons, and therefore of a different race, which contravened Saxon law. Benedict's Rule said nothing about either witnesses or their nationality, but the argument shows how far the Rule had come to be internalised in regional and ethnic law codes. For Gottschalk the central issue was that he had been compelled to take vows, which contravened canon law. As recently as 826 the Council of Rome had forbidden forced entry to monastic life.[82] In response to this seemingly powerful argument, Hrabanus countered that oblation was a gift that could not be taken back.

Moreover, a vow was a vow, however and by whomever it was made, and once made to God could not be contravened. Hrabanus did not deny the force of Gottschalk's argument that the vow made on his behalf had effectively placed him in servitude. But he defended this on two grounds: first, that the Scriptural example of Hannah giving her child Samuel to the Temple was a precedent that validated the practice of oblation; and, following logically from this, that monasticism, which enshrined oblation as a means of recruitment, was instituted by divine authority rather than human invention.[83] The biblical example was particularly important because one of Gottschalk's arguments was apparently that the oblation had been made after his father, Berno, had died and that there was therefore no way of knowing whether it was in agreement with his wishes as head of the family. As for monastic life being *servitium* (servitude), that was a question of attitude: surely all human life on earth was a form of servitude, compared to the liberty of eternal life? As Mayke de Jong has observed, in representing Gottschalk's complaint as an attack on monasticism more generally, Hrabanus reveals how critical oblation was as source of recruitment to monasteries.[84] By *c.* 800 most monks and nuns in Carolingian territories had probably entered their monastery as oblates.

By this period monasteries in the Carolingian Empire were typically much larger than the type envisaged by Benedict in his Rule. Between 826 and 835 Fulda recruited between 100 and 130 very young monks; indeed only two from this date range are known to have entered the monastery as adults.[85]

At the synod of Mainz, the central point of the argument revolved around the age at which an oblate was called upon to take formal vows. This does not seem to have been established as a rule across Carolingian monasteries, still less across western Christendom as a whole. A case in the second half of the twelfth century, in which a canon who had run away from school to enter a monastery but who later thought better of it tried to leave and recover his benefice, shows that by that period fourteen was considered old enough to make a vow binding on oneself.[86] But that was probably a hypothetical case anyway, and matters were not so clear in the ninth century. The implication of Gottschalk's argument, in so far as it can be reconstructed from Hrabanus's text, is that at Fulda this crucial stage of the process was either omitted, or carried out ceremonially at the same time as or soon after the oblation itself, at a time when the child was too young to understand what was going on.[87] An important reforming Council held at the imperial capital, Aachen, in 817 had reiterated that oblates should be asked to confirm their vow, but had not decreed an age at which it was appropriate for this to happen. But even in monasteries where oblates were given proper opportunities to reflect on their vows – which may have been the majority – the implications of a choice to leave must have been daunting. Boys and girls who had been brought up in a monastery knew no life outside its walls; their friendships, sense of security and belonging all depended on the community of which they had been part. In many cases they had probably forgotten or indeed lost their families. Those who chose to leave the monastery had to be sure they had resources or patronage to support themselves, which might mean becoming dependent on other family members. Boys who had grown up in the monastery were probably well educated and trained for a clerical life, but had missed years of preparation or training for other callings. It is hardly surprising that, in western Europe at least, most monks and nuns between the ninth and twelfth centuries had probably been placed in their monastery as oblates and stayed to live out their lives there.

It can be difficult for us to understand the sensibilities of parents who were prepared to give up their children in this way. One historian has remarked that donation to a monastery was at least more merciful than abandonment, a resort to which economic necessity has always forced some unfortunate parents.[88] But for the social classes from which most monks and nuns came, such hardship was probably rare. The demographic of monasticism was, certainly by the turn of the first millennium, largely represented by landowning families rather than the peasantry. In more abstract terms, Peter Brown has remarked that the practice of oblation demonstrates how the laity treated adjuncts to their own piety.[89] This is undoubtedly true, but cases of unhappiness, even desperate misery, on the part of children placed in monasteries must have been far from uncommon. A case of an oblate at St Gall who climbed to the top of the church tower so that he could see the fields where he could no longer walk freely and either fell or jumped to his death illustrates the potential tragedy of oblation.[90]

By and large the Carolingian commentators on the Rule took the same line as Hrabanus Maur on the question of oblation. Smaragdus included the text of the petition in standard use for oblation, which probably derived from the Aachen reform synod.[91] Paschasius Radbertus, like Hildemar a monk of Corbie (d. 859), extended his discussion to include not only girls but also widows.[92] The assumption by the commentators is that monasteries and convents will recruit largely from oblates, and that adult novices are the exception. This state of affairs had profound effects on the character of monasticism. Just as oblates knew no other home than the cloister and were ill prepared for life outside, adult entrants to a monastery or convent were entering a world apart, a world with a completely different set of values and behavioural expectations. Moreover, whereas oblates had absorbed the necessary training in youth, adult novices had to learn everything from scratch. The monastic profession was highly technical, because it required hours of liturgical service in which psalms were sung according to set modulations. During the course of a week, all 150 psalms were sung. Although monasteries owned some liturgical service books, especially in a large community there were never enough in the age before printing to allow monks or nuns even to share one between two or three, so the psalter had to be learned by heart. For oblates, this was part of their daily schooling, absorbed as part of life, but for novices entering as adults, it required the acquisition of wholly new skills. In consequence, many adult recruits never caught up with their oblate brothers or sisters. This could lead to divisions within communities between those who had grown up in the monastery, who had formed friendships and become acculturated to the cultural idioms, language and gestures of the community , and those who had taken vows as adults.[93]

Perhaps the most noticeable aspect of life in which these divisions could become apparent was education, and specifically competence in Latin. The psalter and Mass responses could be learned by heart – an attainment common enough in a largely non-literate society – but monks who had no Latin could not engage in the *lectio divina* demanded by the Rule, let alone study theology. Of course, it is far from impossible to learn Latin in adulthood, but novices who first had to learn to read and write were at a disadvantage compared to oblates. And at the same time, not all monks who had grown up in the monastery had the aptitude for scholarship. But an illustration of the kinds of jealousy that could be provoked by the division between monks who had been oblates and those who had entered later in life is given by Ekkehard IV, a monk of St Gall. He tells the story of how three monks used to meet to discuss Scripture together in the scriptorium in the intervals between the night offices, rather than going back to bed. Another monk, who had entered the monastery as an adult convert, wanted to listen in because he suspected they were simply gossiping, but when the three realised they were being overheard they immediately switched to Latin, which they knew the convert could not understand. (One of their number completed the unfortunate monk's embarrassment by sneaking up to his hiding place and beating him with a stick.)[94]

This story is rich in the kind of circumstantial detail that helps bring the early medieval monastery alive for us. Primarily, for our present purposes, it tells us of a clique of monks who had grown up together in the cloister (*nutriti*, as they are sometimes called), who, perhaps unwittingly, earned the jealousy of a monk who felt excluded from their society. Such a situation may have been very common in medieval monasteries in the period before oblation was finally ended in 1215. By the eleventh century, the distinction between *nutriti* and adult converts might also correspond to a social divide as well, with the latter more likely to be occupied with the practical aspects of institutional life. Oblation guaranteed recruitment not only to the monastery as a community, but specifically to the choir and scriptorium – the heart of the monastery.

In the case of Gottschalk, a compromise was eventually agreed. He was allowed to leave Fulda, but not to take his property with him – the entry offering gifted to the monastery by his mother when the oblation was made. Moreover, he was to remain a monk. For Gottschalk, this was not what he had hoped, since he had demanded the restoration of his liberty and what he saw as his property. Hrabanus Maur's refusal to restore this to him was an embarrassment to the Council, since the bishops had no means of enforcing this over a royal abbey. Gottschalk first entered the monastery of Corbie, but by 845 he was in Italy. By now he was fulfilling his early promise as a scholar, but when Hrabanus read his treatise on predestination he saw an opportunity to reopen the quarrel begun in the schoolroom at Fulda years earlier. As far as Hrabanus was concerned, Gottschalk's departure from Fulda put him in that most abhorrent of Benedictine categories, the *monachus gyrovagus*.[95] In a letter (846–7) to Gottschalk's patron, Count Eberhard of Friuli, he calls him *quondam sciolum*.[96]

Hrabanus's hostility was instrumental in the judgement against Gottschalk's treatise at the synod of Soissons in 849, where he was condemned for his theory of 'double predestination', publicly flogged, compelled to burn the books containing his theology and forced to enter a monastery again, where he died just before 870.[97] Mayke de Jong suggests that the abbot of Fulda pursued a vendetta against the younger monk out of a sense of rejection by him. This may have been aggravated by Hrabanus's sense that Gottschalk was of a higher social status; perhaps also by the precocity of his intellect. It is more difficult to understand what Gottschalk really wanted when he demanded to be released from his vow at Fulda. Initially at least he expected to be recompensed to the value of the entry gift to Fulda made on his behalf by his mother, but when this proved unobtainable he was always going to have to rely on the patronage of others – or entry into another monastery.

Gottschalk's apparent preference for life as a scholarly secular cleric with the freedom of movement and liberty necessary for him to study and write presupposes that such a career was plausible, if not common, in ninth-century Europe. Hrabanus Maur's accusation that Gottschalk was a 'gyrovague' could only have struck home in a religious culture in which Benedict's categorisation of monastic life had become normalised. If this was the case by the middle of the ninth century, it was the result of deliberate policy rather than evolution. In eighth-century Francia, Germany or Italy, the term *monasterium* might have a variety of connotations, the only constant being a communal life. From the middle of the eighth century, the new Carolingian regime under King Pepin III (751–68) attempted to rationalise some of the variety of monastic types that had evolved over the previous 300 years. There were monasteries in which the Irish tradition of the abbot-bishop had a strong grip – which meant that in some dioceses more than one person claimed the episcopal dignity – and 'vagrant' monks travelling without the permission of their abbots.[98] The *Rule of Benedict* was still far from universal in European monasteries, despite the best efforts of missionary monks such as Boniface of Crediton, and practices that the Carolingians found 'irregular' – for example, retention of private property by monks in some monasteries, or freedom to leave the cloister – were indications not only of local variations and customs but also of the endurance of *regulae mixtae*. Reforming bishops such as Chrodegang, bishop of Metz (d. 766) attempted to revive fourth-century 'episcopal monasticism', as pioneered by Augustine of Hippo and later Caesarius of Arles. The founder of a monastery following the *Rule of Benedict*, Gorze, he also organised the cathedral clergy of his diocese into a monastic community according to a Rule of his own design.[99]

Many monasteries in Francia had, of course, originally been founded by bishops. Many of these came under royal control in the eighth century as part of a deliberate policy by the Carolingian mayors of palace – who constituted real authority from the early part of the century – and then kings to break up episcopal control over land and jurisdictions. As we have already seen, the episcopacy tended to represent and be drawn from the ranks of aristocratic elites, so this was a struggle over huge landed properties held by some of the large monasteries, and of course the resources in food and manpower that they supplied. The process was accelerated by Pepin III, but not complete until well into the ninth century. An important staging post was the ruling at the Council of Ver in 755 that all monasteries in Frankish lands must be either episcopal or royal. The status of 'royal abbey' was double-edged. Conferral of royal patronage meant that a monastery was unlikely to fail, and might indeed be guaranteed considerable resources in the future. But it also meant that the abbey had obligations of spiritual service to the royal family through prayer and memorialisation, and that it was potentially open to interference. The extension of royal status mirrors the extension of Carolingian royal authority into new territories.

Consider as an example the abbey of Farfa, a little to the north of Rome in the Sabine countryside. The monastery was founded sometime between 680 and 700 by a Savoyard, Thomas of Maurienne, supposedly following a vision of the Blessed Virgin. By *c.* 720 Thomas had secured papal recognition of the monastery but also embedded it in regional political networks through the patronage of the Lombard duke. Fifty-five years later, Farfa had entered a much wider field of operations. In 774 Charlemagne defeated the Lombard king Desiderius and annexed the crown to Frankish royal territory. Almost immediately Farfa was declared a royal abbey with the same status as abbeys such as Fulda.[100] One immediate consequence was the appointment of Franks as the next three abbots, ruling between 781 and 802. It was also in this period that the *Rule of Benedict* was imposed on the community in place of a mixed Rule. From a local monastery little known outside its immediate region and preserving a distinctive local tradition of its history, Farfa now became part of a great network of monastic observance and learning, as its abbots attended court at Aachen and corresponded with Carolingian literati such as Alcuin and later Hilduin of St Denis and St Medard, Soissons. These connections enabled the monastery to defend its lands and privileges from papal claims in 823, but perhaps the attention of the papacy would never have been drawn to Farfa in the first place without such a rise to influence and power.[101]

If the Carolingian rationalisation of institutional monasticism served political needs, it also had important practical dimensions in the lived experience of monks and nuns. Pepin III's introduction of the Roman liturgy into Carolingian monasteries meant the loss of some liturgical customs that had evolved over time, such as the *laus perennis*, a system that ensured the constant chanting of psalms throughout the day and night by teams of monks. Before the early ninth century, however, the Carolingian reform of monastic life did not necessarily mean the uniform imposition of the *Rule of Benedict*. Indeed, as Scott Bruce has pointed out, in the 790s the Rule was so little understood in Frankish lands that the Italian scholar Paul the Deacon had to send a copy of the Rule with an explanatory letter to Charlemagne to help him understand some of the terminology.[102] By the time of Charlemagne's death in 814, a programme of imposing observance of the Rule throughout Carolingian territories was under way. That programme was cemented at the Synod of Aachen in 817, under Charlemagne's son Louis the Pious. The synod formally declared the *Rule of Benedict* binding on all monks and nuns in the Carolingian Empire, which at that period extended over most of modern France, northern Italy and much of Germany. But the uniform imposition of the Rule should be seen as a means to an end, which was uniformity of ritual and liturgy. Charlemagne's correspondence with Paul the Deacon epitomises a concern for 'textual Christianity' that his biographer Einhard also noted, and that scholars have identified as the wellspring of the cultural movement at his court commonly known as the Carolingian Renaissance.[103]

The agent of Benedictine uniformity was a Carolingian aristocrat who converted to the monastic life in adulthood, and whose personal path in some ways epitomises the reform programme that he led. Benedict of Aniane was born in *c.* 750 in southwestern France, a region not yet under Carolingian domination. He underwent a personal conversion and followed a life of personal austerity that seems to have entailed a devotion to the Desert Fathers on his family estates near Montpellier, before founding a monastery at Aniane where the *Rule of Benedict* was observed. Under Louis the Pious he became something like the archimandrite figure of early Byzantine monasticism, with authority to visit and reform monasteries throughout the Empire. But his role was more than simply corrective. Essentially he was trying to resolve anomalies in communities that were attempting to lead an enclosed life, by helping them either to conform to the Rule or to live as cloistered canons. In some cases he was prepared to allow communities to split up and monks to leave and join other houses, as for example in resolving a dispute at St Martin at Tours.

Although the synod of 817, under Benedict's guidance, formally bound monasteries to the *Rule of Benedict*, it also recognised the evolution of monastic life since the sixth century. Thus manual labour was not normally expected of monks, and the role of monasteries as schools was limited to educating oblates. In addition, innovations were added to the cursus of liturgical prayers from Benedict's time. Specifically, the office of the dead was to be said daily in monasteries, and the ritual content of the liturgy was emphasised through processions to altars. As Mayke de

Jong has remarked, the commemoration of the living and the dead became the 'all-consuming business' of monasteries in the ninth century.[104] These changes underscored the distinctiveness of the monastic profession, but also served to shape monasteries as being intercessory bodies on behalf of the laity. The effect of liturgical and regulatory uniformity was to present to God a united earthly empire of men and women dedicated to prayer and intercession on behalf of the laity. Prayer – a series of formalised petitions to God for general or specific acts of mercy – was understood to be the most powerful function of the monastery. Common observance of the Rule also fostered relationships between monasteries that were expressed through commemorative prayer. These were often recorded in confraternity books: essentially, autograph albums which would be carried from one monastery to another and in which monks and nuns would write their names to bear witness to their enrolment in the Empire's spiritual army. The confraternity book of the abbey of Reichenau, from *c.* 824, records the names of monks and nuns from fifty monasteries.

Common observance of the *Rule of Benedict* demanded fresh understanding of its tenets in the very different social context and environment of the Carolingian Empire. For this reason, a series of influential commentaries on the Rule was composed in the ninth century. Particularly notable are those by Hildemar of Corbie and Smaragdus of St Mihiel, Hildemar's *Expositio* (*c.* 845) being the most extensive.[105] A monk of Corbie originally, Hildemar wrote it for fellow monks in the north Italian monastery of Civate. Central to his conception of Benedictine monasticism was the cloister, which for Hildemar was as much a mental or conceptual space as it was physical. Thus, when Hildemar wrote of a monk 'leaving the cloister', he distinguished between the mental state of taking pleasure in being elsewhere and the rootedness to the state of mind governed by being cloistered. For Hildemar, the cloister lay not only physically at the heart of the monastery but at the centre of the monk's daily existence. The cloister, a place of contemplation and quiet at the architectural centre of the monastery, was a figure for the monk or nun protected from the dangers of the outside world.

The centrality of the cloister to Carolingian ideas of Benedictine monasticism is emphasised in the Plan of St Gall, a remarkable document that probably derived from the synod of Aachen of 817, and which probably, despite its name, originated from the abbey of Reichenau, probably from Abbot Haito (763–836), a keen supporter of the Benedictine reform. The plan survives in a manuscript that also contained on its obverse side a copy of the Life of St Martin, and it has been extensively discussed since the seventeenth century. In the 1960s Walter Horn and Ernest Born constructed a scale model of the monastery based on the plan, and this, together with their detailed commentary, has become highly influential in our understanding of the document and its implications. The plan itself is 44 by 30 inches, drawn with red lead on five calfskin sheets. It contains more than forty buildings, on a scale of 1:192. The purposes of each building, the dedications to each of the altars in the church and even the types of the trees in the orchard are all labelled.[106] Whoever drew the plan was visualising an ideal world. The St Gall of the plan never existed in reality, as the accompanying preface to the abbot of St Gall, Gozbert (816–37), makes clear: 'I have sent you . . . this modest example of this disposition of a monastery, so that you may dwell upon it spiritually.' That the plan conforms neither to St Gall as far as we know it to have existed in the early ninth century nor to Reichenau suggests that Benedictine abbots at the time of the Carolingian reform were reflecting deeply on the nature of the monastery in abstract terms. The plan may be seen as a kind of visual commentary on the *Rule of Benedict* in light of the synod of Aachen of 817.

The plan can be linked to the debates about the Rule that were reflected in the Aachen synod in tangible ways. One such was the place of the abbot as the vital link between the interior and exterior worlds of the monastery, and thus, in practical terms, the siting of the abbot's house. On the plan the abbot's accommodation was separate from the rest of the community's, though linked to the north transept of the abbey church by a passageway. It takes its place among other buildings for external laity, such as the guest house. The synod, on the other hand, specified that the abbot should live as part of the community. Another point of contention was whether monasteries should be permitted to run schools for the children of the laity. The plan has two schools, one a separate building between the guest house and the abbot's house, the other part of the novice quarters. The cloister on the plan of St Gall is not only at the heart of the monastery, it is a secret space cut off from the external world. It is bounded to the south by the refectory, to the north by the abbey church, by the cellar to the west and the dormitory to the east. These are all parts of the monastery to which only choir monks had access; indeed, access to the cloister was gained only through the monks' parlour, a small room adjoining the church to the south. The effect of the plan was thus to create an enclosure inaccessible to the laity: the counterpart, in some ways, to the zone of inner sanctuary in an early Irish monastery. In this way, despite its square design, the conceptual effect of the plan is to produce a circle with the function of the cloister — contemplation, *lectio divina* and study — at its still centre.

The reforms of 817 may have reset the practice as well as the theory of monasticism in the Carolingian Empire, but they were not an attempt to return to the age of Benedict of Nursia. We have already mentioned some liturgical developments that became enshrined in Carolingian practice. Institutionally, too, monasticism had developed since the sixth century in ways that Benedict would not necessarily have approved of. The position and role of the abbot provides a good example of this kind of change. For Benedict, the abbot was the father of the monks, who constituted a new family. He was required by the Rule to teach, encourage and nurture; indeed teaching — using the yeast of his doctrine to enable the dough of the monastic body to rise — can be seen as the primary function of the abbot in the Rule.[107] Yet by *c.* 800 the practice of appointing lay figures as abbots was already widespread in the Carolingian Empire. Abbacies were given to prominent lay people as rewards for service. Because these were usually supporters of the reform, this irregularity was considered justifiable by contemporaries. Thus Einhard, a courtier and biographer of Charlemagne, who had been educated at the abbey school at Fulda but never took monastic vows, received the abbacy of St Peter's Ghent, and indeed others, as reward. Neither Hilduin, who became abbot of St Denis, nor Alcuin, who was abbot of St Martin at Tours, were professed monks. Despite the decree of the Aachen synod obliging abbots to live in community, this practice seems to have been tolerated as long as the lay abbot did not use the resources of the monastery — the *mensa fratrum* — to run his own household — the *mensa abbatis*. During the reign of Louis the Pious, ten abbots controlled thirty monasteries between them, none of whom had been elected freely by the community as mandated in the *Rule of Benedict*.[108] By mid-century the practice had not only become too deeply ingrained but was also seen by kings as serving their interests. After all, monasteries with large landed properties were, from the crown's point of view, most valuable when they were in the hands of trusted supporters. The problem, of course, was that it was open to abuse, and the siphoning of monastic resources for the personal use of the lay abbot could be rationalised when the abbot in question was using them to support the crown's military effort. Just as had been the case in earlier centuries, lay people could found new monasteries; when they did so, they often expected to exercise control over them. Count Atho of Schienen founded two monasteries on his estates, in one of which, in the 850s, he placed his son Lambert when the boy was aged between eight and eleven. At some point Lambert made formal vows before the bishop at the monastery. Later both Atho and Lambert appealed to Pope Nicholas I to release him from his vows – like Gottschalk, on the grounds of irregular process. Atho admitted that he had not followed the *Rule of Benedict* – perhaps he had never intended the monastery to be Benedictine. Although Atho and Lambert appealed because, as they said, Lambert had never wanted to be a monk, and his father had not understood how hard monastic life could be, there were other reasons that did not form part of the appeal but that must have been equally powerful.[109] For one thing, as Gottschalk had found, an oblate had no further claim on his inheritance once he had professed as a monk. In families where older sons predeceased their fathers, leaving the only heir a professed monk, this was potentially disastrous. Mayke de Jong has suggested that Atho had anticipated being able to control the monastery he had founded through his son, with the son fully in control of the resources of the monastery, which amounted to his own inheritance. The bishop, however, had no intention of allowing a monastery in his diocese to remain under the control of the founding family, and opposed the family's appeal to Rome. The family got their way, because Pope Nicholas took the view that there was little difference in terms of profession between a regular canon – the life that Lambert adopted – and an enclosed monk. The difference was readily apparent in other ways, not least because a canon could retain his own property. In later centuries, the difference in *quality* of profession between monk and canon would become a point of contention in religious life.

Another feature of the ninth-century monastery that Benedict of Nursia would have found unfamiliar was the make-up of the typical male monastic community. As already discussed, the kind of monk or nun envisaged in the Rule – the adult postulant – had become the exception.[110] Furthermore, whereas Benedict had regulated for a community in which most monks took vows but were not ordained priests, by the early ninth century the proportions of monks who were also ordained priests had increased dramatically. At Fulda under Hrabanus Maur, the confraternity book of monks shows 70 per cent as ordained. In the ninth century, more masses were celebrated inside monasteries than outside in parishes or even cathedral churches. This was because mass celebration proliferated in monasteries along with the increase in ordained priests. Historians cannot be certain whether the increase in ordained monks was an answer to increased need for votive masses to be celebrated, or whether the multiplicity of masses was instead the consequence of there being more ordained monks. We will look more closely in a subsequent chapter at one reason for the proliferation of masses in monasteries in the tenth and eleventh centuries, which speaks to wider relationships between monasteries and lay society. But in the ninth century occasions for masses and liturgical blessings requiring an ordained priest proliferated. In part this was the consequence of the Carolingian preoccupation with *correctio* and textual accuracy in the liturgy. But it also reflects the concerns of a society coming under increasing pressure in the ninth century from external forces beyond its control. The second half of the ninth century was a period of raiding from the north, south and east by Vikings, Arabs and Magyars. Even if monastic chroniclers were prone to exaggerating some of the effects of such raids, there is no doubt that monasteries were damaged and property despoiled. Prüm was burned by Viking raiders in 882 and 892, one consequence being the inability of the abbot to maintain discipline, so that the monastery came under the control of the local count. Some monasteries were abandoned altogether: in 897, the community at Farfa abandoned the monastery in the face of persistent Arab raids, and although the raiders did not destroy it, local looting resulted in a ruinous fire. When St Gall was destroyed by fire in 937 some monks used the confusion simply to leave and abandon their vows. The uncertainties and dangers of life are reflected in the ways in which monastic liturgies developed. Liturgical prayers and blessings were composed to petition God for deliverance from attack by fearsome pagan raiders, from harm at the hands of predatory neighbours, from flooding and storms, from crop failure and fire. Given that the *opus Dei* absorbed more of a monk or nun's time than any other activity, it would not be far-fetched to think of monasteries as the spiritual engine rooms of Christendom. For contemporaries, it was the prayers, petitions, blessings and processions engendered in monasteries that protected the world outside their walls

It should be obvious that that was hardly what Benedict of Nursia, still less Pachomius in Upper Egypt, had in mind when they founded their monasteries. The monks and nuns of the late Roman Mediterranean were responding to what they saw around them by withdrawing into a closed world of their own devising. Of course, only in the most extreme circumstances were either monastic communities or individual religious completely separate from their surrounds — if they were, we would hardly know about them, for one thing. But the otherworldliness of early monastic life was as much conceptual as physical. Rejection of the values and customs of a world in which Christian teaching was still far from stable lay at the root of early monastic withdrawal. By the ninth century, if not before, monasticism had developed in concert with the needs of a largely Christian society. The cultural currency and framework of beliefs in which monasteries were founded and grew in the period covered by this chapter were fundamentally Christian. The consequence of this shift was profound for monasticism as a way of life. It meant that monasteries became part of the institutional Church's armoury in conversion of non-Christian peoples, for example in Ireland and eastern Germany. But it also meant that monasteries, even though havens from the world, were intimately connected to the world. A monastery or convent might be the surest way to serve God and the safest place to guard against sin, but it was also a site of mediation for the sinful world outside. Monasticism had developed as a tool of society, maintained by bishops, the landowning elites, and kings and queens with the resources to live in such a way as to produce constant prayer.

CHAPTER THREE

Parallel Paths
Monasticism in the Ninth and Tenth Centuries

THE STUDITE REFORM IN CONSTANTINOPLE

MONKS WERE A COMMON sight in the streets of Constantinople in the ninth century, but there was a particular reason why so many were processing through the city on 11 March 843. At the end of the first session of a council convened by the new Emperor Michael III, his mother the regent Theodora and the patriarch of Constantinople, Methodios, the participants walked in solemn procession the length of the city from the Blachernae Palace to the cathedral of Hagia Sophia to restore the icons that had been removed from churches and monasteries for most of the previous century. For two periods, between 726 and 787 and from 815 to 843, the worship and even display of icons in churches and monasteries was prohibited under imperial regimes that considered them idolatrous. The reasons for the imposition of the iconoclastic regime are too complex to deal with here, but needless to say the banning of icons had profound effects on monasticism. The iconoclast Emperor Constantine V, who had become convinced that devotion to icons had undermined God's favour towards the Roman people, tried to eradicate monasticism. According to the contemporary chronicler Theophanes, he cajoled monks into abandoning their profession, sold off monastic property that had come into imperial control, burned liturgical books, and even held parades in the Hippodrome designed to humiliate monks and nuns by forcing them to parade together hand in hand.[1]

Monks and nuns were the group of people in Byzantine society most associated with icons and their veneration. Constantine's opposition to them, and that of other iconoclast emperors, suggests that they must have been a numerous enough group to have caused real concern about enforcing their programme. It has been estimated that in the middle of the fifth century there may have been between 10,000 and 15,000 monks and nuns in Constantinople, at a time when the population was probably around a million. By *c.* 600 the number of monasteries in the city may have reached 150, and despite fluctuations this number remained relatively stable until *c.* 1200.[2] Nevertheless, there were many changes in the institutions making up those numbers. After the initial period of foundation in the fifth and sixth centuries many monasteries probably folded or declined through lack of sufficient funds, particularly in a period in which the population of the city was falling in any case, and periodically under threat of Arab conquest. From the 780s onwards, during the period between the two phases of iconoclasm, there was considerable activity in founding or refounding monastic communities. By the 960s, however, Emperor Nikephoros Phokas was so concerned about the difficulty of maintaining existing monasteries that he prohibited the founding of new ones. Although it is impossible to be accurate, or anything like it, about numbers of professed religious, monastic foundation documents often imply, even if they do not state, the upper limits of numbers in the mind of the founder. Thus, Peter Charanis estimated that there among the total number of monasteries was a group of ninety-four monasteries whose population of monks or nuns fell below one hundred. Of these, the vast majority were very small, with perhaps twenty monks or nuns each.[3] According to Charanis's estimate, there may have been one monk or nun to every hundred people in the Empire during most of the Middle Ages, if we accept an estimate of around 150,000 professed religious in more than 7,000 monasteries, and a total population in the Empire of between 15 and 20 million. If these proportions are even roughly correct, it is easy to see why emperors might have seen them as a powerful group with the potential to motivate and influence Byzantine society. They were also, in demographic terms, an unproductive population, and it is possible that Constantine's public humiliation of monks and nuns was born of frustration at a time of falling manpower.

In the period between the seventh and eleventh centuries, most monasteries were private foundations. Despite the legal prescription that bishops should oversee all religious establishments in their dioceses, monasticism had begun as a phenomenon of lay piety and even where a bishop happened to be the founder of a monastery, there was no strong tradition of foundation by the state.[4] There are of course exceptions, notably Emperor Justinian's foundation of the monastery on Mount Sinai to commemorate the site of the Burning Bush where God appeared to Moses, but this can be seen as a continuation of the tradition of shrine foundations instituted in the fourth century by Constantine. The essentially private nature of monasteries as institutions is borne out by the surviving documentary evidence. Many founders composed *typika* – formulary documents that explain the nature of the life they wish to be observed by the monks or nuns in the community. These vary in quantity and type of detail. Some provide a statement of the circumstances and reasons for the foundation, even a brief autobiographical resumé. Sometimes founders show careful forethought for the monastery's resources and a keen interest in internal discipline and organisation, even details of diet. Some founders composed separate liturgical typika providing the exact specifications of how the important feasts of the Church were to be celebrated. But almost all include some element that functions as a formal and legal instrument of the transfer of the foundation to a successor – either directly named or through a direction to the community to proceed to an election.

We have already seen how in the West different monastic traditions and regulations developed alongside each other during the fifth and sixth centuries, sometimes causing friction between observances and customs. During the early Middle Ages the *Rule of Benedict*, which epitomised many of the currents of thinking about monasticism, gradually came into a position of dominance, achieved not least through the agency of Frankish royal centralisation of the Church. In the Byzantine world no such development took place. In theory, each monastery or convent was regulated as the founder determined, and there was no equivalent of the *Rule of Benedict*. But of course founders did not operate without reference to monastic tradition, and almost all show knowledge of and reliance on the history of monasticism. The two Rules composed by Basil of

Caesarea in the late fourth century provided inspiration for many Byzantine founders.[5] Although it would be wrong to think of Orthodox monasticism – as later medieval western authors often did – as 'Basilian', Basil's ideas, both as enshrined in the Rules and in his Ascetic Treatises, exerted a strong influence on monastic practices. The usual instrument for setting out governance in the Orthodox monastic tradition was the typikon. Typika as a category have been extensively studied by Byzantinists because they give us pictures of monastic life of unparalleled clarity. There are in fact two types of typikon: the liturgical typikon, which specifies the precise form of liturgical offices to be sung on specific feasts, and the founder's typikon, which ordered the running of the monastery as an institution according to the founder's wishes. Although there was in no sense any such principle of associations of monastic communities as we find in the West, still less of monastic 'Orders', the careful scholarship of the past fifty years has shown that links often existed between monastic regulatory principles across the Orthodox world. Besides the *Rules of Basil*, certain typika, such as that of St John Stoudios in the early ninth century and of the monastery of the Theotokos Evergetis in the eleventh, proved to be highly influential as mediators of a reforming approach to cenobitic monasticism.[6]

Among the characteristic features of Basil's regulations that were adopted by many Byzantine monasteries were the practice of manual labour, especially for new postulants; an expectation of genuine communal life; care of the sick – Basil, indeed, recommended that monasteries have a hospital; literacy on the part of the monks; and a degree of communication and contact with other monasteries and even convents. Philanthropy and works of charity were encouraged in his ascetic writings. Other elements of typical Byzantine monasticism, such as the prohibition on the ownership of private property by monks, and indeed the equality to be maintained in principle among the monks, predate Basil's Rules, and in fact are traceable as far back as the Pachomian communities in Egypt.

The earliest typikon known to us is the foundation document for a monastery founded on the island of Pantelleria, off the western tip of Sicily, in the eighth century. The founder, a monk called John, may have been drawn to this remote spot as a way of escaping the iconoclasm in the capital. The monastery probably did not have a long existence. In 806 many of the monks were kidnapped in an Arab raid that presaged the long drawn-out conquest of Sicily and its ruinous consequences later in the ninth century. The typikon shows no interest in constitutional matters, but reveals a community living in strict asceticism, practising manual labour and with strong regulation of behaviour. Particular concern was shown to guard against any suggestion of homoeroticism. 'Nowhere else in Byzantine typika', John Thomas has commented, 'is there evidence of such a grim regime for daily life.'[7] Discipline was also to be enforced during the offices. There was to be no moving around during the liturgy, but every monk was to remain in place throughout. Humility was to be shown bodily through gestures of submission during the offices (such as bowing nine times between prayers). Anyone who presumed to change any of the words or melodies of the chant was punished by having to prostrate themselves face down on the ground. Monks were to fast during the day unless their manual labour for the day involved particularly heavy work, which entitled them to a quarter of a portion. Aimless talk and socialisation among the monks was forbidden, and certainly anything that might lead to particular affection between monks. Perhaps the unrelenting discipline of the house, as much as the conquest of Sicily, hastened the end of the community.

The end of the first period of iconoclasm after the death of Constantine V and the seizure of power by his iconodule wife Irene enabled an intense period of monastic refoundation in the capital. In 799 Theodore, a Bithynian noble, was asked by Irene to become head of a small and nearly moribund community in Constantinople called St John Stoudios. The monastery had originally been founded in the middle of the fifth century, and was notable for being a 'sleepless community', in other words one where the monks operated in shifts so that the liturgy was being said perpetually in the church. By the end of the eighth century, however, this must have been almost impossible for the ten or so monks who were left. Theodore (759–826) was the son of a provincial family of some distinction, but despite the promise of a glittering career in imperial service after his father's death he retired to a family estate with his uncle and mother and eventually became a monk at a monastery founded by his uncle, Plato, at Sakkoudion. By 794 Theodore was co-running the monastery with Plato, but they fell foul of Empress Irene when Plato was revealed as a supporter of her son Constantine VI, who contracted a second, bigamous marriage as part of an attempt to seize sole control of his throne from his mother. Theodore was exiled to Thessaloniki, but after Irene had finally deposed and blinded Constantine in 797 she relented and Theodore was summoned to the capital to reform Stoudios. It was far from an easy experience for him. In 809 and again after 815 he was exiled owing to contentious relations with the patriarch, and the revival of iconoclasm under Emperor Leo V (813–20) meant the dispersal of his community and the influx of an iconoclast-supporting group of monks. It has been said that Theodore treated the monastery as though it were his own property, but in fact before his exile in 815 he was heading three other monasteries at the same time, with the charge of somewhere between 700 and 1,000 monks.

Theodore's typikon for St John Stoudios, and perhaps even more so his other writings, articulate the ideal of restoring 'original' monastic life. The typikon itself is prefaced by a Testament of faith, asserting Theodore's own Orthodoxy according to tradition. There follows a set of pastoral instructions to the superior who will follow Theodore, urging the care of the community like a good shepherd, and three points of general instruction to the brethren about the calling to despise worldly life. Theodore was adamant about the centrality of Basil to his conception of the monastery: 'It is clear that the monastic life must be ordered according to the ascetic rules of the holy Basil the Great and not by half measures so that some in one place choose some rules and let others go.'[8] But his appreciation of monastic traditions is wider than this, and there are also debts to the spiritual writings of the Sinai monk John Klimakos and Dorotheos of Gaza. The purpose of Theodore's monasticism has been characterised as the realisation of older ideals in the creation of 'a Christian village of an essentially practical type'.[9] In such an interpretation, the monastery provides a route to contemplation through work, or *philergia*. The Testament and typikon form only a fraction of his writings on monasticism. In more than 500 letters and catechetical treatises for his monks, his ideas about the meaning and practice of monastic life come alive, in the same way as for Bernard of Clairvaux 300 years later. The so-called *Great Catecheses*, which are the best evidence for how monasticism at Stoudios actually worked, were epitomised into a collection of 134 that was widely disseminated from the 820s onward as the *Small Catecheses*.[10]

Throughout his writings Theodore advocates a consultative rather than authoritarian style of rule. As *hegoumen*, or superior, he was assisted by appointed officials from among the monks with responsibilities for the fabric and estate (the steward), discipline and the conduct of the sacred offices. In advising his successor at Stoudios, Nicholas, he reiterates the need to ensure that the monastery's property should not be misused or fall into the wrong hands. It is not clear what the property comprised, though it is likely to have been land, probably outside the city walls. Manual labour was required, though not daily: on days when no such work was done, monks were expected to collect a book from the library and spend that part of the day in which they were not occupied in the liturgical offices in private reading.[11] The work was both manual labour of a mixed kind, which might include craftsmanship and the copying of books, and social obligations such as care of the poor and sick. The typikon gives a detailed account of how the liturgies are to be observed, beginning with the waking of the brethren for the night office by beating the semantron, a wooden board hung outside the church (a practice that is still largely standard in Orthodox monasteries). Discipline was to be maintained during the offices by the choir monitors, but gentleness was expected alongside firmness. Within the community more widely *epitactae* ('overseers', of whom the Edwardian biographer of Theodore, Alice Gardner, remarked tartly that 'an Englishman would call them spies') supervised general conduct.[12] For the refractory, confinement in a punishment cell on a diet of dry bread awaited. At mealtimes, monks were seated nine to a (marble) table, and ate in silence while listening to a reading from Scripture or a patristic homily. A single main meal was taken consisting of two different dishes: during normal time, liturgically, these might include garden vegetables, beans or other pulses, fish, cheese or eggs, and olive or another kind of oil, but during Lent, Advent and other periods of fast a precise regimen applied that specified limits on quantities and omitted eggs, dairy products and even on some days oil.[13] Such specific detail was to become a common feature of Byzantine founding typika. Postulants to the monastery were to be received initially in the hospice and to stay for two or three weeks to experience monastic life before taking vows as novices. Should they decide to remain, they received as clothing two undergarments, two cowls, a woollen tunic, a scapular (to wear over the tunic), leggings and two pairs of boots. They slept on a goat-hair mat and straw mattress, and were provided with two blankets.[14] The provision of staying in the hospice to experience the monastery was observed in different ways in later foundations that were influenced by the Studite reform. When Leontios was accepted into St John on Patmos in the twelfth century he was instructed by the superior to stay in his cell reciting the offices until he had become used to the way of life.[15]

Theodore was given licence to reform other monasteries along the same lines as St John Stoudios, and before his exile effectively ruled over a confederation of monasteries in Constantinople. This gave him the opportunity not only to impose his vision of monasticism but also to ensure than cenobitism became the dominant form of monasticism in the capital. We must suppose that Empress Irene was in this way setting out her template for monastic life. Earlier ecclesiastical practice, as enshrined for example in the Council of Trullo (692), had permitted solitary living for monks within a religious community, as long as they had served at least four years as cenobitic monks. This effectively permitted a dual path of monasticism even within a single community. Not all founders – Theodore included – approved of this practice, though it never disappeared altogether and was to be revived by some eleventh-century founders. The phenomenon of iconoclasm and the resistance to it both enabled and stimulated imperial ambitions to control monasticism. Just as iconoclast emperors wanted to limit or even eradicate monasticism, so iconodules such as Irene saw monks and monasticism as a means of channelling a particular religious ideology to Byzantine society. But there was more to this than simply the will to impose an ideology. Theodore's Studite reform recognised the need to place monasteries on a firm financial footing. Traditionally, monasteries had either supported themselves by manual labour – the Pachomian model – or relied on cash revenues from patrons or founders. Neither model was without its dangers. Cash funding could be uncertain and sporadic, since the economic fortunes of donors often depended on political fortunes that might alter very quickly. And manual labour was only as reliable as the continuing abilities and willingness of communities to perform it effectively, and in the first place required suitable grants of land. In the ninth century revenues from grants of land started to replace previous models. One consequence was that new monasteries tended to be smaller, since fewer monks could be supported in this manner.

It is perhaps not very surprising, given the importance of being able to ensure adequate resourcing of a community, that most founders were typically from the provincial upper or middle classes: those with land and cash. As Rosemary Morris has pointed out, founders also had to be comfortably enough off that they might be able to allow sons to profess as monks rather than working family estates, and not too powerful to have ambitions of military or governmental leadership on their behalf.[16] A somewhat different calculation applied to daughters, since they could neither – except in the poorest families – work the land nor advance in imperial service. But a family with no prospects of marriage for a daughter might see founding a convent as a solution to provide for her future. Many monks about whom we know from hagiographies were of noble origin – even allowing for this as a trope of the genre. Besides Theodore himself, the tenth-century monastic founder Athanasius the Athonite and the prominent monastic leader of the early eleventh century, Symeon the New Theologian, were also of noble origin. Yet in contrast with monasticism in the West, Byzantine monasticism attracted people from the peasantry as well as the higher classes. Euthymios the Younger, the ninth-century monk on Mount Athos and elsewhere, was from a peasant family, and Ioannikes had apparently kept pigs and then become a soldier before entering a monastery.[17] Unlike in the West, monks recruited from the higher echelons of society were likely to be literate, even well educated. As we have seen, Studite monks were expected to be able to read, and in the tenth century Athanasios became the subject of scorn when he was taken as barely literate. Monasteries had provision to teach basic literacy – the twelfth-century Cypriot monk Neophytos the Recluse, also from a peasant family, only learned to read when he became a monk – but in Byzantine society monasteries did not become important centres of education as they did in the West. There was no need for this: because learning and education were requirements of membership of civic society, a tradition of education persisted among the middle and higher classes.

MOUNT ATHOS

According to the tenth-century Byzantine historian Genesios, among those celebrating the festival of Orthodoxy in Constantinople in 843 were monks from Mount Athos. The earliest monks seem to have settled the peninsula of Mount Athos, the easternmost and most mountainous of the three fingers that protrude from Chalkidike, in the northeast of Greece, in the mid-ninth century. The peninsula takes its name from the pyramidal range rising to over 2,000 metres that dominates its spine. The terrain is forbidding for human habitation, thanks to steep cliffs, rocky shores and a prevailing northeasterly wind that makes the climate continental rather than Mediterranean. Although Mount Athos became the best-known and organised of such monastic sites, other similarly rugged environments had already attracted groups of monks and solitaries, notably Mount Olympus in Bithynia and Mount Latros in western Asia Minor. Such places were understood as the nurseries of aspiring ascetics, where they might further their spiritual training. The first named monk, Peter the Athonite, is a semi-legendary figure about whom we know very little that can be corroborated from sources other than his hagiographical account.[18]

Early Athonite monasticism has been characterised as a microcosm of the same processes of rural foundation and patronage taking place throughout the Empire. The co-existence of cenobitic communities and solitaries already known at Mount Latros seems to have been a feature of the first century or so of monastic settlement on Athos. In c. 972, however, Emperor John Tzimiskes issued a document known as the 'Tragos' (treaty) – essentially a typikon for Mount Athos – in which strong disapproval was voiced for the practice of solitary ascetic living on the peninsula. Given that the Tragos was signed by fifty-five monastic superiors, we can infer that considerable pressure was being exerted against anchoritic living. Since 943 Athos had enjoyed a legally constituted identity and a form of associative government in the shape of a council formed by the superiors of the existing monasteries, one of whom served as the *protos*, or head. The administrative centre at Karyes, the village in the centre of the peninsula, was already serving the purpose that it continues to this day. In some ways the Tragos gives a misleading picture of monastic life on Athos. We should not imagine the fifty-five superiors who signed the document ruling over monasteries of the type of St John Stoudios. Some undoubtedly had substantial buildings and were surrounded by walls, but others may have been little more than a group of wooden huts surrounding a small church.[19] It was in this environment that in 963–4 Athanasios the Athonite founded his monastery, which he called the Great Lavra.

Athanasios was born between 925 and 930 in Trebizond and brought up from a young age by a friend of his dead mother who had evidently taken personal vows of virginity.[20] Two versions of his *vita* were written, that known as *Vita* B by a monk from the Great Lavra between *c.* 1050 and 1150, but probably based on a lost original written closer to the time of Athanasios's death. After his guardian's death, Athanasios – at that time still known as Abramios – was taken by his tutor to Constantinople to live with relatives. He showed early signs of his future calling by living an austere life in a wealthy household, giving most of his food to the servants and eating only barley bread, raw vegetables and fruit, and drinking only water.[21] After a rather bruising attempt at joining the teaching profession, Athanasios determined on a life of ascetic solitude. He became a follower of Michael Maleinos, a monk at Mount Kyminos in Bithynia, and was invested with the monastic habit at his *lavra*. Here he showed the same inclination to personal austerity: 'he mastered every form of ascetic conduct, and accomplished every sort of spiritual contest through constant abstinence, numerous fasts, vigils and standing vigils, genuflections throughout the night, nocturnal labours, diurnal endeavours, and total submission and obedience'.[22] Having proved himself to his monastic teacher, Athanasios was allowed to live alone a mile away from the *lavra* according to a regime designed by Michael: a diet of bread and water every two days, sleeping on a chair instead of on the ground, and prayer vigils on all dominical feast days and every Sunday from sunset to the third hour.[23] When he understood that he was likely to be named as Michael's successor as his master's health failed, he withdrew and settled instead on Mount Athos. At that time, according to his biographer, most monks were living in solitary eremitism or in *lavrae*, often in huts made of grass, surviving off the fruit and nuts they gathered themselves, supplemented by occasional gifts of grain from pious visitors.[24] Athanasios decided that he needed to live incognito because there was a danger he might be recognised by another monk, the brother of a man powerful at the imperial court, Nikephoros Phokas, who knew him from his own visit to Mount Kyminos. Athanasios's attempt to feign illiteracy was discovered at the synaxis, a thrice-yearly celebration of all Athonite monks, and Nikephoros was able to establish contact with him.[25] The relationship between the monk and the imperial general was to prove instrumental in the future of Mount Athos. Nikephoros, believing that Athanasios's prayers had aided in his conquest of Crete, sent him the funds necessary to build a coenobium on Mount Athos.[26]

Although not the first monastery on the peninsula, this was by far the largest and most ambitious in extent. The cross-shaped domed church stood in the centre, 'like an eye visible from all sides', with cells for the monks occupying a rectangular plan around it. The refectory had twenty-one tables of white marble, each accommodating twelve diners. There was an infirmary, a guest house and a bathhouse for the sick. Water was piped in from streams outside the *lavra* to provide for the cells, for a watermill and for the washtubs, gardens and animals' drinking troughs.[27] The typikon assumes a total of eighty monks, but by *c.* 980 the numbers seem to have climbed to 150. The Great Lavra, as Athanasios insisted on naming what was for all intents and purposes in fact a coenobium, attracted many of the solitaries living on the Athos peninsula. But, even allowing for the hyperbole in the *Life*, Athanasios's reputation seems to have drawn men from different parts of the Byzantine world: from Calabria, Georgia and Armenia as well as the heartlands of the Empire. 'Not only ordinary and common people, but wellborn and wealthy men as well; and not only these, but also the superiors of cenobitic monasteries and bishops renounced their thrones and came to him and subjected themselves in obedience to him.' The Patriarch of Constantinople Nicholas was one of the latter, while among the solitaries were the Calabrians Phantinos and Nikephoros the Nude. Athanasios seems to have been seen by such men, experienced solitaries, as a teacher who could acculturate them to community life. Such a role was accentuated by the counselling sessions Athanasios held after each of the liturgical offices, to which he invited any monk to speak to him about the temptations he was undergoing and to receive spiritual advice.[28]

The governance of the monastery bears strong resemblances to Theodore's provision for St John Stoudios. As in the Studite reform, there was a strong emphasis on communality and collective discipline, with similar measures to enforce this: an *epistemonarches* responsible for the chant, for attendance by choir members at offices and discipline in church; and doorkeepers to show latecomers to their places and to monitor the conduct of monks not in the choirs and to check that none left the church without permission. Likewise two monks served as monitors in the refectory, regulating silence, proper attendance and attention to the readings, but also that after mealtimes monks did not drift into each other's cells for casual meetings.[29] Common possession of all property was to be absolutely enforced: monks were to own 'not even so much as a needle' themselves. Manual labour of various kinds was also mandated, which in the early days at any rate must have included the extensive building works. Athanasios was eventually to fall victim to the expansion of the *lavra* when scaffolding collapsed while he was supervising works, killing six monks and fatally injuring him.[30]

Athanasios is often credited, partly on the strength of the testimony in the *Lives*, with having achieved the conversion of Athos from a site of idiorrhythmic (that is, self-governing) solitary monasticism to the kinds of cenobitic norms that had been set by Theodore.[31] Athanasios thought of himself as entirely consistent with the traditions of the fathers, particularly Basil.[32] It has even been suggested, given the presence of some Italian monks on Athos, that the influence of the *Rule of Benedict* can also be detected, though this remains rather speculative.[33] The cenobitic nature of the Great Lavra may appear odd on an initial reading of the *Lives*, in which Athanasios appears as a determined solitary – indeed, as someone who would rather withdraw from a place and start again than become involved in a community. But there is also a clear sense in the typikon of Athanasios's understanding of early traditions of asceticism. Here we see monasticism characterised as an athletic struggle, in language that recalls Theodoret of Cyrrhus, and a more general tone of pessimism at the human condition in the declaration that monks are 'called to mourning, not rejoicing'.[34] The authors of the *Lives* seem to have seen a need to burnish Athanasios's credentials as a solitary, given that his legacy was in fact the first Studite monastery on Athos. The critical point in his career seems to have been the visit he made to Crete in 961 at the behest of Nikephoros Phokas, who was campaigning there at the time, and who persuaded him to return to Athos not to pursue the solitary life he had previously lived but to exercise leadership in bringing cenobitism to the wilderness.

Athanasios was aware of the possibility of tensions arising between the monks he recruited to the Lavra as converts and those who joined after having professed elsewhere and who may therefore have been used to different customs. This may explain his concern to encourage the 'disclosure of thoughts' after the offices as a way of getting to know his monks and their concerns. Likewise his insistence that the superior, though exercising full authority under God, should live a life indistinguishable from the community, can be seen as a means of forming bonds across a diverse community. The provision for 'kelliot' monks to pursue solitary lives as part of the same community as the cenobitic brethren was a departure from the Studite (and indeed the Basilian) model, but was adopted by later cenobitic founders as well, notably Christodoulos of Patmos in the eleventh century.[35]

The Great Lavra shared one particularly important similarity with Theodore's refounding of St John Stoudios: both were the result of imperial patronage. Nikephoros Phokas became emperor in 963 and both in his reign and under his successor John Tzimiskes imperial favour came to be directed towards a single institution – the Great Lavra – as opposed to monastic life on Mount Athos as a whole. Nikephoros, while a high-ranking general in the imperial service, had flirted with the idea of becoming a monk, and as emperor was invested in a particular approach to monasticism that the asceticism of Mount Athos seemed to exemplify.[36] His novel of 964 argues for the incompatibility of wealth with monastic life, and complains that many monks are so preoccupied with the acquisition and maintenance of property that they are scarcely distinguishable from laymen. On the contrary, only strict adherence to the simplicity of life practised by the early monks of Egypt and Palestine constituted 'genuine' monasticism and enabled a monk or nun to fulfil their vows. On one level this might be seen as an early expression of a sentiment that we see articulated frequently in the period between about 900 and 1200 in both Byzantine and western monastic discourse.

Founders of monasteries, hagiographers and chroniclers speak of Egyptian monasticism in particular as a kind of template for authenticity in monastic life. Indeed, it becomes such a common refrain as to be formulaic. In many cases it is surely not intended as a serious programme for living but rather as a routine observance of the supposed genealogy of monasticism, the purpose being to emphasise the conceptual connection between the life lived by the present subjects and that initiated in the Egyptian or Syrian deserts. One reason why it is difficult to take such statements as anything other than this is that, as we saw in Chapter One, early monasticism in Egypt, Palestine and Syria encompassed so many variations on a central theme. In the case of Nikephoros Phokas, however, we can see Mount Athos providing him with a template in which the ideals of primitive monasticism could actually be fulfilled. His own preference was for lavriot monasteries, because they had less need than a coenobium to acquire land, but to ensure that this continued to be the case he forbade *lavrae* from acquiring any beyond the enclosure itself. Mount Athos seemed to provide a solution to a problem that had troubled earlier emperors. Nikephoros understood that land acquisition entailed other kinds of acquisitiveness on the part of monastic communities, not least labour for clearance, building, maintenance and the production of an income from the land through farming. Over the course of the eleventh century these stipulations would be broken as some Athonite monasteries with rich patrons did indeed acquire land grants beyond the peninsula, which in turn entailed ownership of boats and draught animals and an involvement in trade.[37]

ASCETICISM AND EREMITISM, *c.* 800–1000

Most of what we know about Byzantine monks and monasticism comes either from typika or from saints' lives. In different ways both types of source offer idealised versions of the mundane lives of monks and nuns. Typika usually present the monastery according to the intent of the founder, either at a period when the foundation is still quite young or towards the end of the founder's life. In some cases, as for example with Theodore's for St John Stoudios, the typikon looks forward to the fulfilment of the founder's hopes under a chosen successor. In others, such as in the codicil added by Christodoulos to the typikon for St John on Patmos, it gives the founder an opportunity to reflect on a monastic career. Christodoulos's codicil, indeed, shows a state of mind beset by dashed hopes and fears for the future of his foundation.[38] In such moments the typikon can intersect with hagiography, as the founder looks back at – usually his – life as a series of stages on the road to the construction of monastic sanctity. Hagiography is the largest single category of Byzantine literature. The *Bibliotheca Hagiographica Graeca*, which is the nearest thing to an official catalogue of edited saints' lives, contains about 3,000. Since the purpose of hagiography, obviously, was to exemplify the qualities of holiness, we cannot invariably take saints' lives as accurate indications of the inner workings of a monastery, even though such workings are sometimes described in detail. For example, when the eleventh-century hagiographer of Lazaros of Mount Galesion recounts the sometimes difficult relationships between the stylitic founder and his monks, it is invariably the monks who are at fault.

Notwithstanding the need to read them critically, saints' lives cannot be dispensed with as sources for what those from 'within' monasticism thought about authentic traditions of living. Almost all hagiographies were written by monks, often the disciples or followers of founders of communities. One of the most distinctive features of early Egyptian and Palestinian monasticism was the relationship of instruction and training between an 'elder' and a novice monk. This proved to be a feature that endured in the Greek monastic tradition. We have seen it at work already in the *Life of Athanasios*. But although Athanasios may have been the founder of organised monasticism on Mount Athos, he was drawn there in the first place by its burgeoning reputation as a centre for unregulated ascetic life. Most of what we know about Athonite predecessors of Athanasios comes from hagiography. Prominent among such saints' lives is the *Life of Euthymios the Younger*, written by his disciple Basil, who later became bishop of Thessaloniki. Euthymios (823/4–898), a native of Galatia in Asia Minor, can be said to have exemplified the full range of monastic experience: besides his eremitical life on Athos, he was also for a time a stylite on a pillar near Thessaloniki, a cave dweller, and a cenobitic monk and finally founder of a monastery. Euthymios was born into a respectable but far from wealthy family, but his father died when he was young and although he had a desire to be a monk, he had to support his mother and two sisters, and fulfilled his obligation of military service before marrying the woman his mother had arranged for him. One day he simply walked out on his family. His first step in becoming a monk was not, as we might expect, to find a monastery, but to attach himself to a 'holy father'. He met a monk called Ioannikos at Olympus who after testing him in various ways – including subjecting him to deliberate indignity by pretending to recognise him as a notorious murderer – welcomed him into the community of his followers.[39] Eventually Euthymios left his first teacher to go and live with another monk who in 842 tonsured him and sent him for training to a cenobitic monastery. Here he was put to work on a series of menial tasks, first as assistant to the monk in charge of the pack animals, then as a kitchen boy, then assisting the cellarer and finally as ox driver. Only after serving these labouring apprenticeships was he taught to read, so that he could join the choir in the monastery.[40]

A clear progression is traceable in the biography of the ideal monk. As a young man from a peasant family, working with animals would have been second nature to Euthymios, but service in the monastery kitchens often appears in monastic hagiography as an example of subjection to physical discipline, sometimes as a punishment. Basil's Shorter Rules indicate that extreme spiritual need demanded extreme forms of labour, but also that individual regimens of such labour should be designed for each monk.[41] The twelfth-century superior of the monastery of St Euthymios in the Judaean desert was following this mandate when he assigned a regime of hard labour – collecting and carrying wood for the bakery and kitchen fires – to the recalcitrant monk Gabriel, who under the influence of demonic possession had tried to murder another monk.[42] In Palestinian monastic hagiography, volunteering for menial kitchen work had traditionally been seen as a path to virtue. Kyriakos, one of the early Palestinian monks about whom Cyril of Scythopolis wrote, proved himself in the coenobium by chopping wood and carrying water for the kitchen. Another of Cyril's subjects, John the Hesychast, entered the *lavra* of St Sabas in order to escape the burden of his episcopal office, and found a new role in serving as cook and helper for the workers who were building the new guest house at the *lavra*.[43] This trope seems to have made its way into early medieval western hagiography as well. St Adalbert of Prague (d. 997) similarly abandoned his bishopric to become a monk at San Bonifacio in Rome, 'making himself small in the midst of the brethren' by taking on the role of cook and pot washer in the kitchen.[44] And John of Gorze, though founder of an important reforming monastery, not only insisted on taking his turn in the rota of kitchen work but looked for extra work: he drew water from the well, chopped, washed and prepared vegetables and washed all the dishes by himself.[45] There was of course no question of Euthymios the Younger needing to be punished, but the discipline of the coenobium required that he progress through a designated path from menial to intellectual; from stable and kitchen to choir. Similarly the twelfth-century Cypriot monk Neophytos, also a village boy from a humble background, was first put to work in the vineyard of St John Koutsovendis before being taught to read and joining the choir monks.[46]

Physical discipline was necessary as part of the training in endurance. Accompanying the regime of manual labour was self-discipline that enabled a monk to withstand all-night vigils of prayer, intense fasting and concentration of thought that might make a monk 'worthy of heavenly illumination' so that he became 'a beacon of theophany'.[47] In the *Life of Euthymios*, this training was the preliminary to his entry into a different 'wrestling arena', one which bore the same characteristics as Mount Carmel where Elijah found solitude in the Old Testament and the Judaean desert where John the Baptist prepared the way of Christ.[48] A great deal is conveyed by Euthymios's hagiographer in this deceptively simple remark. Basil's use of the term *palaestra* (wrestling arena) consciously recalls the vocabulary of earlier Greek monastic writing, especially Theodoret of Cyrrhus's descriptions of monks in fourth- and fifth-century Syria. Euthymios is, in Basil's view, to be seen in the same tradition as the monks of the 'golden age' of solitary ascetic practices. Indeed, his later brief and unsatisfactory career as a stylite in Thessaloniki was a deliberate evocation on his part of the kind of asceticism pioneered by Symeon.[49] Terminology that at first sight may appear playful in fact points to a deeper purpose. The 'wrestling ground' where Euthymios and a companion, Joseph, stripped for asceticism was Mount Athos, which at that time, over a hundred years before Athanasios, was inhabited mostly by solitaries or small groups of ascetics. But, as the terminology suggests, asceticism might be a competitive business. Early monastic writing is infused with the notion of monks outdoing each other in feats of asceticism, whether the competitive fasting that is such a pervasive feature of Irish hagiography or the feats of self-mortification and endurance practised by Syrian monks. Monks proved their potential through their capacity to withstand pain, physical hardship, hunger and cold.

In Byzantine hagiography the emphasis on inflicting pain on the body is less common than it had been in Syrian monasteries, where monks tied tight bands around their chests to restrict breathing, or suspended themselves from hooks in the ceiling, and rather on enduring hardship. Sleeping on the ground or in a chair – even, in the case of the twelfth-century monk Leontios on Patmos, in a coffin – is a common trope in hagiography. We find it equally in Byzantine and medieval western practice. Lazaros of Mount Galesion (981–1053), a monk from Asia Minor who revived the practice of stylitism, designed a chair in which he could recline to rest but not sleep, and the same idea seems to have occurred to the English anchorite Godric of Throkenholt in his fenland hut in the twelfth century.[50] Self-imposed sleep deprivation was a practice that dated back to the early days of monasticism, but one that Athanasios, in his treatise *On Sickness and Health*, had criticised, suggesting that the principle of constant wakefulness and vigilance should be taken to refer to the sleep of the soul rather than the body.[51] But it is easy to see how observance of the night office, which was a very ancient monastic practice and must have entailed interruption of sleep even for monks not committed to a particularly ascetic programme, could be extended into the more wilful kinds of practices that denied any sleep. Some monastic writers have remarked that observance of the night office need not necessarily mean sleeping less, depending on when monks retired to bed – and doubtless years of rising at 2 or 3 a.m. accustom the monk to a different pattern of sleep.[52] Nevertheless, recent studies have suggested that people who work night shifts may suffer more health problems than those able to organise their days according to natural light.[53]

Euthymios's notion of training for the athletic arena of asceticism on Mount Athos carries a further echo of early Syrian and Palestinian monastic practices. The warm-up exercise, so to speak, was to spend forty days 'purifying our mind', as he explained to his companion, 'and recovering again the quality of being in the image and likeness of the Creator'. But the surprising method by which this was to be achieved was to pretend they were animals rather than humans, crawling on the ground on all fours rather than walking upright, and feeding on grass like cattle.[54] After this period was over, they lived in a cave subsisting on a diet of acorns, chestnuts and wild strawberries. While this is described by his hagiographer as 'gathering the necessary foods from nearby', like the *boschoi* of the fourth and fifth centuries, it was barely enough to live on.[55] The revival of the practice of grazing is partly a textual phenomenon. Granted that solitary ascetics who neither cultivated land to grow food nor begged had little choice in fact other than gathering wild plants, the hagiographer is also signalling something that he expects to resonate with his audience. The decision to graze links Euthymios with a specific period and place – the Near East in the period between Ephrem the Syrian in the late fourth century and Leontios of Neapolis's *Life of Symeon the Holy Fool* in the seventh. Euthymios was therefore bringing the ascetic past of Syria and the Holy Land to Mount Athos: sanctifying it with venerable monastic practices.

Although previous authors such as the fifth-century historian Sozomen had drawn parallels between the practice of grazing and animals, this is a point explored more fully by Euthymios's hagiographer. Sozomen remarked that grazing monks were called *boschoi* because they had no dwellings, and because they fed on what grew in the hills, 'like animals out to pasture'.[56] A story in an anonymous collection takes the relationship between the monk and the animal world further. A grazing monk who lived near a herd of buffalo and shared their pasture asked God how he could perfect himself. God answered that he should go to a monastery and learn obedience there, but in the monastery the monk found himself being pestered by the younger monks constantly telling him what to do, where to go and being generally disrespectful to him. Eventually he could take no more and prayed to God: 'Lord, I cannot serve people; send me back to the buffalo.'[57] This has the ring of an anecdote generated by a tradition that already existed, but it makes the connection between human and animal behaviour a conscious choice on the monk's part rather than an observation by the narrator.

In Basil's *Life of Euthymios* we see the same self-conscious adoption of a way of living that deliberately evokes animal rather than human behaviour. But why would a hagiographer choose to emphasise conscious bestiality? It was a principle of the Christian understanding of the world that humans had been given domination over animal and plant life (Genesis 1.28–30). Mastery over animals, even dangerous ones, was a power exercised by holy men and women in early monastic writing. But, as the anecdotes about monks and lions in Cyril of Scythopolis and John Moschus make clear, such mastery depended on a harmony between humans and the animal world achieved initially by the hard road of domination over human sinfulness. In a story told by Cyril, when the monk who owned the ass that was being guarded by Sabas's tame lion sinned by sleeping with a woman, the lion killed and ate the ass.[58] As Cyril of Scythopolis explained, the charism enjoyed by Euthymios the Great of living with carnivorous and poisonous animals and remaining unharmed was possible for anyone in whom God was present.[59] But until such perfection of life was accomplished, humans could not expect to be able to fulfil the promise made by God. One way of understanding the impetus to live like the beasts, therefore, is that Euthymios the Younger had not yet perfected his monastic training and was therefore still unable to master the animal world – to walk on two feet, so to speak. Progression is part of the narrative design of the hagiography. From crawling on all fours and eating grass like beasts, Euthymios progresses to living in a cave and foraging for edible wild food; eventually, after three years he emerges from the cave 'as if from a holy sanctuary' (echoes of Anthony emerging from the fortress in the desert are obvious here), to be greeted by the other ascetics of Mount Athos.[60] The idea of progression – but also of competition – is given extra force by the recognition in the narrative that not all will be able to reach this point: Joseph, Euthymios's companion, gave up after a year in the cave. Euthymios's progression is marked in stages of accomplishment, the culmination of which is his restoration of the ruined church of St Andrew in Thessaloniki and his gathering of disciples whom he formed into a monastic community.

All solitary religious probably need to forage at some point, but 'grazing' is a more deliberate act of the renunciation of normal human behaviour. The urge to behave bestially rather than like a human brings us to a further dimension of the ascetic role that is recognisable in eastern Mediterranean, and later Slavic, religious culture, but rare in the West. The *salos*, best translated as 'holy fool', set out deliberately to subvert the norms of social behaviour in order to point to its hypocrisies. The idea is found in very early Christianity. In the apocryphal *Acts of St Thomas*, a third-century text, Jesus tells his disciples to strip off their clothes if they want to see the Son of God. The fourth-century *Liber Graduum* explains that the perfect followers of Christ are like angels, and like angels take no care for clothing or food. Pagans who noticed what they considered outlandish behaviour among some Christian ascetics were particularly appalled. 'These monks', exclaimed Eunapius in his *Lives of the Sophists*, 'look like humans but act like pigs. They make a show of their suffering and perform thousands of unspeakably obnoxious acts. But piety for them lies precisely in despising the holy. Thus any man who wears black and wants to behave indecently in public . . . possesses tyrannical power.'[61] If the effect of such antisocial behaviour was to provoke disgust in those who witnessed it, the intent was, as the Sinai monk John Climacos explained, to achieve genuine impassivity to the human condition. Thus, a monk who strove for chastity might take off his clothes in the market place and walk around the city naked without showing any awareness of his condition.[62] Sergey Ivanov has argued that a turning point in the phenomenon of the *salos* was reached when he (and it was usually a man) shifted from a position that might be interpreted as 'leave me in peace!' to 'I will not leave you in peace!' – in other words, when the monk who wished to act in this way deliberately sought a public to whom he might display his foolery.[63]

The archetype of the Byzantine *salos* was the seventh-century Syrian Symeon the Holy Fool, whom we encountered in a previous chapter. Having lived as a 'grazer' in the open air, Symeon announced his status to the people of Emesa by entering the town pulling a dead dog on a rope. This meaningless act of foolishness was merely the preamble to a series of subversions of 'normal' social conduct, which included public nudity and even deliberate entry into the women's section of the bathhouse. Nudity and grazing were often part of the repertoire of the *salos* because both enabled him to demonstrate indifference not only to social norms but also to his own body. For some, stylitism might also sit at the boundary of acceptable and outlandish asceticism. In the *Life of Theodore of Edessa*, a stylite is assumed by some onlookers to be a *salos* even though that is not his intention.[64]

The phenomenon of the *salos* occupied an uneasy space within monasticism. Theodore of Stoudios distrusted the idea, but in the early eleventh century the cenobitic reformer Symeon the New Theologian is described by his biographer as displaying some of the main characteristics of the *salos*, 'having no more feeling with regard to the bodies around him than a corpse has for the dead'.[65] Moreover, onlookers might not agree that a *salos* was genuine. The eleventh-century Greek youth Nicholas, who came to be venerated in Trani, in Apulia, as Nicholas the Pilgrim, might be seen as a holy fool. As a young monk at Hosios Loukas he caused understandable irritation by his apparently uncontrollable habit of shouting *Kyrie eleison* at regular intervals, and was ejected from the monastery. Wherever he went he caused the same reaction, even to the point of having to escape an attempt to drown him. It was only when he left his own land and started wandering through Apulia that he was taken seriously as a holy man.[66] Today we might recognise in Nicholas a man with a condition such as extreme autism, but the contrasting reactions he provoked show how unstable the category of *salos* could be. For the largely Italian population of Trani, with no experience of a *salos*, Nicholas was a man possessed by God, but for his compatriots, fellow monks, even his mother, he fell on the wrong side of the border between inspired behaviour that showed up the follies of human social conduct and simply being an irritant.

Holy fools, or the kind of behaviour associated with them, occur only sporadically in the early medieval West. Similarly, stylites remained a largely, though not exclusively, eastern phenomenon. As we saw in the previous chapter, Gregory of Tours tells the story of the unfortunate Wulfilacius, a sixth-century Frankish hermit who had himself bodily attached to a column outside Trier as a witness to Christianity in a region where pre-Christian rites still prevailed, and where people had to pass by him as they went into the forest to observe them. The local bishops, distrusting him, summoned him to a meeting and while he was there destroyed his column.[67] This would have been less likely in the Greek-speaking world, where the practice, though originally deriving from

Syria, became a recognisable form of asceticism throughout the Empire. In the ninth century, Euthymios the Younger withdrew to a pillar outside Thessaloniki when he realised that his fame as an ascetic had spread throughout the city. Although the practice had been started by Symeon in a rural setting, stylites realised that cities provided ideal opportunities for this kind of detached holiness. If *saloi* attracted attention by forcing people's gaze on their playful acts of subversion, stylites made them stand still and look upwards. Their own stillness demanded a parallel quality of temporarily pausing normal life in order to focus simply on the act of being an ascetic. Of course, as Peter Brown showed, occupying a pillar was no bar to fulfilling the roles of mediator, prophet, enabler and influencer. Nor, indeed, did it necessarily even prevent an ascetic from leading a community. Lazaros, a monk from western Asia Minor, founded a cenobitic community at Mount Galesion in the eleventh century over which he presided from his column. From this vantage point he directed, exhorted and reprimanded monks while retaining his own position of withdrawal from the community.[68] Stylitism remained a feature of eastern Mediterranean monasticism into the thirteenth century. John Phokas, a Greek pilgrim to the Holy Land in the last quarter of the twelfth century, saw a Georgian stylite near the Jordan, and we have already had cause to note Gabriel, the monk of St Sabas who withdrew to a pillar in the desert near the *lavra* before 1183.[69] The crusaders who sacked Constantinople in 1204 found an urban stylite. In the eleventh century, use of the column originally erected by Symeon the Younger at the Monastery of the Wondrous Mountain outside Antioch 500 years earlier caused trouble between Greek and Georgian speakers in the community.[70]

Women are notable by their absence from ascetic sites such as Mount Athos because of the strict separation observed by most monastic founders between men and women. Athos was far from unique in excluding women not simply from monastic enclosures but from the wider area.[71] Christodoulos tried to ban women from the island of Patmos, where he founded his monastery of St John the Theologian in the 1050s, but had to retract when the workmen he had hired to help build it refused to go there to live without their families.[72] In the fourteenth century the Meteora in central Greece would also ban women from the mountain.

Although one of the most enduring archetypes for early asceticism was Mary of Egypt, it was difficult for women to lead the kinds of lives that male ascetics could. Typically, as the careers of the Athonites Athanasios and Euthymios the Younger, and indeed of the Italo-Greek monks demonstrate, ascetics of this period were highly mobile and restless. Athanasios was from Trebizond but ended his life on Mount Athos; Euthymios spent time in Thessaloniki and never settled on Athos; Lazaros professed as a monk in Asia Minor but went to the Holy Land to join the *lavra* of St Sabas in the 990s before returning to western Asia Minor; Elias Speleota and his teacher Arsenios left Calabria to live as ascetics in the Peloponnese before returning to Italy.[73] They also fluctuated between periods of solitary and community living. They founded monasteries and then moved on to evade responsibility or leadership. This manner of ascetic living was simply not possible for women in the Byzantine Empire. Women became nuns, of course, sometimes in the kinds of enclosed household community that are known in the ancient Mediterranean. Property-owning women also donated to monasteries in the expectation of 'sharing in the Holy Mountain'. As one such woman, Maria Tzousmene, expressed it, 'When I heard about the holy mountain, my soul thirsted for the living God, whether I too might have a share in the holy mountain . . .'[74] But where women feature as individuals in the hagiographical sources from this period, it is often as people to whom things happened rather than as those who made them happen. Female relatives – for example Theodore of Stoudios's mother, or Athanasios's foster mother – led enclosed lives because of decisions made by others or circumstances in which they became involved. The monastic careers of the ninth-century Byzantine nuns Theodora of Thessaloniki, Athanasia of Aegina and Theoktiste of Lesbos appear to fit into this pattern of passivity. All three suffered at the hands of Arab raiders. Theodora and Athanasia were forced to flee their native island of Aegina as a consequence of the Arab conquest of the 820s, and both subsequently became nuns. Theoktiste was captured by Arab pirates and escaped to lead a life of solitary asceticism.[75]

When the unfortunate Nicholas the Pilgrim crossed the Adriatic to Apulia he was entering an environment that was still Byzantine. Much of Apulia and Calabria was Greek-speaking and observed the Greek rather than Roman rite. Most bishops were Greek and used Byzantine rather than western collections of decretals in governing their dioceses, and monasteries followed the Greek liturgy.[76] Towns such as Trani and Bari were more mixed in terms of population, with large numbers of Italian speakers whose religious affiliation was Latin. Italy south of Rome was a region where different types of what have been called 'territorial fixity' loosely combined with a lack of overall public authority.[77] As in much of the medieval West in the tenth and eleventh centuries, competing authorities and jurisdictions were interwoven and crisscrossed each other. Religious and cultural affiliations were sometimes, but not invariably, determined by these – and not always in ways that might be expected. As we will see later, Latin territorial lords might patronise Greek-rite as well as Latin monasteries. Apulia was always more closely linked to the Byzantine sphere of influence, and from the 870s Greek-rite bishops were appointed directly from the imperial capital. But although in 970 the emperor established a new administrative system in Apulia with a view to securing fuller control over this province of the Empire, by the 1040s political control was already draining away to local lords. Among these was a small but powerful group of Normans, who over the next couple of generations took more and more control of Italy south of Rome. By 1091 they had conquered the island of Sicily as well as the major cities such as Bari, Otranto and Troia. In the wake of Norman political and territorial control came the *Rule of Benedict*, which had previously been scarcely known south of Subiaco.

Before the mid-eleventh century, however, southern Italy provided a landscape for very similar kinds of ascetic behaviour as other provinces of the Empire. The *Life of Elias Speleota* (c. 866–960: Elias 'the Cave-Dweller') provides a glimpse into the world of Italo-Greek ascetic monasticism.[78] A Calabrian by birth, Elias was born into a family characterised in his *vita* as distinguished parentage. As a young man he lived for a while in solitude as a hermit before making a pilgrimage to Rome. On his return he resumed his ascetic life but this time with an older monk, Aganatus. A little later he took the habit of a monk under Abbot Arsenios at Reggio, but along with Arsenios he transferred to the monastery of Sant' Eustrazio, to escape dissensions among the community. Raiding from Arab-occupied Sicily caused them to flee across the Adriatic to the Peloponnese, where they took up residence in an abandoned tower near Patras. The tower was supposed to have been haunted by a powerful demon whom they were able to vanquish through their fasting and prayers. This brought them to the attention of local villagers, but although they were at first both grateful and impressed, relations soured when Elias was accused of stealing and selling liturgical books belonging to the local church, and when Arsenios was subjected to the unwanted advances of the bishop. They returned to Sant' Eustrazio, where Arsenios died. Elias then joined with a disciple of the Sicilian monk Elias of Enna (822/3–906), whose death is also described at length in the *vita*, and together they built a new monastery in Calabria by hollowing out a vast cave. Here Elias remained for the rest of his life, leaving the cave only to perform miracles of healing and exorcisms on request.

The character of Italo-Greek monasticism was largely eremitical and ascetic: as Agostino Pertusi remarked, 'a perpetual oscillation between a type of anchoritism or hesychastic eremitism and a *lavra* or cenobitic community'.[79] We see this in the *Lives* of Elias Speleota, of Elias of Enna, Vitalis of Castronuovo, Sabas the Younger and Macarius, to name only a few. In the form in which we have it, the *Life of Elias Speleota* is something of a hybrid that expresses in itself the fluid boundaries between religious traditions. This is because it is a Latin translation of the original Greek made in the 1080s at the behest of the Norman abbot of Sta Eufemia, a Calabrian Benedictine monastery founded in 1062 whose endowed property included the cave monastery of Elias.[80] Nevertheless, the *Life* is in many ways typical of Greek monastic hagiography of the period between the ninth and eleventh centuries. One such feature is the linkage of two saints' cults – that of the Cave-Dweller with Elias of Enna – in the text, through the description of the older monk's death. Italo-Greek monastic saints operate within a network, a 'hagiographic intertextuality', as Annick Peters-Custot has characterised it.[81] Each ascetic is described – 'constructed' might be a better term – through the exemplar of an illustrious predecessor. Personal relations are evoked in the *Lives* through episodes in which the sanctity of one ascetic is recognised by another. Thus, in the *Life* of Vitalis of Castronuovo (d. 893), the extent of the subject's sanctity is tacitly affirmed when an older ascetic, Luke of

Armentum, pays him a visit and Vitalis, echoing the practices of the Desert Fathers, gives him hospitality by cooking freshly picked mushrooms for him, which at first the older monk refuses (with good reason, as it turns out, since they make him so ill that Vitalis has to cure him).[82] Ascetic saints frequently invade each other's *Lives* as a form of mutual validation. Vitalis was supposedly the nephew of Elias of Enna. Two other Calabrian Greek ascetics, Nikephoros the Nude and Phantinos, went to Mount Athos to learn cenobitic life from Athanasios in the 960s.[83]

An important factor in the success of an ascetic was the relationships he could establish with local populations. Cooperation between a charismatic ascetic and a local populace can be seen in the *Life of Luke of Armentum*, in which in exchange for protection offered by Luke, villagers provided shelter and sustenance for him and his companions. The capacity to mobilise local people to help in the work of building a monastery was also a feature of the *Life of Euthymios the Younger*. When he started to clear the sheepfold in the ruined church of St Andrew in Thessaloniki in *c.* 871 in order to build a new monastery, curious bystanders joined in to help.[84] But local people were not enough by themselves. Athanasios's relationship with the powerful general – later emperor – Nikephoros Phokas was instrumental in his founding of the Great Lavra. In Apulia, Sabas of Collesano was an intimate of the patrician Malacenes, the Byzantine *strategos* Romanos, the Lombard prince of Salerno, Otto II, and Empress Theophano, wife of Emperor Otto II, who was at his deathbed in Rome. Elias Speleota received a *strategos* of Calabria, Michael, as a monk.[85]

Just as we saw in the case of Athanasios, influences of the literature of early monasticism also pervade Italo-Greek asceticism. The episode in which Elias and Arsenius are attacked by 'panzooic' demons in the ruined tower at Patras – taking the forms and sounds of animals – derives ultimately from the *Life of Anthony*. There may however be a more specific allusion to a passage in the *Dialogues* of Gregory the Great in which Dazius, bishop of Milan, is prevented from sleeping while on a journey to Corinth by the noise of demons who roar like lions, bleat like sheep, bray like donkeys, hiss like snakes, honk like boar and screech like mice.[86] This borrowing, as Vera von Falkenhausen has pointed out, surely indicates knowledge of Gregory the Great's text about Italian ascetics of his day among Greek-speaking monastic communities in the tenth century.[87] In the *Life* of another Italo-Greek monk, Sabas of Collesano, we encounter three modes of Italo-Greek monastic life: anchorites, *lavra* monks and cenobitic monks.[88] But, as in all the examples we have seen so far, these types are not invariably separate, and are commonly combined in the career of a single monk. Like Elias Speleota, Athanasios and Euthymios the Younger, Vitalis founded a monastery observing the *Rules of Basil*, but later withdrew to enter a different community.[89]

Ultimately these types derive from Syrian, Palestinian and Egyptian traditions, but they are also deeply informed by the two new influences from ninth- and tenth-century Byzantium. Tempting as it is to see the hagiographical ideals of asceticism in southern Italy as the result of Greek monks being drawn away from the more urbanised society of Sicily to the more remote and rural Calabria as a result of the Arab invasion of the island, they can also be taken as a reflection of the reach of Byzantine monasticism, and in particular of the Studite and Athonite reforms. Annick Peters-Custot has gone so far as to declare the Italo-Greek monks 'pure products of Byzantine hagiographic culture'.[90] We might also note some traits of urban Byzantine asceticism, such as the gift of tears, and public nudity. But they were far from simply imitators of contemporary monks nearer the centre of the Byzantine world. They also exhibited what might be termed 'universalist' tendencies in their piety. Vitalis, a Greek speaker from Sicily, obtained permission from his *hegoumen* to make a pilgrimage to Rome. He was only one of many Italo-Greek saints following this path, from Gregory of Agrigento in 553. Both Elias of Enna and Elias Speleota also made pilgrimages to the tombs of the Apostles in Rome, as did another ninth-century Sicilian refugee, Sabas of Collesano. The tradition continued well into the tenth century: Leoluca of Corleone made his pilgrimage at around the same time that Athanasios was founding his Great Lavra on Mount Athos. Gregory of Cassano, abbot of Sant' Andrea di Cerchiara, founded the Greek-rite monastery of St Saviour in Rome.[91] Rome, indeed, was something of a centre for Greek-rite monasticism in the tenth century.[92] Other shrines associated primarily with Latin rather than Greek traditions, such as Monte Gargano in Apulia, might also be part of the circuit of a Greek monk's wanderings.[93] This transcultural aspect of the Italo-Greek tradition, which would become more pronounced still in the eleventh century as Latin-speaking monks and patrons encountered Greek monasticism, is distinctive to southern Italian asceticism.

Ascetic monasticism was far less integral to monastic life in the western Church than in the Orthodox world in the ninth and tenth centuries. There are plentiful examples of individual ascetics living an anchoritic life in the Low Countries, Gaul, the Iberian peninsula, England, Germany and Italy in the period up to the eighth century. More than a hundred are known by name from northern France and the Low Countries alone between the sixth and eighth centuries, about a quarter of whom were women.[94] Fifth- and sixth-century Councils (such as Vannes in 463, Agde in 506 and Orléans in 511) attempted to regulate the life of solitary ascetics by restricting the practice to male monks who had their abbot's permission and who occupied a cell within the monastic enclosure.[95] But the pages of Gregory of Tours tell a different story, in which independent ascetic life was clearly possible even though frowned upon by the authorities. In the western Mediterranean world, the Desert Fathers continued to provide inspiration for many. Valerius of El Bierzo (c. 630–695) may be taken as a typical early medieval example. As solitary at first, he was briefly a monk at Compludo but could not settle in a cenobitic community, and withdrew to a small cell attached to the monastery of San Pedro de Montes, where he taught disciples and copied books, but also criticised the cloistered monks and the bishop.[96]

Carolingian ecclesiastical reforms, which as we have already seen showed a preoccupation with standardising practices across Frankish lands, repeated earlier prescriptions against individual solitaries, notably at the Council of Frankfurt in 794. Ascetic life was to be absorbed into institutional monasticism, which was the genuine expression of religious life. This is not to say that all solitaries were monks or nuns. But anyone who, like Liutbirg, the adoptive daughter of a Saxon noblewoman who became her son's housekeeper, wanted to dedicate herself to an enclosed life, had to petition her bishop for permission to be enclosed in a cell near the monastery at Wendhausen. Liutbirg was a contemporary of the unfortunate Fulda monk Gottschalk, who had such a difficult time in trying to escape the confines of the cloister. In contrast, Liutbirg, a pious laywoman, had to convince first her employer Bernhardt and then the bishop to allow her to be enclosed, after which she followed a regulation probably of her own devising but approved by the bishop.[97] Another German anchoress, Wiborad (d. 926), adopted enclosure after making a pilgrimage to Rome with her brother, whom she convinced to profess as a monk at St Gall. She herself became an anchoress in 916, when she was shut in her cell by the bishop of Constance. As with Liutbirg, the enclosure followed a period, unspecified in length, of advice and instruction from the bishop. Although Wiborad remained enclosed in her cell, a community of like-minded women mushroomed around her. She retained a servant who was responsible for ensuring she was provided with food and other needs. Like other enclosed religious, she did not cut herself off completely from the surrounding community, but communicated with visitors through a window in her cell.[98]

Neither Liutbirg nor Wiborad was a professed nun, but the assumption that most solitary ascetics would be professed religious was reinforced by the Rule for solitaries written by the German Benedictine Grimlaic, probably in *c.* 950.[99] Grimlaic recommended at least a year's experience in a monastery and insisted that the recluse obtain episcopal and abbatial permission. Grimlaic's Rule would not have been needed had there not been numbers of men and women interested in leading an enclosed life as a recluse, but our knowledge of these depends on patchy survivals in the sources and on the interest shown by individual bishops in the problem. Bruno, archbishop of Cologne (953–65), regulated that recluses in his province were only to live in cells attached to monasteries or churches, but we cannot tell how many other prelates took this level of interest in anchorites; we know this about Bruno because a contemporary wrote a *Life* of him.[100] Although the regulatory sources from the ninth- and tenth-century West deal with solitary ascetic life largely as a phenomenon of enclosure, this does not invariably correspond to the experience of *vitae*. Individual ascetics might wander from place to place just as much as in the Orthodox world, often but not always in consequence of a pilgrimage. Guy (d. 1016), a Brabantine from a poor family, travelled to Rome and Jerusalem and returned to Anderlecht to live as a hermit.[101] Heimerad (d. 1019), a Swabian priest of servile origins, was chaplain to a noblewoman who after leaving her service made a pilgrimage to Rome and the Holy Land and on his return became a monk at Hersfeld.

He was expelled – according to the *Life* – when he became too critical of the lax regime there, and after unsuccessful periods exercising his priestly ministry in different towns, and being coolly received by Meinwerk, bishop of Paderborn, ended as a hermit in the mountainous territory around Hasungen.[102]

Perhaps a closer example, if we are looking for similarities with the kinds of eremitical ascetic lives so familiar from the Byzantine world, is Lambert, a hermit described in disobliging terms in the *Life* of the tenth-century monastic reformer John of Gorze (d. *c.* 975). Like Nikephoros the Nude and Euthymios the Younger, Lambert drew attention to himself through wearing rags that left him indecently exposed. He fasted and lived a simple, austere life. Despite Lambert's obvious attempt to fulfil the expectations of the solitary ascetic, however, he drew sharp criticism from John for a lack of discipline. Although he was a priest and could therefore say the offices, he did so at erratic times of day and night, simply as it pleased him. He lived in a cell in the forest but wandered into towns and villages on a whim. He might abandon a three-day fast after only two days. Without discipline, John pointed out, Lambert was doing no more than living as any poor man had to. The problem with the kind of life followed by Lambert was that it left too much latitude for the exercise of individual will.[103] 'Impulse', as Phyllis Jestice remarked, 'was the opposite of sound religious life.'[104]

Grimlaic's Rule was premised on prior training in the cenobitic life, from which only the truly self-controlled and disinterested ascetic might progress to a solitary life. Grimlaic, though preferring solitaries to live regulated lives in cells – where there was less scope for individual whims to be indulged – recognised in principle the ideal of living an unattached life in the open, in imitation of the Desert Fathers.[105] As we have seen, this principle of progression was fundamental to monastic ideals from the fifth century onwards, and common alike to Benedict's Rule and the monastic governance of Sabas in the Judaean desert. Nevertheless, the norm for western ascetics was to remain within the wider confines of a monastery, and to be overseen by a bishop. Suspicion attached to the kind of fluidity between states of cenobitic and eremitical life that was a cornerstone of Byzantine monastic hagiography in the ninth and tenth centuries. One reason for this was doubtless that those who opted for a solitary ascetic life could be seen as having abandoned what was intended as a lifelong profession in community. Strict *anachoresis* in imitation of the Desert Fathers needed to be corroborated by external witnesses in order to be taken seriously. But the authorities feared any monk or nun who 'failed' or was unhappy in the coenobium could simply withdraw and set themselves up in solitude, where there would be little opportunity for them to receive guidance. Doubtless monasteries were only too relieved when a particularly troublesome monk decided to leave, but no institution likes to feel that it has failed, and every such case had the potential to undermine the community.

EXTERNAL THREATS TO MONASTICISM

The early Christian writer Tertullian (*c.* 150–225) famously remarked that blood of the martyrs was the seed of the Church. After Christians were no longer persecuted for practising their religion, however, renunciation of the world came to be seen as a substitute for martyrdom. Writing about the holy fool, Sergey Ivanov remarked that this form of ascetic behaviour was only to be found when and where Christians were not suffering persecution or martyrdom.[106] Ridicule and opprobrium from a Christian populace was, in some sense, a substitute for the danger of persecution suffered at the hands of the Roman authorities and sometimes fellow-citizens in the period before Constantine's Edict of Toleration. During the period from the ninth to eleventh centuries, however, monasteries and their inhabitants all over the Christian world came under physical attack. Although the raids carried out by largely disconnected groups of Arabs from the Mediterranean, Vikings from Scandinavia and Magyars from the eastern continental plains were not specifically aimed at monastic life, monasteries, convents and churches were obvious targets because they were more likely to be storehouses of portable wealth. Monks, nuns and ascetics therefore ran the risk of attacks from non-Christians that could be portrayed by hagiographers as a form of martyrdom.

During the ninth century the Aghlabid conquest of Sicily and the resulting attempt at reconquest from Constantinople destabilised the Christian population of the island, causing large-scale disruption and migration from the island to Calabria and Apulia. Raiding on southern Italian and French coastal areas continued into the tenth century. Rome itself was sacked in 846, and Greek islands were subject to frequent attack by Arab pirates in search of slaves. The *Life of Euthymios the Younger* reveals something of the preoccupation with such dangers. Euthymios and two disciples were snatched by Arab pirates while they were on the island of Neoi, and taken prisoner. As often in hagiography, a violent episode furnished an occasion for the ascetic's holiness to be revealed. The raiders were unable to sail away from the island with their prisoners even though there was a favourable wind, and were forced to return them. One of the Arabs beat Euthymios's disciple John Kolobos, which drew from the saint a warning of future punishment, and their ship was duly attacked by a Byzantine vessel when they left the island and the raiders themselves were taken prisoner.[107] The attacks on Sicily and Calabria provide the backdrop to the *Lives* of two Italo-Greek ascetics, Vitalis of Castronuovo and Elias Speleota. The grave of Elias's teacher Arsenios is robbed by Arab raiders in search of treasure, but their attempts to burn the body are unsuccessful.[108] Vitalis's monastery is attacked by raiders but though unarmed he faces them down and they are struck by a thunderbolt; he takes the opportunity to deliver an exhortation to them to desist from their cruelty to Christians.[109] Vitalis is said to have been the nephew of the Sicilian Greek monk Elias of Enna (822/3–906), who was sold into slavery as a child during the Arab conquest of his homeland. Having obtained his freedom much later, he made a pilgrimage to the Holy Land, during the course of which he was accosted by a group of Muslims who interrogated him about the doctrine of the Trinity. He was able to preach so persuasively that they agreed to be baptised.

There was nothing new about monks being represented as suffering at the hands of an aggressive enemy. A vivid account of the destruction of monasteries in Jerusalem by the Persians in 614 evokes the pitiless massacre of monks and nuns.[110] The total number of monasteries in the Holy Land destroyed or abandoned between the seventh and eleventh centuries will probably never be known, but the analysis undertaken by Robert Schick for Palestine suggests that around sixty passed out of existence.[111] Although the Arab conquest of the 630s does not seem to have been especially disruptive to monastic life, sporadic attacks and outbreaks of persecution occurred at periods of political turmoil in subsequent centuries. These were more frequent from the 750s onwards, under the new Abbasid regime. In the governorship of Musa ibn Mus'ab in the region of Mosul, monks were apparently afraid to walk openly in the streets for fear of inciting riots.[112] In 796 twenty monks of St Sabas were killed in a raid during the War of the Watermelon, and in 813 further violence against the desert monasteries, coupled with threats to the Anastasis Church in Jerusalem, resulted in the large-scale flight of indigenous Christians to Cyprus.[113] The main source for these events, the *Chronographia of Theophanes*, was written by a Palestinian monk in Constantinople, George the Synkellos, who formed part of a group of refugees from Jerusalem and St Sabas. Suffering at the hands of a predatory enemy came to be a feature of the self-representation of monasticism in the Holy Land in the period before *c.* 1000.

This discourse drew on and perhaps perpetuated networks across the Mediterranean world. George, a monk of St Sabas, appears in the martyrdom of a group of forty-eight Christians executed by Caliph Abd al-Rahman II in Cordoba in the 850s.[114] In the eleventh-century *Dialogues* of Desiderius, abbot of Monte Cassino, language rather similar to that in the *Life of Vitalis Siculus* is ascribed to SS Peter and Benedict as they observe the Arab raids on Italy in the ninth century.[115] Western monastic communities might also find confrontation with Muslims providing an important component in the formation of a particular kind of sanctity. A local cult grew up at Voghera, in the Po Valley near Pavia, centred on the figure of the tenth-century Provençal knight Bobo, who had devoted much of his life to fighting against the Arabs who had fortified the southern French port of Fraxinetum (La Garde-Freinet).[116]

The most enduring memory of this kind of challenge to monastic life was shaped by the hands of the monks of Cluny over the course of a century and a half. In 972, raiders from Fraxinetum kidnapped the abbot, Majolus, and his travelling household in the Great St Bernard Pass while they were returning from Rome to Cluny, in southern Burgundy. They used Fraxinetum as a slave market and base for such operations from the late ninth century until it was destroyed in the early eleventh century by the duke of Aquitaine, and Majolus was far from being the only prominent figure to suffer this indignity. So concerning were the activities of the Fraxinetum pirates that an imperial German delegation was sent to the emir of Cordoba in the 950s, in which the reforming monk John of Gorze was a member, to ask him to intervene.[117] Majolus was allowed to write a letter to his monks pleading with them to pay the ransom that would set him free. This letter does not survive, but in a *Life* of Majolus written by Syrus, a monk of Cluny in *c.* 1010, the desperation of his plight is evoked: 'The hordes of Belial have surrounded me; the snares of death have seized me.'[118] Over subsequent generations the story was embellished to draw out the symbolic power of the imagined confrontation between the abbot and his Muslim kidnappers. As Scott Bruce has shown, the story of Majolus's kidnap was retold at least four times in the first half of the eleventh century. Majolus emerges as a heroic figure who underwent suffering willingly but also took the opportunity to preach to his Muslim captors in the face of extreme personal danger.

The debate between Majolus and the Muslims of Fraxinetum is, in Bruce's estimate, 'unprecedented in Latin literature composed north of the Pyrenees in the early Middle Ages'.[119] But the scenario of a Christian monk preaching to Muslim captors was far from unusual in monastic writing in other regions. The *Passion of Michael the Sabaite* tells the story of a monk of St Sabas who is summoned to a debate at the *majlis* (court) of an emir in which he argues the principles of Christianity in a hostile environment and suffers martyrdom as a result of being so persuasive and eloquent that the emir fears he will draw Muslims away from their faith.[120] This is only one example of the genre of monastic suffering and martyrdom in Arabic Christian hagiography in the ninth and tenth centuries.[121] Sidney Griffith has argued that the Judaean desert monasteries, particularly St Sabas, provided an identity for the Orthodox Christians living under Islamic rule in the Holy Land. Christians were not systematically persecuted – save for brief periods such as in the early years of the eleventh century – but as *dhimmis* (non-Muslims with legal protection) both Christians and Jews were obliged to pay a special tax and prohibited from certain positions and privileges. In such circumstances monasteries played a special role as the safeguards of Christian practices for communities that might be subject to arbitrary violence in times of political turmoil.

Quite different were the dangers faced by monastic communities in the face of attacks by two other groups of non-Christians in other parts of the Christian world: the Magyars and the Vikings. Until their defeat by the Emperor Otto I at Lechfeld in 955, the Magyars were an unpredictable but potent force in central Europe who caused damage and spread fear largely in German-speaking territories. The conversion of the Hungarian people to Christianity was accomplished in the eleventh century, during the reign of King István I (1000–1038). An anti-Christian reaction after his death resulted in the martyrdom of St Gellert, a Venetian otherwise known as Gerard. Gerard was a Benedictine monk who was travelling through Hungary to the Holy Land on pilgrimage when he was persuaded by István to stay and become bishop of the newly formed diocese of Csanád. In 1046 Gerard was taken to the top of the hill in Buda now named for him – the Gellert hill – and rolled down in a cart into the Danube.[122] By this time the Hungarian threat to monastic communities was only a memory, but for periods in the tenth century they were greatly feared. Wiborad, the anchoress in the diocese of Constance, fell victim to the random violence of the Hungarians in 926. According to her *Life*, she foresaw a Hungarian raid and told a monk from the monastery of St Mang, near her cell, to take the community to safety. The raiders burst into her cell through the roof – since she had been walled in, there was no door – stripped her to her hair shirt, stole her clothes and murdered her with an axe.[123]

Viking attacks on monasteries are well documented in contemporary sources. Lindisfarne, the monastery of Cuthbert, was sacked and burned in 793. This proved to be the start of a period in which monasteries in northern Europe were targeted by Viking raiders for their portable and disposable wealth. News of the fate of Lindisfarne spread to Ireland, where at the end of 794 an entry in the Irish Annals announces portentously the 'devastation of all the islands of Britain by the heathens'. In 795 the monks of Iona fled, but in 806 and 825 Vikings returned and killed many of the monks they found there – sixty-eight in the earlier year. In Ireland, Clonfert and Clonmacnoise were both sacked. Opinions both popular and scholarly still differ as to the real extent of the ruin visited by Viking attacks on Britain and northern France, but there can be no doubt about the fear they provoked in contemporaries. A now famous Irish verse in the margin of a ninth-century manuscript from St Gall still gives us a flavour of this fear:

> The bitter wind is high tonight
> It lifts the white locks of the sea;
> In such wild winter storm no fright
> of savage Viking troubles me.[124]

Attacks on the Frankish lands started in 841, when Rouen was sacked. In 842 and 843 Vikings attacked Quentovic and Nantes and in 844 sailed up the Garonne and then marauded the Iberian coastline. Abbeys along the river valleys of the Seine, Meuse and Loire were easy victims to raids.

Yet the attacks may appear more devastating through the lens of the available sources – largely monastic chronicles and annals – than the reality. Raids were certainly not annual occurrences. As has recently been observed, the *Annals of Ulster* record only seven episodes of Viking activity in the first twenty years of the ninth century, and sometimes raids were repulsed by local defenders.[125] The raids on Frankish lands in the 840s and 850 were far from being co-ordinated attacks, and not all of them resulted in destruction. But when raiders fell on a monastery, they could be brutal in their treatment of its inhabitants and their property. Monastic annals sometimes speak of raids 'depopulating' monasteries and communities. What they mean is that monks and nuns as well as neighbouring villagers were often taken as slaves. Notable monks might be ransomed: when Louis, abbot of St Denis, was captured with his brother on a raid in 858, Emperor Charles the Bald, who was a relative, paid a ransom of 688 lb of gold and 3,250 lb of silver to obtain their ransom.[126]

Violent and destructive though they were, these were not attacks on monasticism, but on owners of wealth. Monasteries were almost the only institutions where easily transportable goods of value could be found. In Ireland, and possibly elsewhere, it was not only the treasures of the church and sacristy – precious objects such as gem-studded chalices and office books with golden covers, or the gold crown from a statue – that might be found.[127] As Viking raiders were well aware, kings sometimes kept their own treasure in monasteries for safekeeping. But monasteries were also particularly vulnerable, not only because they were usually defenceless against sudden and unpredictable attack, but also because of their location. Lindisfarne, Iona and Noirmoutier, off the coast of Brittany, were sited on small islands in sight of the coastline, and inland monasteries were often sited on or near the great rivers along which the Viking longships could easily navigate. But monasteries were also vulnerable for other reasons. The system of the reform of monasteries in Frankish lands had had its day by the middle of the ninth century. As we saw in the previous chapter, lay appointments to abbacies were widespread even during the reform period, and this trend only continued after the death of Emperor Louis the Pious and the political instability that followed as his sons competed among themselves for shares of the empire. Frankish bishops complained to Emperor Charles the Bald in 844 that laymen were being given abbacies against all custom and authority: 'They sit in the midst of priests and levites like abbots and make rules for their life and conversation.'[128] It is not surprising in these circumstances that abbeys that had become prey to raiders lacked the kind of leadership that might preserve the community when its buildings had been robbed and burned. The community of St Philibert of Noirmoutier fled from a Viking raid in 836, and only found another permanent home at Tournus in 875, having taken temporary refuge with five different other monasteries in the intervening years.[129] Similar fates were suffered by monasteries at either end of western Christendom at the hands of raiders. The monks of Lindisfarne wandered through Northumbria, carrying the precious body of St Cuthbert, before finding a place of refuge at Chester-le-Street. The Farfa monks dispersed to three different monasteries in 897, to return only forty years later, and after Monte Cassino was destroyed by Arab raiders in 883, and many of the monks killed, it took some sixty years before the site could be occupied again.

Monks, nuns and monasteries were liable to suffer periodic violence in the ninth and tenth centuries in a variety of ways. Solitary ascetics or monks on the move could be abducted, treated roughly and held for ransom. Monks who came to the attention of hostile authorities might, albeit rarely, be judicially executed. At various periods, monasteries within easy reach of coastlines, navigable rivers or road systems could be sacked and burned, and communities killed, enslaved or forced into flight. The randomness both of the timing and of the violence must have raised the consciousness of such possibilities into the kind of terror that sometimes echoes still in the pages of monastic annals. But the possibility of hostility towards them enabled monks to understand themselves in a new role: not only as supplicants to God on behalf of their wider society, but as the front line of the defence of Christianity against pagans.

'PROFESSION OF A SUBLIME RESOLVE': CLUNY IN THE TENTH CENTURY

When Abbot Berno took twelve monks from his monastery of Baume-les-Moines in the Jura to a small farm in southern Burgundy in 909, he can hardly have imagined that their new home would, within 150 years, become the most powerful religious institution in Europe outside the papacy.[130] By the time the third version of its church was completed in the twelfth century, Cluny boasted the largest church in the Christian world: not to be surpassed until the rebuilding of St Peter's in Rome in the sixteenth century. It is not surprising, given its spectacular rise to influence, wealth and prestige, that no other monastery has stimulated so much scholarly endeavour as Cluny. Modern scholarship on Cluny began with a monumental study of Cluny up to the mid-eleventh century by Ernst Sackur published in the 1890s, and is still gathering momentum.[131] Cluniac studies have produced editions of the customaries (which we may think of as manuals of usage) of Cluny that became highly influential throughout much of the western monastic world, of the prodigious collections of charters associated with the monastery and its dependent priories, and the necrologies that preserve the names of tens of thousands of monks.[132] That we are still far from having as complete a picture of Cluny as the surviving records allow tells us just how important and far-reaching a role the monastery played in the first 300 years of its existence. Because we know this about Cluny in the eleventh and twelfth centuries, it is sometimes difficult not to project its influence back to the first few generations after the foundation. In fact monastic historians are at pains to point out that in the first century or more of its existence, Cluny was little different from many other monasteries in its practices or aspirations, and that much of what we think of as 'Cluniac' can be seen only in the abbacy of Odilo (994–1049).[133]

Berno's monastery of Baume was an old foundation with a Columbanian tradition, but which had been restored from a condition of decline in 904 by Berno. In 910, however, Duke William of Aquitaine presented a *villa* (farm) at Cluny that had been given to him by his sister Ada in 893 to Berno, with a view to establishing a monastery there. Ada is described in terms that may suggest she was in religious life herself, perhaps even head of a community. The foundation charter drawn up, presumably by Berno, to record the establishment, transfers the total property to St Peter, the dedicatee of the new monastery, and through him to Berno and the monks. Cluny's foundation charter has been endlessly pored over by scholars and students of monastic history, with good reason. It remains one of the clearest expositions of the principles of the meaning, purpose and demands of monasticism as it was understood in the early Middle Ages. The charter outlines the reasons for William's foundation, the terms on which the monastery is to exist and its constitutional position. It is firm in its insistence that the *Rule of Benedict* is to be observed and stipulates that future abbots are to be chosen by the monks in accordance with the Rule. The founder formally cedes all rights in governance and ownership to St Peter, denies the bishop of the diocese of Autun or any other regional authority, lay or ecclesiastical, rights of jurisdiction over the community, and places it instead in the hands of St Peter's vicar on earth, the pope. These days scholars are disinclined to see too much originality in a document that once seemed to represent a new movement in monasticism. As has been pointed out, even the reliance on the papacy mirrors what had already been claimed for Vézelay and other monasteries in the wider region. In many ways, the Cluny of 910 can be seen as a rather traditional expression of the Carolingian reform initiated by Benedict of Aniane. But the assurance and clarity with which these principles are articulated in the foundation charter make it a landmark in monastic history, and worth examining carefully.[134]

William begins with an assertion of the power of wealth to assist in obtaining salvation. 'It is clear to all right thinkers' that those blessed with wealth can, by using it well, 'merit everlasting rewards'. Thus he determines, while he is still able, to follow Jesus's advice to 'make the poor his friends' (Luke 16.9) by making a lasting rather than a temporary provision by founding a monastery. An unambiguous relationship is premised between earthly prosperity and eternal life. This does not mean that only those with such wealth can hope to enter the kingdom of heaven, but rather that those fortunate enough to have it have only themselves to blame if they do not use it in such a manner as to give them every prospect of doing so. Wealth brings benefits for the wealthy, but also responsibilities. Moreover, founding a monastery is not simply an act of devotion on the part of the founder, but a practical means of providing a living for those leading a religious life. William clearly regards this as a solemn undertaking in part because it is not simply a gift that may eventually be dissipated, but a permanent commitment. The most important sentence in the document follows – a sentence that perhaps encapsulates the social meaning of monasticism more clearly than any other in the Middle Ages. 'And this is my trust, this is my hope, indeed, that although I myself am unable to despise all things, nevertheless by receiving despisers of this world, whom I believe to be righteous, I may receive the reward of the righteous.'[135] William lived in a society dominated by a militarised aristocracy; a society moreover in which public authority and even justice rested in men (and to a lesser extent women) like him. He was aware that the kind of life he and others close to him lived was dominated by violence that could be spontaneous and cruel; that people less fortunate than he suffered arbitrarily and randomly from the actions of their social and economic superiors, from the vagaries of the climate, from disease and the sheer hard work and endurance needed to sustain a rural existence in pre-industrial Europe. He knew also that eternal justice would redress this imbalance and that those whom providence, in the words of the charter, had favoured in this life would be judged according to how they had used their wealth and power. And judgement, in the religious imagination of the time, resulted in either eternal salvation or damnation – however either of those two conditions were conceived in people's minds.

The phrasing of the charter shows that people in William's position realised what they might do to ensure that they fell on the right side of the scales at the time of judgement: despise the world, or, in other words, enter religious life themselves. This was certainly not impossible for aristocrats – in fact, in the West, monasticism for both men and women was largely an aristocratic profession in the sense that most monks and nuns came from the landowning classes. There are plentiful examples of widows, or men and women past middle age, entering a monastery as a form of retirement from active life. There is a particular poignancy in the recognition by William that he knows what he ought to do in order to be sure of salvation, and yet is unable to renounce what he has in such a radical way. Something of this tension is conveyed by the *Life of Gerald of Aurillac*, a rare hagiographical account of a layperson written by Odo, Berno's successor as abbot of Cluny. Gerald, a knight, was consumed by doubt and guilt over his way of life but could not renounce his responsibilities to those who relied on him for protection, so he adopted a life of personal austerity and chastity, refused to kill even in battle, and prayed constantly.[136] The *Life* may, needless to say, be thought of as wishful thinking rather than reality, but it is an important window into the way that leaders in the monastic world such as Odo wanted laypeople to think about their lives. In some ways the point of the *Life of Gerald* may indeed have been to show how impossible it was to live in the world and at the same time despise it in the manner that would ensure salvation.

Founding a monastery was seen by people such as William as the next best way of dealing with their doubts and fears. But William's expectation of 'receiving the reward of the righteous' was not simply because of the permanent provision of sustenance for a group of monks or nuns, but because of what they would be doing. The foundation charter stipulates that the monks of Cluny must follow the *Rule of Benedict*, which guaranteed to William that they would be living penitent lives shaped by the liturgical offices and governed the qualities of obedience, poverty and humility. But the observance of the liturgy would not be solely for their own benefit. The terms of the foundation name individuals on whose behalf prayers would be said as long as the community remained in existence: William himself, his wife Ingelberga, brothers, sisters, nephews, and the whole family; King Odo of Burgundy; and all those in service to William. The monks would, in other words, be performing surrogate penance for all those named in the charter. The idea that a monastic community had the power to effect penance on behalf of others lies at the very heart of the medieval understanding of what a monastery was for.

Throughout the Christian world, monasteries were usually regarded in this period as the private property of the founders and their families. Although some had been founded by bishops or had developed around the shrines of saints, most monasteries owed their existence to a combination of piety and landed wealth. Not surprisingly, founders and their families had a tendency to view them proprietorially. William – probably at Berno's insistence – stipulated that this was not to be the case with Cluny: 'It has pleased us also to insert in this document that, from this day, those same monks there congregated shall be subject neither to our yoke, nor to that of our relatives, nor to the sway of the royal might, nor to that of any earthly power.'[137] In practice this meant that the monks themselves, rather than any member of William's family, would have sole responsibility for electing the abbot. Insistence on the freedom of the community to choose their head was enshrined in the *Rule of Benedict*, but as we have seen, monastic headships were commonly held by laypeople. But the charter goes beyond this, in denying the bishop any jurisdictional right over the governance of the monastery and placing its ultimate protection in the hands of the pope. Cluny's status as a subject of St Peter was confirmed in a papal grant of 931, along with its privilege to retain tithes from churches in its ownership (a point to which we will return). But since papal authority did not extend to Burgundy, the real authority over Cluny was in fact the abbot, which is presumably what Berno wanted.

The somewhat shadowy figure of Abbot Berno tells us something about the way that Cluny fitted into the tenth-century landscape of monasticism. Already abbot not only of Baume but also of five other monasteries, he assumed charge of Cluny as part of an unofficial association of religious communities in Burgundy. The language of early charters is vague about the practical implications of such links as suggested by the 'familial love' joining Cluny and Gigny. On the other hand, when the monastery of Romainmôtier was given to Cluny by its proprietor, Adelaide, sister of the count of Burgundy, in 929, the gift was accompanied by the demand that 'they should hold in common the decrees concerning divine service, alms and any good work so that whatever is done at Cluny . . . should also be done among us and ours, and they will equally participate in what will be done for us at Romainmôtier in accord with the will of the Lord'.[138] Berno's will, drawn up in 926, emphasises unanimity, poverty, simplicity of food and clothing, attention to psalmody, and silence. These are conventional qualities in the sense that they are embedded in the *Rule of Benedict*, but the value of underscoring them indicates that they could not invariably be assumed as normal practice in monasteries at the time.

We know more about the ideals that shaped Cluny under Berno's successor, Odo, because of the *Life* written by his follower John of Salerno, as well as Odo's own *Life of Gerald of Aurillac*.[139] Odo's view of human life was not optimistic. The chances of attaining eternal life rather than damnation outside the cloister were low. But monasticism offered humans the opportunity to fulfil their highest nature. Those who followed the monastic life were making a 'profession of a sublime resolve'.[140] In his meditational text, the *Occupatio* (924), Odo made a case for monasticism as the final evolutionary stage of the age that had been initiated at Pentecost. But the stakes were high. If monasticism represented a state as close to perfection as the constraints of human nature allowed, failing as a monk incurred greater risks than remaining in a lay state. 'If monks are perfect, they are similar to the blessed angels, but if they revert to a desire for the world, they are justly compared to the apostate angels . . .'[141] Yet, if we accept Odo's view of monasticism as a kind of return to paradise, his view of correct observance looks rather less austere than it might otherwise appear. The renunciation of sex and of anything other than the simplest food and clothing, the insistence on silence as far as possible, and the importance of psalm-singing were not intended to make life difficult or unpleasant. Rather, they were attempts to steer monks towards eternal life by anticipating the time when, as the Gospel of Matthew promised, all humans would be like the angels (Matthew 22.30). Angels were sexless beings and therefore had no sexual desire and no appetite or need for finery. And, as Scott Bruce has brilliantly shown, the rule of silence was a further way of imitating the angels, since the only sounds made by angels were the constant praise they gave to God.[142] This explains the early Cluniac preoccupation with liturgical integrity: the monks' psalm-singing was a marker of their aspiration to be angelic.[143] To this end, Odo extended the regime of psalmody initiated by Benedict of Aniane's reforms, adding psalms to be sung outside the abbey church while pursuing ordinary activities – even while shaving. According to John of Salerno, 138 psalms were sung every day from Odo's abbacy onwards.[144] Because we associate Cluny at the height of its influence with a complex liturgical cursus, it is tempting to locate the seeds of this development in Odo's abbacy. Yet Odo opposed ritualism for its own sake and preferred a simple office with the use of plain chalices and patens.[145] The liturgy at Cluny in the tenth century probably resembled that of other monasteries following Carolingian reform traditions. When the reforming canons of Tours asked him to compose a longer set of antiphons for their liturgical uses, he praised the brevity of their current settings.[146]

When Berno died in 926, Cluny was probably the largest of his monasteries in terms of numbers of monks, if not the wealthiest. By the middle of the tenth century, the original group of twelve (a conjectural number) may have increased to about fifty. The notice of the election of Abbot Odilo in 994 was signed by seventy-six monks, and even fifty years later a list of those monks present in community during Lent gives sixty-four names.[147] Numbers of monks, therefore, reached a stable point in mid-century at which they remained until the second half of the eleventh century. Yet Cluny was already projecting an influence far beyond Burgundy in the tenth century. Odo and his successors as abbot, Aymard (942–54) and Majolus (954–94), were very active as promotors of Cluny's reforming practices. Fleury, Déols and Romainmôtier were all in some way part of the Cluniac sphere of influence by the 930s. The papal privilege obtained by Odo in 931 from John XI facilitated Cluny's reach over other communities by allowing the monastery to accept any monk already professed at another monastery but who wanted to follow a stricter observance.

As we have seen, Majolus's frequent travels landed him in trouble in 972.[148] Both Odo and Majolus were particularly active in Italy, where they were asked to advise on the reform of monasteries that had undergone difficult times. Farfa, north of Rome, provides an example of Cluny's early activity in this respect – but also of the task facing reformers at some monasteries. The community had dispersed to three different sites in 897 as a result of the threat of raids, but in the 930s Abbot Ratfred reinstated a small group of monks at Farfa. In what its modern historian has characterised as 'the most scandalous episode in the monastery's history', Ratfred was poisoned by two of his monks in 936.[149] One of the murderers took over the headship, and refused entry to Odo of Cluny, who was at that time working to reform monasteries in Rome at the invitation of the pope. Only when the *princeps Romanorum*, Alberic, forcibly installed a Cluniac monk as abbot in 947 could the reform process start – until he too was poisoned six years later. Under Abbot John III (966–97) Farfa was restored to imperial protection, and in the early eleventh century the community accepted reform at the hands of Abbot Hugo (998–1039).

GIVING TO CLUNY

For Odo, it was not sufficient for a monastery to exist simply in order to ensure the salvation of its own monks. They also had to be the source of 'floods of grace' for the wider community.[150] Historians have for over a century pondered the relationship between Cluny and its 'public'. In a memorable phrase coined by Barbara Rosenwein to summarise the conclusions of Georg Schreiber, '[t]he monastic liturgy was the key that opened the pocketbooks of the laity.'[151] After the initial foundation and land grant by William of Aquitaine, Cluny developed its property in the environs of the monastery painstakingly over several generations. The best account of how this happened and of the strategies employed by Cluny's monks is Barbara Rosenwein's expert analysis of the surviving charters of the monastery from the tenth and eleventh centuries.[152] She has found that there is surprisingly little evidence, at least before the mid-eleventh century, for what Schreiber took for granted, namely the reciprocity implied in William's foundation charter of 'land for prayers'.[153] But if laypeople were not giving away property in order to be remembered liturgically, what was the reason for their apparently suicidal generosity? In an age when most families' wealth was land, why alienate or give away assets that could be passed on to their heirs; or to put it another way, why disinherit their heirs? One possible and partial answer is that gifts of land guaranteed burial in the monks' own consecrated ground at Cluny, which was more prestigious than a parish church. But this scarcely accounts for the steady and piecemeal acquisition of land by Cluny over the course of the tenth century. Rosenwein asks us to think instead about a different paradigm of generosity, in which the relationships between families and Cluny were paramount. Precisely because this was a period of political fragmentation, interrelations between groups of people, principally neighbouring families, but also institutions, could be underscored by transactions in land. But we must also think of Cluny as contemporaries did. If we take at face value the language of the foundation charter in which the donation is made to St Peter, then the generosity of local landowners can be seen as a pact between them and the saint: the prince of the Apostles, no less.[154] Anthropologists have found that in many societies gift-giving is a powerful means of forging relationships through exchange. In many non-literate cultures, such exchanges often take the form of moveable objects that are imbued with the spirit of something intangible, or that represent hidden protective forces. In early medieval society, grants of land were accompanied and represented by ritual moments in which a piece of turf, or a knife – or, in due course, a charter – betokened the land. But the land itself was possessed not by the spirit of place, but by the protective force of St Peter himself. To give land that your family owned next to an estate, a farm, village or church owned by Cluny was to make yourself the neighbour of St Peter.

Rosenwein noticed discernible patterns of gift-giving to St Peter. Some families gave repeatedly across the generations. But giving to Cluny must be seen as part of a larger matrix of exchange and transfer of rights among a network that included the wider family, relatives by marriage, neighbours and so on. Cluny also entered the land market to build up strategic possessions in some areas. In the Bezornay region of the Mâconnais, 81 per cent of the land purchased by Cluny bordered at least in part the existing property of St Peter. Acquisitions might also be surrendered back to the original owner. In 949, for example, Cluny purchased half of a church at Sennecé-lès-Mâcon, and received the other half as a gift from the bishop of Mâcon in the 960s. (It is worth noting here that churches, which were often owned and had been built by landed families, were a frequent type of gift to monasteries. Recipients of churches were responsible for providing the cure of souls in them but acquired revenue through the tithes payable to every church by its parishioners.) Ten or so years later, Abbot Majolus gave away the church *in precaria*, but in *c.* 1050 it was returned to Cluny in a quitclaim.[155] In pursuing such strategies, Cluny was behaving in a very similar manner to secular families. Some pieces of land in the possession of a family or kin grouping had more meaning to the family than others, and would be retained, while less important properties could be ringfenced for parcelling out for sale or gift. In this way a family remained in control of what was alienated and could keep its inalienable possessions out of the exchange.

Rosenwein has argued persuasively that the critical point for a potential donor was not so much the question of exclusive ownership over property as how links to St Peter might be created through the donation of property.[156] The social fabric created by a gift might be more significant than the value of the gift itself. At the same time, value was calibrated according to social distinction. Obviously, the wealthier and more powerful a donor, the greater the value of gift was expected in order to enter into a meaningful relationship with the saint.

The notion of reciprocity in creating such a social fabric was far from simple. As anthropologists have found, the gift itself might play a relatively unimportant part in the exchange, appearing only as the token of the relationship being established. Even today we retain some sense of the intangible value attaching to certain gifts, even valueless ones, because of who gave them to us. The memory of the occasion, or of the relationship that is celebrated in the giving and receiving, is far more resonant than the object. In the same way, a property given to a monastery should be seen as remaining infused with the identity of the original giver.[157] The recording of the name of the donor in a charter, which then takes on a more permanent life by being copied into a cartulary or registry, is one way in which this dynamic can be observed. Much of the documentary record of monastic communities, as recorded in cartularies – it might be said, indeed, one of the main reasons for the existence of a cartulary – was concerned with the business of trying to protect and defend landed assets from counter claims to ownership. Especially in the first century of Cluny's existence (in fact, until the late twelfth century), there was no single public authority with jurisdiction over the process of giving, receiving and recording. The lack of central authority put the obligation to sustain social cohesion in a given region on the shoulders of the more powerful landowners. Entering into partnership through exchange or sale of property was a particularly resonant method of doing this, because it was public and open. In the absence of the threat of enforcement, the sense of transgression and the social shame resulting from it were of great importance. Being St Peter's neighbour brought prestige and assurance of the saint's protection, but also carried obligations to be a good neighbour.

While abbots and monks might come and go, St Peter was a permanent fixture in his corner of southern Burgundy, and increasingly, throughout a much wider area of western Europe. If the concept of neighbourliness explains why local families were so ready to detract from their own landholdings in order to enter into partnership with Cluny, it is less easy at first sight to see why those outside the immediate region would also be so willing to do the same. One of the most striking examples of this far-flung reach is the extensive giving by the tenth-century kings of Italy. The aristocracy of the tenth century – indeed, for most of the Middle Ages – was transnational and highly inter-related. The kings of Italy were a dynasty that came to power under the Carolingians, and were closely connected with the nobility in Frankish lands. Intersecting relations between aristocratic families brought new potential donors into Cluny's orbit. Agnes, daughter of the duke of Burgundy, married William V, duke of Aquitaine, the descendant of the founder. Agnes was also related to another Cluny benefactor, Leotald, count of Mâcon, and William V had a diplomatic relationship with Sancho, king of Navarre (1000–35), which led Sancho to become a 'familiaris' of Cluny. After William V's death, Agnes married Geoffrey Martel, son of the count of Anjou, and the new couple co-founded the monastery of Holy Trinity at Vendôme soon after 1032. Fifteen years later, having succeeded to the county, they co-founded a nunnery at Saintes. Patronage to Cluny and its affiliates did not necessarily mean that a family did not support religious men and women elsewhere as well. Marriage alliances meant that women were often the mediators of this international dynamic of piety and gift exchange within the aristocracy.[158]

REFORM IN THE 'AGE OF IRON'

'The tenth century has a bad name; but good things came out of it.' Helen Waddell was thinking specifically of Latin culture, but her dictum holds true for religious life more generally.[159] The foundation of Cluny is only the most prominent example of a wider urge to reform monasticism in the tenth century. In Flanders, observance of the *Rule of Benedict* was restored at St Bavo in Ghent, St Amand and other monasteries by Gerard of Brogne, a protégé of Arnulf I, count of Flanders. In 933 the abbey of Gorze in Lotharingia, an eighth-century foundation that had fallen into disrepair physically and spiritually, was reformed by a young monk, John, and Einald, archdeacon of Toul, under the authority of the bishop of Metz.[160] John, an accomplished administrator from a well-heeled family, was already as a young man intimate with the count and bishop of Verdun. He had a reputation for vigorous practical management and was apparently blessed with a remarkable memory and a head for figures.[161] These reforms developed largely independently of each other as responses to local situations. Nevertheless, like Berno at Cluny, both Gerard and John took their inspiration from Benedict of Aniane's reforms of the early ninth century – not only in the ambition to observe the *Rule of Benedict* uniformly, but also in the leadership that each assumed over a group of monasteries. John's revival of Gorze led to a federation of reformed monasteries in the region, notably St Vanne at Verdun and St Maximin at Trier, and a wave of new foundations in southern Germany. Nor was Cluny even the only direct agent of monastic reform in Burgundy. William of Volpiano, an oblate at the monastery of Lucedio, near Vercelli, became a monk at Cluny after meeting Abbot Majolus on one of his Italian journeys. In 989 William left for Dijon, where he introduced Cluniac customs to St Bénigne. From this base he influenced a monastic revival over two regions – the Piedmont and Normandy – without directly associating his new foundations or refoundations with Cluny.

Individual enterprise lay at the heart of the dissemination of reform. A monk at Einsiedeln, the former head of the cathedral school at Trier, Wolfgang, introduced the Gorze customary to St Emmeram, in Bavaria, in 972. This became the centre of a federation of associated monasteries for men and women using the same customary. The customary – the practical manual of everyday usage in the monastery – lay at the heart of this federation. But there was little or no formal bond between the monasteries, and unlike Berno at Cluny, John did not expect to run different monasteries concurrently. Association was formed more loosely, through prayer for each other's dead brethren. This practice can be glimpsed in the ninth-century necrologies at abbeys such as Fulda, so it was nothing new in German-speaking lands. And unlike at Cluny, there was no attempt to separate the monastery from episcopal jurisdiction; indeed partnership between reform-minded bishops and enterprising monastic leaders was the hallmark of the Gorze reform. Ascetic practices among the episcopate were, if not widespread, at least familiar as an idea. Archbishop Frederick of Mainz (937–54) followed an ancient custom of retiring every Lent to live with hermits and solitaries.[162]

A close alliance of bishops and crown achieved the reform of monasteries in southern England in the second half of the tenth century. The great monasteries of the early English period had been decimated by the tenth century. Asser, the biographer of King Alfred of Wessex, made a distinction between the continuing existence of monasteries as institutions and the failure of regular life in them: 'for many years past the desire for the monastic life had been totally lacking in that entire race . . . although quite a number of monasteries still remained, none held to the rule of monastic life in an orderly way'.[163] Some of the damage was done by the Viking attacks of the ninth century. Even monasteries in the heartland of Wessex, such as the convent at Sherborne founded in 705, might be prey to such attacks and have to be abandoned. Yet not all of the damage to monasteries was done by axe-wielding invaders. The *Regularis Concordia* (Monastic Agreement of the Monks and Nuns of the English Nation) of 970 explains the need for the reform undertaken by King Edgar (959–75) as the restoration of monastic lands from the hands of laypeople. The synod of Winchester in 964, at which the reform was promulgated, forbade monasteries to acknowledge *saecularium prioratum* (secular domination), which had led to ruin in the past.[164] There is no mention at all of the Danes and their notorious raids: the enemies of monasticism in the eyes of the reformers were secular lords who sought to run monasteries for their own profit.

The partnership between the king and reforming monks can be traced back to the appointment of a monk, Aelfheah, as bishop of Winchester in 934. His protégé, Dunstan, was given the monastery at Glastonbury to reform in 940 in a volte face by the king, Edmund, who had initially banished him.[165] The temperature of reform was still cool at this point. In 944, Bath Abbey was given to a group of secular clerks who had left St Bertin in Flanders when Gerard of Brogne started enforcing the *Rule of Benedict* there. Even at Dunstan's Glastonbury reform proceeded slowly. One of his monks, Aethelwold, who was to emerge as the driving force behind the reform movement, intended to leave for the Continent in search of 'a more perfect monastic discipline', and was dissuaded only when he was offered the opportunity to found his own *monasteriolum* at Abingdon.[166] After Edmund's death in 955 his sons Eadwig and Edgar succeeded in Wessex and Mercia respectively. A new reign in Wessex that did not at first appear conducive to monks paradoxically gave impetus to the reform. Dunstan, exiled from England, went to the abbey of St Peter's in Ghent, while his nephew Oswald became a monk at Fleury-sur-Loire, recently reformed by Cluny. Their exposure to full observance of the *Rule of Benedict* was to prove crucial after Eadwig's early death without heirs in 959, which allowed Edgar to become king of Wessex as well as Mercia. Abingdon's first copy of the *Rule of Benedict* was sent from Fleury. As Eric John observed, with Edgar's accession 'the monks came to power'.[167] Dunstan was enthroned as archbishop of Canterbury in 961, while Oswald became bishop of Worcester around the same time. From the 960s onward, several older monasteries were refounded or restored, among them a number of early English foundations in East Anglia such as Thorney, Crowland, Ely and Peterborough. Smaller informal communities were also brought into the Benedictine sphere, such as the hermitage supposedly founded in the ninth century at Cerne Abbas in Dorset by the brother of the martyred King Edmund of the East Angles. The driving force behind much of the practical reform was Aethelwold, the 'father of the monks' as he was known to contemporary admirers.[168] His translation of the *Rule of Benedict* into Old English enabled its spread even among relatively untrained recruits.

The critical moment in the reform, however, was Dunstan's Winchester synod of 964. Much of the business was later articulated in the *Regularis Concordia*, which there is good reason to suppose was drafted by Aethelwold. According to the biography of Oswald by Eadmer, a monk of Christ Church Canterbury writing in the late eleventh and early twelfth centuries, the synod decreed that 'all of the canons, all of the priests, and all of the deacons and sub-deacons should either live in chastity or lose control of the churches that they held, together with the goods belonging to them'.[169] This is almost certainly a rose-tinted as well as an over-simplified view of what the synod achieved. But Eadmer puts his finger on the problem as perceived by the reformers. Cathedrals and minster churches that were staffed by canons leading an unregulated life, holding prebends with landed endowments and usually married, were to be swept clear and the canons replaced with celibate monks. Secular canons were evicted from Winchester, Worcester, Chertsey, Milton Abbas and New Minster (Winchester). The process is revealed at its most radical in the language of the 'Oswaldslow Charter' with which Oswald reformed Worcester. Here Oswald ruled that the 'degraded and lascivious' clerks at Worcester cathedral must renounce either their prebends or their women: in other words, if they wished to continue living with women, they were obliged to give up their livelihoods. If they chose to stay at Worcester, they could do in a new role as celibate monks following the *Rule of Benedict*.[170] This was the beginning of a peculiarly English tradition, which continued until the Reformation, in which many of the cathedrals were staffed by Benedictine monks rather than canons. By *c.* 1100 this was the situation at Christ Church Canterbury, Durham, Norwich, Ely and Rochester as well as Winchester and Worcester.

The enforced adoption of the *Rule of Benedict* amounted to a revolution with far-reaching consequences. The vocabulary of the reformers is the language of the victors. The 'degraded and lascivious clerks' were probably perfectly respectable according to the usual practice in England and much of the Continent not only in the tenth century but in the pre-Viking past. Moreover, there is every reason to suppose that contemporaries regarded priests staffing a cathedral or minster and supporting families on landed endowments as monks. We have already seen very wide variation in contemporary use of the term from the earliest days and in different parts of the Christian world. The *Rule of Benedict* was only one method of observing monastic life. The homilist and sometime monk of Cerne Abbas, Aelfric, writing in the early eleventh century, saw the main elements of monasticism as being the common holding of property and communal eating on the part of monks. Although these requirements would exclude the canons expelled from Worcester and other English churches, they would still allow for wide variation in observances not necessarily based on Benedictine profession; for example, the reformed communities of canons founded by St Chrodegang of Metz in the eighth century whose way of living was prevalent in cathedrals in Lotharingia and eastern Francia. In reforming Fleury in *c.* 930, Odo of Cluny stripped back to three essentials the Cluniac observances: living frugally, eating communally and owning no property as individuals.[171] What was revolutionary about the tenth-century reform in Wessex and Mercia was that the abolition of proprietary incomes freed up resources for the monastic community as a whole. And with no families or separate establishments to maintain, a reformed monastery became a powerful corporate landowner. Moreover, as the *Regularis Concordia* makes explicit, monasteries were to be run by abbots according to the Benedictine Rule rather than – as had also been common practice on the Continent – by members of the founding family. Naturally, families that had founded monasteries and become used to treating their prebendary endowments as private property to be distributed to kin or supporters sought ways of blocking what they saw as unjustified seizures. Edgar's safeguard against this was to transfer local jurisdictional rights to abbots, who effectively became agents of the crown in their localities. Enforcement of the *Rule of Benedict* was thus accompanied by – and indeed made necessary – 'a swingeing attack on entrenched and traditional local interests'.[172]

Even a superficial reading of the *Regularis Concordia* cannot fail to bring to our attention the prominent place of the king and queen. Monks and nuns in England were to be entrusted to the protection of the king and queen, who alone among the laity had open access to monasteries. After the night office, psalms and prayers were said specifically for the health and salvation of the king and queen.[173] This was reform underwritten by royal authority. Edgar, who had 'not merely grown up with the monks, [but] had been brought up by them', must have realised the immense advantages this could bring to the crown.[174] Unlike a lay abbot, an Aethelwold or an Aelfric had no heirs, and therefore no possibility of conferring the properties or jurisdictional rights of the abbey to a locally powerful family of which he might be a member. On the contrary, the more powerful a monastery became in a given locality, the less powerful, in principle, were local notables. Promotion of reformed monasticism, reliant as it was on the crown, could thus be a valuable tool of maintaining royal interests. Moreover, the king was the guarantor of monasteries abiding by the *Regularis Concordia*, which by implication meant that he could intervene in the operations and conduct of a monastery that failed to do so.[175] Although in practice the situation was far more nuanced than this, such was an important principle not only in England but wherever there was a strong monarchy. It is no surprise to see the Ottonian imperial dynasty in Germany acting as sponsors of monastic reform in very similar ways. Emperor Henry II (973–1024), for example, was responsible for enforcing the Gorze customary at Fulda.

Cluny in the tenth century was a largely male sphere. The early Cluniacs had little apparent interest in extending their observances to women's convents – the first Cluniac house for women, Marcigny, was founded only in 1055. For this reason it has sometimes been assumed that women had little role to play in monasticism in the tenth century. Such a view appears to be supported by the paucity of new foundations. As far as we know, not a single nunnery was founded in Frankish lands between *c.* 900 and *c.* 930, and only one apiece in southern England, Lotharingia and Poitou. As a recent study of female monasticism in Lotharingia has shown, documentary evidence of a traditional kind is very sparse.[176] It has been estimated that there were around seventy active convents for women in the whole of England and France in *c.* 1000.[177] Nuns suffered just as much as monks from Viking attacks. The nuns of Fécamp in Normandy apparently took their own lives rather than be subjected to the full force of a raid, and when the convent at Ely was destroyed, 'the company of nuns was sacrificed like an innocent victim'.[178] Moreover, some nunneries that did not survive the Viking attacks, such as Sherborne and Ely, were refounded not as convents for women but as male communities – in the case of Sherborne as secular canons. Fécamp was refounded by William of Volpiano for monks at the end of the tenth century, and Vézelay, originally founded in 867, was given over to monks after its refoundation because it was considered too unsafe from potential Magyar raids.[179]

Yet women were far from invisible in religious life in this period. Some nunneries, especially in inland areas, survived the invasions, even where – as at Leominster in Mercia in the mid-eleventh century – the abbess was abducted.[180] And new convents for women were founded even during the Viking period: Alfred, king of Wessex founded Shaftesbury for his daughter Aelfgifu to serve as abbess, Wilton and

Nunnaminster at Winchester. Barking, destroyed in the late ninth century, was restored in *c.* 950, and Romsey in the 960s.[181] In some ways nuns' influence was out of proportion with their numbers. According to his *Life*, Dunstan's inspiration for the monastic life came from Aethelflaed, a widow who occupied a cell as a solitary near the abbey at Glastonbury in the 930s. It is telling that even though the number of functioning nunneries in England was still small at the time, the *Regularis Concordia* specifically includes and addresses nuns as well as monks. This may also be a sign that the house of Wessex found the promotion of female monasticism particularly appealing. Karl Leyser showed that during the tenth century nunneries were founded in preference to male monasteries, and this in itself suggests that the impetus often came from wealthy widows, in a society where women's life expectancy was longer than men's, and where inheritance customs enabled women to hold on to their own property more easily than in, for example, the Frankish lands.[182]

Needless to say, however, new convents were also founded for women in tenth-century France. The reform movement in Lotharingia may have provided the impetus for the founding of the nunnery of Bouxières-aux-Dames in Lorraine in 930, and there were also new foundations in other dioceses in the region. As with Alfred's Shaftesbury, this had a distinctly aristocratic character. The founder, Gauzelin, bishop of Toul, placed relatives in the convent, and this may have been an underlying reason for the foundation.[183] Nuns in Lotharingia sought direct connections with royal and imperial figures, achieved partly through emphasis on unique saints' cults and their shrines.[184]

Bishops were also behind the founding of the nunnery at Épinal, in the diocese of Metz, and indirectly of Vergaville in the same diocese in the 960s; and of St Maur soon after 1000 in the diocese of Verdun. What observances these foundations followed is not always clear, though the foundation charter of the new nunnery of the Holy Trinity at Poitiers, founded just before 980, specified that the endowment was large enough to enable the nuns to follow the *Rule of Benedict*.[185] This point serves to remind us of the resource required to establish a new community. Nuns had no income other than that provided by rentals or the produce of the land owned by the house. But where such resources were not readily available, women found ways of leading religious lives, sometimes in the orbit of a monastery. Between the solitaries enclosed by bishops such as Liutberga and a foundation with an endowment, there must have been many semi-official ways for pious women (*religiosae feminae*, as they are often referred to in sources) to live in community.[186] Sometimes, as we saw in the case of secular canons in English cathedrals, such communities were judged by reforming bishops to be unsustainable or unworthy; thus, the nunnery at Homblières in Picardy was transferred to monks in 949 because the nuns were considered not to be living according to a Rule.[187]

During the ninth and tenth centuries, in both Latin- and Greek-speaking worlds, monasteries occupied ground that could be uncertain. Most monasteries were private foundations made by individuals or families. They might be made because members of a family had a vocation or need to retire from the world – perhaps after being widowed, or withdrawing from public life, or because the family did not want to support them any longer. If this appears overly cynical, it does not mean that founders were not also motivated by genuine piety or the conviction that establishing a community to lead a religious life was the 'right' thing to do. The foundation charter of Cluny expresses sentiments that must have informed all founders in some measure. Not all monasteries were founded by laypeople. In both East and West, bishops were responsible for the maintenance of religious life in their diocese, and for some this was best accomplished by founding religious communities. Bishops often worked in partnership with prominent lay families – often ruling dynasties – to found and endow monasteries. But religious communities sometimes evolved in less clearly defined ways than through an act of foundation. Individuals in search of a path to understanding God, or in flight from the world, banded together in loose associations in uninhabited and often inaccessible locations – Mount Athos is an obvious but far from unique example – out of which a community could emerge. In the Greek-speaking world the relationship between this kind of religious life and the formalised life of an institution with a typikon was particularly fluid, at least for men. Prominent holy men wandered in and out of institutional life, apparently – at least in their hagiographies – much as it suited them. They might found communities by gathering like-minded men around them, then leave them for periods of solitude, sometimes shifting their location to found another. This pattern is particularly discernible in the Byzantine provinces. Sometimes such communities developed into enduring monasteries, as for example at Elias Speleota's cave monastery in Calabria.

All monasteries needed some form of endowment or a regular income stream. This meant that the founding of a monastery required a partnership between spiritual leadership and the wealthy. The ideal of the 'desert monks', espoused by Benedict's Rule and prevalent in the early centuries of monasticism, of religious communities supporting themselves from their own labour, had eroded by the ninth century. We find it surviving only among individuals or very small groups who relied on their own ability to plant and harvest. At one extreme, monks' desire to exist independent of any support from external agency could determine their manner of life, as we see in the early career of Euthymios the Younger on Mount Athos. But most monks and nuns accepted that monasticism was a partnership between those following a religious life and those with surplus disposable property. The relationship was regarded as beneficial not only for those engaged in the partnership but for wider society as a whole. Both partners in the relationship brought power, of a sort. But relationships with the powerful could not protect monasteries from all eventualities. For periods in the ninth and tenth centuries (especially *c.* 850–970), monks and nuns ran the risk of random violent attacks from pirates and raiders. If no more vulnerable to such attack than the rural poor, the settings in which they lived were more likely to attract raiders looking for disposable wealth. Even where monastic communities were not wholly destroyed, an attack could destabilise it to the point where it was unviable. Moreover, wider instabilities in society undermined the continuing capacity of families of founders to continue funding monasteries. Much of Europe, east and west, experienced weak public authority as a result of overstretch, ideological division or economic malaise. These uncertainties, however, did not prevent the vigorous renewal in monastic life in both Latin- and Greek-speaking worlds in the tenth century. As we will see in the following chapter, after the year 1000 a fresh tide of reform would gather force strengthened by an ideological commitment to the fundamental principles of poverty and simplicity.

CHAPTER FOUR

'There Are Angels Everywhere'
Reform in the Eleventh and Twelfth Centuries

> Walk cautiously, since there are angels everywhere: according to the commandment given them, they are in all your ways.
> Bernard of Clairvaux, *Sermon on Psalm 90*, XII, 6

CENOBITIC MONASTICISM IN THE ELEVENTH CENTURY: A SNAPSHOT

IN THE SECOND HALF of 1091 a Byzantine monk known to history as John the Oxite arrived in Antioch to take up his new office as patriarch John IV. He had been appointed two years previously while in Constantinople to attend a synod on the reunion of Greek and Latin worship. John had a wretched time as patriarch: tortured by the Seljuks during the crusaders' siege of the city in 1097–8 by being suspended in an iron cage from its walls, he was thrown out by the new crusader ruler Bohemond in 1100 in favour of a Frankish bishop, a victim of the failure of Byzantine–Latin diplomacy, and retired to a monastery in Constantinople. John was something of a controversialist, who wrote polemical treatises against Roman ecclesiastical practices and against the Maronites of Lebanon. But he recognised the universal quality of monasticism as a force for salvation.

In a treatise written before his election, John IV traced the evolution of monasticism from the early days of the Christian Church. Some followers of Christ, he wrote, realised that the ascetic life was the only reliable way to serve one maser, and to follow Jesus's injunction to follow him exclusively. As their fame spread throughout the regions where the name of Jesus was revered, many joined them, and these became the first monasteries. Thanks to their example, the whole world can now rely on salvation by taking flight from the world and its goods. It is not only in Constantinople that this is taken for granted, but in Egypt, Palestine, Syria, Persia, the Caucasus and in western territories obedient to Rome. Nor is this practice confined to men, for it is also women who understand the benefits of monasticism. The world is no longer divided between men and women, John announced, but between the chaste and the unchaste.[1]

John's treatise was aimed against the practices of lay ownership and direction of, and profit from, monasteries. We will examine the reasons for his stand and why he thought it necessary in the course of this chapter, but his brief account of the origin of monasteries serves as a valuable reminder that, at a time when relations between the great powers of the Christian world in Rome and Constantinople were worsening, monasticism was seen by some contemporaries as a universalising force. This is not to say that monasticism followed a similar path, or was even necessarily very similar in terms of practices or institutional setting, in eastern and western parts of the Christian world. But, as we shall see, the differences did not preclude a general acceptance that the underlying ideals and fundamental job of the monk was essentially the same.

A snapshot of two monasteries – one Latin, the other Greek – in the 1060s serves to highlight both some essential similarities of principle and important differences of approach. In 1063 Peter Damian, a monk from an eremitical community in Italy, Fonte Avellana, was dispatched by the pope to Cluny to resolve a long-running dispute between the monastery and the bishop of Mâcon over jurisdiction. As we saw in the previous chapter, the foundation charter of William of Aquitaine demanded freedom from episcopal jurisdiction, even though it was of course not a lay founder's prerogative to do so. Understandably frustrated at successive renewals of the abbey's exemption from just about any episcopal right, Bishop Drogo of Mâcon claimed the right of visitation of the monastery in person, but was refused entry by the monks.

Abbot Hugh (r. 1049–1109) appealed to the papacy, and Peter heard the case at the Council of Chalon, finding in favour of the monastery – not surprisingly, given papal bulls of 990 and 1027 that confirmed the claims to exemption made in the foundation charter.[2]

At around the same time, a new monastery dedicated to the Mother of God (Theotokos) was being built in a suburb of Constantinople on an estate belonging to a nobleman called Paul Evergetinos. Paul had died in 1054, leaving the monastery comprising only a few small cells occupied by a few monks. His chosen successor Timothy endowed the monastery with more land, built a church and new accommodation, and wrote a typikon. This document was to become the most influential programme for the reform of Byzantine monasticism over the next two centuries.[3] One reason for its influence with other reforming founders was a clause that bears comparison with Cluny:

> We instruct all in the name of our Lord God the Ruler of All that this holy monastery is to be independent, free of everyone's control, and self-governing, and not subject to any rights, be they imperial or ecclesiastic or of a private person, but it should be watched over, steered, governed, and directed only by the Mother of God Evergetis who is worthy of all praise, by the prayer of our most blessed and holy father, and by the one acting as superior in it.[4]

Just as Cluny secured confirmation of its independence in the form of papal bulls, so Evergetis was already at the time of the final version of the typikon supported by imperial chrysobulls.[5]

In a letter written to the community after his return to Fonte Avellana many months later, Peter expressed his admiration of what he had seen.

> Thinking back, moreover, on your strict and totally occupied order of the day, I consider it to be not the result of human invention, but something devised by the Holy Spirit. For such was the extent of your continuous effort to observe the Rule, especially your constant participation at Mass and in choir, that, even in the great heat of June and July, when the days are longest, there was hardly half an hour

throughout the day in which the brethren were unoccupied and permitted to engage in conversation.[6]

The constant occupation, and absence of periods of spare time, removed occasions for the monks to sin. Peter thought that this showed remarkable foresight on the part of Benedict in drafting the Rule, but also suggested that the *horarium* (daily round of offices) took inspiration from Scripture. The complex set of prescriptions followed by the Israelites of the Old Testament had been laid down by God at the time when they were on their journey from captivity in Egypt to the Promised Land. With no permanent homes, and thus no regular economic occupation, the Israelites needed a ritual to keep themselves busy about the affairs of God. This, Peter argued, was also what lay behind Cluny's tightly controlled *horarium*.

This passage from Peter's letter is often taken as evidence that Cluny had so far extended the liturgical hours as to leave no time for the monks to do anything else. In fact, this is not quite what Peter says. According to him, 'constant participation at Mass and in choir' was one way in which Cluniacs continuously sought to observe the Rule. What he wants to draw attention to is the tightness of the structure of daily life, that removes unused time.[7] Indulging in conversation was particularly undesirable. Nevertheless, it seems clear that in the early eleventh century, the liturgy was developed in such a way as to lengthen it considerably.[8] The Council of Anse (994) can, in retrospect, be seen to have ushered in a new period of Cluniac history characterised by the expansion of its association with other monasteries and their dependence on Cluny, increased assertions of independence, and economic consolidation. The growth of the liturgy and the writing of its customaries were an expression of these developments. Ulrich himself acknowledged that at Cluny the number of psalms sung at the offices greatly exceeded that prescribed by Benedict, especially during Lent. Monastic psalmody was a collective sung recitation by all choir monks, which obviously took a good deal longer than simply saying the words.[9] Moreover, Cluny was simply following what had already become standard practice in many Benedictine monasteries by the mid-eleventh century. One reason for this was the simple passage of time. Anniversaries for deceased monks were easy enough to incorporate into the *horarium* in a community's early years, but by the late eleventh century the practice of singing psalms to commemorate an anniversary after daily chapter, as well as special vigils comprising psalms and readings, took up increasing amounts of time. Abbot Hugh eventually introduced a collective anniversary commemoration for all dead Cluniacs in order to free up time.[10] Another factor was the increasing number of monks in monasteries. After the death of a monk, the whole psalter was sung during the night vigil in the presence of the body, and at requiem masses up to ten special collects might be said. These traditions had been established in times when smaller numbers of monks meant that these extra observances did not take up so much time as to unbalance the liturgy, but as recruitment to monasteries increased in an age of expanding population, monastic communities might find that observing the proper liturgical rites for the deceased created a log-jam in the day. Many anniversaries were of benefactors rather than monks. The implication of observing these was to change the way in which a mass was understood within the community: not so much a celebration of the entire community, on behalf of the wider Church, with Christ, but rather a private gift, for which a counter-gift was to be expected from the families or individuals who made them. But everything must have taken longer in a larger community: liturgical processions, the feeding of monks in the refectory, the public accusations and punishments of refractory monks at daily chapter.

Peter Damian was not the only observer to draw attention to the liturgically overfreighted *horarium*. The eleventh-century monk of Bec and later archbishop of Canterbury, Anselm, rejected the idea of a vocation at Cluny because he thought there would be insufficient opportunity for private study.[11] In 1189, in a letter to a correspondent who wanted to become a Cluniac, Peter of Blois criticised the formalism of the Cluniac liturgy, which he contrasted unfavourably with both the Carthusian approach of gathering the hidden manna from the desert and the 'busy austerity' of the Cistercians.[12] The liturgical intensity of the *horarium* at Cluny contrasts with Evergetis, where liturgical offices in the church during day and night were balanced with private offices said by the monks in their cells. In general, the Evergetis typikon held the relationships of mutual service in the community to be higher than public observance of the liturgy.[13]

'THERE ARE ANGELS EVERYWHERE'

Scott Bruce has argued that both the effect and, in part, the prior intention of liturgical development was to reduce opportunities for casual conversation between monks, in order that the community could fulfil the ideal of becoming truly angelic.[14] Monks should be like the angels, who were silent except for the noise they made in praising God. Similarly, in legislating for the conduct of Evergetis monks, Timothy required silence and attentiveness in church and refectory. Monks were to leave the offices in silence and return quietly to their cells without any conversation among them.

> For what comes of such things? Clearly, the lapsing into disgraceful talk, abuse, and condemnations because your mind is relaxed by this and you forget what is really good, and reaching your cells in a dilatory and lazy frame of mind you sink at once into a sleep of *akedia* and pass almost all the day in idleness without engaging in any beneficial activity whatever . . .[15]

Some monks were to be appointed to check that there were no covert meetings among members of the community in individual cells. All opportunities for casual conversation were to be avoided. At Cluny, as at other large monasteries in the West, the monks responsible for checking idle conversation were known as *circatores* ('roundsmen'). Their task was to patrol the monastery checking for infringements against the rule of silence. The eleventh-century Customary of Ulrich recommends that they make random patrols 'so that there is neither a place nor a time in which any brother . . . may be unconcerned by the possibility of detection'.[16] In principle it should have been more difficult for Benedictine monks to indulge in idle conversation, since unlike Greek monks they had no private spaces. But monks found ways and means. The moral of the story told by Ekkehard IV of St Gall about the learned monks who used to meet in the scriptorium to discuss the Scriptural readings for that day's offices makes sense because of the jealous monk who suspected that they were secretly gossiping.[17] But despite the different living arrangements in western and eastern monasteries, cenobitic regulators in both were concerned with the problem of idle and underemployed monks.

Benedict might have been surprised to learn that this was a problem in monasteries following his Rule, which was designed to provide a balance between types of activity, worship and quiet study throughout the day and night. But by the eleventh century, little useful manual work was being done in Benedictine monasteries. The Cluniac customaries prescribe a single period of work during the day for most of the year (between Tierce and Nones, broken by Sext, in other words from about 8.30 a.m. to 2 p.m. with a break at noon), but it is unlikely that much of this was *necessary* work of the kind that sustained the economy of the monastery. The *Regularis Concordia*, heavily dependent on both Cluniac and Gorze customaries, expected all able-bodied monks to be on the kitchen and bakehouse rota. But the designation of specific psalms to be sung by monks while they worked in the fields suggests that this was already a ritualised form of activity.[18] The twelfth-century Benedictine Boso of Prüfenung thought that manual labour was useful only so far as it might aid contemplation.[19] This situation was in many ways inevtable. Even a small or medium-sized monastery – for example, one with under a hundred monks – needed considerable agricultural labour to feed the community. If a monastery's landed property was largely arable, the labour was seasonal: very heavy at times of ploughing, sowing and harvest, less so at other times. Livestock and fish farms, on the other hand, needed frequent care and attention. The work was not only demanding but also required a degree of know-how. The maintenance of the monastic estate – repairs and upkeep – was constant. Then there were the workshops needed by any establishment or household to forge iron, shoe horses, make everyday items for use in the kitchen and refectory from wood or leather, and so on. Most western monks, who came from the propertied classes, did not possess the skills, experience or muscle to accomplish all this work without outside help. There cannot have been a monastery that did not make use of paid servants. But the possession of land in medieval society also implied the legal possession of the labour of those who lived on the land. As an early twelfth-century foundation charter expressed it,

> I donate, give, and concede to God Almighty and to the holy Trinity at Savigny, and to the abbot of that place, all my forest of Furness,

> Walney, with all the hunting [rights] that go with it, Dalton and all my lordships below Furness, with all the men [living there] and everything pertaining to them, that is to say, in woods and meadows, on land and water . . .[20]

It was 'all the men living there', not the monks, who did the manual labour that yielded food and other kinds of income from possession of land. Monasteries, in this respect, were no different from any other property owners.

This does not mean that no work at all was done at most monasteries; rather that it was of a more specific sort than probably envisaged in the Rule. Study, writing, copying and illuminating manuscripts were all forms of work – writing on vellum, indeed, was nothing if not intensely manual. In addition there were other forms of skilled work associated with the care and supply of liturgical equipment, such as turning wax harvested from beehives into candles, that might fall into this category. The Byzantine tradition of monastic labour developed in analogous albeit rather different ways. Following the Studite Rule of the ninth century, Timothy Evergetinos assumed a role for manual labour without being very specific about the kind of work done. Cellarers, bakers, cooks and muleteers are mentioned with the strong implication that these roles were to be undertaken by monks. Inclusion of those serving as stewards of estates carries with it an implication that they must have been supervising agricultural workers who were not part of the community.[21] Many, perhaps most Byzantine monasteries had some unlettered monks whose backgrounds may have qualified them to be effective in such roles. Some monastic regulators, such as Nikon, specifically endorsed manual labour, though this might take the form of a skilled craft. Nikon's template for a monastery on the 'Black Mountain' (Jabal Lukkam, northwest of Antioch), written between 1055 and 1060, followed the Basilian Rules carefully in articulating the importance of manual work.[22] Basil's view of manual labour was that it should function as a social leveller; thus, monks of high social status might be tasked with heavy work as a test of their humility.[23] It was the superior's responsibility to match the job to the spiritual as well as spiritual state of the monk. Monks should not be set work that they would necessarily find easy or amenable, which would be of less benefit to them than more unfamiliar work. In Nikon's typikon, monks who were assigned to heavy work were given fewer hours of manual labour than others. Crafts were encouraged, and a cell in the monastery was to be set aside for such work under supervision.[24] Some work, such as kitchen and bakery jobs, were to rotate among the monks. But Nikon was also careful to advise that although manual work of some kind was necessary for all monks, it should not obstruct the liturgical offices, either in the church or those said privately by monks in cells.[25]

Perhaps what Cluny and Evergetis had most in common from the middle of the eleventh century onwards was that both offered a template for cenobitic monasticism. In both cases, this was conscious and intentional. Two important customaries were produced at Cluny in the eleventh century, by the monks Bernard (probably in or soon after 1078) and Ulrich (1079–84).[26] These were detailed compilations of information about how the liturgy was celebrated, how daily life was regulated and by whom. They represented the practical application of the Rule in a particular community. As some historians have pointed out, like all legislative documents they display an ideal rather than, necessarily, the messy daily realities. Historians who have studied monastic customaries in detail have proposed that they should be subdivided into different types: those written for the use of the community itself, with the intent of underlining or enforcing existing customs, and those produced as information, or even instruction manuals, for other communities.[27] As we have seen, only a few years after its founding the abbots of Cluny were already providing such advice for other monasteries, and the network of influence established by Odo, Majolus and Odilo continued to grow in the eleventh century. In *c.* 1000, Farfa used Cluny's old customary to re-establish cenobitic monasticism after a period of decline, and by the 1050s had more than 500 monks in the abbey and its dependencies.[28] In analogous fashion, although without the contemporary fame of Cluny, the typikon of Evergetis provided a template and exemplar for subsequent Greek monastic foundations. It has been described as 'undoubtedly the most influential Byzantine founder's typikon ever written', to the extent that a summary of the influence on later monasteries would essentially be a summary of Byzantine monasticism from the mid-eleventh to the fourteenth centuries.[29] Some typika, such as the Sebastokrator Isaac Komnenos's monastery of the Mother of God Kosmosoteira (1152), borrowed directly but without attribution from Evergetis, while others such as Empress Irene's convent of Kecharitomene (1110–16) borrowed more indirectly. Evergetian customs were incorporated into a number of twelfth-century foundations, such as Emperor John II's foundation of Pantokrator (1136), and Athanasios Philanthropenos's monastery of St Mamas in Constantinople (1158). The influences exerted by Evergetis were primarily textual rather than personal. Evergetis was not particularly well known or celebrated as a monastery in Timothy's own day, and it is the typikon rather than personal leadership or example that provided continuity.

It is tempting to read into this contrast with Cluny an inference that Byzantine monasticism developed in a more textual manner, through the preservation and reading of materials such as typika, whereas western cenobitic practices were conveyed through personal example. This would not be entirely wrong. The attempt to impose up-to-date reformed cenobitic life in Byzantine Syria in the 1050s by the Constantinopolitan monk Nikon provides an extreme example of this textualised approach to monastic regulation.[30] Nikon was offered the position as archimandrite of the Antioch region by the patriarch, Luke Anazarbos, with a mandate to bring contemporary metropolitan practices to a province that had been restored to the Empire in 969. His enormously detailed typika for a monastery on the Black Mountain near Antioch and for another (the Monastery of the Pomegranate) in an as yet unidentified area under Armenian control reveal his voracious reading of previous monastic, canonical and patristic texts.[31] Yet it is not even certain whether the Black Mountain monastery ever existed in reality, and Nikon himself later testified to his disappointment in being less successful than he had hoped in bringing about cenobitic reform based on deep textual integrity. In contrast, Farfa had help in re-establishing cenobitism not only from Cluny's customary but also from the monks sent there by Romuald, abbot of Sant' Apollinare in Classe, and by the former Cluniac William of Volpiano. The method of William of Volpiano's reform of Fécamp in the early eleventh century was simply to import a large group of his monks from St Bénigne, Dijon, to live alongside and teach the 'inconsequential little congregation' of resident secular canons.[32] But this does not tell the whole story. There are plenty of examples of eleventh- and twelfth-century Byzantine foundations established through personal example. The two twelfth-century Cypriot foundations of Makhairas and Neophytos's Enkleistra provide contemporaneous but very different such examples. Moreover, as we shall see, monastic reform in the West could also be deeply textual, as William of Malmesbury's account of the role of Stephen Harding in the founding of Cîteaux in 1098 testifies.[33]

BYZANTINE CENOBITIC REFORM

If Cluny and Evergetis both appear to represent the dominance of regulated cenobitic monasticism in the Greek- and Latin-speaking worlds in the middle of the eleventh century, they also suggest the availability and attraction of other monastic paths. Timothy was insistent that monasticism meant a communal life, yet he himself preferred to live as a recluse in a hermitage attached to the monastery.[34] His original intention was for the monastery to have two superiors, the recluse and a partner living 'unconfined' in the community. On the death of the recluse, his partner would then assume his role in a cell and his place would be taken by another monk in the community. But by his own acknowledgement, it would go against the spirit of uniformity and charity to enforce seclusion on the monks' choice of superior against his will, so he abandoned this design and simply left it to the choice of his successor whether he wished to be secluded or not.[35] The overriding point, for Timothy, was to preserve unity in the cenobium, even if it meant electing a less capable superior.

> But if . . . you yourselves resort to strife and discord, the bad steward himself will become your superior to avoid uproar and dissension. For when two evils lie before us then the less bad one is preferable, and it is better for you to be exposed to a little danger during the leadership of this worthless man, than to be rendered completely useless by resorting to discord and quarreling or even the remembering of injuries. For if you are living in peace and preserving good order, it is impossible that even a little harm should come to you

from the leadership of this worthless man. But if you indulge in discord and quarreling, every evil will follow.'[36]

Counterintuitive though it may seem, this model of a recluse as superior was not unique. Lazaros of Mount Galesion founded a monastery in western Asia Minor earlier in the eleventh century over which he presided as a stylite. Nor did a reclusive superior abdicate from close governance. A number of incidents in the *Life* written by one of his monks demonstrates his concern to keep a watchful eye on his monks' activities. Any monk who had permission to leave the monastery on official business had first to report to him. In fact, some monks found him overly authoritarian in his approach.[37] Similarly, about a hundred years after Timothy at Evergetis, Neophytos remained in the cave-cell he had hollowed out as his home even after founding the Enkleistra community on the flat shelf below his cliff. He assumed that his successor – his nephew – would continue the reclusive tradition, and remain out of direct contact with the community. 'Do not converse with many, and in particular with fools, maintaining circumspection and power over your thoughts.'[38] Personal self-restraint was the fundamental requirement for anyone in authority.

Both Lazaros and Neophytos were mavericks. Lazaros was on bad terms with his bishop, whose jurisdiction he denied, while Neophytos had been persuaded against his better judgement to convert his hermitage into a cenobitic community. But both represent a new wave of independent self-governing foundations in the Byzantine world in the eleventh and twelfth centuries. Most monasteries in the earliest period had been independent foundations because the prestige of being a *ktistes* ('founder') matched closely with late Roman patterns of patronage. The tensions implicit between this impetus for privately funded foundations and the sixth-century imperial legislation requiring monasteries to be under the jurisdiction of bishops were eventually snapped by Emperor Leo VI in the tenth century, who removed the last vestiges of the restraints in the Justinianic code. Now founders sought to establish monasteries that would be immune from state or imperial control. By the 960s, however, reaction was already setting in. Emperor Nikephoros Phokas discouraged new foundations, preferring donors instead to repair dilapidated monasteries. He was responding to the growing problem that many monasteries, founded through the generosity of bygone patrons, languished on large estates that provided insufficient income but from which they could not profit through sale. Like landed families in Victorian Britain, they had land and prestige but no capital assets. It was in these circumstances that in 996 Emperor Basil II instituted the phenomenon known as the *charistike*.

The *charistike* has been defined as 'a public programme sponsored by the emperor and the ecclesiastical hierarchy for the private management of religious institutions'.[39] In essence it was a public–private partnership in which lay patrons were encouraged to shoulder the burden of restoring failing monasteries by making grants that were intended to be temporary, lasting perhaps for one or two lifetimes. In many cases it doubtless worked as intended. A monastery that had been founded on private land by a family that had died out or whose original endowments had been exhausted could not, by canon law, be supported through diocesan funds, so partnering with a rich patron was an elegant solution. Basil II even offered inducements in the form of sharing the income from improved estate management. It was this that led to abuses in the system, as lay patrons could use the *charistike* to muscle in on monasteries that did not really need their financial support but which they could treat as cash cows from which they might profit.[40] Eventually the logic of the *charistike* led to private foundations that were designed to remain in the control of the founding family. A good example of such is the almshouse (*ptochotropheion*) founded in 1077 at Rhaideros, on the Sea of Marmara, by Michael Attaliates. This was one half of a pair of foundations, the other being the Panaiktimos monastery in Constantinople. Both shared governance and administration, and drew on a common revenue provided through the founder's endowment. Clearly the almshouse was always intended as private familial property, since the typikon bequeaths ownership to Michael's heir: only once direct and collateral heirs died out was the property to become independent. The arrangement allowed heirs to receive two-thirds of the revenues from the property, after all expenses, including maintenance of the property, had been discharged. As Thomas has pointed out, Michael also allowed for the siphoning off of revenue for other monasteries of which he or his son was the *charistikarios*.[41]

This was precisely the kind of situation against which John the Oxite, with whom this chapter started, was reacting when he wrote his treatise examining the origins of monasticism. As John rightly saw, arrangements such as those that Michael instituted meant that the spiritual superior effectively lost control of the institution's finances, and thereby of its daily administration. Even a well-intentioned *charistikarios* diffused the authority of the superior by acting as a counter-balance against him, to whom dissatisfied monks might appeal. Some *charistikarioi* assembled multiple such appointments, which resulted in their placing agents in monasteries to represent them, who could easily act beyond their control. John knew of cases where *charistikarioi* and their families took up residence in monasteries whose fortunes they had been appointed to restore, thereby burdening the institutions with further unnecessary costs.[42]

By the end of the eleventh century, other reformers had joined their voices to John's, and an imperial novel issued by Emperor Alexios I in 1096 sought to redress the balance by restoring patriarchal rights of oversight and correction to all monasteries within his jurisdiction, regardless of the circumstances of foundation. It is too simplistic to think of 'reformers' as being invariably anti-*charistike*, and assume that those who supported the institution were 'unreformed'. After all, Nikon of the Black Mountain, whose reforming credentials are impeccable, made provision for the upkeep of his monastery of Roidion through an arrangement that, while not using the term, looks very like the appointment of a *charistikarios*. And opponents of the *charistike*, such as the late twelfth-century canonist Theodore Balsamon, might themselves be owners of private monasteries. Nevertheless, the rise of independent autonomous monasteries such as Evergetis in response to the abuses of the *charistike* system strengthened the hand of reformers who wished to emphasise the strict observance of cenobitic monasticism. Consequently, one of the hallmarks of the Byzantine cenobitic reform movement of the eleventh and twelfth centuries was the strict separation of monastic and lay life. Christodoulos, the founder of St John of Patmos, specified in his typikon that the monastery was not to come under imperial or ecclesiastical authority, nor to be granted away under a *charistike* arrangement. Although, somewhat confusingly, he made use of lay patronage through someone to whom he referred as a *charistikarios*, he was careful to limit his powers, for example by prohibiting the introduction of any of his relatives into the monastery.[43] Such was his fear of contact with family life that he even tried at first to ban married men from among those settling on the island to cultivate the land, though this plan had to be abandoned.[44] Nikon forbade women from entering the property of the monastery altogether, and the twelfth-century foundation of Makhairas on Cyprus repeated this injunction, ruling out even the possibility of aristocratic women entering the church to attend liturgies, which Evergetis had permitted.[45] But even monasteries whose typika might be fairly relaxed about the incursion of outside life into the community insisted on certain fundamentals of cenobitic life. Thus, for example, the foundation made by the former soldier Gregory Pakourianos at Petritzonitissa in Bachkovo (Bulgaria) in 1083, while eschewing some of the stricter measures of Evergetian reform, demanded that all monks eat the same food at a common table, that no private pursuits were followed, that no animals were privately owned and no food stored privately in monks' cells.[46]

Cenobitic reform was a response to the *charistike* in the broad sense that every increase in lay influence in a monastery was more likely to lead to the erosion of strict communality in favour of individualism. Reformers thus emphasised the need for strict communality as a way of countering its effects. Until the end of the eleventh century, the *charistike* was of course still part of imperial policy, so even its critics had to find ways of resisting its effects that did not leave them open to charges of disloyalty. Twelfth-century founders could afford to be less circumspect. In contrast to Evergetis, which simply requires administration of the monastery's estates to be carried out by reverent and discreet, preferably elderly people, Neilos's monastery of Makhairas in Cyprus specifies that all properties were 'administered by us', and forbids laymen from supervising a daughter-house.[47] Cenobitism was, in minds of Byzantine reformers, intimately connected with the autonomy and independence of the monastery.

REFORM IN THE WEST

Peter Damian, although effusive in his compliments to Cluny, had chosen a very different kind of monastic life himself. At the time of his visit to Cluny he had for the past twenty years been prior of the eremitical community of Fonte Avellana in the Apennines, which he had joined in 1036–7. In the *Institute for the Order of Hermits* that he wrote as a direction for like-minded communities, Peter described a regime based on a life of consistent personal mortification lived in a small group broken down into pairs sharing a cell. Summer and winter alike the monks went barefoot, underwent frequent flagellation, and fasted on bread, water and salt four days a week. At around the time he became prior, he also wrote a *Life* of Romuald of Ravenna, the founder of an eremitical monastery at Camaldoli (1012–14) whom he regarded as his exemplar. Unlike most hagiographical texts, this *Life* was a record of Romuald's *conversatio*, a word that has been paraphrased as 'his life in orientation to God'.[48] The need to write such a work can be taken as an indication of a debate among those leading a religious life about the relationship between cenobitism and an eremitical life.

Many historians have viewed this relationship as one of tension, and eleventh-century Italy as its proving-ground.[49] The narrative arc of western monasticism is usually seen to take an eremitical turn in the eleventh century, as reforming figures such as Damian at Fonte Avellana, Romuald at Camaldoli, John Gualbert (985–1073) at Vallombrosa (1036) and others sought to restore an eremitical element to monastic life that they considered had been lost. In so doing they were not overthrowing or discarding Benedictine monasticism; Damian, indeed, thought that Benedict was a hermit whose Rule was a first stage towards a perfect monastic life characterised by a kind of communal eremitism. The Italian reformers, in most received accounts, in turn gave rise to a generation of reformers in France such as Bernard of Tiron (1046–1117), Robert of Arbrissel (*c*. 1045–1116), Vitalis of Savigny (1060–1122) and Robert of Molesmes (1028–1111), who founded monastic communities based on what they considered to be eremitical principles.

What 'eremitism' meant in such communities is not always obvious. It is tempting to follow the logic of an apparent tension between eremitism and cenobitism as part of the 'story' of reform.[50] According to this logic, new reforming communities often arose out of such tensions in existing monasteries. In an important and influential book, Henrietta Leyser showed that many of the new foundations of the eleventh century in France had 'unofficial' or eremitical origins: in other words, that rather than being the result of conscious foundation by a family or patron, or an offshoot of an existing monastery, many developed out of a small group who were dissatisfied with monasticism on a larger scale. Many were already monks in established monasteries, though some were cathedral canons, secular priests or laypeople.[51]

The urge to leave their current existence and start afresh was characterised by certain shared assumptions and aspirations about what constituted original, and therefore 'correct', monasticism. Poverty, simplicity of life and manual labour were instrumental in recovering monasticism. A classic example of this tendency is the series of events at Molesmes, an eleventh-century Benedictine house in Burgundy, that gave rise in 1098 to the departure of the prior, Robert, and several monks, to form a new community at Cîteaux – the community from which the Cistercian Order would emerge in the twelfth century. Such foundation narratives often seem to be as much literary trope as reality, even when the basic outline of facts seems to be accurate. But reformers invariably identify themselves in contrast to a prevailing tendency, often as heroic visionaries contending against entrenched interests. Thus, reformers wished to present themselves as restorers of 'original' monasticism as against the complacency of the mainstream that had forgotten what the *Rule of Benedict* – let alone the desert parents – really meant. This narrative of a 'return to poverty and simplicity', though understood by historians to be a simplification of reality, is nevertheless still found in most treatments of western monasticism in the eleventh and twelfth centuries. This is supported by much of the contemporary monastic discourse, in which we frequently find terms such as *renovatio*, and where religious describe themselves and others as being in the process of *recalescere* and *recuperari*. The notion of 'recovery' of an idealised past is prevalent in much of the writing by reformers.[52]

The picture as it must have seemed to most contemporaries was far more nuanced and slippery. Three points are worth making briefly at the outset. First, 'reform' did not mean the same thing to everyone. According to the eleventh-century Cluniac writer Ralph Glaber, the reformer William of Volpiano considered the essence of reform to be not a 'return' to an original form of living, but liturgical accuracy. Second, monastic simplicity of the kind that infused Benedict's Rule could be found in surprising places. When Peter Damian visited Cluny in 1063, its abbot, Hugh the Great, was one of the most powerful men in Christendom: the godfather of the German emperor, a man at ease in the courts of kings, who controlled directly or indirectly a huge network of landed properties, and who was on the point of rebuilding the abbey church on a scale greater than St Peter's in Rome. Yet Peter was astonished to discover that Hugh had no private bedroom of his own, and slept with his monks in the common dormitory.[53] In a similar way, Bury St Edmunds, one of the wealthiest and oldest monasteries in England, was not necessarily the place we might think of looking for 'reform'. Yet Samson, abbot of Bury in the late twelfth and early thirteenth centuries, was characterised by his biographer, the Bury monk Jocelin of Brakelond, as a reformer, by virtue of the moderation of his way of life, specifically at the table.

Third, and related to the second, the dividing line between reform and tradition could be porous. Romuald may have founded an eremitical community, but he advised both the founders of Fonte Avellana and the Cluniac monastery of Farfa. John Gualbert, who became associated with the eremitical house at Vallombrosa, was initially (in *c.* 1030) a Benedictine monk at San Miniato. It was not the observance or lack of it of the Rule that caused him to leave, first for Camaldoli and then to found a reformed cenobitic monastery at Vallombrosa in Tuscany, but the simony of his abbot.[54] Moreover, eremitical reforming communities could behave in ways that appear rather similar to 'traditional' monasteries. Fonte Avellana and other such communities owned land and made agreements with local landowners about boundaries in the same way as an established monastery. Similarly, when Heloise sought the advice of her former teacher and lover Peter Abelard to help her reform her community of Benedictine nuns, who had recently been forced to move from their house at Argenteuil to new accommodation at Abelard's hermitage of the Paraclete, it was not a simpler or 'purer' way of life that she wanted. For Heloise, reform was necessary because the *Rule of Benedict* was simply not inclusive enough: it treated women as 'exceptions' to a norm, who might be exempted from some of the stipulations of the Rule, rather than as central subjects of the community.[55] There were many different pathways to reform.

One such pathway was through study of the monastic past. In his classic account of the split at Molesmes that led to the founding of Cîteaux, the Benedictine monk Orderic Vitalis recounted a debate at the monastery in which the reforming prior, Robert, recommended to his monks that they read 'the accounts of holy Anthony, of Macarius, of Pachomius, and above all, of Paul the Apostle, the teacher of the gentiles'. In other words, Robert was claiming the authority of a body of literature about the origins of monasticism, including Scripture. Guibert of Nogent, recounting the founding of La Chartreuse by Bruno of Cologne in 1089, remarked how apt it was 'that one of the learned should also draw after him a crowd of men'.[56] William of Malmesbury, writing about the founding of the breakaway reforming community at Cîteaux, portrayed the reform as simply the application of reason to the practice of monasticism.[57] As John Thomas observed in relation to Byzantine monastic reform, not the least influence of Evergetis on a generation of reformers, including John the Oxite, was its comprehensive library of ascetic literature.[58] In both East and West, reform was in some measure driven by religious men and women reacquainting themselves with monastic history through reading.

Similarly, in William of Malmesbury's account of the same events at Molesmes, the protagonist of reform, Stephen Harding, is shown as studying the *Rule of Benedict* intensely for a long time, then encouraging the monks at Molesmes to do likewise. The reformers of the eleventh century were imbued with the 'literature of the desert', to the degree that one of the retrospective accounts of the founding of the Cistercians, written at the beginning of the thirteenth century, traces the origins of the congregation directly from the monks of the Egyptian desert to Cîteaux in 1098.[59] An admirer of the early Cistercians – and later a postulant to the Order – William of Saint-Thierry said after a visit to the new Cistercian foundation of Clairvaux in the 1120s, 'Wherever I turned my eyes I was amazed to see as it were a new heaven and a new earth, and the well-worn path trodden by the monks of old, our fathers out of Egypt, bearing the footprints left by men of our own time.'[60] A colourful if literal example of the adherence to tradition was witnessed by Aelwin, prior of Durham in 1151, while he was in retreat on Cuthbert's island of Inner Farne. Another Durham monk, Bartholomew, turned up on the island dressed in a long-sleeved tunic of animal skins and a separate hood, over which he wore a black cloak. Dressed thus, 'he showed to all who saw him the figure of the ancient fathers'. Bartholomew's clothing was a studied approximation to the appearance of the monks of Egypt, as described in John Cassian's *Institutes*.[61]

It must have been relatively simple for monks and nuns to find out for themselves how 'the ancient fathers' had lived from their own reading. John Cassian (either the *Institutes* or *Conferences* or both) was in the libraries of several English monasteries by the early thirteenth century: Burton, Bury, Christ Church Canterbury, Flaxley, Glastonbury, Peterborough, Reading, Rievaulx, Rochester and Whitby, and the collection known as the *Vitas Patrum* was in most of these, and in others such as the London house of Holy Trinity, Aldgate. Manuscripts of the *Rule of Basil* were so common in European monasteries as to be virtually ubiquitous. From at least as early as the eighth century it could be read at Bobbio, Corbie and Fleury; in the ninth at St Gall and Lorsch; by the eleventh Stavelot and Monte Cassino; and in the twelfth St Amand, Anchin, St Bertin, Fécamp, Santa Maria in Florence, Chartreuse, Grandmont, Cîteaux and its daughter-houses. At Cluny, the Rule was read in the refectory during Lent.[62] But this is only a brief indicative, not a comprehensive list. The *Rule of Benedict* itself recommended the reading of Cassian, and other common texts such as the letters of Jerome also enabled familiarity with the idea of an 'original' monasticism.[63] Other, less well-known texts from early monasticism were known patchily, especially in areas that retained strong Byzantine influence. Leo, archbishop of Ravenna (999–1001), gave as examples to hermits in his diocese who were trying to follow the *Rule of Benedict* Cyril of Scythopolis's *Lives* of St Sabas and St Euthymios, but this is a rare example of knowledge of a text from outside the Egyptian tradition in the Latin West.[64]

Another way for monks to connect to earlier traditions was to observe other monastic settings where practices associated with 'original' monasticism were still followed. The *Chronicle of Monte Cassino* provides an illustration. In the 990s a group of monks left Monte Cassino on pilgrimage to Jerusalem, visiting Mount Athos on the way back to Italy. On their return to Monte Cassino in 998, one of the monks, Liutulf, founded a dependent cell of the monastery at Albareta, 2 kilometres away, where he established a community of thirty reforming monks. They devoted themselves to lives of asceticism that included manual labour such as grinding and sifting the flour for their bread. The surprise that this provoked in the chronicler and his contemporaries reveals how unusual they considered this kind of work for monks.[65] Eleventh-century Italy, indeed, was something of a mixing-bowl for monastic reformers.[66] Romuald, as a native of Ravenna, a region of strong Byzantine influence, was familiar with the ascetic spirituality of Orthodox monasticism, so it is no surprise that traditions such as fasting, spiritual kinship and struggles against the demonic were prominent in his monastic formation.[67] Other individual Greek monks made an impression in Italy. Nilos of Rossano, born in 910 in Calabria, abandoned a marriage in order to become a monk. His early career follows a pattern familiar from earlier Calabrian hagiography: flight from Arab raids; hostility to monks from the local governor; persistence in study as a cenobitic monk; withdrawal to a cave and the adoption of an anchoritic life characterised by self-mortification, fasting by eating only raw food; the endurance of horrible clothing. Towards the end of his life, he founded the Greek monastery of Santa Maria di Grottaferrata in Rome (1004). By this time he had he already become well known among Latin monks from a famous visit to Monte Cassino, where he presided over a conference held to discuss differences between Greek and Latin monastic practices.[68] While conscious of his difference from Latin monks – as he told Adalbert of Prague, his habit and beard proclaimed him as Greek – he saw Benedict as an ascetic exemplar, and wrote a hymn honouring him for the Monte Cassino monks.[69] The differences they explored, according to Nilos, related to practical observances rather than matters of principle: abstention from meat; why Greek monks fasted on Saturdays in Lent; and so on.[70]

These were important, but not insuperable distinctions, and Latin and Greek monks were often prepared to adapt to each other's practices. This did not necessarily entail a change of confession, nor did it have to be a permanent choice. John of Matera, a Latin-speaker from a distinguished Italian family, joined a Greek monastic community on an island near Taranto in *c.* 1100, but left in search of a more complete solitude, before eventually attracting followers and in 1129 founding a new community at Pulsano, near Monte Gargano in Apulia.[71] Western monks in search of ascetic practices sometimes adopted behaviours that were long entrenched in eastern tradition. Liutulf of Monte Cassino's work in the bakery is a case in point. In Cyril of Scythopolis's portraits of Palestinian monks, working in the bakery was often given as an example of particular humility, and kitchen work in general was also praised by Latin authors for this reason. When Adalbert of Prague abandoned his see to become a monk at San Bonifacio in Rome, he 'made himself small in the midst of the brothers' by washing the pots, preparing the food and doing every menial job in the kitchen.[72] John of Gorze, likewise, had inserted himself into the kitchen rota more than the other monks, drawing water from the well and carrying it into the kitchen, chopping the vegetables and washing up after the meal.[73] Were these deliberate imitations of eastern practices? If so, they can hardly have come from literary example, since Cyril of Scythopolis's work was scarcely known to a Latin audience. They may therefore show the transmission of practices through observation or hearsay rather than reading. But it is also possible to take a more reductive view of such practices. Manual labour was practised at some early eleventh-century monasteries, such as Bec in Normandy, founded by the pious layman Herluin, without any apparent reliance on any specific influence.[74]

Not all institutional practices common in the Orthodox world were less acceptable to western reformers. Abbot John III of Monte Cassino may have been influenced by Orthodox customs relating to the transfer of authority in monasteries when he tried to impose a relative on his community as his successor. This may have been one result of his tour to the East, though there were more local examples at hand as well.[75] Latin reformers were not uncritical adopters of eastern monastic practices, and sometimes may even have been imitating them without realising their debt. The career of Dominic of Sora (*c.* 960–1032) is a case in point. Although less well known to historians than his contemporary Romuald, Dominic was the subject of four hagiographical accounts as well as other biographical material composed from the 1060s to the 1090s.[76] In many ways Dominic epitomised contemporary currents in reform in such a way that he defies strict categorisation. Although he was a Latin rather than a Greek monk, his career followed a pattern that combined solitary eremitical life, wandering from place to place, restoring ruined churches, gathering followers and leading communities through personal charisma, that is entirely familiar from Orthodox contemporaries and predecessors. His remote supervision of communities recalls the example of his contemporary in Asia Minor, Lazaros of Mount Galesion, as well as of Romuald in Italy.[77] Yet although the 'Sora Life' recalls some Greek reflexes of expression (for example, the use of the term *exenia*, from the Greek ξενια, to denote gift offerings from patrons), there is nothing overtly 'Greek' as opposed to 'Latin' in his career. Indeed, the career of Dominic may be said to skirt the whole question of whether a given practice or way of conducting oneself was 'Greek' or 'Latin'. More surprising still is the relative difficulty of identifying the *type* of monasticism that he promoted. Although Dominic seems to have first taken the habit at a Benedictine foundation near Farfa, as John Howe has pointed out, he was remarkably relaxed about breaching the Benedictine Rule when it came to the governance of his own foundations.[78]

Equally difficult to label is the foundation made by Bruno of Cologne at Squillace in Calabria in 1090. Bruno was already the founder of a monastery in the Alps, La Chartreuse (1089), espousing a cenobitic way of life not based on the *Rule of Benedict*. In a letter to a companion, Raoul the Green, Bruno described Squillace as a 'desert' far from all human habitation, but agreeably situated.[79] This letter, written at some point between 1096 and 1101, gives the impression that Squillace was a hermitage whose inhabitants lived a virtually solitary existence. Bruno's concept appears to have been an establishment grouped around a church but living collectively as hermits. The earliest deeds generated by the foundation (from 1094 to 1101) use the term *eremita* rather than 'monk', but it is possible that this was the designation chosen by the Italo-Greek scribe rather than by Bruno himself.[80] Bruno's letter to Raoul speaks of the 'brothers in religion' (*fratribus religiosis*) with whom he lives.[81]

It is tempting to try to find parallels with other foundations, not least La Chartreuse itself, or for that matter with Fonte Avellana. In the end, however, it may be wisest to understand Squillace as the unique establishment made by a charismatic monastic leader in very specific circumstances.[82] Before the arrival of the Normans into southern Italy, the *Rule of Benedict* was unknown in Calabria or Apulia. The first Benedictine monastery in Calabria, Santa Eufemia, was founded in *c.* 1062 by Robert of Grandmesnil, formerly abbot of St Evroult in Normandy.[83] The endowment given by its patron, Robert Guiscard, included the property of the cave monastery founded in the tenth century by Elias Speleota at Piana di Gioia Tauro. The Norman rulers became enthusiastic patrons of Greek-rite monasteries, sometimes refounding those in ruinous condition. San Filippo di Fragolà in Sicily was refounded in 1090 with the aid of Roger I; his widow Adelaide continued to support it with gifts in 1101.[84] But they were also sometimes indispensable in founding new houses: San Salvatore in Messina was built in 1122–32 for the Greek monk Bartholomew of Simeri with the support of Roger II.[85]

Before settling in Calabria, Bruno had already founded a previous community in a remote setting. Like many reforming founders, Bruno left a settled life for a more precarious existence as a result of an inner conversion. Master of the cathedral school at Reims, he joined a group of hermits living in forests in *c.* 1080, and later settled 'on a high and dreadful cliff' in an Alpine valley on land granted him for the purpose by the bishop of Grenoble.[86] After only a couple of years, however, Urban II, whom Bruno had taught at Reims, took him to Rome, and he never returned to his new foundation of La Grande Chartreuse. But in 1109 the dean of Grenoble, Guiges du Pin, who had joined the community a few years earlier, was elected prior. Guiges was well networked, with a circle of correspondents that came to include both Peter the Venerable – who also made regular visits – and Bernard, abbot of Clairvaux. This enabled the community and its distinctive style of monasticism to become well known – a development that was also helped by their move further down the valley after an avalanche had killed some of the monks in 1132. The Carthusians, as they were known from the name of the foundation, were described in admiring terms in other contemporary writing, notably in Guibert of Nogent's memoir. Guibert described the Carthusian way of life in terms framed by the architecture of the monastery. There were thirteen monks, who occupied individual cells around a cloister, and who worked, slept and ate in their cells rather than living together like other monks. Every Sunday the cellarer provided a week's supply of food for each monk, who then prepared it daily. Each cell must have been provided with a hearth for cooking the vegetables that, according to Guibert, comprised the only accompaniment to the weekly ration of bread. Drinking and washing water came from a conduit that ran through each cell. Daily offices were said in each monk's cell, but on Sundays and feast days they worshipped together in the plain, undecorated church. Silence was almost universal throughout the community.[87] Poverty was strictly maintained, but the monastery accumulated a library through assiduous borrowing and copying of books.[88] The Carthusian style of monasticism, whether consciously or not, imitated the *lavra* communities of the Holy Land and Syria; in general, it shared characteristics with monasticism in the eastern Mediterranean, and perhaps also the Celtic world. The emphasis lay on individual contemplation, study and prayer. Each cell had a little patch of garden, which monks could use to grow their own vegetables. Hugh, later bishop of Lincoln, kept birds in his garden at the Carthusian house at Witham. There was no Rule as such, but Guiges du Pin compiled a set of simple statutes and spiritual guide for the monks. Carthusian spirituality centred on the monk's cell: his moral and imaginative universe. Carthusian monasticism was demanding, and perhaps unsurprisingly the number of foundations was always small. Moreover, each house was limited by Guiges's statutes to a dozen monks. When Stephen of Obazine went to ask permission to establish his monastery as a Carthusian house, he was told, regretfully, that he had already accepted far too many men and women to be considered as a Carthusian foundation.[89]

How were new religious communities founded? In both the Greek and Latin worlds, any private individual could found a monastery or convent. The prerequisite was, of course, to have a suitable location. Eadmer, the biographer of Anselm of Bec, reports that Hugh, earl of Chester asked Anselm to come to England in order to view a possible site and advise on its suitability.[90] Some kind of property was also necessary, of course. Herluin, founder of Bec, like many other founders, used his own landed inheritance to found his monastery.[91] But one might also be given land on which to found a community: Robert of Arbrissel, for example, founded Fontevraud in cleared woodland given him by local landowners, which happened to lie in the borderland both of dioceses and of secular lordships.[92] The Cistercian monastery of Garendon, in Leicestershire, was likewise founded on disputed land between two lordships. In certain circumstances, donating the land on which to found a religious community might be a means of defusing political tensions between antagonistic neighbours by 'sanctifying' the territory under dispute.[93]

But not all monasteries were planned as communities from the start. A trope of monastic hagiography, in both Greek East and Latin West, was the monastery that grew from individual eremitical origins, as for example in the case of Obazine.[94] Hagiographical accounts, however, often reflected realities verified by documentary sources. In mid-twelfth-century Cyprus, the hermitage of a monk who had fled the Holy Land grew into the monastery of Makhairas, while at the other end of Europe, Cockersand Abbey on the Lancashire coast similarly developed from the following coalescing around a single hermit who had settled overlooking the Irish Sea.[95] These are just two examples, that could be multiplied several times across Europe. The moment at which a group of eremitically minded individuals became a community differed from case to case, of course, and the language employed by reformers does not help to make the distinction clearer. William of Saint-Thierry must have been choosing his words carefully when he described the community at Clairvaux as he knew it in its early years as 'a crowd of solitaries'.[96]

A striking aspect of eleventh-century reform is the physical building and restoration of churches. Reform in its widest sense entailed construction and reconstruction. Dominic of Sora, who built a network of monasteries and hermitages, is a case in point. Some of these were new human plantations appearing in an apparent wilderness. Ralph Glaber, a Cluniac monk writing in *c.* 1040, was rather disparaging about the rush to rebuild churches even when existing ones were 'not in the least unworthy'. He attributed the vogue for new building to emulation and a sense of wanting to leave an older world behind.[97] Much of the discourse of reform made use of the idea of rebuilding ruined churches and repopulating abandoned monasteries with religious men and women. We have already seen the importance of this pragmatic facet of reform in Byzantine hagiography, for example as in the case of Euthymios the Younger. Naturally, restoring ruined churches was a particularly powerful metaphor for restoring monasticism itself. Northern England, so important in the development of monastic life in the early Middle Ages, had lost almost all its functioning monasteries by the late eleventh century – the long-term effects of the Danish invasions and resettlement. In 1068–9, a Norman force sent to the north by William the Conqueror to suppress uprisings against his rule caused widespread destruction to property and agriculture. One of the soldiers, Reinfrid, was so affected by the sight of the ruins of Whitby Abbey that he later became a monk at Evesham under its English abbot Aethelwig. With another Evesham monk, Reinfrid later travelled to the north and settled at the site of Jarrow, attracting local recruits to their way of life. Reinfrid then moved to Whitby while his companion, Aldwin, resettled Melrose. Eventually Aldwin restored Bede's old monastery at Monkwearmouth, and in 1083 this community replaced the secular clerks at Durham Cathedral, making it a monastic chapter.[98] The evocation of past monastic observance through ruins was thus a powerful force in the revival of regular religious life in Britain.

Since monasteries were in theory subject to the jurisdiction of the diocesan, bishops often played a role in confirming a new foundation. At an early stage in the establishment of his community in the Limousin, Stephen of Obazine asked the bishop of Limoges to confirm his foundation by blessing a cross for it.[99] But not all founders welcomed the involvement of a bishop, which implied a jurisdiction that they did not necessarily wish to acknowledge. Neophytos, the founder of a hermitage known as the Enkleistra, in western Cyprus, was informed by the bishop of Paphos that he would only be permitted to live there if he consented to accept ordination and a companion to live with him: a number that eventually grew to eighteen.[100] Bishops might themselves be the founders of reforming foundations: such was the case, for example, with Waverley in Surrey, the first Cistercian house in England, founded by the bishop of Winchester in 1128.

But some contemporaries witnessing what appeared to them to be a new wave of monastic vocations thought that building was necessary in order to accommodate them. Guibert of Nogent, looking back in the first decade of the twelfth century at the phenomenon of widespread reform, wrote that new monasteries had to be built because 'nowhere but in the oldest monasteries was there room for many of the monks'.[101] Notwithstanding the narrative arc of reform arising from dissatisfaction with established monasteries, Guibert suggests that the eremitical origins of new monasteries may have arisen from more pragmatic causes. Because new building was expensive and not always practical, promoters of 'new monasticism' settled in smaller groups for which accommodation and food supplies could be more easily arranged. 'Consequently, in manors and towns, cities and castles, and even in the very woods and fields, there suddenly appeared swarms of monks spreading in every direction and busily occupied, and places which had contained the lairs of wild beasts and the caves of robbers were suddenly devoted to the name of God and the worship of the saints.'[102] In Guibert's famous picture, the enthusiasm for new monastic settlement extended to include the nobility, who 'stuffed the monasteries they entered with the goods they had given up', and induced others to do the same. Wives abandoned marriage and children to enter convents, or supported monastic foundations materially. Guibert conjures up a cycle of reform in which monks and nuns who start out by rejecting material goods become, after a generation or so, unthinking recipients of wealth. The result is that 'every day there seems to be a falling away from the conditions which flourished then'.[103]

Guibert's scepticism about reform reflects his disappointment in human nature, but he was not hostile to the idea itself. As he acknowledged, the trouble with monasticism in his day was that too many monks – like himself – had been in the cloister since childhood, and consequently considered themselves to have attained perfection already. He saw little zeal in the monastery in which he grew up or the one of which he later became abbot, at Nogent-sous-Coucy.[104] A younger contemporary Benedictine, Orderic Vitalis, was more sceptical about reform in principle. His account of the origins of Cîteaux brilliantly encapsulates the motif of reform contending with tradition. Molesmes, founded in 1080 under Cluniac liturgical observance, had grown rapidly and by *c.* 1100 was associated with at least forty other monasteries. According to Orderic, its prior, Robert, was dissatisfied with the customs observed in the monastery, and suggested to the monks that they had deviated too far from the *Rule of Benedict*. Two practices in particular troubled him: first, that they did not undertake any manual labour, though this was specified in the Rule; and second, that their income came partly by way of tithes through ownership of parish churches.[105]

Molesmes was far from unusual in no longer performing manual labour of the kind that Benedict had envisaged. Benedict assumed circumstances in which religious communities would survive on what they produced themselves, in the way that Egyptian and Syrian monasteries – and some early western communities – had done. But these circumstances no longer applied once monasteries had come to depend on property donations. As we saw in the last chapter, monasteries were now part of a complex ecology of gift, transfer and sale. At best, monks might perform some token labour of this kind, such as the weeding in the kitchen garden known to have been done at Cluny. But in a monastery of any size, monks had neither the time nor the expertise to carry out such work. Other sorts of manual labour necessary for the community – repair of the fabric, ironmongery, leather-working, etc. – were likewise best left to those who had the experience and knowledge. The kind of labour that could be done by monks or nuns might involve gardening, apiary, candle-making, manuscript copying and illumination, and other craft work. But this was apparently not the kind of work that Robert thought was commensurate with the Rule – or with his literal interpretation of the Rule.

Monastic tithe is a fearsomely complex subject, but in essence it relates to the ownership of property by monasteries.[106] As we have already seen, it was difficult for monasteries to avoid ownership of landed property since this was the means of exchange and support between them and the laity. And where such ownership, as it often did, included villages with parish churches, the tithes payable by all parishioners to the parish priest went ultimately to the owner, in other words the monastery. Robert professed to be horrified by the realisation that they were living off what he classed as the legitimate earnings of parish priests. Robert therefore suggested that they should earn their keep through their own labour – in other words, cultivate the land themselves – and that they should no longer rely on tithes. Although in principle these were two separate principles, as Orderic realised, they were intimately linked through the ecology of the monastic system. If monks refused to accept tithes, their income would be reduced to the point where they would have little option but to feed themselves through their own labour. For good measure, Orderic makes Robert also ask his monks to forswear the use of secular – by implication, luxurious – clothing.[107]

The response made by the monks to Robert can be assumed to represent Orderic's own views: 'The community of monks did not agree with these words.'[108] The imitation of the Egyptians of the Thebaid was unnecessary, they argued, because that kind of monasticism had developed in a period of persecution when circumstances were very different. The way of life they followed was what had developed over the course of centuries, and could be traced directly back to Benedict from his own follower Maur, who according to tradition had brought the Rule into Gaul. Over the intervening centuries the practices of the original monks – to which Benedict himself had been an heir – had been rendered irrelevant either by geography or societal change. There was no point in monks in France pretending they lived in the Egyptian desert in the fourth century, and therefore no point in trying to reproduce a form of living that was unique to that period and stage of development in Christian life. Monasticism had developed the characteristics it now enjoyed as part of the way that Gaulish society itself emerged. Kings and lords dominated a peasant agricultural labour force, and maintained monasteries in which monks and nuns sang the psalms, and meditated on divine law. 'In the West monks have done these things until now and everyone knows and attests that this should be their sort of undertaking.'[109] The intense conservatism of this argument is of course no less a caricature than the radical proposal put in Robert's mouth that the monks should give up their accustomed clothing in order to dress like the monks of Skete and Nitria.

Notwithstanding Orderic's caricature of Robert's position, the idea of a direct conceptual genealogy between the early monks of Egypt and those of the present day came to be enshrined in Cistercian ideology, in what one historian has felicitously called the 'myth' of the desert.[110] In the early thirteenth century, the *Exordium magnum*, which traced the history of the founding of Cîteaux, began its account of the monastery's origins with John the Baptist, the apostles and the first monks of Egypt.

Orderic lays bare the tensions between the forces of change and the status quo. If they were going to carry on conducting the liturgy in such a way that commemorated benefactors, studying and teaching younger generations, and living out penitential lives on behalf of others, they needed material support. Recalibrating the nature of their penitential lives so that it was more like those in the pages of Cassian or Jerome would upset the symbiotic balance between monasticism and the society that produced it. Monks who worked the land to feed themselves had no need of a peasant workforce, but by the same token they had less time to devote to commemoration of benefactors in a complex liturgy. Like the monks of the early Church, then, the austerity of their lives was for their good rather than for others. Withdrawal and solitude, as the benchmarks of the 'new monasticism', entailed – in principle at least – cutting the web that been spun around monastic life in previous centuries.

THE CISTERCIANS AND REFORM

Robert left Molesmes in 1098 with some of the monks – twenty-one, according to tradition – who shared his vision of a more austere observance of the *Rule of Benedict*. The first requirement for monks who wanted to found a new community was to find a suitable location. Given Robert's desire not to be drawn into the relationships that followed from accepting property, this logically should have meant a location that was not already part of someone else's land, or that was unsuitable for agriculture or habitation. In fact, Robert and his monks settled in a marshy area near woodland south of Dijon that was gifted to them as wasteland. The rigours of building shelter and a church on land that had to be drained dominated the first years of the new foundation, before the duke of Burgundy offered financial help to finish the building and to provide livestock. The opening lines of the *Exordium parvum*, a later account of these circumstances, refers graphically to the monks who had 'tirelessly borne the burden of the day and the heat'. The passage is intended to be a figurative evocation of the rigours of Benedictine observance, but it carries a note of authentic experience. The first threat came when the community at Molesmes insisted on Robert's return. Although the *Exordium parvum* is at pains to show that the initial settlement was made with the approval of the diocesan, Archbishop Hugh of Lyons, Molesmes appealed to Rome and eventually Robert succumbed, taking about half of the new settlers with him.[111]

Subsequently he reformed Molesmes according to the *ordo* that was emerging at Cîteaux. A crucial moment in the new monastery's existence occurred when Robert's successor at Cîteaux, Alberic (d. 1108), secured a privilege from Pope Pascal II, giving it protection under the holy see although not removing it from the jurisdiction of the bishop of

Chalon.[112] But the major figure to emerge from early Cistercian history was one of the twenty-one, the English monk, Stephen Harding. Stephen had been an oblate at the monastic cathedral chapter at Sherborne in Dorset before becoming a Benedictine at Molesmes after a period of study in France.[113] Under his leadership after Alberic's death, in 1113 Cîteaux founded the first of its direct daughter-houses, La Ferté, to be followed by Morimond, Clairvaux and Pontigny.[114]

The original community at Cîteaux used the liturgical books that Robert had brought from Molesmes. Moreover, despite Orderic's characterisation of his ideas, the land they first settled had serfs attached to it.[115] We should see this not as applying double standards but either as the slow evolution of the ideas that eventually came to characterise the Cistercians, or indeed as evidence that those ideas were a kind of post-hoc manifesto with the intention of establishing a distinction between them and other Benedictines.[116] But it is clear that the early Cistercians developed a more reduced office than what they had previously been used to. This must have been necessary in any case, since the serfs who came with the land presumably worked it for food production on their behalf, but could not be expected to do all the clearing and building of the new monastery as well. The liturgical offices marked the seasonal difference between longer and shorter days, allowing for more time in manual labour in the summer. The biggest difference between Cîteaux and its daughters and more established monasteries, however, was the same as with most new houses. There were few patrons in the early years, and therefore little commitment to commemoration of dead benefactors; no relics to attract pilgrims; no oblates and no school. Stephen Harding's attitude to monasticism, as William of Malmesbury noticed, was marked by his scholarship. He worked on a reliable edition of the Bible (at a time when a canonical version and commentary was only just being made by theologians), and arranged a new hymnal and antiphonary for the Cistercians based on the hymns composed by Ambrose in the fourth century and still in use in Milan, and the chants in use at Metz, which he considered the most authoritative.[117]

There was no intention to start a new kind of monasticism. Where the early Cistercians differed from other reforming communities of the same period was that unlike Vallombrosa or Camaldoli in Italy, or Tiron or Savigny in France, which also emphasised communal austerity, fasting, poverty, simplicity of liturgy and separation from the world, they insisted on the strict observance of the *Rule of Benedict* rather than looking for adaptations or new Rules. Stephen Harding is credited in the traditional historiography of the reform movement with the articulation of a monastic way of life, but according to William of Malmesbury his primary aim was to apply the Rule, which 'brought back the deviations of nature to reason'.[118] Older books on monasticism tended to take at face value the early history of the community as presented by Cistercians writing later in the twelfth century. According to this version of events, Stephen drafted the earliest historical account of the events of 1098–9, the *Exordium parvum*, probably in *c.* 1120.[119] This was reworked and expanded into the *Exordium magnum* by the Cistercian monk Conrad of Eberbach in the early thirteenth century. Another document, the *Charter of Love*, traditionally ascribed to Stephen and dated to before 1118, has been seen as the foundation of a new constitutional Order. According to this view, the Cistercians developed from the start a clear and coherent organisation based on a hierarchy in which Cîteaux stood at the top and its four daughter-houses below. The Cistercians are seen as early developers of managerialism, even as the protagonists of an international corporation. Centralised governance was assured through the *Charter of Love* and through annual chapter-generals attended by abbots and abbesses of all daughter-houses across the Cistercian 'empire'.[120] The *Charter of Love* emphasised uniformity of liturgical observances across the abbeys dependent on Cîteaux. The discipline required for such a regulatory framework to be effective was provided by *caritas* – the spiritual love that bound the different communities of those professing obedience to the abbot of Cîteaux. Such at any rate was the standard view – prevailing, at least in the teaching of students, well into the 1990s. Moreover, this early centralisation – springing apparently ready-formed from the mind of Stephen Harding – has also been given as an explanation for the success of the Cistercians in spreading so rapidly across the western Christian world. This success is represented on maps showing the number of Cistercian foundations, sometimes in comparison with Cluniac monasteries.[121] The effect of this kind of representation is to show what one critic of this historiography has called 'corollary conclusions about Cistercian singlemindedness and unanimity'.[122]

Although many monastic historians were sceptical about the simplicity of this narrative, and suggested a more nuanced view of the relationship between the ideals presented in the early documents and the reality on the ground, the essential reliability of the documentation on which the narrative was based was assumed until the beginning of the twenty-first century. In 2000, Constance F. Berman's *The Cistercian Evolution: The Invention of a Religious Order in Twelfth-Century Europe* presented a fundamental challenge to this consensus. Berman argued that the whole notion of the Cistercians as an 'order' with an organised mechanism for establishing uniform observances and propagating new daughter-houses was anachronistic and misleading. Such a notion depended, she argued, on a fundamental misunderstanding of the nature of the documentation from which historians had been working. As she pointed out, the earliest manuscripts of the documents dated from later in the twelfth century, and there was no verifiable witness to their existence before the 1160s at the earliest. Moreover, the fact that the earliest manuscripts packaged the *Charter of Love* together with the *Exordium parvum* – and indeed, an earlier document, the *Exordium Cistercii*, which had been unknown before its discovery in the twentieth century – pointed, in her view, to the post-hoc creation of a dossier with the intent of making it look to people as though the Cistercians had existed as a coherent monastic Order well before 1120. The reality, she argued, was very different. Instead, the Cistercians were a group of loosely organised reforming communities much like many others. The growth of the 'order' came about less through the deliberate 'planting' of strategic new foundations than from the more random process of absorption of existing reforming communities that were in danger of becoming unsustainable without external support.

Constance Berman's arguments have had a mixed reception from monastic historians. The least convincing part of the case, ironically, is forensically the strongest. Some critics have questioned the re-dating of the manuscripts to the later twelfth century, but in a way this is less important. Only a small proportion of medieval writing survives in 'autograph' form, in other words in the original manuscript, and it is far from uncommon for the manuscript of an authentic original work to be dated to generations later than the date of its composition. Moreover, institutions such as monasteries tended to gather together documents relating to their history as a defence against rival claims or interventions, which explains the contrived nature of the 'dossier'. Part of Berman's scepticism about the Cistercians arose from the absence of explicit reference to the supposedly foundational documents in other Cistercian writing before the 1160s. Other historians have pointed to formulations of ideas and words that show knowledge of the *Charter of Love*, for example in letters by and between Cistercians and in theological commentary. We will have occasion to look in more depth at one such case in due course in this chapter.

A degree of scepticism about the traditional narrative of Cistercian expansion, however, is certainly merited. Many monasteries entered the Cistercian family through methods other than that assumed in the *Charter of Love*. Furness Abbey in Cumbria may serve as an example. Founded in 1124 (originally in Tulketh, now a district of Preston, Lancashire), the community moved to the Furness peninsula in 1127, on land donated by Stephen, count of Blois.[123] The community was a foundation of the Savigniac community. Vitalis of Mortain, a secular clerk, had established a hermitage at Savigny, a Norman forest, in *c.* 1089, where, as often happened in such cases, he was joined by like-minded followers. At some point between 1112 and 1115 the community was recognised as a monastery, and by the 1140s there were thirty-three houses claiming to be Savigniac. What this meant in practice is not clear. Vitalis wrote a simple Rule based on the *Rule of Benedict* but designed for a smaller community of simple hermits, but this could hardly have served once Savigny became a monastery, let alone after it expanded outside Normandy. But by 1147 the Savigniac congregation had run into problems of sustainability, and Furness and other houses adopted Cistercian customs.

What did it mean to 'become Cistercian'? In the 1130s, a reforming community at Palmaria in the Galilee region of the kingdom of Jerusalem explored the possibility of adopting Cistercian customs. The abbot of Palmaria, a cell of the Benedictine monastery of Notre-Dame de Josaphat just outside Jerusalem, was a former hermit with a pedigree of asceticism. At this date there was no Cistercian presence in the Holy Land, but Abbot Elias managed to secure the services of two Cistercians from the West to teach the community their customs. According to our contemporary witness to this episode, Gerard of Nazareth, the experiment failed because the monks refused to tolerate the heavy European woollen habit. If this was indeed the case, it suggests that the literalist approach to monastic customs caricatured by Orderic Vitalis may have had some truth to it, but it just as likely that Gerard, who was sceptical of extremes of ascetic behaviour, was showing an ironic hand.[124] But clearly, for contemporaries, being 'Cistercian' was a question of practices rather than membership of a complex structure.

The process by which a monastic community might become Cistercian is shown at greater length in the twelfth-century *Life of Stephen of Obazine*. Stephen left his Benedictine monastery in the Limousin in search of a more austere and simple observance, and with a companion settled in dense woodlands. After a series of adventures in survival that will be familiar to connoisseurs of the genre of eremitical hagiography, including near starvation, the kindness of local villagers and the threat posed to their credibility by a 'false anchorite' in the same woods, Stephen began to attract both men and women to build a community. They built a church and separate living quarters for monks and nuns, and the foundation was duly recognised by the bishop. The *Life* describes building, communal life, the simplicity of the food and faithfulness to the principles of 'original' monasticism.[125] But they had no written Rule. Perhaps echoing the words of the reformer Stephen of Grandmont, who when asked what Rule he followed, replied simply that it was the Gospel, Stephen of Obazine considered that his personal example was sufficient. But as the community grew, his followers pointed out that he was not immortal and that without a written formula it would be liable to collapse after his death. Stephen embarked on a process of visiting and observing other reforming communities, including the monks of La Chartreuse, to seek inspiration and advice. The rather anticlimactic result was that he recommended to his monks and nuns that they adopt the *Rule of Benedict*. Obazine eventually became part of the Cistercian congregation in 1147.[126]

The *Life of Stephen of Obazine* shows us how a reforming community could slip almost without noticing into Cistercianism. Stephen and his followers had an idea of what they did not want – landed wealth and the ties and way of living that resulted from it – but little idea of what might take the place of their former monastic experience. The community they built must have looked, for all intents and purposes, simply like a new cenobitic monastery, rather than a new *type* of community. But another important aspect of Obazine was that it had men and women. As Constance Berman has shown in a landmark book on Cistercian nuns, much of the expansion of the Order came through absorption of existing women's communities. This process seems to have begun early on, for even before the founding of the convent of Le Tart in the 1120s, the nuns of Jully had been in contact with Bernard, founder of the daughter-house of Clairvaux. But Le Tart's own daughter-houses in the Ariège and Languedoc regions of southern France were in fact local independent houses that may have been part of regional networks but were not founded as part of a centralised mission from Burgundy.[127] Yet from the middle of the twelfth century onwards there was a perception that the Cistercians did not include women as part of their congregation. The *Book of St Gilbert*, a hagiographical account of the reforming founder Gilbert of Sempringham, shows Gilbert attempting to secure absorption for his double houses of monks and nuns into the Cistercian Order in the same way as the Savigniacs, only to be told at the chapter-general in 1147 that it was impossible because the Cistercians did not include women.[128] Berman suggests that later medieval Cistercian historiography erased the role of women in the congregation from the earliest stages, just as it pushed the orthodoxy of a centralised Order emanating from Cîteaux.

Another orthodoxy perpetuated in the dossier of constitutional documents was the rejection of tithes by the Cistercians. This is clearly stated in the earliest set of statutes traditionally dated to 1134: 'Churches, altars, sepulchers, tithes from the labor or husbandry of another, rural domains, serfs, land rents, revenues from ovens and mills, and other such things contrary to monastic purity are excluded by virtue of the institution of our name and our Order.'[129] Yet, as Giles Constable has shown, it proved impossible in practice to hold the line on such an ideology.[130] The fundamental principle was that ownership of tithes were simply not an issue for the Cistercians because they accepted land that was not already in agricultural use, which therefore yielded no tithe anyway. But houses that were absorbed into the Cistercian congregation – Savigny, for example – were disinclined to give up the practice of accepting tithe as an income stream. As we have already observed, the question of tithe was closely related to manual labour. Where a monastic community worked the land itself, tithe was not an issue. But the prohibition on tithe did not work for female communities, which could not support themselves through their own agricultural labour – and as we have seen, the Cistercian congregation did include female communities from early on. Constable concluded that while acceptance of tithe was indeed frowned on by the Cistercians, it was happening probably as early as the 1130s and was quite common from the 1150s onward.[131]

There were, however, genuine points where the Cistercians sought to depart from existing Benedictine practices. One was their avowed refusal to accept oblates, which meant in practice that most Cistercians were – like Bernard himself – adult converts to monasticism, and consequently did not have the same level of liturgical education as most Benedictine monks. Clearly this played a role in the simplification of the liturgy. Another difference was the extensive use of lay brothers (*conversi*) in manual labour. The concept of *conversi* was not new, but it usually referred to adult entrants to monastic life. Cistercian *conversi* were members of the congregation but were not 'choir monks'; in other words they did not take part in the liturgical chanting at the offices, though they were present at some of them in the nave of the church. The Cistercians were not the first reformers to create a distinction between the choir monks and the men of 'inherent simplicity' who performed manual labour but who were considered members of the community in its widest sense. Camaldoli and Vallombrosa had already pioneered the idea of recruiting for the jobs of 'cobblers, cowherds, stablemen, masons, smiths, reapers and vine-growers' (as one Cistercian monastery was to list them) men who would benefit from the spiritual communion of the monastery.[132]

Cistercian *conversi* were regulated by a separate set of ordinances developed in the first half of the twelfth century, known as the *Usus conversorum*.[133] They took vows of obedience like choir monks but were not tonsured and could grow beards. In the early years of the Order, there was something of a vogue for aristocratic converts to the Cistercians to opt to be *conversi* rather than choir monks out of a sense of humility – Alexander, a member of the Scottish royal family (d. 1229), became a *conversus* at Foigny – but this was discouraged from 1188 onwards.[134] Most *conversi* were from the local peasantry, although as the Order expanded eastwards into Poland they brought German-born *conversi* with them because of the lack of native vocations to the role.[135] Some houses allowed married men to become *conversi*, but not all, and perhaps many were widowers. The distinction between *conversi* and choir monks was reinforced by the nature of the profession as a *conversus*, which all but ruled out becoming a choir monk at any stage. Thus the *conversi* were in no sense encouraged to see themselves as trainee monks or on a possible path to 'promotion' to the choir. They lived in separate quarters with their own dormitory and refectory at the west end of the monastery.[136] Much of their work was concerned with the maintenance of the monastery and its workshops, but they were also responsible for the granges, or farms that provided the monastery's food supplies and income.

The Cistercian claim to have done manual labour as demanded by the Rule, therefore, depended on the division of each community into contemplative choir monks and active *conversi*: in practice it was the latter who did the manual labour. Critics of the Cistercians pointed out that this labour force was typically generated not only from willing recruits to their ranks but also from villagers who had been turned off land they had previously rented and farmed when a Cistercian monastery was given it.[137] The Cistercians experienced increasing difficulties in regulating their *conversi* in the later twelfth and thirteenth centuries.[138] In a famous episode recorded in Conrad of Eberbach's *Exordium magnum*, in 1168 the *conversi* of Schönau revolted against the abbot by plotting to destroy the new boots given out to the choir monks at Christmas, in fury at his refusal to allow them to have new boots as well.[139] That the custom of giving boots to the *conversi* had developed at Schönau, contrary to regulations, points both to the difficulty of enforcing universal rules and also to a growing sense of dissatisfaction at attempts to enforce the lower position of *conversi*. In 1230 the abbot of Meaux removed the *conversi* who had charge of the abbey's granges, demoting them from supervisory roles to cutting stone, ploughing and feeding the pigs.[140] Later in the century, Abbot Brockhampton of Evesham (1283–1316) complained that the *conversi* had ruined the abbey's granges. Numbers of *conversi* declined in the thirteenth century, and recruitment suffered even more as a result of the labour shortages across Europe after the Black Death.

1. The *lavra* of St Sabas was founded in the late fifth century in the wadi Kidron. Sabas, originally from Asia Minor, had been trained in monastic life by his precursors in the Judaean desert, Euthymios and Theoktistos. The original cells of the *lavra* were in the rock face of the wadi, but the church has been on the ledge overlooking the wadi since Sabas's own day.

2. The monastery of Mount Quarantana (Jebel Quruntul), just to the north of Jericho, was originally a sixth-century foundation. The cells are built precariously along the rocky ledge of the cliff which was identified as the place where Jesus was tempted by the Devil in the New Testament. In the twelfth century a group of Frankish hermits occupied the site.

3. The monastery of Our Lady of Saidnaya, a convent founded according to tradition by Emperor Justinian in the sixth century, is located in a hilltop town about 17 miles north of Damascus. The monastery's fame is based on its possession of an icon of the Blessed Virgin that exudes a supposedly miraculous oil used for healing. It has always been a place of veneration for Christians and Muslims.

4. Vatopedi, founded before 985, is the second oldest and one of the largest monasteries on Mount Athos. Parts of the building, including the refectory, date to the eleventh century. Like most of the larger Athos monasteries, it is located on the coast of the peninsula and most easily accessible by sea.

5. San Vittore alle Chiuse di Genga, founded in the early eleventh century, retains the architectural form of the building campaign between 1058 and 1098. Occupying an isolated position in the Apennines of the Marche, it represents the interchange between Byzantine and western monastic forms often found in southern Italy.

6. Clonmacnoise, founded by the monk Ciaran with the support of King Diarmait Uí Cerbaill, enjoyed a golden age between the eighth and twelfth centuries. Although largely in ruins today, enough survives to show the distinctive concentric plan of the monastery, so unlike the normative model in western Roman monasticism.

7. The convent of Sant Joan de les Abadesses, Catalonia, was founded by Wilfrid the Hairy, count of Barcelona, in 885, and his daughter Emma served as the first abbess. In 1017 the bishop of Besalù installed a community of monks, and in the twelfth century, after a brief interlude when nuns were once again in residence, it became a monastery of Augustinian canons.

8. Rievaulx Abbey, founded in 1132, was one of the earliest Cistercian monasteries in England. Walter Daniel, the biographer of the celebrated abbot Ailred, described the monastery in terms of the natural beauty of its setting in a wooded valley surrounded by hills.

9. Dormitory of the Cistercian monastery at Alcobaça, Portugal, founded in 1178. The *Rule of Benedict* required monks and nuns to sleep in a dormitory in which a light was always kept burning. The dormitory was usually located on an upper storey and was often directly connected by a staircase to a transept of the abbey church for ease of access to the choir for Prime.

10. Cloister of St Peter, Moissac, Tarn-et-Garonne. The monastery was a seventh-century foundation that was reformed by Odilo of Cluny in the eleventh century. The cloister, often decorated with complex iconographic programmes, was the heart of the monastery or convent. Cut off from the external world, it was a space for reading, contemplation and exercise.

11. Decorative stone relief in the chapter house at the Cluniac priory at Much Wenlock, Shropshire (*c.* 1140). Often located off the cloister and close to the abbey church, chapter houses were fitted with stone benches around the internal walls as seating for the monks. Chapter was the occasion for daily pastoral and disciplinary instruction, and for the community to meet for formal occasions.

12. Monks at work splitting a felled log as part of a building project, an illustration from Gregory the Great's *Moralia in Job*. Monks at many reforming communities are described as participating in the building work of new monasteries.

13. Many monasteries farmed fish in order to maintain a ready supply of permitted food. The 'fish house' at Meare Abbey, in Somerset, was built in an area of natural wetland. Fishing was sometimes done from boats, as at Clairvaux. The two-storey building probably had facilities for gutting and preparing fish and storage for nets and rods.

14. These clay jars excavated at Melrose Abbey, a Cistercian house in the Scottish lowlands, were probably used as portable urinals. Like most monasteries, Melrose had communal toilets, but chamber pots such as these were used in dormitories to avoid the need to leave the building at night.

15. A bishop accepts the vow of a Benedictine nun in this illuminated initial from a thirteenth-century ordinal. Both male and female novices made formal profession of their vows before bishops, who were responsible for monasteries in their dioceses.

16. Tomb effigy of Rowland Leschman, prior of Hexham Abbey (1480–91), originally founded in the seventh century and from the twelfth century onwards home to a community of Augustinian canons. The cowl pulled down to cover the upper part of the face is a distinctive way of depicting dead religious figures.

The doubts cast on the accepted narrative of Cistercian growth and expansion by the last generation of scholarship have had the effect of making monastic historians confront the meaning of some words that had previously been used very freely – none more so than *ordo*, usually rendered in English as 'order'. It is tempting, if unhelpful, to subdivide monastic congregations and communities and to place them categorically into silos. This tendency is found in monastic discourse from about the middle of the twelfth century, as monastic writers wrestled with the questions of distinction between different types of observance and way of life. Thus, for example, in a contrived 'dialogue' between a Cluniac and Cistercian written by the German Cistercian Idungus of Prüfenung, the argument revolves in part about whether not only they but also other forms of monastic life such as regular canons constitute an *ordo* within the Church.[141] An unnamed cleric from the Tournai region wrote a remarkable treatise on the diversity of religious lives in his day, and what they represented.[142] But in the early days of the Cistercian experiment – say before the 1130s at the earliest – the terminology of an *ordo* conjured up in people's minds how religious communities lived and what, if any, Rule they followed, rather than membership of a rigidly defined structure. In the Greek-speaking world, indeed, this idea was never accepted.[143]

BERNARD OF CLAIRVAUX

In the early 1120s the Benedictine abbot William of Saint-Thierry spent several months at Clairvaux, one of Cîteaux's daughter-houses, to recover from what may have been a breakdown. This was the start of what was to become a deep friendship with his host, Clairvaux's young abbot Bernard. 'So deeply affected was I by the aura of sweetness surrounding the man, so intense was my desire to live with him in that poverty and simplicity that, had the choice been given me that day, I should have wished for nothing more than to stay with him there for ever and wait upon him.'[144] Bernard was a man of genuine charisma who was able to inspire and motivate others, often to follow a course of action that radically altered their lives. Through his own voluminous writing and contemporaries' perceptions of him, we know, or think we know, a great deal about him as a person.[145] He has probably been the subject of more biographical studies than any medieval figure other than Francis of Assisi, and he continues to divide opinion scarcely less than he did in his own lifetime. He embodied contradictions. Highly articulate, Bernard was capable of both lyrically beautiful passages of biblical commentary and heavy sarcasm in his writing. He must have been a man of considerable personal warmth, yet he could be vindictive towards those he cast as enemies or who thwarted him. Like many charismatic religious leaders, he was often convinced of his own rectitude. Although he often complained in his letters of the demands that broke in on his quiet contemplation, he actively courted controversy and argument. And although he never held episcopal office, he had considerable influence over bishops, kings and queens, and even popes.

Bernard was one of six sons of a vassal of the duke of Burgundy and Aleth, daughter of the count of Montbard. He was probably born in 1090, and educated – rather thoroughly for the son of a knightly family at that period – at a house of Augustinian canons. At around the age of twenty-two he appeared with a group of young men, including four of his brothers and other relatives, at Cîteaux to seek entry to the community. Just three years later, he had begun the foundation of Clairvaux. The first phase of his monastic career, from 1115 to 1130, was devoted to building up his community and his own spiritual understanding. Among his earliest writings, dating from the early and mid-1120s, were the long letter he wrote to a relative, Robert, who had abandoned Clairvaux for Cluny, and a follow-up treatise known as the *Apologia to Abbot William*, and addressed to his friend William of Saint-Thierry.[146]

In these works, and in the more reflective *On the Steps of Humility and Pride*, Bernard began to develop and express a distinctive monastic identity. At first this was forged in relation – in opposition, even – to others. The *Letter to Robert* presents Cluny as the dialectical opposite of Clairvaux: rich where Clairvaux was poor; luxurious where Clairvaux was austere; arrogant in its assumption of its importance in contrast to Clairvaux's humility. Bernard's fury and disappointment burns through the pages. Robert had betrayed him by opting for Cluny over his own monastery, and Bernard could feel only resentment and a sense of unfairness. He dismissed the argument evidently made by Robert and the Cluniacs that as a child Robert had been promised to Cluny, and that his entry to the cloister there was simply the acknowledgment of an oblation. The behaviour of the Cluniacs was predatory: the prior of Cluny, Bernard wrote, descended on Clairvaux like a wolf in sheep's clothing. Robert had been lured by the promise of a life of greater comfort, finer food and clothing; the comforts of prestige. But these were promises fraught with spiritual danger: 'the soul', Bernard warned, 'is not fattened out of frying pans.' Beneath the anger, a sense of frustration in the face of power is also apparent. Bernard casts Cluny as the monstrous devourer of weaker but more authentic communities. In fact, Cluny in the 1120s was hardly in the position that Bernard pretends in the letter. The building of the new church begun by Abbot Hugh had dug deep into the monastery's finances, but attempts by Abbot Pons to curb spending to meet these costs made him so unpopular that in 1121 he abdicated and left on a pilgrimage to the Holy Land. His successor, Peter the Venerable (1122–56), under considerable pressure from Cluniac 'alumni' to maintain the monastery's traditions, had to find new sources of revenue. The affair of Robert seemed to unlock latent tensions between forces of tradition and reform principles.

In the *Apologia*, Bernard expanded the argument to encompass a wider field of monastic conduct. Here the anger has subsided, and the bitter invective has become scornful irony. Cluny may still have been within Bernard's sights, but the treatise has much broader application, and must have brought many other examples of traditional 'unreformed' Benedictine communities to readers' minds. St Denis, the monastery patronised by the Capetian monarchy and the dynasty's burial place, has been suggested. The best-known passages in the *Apologia* are those where Bernard fulminates against material wealth in established monasteries. 'Tell me, "poor men", if you are really poor, why is there gold in your churches?' He professes astonishment at the sophistication of the food served in refectories, in defiance of the *Rule of Benedict*'s injunction that two simple dishes should be served at the main meal.

> To take a single example: who could describe all the ways in which eggs are tampered with and tortured, or the care that goes into turning them one way and then turning them back? They might be cooked soft, hard, or scrambled. They might be fried or roasted, and

occasionally they are stuffed. Sometimes they are served with other foods, and sometimes on their own. What reason can there be for all this variation, except, the gratification of a jaded appetite?[147]

Doubtless Bernard's eloquence found its mark among a readership prepared to agree with him. In fact, it is easy to overlook the underlying message of the *Apologia*, which is a plea for unity among those who follow the *Rule of Benedict*. While pointing out the faults of unreformed monasteries, Bernard also urges those more aligned to his way of thinking not to judge others – a rather awkward dual message that reflects the commission from William of Saint-Thierry to write the piece. This explains the divided structure of the work, the first half restraining criticism by Benedictines of others following the same Rule, the second enumerating precisely the reasons why some Benedictines were so critical of others. Although Bernard protests that he does not want to cause scandal, that is exactly what he accomplished. The dissemination of the *Apologia* was wide enough for the criticisms initially made by Bernard to appear in more than ten other treatises over the next century. Peter the Venerable responded to the critiques on behalf of Cluny in a letter to Bernard that opened a correspondence between them that would continue until Bernard's death in 1153.[148] Much of the traditional historiography of the Cistercians in the twelfth century revolves around the controversy with the Cluniacs generated by Bernard's *Letter to Robert* and *Apologia*. The notion of a dispute between them appears to be validated by the provocative language used by Bernard, but much of this was for rhetorical effect. As Giles Constable has noted, the supposed dispute did not really become institutionally bitter until the second generation, after Bernard's death.[149] Even Peter the Venerable, while defending the dietary practices attacked by Bernard, acknowledged that there were areas in which Cluny could reform.

Whether or not it was his intention, the *Apologia* brought Bernard to wider attention, and in 1128 he was invited to the council of Troyes, where the Knights Templar were confirmed as an Order in the Church. He would later write a treatise, *In Praise of the New Knighthood*, to solicit support for the new Order. By the time he started to intervene in the disputed papal election of 1130 he must already have been well known in important circles, and his activities over the next decade made him more so. Besides increased responsibilities arising from the expansion of the Cistercians into England, Spain, Flanders and Germany, with resultant daughter-houses to be overseen, Bernard also became involved in wider problems in the Church and even international politics. In 1135 he was present at the Diet of Bamberg, where he met Emperor Lothar, whom he encouraged to campaign against Roger II of Sicily. Travelling on to Italy, he attended the Council of Pisa (where he met Peter the Venerable in person). He was to spend a whole year in Italy two years later, combining the plans for the foundation of new houses with support for Innocent II in his ongoing struggle with his rival for the papal see, Anacletus II. In the following decade he was active in preaching the Second Crusade (1147–9) on behalf of Pope Eugenius III (r. 1145–53), whom he had first met at Pisa in 1135 and whom he had received into the cloister at Clairvaux and then sent back to Italy to found Tre Fontane, near Rome in 1140. Two examples of other activities in this decade provide an example of his range of interventions. In 1141 he accused the scholar and monk Peter Abelard of heresy at the Council of Sens on the basis of his writing about the Holy Trinity, and in 1145 he advocated for the election of Henry Murdac, abbot of the Cistercian monastery of Fountains (Yorkshire) to replace the deposed William Fitzherbert. In both cases Bernard combined passionate invective – with heavy doses of irony – with eloquence and persistence. He had no qualms about bombarding bishops, cardinals and, of course, his former protégé Pope Eugenius with unsolicited and sometimes peremptory advice. His pursuit of what he considered the right path could reach the point of looking uncomfortably like persecution – certainly in the case of Abelard, the depth of whose theology he probably did not wholly grasp. Throughout his career, Bernard wrote busily. His sermons and commentaries for the monks of Clairvaux and other monasteries, notably the sermons on the *Song of Songs* begun in 1132 but not completed until after 1147, probably show him at his most inspiring. Between 1148 and 1152 he also wrote *De consideratione*, a book of advice for Eugenius III, and in 1150 a *Life* of Malachy, the abbot of Armagh who had died at Clairvaux while on pilgrimage.[150] He also wrote letters constantly, of which almost 550 have been edited. As Beverley Kienzle has put it, letters 'to every person of note or influence in the west were pouring from his pen'.[151] Or rather, they poured from the pens of the secretaries he appointed from among his monks as he dictated to them – according to one observer, more than one simultaneously. Letter-writing was both an essential means of communication for conducting business across long distances and also a diplomatic and rhetorical exercise. As for many other monastic leaders – Anselm, Peter the Venerable, Peter of Celle and Adam of Perseigne to mention four others – letter-writing was for Bernard a means of creating and maintaining a friendship circle. But he also wrote letters to people he did not know, informing, pleading or advising. To Melisende, widowed queen of Jerusalem, he wrote with advice – perhaps unsolicited – on whether or not she should remarry. His intrusion into Abelard's case was announced with a flurry of letters to cardinals and bishops demanding that Abelard be censured. To Alexander, bishop of Lincoln (1123–47), he wrote a letter that epitomises both his view of Cistercian spirituality and at the same time his own spiritual certainty. In the letter he informs the bishop of the safe arrival of his clerk, Philip, who had set out on a pilgrimage for the Holy Land – but his arrival at Clairvaux, not Jerusalem. He had stopped there for hospitality, and got no further. As Bernard clearly enjoyed telling the bishop, in the cloister at Clairvaux Philip was now closer to the heavenly Jerusalem than he would ever have been had he completed the pilgrimage. In fact, he continued, the bishop would do well to follow in his footsteps to become a Cistercian himself. If Alexander replied, his letter sadly does not survive.

Bernard was preoccupied with the relationship between the heavenly and earthly Jerusalem. It was a trope in monastic discourse to see the cloister as a foretaste of Paradise, but in 1124 Bernard confronted the question of this relationship in a more immediate way. It came to his attention that Arnold, abbot of Morimond, one of the four daughter-houses of Cîteaux, was planning to take a group of his monks to the Holy Land, probably with the intention of founding a Cistercian monastery there.[152] Bernard was opposed to the idea on several grounds. In 1131 he declined an invitation to found a monastery in the kingdom of Jerusalem; indeed, the first Cistercian house in the Holy Land would not be founded until 1157, four years after his death.[153] In the event, Arnold, who seems to have been undergoing a difficult time as abbot, died in 1125 without having been able to put his plan into effect. In a letter to Arnold before his death, and in subsequent letters to the abbot of Clairvaux and to Adam, one of the young monks of Morimond whom Arnold had singled out to accompany him, Bernard laid out the grounds of his objection. One was that in abandoning Morimond just because things seemed difficult, Arnold was undermining the wider Cistercian community, which was already suffering 'the heavy burden of scandal caused by your departure, and feared more to come'.[154] Specifically, Arnold was abandoning his responsibilities to his own flock by leaving them alone to 'prowling wolves'. This meant not only the monks of Morimond but also those of its daughter-houses, Bellevaux, founded in 1120, La Creste, in 1121, and Vieux-Camp in 1123. Morimond, as the only one of Cîteaux's original daughters founded in German-speaking territory, was at the forefront of Cistercian expansion eastwards, and the loss of its abbot would undermine these 'new plantations of Christ'. Furthermore, there was the danger of the journey to the East with young and inexperienced monks to be considered. The kingdom of Jerusalem in the 1120s was the eastern frontier of Christendom. A few years earlier, in 1119, a party of unarmed pilgrims had been attacked by bandits while travelling from Jerusalem to the Jordan. The Templars, whom Bernard was to support, were founded as a military escort for pilgrims in response to these dangers.[155] Bernard may have been aware that in 1124 King Baldwin II was a captive of a neighbouring Turkish emir, and that the kingdom was leaderless. It hardly seemed a promising location for new monastic foundations. In fact, Bernard argued that Arnold's sense of priorities was mistaken. What the Holy Land needed was fighting men, not chanting monks. In his letter to Adam, which is essentially a short treatise, Bernard developed some of these ideas further, discussing the principle and limits of a monk's obedience to his abbot.[156]

The case of Arnold of Morimond is important for us not simply as a clue to the development of Bernard's ideas about the relationship of monastic life to earthly events. As Michael Casey has argued, the whole affair is crucial to our understanding of what 'Cistercianism' meant to monks of Cîteaux and its daughter-houses a generation after Robert's fateful departure from Molesmes.[157] Bernard's fear that Arnold's departure would cause scandal is very revealing, given the circumstances of Cîteaux's founding in 1098. Clearly the memory of Molesmes's demands for Robert to return was still a source of potential embarrassment; indeed, the *Exordium Cistercii*, the Cistercian version of those events, was probably edited at Clairvaux around that time.[158] There were other considerations as well. Adam was the son of a prominent German noble, and the fear that the Cistercians might be held responsible for his possible death on the journey, at a time when they needed the support of powerful patrons, was probably very real. But above all, the case enables us to observe the workings of Cistercian structures at a time when, according to Constance Berman, there was as yet no Order. Besides the letter to Arnold, Bernard also wrote to the pope asking him not to grant the licence that the abbot would canonically need in order to leave his monastery.[159] One may wonder why, given the strict hierarchy represented in the *Charter of Love*, Bernard took this responsibility on himself rather than leaving it to the abbot of Cîteaux, the head of this hierarchy. The absence of the abbot from Cîteaux on business was mentioned by Bernard in his letter to Arnold: in fact, he accused him of waiting for an opportune moment before taking action he knew was against the interests of the community, and in his letter to Pope Calixtus II he implies that the abbot of Cîteaux would have intervened directly with the pope had he been able to. Bernard's use of the term *ordo* in his letter to Arnold may not be decisive, given the uncertain meaning of the word at this juncture, but the whole tenor of his argument implies the sense of a collective body, and the threat posed to that body by the indiscriminate action of one important constituent member. Perhaps the most likely inference to draw from the affair is that the main players in the Cistercian congregation understood the *principle* of a coherent structure but that it was not yet effective in practice.

Bernard of Clairvaux is synonymous with early Cistercian history. Inescapably this is partly because both he – through his interventions, his writing and his general energies – and his admirers saw to it that he was identified with the growth of the congregation. As early as 1147, six years before his death, William of Saint-Thierry began working on what would be a collective hagiography of Bernard, known as the *Vita prima*. Other sections were written by Arnold, abbot of Bonneval, and, after Bernard's death, by Geoffrey, bishop of Auxerre.[160] At the Council of Tours in 1163, Pope Alexander III was asked to canonise Bernard on the basis of the *Vita prima*. After a revision to the text, and a subsequent *vita* written by Clairvaux monks in the 1160s, Bernard was eventually canonised in 1174. A collection of miracles attributed to Bernard was also composed at Clairvaux. It is hardly surprising, in the face of Bernard's capacity for leadership, that it took so long for the sense of an Order to emerge from his shadow.

THE AUGUSTINIANS

In 1108, a teacher at the cathedral school of Notre-Dame in Paris, William of Champeaux, gave up his job to retire to a small hermitage at the foot of the hill known as Mont Ste Geneviève in Paris. It is possible that his decision to withdraw from teaching was partly the result of his experience of being bested in argument by one of his pupils, the precocious and arrogant young Peter Abelard, but since the confrontation between the two of them is known largely from the testimony of Abelard, a man never afraid of proclaiming his abilities, it is perhaps just as likely that he had decided on a life of contemplation. The community became a house of Canons Regular. In 1113, William was made bishop of Châlons-sur-Marne, but under his guidance the hermitage, dedicated to St Victor, became a house of study and learning.[161] During the twelfth century it attracted some of the most influential intellectuals in France. At around the same time that William was bishop of Chalons, a royal clerk in London, Rahere, founded a hospital dedicated to St Bartholomew in London. According to a later tradition recorded in the *Book of Foundation*, Rahere was a court entertainer who attracted the patronage of King Henry I. In reality he was probably a prebendary of St Paul's cathedral, and therefore a secular canon, but by 1123 he had become the first prior of the religious community attached to his new hospital.[162] About twenty years later, in 1134, the church of St Mary on the south bank of the Mersey estuary near Runcorn in Cheshire, and the canons living a regular life there, were given a parcel of land and the rights pertaining to it by William, constable of Chester. The canons, who had recently moved there from Runcorn, were to receive not only arable land but also fisheries and weirs, mills and ovens: in other words, the usual sources of income enjoyed by property owners.[163]

One feature linked these three otherwise very different early twelfth-century monastic foundations: they were home to religious following not the *Rule of Benedict* but a quite different formula for living, the *Rule of Augustine*. As we saw in a previous chapter, Augustine advocated a celibate communal life for the clergy of his diocese in North Africa. The document known as the *Rule of Augustine* was codified in the late eleventh century from three different writings of Augustine: two sermons (355 and 356) addressed to the clergy of his diocese, and especially a letter (211) written for a community of women that included his sister and a cousin. Letter 211, written in 423, is abstract and generic in tone, emphasising the virtues of moderation, obedience and charity rather than legislating in precise detail for how the community is to live.[164] Particular stress is laid on poverty and communal harmony as the conceptual foundations of the community. Although Augustine's monastic prescriptions were known in the early Middle Ages, it was in the context of eleventh-century clerical reform that they enjoyed new attention. The Lateran Council held by Pope Nicholas II in 1059 adopted observance of the *Rule of Augustine* for cathedral or collegiate canons living in communal life. As ordained priests, canons were part of the Church's ministry, in a way in which monks did not usually seek to be.[165]

The *Rule of Augustine* in its collated form is significantly more concise than the *Rule of Benedict*. It was divided into eight short chapters, with further subdivisions into sentences or sections. In a modern English translation, it is around 3,200 words.[166] The Rule begins by reminding monks of the reason they have associated together in a community: 'to live harmoniously, intent upon God in oneness of mind and heart.' From the outset, the emphasis is on the unity that can be accomplished by communal focus on God. The Rule proceeds to insist on common ownership of all property, regardless of what the members of the community may have owned in the world outside. A gentle admonition reminds those who had been poor that joining the community should not be seen as a way of enjoying more than they had been used to in their previous life. There seems to be an acknowledgement that the potential appeal of joining an Augustinian house might have included the provision of food and clothing previously unavailable to some. Equally, however, those who were used to wealth and ease should not condescend toward those who were not so accustomed. For Augustine, common ownership did not necessarily mean absolute equality in monks' use of provisions. The Rule accepted that some would eat more than others. This was natural, and to be expected in a community in which some individuals would suffer worse health or enjoy better appetite than others. Likewise, brethren and sisters were urged to be understanding of those who had always been used to the finer things in life, and to accept that some accommodation in learning how to support greater austerity was needed. Although poverty was upheld as a communal ideal, Augustine was wary of allowing self-denial to become an end in itself. He was particularly alive to the problems that could be caused in a community by jealousies and rivalries over observance of the Rule. Those who saw faults in others' conduct were encouraged to point them out, but in a loving rather than accusatory manner, and for the purpose of amending the community's spiritual health rather than to score points off others.

For founders, the *Rule of Augustine* offered several features that distinguished it from the *Rule of Benedict*. Its inherent flexibility allowed for different types of community to live in observance of a Rule in ways that would not have been possible under the strict enclosure of the *Rule of Benedict*. Thus the Rule envisages that religious following the Rule will need to leave the confines of the monastery for legitimate purposes connected with the profession — for example, to exercise their priestly ministry. This had consequences for the underlying spirituality of the monastic life. Canons regular were visible in the public sphere, so how they conducted themselves was particularly important. Here Augustine encouraged canons to please not by their dress but by their behaviour. Under this ruling, an influential twelfth-century commentator on the Rule explained that 'these are specially rebuked who, rejecting the common allowance of food or clothing, demand for themselves articles of food or garments which, in comparison with those of the brethren among whom they live, are choicer or more austere'.[167] Anyone who fetishises self-denial so as to exceed 'the custom of the good people among whom his life is spent' is deliberately drawing attention to his own supposed merits. Drawing on contemporary ethical teaching, Robert of Bridlington explains that it is not use of earthly things in themselves that is sinful, but the interior mental state of the user. Gerald of Wales (*c.* 1145–1223), describing the monasteries of Wales in the later twelfth century, thought that the Augustinians were 'more content than any of the others with a humble and modest mode of life'. Although they lived among laypeople, they avoided the notoriety for gluttony, drunkenness or lechery that appeared to attach to other Orders.[168] Gerald, who was unimpressed by Cluniacs and Cistercians alike, thought that the Augustinian Rule was preferable to any other.[169]

In the polemical *Dialogue of a Cistercian and a Cluniac*, written by the German Cistercian Idungus of Prüfenung in the 1150s, the point on which both interlocutors readily agree is that all those who follow the *Rule of Benedict* are proper monks, while those following other Rules have no claim to that title. Yet it is far from clear that such hard and fast distinctions always existed in the minds of potential founders or recruits at the time. The first reader of Bernard of Clairvaux's *Apologia* – to whom he sent his text for friendly criticism – was a canon regular, Oger of Mont-Saint-Éloi.[170] If we take one example of a prodigious founder of monasteries, King David I of Scotland, it is difficult to infer a consistent strategy from his investments in monastic life: he founded or supported Tironians at Kelso, Cistercians at Melrose and Newbattle, and Augustinian canons at Holyrood and Jedburgh.[171] As Christopher Brooke has pointed out, Gilbert of Sempringham saw no apparent need to explain why, in his double houses for men and women, the enclosed women were obliged to follow the *Rule of Benedict*, the men the *Rule of Augustine*.[172] Nor can we make assumptions that communities following the *Rule of Augustine* were less austere or 'reforming' than, for example, the Cistercians. Some monastic communities that developed into Augustinian houses had eremitical origins: Cockersand Abbey on the north Lancashire coast, and Llanthony in Breconshire being two such examples.

At the same time, those within the profession were alive to competition with others. St Martin's at Dover, originally a house of secular canons, was reformed as a monastery of regular canons by William of Corbeil, himself an Augustinian, after he became archbishop of Canterbury (r. 1123–36). While William was dying, however, the prior of Christ Church Canterbury, which had a claim to the property, installed Benedictine monks from their chapter instead of the monks from St Augustine's, Canterbury. During the two-year vacancy of the archbishopric of Canterbury, the papal legate Henry of Blois (a former monk of Cluny) had removed the monks, but in 1139, very shortly after his election as archbishop, Theobald of Bec restored the Christ Church monks. Theobald, a Benedictine, even secured a bull from Pope Innocent II – and subsequently from his successors – confirming that the disposal of the affairs of the priory lay solely in the hands of the archbishop of Canterbury.[173] The issue at stake might at first sight be explained in terms of the property of St Martin's, which the rival Canterbury communities clearly wanted for themselves. But the terms of the papal bull make clear that the grant was in favour of Theobald and his successors in the archiepiscopal see, and the conformation by Pope Adrian IV explicitly prohibited the prior and monks of Christ Church from exercising authority over the community.[174] This makes it look as though Theobald had a personal stake in the community being Benedictine, at least during his lifetime – since presumably a subsequent archbishop who favoured canons regular could restore them to St Martin's.

One reforming congregation that adopted the *Rule of Augustine* was the Premonstratensians, founded by Norbert in 1120 in the diocese of Soissons. Originally a canon of Xanten Cathedral of aristocratic birth, Norbert underwent a personal conversion to a penitential way of life and as a result spent some years as a wandering preacher. Denounced for unlicensed preaching, he personally petitioned Pope Gelasius II to be permitted to continue, before founding a community at Prémontré in northeastern France that followed the *Rule of Augustine* overlaid with his own customs, and other houses at Floreffe, Laon and Cuissy.[175] In 1126, Pope Honorius II recognised them as a distinct Order living according to the *Rule of Augustine* and in accordance with the way of life of Prémontré. In fact, it was Norbert's successor, Hugh des Fosses, who compiled the *Liber Ordinarius*, or liturgical guide for all houses in the Order. Like the Cistercians – at least in principle – with whom they shared certain common principles, the Premonstratensians established a hierarchy of governance based on the 'head' abbey of Prémontré, its daughter-houses and then other foundations, linked by an annual general chapter. Monasteries were exempt from episcopal jurisdiction, even though Prémontré had itself been founded through the patronage of Barthélemy, bishop of Laon. Like the Cistercians, Premonstratensians also absorbed existing houses. In 1112, three priests in the diocese of Troyes were given permission to establish a small monastery which in 1140 became the Premonstratensian monastery of Beaulieu, with the encouragement of Bernard of Clairvaux. The double house of Basse-Fontaine, in the same diocese, was founded by the countess of Brienne in 1143 and affiliated with Beaulieu.[176]

Norbert was essentially a missionary, and the Premonstratensians found plenty of work – sometimes alongside Cistercian communities – in 'frontier' areas of Christendom where the parochial system was still in its infancy. The reluctance of the Cistercians to found any houses in the Levant (at least until after the death of Bernard of Clairvaux in 1153) allowed the Premonstratensians to accept an invitation from Baldwin II, king of Jerusalem, to found a monastery dedicated to the prophet Samuel, and a second house followed dedicated to Habakkuk.[177] Premonstratensians and Cistercians were both to be found in German- and Polish-speaking regions in the twelfth century, accompanying the eastward advance of the Latin Church.[178] It was not only in mission areas that they flourished: the founding of small Premonstratensian houses in under-inhabited regions of the northwest, such as Shap in Cumbria (founded 1199), and Tongland in Galloway (1218), demonstrates their usefulness in supplementing the thinly stretched parish priesthood. But in the middle of the thirteenth century they were still associated in the minds of many with preaching connected to crusading. In a letter to his archbishop written in 1241 or 1242, a disgraced priest of Narbonne called Yvo described his sighting of the Mongol army that had swept through Hungary and briefly threatened to cross the Danube. In despair, he called upon the preaching friars and the 'Norbertines', whose job it was to assemble forces for a holy war of deliverance from the apocalyptic threat he thought these 'inhuman' forces posed.[179]

HOW SIGNIFICANT WAS 'REFORM'?

Contemporary accounts of the eleventh and twelfth centuries, especially narrative and hagiographical sources, often give the impression that monastic life was a whirlwind of new foundations, reform and renewal. Expressions of a yearning for a simpler form of monasticism than that to be found in a large, well-endowed monastery deeply implicated in landholding networks have been picked up by modern historians of monasticism in the writings of many eleventh-century monks.[180] The inference drawn by many historians has been that, as John van Engen characterised it, 'something must have gone deeply wrong with Benedictine monasticism'. As he observed in a characteristically astute essay, however, the disruptions of 'reform' were the exception rather than the rule in western monasticism. Although the term 'crisis' has been liberally used by historians of monasticism to explain the phenomenon of reform, it is not a term found in contemporary sources.[181] Moreover, many accounts of 'breakaway' reforming communities were produced by new foundations in order to justify disruption by emphasising the unsatisfactory state of observance against which reformers were reacting. This is clearly the case with the early Cistercian documents, or with a hagiographical 'foundation text' such as the *Life of Stephen of Obazine*. Other representations of reform have become part of a standard narrative because they occur in texts that have become highly influential as part of a wider understanding of the period. Such is the case, for example, of William of Malmesbury's account of Stephen Harding's role in the founding of Cîteaux, or Guibert of Nogent's observations on the indifference of many of the monks of his experience.[182] Recently, Steven Vanderputten has also cast doubt on the chronology of reform as it appears in twelfth-century accounts, arguing that the apparently spectacular changes of the later eleventh century were often in fact the result of generations of patient 'process-driven' reform in communities in the tenth and earlier eleventh centuries. At St Bertin in Flanders, for example, patient work by a series of abbots in the later tenth and early eleventh centuries meant that a 'reformed' community developed without the need for intervention or disruption.[183] Such must have been the norm; the type of situation described at Molesmes the exception.

Most monks and nuns probably lived most of their lives in monasteries or convents – whether happily or unhappily – untouched by currents of reform. All institutions undergo cycles of renewal as leaders change and as new agendas are drawn up to reflect their ideas and aspirations. As observed above, practices of individual austerity often associated with reforming houses might also take place in 'unreformed' monasteries.

Jocelin of Brakelond's picture of Abbot Samson of Bury St Edmunds, for example, could very well have been written about a 'reforming' abbot, even though nobody would characterise Bury as a reformed house. Van Engen is surely correct to emphasise that the period from c. 1050 to c. 1150 was one of expansion and growth for what we might term 'Benedictine normalism', as well as being a period of reform and change: in other words, reform was a sign of the health of cenobitic monasticism rather than of crisis.

Another cause for some scepticism about the dramatic nature of reform lies in the language deployed by reformers. William of Saint-Thierry famously described Clairvaux, a few years after its foundation, as 'a community of solitaries', and reformers were prone to bring out those elements of new foundations that underscored their remoteness and solitude.[184] Romuald's hermitage of Sitria was said by his biographer, Peter Damian, to be like Nitria in more than name only. Later, while at Camaldoli, Romuald used to withdraw to nearby mountainous countryside with a few companions 'to make a desert there'. Perhaps he was recalling the practices of the monks of the Judaean desert. Although Damian does not make this connection explicitly, he makes a general allusion to early monastic exemplars when he exclaims, 'Oh golden age of Romuald, which although it did not suffer the torment of persecution, yet did not lack martyrdom!'[185] Yet the need to make such comparisons to some extent shows how much of a contrivance this was on the part of reformers and their supporters. Cîteaux lay not in an inaccessible desert or the depths of a tangled woodland but on a crossroads. Fonte Avellana liked to think of itself as living in solitude, but this was to some degree engineered by the creation of buffer zones between its own *terroir* and that of neighbouring landowners. The 'myth of the desert', as Benedicta Ward termed it, was created in order to make apparent the comparisons that reformers wished to be drawn between themselves and the Desert Fathers.[186] Orderic Vitalis's scathing commentary on the schism at Molesmes shows that, to some degree, this association had worked.

Perhaps a more striking problem generated by a focus on reform-as-disruption is that it does not work for both male and female monasticism alike. The movements in western religious life that most clearly shaped monasticism – the rise and growing influence of Cluny, and the return to the literal observance of the *Rule of Benedict* – were male-centred, and drew women along in their wake. For this reason, Bruce Venarde has suggested, female monasticism in this period has generally, but misleadingly, been seen as subordinate to male. In fact, female monasticism was no less shaped by reform tendencies, by new projects and by the questioning of contemporary practices, but because these did not align exactly with what was happening in male monasticism, they have been less clearly understood.[187]

The abbey of Fontevraud in Anjou (northwestern France) provides a good example of Venarde's point. In many ways its foundation follows a familiar story of a charismatic male founding figure – the studious archpriest turned ascetic preacher, Robert of Arbrissel – who in 1101 gathered a group of followers and settled them in a location provided by lay supporters. The monastery was founded on land given separately by Adelaide Rivière and Gautier of Montsoreau, on either side of the Loire. The charter confirming the abbey's possessions issued by the bishop of Poitiers in 1106 attested that Robert had 'gathered many women, whom he made nuns, so that they might live the regular life there'.[188] Although Robert's followers included both men and women, Fontevraud was run by two women, Hersende, Gautier's widowed mother-in-law, and Petronilla of Chemillé, a well-connected laywoman who became the first abbess in 1115.[189] Moreover, some of those whom Robert 'made nuns' appear to have been women left behind by the movement of clerical reform in the Church. In the last quarter of the eleventh century, some bishops, especially in northern France and Italy, began to implement reforms of clerical life, of which one outcome was the emergence of the *Rule of Augustine*. One dimension of such reform was the enforcement of clerical celibacy, which although always an ideal in the early Church in the West had never been practised universally. In dioceses where bishops took an energetic lead in enforcement, women who had married or lived with men in Holy Orders might find themselves homeless almost without notice. Such a diocese was Rennes, where Robert of Arbrissel had been a diocesan official tasked with implementing clerical reform. Although he supported clerical celibacy as an ideal, he did not share the view that men and women could not share a common religious life.[190] Some of the early vocations at Fontevraud appear to have been women who had lived as the wives of priests and were left with no means of support as a result of the energetic pursuit of clerical reform.

In the previous chapter the scarcity of convents for women in *c.* 1000 – seventy in the whole of England and France – was noted.[191] In the hundred years after *c.* 1050 this situation changed radically. As Venarde notes, many scholars used to assume that the wider reform movement was hostile to the possibilities of women in positions of genuine participation in religious life.[192] But the estimates he gives – from about 100 convents in northwestern Europe *c.* 1070 to about 400 by 1170 – indicates that this was not the case. On average, at least fifty new convents were founded in each decade between 1121 and 1160. What is particularly striking, moreover, is that only a quarter of these were affiliated to a reform congregation of the type that has been discussed in this chapter.[193] Of the 310 convents known to Venarde and founded between 1101 and 1175, 'nearly 140 were autonomous houses following the Benedictine or Augustinian Rules, and another 65 were affiliated with the female-centred Orders of Fontevraud or Sempringham'.[194]

The implication of these statistics is that women's participation in and leadership of monastic life was not dependent on the kind of reform that we have encountered in this chapter. If the reasons for the momentum in women's monasticism so noticeable after *c.* 1050 had other causes, what could they have been? One place to look for an answer is a new convent that started as an obscure hermitage in Hertfordshire. Markyate, near Dunstable, grew, like many reforming houses, out of a hermitage. Its founder was a monk of St Albans, Roger, who had retired there with five other hermits.[195] In *c.* 1131, however, an anchoress called Christina (*c.* 1096–*c.* 1160) made a formal profession as a female religious at St Albans with the encouragement of Abbot Geoffrey of Gorron (d. 1146), and after Roger's death moved into the hermitage as the head of a small, as yet unregulated community. The informality of the arrangements at Markyate, as conveyed in the Life of Christina written by a St Albans monk, are typical of the character of much of reform monasticism. Christina, the daughter of an aspirational English family from Huntingdon, wanted to profess as a nun but was forcibly dissuaded by her parents, who even conspired in her attempted seduction at the hands of the bishop of Durham, Ranulf Flambard. Christina was able to evade the bishop but not his influence, and she was given in marriage instead to the son of a neighbour, Burthred. It is not clear whether Christina was in fact legally married to Burthred, but she escaped from him before the marriage could be consummated, and was hidden by a network of hermits in the region, eventually ending up at Roger's hermitage.

Markyate was established as a convent in 1145, according to the St Albans chronicle known as the *Deeds of the Abbots*, with the energetic help and encouragement of Abbot Geoffrey. Geoffrey himself is a somewhat equivocal figure. A native of northwestern France, he was master of the school at Dunstable at the time of his appointment as abbot of St Albans in 1119. As abbot, he founded a leper hospital, built an impressive new shrine for St Alban, and improved the abbey's finances.[196] But he was accused of maladministration by his monks, and according to the *Life of Christina of Markyate*, underwent a personal transformation through the ministrations and friendship of Christina, who became his spiritual adviser. His material help in refounding Markyate as a convent seems to have been a way of making amends for his lapses. According to the *Deeds of the Abbots*, Geoffrey had initially become a monk in remorse at his negligence in accidentally destroying vestments to have been used for a liturgical drama on the passion of St Katherine of Alexandria that he had written for his students at Dunstable.[197] Geoffrey seems to have had a devotion to the martyr saint, whose popularity in the Norman world was already well established before 1100; indeed, he chose 25 November, Katherine's feast day, as the day of his ordination as abbot.[198] His friendship with Christina is far from coincidental given this personal devotion. Katherine was a popular saint because, besides her spectacular and glorious martyrdom, she was also a pattern of the learned and contemplative woman. Her learning was established by her refutation of the pagan philosophers sent to dissuade her from her Christian faith, while the period she spent in prison awaiting martyrdom was associated in medieval piety with monastic seclusion. Moreover, like Christina, Katherine chose a life of holy virginity by refusing to marry against her will.[199]

Christina and her foundation at Markyate offer a different view of reform, in which a woman leading a regulated religious life of her own volition provides the inspiration for a monk from the Benedictine mainstream. Geoffrey, perhaps finding in Christina an embodiment of the focus of his own devotional piety, becomes the enabler of new reforming communities for women – he also founded a hermitage for enclosed women at Sopwell, near St Albans. An analogy of a kind can be made with Heloise (*c.* 1100–1163) and her community of the Paraclete, founded in 1129. Heloise, after a love affair with the celebrated Paris teacher Peter Abelard had ended, took vows at the Benedictine convent at Argenteuil where she had previously been brought up. In 1122, however, the community was evicted by Suger, abbot of St Denis, who was able to prove to his own satisfaction that the land on which the convent was built belonged to St Denis. It was fortunate that Abelard, having first himself taken vows at St Denis, was able to put at Heloise's disposal a property by the river Ardusson near Troyes, in Champagne, where he had built an oratory and founded an eremitical community for scholars. When he left this foundation, which he called the Paraclete, to take up the abbacy of St Gildas in Brittany, he effectively became the refounder of the Argenteuil community.[200]

In a series of brilliant letters, sometimes passionate, sometimes tragic, always deeply learned and intelligent, Heloise and Abelard explored the meaning of monastic life in the context of their shared memories and feelings. In the third letter to Abelard, Heloise asks him for two things: to explain for the benefit of her nuns the historical origin of women's monasticism; and to write a Rule specifically for women to follow. In her words, the necks of bullocks and heifers cannot be joined to the same yoke, yet the *Rule of Benedict* was written with men in mind. In so far as women follow the Rule, they are compelled to do as exceptions to the norms expected of men.[201] As Felicitas Corrigan has remarked, it is surprising that neither Heloise nor Abelard appears to have been familiar with Caesarius of Arles, who, as we saw in an earlier chapter, wrote one of the earliest Rules known to us for his sister and her female community.[202] Abelard refers to the abbess as *diaconissa*, implying that he acknowledges a liturgical role for the head of the community. Other officials should comprise the gatekeeper, cellarer, needlewoman (to make the nuns' habits), infirmarian, cantor and sacristan. Most of his rather lengthy and turgid Rule deals with the practical administration of the community – almost as though he was deliberately ignoring her hint that the Paraclete should embrace a simple and poor life and prioritise the spiritual training and development of the sisters. But he also wrote hymns (133 in all), lamentations based on biblical narratives, homilies and a commentary on Creation. The demand for a separate Rule for women reveals Heloise as an astute and thoughtful critic of monasticism. She was also a founder in her own right: the Paraclete eventually had six daughter-houses of its own. She was celebrated for her spiritual wisdom and learning; Peter the Venerable told her in a letter that she had 'surpassed all women and outstripped almost all men'.[203] The basis for comparison with Christina may be slight when we consider their respective situations and especially their accomplishments. Nevertheless, like her contemporary, she was both the inspiration for and at the same time dependent on a male monastic figure in trying to recreate monasticism.

Christina of Markyate is only one example of a large number of men and women who chose anchoritic lives in the eleventh and twelfth centuries. As we saw in the previous chapter, many hermits and anchorites developed or maintained relationships with established monasteries. Wulfric of Haselbury, an anchorite in a Somerset village, received his food as a gift from the Cluniac abbey of Montacute.[204] Godric of Finchale, who occupied a cell on the River Wear, was a member of the Benedictine confraternity of the cathedral priory at Durham, and in the eleventh century the Greek monk Anastasius had lived as an anchorite while a member of the community at Cluny by permission of Abbot Hugh.[205] Living in a self-imposed wilderness, such as impenetrable woodland, or in the reclusion of a cell, did not mean that a hermit cut him- or herself off from society; indeed, in many ways the essence of the eremitical life was the capacity to love the world one had left.[206] But the case of Christina also shows that the new beginnings in monastic life in the twelfth century might come about from different sources and different kinds of relationships than those suggested by too singular an attention to 'reforming' communities.

CHAPTER FIVE

The Mill and the Grindstone
Monasteries and the World, *c.* 1100–1300

The whole life of man can be compared to a mill built over a swift-flowing river. In this mill, suppose that there is a millstone with which men grind for their own use . . . The grindstones are their actions. For as the grindstone goes round and round over the same course while it is grinding, so human actions repeat themselves as their time comes round . . . Now see the . . . men leading a monastic life. Here is a monk placed under the rule of his abbot, having promised obedience in all matters which are laid upon him . . . Now see; he comes to the grindstone; he must perforce set about grinding. On all sides he is beset with complaints, with pleas, with lawsuits. But, let him like a wise monk, hold on to his flour, and store it carefully in his bin lest it be carried off by the river. And how, you ask, will he do this? By doing nothing for vainglory; by doing nothing that God forbids because of any hope of gain; by so carrying out the task enjoined on his obedience that he both protects and preserves the goods of the church manfully and justly against all men, and yet tries to bring nothing belonging to another into his church's possession by injustice.[1]

IN A LONG EXTENDED metaphor, the Christ Church Canterbury monk Eadmer explains how Anselm, as abbot of the community and archbishop, advised his monks on how to balance the demands of a contemplative life following the *Rule of Benedict* with the obligations laid on many monks to help conduct the business of the monastery. Anselm, who had been a monk and abbot at Bec, assumed that for most monks such obligations came as unwelcome distractions from the liturgical and prayerful life. How were monks to negotiate the outside world and still remain obedient to the Rule? In the metaphor, some men waste the flour that they mill through neglect, while others keep enough not only to feed themselves but to store some for the future. Those who waste their flour are those who work only for worldly gain, and who find at the end of their lives that they have lost everything to 'the flux of worldly desires'. Others – those who manage to save some of the flour from waste – are the laypeople who give alms to the needy, go to church and perform some good works, but are also prey to human weaknesses. The monk, however, keeps all the flour he grinds safe because the work he does is not for personal gain but to fulfil the needs of the community.

Clearly some dispensation from the strictest demands of the Rule, particularly those relating to stability and regular observance, was needed for monasteries to conduct their normal business, whether that entailed monks leaving the monastery or laypeople entering its precincts. Large monasteries held lands that might be scattered over several regions, and might include dependent priories. In some parts of Europe, they might owe obligations of service – sometimes military service – to the crown. Even smaller monasteries had to cultivate and maintain relationships with neighbouring families, with tenants and the peasantry working their lands or townspeople. If a monastery maintained a shrine with relics of a saint, they could expect pilgrims who would require accommodation; if it was situated on a main road, a stream of travellers and guests. Provision of food and other supplies required logistical supply chains to be established and maintained. Tensions and conflicts over jurisdiction and rights arose constantly with bishops and powerful neighbours. An abbot or abbess was – whether welcome or not – running a business. As such, the points of contact with 'the world' were varied and demanded constant attention. This chapter examines the nature of such contacts with the world outside the monastery in the central medieval period, and some of the ways in which these contacts shaped and changed monastic communities themselves.

In both the Byzantine and western worlds, monasteries were by the twelfth century fixed and immutable points in political culture. They were found in the centres of towns and cities as well as in remote areas of countryside. Abbots, and to a lesser extent abbesses, were regular attenders at royal and aristocratic courts. Possession of landed property brought not only responsibilities to those who made a living on the land but also obligations to the running of political society.[2] Monasteries provided knights and soldiery for war, and abbots sometimes took up arms themselves. Monasteries also performed multiple and varied functions for wider society. In an age where there was no systematic governmental support for the disadvantaged, they offered relief for the poor through alms. In place of hotels and restaurants they provided hospitality for travellers and pilgrims; schools for the children of the influential; or accommodation for refugees, political exiles or the retired. As businesses, they were employers and sources of labour, and commanded a secondary economic chain as both purchasers and suppliers of goods. As such, they attracted criticism as well as commendation from contemporaries. What were the implications of the role monasteries played for the communities themselves, how they were organised and regulated; and how they absorbed and reflected wider changes in external society?

The increase in business experienced by monasteries is not unrelated to wider societal developments. The development of papal bureaucracy lies outside the scope of this study, but it is clear that the twelfth century saw a huge increase in administrative business transacted by the papal curia. From around the middle of the twelfth century, the practical dimensions of the centralisation of papal governance began to take shape, especially with the creation in the 1140s of a new codification of canon law, the so-called *Concordance of Discordant Canons* by Gratian – known as Gratian's *Decretum*. The pope in whose reign the effects first started to be most fully experienced was a Cistercian monk.

In the early weeks of 1145, the pope, Lucius II, was seriously injured during a riot in Rome. Popes were often unpopular with the Roman people, and in the 1140s a campaign to recreate the Senate with powers of urban governance set the papacy against the city. In February Lucius died of the injuries sustained during an attack on the Lateran palace. So hostile was the situation that the cardinals fled the city. The election of the new pope, and his consecration, had to be held away from the symbols of papal power and authority in Rome. These crucial events took place instead at the Cluniac monastery of Farfa. The man elected was an Italian from Pisa, Bernardo Paganelli, who took the name Eugenius III. Bernardo had been a prominent clerical administrator in the archbishopric of Pisa until, in 1138, an encounter with Bernard of Clairvaux changed his life. Bernardo followed Bernard back to Clairvaux and took the habit there. A few years later he was back in Italy, leading a group of Cistercians to refound a former Greek monastery near Rome, Tre Fontane, as a Cistercian house. His sudden elevation to the seat of St Peter must have come as a considerable shock to Eugenius, as indeed it did to Bernard, who wrote a letter to the cardinals in which bewilderment competes with outrage.[3]

The election of Eugenius is often seen as a moment of affirmation for the Cistercians – the moment when the new Order scaled the heights of the Church hierarchy. But we may also see it as an occasion of wider significance for what it tells us about the role of the monastery in the Church and political life more generally in the mid-twelfth century. At a time of crisis for the papacy as an institution, it was a monastery that provided a consecrated safe space for the election to take place. No less important was that there were probably few buildings or complexes that could accommodate and feed the cardinals and papal household. In 1147 Eugenius – still unable to live safely in Rome – undertook a grand tour of France and the Empire. He met King Louis VII of France and Emperor Conrad III, held Councils, and sat in judgement over theologians accused of error. When he visited Louis in Paris at Easter in April 1147, it was at the monastery of St Denis that Eugenius and the papal curia were received and entertained, with tables being set up in the cloister because the refectory could not accommodate everyone.

IN THE HOUSES OF PRINCES: MONASTERIES AND RULERS

The use of a monastery to hold a celebratory feast marking such an occasion was far from unusual. Kings might hold court or council in monasteries. In 1215, for example, King John held his council in the chapter house at the abbey of St Albans.[4] Lanercost Priory served as a base for Edward I of England to convalesce during his Scottish campaign in 1307. Given the purpose of a monastery as a 'factory of prayer' and a site of withdrawal from the world, the prominence of monasteries in the public sphere might at first glance seem odd. But there were practical reasons for this. From a king's point of view, a monastery could be one of the few sites with the physical capacity to accommodate a large household. Few other structures – even castles and manor houses – possessed a purpose-built room for feeding large numbers at the same time, and monasteries had a duty to provide hospitality for visitors. It has been estimated that Eugenius III's travelling household in exile may have comprised more than a hundred people, including eighteen cardinals.[5] The convenience of a monastery's permanent buildings sometimes meant that a monastery was actually located at an existing centre of secular power, as for example was the case when Aubrey de Vere, earl of Oxford, founded the convent of Castle Hedingham at his castle.[6] More pertinent, perhaps, a monastery might have a customary obligation to provide victuals and accommodation to the king at various points in the year, and calling in such an obligation was a useful way of reducing the royal household's own costs for a period of time. This was an especially valuable right in an age when kingship was still largely peripatetic, as it was for much of western Europe before the thirteenth century. Sometimes kings took this too far. The English chronicler Roger of Howden bluntly recorded how King John, as regent of England during his brother Richard the Lionheart's crusade, abused his authority by lodging in any religious house he pleased 'with such a vast array of men, horses, hounds and hawks, that a house where he took up residence for only a single night was scarcely able to recover for three years afterwards'.[7]

A monastery might also provide a valuable 'neutral' space for delicate political negotiations, and monks themselves were used as representatives of kings and governments, at a time when professional diplomacy did not yet exist in the sense that it had come to do during the fifteenth century. Geoffrey, abbot of the Augustinian house of the Temple in Jerusalem, was sent as an ambassador along with the bishop of Bethlehem and a prominent lay magnate to Emperor John II Komnenos in 1142, because he could speak Greek.[8] He was selected for a similar mission in

1158 to negotiate protocol for a meeting of Emperor Manuel Komnenos with King Baldwin III.[9] It is perhaps not very surprising to find Arnulf, abbot of Melrose, as part of the delegation sent by William the Lion, king of Scotland, to Rome in 1181 to appeal the sentence of excommunication against him.[10] But in 1192 it was a monk, the prior of Hereford, who was entrusted with the delicate task of travelling to the Holy Land to inform Richard I that the administration he had put in place to govern England while he was on crusade was collapsing, and that he would be well advised to abandon his dream of recapturing Jerusalem and attend to matters at home.[11] Likewise, when Richard was in captivity in Germany a year later, having been taken on his way back from the crusade, it was two monks, the abbots of Boxley and Pont-Robert, who were entrusted with the even more difficult assignment of locating him in his unknown prison.[12] Kings might use monks as informants or spies as well as diplomats. It was a monk, Ubaldo, who informed Emperor Henry VI of the plot against him by the adherents of the deposed Tancred of Lecce in Sicily in 1194.

For a monastery, too, there were benefits as well as costs in such a relationship. Royal protection might take a direct form such as intervention on behalf of a monastery, for example in cases where monks had a complaint against a superior. In the early thirteenth century, the subprior of Montacute Abbey, a Cluniac house in Somerset, complained directly to King John about the behaviour of the prior, which prompted a visitation from the diocesan, Jocelin, bishop of Bath, to investigate the case. But a royal connection could be helpful in less direct ways as well. The prestige of royal burials in the abbey church elevated the status of St Denis, carefully cultivated by Abbot Suger (1081–1151). Suger acted as regent for Louis VII while he was on crusade (1147–8), on which a monk of St Denis was among the royal household.[13] Some English monasteries – St Albans, Westminster, Christ Church Canterbury, Glastonbury, Bury St Edmunds – were regarded as traditional guardians of the monastic Order in England not only because of their age but also by virtue of royal patronage over centuries.[14] The St Albans chronicler Matthew Paris (d. 1259) had access to letters and papers that circulated at the court of Henry III, as well as to distinguished visitors and guests on their way to or from Westminster. Monks might be in direct contact with members of ruling dynasties: William of Malmesbury, for example, was encouraged to write his *History of the Kings of England* by Maud, the wife of King Henry I, to whose daughter Matilda he addressed a prefatory letter.[15]

The nature of royal patronage to monasteries differed across the Christian world. In the Byzantine Empire, the tradition of the imperial founding of monasteries went back to the sixth century, when Justinian established several monasteries, including the one on Mount Sinai that would later be dedicated to St Katherine.[16] This tradition was revived in the early twelfth century during the programme of cenobitic reform in the Empire. The long gap did not mean, however, that imperial patronage was lacking in the intervening centuries. As we saw in Chapter Three, Emperor Nikephoros Phokas was a keen supporter of Athonite monasticism in the tenth century. Imperial patronage of individual holy men who were encouraged and materially supported in establishing monasteries according to their own pattern was far from uncommon.[17] But under the Komnenos dynasty (1080–1185), direct and indirect imperial patronage became more evident. The monastery of Our Lady of Kykkos, which was to become the most prominent of Cypriot monasteries by virtue of the ikon it possessed supposedly by the hand of St Luke, was founded in the 1090s by Alexios I Komnenos's general Manuel Butumites. This foundation follows the pattern outlined above, if a later tradition that the site of the monastery had been the hermitage of an ascetic who cured Butumites, and later the emperor's daughter, of sciatica is to be believed.[18] Another of Alexios's generals, Eumathios Philokles, founded St John Chrysostom at Koutsovendis, in the north of Cyprus. Also in the 1090s, Alexios Komnenos was a generous donor to the recently founded monastery of St John on Patmos, to which he assigned an annual portion of the public tax revenue in coin and in wheat.[19] In the mid-twelfth century, the monastery of Makhairas in Cyprus – also originally a hermitage – received generous patronage from Manuel Komnenos. Emperor Alexios Komnenos's wife Irene founded a convent for nuns in Constantinople in 1110–16, dedicated to the Mother of God *Kecharitomene* ('full of grace'). This was part of a double foundation, with a male community attached to it. Empress Irene herself retired to the convent in *c.* 1123, as did her daughter Anna Komnene, and it was within its walls that the latter wrote her celebrated *Alexiad*, the history of her father

Alexios's reign in the 1130s.[20] It seems probable that the empress herself was the author of the surviving founder's typikon, which attests to the close concern she gave to the project.

Komnenos dynastic activity in founding monasteries looks particularly striking when contrasted with the type of patronage typical of royal dynasties in the West. Typically, kings or members of royal dynasties founded monasteries in order to emphasise dynastic authority, often in newly acquired territories or in regions with multiple religious affiliations. Géza I of Hungary's founding of Pannonhalma at the end of the tenth century, the first Benedictine monastery in Magyar territory, is a case in point. Almost two hundred years later, between 1179 and 1196, Béla III founded five Cistercian monasteries: Egres (1179, now in Romania), Zirc or Cikádor (1182), Szentgotthárd (1183), Pilis (Pilisszentkereszt, 1184) and Pásztó (1191). A sixth, Borsmonostor (Klostermarienburg, 1194), was founded by a royal official.[21] King Roger II of Sicily seems to have elected to found a new Greek monastery on the island as a means of drawing together idiorrhythmic practices into a single community, with the Greek monk Luke of Messina at its head. The Norman aristocracy in Greek-speaking southern Italy had already been patronising local Orthodox establishments for a few generations by the mid-twelfth century. As count of Sicily, Roger I (1072–1101) had begun to extend patronage to the ancient monastery of Fragalà in the Val Demone in the 1060s, and confirmed his privileges in a charter of 1090.[22] William the Conqueror founded, and generously endowed, Battle Abbey in Sussex as a public penance for the English blood he had shed at Hastings, and his son Henry I's foundation of Reading Abbey may be seen in a similar fashion as a means of moulding a distinctively Norman Church in England. Reading, an Augustinian house, represented continental directions of monastic spirituality, doubtless to be understood as standing to one side of traditional English monastic centres. Kings of Scotland likewise founded or supported continental reform monasteries – for example, the Cistercian houses of Melrose (1136) and Dundrennan (1144) by David I, and the Tironian houses at Kelso by David, earl of Huntingdon and later king of Scotland, in *c.* 1113, Lesmahagow, also by David I in 1144, and Arbroath by William the Lion in 1178. The Cistercian houses were planted in a region over which his dynasty had recently stamped its control. Planting a monastery – to use the horticultural metaphor of the times – was a way of telling the world that the land on which it was founded was yours to give to God's servants. Sometimes an existing monastery might serve as a means for the crown to establish its authority. In the 1220s, Louis VIII of France (1223–6) built a fortress on the western side of the Rhône opposite Avignon, a town that at that point lay outside the border of the French kingdom. Rather than occupying a new site, he contracted with the abbey of St Andrew, which lay on the hill overlooking the river, to fortify the hill, thus encompassing the monastery within the fortress. In return, the monastery withdrew from the jurisdiction of the bishop of Avignon. A further contract was drawn up between Philip IV and St Andrew in 1290 when the king founded the town of Villeneuve below the fortress. The great age of royal monastic foundation in the West was largely past by *c.* 1200, though there are striking and apparently anomalous examples in the thirteenth century. Edward I of England's foundation of Vale Royal in Cheshire – in fulfilment of a vow made during a stormy Channel crossing – may have been a deliberate echo of Louis IX's founding of the Cistercian house at Royaumont (1228–35) and his mother Blanche's new convents at Le Lys (*c.* 1241) and Maubuisson (*c.* 1236).[23] Louis's younger brother Charles of Anjou chose new Cistercian foundations at Realvalle and Vittoria as the way to celebrate his victories over the Hohenstaufen in Italy in 1266.

Imperial subjects who visited the Holy Land as pilgrims noticed the reach of the imperial arm. The Cretan monk John Phokas, who made a pilgrimage in the Holy Land probably in 1177, noted that images of the Emperor Manuel Komnenos (1142–80) hung in the Church of the Nativity in Bethlehem to mark his patronage of the church, and that Manuel had subsidised the rebuilding of other monasteries in the Judaean desert and by the Jordan. The monastery of St Elias, near Bethlehem, and St John the Forerunner, on the river Jordan, a famous imperial foundation of the sixth century, had both suffered destruction in earthquakes.[24] The Holy Land had been a province of the Roman Empire until the Arab conquests of the seventh century, and most Christians in the region, though Arabic speakers, were Greek Orthodox in religious affiliation. Between 1099 and 1187, Jerusalem, Bethlehem and the areas where Phokas noted restoration of Orthodox monasteries lay in the Kingdom of Jerusalem, which since the conquest of Jerusalem on the First Crusade in 1099 had been under the control of a Frankish dynasty. Likewise, the Franks had established a Latin Church hierarchy and taken over the running of most of the major shrine churches in the Holy Land. The attitude of the political and religious authorities toward Orthodox monasteries was largely one of laissez-faire, though, unlike in Norman Sicily, there was no interest on the part of the Franks in supporting, let alone founding, Orthodox monasteries. On the other hand, they made no objection to the intervention of the emperor. Other Orthodox princes also found the Holy Land a receptive place for establishing new monasteries. In 1229–30, Savvas of Serbia consulted the *hegoumen* of St Sabas, Nicholas, for advice on a suitable location to found a monastery, and Athanasios II, Orthodox patriarch of Jerusalem who was at that time in residence, provided the church of St John on Mount Zion, which became the oratory of the new monastery.[25]

Giving material support to monasteries for building or repairs was of course far from unusual throughout the Christian world. Kings frequently made gifts of building materials, such as timber from their woods, for religious houses. Moreover, there was earlier precedent for imperial aid to the shrine churches of the Holy Land, since Emperor Constantine IX had subsidised the rebuilding of the Church of the Holy Sepulchre in Jerusalem in the 1040s after its earlier destruction at the hands of Caliph Al-Hakim (1009).[26] But the significance of imperial intervention in rebuilding the fabric of damaged monasteries in the Holy Land was surely not lost on the Christian population of the kingdom of Jerusalem. This was Byzantine imperial 'soft power' reaching across territorial borders and political frameworks, to remind the Orthodox population where their loyalties and affiliations should lie. Monasticism thus provided openings for Byzantine imperial authority to be understood and felt at a distance and without the need for direct intervention. The symbolism of restoring a monastery was particularly powerful to a community that had been subaltern to other powers for centuries, and as such had endured periods of persecution and hostility. For the Christians of the Holy Land, the continuity of monasteries founded in the 'golden age' of Chariton, Euthymios and Sabas provided an identity and an assurance of spiritual support in the absence of autonomy.[27]

Paradoxical though it may seem, the monastic landscape often reflected dramatic political changes. The conflict between the papacy and German emperors, which was periodic in the eleventh and twelfth centuries, had a serious effect on some communities. The monastery of St Vanne at Verdun was dispersed in 1085 because of splits between the community and the abbot over their imperial or papal allegiances. Papal-supporting monks, such as the chronicler Hugh of Flavigny, were taken in by other monastic houses.[28] During the pontificate of Gregory VII (1073–85), factions arose among the monks at Farfa. Abbot Berardus II (1100–19) was aligned with the imperial cause – not surprisingly, perhaps, given the imperial connection with the abbey's early years – and the anonymous treatise *Orthodoxa defensio imperialis* was composed at Farfa during this period. But his successor, Adenolfus (1125–44), sided with Innocent II rather than the imperially backed Anacletus in the papal schism that occupied much of the 1130s. This support, although damaging to Farfa's landed estates, which were ravaged by imperial supporters, must have been a reason for the choice of the abbey by Eugenius III for his consecration in 1145. When Emperor Frederick I (1152–89) was trying to impose imperial authority over Pope Adrian IV in the 1150s, Farfa lay directly in his sights. His visits to the abbey in 1155 and 1159 may be one reason for the support shown by Farfa to the imperial candidate for the see of St Peter, Victor IV, instead of Alexander III in the 1160s. As popes secured a firmer hold over the regions around Rome with the creation of the so-called Papal States, however, Farfa came to lie much more closely within the papal sphere. By 1261 Urban IV's declaration of papal protection over Farfa and its possessions recognised the fait accompli.

Conquest of new territories also brought new monastic settlement in its wake. After the conquest of Constantinople by the Fourth Crusade and the establishment of the Latin Empire of Constantinople, the Cistercians founded monasteries in Greece.[29] Similarly, the Cistercians followed territorial expansion into the peripheries of Latin Europe in the Iberian peninsula from 1123 onwards, central and eastern Europe from the 1140s and the eastern Mediterranean after 1153.[30] In northeastern Europe especially, Cistercians and Premonstratensians came to be associated with the conversion of non-Christians through preaching. Berno, a monk of Amelungsborn Abbey in Saxony, was made bishop to the

Obodrites of the south Baltic coast in 1155, and supposedly joined the king of Denmark's conquest of the island of Rügen, still inhabited by pagans, in 1168.[31]

The Norman Conquest left ineradicable marks on monasticism in England. It was not simply that many new monasteries – Battle, on the site of the decisive encounter in October 1066 being the most obvious example – were founded by the newly dominant Norman monarchy and aristocracy. Within a few years after 1066, some English abbots were being removed from their monasteries in favour of Normans, though most were simply replaced by Normans when they died. Godric was replaced as abbot of Winchcombe by a monk of Cérisy as early as 1066. In 1070 William the Conqueror deposed a number of English abbots at a council at Winchester; in 1071 Ealdred, abbot of Abingdon was replaced by a monk of Jumièges; and in 1085 the abbot of Crowland was similarly deposed. All of these depositions were probably punishments for the support of these monasteries given to rebellions against William. But whether it happened suddenly or gradually, by William's death in 1087 almost all the headships of monasteries were in the hands of Normans, French or Italians.[32]

The effects of these changes went far beyond the question of the nationality of the head of a religious house. Lanfranc, who as archbishop of Canterbury from 1170 was also head of Christ Church, introduced a new set of constitutions which were also adopted at St Augustine's Canterbury, Rochester, St Albans, William's new monastery at Battle and Durham. At St Albans, Abbot Paul, a nephew of Lanfranc, reintroduced the strict observance of the *Rule of Benedict*, including maintaining silence and a total prohibition of meat. He was also remembered at St Albans for his devotion to the eastern pioneers of monasticism.[33] It used to be thought that Norman abbots were disrespectful towards English saints with whose stories they were unfamiliar, partly because of a famous case in which Lanfranc removed the early eleventh-century martyred Archbishop Aelfheah from the Canterbury calendar. But this was soon corrected by his successor Anselm, and most Norman abbots were energetic in promoting the causes of their local monasteries' saints.[34]

This is not to say that the influence of the Conquest on English monasticism was entirely negative. As we saw in the previous chapter, from the 1070s, the refounding and rebuilding of monasteries in the north was triggered by the effects of Norman power; more generally, it may be said, by the enforced political unity imposed by the Normans. Historians still debate the extent of the economic effects of the Conquest on English monasteries. The traditional view is that financial obligations in the form of knight service were a new financial exaction imposed on English monasteries – since the knights provided, obviously, had to be given maintenance of some kind by the monastery. It is far from clear that this was in fact a wholly new system, and it is possible that what we see is an increase in the nature of the obligation on monasteries. But it does seem undeniable that there were huge differences in the amounts at which monasteries were assessed. Based on data from a century after the Conquest, the obligations fell arbitrarily on English monasteries, with Peterborough and Glastonbury at the top end. Glastonbury's quota of sixty knights was reduced to forty even though its assets were somewhere between two and three times those of Peterborough.[35] The most burdensome levies seem to have fallen on the older English houses, whereas post-Conquest foundations such as Battle got away more lightly. It is possible that the rationale behind the levies was related to strategic needs – for example, Glastonbury's location near the mouth of the Severn, and Peterborough's near the Fenland, both made them valuable assets for the defence of regions that might come under threat.

The political importance of monasteries is underscored by the frequent presence of heads of religious houses at royal and ducal courts. If we take as a representative example the Temple of the Lord in Jerusalem, a house of Augustinian canons founded on the site of the Jewish Temple, its abbot Geoffrey appears in witness lists to charters in 1138, 1144, 1146, 1149, 1150/1, 1155 (three times) and 1160, in the reigns of Queen Melisende of Jerusalem (r. 1131–62) and her son Baldwin III (r. 1147–62).[36] This example could be amplified countless times by others from almost any royal or ducal court in Europe for which a series of *regesta* or acts survives. The presence of an abbot of a notable house such as Geoffrey tells us more about the operation of royal government than about the monastery itself. Although there were occasions when intervention or favour might have been needed at court, on the whole an abbot's presence was for the benefit of the smooth running of governmental business. Senior clergy were indispensable for giving advice on policy matters that touched on the Church, but also for the more mundane business of witnessing deeds, contracts and charters. Typically, a mix of secular nobility and senior clergy, often with one or more royal officials, would constitute the witnesses to such business. The clergy, of course, had the advantage as far as the issuers and recipients of deeds were concerned that they could read and attest to the wording of the document.

Intensive relationships between a monastery and the crown were usually, of course, greatly to the advantage of the monastery. Royal patronage of Westminster, founded by Edward the Confessor and dependent on the crown, elevated it above other monasteries in terms of shares of resource. In England, the reform of monastic life in the tenth century had been accomplished through direct royal initiative. The king was even envisaged in the *Regularis Concordia* as being the guarantor of monasteries abiding by its stipulations.[37] But closeness to the crown had its drawbacks as well. A monastery under royal patronage could less easily escape notice when it got into difficulties. Henry II sent a royal servant to Bury St Edmunds to investigate its finances when it got into debt in the 1180s.[38] When the monks had to elect a new abbot in 1182, the process involved first choosing a group of twelve of them to make the election in the king's presence.[39] St Albans may have benefited from the prestige and inside knowledge to be gained from its closeness to the crown, but by the early fourteenth century the strain of having to accommodate Parliament at the king's pleasure was telling on the abbey's resources. An appeal to Rome appealing for the reinstatement of exemptions from providing royal obligations followed.[40]

MONKS AND THE LAITY

Anselm's metaphor about the grind of worldly life wearing away at the monastic profession drew directly on his own experiences in the world. As abbot of Bec, he was a frequent visitor to noble households while conducting visitations of his monastery's new estates in England. His biographer Eadmer stresses the care he took to be approachable to his hosts, 'conforming himself, so far as he could without sin, to their various habits'. This doubtless meant that he had to turn a blind eye to those who 'lived in many respects without even the law of Christ'.[41] The reason for this absorption in the external world was to be able to instruct them, just as he also instructed his own monks and clerks. Anselm regarded his profession as a ministry not only to his own community but to the whole of humanity. Eadmer sees Anselm's 'colloquy' as a particular kind of blessing for the laity, but it had important consequences for Anselm – and, according to Eadmer, for the political culture of England as well. Even William I, who seemed terrifying to everyone else, became agreeable in Anselm's company.[42] The consequence of Anselm's readiness to mingle with the lay nobility was that he became well known and well liked among the Anglo-Norman aristocracy – ultimately with the result of his appointment by William Rufus to the vacant see of Canterbury in 1093.

The 'friendship circle' that Anselm established in the twenty years before this appointment, expressed through correspondence, was mostly conducted with other monks or clerics. The range of his correspondents widened in his later letters, however; especially significant is the inclusion of women.[43] Richard Southern has shown that his most intimate expressions – indeed, understanding – of friendship were reserved for those in the monastic profession. Thus, even when commending men and women who practised virtue in their secular lives through being just, giving alms and living moderately, Anselm used such letters as ways of reminding them that full service to God entailed a monastic vow. In a characteristic parable, he identifies the monk or nun with the orchard owner who hands over the orchard and its produce once and for all to his lord, in contrast with the virtuous secular who simply renders an annual return of the produce.[44] Moreover, he was uncompromising in his conviction that only a monastic life enabled the fullness of an experience of God. Yet, perhaps surprisingly, this did not translate into contempt for all forms of secular life. In fact, Anselm 'looked benignly', in Southern's words, on human institutions: 'all associations and authorities which enlarged the area of peace, justice and charity partook in some degree of the monastic purpose.'[45] One might say that since, to him, the whole world outside the cloister was by definition at a remove from God, equal levels of compassion were required in supporting it.

Anselm's genius for friendship lay in his ability to demand and retain the most exacting standard of spiritual virtue while expressing this in terms that conveyed warm sentiments to his correspondents.[46] When he was in lay company, what did he talk about to his lay hosts? According to Eadmer, he acted as a kind of marriage counsellor, encouraging married couples to act and think together in both spiritual and worldly affairs. Of course, the kind of advice he gave conformed to the expectations of marriage of his own day.[47] Husbands should be sexually faithful to their wives but also free of jealous suspicion; wives should subject themselves to their husbands lovingly, encourage them to act virtuously, and act as a brake on their tempers.[48]

At first sight it might appear surprising, given that most monks had no experience of the married state, that this should have been the subject of Anselm's advice. But he was far from being the only male monk from whom married laypeople took such advice. The Cistercian abbot Adam of Perseigne developed an epistolary friendship with the countess of Perche in which he responded to a request from her for advice about her marital relations. The countess's letter does not survive, but we can infer from Adam's reply that she was wrestling with her conscience over her husband's sexual demands and her own spiritual status. Adam's advice, which may not have provided much comfort to her, was that while she was obliged to submit to her husband in all bodily matters, in matters of the soul she should remember that she was Christ's daughter.[49] Adam's teaching implied a separation between body and mind, but also contemporary teaching about intent and action. In pastoral terms, however, the significance of such advice lies in his sensibility toward the plight of a young, perhaps lonely wife married to an older man whom she had almost certainly not chosen as a partner. Monastic advice to married couples reflected concerns about the good behaviour of husbands toward their wives, in a social context in which members of the aristocracy might have been chosen as marriage partners at a very young age without having any say in the matter. Naturally such advice encompassed marital fidelity, but also gentleness, courtesy and consideration.[50]

A different kind of marital advice was offered by Bernard of Clairvaux to Queen Melisende of Jerusalem after the death of her husband King Fulk in 1143. The correspondence appears one-sided, partly because all four surviving letters come from Bernard, but also because it is apparent from one letter that he had not received an expected reply from the queen. While commiserating with her on the death of her husband, Bernard seeks to encourage Melisende to 'act as a man . . . so that all may judge you from your actions to be a king rather than a queen'.[51] In a subsequent letter, Bernard admits his disappointment at not having received a response. Getting straight to business, he chastises her on account of rumours that have reached him of her conduct, though at the same time admitting that he has had other reports of her virtue. Although Bernard does not indicate openly that the rumours concerned sexual propriety, this has been assumed by historians, because he then goes on to discuss widowhood and remarriage. Melisende is a widow, but need no longer remain one if she does not wish it. But if she remains a widow, she must remember that her concern is 'to please not a man but God'. In order to do this, she must learn self-control. She cannot be a good queen if she is not also a good widow.[52]

Our first reaction on reading a letter such as this might well be to reflect that it was scarcely a surprise that he had received no reply from his earlier approach. In the context of the political situation in the Levant, however, perhaps it is more comprehensible. As Bernard observed in his first letter, the reason that Melisende needed to be a king rather than a queen was so that the kingdom's enemies – the Seljuqs and Fatimids – would not feel licensed to take advantage of weak rulership. In Bernard's mind, strong leadership was best provided by kingship, and the best solution would be for Melisende to remarry suitably. If that was not going to happen, then she had an obligation to live virtuously as a widow. In the minds of many in western Europe, the fate of the kingdom of Jerusalem was tied to the moral standing of its inhabitants. As queen, Melisende had the greatest share of responsibility for moral leadership; if she failed to provide it, God would use the kingdom's enemies as an instrument of punishment for sinfulness.

Although this kind of epistolary friendship between monks and prominent laity was an important feature of the monastic social landscape, it was not the kind of relationship with the outside world that most preoccupied monasteries. Far more time and effort were expended in the kinds of relationship outlined in the two previous chapters, in regard to donations, bequests and the balancing of spiritual favour with social and financial capital. One of the most helpful guides to understanding the interactions between monasteries and the lay world is Orderic Vitalis, a monk for most of his life at the Norman house of St Evroult. We have already encountered him as a critical observer of the early Cistercians through his vivid imagined reconstruction of the arguments between Robert of Molesmes and his monks in the 1090s leading to Robert's departure and the founding of Cîteaux.[53] In a long passage Orderic describes how his monastery acquired property in Ouche, in Normandy. Two Norman knights who were tenants of St Evroult, Anquetil of Noyers and Theodelin of Tanaisie, stole money and treasure that had been entrusted to them by Duke William to bring back to St Evroult from Norman settlers in Apulia. When the abbot of St Evroult asked for a full rendering of accounts, Anquetil admitted that he had spent some of the money as travel expenses, and deposited the rest at Rheims on the advice of another monk. Eventually, despite the assistance of the archbishop of Rheims, all that St Evroult was able to recover of the treasure was two chasubles, a silver chalice, an elephant's tooth and a griffin's claw. Summoned to judgement at the court of St Evroult, Anquetil was – unsurprisingly, given that the plaintiff was also the judge – sentenced to lose his fief. The most significant part of the story, however, is how the matter concluded.

> Finally, through the mediation of friends, an agreement was made between the two parties. Anquetil publicly confessed his guilt, gave pledges to Abbot Thierry, and humbly begged the monks for pardon; and as compensation for the loss they had sustained through his fault he granted to St Evroul before many witnesses the third part of the town of Ouche, which he had as his inheritance from his father, in token of which he laid on the altar a silken cloth which was used to make a cope for the cantor. Moved by this pious gift the monks charitably forgave his misdeeds, and graciously allowed him to keep the whole of his fief except the part that he had surrendered by the amicable compromise.[54]

The important point as far as the monks were concerned was that Anquetil should admit his fault in a public manner, and testify to it through a gift. There was probably no real sense in which the monastery wanted to deprive Anquetil of his fief in reality, which might have driven him to despoil its lands in the hope of recovering it. It was far better for both parties to come to an accommodation, and the 'mediation of friends' indicates that this was probably the expectation of all concerned. Although a great deal of surviving evidence indicates that monasteries frequently needed to protect their lands from neighbours' claims, there is no reason to suppose that monastic communities sought disputes as a means of increasing their holdings. In this case, Anquetil was likely to have been a better neighbour if left in possession of most of his fief – that is, had he not been killed soon afterwards.[55]

Sometimes monasteries formalised agreements through receiving into confraternity a layperson with whom they had previously been in dispute. In the early twelfth century (either 1114–17 or 1121–6), Robert de Ferrers paid 20s for ownership of woodland near the monastery of St Modwenna at Burton-on-Trent, and was received into the abbey's confraternity, as a way of concluding a resolution to a long-standing dispute.[56] What did the status of a *confrater* mean? This must have differed from one monastery to another even where the same terminology was employed. In 1089, Hugh, earl of Chester was admitted to confraternity at Abingdon Abbey 'so that I may become your brother, and likewise my wife and my father and mother . . . and so that we shall all be recorded in the Book of Commemoration'.[57] Guidelines for admitting laypeople to confraternity were laid down by Lanfranc in his *Constitutions*, and probably, like much else in them, derive ultimately from Cluny's customs.[58] It is probably more difficult to be precise about what it meant for the Greek Orthodox monk Meletos, the coadjutor archbishop of Gaza in the kingdom of Jerusalem, to be admitted to the confraternity of the Hospital of St John in the 1170s. According to the charter in which Meletos was given control over the monastery of St George at Bethgibelin as a base from which to exercise his office, he was also entitled to burial as a *confrater* of the Hospital.[59]

Anquetil's admission of guilt over the purloined treasure was designed to shame him not only in front of 'many witnesses' – presumably other tenant knights of the monastery and local ecclesiastical dignitaries – but also to St Evroult himself. As we saw in a previous chapter, Benedictine monasteries regarded themselves as communities of prayer under the protection of the saintly dedicatee of the monastery. The language employed by monastic chroniclers often reflected this, but it was in the context of threats to a monastery's property that it became most obvious. Geoffrey of Burton's *Life and Miracles of Modwenna* shows how a relatively small and obscure English monastery used a largely invented *vita* of the saint to list a set of miracles whose message was that the saint was a figure of power who was capable of protecting her servants. Many of the miracles concern acts of punishment or vengeance by the saint against those who tried to harm the material goods of the monastery, which of course belonged not to the abbot and monks but to the saint herself. A goldsmith who tried to cheat the saint of the gold and silver around her shrine on the pretext of selling it to provide alms for the poor but ran off with it himself managed, through the saint's intervention, to impale himself fatally on his own spear.[60] A royal official, Aelfwine, 'had no reverence for the virgin' and 'wished to injure her monks as much as he could' through the abuse of his authority. The saint took her revenge by causing him to poke out his own eye while drunkenly boasting one night to his friends of his latest misdeeds.[61] But perhaps the clearest indication of the intimate identification of the saint with the monastic community in this context occurs in the strange tale of the serfs of the village of Stapenhill. When two serfs of the monastery fled from its lordship to a neighbouring village, the dispute between the abbot and the neighbouring lord became violent. The community's response to the seizure of its food stores from the barns at Stapenhill was to involve St Modwenna directly through the ritual act of the humiliation of her relics by placing the shrine containing her bones on the ground.[62] This act had the desired effect: not only were the monastery's ten knights able to force the sixty of the neighbouring lord to flee 'through the merit of the virgin [i.e. Modwenna] and the power of God', but justice was eventually served to the runaway serfs. Most disputes between monasteries and their neighbours were on a less dramatic scale than this, of course: pigs loosed in another landowner's woods and feeding at his expense, cattle straying, and so on.[63] But anyone whose lands abutted those of a monastery could be reminded that they were dealing not only with unarmed religious but also with heavenly powers.

Monasteries in both East and West were indispensable as part of the social order in another important respect: charity. The *Rule of Benedict* assumed that a guest house would be a feature of every monastery, in accordance with Christian obligations of hospitality. Early Christians were aware that obligations of hospitality were also a feature of non-Christian society, but sought to differentiate between them. The fourth-century apologist Lactantius argued that when pagans offered hospitality it was part of a reciprocal relationship for advantage, whereas Christians gave hospitality especially to those who had nothing to offer in return.[64] In the Rule, particular honour was to be paid to the needy and to pilgrims. The abbot was to wash visitors' hands and feet personally and to take responsibility for feeding them, even to the point of breaking his own fast, so that the routine of the monastery was not disturbed.[65] In practice, this function was deputed to a guest master who ran a separate establishment within the monastery, though abbots might also take it on themselves to feed guests at their table and from their own income.[66]

The principle that monasteries should offer hospitality was already widespread in the sixth century, so there was nothing innovative about its inclusion in the Rule. Archaeological and literary evidence of *xenodochia*, or guest houses, at monasteries in the Judaean desert in the fifth century is plentiful from both cenobitic houses and *lavrae*. The Great Lavra of St Sabas had a *xenodochos*, or guest master, initially an office combined with that of cook.[67] In a *lavra*, the duties of cooking for guests may in fact have been more onerous than of providing meals for the monks, since for most of the week the monks prepared their own food in their cells. Some cenobitic monasteries in the region had more than one guest house. St Theodosius had three: for pilgrims of high status; for the poor; and for visiting monks. At St Euthymios and St George Choziba there were also guest masters. In most cases the visitors would probably have been pilgrims on their way either from one monastery to another as part of a spiritual exploration of the desert, or to or from Jerusalem.[68] The monastery of the Roidion refounded by Nikon in the late eleventh century in an as yet undetermined location in north Syria had a *xenodochium* for pilgrims on their way to the Holy Land. This was a route well known to monks from Asia Minor, but the timing of the foundation may also owe something to the First Crusade, and the typikon of the monastery makes allowance for Latin as well as Orthodox pilgrims. Indeed, Nikon's refounding of the monastery was designed around the hospice, the steward of which was the main administrative officer in the community.[69] The term *xenodochium* was also used to describe hospices for pilgrims maintained by monasteries in other major pilgrimage locations or routes, particularly on the routes to Rome and Compostela from the eleventh century onwards. The Augustinian monastery of San Juan de Ortega in eastern Castile was founded in 1150 as a resting place for pilgrims as they crossed the Oca range on their way towards Burgos and onwards to Compostela.

By the late tenth century, the *Regularis Concordia* stipulated daily alms-giving and the provision of food for the poor at the monastery gates. The alms were to be given to three poor men chosen daily from among those who were regularly fed by the monastery. The food itself was to be identical to that eaten by the monks, and to be brought out by the monks according to a rota.[70] Funding of the functions of the guest house might come from one of the manors or estates, or, as in Carolingian practice, from specific tithes.[71] The observances for the Hospital of Barnwell, an Augustinian foundation near Cambridge, specified that the guest master must be a man with 'elegant manners and of respectable upbringing'. But he should be no pushover: one of his functions was to watch out for guests 'accidentally' taking away with them property belonging to the priory.[72] Monasteries and individual abbots also sometimes went beyond regulatory expectations in special acts of charity. A severely disabled woman was supported by the monastery of Burton, and a disabled boy fed by the Malmesbury monks.[73] Abbot Aethelwig of Evesham (d. 1077/8) provided food for thirteen poor men daily from his household, as also did Abbot Samson of Bury St Edmunds a century later.[74]

Even monasteries that did not lie on pilgrimage routes might find themselves expected to provide hospitality, in the absence of a network of inns. Simply being located on or close to a road or port could make demands on a monastery to provide hospitality. The priory of Birkenhead, on the Wirral, complained to King Edward II that the burden of being the only place where travellers waiting for the ferry across the river Mersey could stay weighed too heavily on it.[75] A Chester chronicler remarked that the seats at the guest-house table had become worn through the numbers of travellers crossing the Irish Sea who needed to be fed in the monastery.[76] In thirteenth-century northern France and Flanders, nuns came to be especially associated with care of the chronically ill. Cistercian convents in particular were sometimes founded near or coalesced around existing hospitals. Anne Lester has suggested that an association between Cistercian nuns and active care-giving was cultivated by the nuns themselves, partly to emphasise what they *could* provide themselves rather than what they could not, namely offering masses.[77] The convent of Val-des-Vignes, near Bar-sur-Aube in Champagne, began in the 1230s to accumulate parcels of land near the small town of Ailleville, where there was a leper hospital.[78] The convent of La Cour-Notre-Dame de Michery, in the diocese of Sens, grew from a looser association of women living in a grange and ministering to a group of lepers. In this case, the leper hospital already existed, and in 1225 the nuns were recognised by the archbishop as a Cistercian community with a particular devotion to lepers.[79]

Monasteries that had important relics naturally attracted pilgrims. Even where there was no expectation of providing lodging for pilgrims, their presence entailed work for a monastic community. At St Foy in Conques, the monks took turns to stand guard over the reliquary while pilgrims kept nightly vigils in front of them.[80] Bernard of Angers, who made three pilgrimages to Conques in the eleventh century and recorded the miracles he had seen or heard about at the shrine of St Foy, complained to the monks about the 'little peasant songs and other frivolities' of the pilgrims during these vigils. The monks told him that in the past they had tried to keep the doors of the abbey church closed at night, allowing entry only to those they considered serious pilgrims who could chant the office, but the pilgrims noisily demanded to be let in. When the monks filed into the church for Matins they found that the bars holding the doors shut had miraculously been opened and the church was so full of people that they could hardly get into the choir. They concluded that it was the saint's wish to be honoured by the illiterate and frivolous as well as the learned.[81] When the newly discovered relics of SS Cuthbert and Oswald were displayed at Durham Cathedral Priory in 1104, there was 'a long queue of people going and coming back, and a great press of those jostling each other at the door, for they took delight in seeing over and over again what they had already seen once.'[82] The Durham monks were spared only by a rainstorm that dispersed the crowds. Suger, abbot of St Denis, wrote that the enlarging of the abbey church in the 1140s was necessary because it was too small for the mass of pilgrims crowding in to venerate the relics of the saint. On one occasion the monks fled the church through the window clasping the casket with St Denis's bones, in fear for their lives from the crush.[83]

Monasteries encountered the laity in many circumstances: as friends to be cherished and encouraged; as neighbours to be cultivated or kept in check; as travellers or supplicants in need of shelter and food; as pilgrims expecting to venerate the relics of the patron saint. The relationships between monastic communities and their tenants could be fraught, especially where monasteries exercised lordship in heavy-handed ways. But it is probably also the cases of disharmony or conflict that stand out in the sources rather than the more mundane neighbourly relations characterised by memorial prayer and masses, confraternity and mutual aid in times of need.

ECONOMY AND LAND MANAGEMENT

When Anselm talked of the cares and responsibilities of monks outside the cloister, he was thinking primarily of the problems associated with land ownership and management. The range of dealings that monasteries had with lay society as a result of land ownership was huge. As we have already seen, possession of landed estates meant ownership of villages and manors, and of the people living in them. Any monastery that owned land either had tenants whose labour made the land productive, thus providing the monastery's main income stream, or it had to find a way of doing the labour itself. The 'conjunction of worship and lordship', as James Clark memorably phrased it, meant both that monasteries became centres of administrative business connected with their estates, and also that they transformed the economic landscape of their regions.[84] Almost all monasteries and convents needed some kind of landed endowment in order to subsist, but the differences between the very wealthiest in terms of property, such as Cluny, Monte Cassino or Glastonbury, and a recent foundation with a few arable fields such as

St Evroult, Normandy, could be vast. The period between the later eleventh century and the later thirteenth marked a peak in the acquisition and exploitation of land by monasteries, especially Benedictine. By c. 1300 new acquisitions were limited by law in England through the Statute of Mortmain (1279), and throughout much of Europe by the effects of other types of legislation.[85] Patterns of giving to religious Orders also changed profoundly in the thirteenth century after the emergence of the mendicant Orders of friars. Although they do not form part of this book, it is worth noting briefly here that benefaction to mendicants was on the whole less demanding on the pocket. Since the friars typically owned smaller urban properties, they expected to run their operations from donations and bequests that probably came from a wider segment of society but that might range from a few pence to hundreds of pounds. In a society that was becoming increasingly urbanised and cash-using, the agility of the mendicants as active urban pastors marked them out in contrast with the monasteries.

It would be a mistake, however, to think of monasteries as mainly rural in contrast with urban friaries. Many towns, markets and villages owed their existence to monasteries and their patterns of land ownership.[86] Some of the largest and wealthiest monasteries – Bury St Edmunds being an obvious English example – effectively created towns around them. Even monasteries founded in pre-existing urban environments, such as St Albans in Roman Verulamium, altered the centre of economic gravity and patterns of activity.[87] Some monasteries – Westminster in England, Evergetis in Constantinople being two obvious examples – were deeply entrenched in cities. Just as monasteries gave many towns life in the first place, they also controlled their development. St Albans established a public school in the town to which tenants of the monastery who wanted their children to be educated to an elementary level were obliged to send them, in preference to any other school; in due course, this was reinforced by a ban on any other school in the town.[88] A tangible sign of monastic economic control over commercial enterprise in twelfth-century Jerusalem can still be seen in the inscription SCA ANNA carved into the stonework of a shop front, to mark ownership by the Benedictine convent of St Anne. In some respects this led to the curtailment of economic activity. At Bury St Edmunds, for example, the monastery's insistence on controlling the townspeople's supply of bread through its ownership of mills was an economic right that came to be greatly resented from the later twelfth century onwards. When Abbot Samson heard that a windmill had been set up within the area of the abbey's jurisdiction, he immediately sent carpenters to tear it down. The perpetrator – a rural dean – protested that he owned the corn and held his fief freely, and that the wind was free for anyone to use. Samson did not deny that the land was the dean's but argued that the right to erect and use a mill came under the 'liberties' of St Edmund. As he pointed out, the action the dean had taken was to the monastery's economic detriment, since the townspeople would be able to take their corn to his mill to be ground, which would mean a financial loss of mill fees to the monastery.[89] The early Cistercian statutes treated mills in the same way as tithes, and prohibited deriving an income from them, although mill ownership was permitted for the needs of milling the community's crop. Although the statute was repeated in the early thirteenth century, a papal bull of 1228 shows that some Cistercian monasteries were regularly infringing it through exploiting ownership of mills and ovens, which suggests that the income generated from them was too important to be given up.[90] When the townspeople of St Albans rebelled against the abbey's lordship in 1274 by using hand mills to grind their wheat rather than taking it to the mills, and refusing to take their cloth to the abbey's vats for fulling, the monastery sent agents throughout the town to find and confiscate or destroy the hand mills.[91] In 1326 the townspeople rioted, demanding the use of 'common custom' rather than proprietary lordship in woods, lands and fisheries belonging to the abbey. Although the rioters were successfully driven away by the monastery's 200 men at arms, Edward II subsequently ruled in the townspeople's favour in all measures save the use of hand mills.[92]

Abbot Samson proved to be a zealous advocate of the monastery's rights in the town. Jocelin of Brakelond gives as proof of his *probitas* (which could be translated as 'upstanding excellence') his expulsion of the Jewish community from Bury, on the grounds that 'everything that is in the town of St Edmund or within its liberties belongs of right to St Edmund: therefore the Jews must either be St Edmund's men or expelled from the town.'[93] As abbot, Samson even controlled entry to and egress from the town. When, after 1194, tournaments were permitted by Richard I, Samson refused to allow a group of eighty knights who had come to Bury for a pre-arranged tournament to leave the town to fight, and had the town gates locked and barred.[94] In the fourteenth century, the resentment of the town provoked rebellion against the monastery's lordship.[95]

The effects of monastic lordship on the landscape were often profound and far-reaching. As Jocelin of Brakelond said of Abbot Samson, 'he restored old halls and ruinous houses through which kites and crows were flying'. In addition, he built chapels and houses where previously there had only been barns, and created deer parks. The significance of these remarks by Jocelin is considerable, because such activities were not 'neutral' in terms of their effects on the social and economic landscape. The creation of deer parks entailed the enclosure of large tracts of land, usually mixed heath and woodland, for the exclusive use of the monastery and its guests. As Jocelin explained, Samson himself rarely ate venison (or any other kind of meat – his favourite foods were milk and honey!) but the obligation to feed guests to the monastery demanded a regular supply of meat.[96] The construction of chapels, likewise, meant the implanting of the monastery of Bury St Edmunds on to the landscape. Building a chapel meant establishing a priest to say Masses, thereby exercising the abbey's rights in ways that overlapped with the parochial structure. Samson was maximising the potential of the monastery's existing land by exploiting its use in new ways.

For most monasteries, especially Benedictine, revenues came mostly from agricultural surpluses. In this way, they were no different from secular landowners. The forms taken by agriculture naturally differed across Europe and the Mediterranean: in France and Flanders, southern England and most of the Byzantine Empire, this largely meant arable farming or viticulture, but in Germany, northern England and parts of Italy monasteries kept substantial herds and flocks, as also did some Byzantine monasteries. The monks of St John Patmos kept livestock on a neighbouring uninhabited island. These seem to have included beef cattle that were slaughtered every summer for sale on the commercial market.[97] Both in the West and in the Orthodox world, the predominant method of exploiting land ownership was through rentals to tenant farmers (*paroikoi* in the Byzantine world). In the thirteenth century, many landowners, at least in the West, opted to farm their estates directly rather than renting them out, to try to maximise income from agriculture at a time of inflation but fixed rents.[98] The organisation of the estates of Peterborough Abbey in the twelfth and early thirteenth centuries has been thoroughly studied, and provides a valuable window on to the mixed agricultural economy of an English monastery. At the monastery's grange at Biggin in 1310, for example, there were three officials – a reeve, forester and hayward – in charge of three carters, twelve ploughmen, four shepherds, a cowherd, a swineherd, a woman running the dairy and three casual labourers. Obviously these twenty-eight needed to be supplemented by piece-workers to reap, make hay, thresh the grain at harvest and so on, but labour services were also provided by villeins in villages in the monastery's ownership. The wage bill for this grange in 1310 came to £50, and included food for the workers' families.[99]

Anselm's metaphor of the mill and the grindstone shows how important the technological innovation represented by watermills (and to a lesser degree windmills) was to the monastic economy. In drier climates, monasteries obtained licences to irrigate lands by diverting water courses, such as when the Cistercian house at Staffarda in the Piedmont cut a channel from the Po in 1176.[100] Monasteries were heavily involved in the reclamation of marginal lands through deforestation (assarting) and wetland draining in areas such as East Anglia and the marshes of the Camargue.[101] But forests were also valuable natural resources for monasteries, especially for building, fuel from woodland undergrowth and beeswax for candles.[102] Likewise, rivers and wetlands could provide fish both for the refectory and for commercial resale, and other resources such as rushes and willows for making baskets.[103] Marsh land might also be valuable for grazing: at Meaux, 2,000 sheep grazed on the freshwater marshes of Wawne and Sutton.[104] Monasteries as remote from each other as Germany (Tegernsee and Niederaltaich) and Cyprus (Agios Nicolas near Limassol) benefited from the exploitation of salt – mines in the German examples, pans in Cyprus. Fulda and St Gall, in modern Switzerland, were involved in mining iron, Tavistock in Devon mined tin.[105] It is well known that Cistercian monasteries in England and Wales accrued great wealth from sheep farming, especially from the sale of wool, but the range of types of land utilisation was considerable. The type of farming depended on local conditions and soil types. Although wheat was the favoured cereal crop throughout Europe, Beaulieu in Hampshire grew oats as well as wheat, and Aubepierre largely rye, which was more productive on its assarted land. The German Cistercian monastery of Schöntal likewise grew more rye than wheat, and Pásztó in Hungary mostly barley.[106]

Exploitation of land and resources needed substantial investment and management. Constructing a watermill, for example, meant acquiring timber for the mill itself, quarrying the millstones, and in many cases also flooding a riverine area to form a mill-pond, and putting in a path for access. All this required expertise and the ability to manage a workforce. Monasteries were often regarded by their neighbours as especially expert in land management, and their advice was sought out.[107] But some monastic congregations developed a reputation for particularly canny land management, in contrast with others. In a typically waspish passage that has become celebrated as a contemporary perception of different styles of monastic land use, Gerald of Wales observed that whereas the Cluniacs ruined landed estates, the Cistercians enriched them:

> Give the Cluniacs today a tract of land covered with marvellous buildings, endow them with ample revenues and enrich the place with vast possessions: before you can turn round it will all be ruined and reduced to poverty. On the other hand, settle the Cistercians in some barren retreat which is hidden away in an overgrown forest: a year or two later you will find splendid churches there and fine monastic buildings, with a great amount of property and all the wealth you can imagine.[108]

As with all such generalisations, there is a good deal of exaggeration for effect here. Gerald was writing in the early thirteenth century, after a long career in the administration of the Church in south Wales, as archdeacon of St David's, and extensive travel throughout Wales. The timing is significant both on a personal level and in terms of the wider observation. Gerald's disappointment at being passed over for preferment made him rather a jaundiced commentator on the Church, and much of his irritation was directed at monasteries and their communities, many of which he considered to be lazy, lax in following the Rule, or exploitative. But there is also a streak of realism in his remark. The later twelfth and early thirteenth century was also a period of high inflation across Europe in which landowners who relied for their income on rents from tenancies suffered economically. Because most Benedictine monasteries were probably in this position at this period, Gerald's remark about ruination and poverty is a reflection of the difficulty of making a profit from land ownership. A 'tract of land covered with marvellous buildings' sounds like an evocation of the typical landed estates of monasteries that included agricultural tenancies, and it was precisely these that monasteries found such a financial drain. At least in the West, the thirteenth century saw a return to more widespread direct cultivation of estates on the part of landowners. In a sense, the Cistercians were ahead of this trend, since, as we saw, the particular ideological understanding they conferred on the *Rule of Benedict* did not permit them to accept land that was already in cultivation or settled by existing habitation.

Cistercian land management was based on the grange, which was essentially a model farm staffed by *conversi* and other agricultural labourers.[109] Some were a considerable distance away from the monastery, despite the ruling that they should be located no more than a day's walk so that *conversi* could observe Sundays and feasts at the monastery. Grandselve had a grange for livestock that was 140 km from the abbey; Øm had one with a limestone quarry 90 km away.[110] Consequently *conversi* were sometimes based there during the critical periods of sowing, harvest, lambing and so on, depending on the type of agriculture. Granges might form a compact bloc of farmland or be scattered across a wide region and disconnected from each other. Many were typically located on the edges of parish boundaries, but they could also cross into parishes. As Gerald of Wales was aware, Cistercian ideals and practices with regard to land management were often achieved at the expense of local communities. The Welsh Cistercian abbey of Dore created its granges by destroying villages on its lands, and the same happened at Melrose in the Scottish borders and Fountains in Yorkshire. Nine villages were displaced to create granges for the monastery of Plasy. At

Kirkstall, also in Yorkshire, the abbot even pulled down a parish church and ejected tenants in the village served by the church on the grounds that their presence interfered with the monastery's solitude. A subsequent appeal to the archbishop of York proved useless; both the archbishop, Henry Murdac, and Pope Eugenius III were Cistercians and upheld the abbot's decision.[111] This kind of practice led one early thirteenth-century commentator to remark tartly that, 'In churchyards, over men's bodies, [the Cistercians] have built pigsties, and their asses lie where men used the chant the Mass.'[112]

Other examples show more concern for populations that might be displaced by Cistercian practices. King John intervened on behalf of villagers threatened by grange creation or extension by Neath and Kingswood.[113] It is difficult to assess the overall effects of this apparently harsh policy across Europe. At Byland (Yorkshire), displaced villagers were resettled elsewhere; at Lubiąz the villeins became free, but presumably still had to relocate; while at Margam in Wales they became *conversi*, and at Furness simply hired labour for the monastery.[114] Conrad of Eberbach, who composed the *Exordium magnum*, an important text for understanding how the Cistercians saw themselves in *c.* 1200, thought that many peasants were forced into becoming *conversi* by necessity. It is impossible to know whether, by and large, the peasantry might have benefited from these changes of status and location, as has been suggested was sometimes the case.[115] But it is difficult, on a human level, not to see Cistercian policy as an ideology imposed on people by an aristocratic elite without much thought for rural populations.

In practice, there were many exceptions to the implementation of Cistercian policy. For one thing, many of the Cistercian houses were not originally founded as such, but absorbed from other reforming congregations that had collapsed, such as the Savignacs. These houses, like Furness Abbey in Cumbria, or virtually all the convents for women that came to be absorbed into the Cistercians, had been founded with substantial landed endowments that formed the basis of their income, and it would have been impossible to do away with these.[116] Besides this, there were plenty of occasions on which Cistercian houses seem simply to have bypassed or ignored restrictions. Before the end of the twelfth century some Cistercian houses were already behaving in the way they criticised in traditional practices, and leasing land out to non-monastic communities. In 1180 for example, Poblet, in Aragon, leased out a grange to the bishops of Huesca and Pamplona for an annual rent of 500 measures of wheat and barley, and from the 1190s Fountains, North Yorkshire, was also leasing out lands.[117] In the first quarter of the thirteenth century the chapter-general of the Cistercians tried to deal repeatedly with the problem through regulation and concession.[118] What might happen to communities that relied on direct farming alone is demonstrated by the cases of Meaux in 1155 and Waverley in 1203 and 1210, both of which had to disband temporarily when their harvests failed.

Such lapses from their own regulations have led some historians to view the statutes as simply ideological rhetoric with little reflection of the reality in the fields. Gerald's observations of Cistercians in England and Wales, however, would seem to suggest that there was more to it than this. In the passage quoted above, he evokes the picture of a 'typical' Cistercian settlement in barren, uncultivated land. In this picture, the implication is that the work of clearing, building and planting has been accomplished by the monks themselves through the sweat of their brow, which conforms to the ideological imperative in early Cistercian sources about a return to manual labour. There is some evidence in early sources that monks engaged in founding new reforming communities did clear land and contribute to the construction of the first monastic buildings.[119] But the system of *conversi*, or lay brothers, was designed to enable the Cistercians to make the claim that the Order performed manual labour, even when most of it was not done by the choir monks. As we have already seen, manual labour was largely a symbolic act in most established western monasteries by *c*. 1100, so the Cistercian system was very much in line with contemporary norms. Where land was leased out for rent, however, we can probably assume that this was because even with *conversi*, the extent of land was simply too great to be farmed entirely by the community. *Conversi*, indeed, seem already by the later twelfth century to have served in a supervisory capacity on the granges, partly because they were skilled labourers and partly because they were outnumbered by hired seasonal labour.[120] It is difficult to know the extent of the *conversi* labour force, but the proportion of 140 monks to 500 *conversi* reported at Rievaulx in the abbacy of Ailred (1147–67) seems rather high, and by the 1280s in any case at some German houses they had shrunk to somewhere between parity and 1:2.[121]

Most of what we know about land management and use in Orthodox monasteries comes from the foundation typika, though here the information is often sparse or highly generalised.[122] Konstantinos Smyrlis has suggested that typika across a wide geographic spread, including Bulgaria, Asia Minor, Cyprus and Sicily, show an increased interest in the economic well-being of monasteries from the eleventh century onwards, and the development of more complex techniques of financial management.[123] This corresponds, of course, to the period in which cenobitic monasticism was undergoing more widespread reform. The basic model of estate management was a division between the central administration of the monastery, in the hands of the *hegoumen* or in practice more often the *oikonomos* or steward, and local superintendents at the estates or *metochoi*. The delegated management of estates might, in the case of larger monasteries, be carried out by laymen under the supervision of the steward. A local *metochiarios* or steward of a dependent estate usually lived there, often with monks or lay servants assigned to it. Sometimes, as was the case with St John Patmos, a monastery founded in a remote location had to import estate workers. The founder, Christodoulos, initially wanted to use only unmarried male workers but found that in order to provide sufficient labour he was obliged to found a colony of lay workers with their families at the far end of the island from the monastery. The families were confined to their part of the island while the workers spent the week at or near the monastery.[124] The monastery of Pantokrator, an imperial foundation, was endowed with estates that already had their own system of management, which it retained.[125] The intention was probably to ensure that monks did not have occasion to leave the monastery for purely administrative reasons. In general, monasteries founded by monks or that developed organically, whether from cenobitic origins such as Evergetis or eremitic like Makhairas, tended to reserve management for the monks rather than outsourcing to laity. Like western monasteries, they also sought to make the land in their ownership as productive as possible, which included purchase and settlement of peasant workers. Monasteries bought, sold and exchanged land. Neophytos the Recluse, somewhat reluctantly, bought enough land for cultivation to require building a grain store, and also some livestock, in order to provide an income stream for the Enkleistra in the 1190s, when as a result of the Latin Conquest of Cyprus and the impoverishment of local landowners, the monastery could no longer rely on donations from its previous patrons.[126] St Sabas in the Judaean desert sold three villages that had originally been gifted by Queen Melisende to the Augustinian community of the Holy Sepulchre in 1163/4, and with the proceeds purchased a property from the crown of Jerusalem. The term used in the Latin charter, *vastina*, implies in the context of the Levant either arable or pasture.[127] The pilgrimage account of John Phokas (1185) notes the arable land owned by the Orthodox monasteries in the Jordan Valley. Arable land, of course, required some livestock in the form of draft animals for plough, and some typika specify numbers of animals. Pakourianos owned forty-seven pairs of oxen, which would seem to indicate extensive arable holdings.[128]

Whatever practices a monastery adopted in managing its estates entailed interactions with wider society. The ownership and use of land meant dealing with tenants, villeins, estate workers and families; ensuring that farms and houses were maintained and that wages were paid; and that rents in kind and coin were collected. Even where *conversi* rather than monks managed granges or farms, the liaison between monastic officials and estate management entailed internal processes that overlaid the core profession of the monk, and especially the *opus Dei*, in exactly the manner that Anselm tried to communicate in his extended simile.

BISHOPS AND MONASTERIES

Soon after the death of Pope Innocent II in 1143, a Mass in the parish church at Ligio, in the Galilee region of the Holy Land, was interrupted violently one day when a clerk of the archbishop of Nazareth burst in at the moment of the elevation of the Host and assaulted the celebrant. Only the intervention of the congregation saved the priest from suffering serious injury. The celebrant was either a monk of the Benedictine monastery of Notre-Dame de Josaphat, or a chaplain appointed by the monastery. When the monks threatened to appeal to the archbishop's superior, the patriarch of Jerusalem, they were taunted with the retort:

'What good are your Roman privileges to you now? The pope [who granted them] is dead, and unless you make peace with [the archbishop], you will have nothing.'[129]

This was the culmination of a long-running dispute between the monastery and the archbishopric of Nazareth. Notre-Dame de Josaphat, situated just outside the eastern wall of Jerusalem in the Kidron Valley, was one of the wealthiest and most prestigious monasteries in the Holy Land.[130] The shrine served by the monastery, the tomb of the Blessed Virgin, had been venerated by Christians since the fourth century, but the monastery was founded and generously endowed by Godfrey of Bouillon after the First Crusade for a group of monks he had brought with him.[131] A papal letter of May 1145 confirms Notre-Dame's possession of the two churches of Ligio and Thanis in the Galilee, with their tithes.[132] Robert, the archbishop of Nazareth, refused to accept their rights, and at one point had the locks of the church broken and the monks who served the church ejected, only to be brought to heel by the patriarch after a plea by the monks to Rome.[133] After Innocent II's death, the archbishop installed his own chaplain in the church to serve as parish priest. For a short while the church seems to have been used by both the monks and the archbishop's chaplain, but this compromise clearly broke down, and Pope Eugenius III was asked by Notre-Dame to reconfirm the original grant of tithes and property. The case was not settled until 1161, when a successor as archbishop of Nazareth recognised the right of Notre-Dame to administer the parish through its own monks, but at the same time insisted on the right of canonical obedience from any priests appointed to serve the church.[134]

The grant of parish churches and their income to monasteries cut into the main source of diocesan income: parochial tithes. In fact, they were especially important in the Latin East, because there were far fewer parish churches than in the West, which meant dioceses were often in financial difficulties. Notre-Dame, one of the wealthiest monastic establishments in the East, had only thirteen parochial benefices throughout the kingdom of Jerusalem, the county of Tripoli and the principality of Antioch, but by *c.* 1150 it already owned thirty-three churches in southern Italy.[135] Monasteries such as Notre-Dame, which could appeal to pilgrims because it contained the important shrine of the Tomb of the

Blessed Virgin, were able to compensate for the shortfall in tithe income in Outremer with substantial bequests and grants in the West. The loss of parochial tithes probably meant more in financial terms to the archdiocese of Nazareth than did the gain to the monastery, as implied in the archbishop's demand that he would not agree to any accord to end the dispute unless Notre-Dame guaranteed compensation of half the tithes, or a mark of gold.[136] Eventually the monks of Notre-Dame seem to have agreed to pay an annual sum of a mark, together with a roll of wax and one of incense.

A similar though less contentious case arose from Notre-Dame's possession of a church dedicated to St George outside the city of Tiberias.[137] In a concordat drawn up in 1178 the monks were accused of drawing parishioners away from the cathedral parish, thereby threatening its financial health. The concordat prohibited the monks serving St George from conducting baptisms, marriages or the purification of women, and permitted burials only of monks or Orthodox Christians in the cemetery of St George's.[138] These details are important because they show precisely what was at stake between bishops and monasteries with ownership of parish churches: all of these rites carried extra fees or offerings from parishioners that would normally have gone to support the parish priest, but which would also contribute to the running of the diocese. In both the Ligio and St George cases, the monks seem to have built up strong congregations – at Ligio, one that was prepared to take the monks' side and stand up to the violence offered by the archbishop's chaplain. This *may* attest to the greater appeal of monks as parish priests than those appointed by bishops, though this would be difficult to prove.

The Ligio–Nazareth case emerged in the pontificate of Eugenius III. Of the thousand-odd surviving privileges datable to Eugenius's reign, 367 were to monasteries, and most of these, like the case of Notre-Dame, were responses to petitions from monastic communities asking for protection of property or rights.[139] Given that Eugenius was a Cistercian monk, but had before that been for many years a diocesan official, it would be interesting to know whether such petitions suggest that communities expected to find him sympathetic to their problems. The Notre-Dame case bears some general similarities with a more complex three-cornered affair centred on the Cluniac monastery of Vézelay, in Burgundy, which seems to have begun in earnest in 1146.[140] The Vézelay monks were defending their possessions against the count of Nevers, and their exempt status against the bishop of Autun. The bishop's argument was that since he performed ordinations of Vézelay monks to the priesthood, consecrated its altars and had rights of visitation, exempt status was inappropriate for the abbey. This may have followed similar claims made by French bishops over monasteries in their dioceses at the Council of Rheims in 1148.[141] Although at the Council Eugenius had dismissed all these claims, three years later he tried to reconcile the Vézelay case by appointing judges-delegate to examine the documentation provided by Abbot Pons in support of the monastery's claim to exemption and to take depositions from the bishop's witnesses.[142] When the judges decided in Vézelay's favour in 1151, the bishop joined forces with William, count of Nevers, in resuming a campaign of harassment: stealing horses and oxen belonging to the abbey; kidnapping servants; injuring men and damaging property. William argued that the monastery had undermined comital authority in the first place by levying tolls on roads leading to Vézelay.[143] At one stage Abbot Pons was forced into exile by a direct assault on the monastery, and Eugenius placed the town under interdict. The whole affair remained unresolved on Eugenius's death in 1153.[144]

The development of papal bureaucracy lies outside the scope of this study, but what we see in these cases is the huge increase in administrative business transacted by the papal curia. From around the middle of the twelfth century (and the pontificate of Eugenius III may have been a critical phase) the practical dimensions of the centralisation of papal governance began to take shape. We have focused here on a couple of examples in depth to illustrate the wider problem, but almost any number of similar cases could be deployed to make the same point. To put it bluntly, bishops almost always had problems with monasteries in their dioceses; or vice versa. Often it is difficult to know which side in an argument was in the right.

Questions of jurisdiction and authority were not restricted to Latin Christendom. Despite the clear ruling of the Council of Chalcedon (451) placing monasteries under the jurisdiction of the diocesan, Byzantine emperors could enable favoured monasteries to evade this oversight. Manuel Komnenos, for example, instructed the diocesan to grant 'stauropegial' status to the monastery of Makhairas in Cyprus (1178/80), which meant that it was removed from his jurisdiction and placed directly under the patriarch of Constantinople.[145] This – along with a generous financial stipend – was the outcome of an appeal in person to the emperor by two of the monks immediately after the death of the founder. In contrast, another Cypriot monastery founded around the same time had a very different relationship with the diocesan. The monastery of the Enkleistra was founded in 1159 by the solitary monk Neophytos. Previously a novice at the monastery of St John Chrysostom at Koutsovendis in the northeast of the island, Neophytos became a wandering solitary in the Holy Land in his twenties, then returned to Cyprus where he started to occupy, then enlarge, a cave in the cliffs near Paphos in the west of the island. In 1166, the new bishop of Paphos, Basil Kinnamos, started to take an interest in Neophytos and his cave cell and church. After four years of (in Neophytos's view) ceaseless urging, Neophytos agreed to be ordained, and to take in other monks rather than living as a solitary.[146] This effectively created a monastery rather than a hermitage at the Enkleistra, and over the next twenty-five years the monastery developed into a community of possibly as many as two dozen.[147] As we saw in a previous chapter, the process of founding a monastery in the Byzantine world was such that the Chalcedon canon requiring episcopal consent was not invariably followed. In practice, any layperson could declare private property to be a monastery. The eleventh-century monastic founder Lazaros never received permission from the metropolitan of Ephesus to found his monastery at Mount Galesion, and in his final years he had to resist pressure from the later holder of that office to close down the monastery and send the monks elsewhere.[148]

Matters were more complicated in regions where Greek monasteries existed under the Latin Church hierarchy. In 1133 Roger II of Sicily created a system in which his kingdom's Greek monasteries were subordinated to the head of the newly founded monastery of San Salvatore, Messina, who was given the title of 'archimandrite'. The *hegoumenoi* of the subordinated monasteries continued to rule them, but the archimandrite had rights not dissimilar to those of visitation in the West.[149] In the kingdom of Jerusalem, an attempt was made in the 1170s to assign to the *hegoumen* of St Sabas supervisory rights over Orthodox populations in the southern parts of the kingdom, but nothing comparable to the position of archimandrite seems to have been created. In principle, Orthodox monasteries came under the oversight of Latin bishops. This was because the Latin and Orthodox Churches were technically in communion and there could therefore only be one bishop for each diocese. In practice in the Crusader Levant this was almost always a Latin, unlike in southern Italy, where Greek-rite bishops were common well into the thirteenth century.[150] In Cyprus, a conquest made by Richard I in 1191, a Greek episcopal hierarchy – albeit reduced – was permitted to co-exist along lines not dissimilar to the situation in Italy, but after 1231 the Latin Church hierarchy assumed greater powers, including over Greek monasteries on the island. In a notorious episode, thirteen monks of the monastery of Kantara were judicially executed for refusal to recognise Latin ecclesiastical authority, but this was an extreme and anomalous case.[151]

The most contentious issue in the West was over the rights of bishops to 'visit' – effectively, to inspect – a monastery. A protracted case involved Evesham Abbey, Worcestershire, and Mauger, bishop of Worcester, between 1195 and 1206. According to the *Evesham Chronicle*, visitations could take place as often as the bishop wanted. Mauger would descend on the abbey with his servants and officials, stabling and feeding their horses at the abbey's expense, and expecting to be lodged and fed in the abbey guest house.[152] Episcopal visitations became more common after 1215, when the Fourth Lateran Council confirmed what had in fact been canonically the case since the fifth century, namely that bishops had rights of oversight over monasteries in their dioceses.[153] Even so, bishops seem to have exercised their rights patchily in different parts of Christendom. In Italy, for example, we know about visitations undertaken by bishops in the dioceses of Pistoia between *c.* 1225 and 1250, at Città di Castello in 1230 and Brindisi in 1245. In Germany there were visitations in the dioceses of Cologne in 1261, Mainz between 1271 and 1300 and Passau from 1258 to 1301. The lack of much evidence for visitations from the Iberian peninsula, however, suggests that they were rare.[154] It is difficult to arrive at firm conclusions because our knowledge of visitations depends on the survival of episcopal records. There is a remarkably full record of hundreds of visitations of monasteries and convents undertaken by the archbishop of Rouen, Eudes Rigaud, between 1248 and 1269, and we may surmise that he is unlikely to have been the only French prelate exercising this right even where other diocesan registers do not survive.[155] But both the frequency and scale of visitations, and their recording in registers, must also have depended to a degree on the conscientiousness of the bishop. Sometimes a visitation might be requested by a monastery, as for example when Jocelin, bishop of Bath, visited Montacute in response to a complaint to King John about the prior from the subprior. In general, however, there seems to have been suspicion and scepticism about the process.

Given that the canonical principle of episcopal jurisdiction was of such long standing throughout the Church in both East and West, we may well wonder why monasteries expended so much energy in resisting it. As Peter of Blois, humanist scholar and civil servant, expressed it in a letter to Pope Alexander III in 1180 on behalf of the archbishop of Canterbury, abbots resented having someone set over them to correct their excesses; on the other hand, to allow them to act without oversight was tantamount to inciting rebellion, and 'the arming of sons against their parents'.[156] The exact opposite point of view was articulated by the Vézelay chronicler Hugh of Poitiers, describing the attempts of the bishop of Autun to enforce visitation and to 'reduce [the monastery] to the status of a subordinate parish within his diocese . . . and to make it obedient to his synods'.[157] These inflammatory words show what was at stake for monastic communities. They were resisting arbitrary exercise of authority that would make 'cowled champions' – the spiritual army of God, the servants of the saints, the inhabitants of the heavenly Jerusalem – indistinguishable from parish priests. The capacity of monks and nuns to resist episcopal authority was centred on precisely this sense of their spiritual power. When the archbishop of Bourges tried to keep the body of the recently deceased Robert of Arbrissel for burial at Orsan, where he had died, the nuns of Fontevraud went on hunger strike until he relented and agreed to release the body to the abbey he had founded: 'We are no longer your daughters and will no longer pray for you and yours until you return our good father to us.'[158]

What happened in practice when a bishop 'visited' a monastery in his diocese? When Robert Winchelsey, archbishop of Canterbury, visited

Christ Church in 1296, he went first into the chapter house and preached to the community. He then announced his intention to interview each brother in turn in the presence of his chancellor and clerk. On the grounds that these officials were 'seculars', the chapter refused to admit them, and a compromise was reached whereby the witnesses were the archdeacon of Middlesex and Archbishop Winchelsey's chaplain, both of whom were ordained priests. Questions were limited before these witnesses to issues that pertained to the whole community, but once the archdeacon had withdrawn, Winchelsey questioned each monk more personally. A month later the archbishop returned and held a conference with the obedientiaries in which he made corrections to various practices and levied penances. A series of written complaints was read out to the prior, to which he responded orally.[159] So much for the procedure. To know more about the nature of such an inspection, we can do no better than take an example of a visitation from Archbishop Eudes Rigaud's register. On 16 July 1265, for example, the archbishop went to the Cistercian convent of nuns at St Saëns, in Normandy. The register records that he 'found the nuns living in disorder and not according to the Rule'. Among his criticisms were that they often recited the offices, even on Sundays, 'without modulation' (i.e. not chanting). They ate in separate groups rather than together, and they were infrequent in confessing. Their finances were in a poor state and they had inadequate supplies of grain to last until the harvest later that summer. The archbishop instructed the prioress to ensure that the chapel of a manor in their ownership was provided with a regular chaplain. The next day, he assembled the nuns in the chapter house and received their submission, which was put in writing and sealed by the prioress and the archdeacon.[160] This was not the archbishop's first visit to St Saëns. On his first visit, in January 1250, he remarked on their custom of receiving presents – presumably from lay donors. By 1259, worse had been revealed, including two pregnancies of one of the nuns and the irregular reception of nieces of members of the community as novices. On his visitation that summer he lost his temper and in the chapter house tore up the letters on which the promises to the girls had been made.[161]

Prelates on visitations generally had little compunction about using ceremony to make their authority felt. The monks or nuns were expected to turn out in force, singing psalms and processing outside the gates to greet him and escort him inside the precinct. Penelope Johnson has rightly remarked that the ceremonial surrounding the visitation probably marked a welcome break in the routine for many communities; on the other hand, the whole tenor of the occasion, culminating in the act of submission, was clearly designed to assert the kind of authority articulated by Peter of Blois.[162] Yet, as she observed, the case of St Saëns may also make us wonder whether any of this had much effect on the way the community conducted its affairs. The example of the Norman convent of Montivilliers is a case in point. In 1215 the nuns walked out of the chapter house when during an episcopal visitation the archdeacon started to preach a homily.[163] This was the denouement of a long-standing dispute over the convent's supposed exemption from the bishop of Fécamp: specifically, over its rights to place its own clerics in churches whose ownership it claimed. Subsequently, the nuns resisted the rights of Eudes Rigaud to visit them at all.[164] To put this into perspective, Eudes Rigaud's register records visitations of eighty-two monastic communities over the years between 1248 and 1269, of which sixty-one were for men, fourteen for women, and seven were mixed hospitals. Johnson's analysis of the register suggests that although Eudes usually found faults whenever he made a visitation, on the whole he was more critical of women's convents than male monasteries.[165] This may be because, consciously or otherwise, he held nuns to a higher standard of conduct than monks; on the other hand, it may also signal the sorts of difficulty to which Heloise had drawn attention more than a century earlier that nuns encountered in trying to observe a Rule written with men in mind.

The process of visitation, regardless of consequences, seems to have made some communities suspicious about any attempt by bishops to exercise leadership. In 1248, Matthew Paris, the St Albans chronicler, complained about the bishop of Durham's apparent violation of St Albans' exempt status by visiting the abbey's dependent priory at Tynemouth. Two years later he recorded an unrelated episode in which Robert Grosseteste, bishop of Lincoln, demanded that all monks in the diocese assemble to hear a papal mandate. Matthew observed caustically that this was really a pretext for getting revenues in the hands of monasteries back into episcopal control.[166] This was a common suspicion, expressed in a variety of circumstances. For wealthy monasteries, it was sometimes well founded. Roger, bishop of Salisbury (1125–39), managed to 'annex' Malmesbury Abbey into his see on the grounds that it had once been an episcopal seat, and his successor used this as a pretext for exacting payments for dedications.[167]

ABBOTS AND THE GOVERNANCE OF MONASTERIES

It was not only external intervention that distracted monks and nuns from their routine. As prior and then abbot, Anslem understood only too well the demands on the time and concentration of heads of monastic communities. The abbot or abbess was ultimately responsible for the material as well as the spiritual health of the community, which meant that skills in leadership were indispensable. Perhaps as a reflection of the burdens of responsibility on heads, during the period after 1100, the relationships between abbots and their communities started to change. In the later eleventh century, even the abbot of the largest and most influential monastery in western Europe, Cluny, lived with his community and slept in the dormitory. By *c.* 1200 this can only rarely have been the case, as abbots became increasingly distant physically from their communities. As early as *c.* 1110 Faricius, the abbot of Abingdon, is reported as dining apart from his monks, though like Anselm he invited selected monks to dine with him at his table.[168] As Knowles suggested, we can probably assume that abbots also stopped sleeping in dormitories at the same time as they took meals separately.[169] The Benedictine chapter of the Canterbury province held in 1218–19 reminded abbots that they should try as far as possible to attend chapter (which, of course, they were supposed to run) and the offices, and to be present in the cloister and refectory 'for brotherly consolation' whenever possible. The inference of such an injunction is that this was far from often the case.[170]

In the English context, this development may have arisen from the practice of separating the income and assets of the monastery to provide abbots with a different income stream from that of the community. In the past, this development has been attributed to the need to protect monastic estates from their use by the crown. In the 1090s, William Rufus claimed the rights to enjoy the income of monastic estates during a vacancy (in other words, in the gap between the death of one abbot or abbess and the election of another). Separation of income streams meant that if the king could enjoy the abbot's revenues, at least those going straight to the community could be protected.[171] Consequently, abbots established separate households who also had to be housed and fed, and this led to the full separation of abbots from their communities. This is certainly what seems to have happened, but as we have already seen, it was not only in England that monasteries could be exposed to the claims of powerful lords. The development of separate establishments for abbots and abbesses seems to have been common across most of western Europe, even among abbots who regarded themselves as reformers.

'It is an arduous task to rule souls, and to adapt oneself to so many dispositions,' observed Richard of Wallingford, the fourteenth-century abbot of St Albans.[172] Elias, a twelfth-century abbot of the Cluniac priory of Palmaria, in the kingdom of Jerusalem, would have agreed wholeheartedly. Having originally come to the Holy Land as a pilgrim, probably in the 1120s, Elias lived as a hermit before joining the monastery of Notre-Dame de Josaphat. He was elected prior of Palmaria, which seems to have been a monastery with eremitical foundations. His rule as prior was so disastrous because of his inability to deal with financial affairs that he appealed to Queen Melisende to be allowed to resign and return to Jerusalem, but was later forcibly reinstated at Palmaria by the archbishop of Nazareth.[173]

A complete picture of how a twelfth-century abbot managed his community and the monastery is provided by the remarkable account of Samson, abbot of Bury St Edmunds (1135–1211) by the Bury monk Jocelin of Brakelond.[174] Samson became abbot in 1182, inheriting a large and ancient monastery with a prestigious shrine to the martyr St Edmund, king of East Anglia, but burdened with debt as a result of poor administration. One of the problems that Samson attempted to reform was the tendency not only to split income streams between abbot and community, but to further assign an income stream from different estates to each obedientiary (officeholder) in the monastery. Thus the cellarer, guest master, sacristan, and so on, each funded the operations of their office from the income of estates that they controlled. Similar arrangements were in place in most large houses during the twelfth century and beyond. The *Waltham Chronicle* lists the arrangements for supplies of food to the canons, according to which the different prebendaries provided for set periods of weeks each year.[175]

In principle the idea of separate budget-holding may have made administrative sense, and it is easy to see how such a system developed out of the initial development of the separate abbatial household. But it turned out to be disastrous at Bury, because it meant that obedientiaries could conceal their financial activities from the abbot. The cellarer in particular was constantly in debt, because he arranged private loans to make up the shortfall from his mismanaged income in order to be able to feed the community.[176] Eventually Samson dealt with this by appointing a clerk from his own household to oversee the cellarer's activities. At one point he even took back into his own hands all the seals of the obedientiaries and tried to run their offices through the monastic chapter, though this proved to be too great an administrative burden.[177] According to Jocelin, relations between Samson and his monks deteriorated so far in 1199 that he stayed away from the monastery for fear that they would murder him.[178]

Bury was certainly not the only monastery in the later twelfth and early thirteenth centuries where tensions arose between abbot and community over the domestic economy. Sometimes these were provoked by mismanagement from the head of the community rather than officeholders. In the thirteenth century Prior John de Tycford ruined the Cluniac house at Bermondsey through accepting loans from a moneylender, then when he moved to Wenlock in 1272 proceeded to sell off the house's wool futures for the next seven years. William Somerton, the early fourteenth-century prior of Binham, in Norfolk, a dependent priory of St Albans, wasted the priory's resources by investing in a fraudulent get-rich-quick scheme – giving money to a mendicant alchemist who promised he would turn base metal into gold.[179]

But a particularly notorious case arose at Evesham in the last year of the twelfth century. Roger Norreis (d. 1223) had been a monk at Christ Church Canterbury, where he incurred the odium of the community by betraying their trust when in 1187 he was sent on a mission to Henry II to appeal the monastery's case against Archbishop Baldwin, who was trying to found a house of secular canons in Canterbury. He allowed himself to be suborned by Baldwin – who as archbishop was of course abbot of Christ Church – in return for the appointment as cellarer. The furious monks refused to accept him and imprisoned him, but he escaped through the sewer, thus acquiring the nickname Roger Cloacarius ('Drain-Cleaner'). Archbishop Baldwin, in an act of deliberate provocation, tried to appoint Roger to the vacant position of prior, but the monks appealed to the pope against him. By the end of 1189, Roger had been 'elected' to the abbacy of Evesham, evidently through the support of Baldwin and the new king, Richard I.[180] As abbot of Evesham, Roger seems to have behaved as badly as the Christ Church monks had feared he would at Canterbury. He got drunk, openly consorted with women and even abandoned the monastic habit for secular clothing; he also appropriated estates belonging to the community for his own use. Roger may have thought that he could get away with this high-handed behaviour because the monks, although despising his lack of monastic dignity, shared a common interest with him in resisting the attempts by Bishop Mauger of Worcester to conduct visitations of the monastery. Indeed, in 1205 when Mauger tried to excommunicate Roger the monks stood by him despite their mutual antipathy. Although the abbey's exemption from visitation was upheld on appeal to Rome, a full investigation by the papal legate in 1213 revealed the extent of Roger's mismanagement of his office. One of the monks, Thomas of Marlborough – on whose account in the *Evesham Chronicle* most of our knowledge of the affair rests – gave a long public testimony to the legate in which he enumerated Roger's failings.[181] The main elements of the monks' complaint were that he had been 'intruded' into the community against their will and uncanonically, that he committed simony and that he had deprived the monks of adequate food and clothing.[182] As a result of Thomas's testimony, Norreis was deposed as abbot and sent to the abbey's dependent cell at Penwortham, now a suburb of Preston in Lancashire.

The case of Roger Norreis is doubtless unusual in the scale and wilfulness of his depredation. The chroniclers at both Canterbury and Evesham leave no doubt that Roger abused the position of authority in order to enrich himself and to follow a way of life that contravened the Rule. But many abbots and abbesses must have failed in their role, like Elias of Narbonne, simply because they were inexperienced or ill equipped for the task of running what was in effect a small (or sometimes large) business. After all, few monks or nuns who found themselves elected to the office can have had the opportunity for such experience. In this matter, Petronilla, the nun whom Robert of Arbrissel appointed as his successor to rule Fontevraud, was an exception. Not only was she a widow, she was also, according to Baudri of Bourgeuil, an expert property manager.[183] Robert was aware that such an appointment was unorthodox, and took advice from the papal legate, Gerard of Angoulême, as to whether this would be acceptable. After all, as Andreas of Fontevraud, author of the 'Second Life' of Robert expressed it, 'how will any claustral virgin, who knows nothing except how to chant the psalms, be able to manage our external affairs suitably?' Gerard, in reply, acknowledged that 'many monasteries were destroyed through the negligence and inexperience of abbesses raised in the cloister' – and the same applied, of course, to male monasteries.[184] Frances, elected abbess of Holy Trinity, Poitiers in 1297, was described as 'trained over a long time in honesty of speech and life and in spiritual things, and circumspect in handling temporalities'.[185] As in many other aspects of monastic life, Jocelin of Brakelond provides us with a vivid picture of the atmosphere after the death of an abbot, as open debates and whispered discussions carried on among the monks about his likely successor, and especially the qualities needed for the role. Would they be better off with a competent administrator who knew the Rule but had no special spiritual gifts? As one monk observed, 'Abbot Ording was an illiterate man, and yet he was a good abbot and ruled this house wisely.' Others suggested the advantages of a learned and eloquent man who could preach in chapter and explain the Scriptures; or of an affable and kind man who would care for the community.[186] It was through unofficial conversations such as these that soundings were taken within the community before any official election was made.

Given these considerations, how did communities arrive at the choice of abbot or abbess? The *Rule of Benedict*, rather elliptically, says simply that a new superior should be chosen either with the unanimous consent of the community or, in the case of partial consent, by 'wiser counsel'.[187] As we have already seen, in some cases superiors were imposed on them from outside, by powerful lay or ecclesiastical interests. A notorious case was that of Robert, 'a contemptible little man', according to

Orderic Vitalis, who became abbot of St Pierre-sur-Dives in Normandy in 1106 by paying a large sum to Henry, duke of Normandy. His introduction of a troop of knights into the abbey, presumably to live at its expense, caused the monks to flee and the community to disperse.[188]

Elections to abbacies could be mysterious even to those so chosen: Guibert of Nogent admitted that his election had been 'made by men from afar who were utterly unknown to me'.[189] Guibert had probably attracted the attention of the monastery of Nogent-sous-Coucy because of his reputation for learning. A reputation for piety, as in the case of Elias of Narbonne, might also prompt an election from outside. Some observers, Jocelin of Brakelond among them, thought it was preferable for a superior to be chosen from outside the community.[190] The Fourth Lateran Council (1215) affirmed three methods of election: acclamation by the community; scrutiny (by individual secret balloting); or compromise, in which the senior monks or nuns would decide among themselves. In practice, where matters were genuinely left to the community, processes of election could be complex, as befitted the importance of the task of election.

Jocelin of Brakelond's account of the election of Samson as abbot of Bury in 1182 gives us an example of how an abbatial election might work in practice. First, twelve monks of the community at Bury were chosen by the prior as electors, and they appeared along with him in the presence of the king to make their choice. King Henry II then asked the thirteen to nominate three among them. The monks had worried what might happen if the thirteen could not agree on a candidate, and had followed the advice of Samson, at that point the sub-sacrist of the abbey, to choose six monks to hold a secret mock-election among themselves of the three candidates they thought best suited for the office of abbot, the names to be written down and enclosed under seal. When the king asked them for three names, therefore, the thirteen electors broke the seal and found the names of Hugh, the 'third prior' (deputy subprior), Roger the cellarer and Samson. The king then asked for three more names, since he did not know any of these men, and the names of the prior, the sacrist and one other monk were hurriedly added. Then three more names, this time of monks from other monasteries, were demanded by the king, and these too were added. Then the process of elimination began, as the electors were asked to strike out three names, and chose the 'aliens'. The sacrist withdrew his own name, and the king removed three others (according to criteria that Jocelin does not reveal). Only the prior's name and Samson's were left. At this point the king consulted with his intermediaries, the bishop of Winchester and the chancellor of York (later himself archbishop of York). Pressed by these two, the electors eventually admitted that they thought Samson, despite his relative inexperience, was better equipped to take on the role, and Henry accepted the choice.[191]

It is clear from Jocelin's narrative that Samson became an increasingly influential figure during the complicated process of election itself: it was he who suggested the strategy of the secret ballot for the three names in case of an indecisive election, and he who further advised on the process in the event of no name being acceptable to the king. The overlooking of senior obedientiaries in favour of the sub-sacrist suggests that, even when the crown was as heavily involved as was the case at Bury, there was room for talent to emerge.[192] Variations on the same principle of selecting electors to make the final choice were common elsewhere. At the convent of Holy Trinity, Poitiers, in 1297, all the nuns assembled in the chapter house to pick seven electors who were then mandated to choose an abbess in the length of time that it took for a candle to burn out. At St Albans in 1235, three or four confessors among the community chose twelve of the monks as electors, but they were restricted in their election to a member of chapter or of a dependent cell of St Albans. Because the Fourth Lateran Council (1215) had ruled that newly elected abbots of houses exempt from episcopal jurisdiction had to be confirmed by the pope, the community then had to record their assent to this election in writing in a sealed letter that was taken to the papal curia by two of the monks. The pope heard a verbal account of the process from the monks and then tasked two English bishops to confirm the suitability of the man elected.[193]

By the thirteenth century, therefore, it must have been a very rare event for a vacancy in a monastery or convent of any importance to have been filled without some involvement from external influences. Given the responsibilities of the superior over property that was often extensive and from which the community derived its main sources of income, sometimes over entire villages and manors inhabited by the monastery's tenants, it was scarcely surprising that secular rulers wanted to know what kind of person was taking on these powers. As Henry II observed about the candidates for Bury in 1180, none of those on the list presented to him was known to him. By virtue of their status as landholders, abbots and abbesses might also owe knight service or its equivalent to a secular lord. From repair of roads and maintenance of bridges to the education of the young, monasteries were so indispensable that rulership was impossible without their complicity. Popes, likewise, had an interest in knowing that monasteries were being run competently and without scandal. But there were other reasons for papal concern over elections. In much of Europe – though less so in England after *c.* 1300 – the stipulation of approval for vacancies in exempt monasteries gave popes opportunities to dispense patronage by actually making an appointment rather than simply confirming an election. This system of 'providing' to a vacancy was prohibited by statute in England in 1350 but not elsewhere in Europe. In practice it often meant that there was no abbot in residence, since the individual 'provided' might be a cleric in need of a benefice or income who had no intention of actually taking up the office in person. In this respect, it was similar in effect, if not intention, to the Carolingian system of lay abbacies.

In the Greek-speaking world, the question of a superior's relationship to the community, and indeed the process by which a *hegoumen* came to office, was much less uniform than in the West. Since there was no universal Rule to legislate for elections, the only guidelines were those that might arise from canon law or patristic writings. The most influential of these was the so-called *Rule of Basil*, in which the superior (literally, *proestos*, or 'the one who stands before') is a spiritual father to all monks rather than a manager or ruler.[194] Theodore the Studite wanted the superior to form a committee of the more experienced monks to guide him in running the community, and this system appears in many of the monasteries influenced by the eleventh-century Evergetis reform subsequently. At Evergetis, the older monks were effectively given responsibility for the succession by choosing the steward, who would become the next *hegoumen* after the incumbent's death.[195] Not all founders understood the role of the superior in this way. Christodoulos, for example, specified in his *Testament* that the superior of his monastery on

Patmos, founded in the late eleventh century, was 'to have all authority and [right of] dominion over [the monastery] and all its possessions'.[196] He also reserved the right to pass on the same full authority as he enjoyed to his chosen successor, whom he names in the *Testament*. Christodoulos's justification for this authoritarian approach was that he had been given absolute authority not only over the community but, as superior, over the island of Patmos, by the emperor and that it was therefore incumbent on him to pass this on. Certainly he could argue that the conditions posed by the Seljuq advance into Asia Minor meant that strong leadership was needed to keep the island, only a few miles off the west coast, safe.[197] Authoritarian leadership may have been a particular hallmark of monasteries on the fringes of the Byzantine world. We see the same tendency towards an emphasis on authority in Nikon's *Taktikon*, where it may be in part a response to something of a crisis in monastic leadership in eleventh-century Syria in the face of Seljuq advances.[198]

Different kinds of relationship were established by superiors according to the nature of the community. In early monastic tradition, authority was typically shaped by the master–disciple relationship so redolent both of Egyptian kelliot and Palestinian *lavra* monasticism, and this pervaded the flavour of Athonite and Italo-Greek ascetic monasticism. But superiors even within this tradition were capable of imposing authoritarian discipline, as for example in the 1180s when the *hegoumen* of St Sabas threw the Georgian monk Gabriel out of the community for infringing his authority in leaving the *lavra* temporarily to pursue a more rigorous discipline: a choice that went disastrously wrong and almost resulted in his murder of another monk.[199] Two charismatic founders who came from a solitary monastic tradition, one of the eleventh century, the other of the twelfth, offer different perspectives on how authority might be perceived in action. Lazaros, founder of a cenobitic community at Mount Galesion in Asia Minor, remained living on the pillar at the centre of his community, from where he could act as a focal point and – like a human panopticon – as the all-seeing eye over the monastery. From this vantage point he exercised a firm grasp of the administrative operation of the monastery, though in practice this was exercised on his behalf by the steward. Nevertheless, any monk leaving the monastery on official business was obliged to report to the pillar first.[200] About a century after the *Life of Lazaros* was written, in 1159, Neophytos the Recluse founded his cave monastery of the Enkleistra. Like Lazaros, he maintained a physical distance from his monks, although in his case by remaining effectively walled up in his cave-cell. His idea was that the authority needed to direct the community derived from the spiritual exercise of anachoresis, and he recommended that his successor (he named his nephew) should continue the policy: 'do not converse with many, and in particular with fools, maintaining quiet circumspection and power over your thoughts'.[201]

This kind of advice would have been useless for the *hegoumen* of a large property-owning monastery such as Makhairas. Founded in Cyprus at around the same time as the Enkleistra, and also from eremitical origins, the two monasteries pursued very different paths. Like Christodoulos, Makhairas's legislator Neilos, the author of the Rule, sought and obtained an imperial chrysobull. As a twelfth-century cenobitic monastery deriving from the Evergetis tradition, Makhairas provides a valuable example of the running of a more typical Orthodox community. The *hegoumen* was elected by the monks, but once elected remained quite a remote figure. He had the authority to inspect monks' cells, and all monks were obliged to make a spiritual confession to him on penalty of expulsion, but otherwise he had little to do with the daily running of the community.[202] Most of this was carried out by the steward, whom – in contrast to the Evergetian Rule – the *hegoumen* himself appointed and could remove from office. In the Orthodox world, the position of the superior was further complicated in some cases by the *charistike* movement and its lingering effects on the establishment of some private foundations. Even a foundation such as that of Empress Irene in Constantinople (*c.* 1110–16), which disavowed the *charistike*, saw a need for protection from a powerful advocate – in this case, a daughter Eudocia, who was a nun, and after her death another daughter, with the intent of passing the line of protection down the generations within the same family. This system, known as *ephoreia*, was not intended to impinge on the autonomy of the superior of the community, however. The superior was to choose all the important office-holders in the convent, and to have the power of dismissing them if necessary. She was to contribute towards the selection of her successor, where possible. As in many other Orthodox examples as well as in the West, this was done by election, but unlike in many other monasteries, the whole community acted as electors. The names of three nuns were to be chosen for piety and intelligence by secret ballot and left on sealed papers on the altar. One paper was chosen at random by the priest who officiated at the liturgy. If the superior died suddenly, it was the role of the protector to help the nuns make the choice of three.[203]

Whether superiors of monasteries and convents were elected from within or imposed from outside, the demands of leadership increased, even exaggerated, distances between them and their communities. By the thirteenth century, abbots and abbesses were often grand figures quite far removed from the daily routines of the community. Early monastic regulation and custom saw superiors as father figures whose most important responsibility was to nurture and encourage the community. Of course, there were still superiors who were able to combine the business of running an economic enterprise with spiritual guardianship, but for many monasteries their superior was a remote figure more preoccupied with affairs of state, diplomacy or accountancy than with hearing confessions, teaching and leading worship.

VIOLENCE, REBELLION AND STRIFE

In any community of men or women drawn together by professional ties of cooperation, tensions as well as alliances develop and sometimes express themselves in acts of violence. Enclosed communities of monks and nuns were no less prone to disturbances of this kind than any other. In many cases these arose from resistance to authority. In a notorious incident in 1083, the monks of Glastonbury were so outraged by Abbot Thurstan's attempt to introduce a new style of chant from Dijon that he resorted to bringing in armed soldiers to impose his will. The monks barricaded themselves inside the abbey church but were unable to prevent the soldiery from loosing off arrows and spears, wounding some of them. The widespread reporting of this incident, initially in the *Anglo-Saxon Chronicle* and subsequently in a range of twelfth-century monastic chronicles, indicates that it was a cause célèbre for some time.[204] The imposition of new forms of monastic customs and liturgy in English monasteries exposed fault lines in monasteries, which sometimes erupted into violence within communities.

It is tempting to see this episode solely in the context of the changes imposed on English monasteries by the Normans, which is how it was deployed by monastic reporters such as William of Malmesbury and has been retold by modern historians. But violence in monasteries was neither new nor invariably concerned with resistance to political authority. In some ways it should not be particularly surprising that monks, like any other people, let their anger boil over into expressions of violence. Monasteries were, after all, cross-sections of the society from which they recruited. On the other hand, monks and nuns constituted an elite group who underwent constant spiritual training to develop the mental discipline required for proper observance of a Rule. As Symeon the New Theologian (949–1022) had expressed it, a monk had to think with the mind inside his heart, observing freedom from care and complete absence of passionate attachment. And, as we saw in Chapter One, anger was the sin that, according to the *Apophthegmata Patrum*, the early Egyptian monks most feared.

Monks frequently protested against their abbots in ways that led to violence. Sometimes this was simply because of their previous associations. At St Augustine's Canterbury, just four years after the Glastonbury debacle, the election of a Christ Church monk, Wido, as abbot proved so unpopular that the new abbot-elect had to flee back to Christ Church. The St Augustine's community was forcibly dispersed as a result as punishment. Christ Church monks could be an unruly bunch. Between January 1188 and August 1189 Baldwin of Forde, who as archbishop of Canterbury was nominal abbot of Christ Church, blockaded the monks inside the monastery for resisting his attempts to found a college of secular canons in Canterbury. Unable to leave the conventual buildings, the monks were cut off from observing the liturgy in the cathedral.[205] The opposite happened to Abbot Pons of Cluny in 1122, when the monks shut the doors of the abbey against him, on the grounds that by leaving to go on pilgrimage to the Holy Land he had abdicated his office, and they had in the meantime elected Peter the Venerable as his successor.[206]

Rebellious protest against an abbot by his monks was sometimes the consequence of what was seen by the community as damaging action by him; in Pons's case, attempts to reform the monastery's finances after heavy expenditure on building the new abbey church in the abbacy of Abbot Hugh the Great. This kind of thing was as likely to happen in the Byzantine monastic world as in the West. When Symeon the New Theologian was superior of St Mamas in Constantinople in the 990s, on one occasion he was attacked by a group of thirty monks at the *orthros* (early morning) liturgy, and had to appeal to the patriarch for protection. In this case the monks were protesting against what they saw as his authoritative style of leadership. Peter Abelard, as abbot of St Gildas, was persecuted to the point of attempted murder by poison at the hands of the monks because – as he complained in his *History of My Misfortunes* – he was trying to reform their slack practices.[207] How far can episodes such as this be taken at face value? Without suggesting that Abelard was inventing what happened to him, we should note that the episode is strikingly similar to one in the *Dialogues of Gregory the Great* about St Benedict, who also supposedly survived an attempt by his monks to poison him. One might say it was almost a mark of abbatial distinction to have an attempt on one's life; at any rate, it was a way of signalling one's own reforming credentials in contrast to an intransigent community.

Sometimes, however, the reasons for revolt against the head of a community are less obvious. The monks of Dover Priory, who kept Prior Richard Wenchepe (1168–73) locked in his rooms for seven weeks after his return from Rome where he had been trying to resolve a dispute with the priory's mother-house, may simply have fancied the freedom of spending the abbey's revenues themselves and riding his horses, but the fact that they allowed the subprior to install himself in his place suggests that they were not unwilling to place themselves under discipline entirely.[208] In 1276, a monk of the Cluniac abbey of Wenlock Priory in Shropshire absconded in order to collect an armed troop for the purpose of forcibly evicting the unpopular prior John de Tycford, but he was captured and imprisoned.[209] Almost seventy years later, in 1342, the abbot of Buildwas was murdered by one of his monks, Thomas de Tong, who was likewise imprisoned but later escaped. It is not always clear what lay behind attacks on heads of monasteries, but personal animosities can build up and take root in extreme forms in communities for reasons that are now difficult to recover. Sometimes abbots caused resentment simply through the exercise of legitimate authority. Hugh of Eversden, abbot of St Albans, incurred the wrath of the monks of the abbey's dependent cell at Binham, Norfolk, when he tried to visit the priory and live at its expense for a period in the early fourteenth century. The prior and monks of Binham were brought to St Albans and forced to participate in a procession in chains, like captives of war.[210] The stakes were raised when William Somerton, the rebellious prior of Binham, appealed to the papal curia against Hugh, but as he was on the point of embarking at Dover to defend himself in front of the curia in person the abbot was arrested by agents of the king, for breach of the law forbidding prelates and abbots to attend the papal court without permission.

Abbots and priors had considerable authority over their monks, and as fathers were obliged to exercise discipline through the daily chapter, which might extend to publicly administered corporal punishment or degradation. Abbots might defuse the possibility of such violence by getting rid of troublesome monks. Abbot Samson of Bury St Edmunds sent recalcitrant monks who had expressed public criticism of his governance to the monastery's dependent cell at Acre to keep them from fomenting rebellion at home.[211] It is perhaps not surprising that when monks were humiliated in such fashion, the spiritual injunctions in the *Rule of Benedict* about the importance of humility to the monastic profession were difficult to remember. Of course, not all dissent against an abbot resulted in violence. Dissent between the monks and abbot of Westminster in 1249, and likewise at Peterborough, was resolved through the intervention of the king.[212] We cannot know how often the advice of Jocelin of Brakelond, that the supreme duty of the monk was to be silent and shut his eyes to the transgressions of his superior, was followed.[213]

Violence in the cloister could be random and unpredictable. In the mid-eleventh century, the abbot of Fleury was asked to reform a monastery in Gascony. While he was there, he heard a fracas break out in the courtyard, went to investigate and was accidentally killed by a spear thrust.[214] Riots between the monastery and local townspeople were sometimes the outcome of proprietorial relations between them, and could result in violence with tragic consequences. Artaud, abbot of Vézelay, was killed in 1106 during a riot caused by his attempt to spread the financial burden of accommodating the abbey's guests throughout the town.[215] In 1229 there was a revolt by the townspeople against Dunstable Priory over payment of tallage, and in 1309 the abbot of Combermere was assaulted by the townspeople of Nantwich and one of his monks was killed.[216] Vale Royal, the Cistercian abbey founded by Edward I, was subjected to an outbreak of local violence in the fourteenth century. In 1330 a servant of the abbey was beheaded by a group of locals who proceeded to play football with his head, and ten years later the abbot himself was murdered. These were occasions on which friction arose because of the monastery's position as landowner, employer and local source of power, rather than being attacks on the monastery as a monastic community.

Sometimes violence was a consequence of communal action by monks to defend the community against perceived external threat. Often, this threat came from within the Church – as, for example, in the case of Christ Church monks protesting against Baldwin of Forde. English monastic cathedrals were special cases, because the abbot was always the bishop of the diocese. The arrangement whereby a cathedral chapter was a Benedictine community rather than canons regular was unique to England, though not the case for every diocese. More often, conflict arose between the monastic community and the bishop – often over issues that probably strike us as very minor, or the significance of which for participants at the time is obscure to us. A striking example is the violent incident at Rouen in 1073, when the monks of St Ouen rioted against the archbishop of Rouen. The cause of their anger was Archbishop John's attempt to uphold his right to celebrate Mass at the high altar of the monastery church on the patronal feast day. At the point of the Mass where the opening of the Gloria was being intoned, a group of monks chased him from the altar wielding candelabra. The archbishop was forced to flee the monastery precinct, and brought a case to the ducal court against St Ouen. The result was that the monks responsible for the violence were distributed among different monastic prisons at Fécamp, St Wandrille and Jumièges.[217]

That the exercise of apparently obscure rights such as that claimed by the archbishop in this case could arouse such passions may appear outlandish to us. But the archbishop knew exactly what he was doing when he attempted to insert himself on the feast of St Ouen, the day that symbolised the community's very identity and reason for existence. It was a deliberate reminder of the jurisdictional rights of the bishop over a monastery in his diocese. These rights were critical to the relationship between monasteries and the regulatory framework of the Church and Christian society more broadly. In a case occurring in 1250 and described by Matthew Paris, the thirteenth-century chronicler of St Albans, it was the bishop in question who caused violence. Boniface, archbishop of Canterbury, went to St Bartholomew's Priory, London, to exercise his rights of visitation. On being told by the canons regular that they had their own diocesan, the bishop of London, to do that job, he flew into a rage and punched the subprior. According to Matthew, he was wearing a mail shirt under his vestments, which suggests that he was expecting, even deliberately provoking, violence. He then asked for his attendants to bring him his sword, and shouting, 'This is how English traitors should be treated!', pushed the unfortunate subprior against a pillar and crushed him so hard that he caused internal injuries.[218] The alleged outburst against 'English traitors' reveals an agenda in this case that may not otherwise be apparent. Boniface of Savoy was the uncle of Queen Eleanor and one of the group of her relatives who were unpopular with the baronage because of their influence over royal government. Matthew, whose sympathies generally lay with 'the English', was hostile to any form of interference in the English Church from outside, including even the papacy; as a monk, moreover, he understood the threat that sweeping claims to jurisdictional oversight could pose to a monastic community.

Violence could break out in the cloister, or against a monastery, for a multitude of causes. These might be related to the internal governance of a monastery, or to difficult relations between the superior and the monks, or to the role of the bishop; even to the wider social and economic context. All the cases discussed here, however, testify to the centrality of monasteries as institutions in society. It was because they lay at the centre of medieval life that, in a violent age, monks were just as subject to acts of violence as anyone else.

MONKS, PILGRIMS AND CRUSADERS

The case of Boniface of Savoy reminds us that most members of the higher clergy in the central medieval period were of aristocratic origin.

This did not, of course, make them all violent by nature, but in some cases it meant that they had grown up in a setting in which martial pursuits were constantly present. The Savoyard archbishop in the mail shirt may have been rather an anachronism by the middle of the thirteenth century, but well into the twelfth century bishops and abbots could sometimes be found accompanying armies and even sometimes assuming a military role. Simon, prior of St Foy at Conques, kept his weapons and armour from his previous life when he entered the monastery as an adult recruit, and even maintained a warhorse in the monastery stable. When the community was threatened by a hostile neighbour, he saddled his horse and led the small force of dependent knights of the abbey to defend it.[219] Examples of monks who are known to have taken arms, or at least to have assumed military roles, are plentiful. They include Henry of Blois, monk of Cluny, who as bishop of Winchester in 1136 crowned his brother Count Stephen of Blois as king of England, and Roffred, abbot of Monte Cassino who accompanied Emperor Henry VI on his invasion of Sicily in 1194. Abbot Samson of Bury St Edmunds led the abbey's tenant knights at the siege of Windsor in 1194 under his own standard – although his biographer remarks that his counsel was more useful than his military skill.[220] Although canon law prohibited the clergy and monks from shedding blood, there were precedents from hagiographical tradition of military men who had abandoned a life of warfare for monastic austerity.

One of the most influential of these was the *Life of Gerald of Aurillac*, a tenth-century knight who, though he realised that his role as a defender of the poor and non-combatants obliged him to use weapons, would only use the flat of his sword so as to avoid killing. The *Life of Gerald* was a product of Cluny's scriptorium, and represented the kind of influence that tenth- and early eleventh-century Cluny sought over knightly ideals of the period.[221] The advent of reform monasticism in the eleventh century changed the relationship between monasticism and warfare, because in the new disposition those who entered monastic life – often as founders of new communities – were often adult converts. The Cistercians, who would not take oblates but encouraged adult postulants instead, numbered among them many monks who had previously been active knights – Bernard of Clairvaux's own brothers among them.

This is one reason why the language of war came to be so prevalent in monastic discourses.[222] This could also be a feature of Orthodox monasticism, even though it was less institutionally entrenched since the practice of oblation was itself irregular. But we encounter Orthodox monks who took the cowl after having had military careers: for example, Nikon of the Black Mountain in the eleventh century, and the Cretan monk John Phokas in the twelfth, who alludes to having served under the banners of Emperor Manuel Komnenos. Finding Orthodox monks who took up arms as monks is more difficult, but not impossible. The Greek-rite bishops of Troia and Acerenza, in Apulia, were killed in battle against the Normans at Montemaggiore in 1047, and the Greek-rite bishop of Cassabo, in Calabria, similarly led armed resistance to the Normans in 1059.[223] The significance of these acts is that in the Orthodox Church, bishops were elected from the monastic rather than the clerical Order, so these men were monks at the time of their election.

In fact, military vocabulary and concepts were never far from monasticism even before the reform period, deeply embedded as they are in the New Testament and patristic writings. Orderic Vitalis referred to monks as 'cowled champions' whose role was to defend the locality of the saint through spiritual warfare. When Anselm spoke of monks as acting 'in God's military service' (*Deo militaturi*), he was echoing a phrase about serving in the army of God from St Paul's second letter to Timothy, but probably also drawing on Benedict's reference to monks taking up the arms of obedience to fight for God.[224] Anselm continued to explain, however, that in every army there was a difference between those who fought for their king out of military service owed for their lands, those who served in order to win back lands that had been confiscated, and those who fought for pay. It was the same in God's army. Monks had to be sure they were taking up arms for the right reasons. How much such imagery meant to a cloistered audience is difficult to gauge. But there must have been a particular resonance in the uses made by Bernard of parables and examples drawn from military language in addressing a congregation of monks who had lived experience of the siege, the campfire and the screams of battle.[225]

So far, so traditional – this is after all the familiar language of Carolingian monasticism. But at the end of the twelfth century, the separation between the metaphorical language of spiritual warfare waged by monks and nuns and the practice of actual warfare narrowed. Like rail tracks, they ran in parallel for a long time but crossed over at a critical point. In 1095, Pope Urban II initiated an armed pilgrimage to the Holy Sepulchre in Jerusalem with the purpose of removing the holy places from the possession of the Seljuq Turks (in fact by the time the crusade armies reached Jerusalem the city had been reconquered from the Seljuqs by the Egyptian Fatimids) and extending Christian protection over them. There was no intention in Urban's mind that monks, let alone nuns, should have anything to do with this military expedition. He seems to have gone so far as deliberately prohibiting monks from taking the cross, and some ecclesiastical leaders policed this conscientiously.[226] Anselm, as archbishop of Canterbury, had to write to restrain the abbot of Corfe, in Dorset, from fitting out a boat to take a group of his monks across the English Channel to join the expedition.[227]

In fact, however, both monks and nuns can be found as participants on the crusade. It is impossible to estimate numbers, or to know under what circumstances most of them took the cross. Presumably most either did not know of Urban's prohibition or were not bothered by it. The first Latin archbishop of Caesarea, according to Guibert of Nogent, was an abbot of an unnamed monastery in the West who had not only taken the cross but cut a cross in his forehead, claiming that it had been incised there by God.[228] Guibert seems to have been confusing Baldwin of Caesarea with Hugh, abbot of Notre-Dame, who was probably one of a group of monks who accompanied Godfrey of Bouillon's army, drawn from the monastery of St Hubert-en-Ardenne and St Lawrence, Liège.[229]

Some of the recent historiography of the First Crusade has revived the idea that participants saw the expedition in millenarian terms, and it is possible that monastic participants were swept up in a wave of popular enthusiasm.[230] One of the features of the Crusade was its sporadic and uncoordinated nature as an expedition. Leaders of contingents assembled their armies in a variety of ways, without much in the way of centralised communication or leadership, so it is likely that those who abandoned cloisters and followed the armed pilgrimage did so in ignorance that their actions were frowned upon. In some instances, we can only guess at how a monk or nun found themselves on the crusade. Albert of Aachen, writing his account of the crusade in *c.* 1120, tells the story of an unnamed nun from the convent of St Mary of the Granary in Trier who was captured by Turkish soldiers in Asia Minor. She was freed after a further skirmish and reported that she had been raped while in captivity, and obliged to undergo a penitential purification.[231] Albert's telling of the incident has inescapably misogynistic overtones for readers today, especially since the conclusion to the story has the nun returning secretly to Turkish lines on the grounds that her captor's treatment of her was better than that of her own people. There is no explanation of how the nun came to be on the crusade in the first place, but the context of the incident suggests that she had joined the so-called Popular Crusade, the contingent largely recruited from German-speaking lands led by Peter the Hermit and Walter Sans Avoir. If not quite the rabble that earlier historians depicted, these were certainly less subject to the same kinds of control as the contingents led by more established lords.[232] If that is the case, it helps to explain the absence of constraint on her participation.

There was a good reason, however, why monastic figures might have considered participation on the crusade as appropriate. The expedition was a pilgrimage, and Benedictine monks had been prominent in leading and popularising pilgrimages to the Holy Land since the late tenth century. Catalan abbots may have been early adopters of the practice. In 955, Laufred, abbot of Besalú, left on pilgrimage for Jerusalem but apparently never returned, while Guarin de Lézat, abbot of Cuxà, went twice, in 978 and 990, on the latter occasion staying in Jerusalem for three years.[233] Guarin probably just missed the stay of John, abbot of Monte Cassino with his fellow-monks Liutulf and Leo in the holy city, as part of a longer tour of eastern Mediterranean monastic centres that included Mount Athos. At around the same time Romuald expressed the desire to go but was dissuaded by his eremitical companions.[234] Perhaps with knowledge of the earlier Monte Cassino pilgrimage, Alfanus of Salerno accompanied Duke Gisulf II on a pilgrimage to the Holy Land in 1062. As we saw in an earlier chapter, there was a long-standing tradition of pilgrimage to the Holy Land in Italo-Greek monasticism, and this continued into the eleventh century. In 1059, Luke II, abbot of St Elias Carbone, left the abbey in the care of a relative, Blasius, when he set out for Jerusalem.[235] But the list of known monks from French-speaking lands who made pilgrimages to the Holy Land in the eleventh century far exceeds that from any other part of Christian Europe. Normandy seems to have been a particular centre for monastic pilgrimage. Ralph, abbot of Mont St Michel resigned the abbacy to go on pilgrimage in 1054; Thierry de Mathinville, abbot of St Evroult, did the same in 1057, dying in Cyprus on his return, and Nicholas of St Ouen died in 1092 on his return from Jerusalem. A stay in Jerusalem following a pilgrimage was part of the experience for some Benedictine monks, such as Emirardus, a monk of the Cluniac daughter-house of Anzy-le-Duc, who lived there for seven years in the 990s.[236]

Given how young the shoots of Benedictine monasticism were in Normandy, this enthusiasm for the Holy Land is especially striking. As Marcus Bull demonstrated, connections between pilgrimage and crusade can be traced in patterns of lay piety in the generations before and after the First Crusade.[237] Families in which traditions of pilgrimage to the Holy Land were already established were more likely to be participants in crusading. Monasteries, moreover, were the vital linchpin in this motor. The Norman abbey of Troarn, founded in *c.* 1050, provides an example. Troarn's first abbot, Durand (1059–88), had been a monk of Fécamp before entering Holy Trinity Rouen, itself a foundation of *c.* 1030. At least three first crusading families were supported financially by Troarn, among them the Milly family, who would become prominent barons in the twelfth-century kingdom of Jerusalem.[238] But monastic pilgrimage was a phenomenon found across all French and Occitan-speaking speaking regions, from Champagne to the Mediterranean.[239] In a famous passage, Ralph Glaber, the eleventh-century Cluniac monk, described the year 1033 – supposedly the millennium of Christ's resurrection – as a time when people from all across the world flocked to Jerusalem on pilgrimage. Benedictines were also at the forefront of the movement of massed pilgrimage to the Holy Land that developed in the eleventh century. Richard, abbot of St Vanne in Verdun, led a pilgrimage with Duke Richard II of Normandy in 1026–7. The fashion for massed pilgrimages seems to have been common to different regions. Berenger, bishop of the Pyrenean diocese of Elne, also led one in the eleventh century, and in 1064 a group of German bishops got themselves and their charges into serious trouble when they fell foul of a dangerous armed gang who besieged them in Ramla.[240]

What was the effect of these monastic pilgrimages on their communities and the local society around the monastery? Obviously the removal, sometimes the death, of the abbot could create disruption in the community. But monks also brought material memories home from pilgrimages, and these sometimes altered the physical shape and appearance of the monastery. Fulcher, abbot of Flavigny, brought back relics from the Holy Land 'with which he enriched his church', and Mainard, abbot of St Cybar in Angoulême, built a new oratory dedicated to the Holy Sepulchre in Jerusalem, in which he placed the relics he had brought home with him.[241] A later abbot of St Cybar, Richard, died near Constantinople accompanying the count of Angoulême on pilgrimage. Deaths on pilgrimages are a reminder of the privations of travel,[242] but sometimes monks were attacked and suffered at the hands of locals. Geraud, abbot of St Florent, Saumur, was captured, tortured and put to death when he refused to abjure his faith, but two monks accompanying him escaped to tell the tale.[243] William Firmat, a solitary monk from Mortain, was imprisoned near Jerusalem and suffered torture from the 'enemies of the cross', but escaped and was able to go to Constantinople to venerate the tombs of the Apostles.[244] It was not always Muslims who attacked monks: Thierry, later abbot of St Hubert-en-Ardenne, set out on an ambitious pilgrimage to Rome, Monte Gargano in Apulia, Constantinople and Jerusalem, but was captured by brigands in Hungary.[245] This suggests that – as we saw in a previous chapter – most of these episodes did not have a religious motivation but simply targeted people who happened to seem vulnerable and unlikely to be able to defend themselves.

By the middle of the twelfth century, the relationship of monasticism to the business of crusading had become more intertwined. In part this was because western monks and nuns were among the immigrants to the new states established in the wake of the first crusade. Virtually all of the shrines in the Holy Land were served by communities of either monks, nuns or canons regular, and in addition other monasteries were founded in locales either associated with the life of Christ or considered to be suitable simply as deserted places in which austere reformed monasticism would be practised. The impetus to reform that was so noticeable in the eleventh- and early twelfth-century West, typified by the desire for new beginnings, poverty and unfettered settlement, was well met by the 'frontier territory' of the Near East, where religious, cultural and political boundaries overlapped. This did not meet with approval from all monastic leaders. Peter the Venerable, in a letter to the Cluniac monks of Mount Tabor, reminded them that they should not think of themselves as holier than their counterparts in the West by virtue of living in the Holy Land; indeed, the more blessings one received from the Lord, the more was expected by way of service and proper observance.[246] As we have already seen, Bernard of Clairvaux was adamant that Cistercians should not be involved in pilgrimage to the Holy Land, and opposed the establishment of a Cistercian community there.

This did not mean, however, that either of them was opposed to the idea of the Crusade. Bernard preached the Second Crusade energetically in France and Germany in 1147 and 1148, to the extent that he acknowledged that he was to some degree associated with its eventual failure.[247] The presence of kings as leaders of the armies of crusades disrupted the rules that Urban II had put in place. Louis VII of France included in his entourage a monk of St Denis, Odo of Deuil, who wrote an account of the journey of the French army to the East in the form of a letter to his abbot, Suger.[248] Likewise, Cistercian monks were apparently part of Richard I's crusading army in the Holy Land in 1191–2.[249] Monks were not only mobilised to preach the message of holy war, but by the early thirteenth century there no longer seemed to be an expectation that they would remain uninvolved in the 'business of the cross'. Martin, abbot of the Cistercian monastery of Pairis in western Germany, accompanied the army of the Fourth Crusade (1202–4) and played an enthusiastic role in the despoliation of relics from Constantinople.

In sharp contrast with the evolution of western monastic involvement in crusading, Orthodox monks remained determinedly opposed to such participation, on the basis of the teaching of Basil of Caesarea against the shedding of blood by those who had taken monastic vows.[250] Even the 'friend of monks', Emperor Nikephoros Phokas, was unable to persuade the bishops – all of whom, of course, were elected as monks – to declare soldiers who had fallen in wars against Muslims martyrs. Indeed, one of the objections made to union with Rome by some

Orthodox clergy in the twelfth and thirteenth centuries was the western clergy's apparent willingness to break the Council of Chalcedon's edict against clerical shedding of blood. As one historian has recently observed, monastic chroniclers writing about the First Crusade tended to see violence inflicted by the crusaders as justified, as against the illicit violence of the Turkish or Fatimid enemy.[251]

Finally, it is important to remember that many monks, whether western or Orthodox, had previous experience of war, or being trained for war, from before entering the cloister. Even those who had been monks from childhood had relatives or close family who fought. The results of war were also hard to avoid, from frightened non-combatants taking refuge in their nearest monastery to the devastation that war could bring to the agricultural economy through the burning of crops. The notion that monks and nuns could entirely avoid the realities of war and violence by immuring themselves in a monastery does not stand up to scrutiny. War was endemic in medieval society, and however they felt about it, monks and nuns were implicated in its consequences if not its practices.

Monks and nuns thought of their profession as embodying purity and holiness. They were angels, living in spaces that were the closest representations on earth to the heavenly Jerusalem. As such, they were entitled to worldly as well as spiritual benefits. Indeed, human society owed them the means of material support so that they could continue to serve it through mediating on its behalf with God and the saints. This transactional relationship, though universally understood and rarely challenged in its fundamentals, was nevertheless subject to constant friction. Negotiating the terms of the relationship required varied and constant interaction with external society. Monasteries were obliged to establish a presence in political society, locally, regionally and even beyond national borders; they had to defend their property and their rights from neighbours and from episcopal jurisdiction; they had to develop systems of governance and domestic economy to manage the properties entrusted to them; and they had to find a response to the demands of national and transnational politics in which the spiritual was invoked in service of territorial defence or expansion.

CHAPTER SIX

Fruit in Its Season
Late Medieval Monasticism

> He shall be like a tree Planted by the rivers of water, That brings forth its fruit in its season, Whose leaf also shall not wither; And whatever he does shall prosper.
>
> Psalms 1.3

ON A PILGRIMAGE TO the Holy Land in 1483, the German friar Felix Fabri (1441–1502) visited the Greek Orthodox monastery of St Sabas in the Kidron Valley. From his observation of the way of life of the monks, he remarked that the resources needed for twenty monks in the West would support a hundred in the East, because of their lower expectations of comfort and their simpler way of life.[1] This western visitor clearly considered Greek-rite monks to be more 'monastic' than their western counterparts. One simplistic response to this observation might be that Fabri's remark should be seen as a dig by a Dominican friar against his Benedictine counterparts. Doubtless there is some truth in this, but his remark raises more profound and interesting questions about the state of monasticism in both East and West at the end of the medieval period. How far had monks and nuns in the West and East diverged from each other in both style and substance of regular living? Why did the monks of St Sabas appear to be living with lower expectations of material comfort, and was this a reflection of the resources at their command as much as of their perceptions of monastic life? If they were so much poorer than western monks, why was this the case – and was this apparent plainness of living specific to the cradle of monasticism in the Levant, or the wider Orthodox world? Conversely, what had happened to monastic life in the West to elicit the comparison in Fabri's mind, and why did monks and nuns in the West live in such comfort?

More than fifty years ago, Richard Southern compared the career of a typical late medieval Canterbury monk, William Chart (d. 1418), with that of a nineteenth-century canon of Durham Cathedral, William Greenwell (d. 1918). Southern drew attention to essential analogies in careers separated by 500 years: both were public servants of the Church, occupying positions of responsibility in their communities. Chart, warden of the Benedictine college in Oxford, canon lawyer, subprior, 'a man of note in the monastery' according to the obituary by a fifteenth-century antiquary, enjoyed 'a career bathed in the late sunshine of the medieval Benedictine life'; a career characterised by ceremony, performance of liturgy and the maintenance of traditional relationships with lay patrons. Greenwell represented the same type in the Victorian cathedral close: besides being a canon of long standing, he was a Fellow of the Royal Society, Justice of the Peace, an antiquarian, an archaeologist and an angler.[2] The astuteness of the comparison is beguiling, perhaps dangerously so. Views of late medieval monasticism have been coloured by the knowledge of what happened in the sixteenth century, when the European Reformation brought a sudden end to monasticism throughout reformed countries, and across Latin Europe as a whole more than half the monasteries disappeared. Assumptions have often been made that the Reformation swept away an institution and way of life so easily because it was an anachronism, or in some places even a relic of a feudal culture that was no longer relevant to the social landscape. More recent appraisals of late medieval monasticism have shown that the picture is much more complex and difficult to read.[3] Monasticism did not stay the same in any single phase of its existence. Although many of the essential forms of monastic life in the 1530s would have been recognisable to a monk or religious sister in the 530s, monasticism was no less subject to changes in the direction of thought, feeling and expression than any other dimension of religious and cultural life. Monasticism had undergone considerable change during the years before Fabri's pilgrimage, much of it directed towards reform of monks' and nuns' way of life and understanding of their profession. The late fourteenth and especially the fifteenth centuries saw change in monasticism through new reform movements on a scale unknown since the early thirteenth century. In order to understand what these changes meant and why they occurred at that juncture, we need first to go back to an event that took place in Rome in November 1215: the Fourth Lateran Council.

MONASTIC ORGANISATION AFTER THE FOURTH LATERAN COUNCIL: PROVINCIAL CHAPTERS

Innocent III became pope in 1198 at the age of thirty-seven, after a series of short-lived elderly popes. Born to an aristocratic Italian family, educated in theology at Paris and law at Bologna, Innocent proved to have natural gifts for leadership. His pontificate (1198–1216) can be seen as the high-water mark of the medieval papacy, and the clearest expression of this was the Fourth Lateran Council, attended by more than twelve hundred bishops and archbishops from across Latin Christendom. In seventy decrees, the Council dealt with a sweeping array of business that touched almost everyone, clerical or lay, male or female. Besides questions of doctrine, theology, discipline and pastoral care, the Council dealt with the phenomenon of the multiplication of new Orders and congregations within the Church. As we saw in a previous chapter, the reform tendencies of the eleventh and twelfth centuries brought into being not only fresh ideas about how religious lives should be conducted, but also new associations and orderings of communities.

But in the early thirteenth century completely new ways of thinking about how people might live a regulated religious life evolved. The Humiliati emerged in the mid-twelfth century from reform principles that took hold among the laity in northern Italian towns. The idea was that pious laypeople might live a communal life, in imitation of the practice of the early Church described in the Acts of the Apostles, even while still married and leading outwardly 'normal' professional lives. The Humiliati were condemned for heresy in 1184, lumped along with Cathars, Waldensians and others, but Innocent III drafted a Rule that offered them a way of living within the Church's discipline.[4] Early in the thirteenth century, two other models of religious life that diverged from existing monastic traditions also emerged, both of which were supported by Innocent (even though formally approved only by his successor Honorius III). Francis of Assisi (*c.* 1181–1226), the son of a cloth merchant, came from a similar background to the Humiliati, and like them wanted to find a way of living as a religious layman. The group of brothers he gathered as followers – whom he called the 'Minors' or 'Lesser Brothers' – lived as far as possible as Francis understood the disciples of Christ to have lived, to the extent that this is described in the Gospels. This entailed mobility in order to preach and to live out exemplary lives of poverty. Although Francis was never ordained priest, remaining a deacon throughout his life, and could therefore not administer sacraments, Innocent saw the potential for a movement such as his to supplement the pastoral care offered by secular clergy. Nevertheless, although they did not take monastic vows, the Friars Minor followed a Rule of Francis's own devising: in its first iteration, a document of extreme simplicity, even of conscious naivety.

More or less contemporary with the Friars Minor, another reforming initiative emerged in the region in which Catharism was perceived by ecclesiastical authorities to be the biggest threat to the Church. Dominic, an Augustinian canon of Osma in northern Spain, developed the idea of forming a group of dedicated preachers to combat heresy. They lived a common life according to a Rule – essentially an adaptation of the *Rule of Augustine* – and were organised into houses based in towns where they might be most effectively deployed in response to Cathar or Waldensian preaching. A fundamental point of difference between the Order of Preachers (Dominicans) and the Friars Minor was that in order to preach, they had to be trained both as theologians and as debaters. Dominic had observed that those usually commissioned to preach against the heretics were monks – often Cistercians – who, no matter how learned, found it difficult to establish a connection with their audience. As we have seen, abbots were by *c.* 1200 often remote figures whose preoccupations and business were on a large scale. By the second half of the thirteenth century both the Dominicans and the Franciscans (less obviously so and despite considerable internal tensions in the Order) were a significant presence at the universities, and had their own study houses for training the brothers.

The full emergence of the mendicants, as they are known, took place over a number of years, but the rise of alternative forms of religious life was one of the drivers for the Council to consider the processes governing monasticism. As we have already seen, the question of oversight and jurisdiction was a constant problem. Specifically, problems arose over the rights of bishops to 'visit' monasteries, in other words, to carry out inspections involving interviews with monks and nuns, to hear grievances from them, to check that the Rule was being followed, that the house was being run in such a way as to ensure financial stability, and to make recommendations or impose punishments where needed.

The Lateran Council reiterated the rights of bishops to visit monasteries. This should be seen as part of the wider tone and thrust of the Council's agenda to invoke a moral regeneration of Christendom. The intent was not to weaken monasteries but to strengthen the authority of bishops and papal legates as a way of binding Christian society together. More far-reaching, however, was the stipulation, in the decree *In singulis* of the Fourth Lateran, that Benedictine and Augustinian monasteries should hold general chapters every three years. These were to be held within each province (archiepiscopate), and to comprise the heads of the monasteries and convents.[5] In England, where we have the most complete record of such chapters, the first was held at Oxford in 1218/19, jointly presided over by the abbots of St Albans and Bury St Edmunds. Chapters of the Augustinians took place in England from 1220 onwards. As with the Benedictines, they were divided into provinces. In 1265 an attempt to produce a uniform set of regulations for all Augustinians in the province of York was abandoned in failure, but in 1325 the houses in the province of Canterbury came up with a set that proved acceptable to all.[6] The issues raised at Augustinian provincial chapters were similar to those for the Benedictines, albeit with the fundamental difference that there was no papal programme of reform governing Augustinian chapters beyond the initial mandate in the Fourth Lateran.

The main points of discussion concerned issues of finance and property: the expenses incurred by heads of houses in relation to the income of the house, and maintaining a ban on monks owning private possessions. Subsequent chapters in the thirteenth century dealt with similar issues of practical concern: residence outside the monastery; regulation of the correct minimum length of the novitiate; financial accountability; keeping the regular *horarium*; and – a perennial issue to which we will return – meat-eating. Clothing was also an issue of repeated concern. The provincial statutes of 1363, for example, observed that monks were wearing habits of bespoke cut and style: some with the very wide sleeves fashionable at the time, or with slits in the side; others copied secular fashion by wearing a short overgarment. Hoods were sometimes lined with fur or silk.[7] It was not only Benedictines who felt the need to reinforce such observances. A series of reforming statutes were issued for the Premonstratensians by Pope Gregory IX (r. 1227–39) that specified, among other things, that fur was not to be used to line monks' cloaks or scapulars and that greaves for the legs and gloves with fingers were prohibited.[8]

Provincial chapters did not take place as regularly as intended by the council fathers. In 1222, one of the nominated presiding abbots failed to appear, and the meeting was cancelled. In any case, attendance was patchy and tended to be unrepresentative of the provinces. In 1225, only fifteen out of the more than sixty eligible heads of houses attended; in 1246 the chapter was cancelled again, and in 1253 more heads sent deputies than actually appeared in person.[9] Some monasteries simply refused to participate on principle, rejecting the implication that monasteries did not enjoy total autonomy of governance. These included Christ Church Canterbury but also Battle, a royal foundation, and Faversham. Perhaps unsurprisingly, it was the larger monasteries that tended to dominate both the rotating presidency and the direction of policy, so the chapters came to represent the interests of powerful houses such as Westminster, St Albans and Bury; but also a couple of the older foundations such as Ramsey and Chertsey. How far decrees were implemented or obeyed in individual monasteries once the abbots returned home is difficult to assess. Doubtless abbots encountered opposition in practical implementation of some of them. Although the decrees of the provincial chapters had canonical force, they were sometimes also supplemented and enforced by papal legates on visitations; hence in 1238 Cardinal Ottobuono approved the chapter's decree on the consumption of meat.[10]

If this gives a rather negative picture of the usefulness of the provincial chapters, the chapters did also result in significant changes. The 1249 chapter produced a set of constitutions notionally binding on all monasteries in the province of Canterbury (in other words, most of England).[11] By the later thirteenth century the logic of the provincial chapter system produced a reform momentum of its own. A further body of legislative constitutions from 1277 to 1279 shows that monastic leaders were interested in reform. William, abbot of St Albans, proposed a reduction of the complex sung liturgy to allow more time for other activities, including study, and this was adopted by the chapter of 1277. The emphasis was on ensuring that what was retained of the sung liturgy should be sung with proper devotion. The statutes of this chapter also articulated more clearly the meaning of manual labour in Benedictine monasteries. There was no longer any suggestion that monks should engage in labour in the fields or of a purely manual nature: instead study, writing, illuminating and binding books were considered appropriate work.[12]

Another issue confronted by the chapters, and eventually addressed specifically by Pope Boniface VIII, was enclosure. In 1298, the papal decretal *Ut periculoso* reinforced the demands of stability and enclosure on all women following a monastic Rule. Historians have sometimes seen the decree as an attempt to control female sexuality, since the wording refers implicitly to notorious cases of scandalous conduct by some nuns.[13] But in a wider sense the decree was also a response to the diversity of religious experiences and ways of leading regular lives by the end of the thirteenth century. The multiplication of religious Orders had continued apace during the thirteenth century despite papal attempts to restrict this at the Second Council of Lyons in 1274. By the 1290s, the Franciscans and Dominicans had established themselves firmly in towns across the whole of Latin Christendom and areas that had come under western dominion, but they were now competing with other mendicant Orders, the Carmelites and Augustinian friars, and with groups such as the Beguines in the Low Countries.[14] The decree was intended to reinforce the difference between enclosed religious and those following vocations that permitted leaving the cloister, or indeed for which such mobility was an essential aspect of their profession.

Sometimes it has been assumed that the decree was particularly directed at women's convents, and that it addressed a specific problem of nuns transgressing the terms of their enclosure. More recently it has been shown that enclosure, far from being resisted or transgressed, was actually welcomed and celebrated in some female communities, especially of Cistercian nuns, as a way of benchmarking the difference between themselves and other groups such as Beguines.[15] Naturally, for reasons that we have already seen in a previous chapter, there were many occasions on which nuns, just as much as monks, might legitimately leave the cloister on the business of the house, or on which laypeople might need to enter the convent. As recent research on German nuns' letters from the fifteenth and sixteenth centuries has shown, correspondence between convents was also a means of both emphasising their enclosure and at the same time indicating their openness to the exchange of ideas and willingness to be part of a network of prayer and study.[16]

The papal decree helped to demarcate legitimate and illicit forms of leaving the convent walls. In the fourteenth and fifteenth centuries, nuns in some communities developed devotional programmes that emphasised their enclosure by embracing paradox. Since pilgrimage for enclosed women had become, in principle at least, an impossibility after *Ut periculoso*, the practice of mental rather than actual pilgrimage – 'the act of imagining oneself on pilgrimage while being somewhere else'[17] – was a particularly valuable devotional resource. As Kathrynne Beebe has shown, the practices involved in such devotions varied from the purely mental exercise of the imagination to meditation on words or images in books, or sacred objects. The practice of imagined pilgrimage was not unique to enclosed religious, but women's communities were probably the most intensive users of this kind of devotion. At its most practical, it was a means for anyone incapacitated or otherwise prevented from making a physical journey to enjoy the spiritual benefits of pilgrimage. Special recognition was given to the position of enclosed women. Thus a papal bull of 1487 allowed the nuns of the Dominican convent of St Katherine in Augsburg an indulgence if they made a spiritual pilgrimage to the main churches of Rome by saying nine Ave Marias and nine Pater Nosters.[18] The means by which this was done is revealed in a remarkable series of illuminated books that circulated in northern European convents as guides to pilgrimage. Through visual and tactile exploration, nuns could transport themselves mentally to the holy places of Rome or Jerusalem.[19]

Among the issues that regularly appeared in the decrees of the chapters of the Canterbury province was the question of meat-eating in monasteries. Although only one aspect of the attempt to enforce observance, this is worth some consideration, not only because it obviously preoccupied monks at the time, but also because it offers a window on to the process by which lapses from observance occurred, and indeed the wider cultural context that allowed for them. Both reform polemic – most famously articulated by Bernard of Clairvaux – and varied archaeological evidence indicates that meat was regularly served in some monasteries in the twelfth century: perhaps as early as the eleventh century at Monte Cassino, according to a story in Desiderius's *Dialogues* of robbers who broke into the abbey cellars but were miraculously prevented from carrying off barrels of cheese and meat.[20] Reformers, of course, were adamant that meat had no place in the monastery: the statutes of Fontevraud, for example, forbade it entirely.[21] But in some monasteries it seems to have become a normative relaxation of the *Rule of Benedict*, openly recognised as such even in grants and deeds. Peter the Venerable acknowledged that at Cluny all kinds of meat were eaten, from livestock to game birds.[22] In 1182, the nuns of Sully were given a vineyard by the countess of Nevers, for the express purpose of using the proceeds of the sale of the wine to buy meat.[23] The *Rule of Augustine* was less restrictive than the *Rule of Benedict*, and meat was permitted within moderation. But even Benedictines found arguments to evade the spirit, if not the letter, of the Rule, and the increasing appearance of the issue of meat-eating indicates that it was an area of monastic practice that changed substantially from the thirteenth century onwards.

The Oxford chapter of 1219 implicitly recognised the change of practice with its ruling that monasteries should provide a room off the cloister in which monks could eat whatever they wanted, presumably including meat. Such a room came to be known as the 'misericord', or 'place of mercy': an established and permitted place for relaxation of the Rule. St Augustine's Canterbury even had a papal concession to eat meat in other places in the monastery. As we have already remarked, monasteries were unique in having refectories – rooms dedicated only to eating – and eating together was recognised as the benchmark of cenobitic monasticism in both eastern and western traditions. The concession to eat elsewhere – which was specifically prohibited in many Orthodox typika – seems to have been accepted as a necessity in the West by the time of the Fourth Lateran. The *Rule of Benedict*, assuming that *all* eating will take place there, casts the stipulation against meat-eating in the context of the conduct of the refectory, thus leaving a loophole hypothetically permitting the eating of meat elsewhere in the monastery. On his visitation of the convent of Almenêches in 1260, for example, Eudes Rigaud found that the nuns were eating meat 'here and there in . . . groups of twos and threes', and that the refectory was empty.[24] The Rule, moreover, only specified that the 'flesh of quadrupeds' was not to be eaten. This left open, for those accustomed to the finer points of interpretation and exegesis, a wide range of what we would consider meat. Fowl and birds could be eaten with impunity, but also animal products that were not strictly speaking 'flesh': offal, brains, or 'meaty food' such as sausage. Barbara Harvey's monumental study of Westminster Abbey in the medieval period shows in detail how both these loopholes became normative in a prosperous monastic community.[25] The misericord was a feature of community living from *c.* 1230, when it is referred to in the abbey's customary.[26] Yet ecclesiastical authorities still tried to limit, if not prohibit, meat-eating on the part of monks and nuns. At the special visitation of Benedictine, Cistercian and Premonstratensian houses ordered by Pope Gregory IX in 1237–8, the prohibition on meat-eating was confirmed, and promulgated by the papal legate Ottobuono in England in 1238. Even so, attempts to enforce it met with resistance: for example, at Peterborough Abbey, when the diocesan bishop Robert Grosseteste tried to restrict the consumption of meat to the abbot's house. By the end of the thirteenth century, however, the regulations at many abbeys – Malmesbury under Abbot William (1260–96) being only one example – not only assumed the regular use of a misericord but incorporated a rota system to ensure that the refectory was not abandoned, as at Almenêches. Half of the community was to dine in the refectory and half in the misericord at any one time (not including those who had been invited to dine with the abbot and those in the infirmary), as long as there was a minimum of thirteen in the refectory at all times. No monk was to eat meat two days running in the misericordia. The implication here is that meat was usually if not always available in the misericordia, but another difference between the food served here and in the refectory was the variety of dishes: three instead of the customary two at dinner.[27]

Meat-eating in monasteries, and the anxieties that it clearly caused among ecclesiastical leaders, look on the surface like an indication of how far standards of observance were slipping in the later Middle Ages. Why this should have been so is not difficult to understand. Monasticism in the West was largely an aristocratic profession, at least in the sense that most monks came from the landowning classes. There are signs that more monks of lower social origins may have been entering monasteries in the later Middle Ages, but this is probably also a function of the rise of a middle class and the relative decline of oblates as a source of vocations. As members of a social elite, monks and nuns were conscious of the material comfort enjoyed by those of their status outside the monastery. Moreover, the standards and quality of material comforts had improved over time. By the thirteenth century, the variety of foodstuffs and domestic consumables available for those with purchasing power was far greater because of the expansion of long-distance trade than it had been 200 years earlier.[28] Large monasteries and convents, as institutions with both liquid and landed assets, were in a position to capitalise on the aristocratic drive for greater conspicuous consumption. This is perhaps most obvious to us in new building projects, but the monastic table also benefited from rising expectations among the elites.

One example of the loosening of the hold that the aristocracy had over monasticism is the rise of Pope Benedict XII (r. 1334–42).[29] Although probably from an obscure family, he joined the Cistercian monastery of Boulbonne in the Haute-Garonne and benefited from the drive to improve education in the monasteries by being sent to Paris to study theology. In 1311 he became abbot of Fontfroide, near Narbonne, then bishop of Pamiers (1317) and Mirepoix (1326), with a reputation for the successful interrogation of heretical suspects. As a bishop active in southern France, he had come to the attention of Pope John XXII (r. 1316–34). Since 1305 the popes had been resident not in Rome but at Avignon. Initially this was a temporary move at a time when French cardinals were in the ascendancy and Italy was in political tumult, but by the 1330s the papal curia was entrenched in its enclave just across the Rhône from territory under the control of the French crown. Elected pope on the death of John XXII, Benedict differed from his predecessor John in many ways, not least in that he was an accomplished and respected theologian, whereas John's interventions in speculative theology had been received with scepticism. Benedict brought monastic rigour to the curia, particularly in regard to financial accountability, clerical preferment and the issuing of indulgences. His decree *In agro dominico* (1338) defined the scope of dispensations and indulgences more clearly than before. He also tried to end the practice of *commendam* appointments, a method of allowing favoured candidates for ecclesiastical office to hold a benefice and enjoy its revenues without actually doing the job – although as we shall see, this proved more difficult to stamp out. Among the most important of Benedict's attempts to reform what he considered abuses in ecclesiastical practices was his decree to reform monastic observance, *Summi magistri* (1336). This was a set of Constitutions to be followed by all Benedictines. The main thrust of the decrees was to enforce enclosure against monks who left their houses for unacceptable reasons, to reinforce the system of provincial chapters – which seem to have lapsed in most areas of Europe with the exception of England – to confirm the obligation of bishops to conduct visitations, and to support houses of study. Although these had some traction in parts of Latin Europe – their influence can be seen, for example, in the English Benedictine provincial statutes[30] – they proved either impossible to enforce or foundered on the rock of neglect and lack of interest from subsequent popes.

LEARNING AND SCHOLARSHIP IN LATE MEDIEVAL MONASTERIES

Historians have long noted that a number of abbots in the second half of the thirteenth century were accomplished scholars or noted for their piety: even looking only at England, Abbot Roger of St Albans (1260–90) was a distinguished canon lawyer; Richard of Ware, abbot of Westminster (1259–83), had been at the papal curia for some years; Nicholas de Spina, abbot of St Augustine Canterbury (1273–83), was known for his piety; and Abbot John of Glastonbury (1274–91) was, to judge from his library, familiar with recent works in scholastic theology.[31] It is surely no coincidence that one area in which reform tendencies can most clearly be seen is learning.

Monasteries had been instrumental in a revival of learning in western Europe from the later eleventh century onwards. Some, such as the Augustinian house of St Victor in Paris, were founded specifically as centres of biblical study; others – Bec in Normandy being an obvious example – developed a tradition of learning because of the presence of a remarkable teacher, such as Lanfranc or Anselm.[32] Even a college of secular canons, Waltham, could develop a reputation for learning.[33] Some of the most prominent theologians and biblical scholars of the twelfth century came from a monastic milieu: Hugh, Andrew and Richard of St Victor; Gilbert Crispin of Westminster;[34] Gilbert Foliot at Gloucester; Bernard at Clairvaux; Ailred at Rievaulx; William of Saint-Thierry; and many others. Although in terms of theological innovation monastic learning lagged behind the cathedral schools and the universities that began to emerge from them towards the end of the twelfth century, the traditions of biblical commentary and the related discipline of history-writing remained strong in monasteries. Some of the most outstanding examples of historical writing of the twelfth and thirteenth centuries came from monasteries or were written by former monks: Otto, bishop of Freising, had been a Cistercian monk; William of Malmesbury, Orderic Vitalis, Roger of Wendover and Matthew Paris were Benedictines; William of Newburgh an Augustinian. Monks and nuns communicated through the exchange of letters that were often infused with biblical learning; sometimes, indeed, such correspondence could be a means of trying out ideas. Peter the Venerable's celebrated correspondence with Bernard of Clairvaux began as an exchange of views about specific aspects of monastic reform, but developed into a more reflective intellectual encounter.[35] Peter of Celle used letter-writing as a way of maintaining a network of contemplative friendship based on the shared exploration of ideas about monastic life.[36]

The rise of the universities, however, shifted the centre of gravity away from monasteries. A young man interested in intellectual advancement at the time of the Fourth Lateran would find a more dynamic and exciting environment at a school or university, where a liberal arts syllabus based on Aristotle was becoming the normative approach to biblical and theological study. There were, of course, monks celebrated for their learning, but often this meant knowledge of the Scriptures rather than analytical learning or experimental knowledge. It is true that Abbot John of St Albans (1195–1214) was commended in the monastery's tradition for being learned in the secular arts of grammar and geometry as well as a contemplative.[37] But basic ignorance among even senior monks was, if not widespread, not unusual. When we hear of such examples, they are usually cited in terms of disapproval, indicating awareness that this was not a state of affairs to be expected. The precentor of Bury was reluctant to become prior because of embarrassment at his lack of learning.[38] Gerald of Wales – perhaps not a wholly reliable witness – tells the story of how Abbot Robert of Malmesbury was accused by his own monks of illiteracy, on grounds of which they sought to have him removed. Pope Alexander III appointed two bishops to assess the truth of the allegation. Sadly Robert failed the test of translating a passage of Latin, but one of the bishops argued that his ability in managing affairs nevertheless made him a good abbot – as long as he agreed to be taught proper Latin by his monks.[39] Perhaps a more telling indication of knowledge of Latin is that Simon of Beaulieu, archbishop of Bourges, apparently preached to the canons of Clermont in Latin, the monks of St Jean-d'Angély in Latin and French, and the nuns of Holy Cross, Poitiers, in French only.[40] Eudes, archbishop of Rouen, found on a visitation to the monastery of St Georges that the abbot regularly absented himself from the offices because of his inability to follow the scriptural readings.[41]

Perhaps in response to the friars' presence at universities, in 1245 the Cistercian chapter-general took the decision to send monks to university for theological study.[42] When one considers the resolute opposition of Bernard of Clairvaux to the teaching in cathedral schools a hundred years earlier, this marks a major change of direction. In 1269 Yves de Vergu, abbot of Cluny, founded the Collège de Cluny in Paris – now home to the celebrated Musée de Cluny – to house novices studying at the university.[43] In England, the 1247 Benedictine chapter in the Canterbury province decreed a daily lecture on theology or canon law for monks with an aptitude for learning who would benefit from it.[44] By 1277 this idea had been developed much further, into the decision to establish a permanent Benedictine house of studies at Oxford, to be maintained financially by a tax imposed according to means on all Benedictine houses in the province. Agreement to participate was not universal. The abbot of Bec opposed it on behalf of the English dependencies of the monastery, enlisting the support of John Pecham, the archbishop of Canterbury (1279–92), in his resistance, perhaps enhanced by the fact that Pecham was a Franciscan who did not welcome the rivalry of another regular house of studies at Oxford. Financial cost may also have been grounds for scepticism. St Albans generally maintained between four and six monks a year at Oxford, the expense of which required a levy of £25 to provide for stipends for the students, and additional amounts from dependent priories.[45] In 1283 a private benefactor donated a property in Oxford for use of Benedictine monks, and in 1298 what came to be known as Gloucester College opened with a few Malmesbury monks, to be greatly expanded over the course of the next generation.

One of the results of monastic involvement in the universities was felt in preaching. Monks who had been sent to university naturally returned with a different approach to the study of Scripture and patristic writings. This had been noticeable as early as the twelfth century. Abbot Samson of Bury St Edmunds, who had studied in the Paris schools, was eager to disseminate his theological knowledge by preaching in English – in a broad Norfolk accent – to the laity.[46] The sermons composed by university-educated monks have been described as 'a self-conscious symbol of a new monasticism positioning itself at the head of the Church militant'.[47] Preaching – the art of expounding the word of God – was stated by the Benedictine chapter-general of 1363 as one of the reasons for sending monks to the university. But preaching was also one outcome of the educational reforms enacted in some monasteries following the Subiaco and Melk reforms of the late fourteenth and early fifteenth centuries. The 'claustral sermon' became a valuable means of educational instruction, and collections of sermons such as those by the Bursfeld monk Bernhard of Waging (c. 1400–1472) became influential throughout German congregations. But more sophisticated preaching in the cloister was not only due to academically educated monks. Women from aristocratic families were by the later Middle Ages increasingly likely to be better educated before entering the cloister, and to have expectations not only of becoming learned but also of sharing and disseminating knowledge in similar ways to men. Advanced preaching and teaching was a feature of convents as well as male monasteries.

The reputation of late medieval monasteries as centres of innovative learning has been restored in recent years. The work of James Clark and others on St Albans Abbey in the fourteenth and fifteenth centuries has demonstrated that a series of able and gifted monks showed more intellectual ambition and curiosity than suggested by assumptions of decline and parochialism.[48] The books known to have been in the monastery's library include an impressive collection of scientific works, with a particular bent for astronomy. Examination of the books themselves shows that they were being read frequently in the later fourteenth century and into the fifteenth. Manuscripts were repaginated, rebound and repaired, and there is evidence of note-taking and rubrication. Previous astronomical works by St Albans monks, such as Matthew Paris's anthology of charts and tables, formed the basis for new writing on the subject. A new version of the *Tractatus Albionis*, a book by the former abbot Richard of Wallingford (d. 1366) about the mechanical clock that he had built, was written by the monk John Westwyke in the fifteenth century.[49] Standard theological works such as Peter Comestor's *Historia Scholastica* and Peter Lombard's *Sentences*, reference works of the twelfth century drawing on pre-existing scriptural commentaries, were frequently consulted, to judge from signs of use. Dictionaries of Greek and Hebrew appear in the list of borrowers from the later Middle Ages, which indicates an interest in the kind of humanistic scholarship that was becoming particularly important in the fifteenth century. But there was also interest in literary and historical works, especially those with a focus on English history and what we would now consider legend.[50]

The breadth of intellectual interests represented in reading by late medieval monks fed into new kinds of composition. The twelfth and thirteenth centuries are rightly seen as a golden age of historical writing in monasteries, but the work of a monk such as Thomas Walsingham (*c.* 1340–1422) indicates that monasteries in the fourteenth and fifteenth centuries were also able to provide the kind of intellectual ambience that stimulated innovative writing. Walsingham's writing was eclectic, though historical in direction. He wrote a history of Normandy for Henry V, a history of Alexander the Great, a commentary on ancient and medieval Latin poets, a version of Dictys of Crete's account of the Trojan War, and among other works, contributed to the St Albans *Gesta Abbatum*.[51]

Although history had always been a particularly monastic literary preoccupation, new kinds of historical interests are noticeable in fourteenth-century monasteries. By the 1370s, monks were becoming involved in debates that had been current since earlier in the century among mendicants over which Order in the Church was oldest and most 'genuine'.[52] Treatises on the origins of the monastic profession written at English Benedictine monasteries – notably Durham, Bury St Edmunds and St Albans – suggest a lively interest in the question, as also do the new commentaries on the *Rule of Benedict* by Richard of Wallingford and John of Beverley, a Durham monk active in the 1340s.[53] This kind of writing was not an exclusively English phenomenon. The treatise *De origine, fundatoribus et regulis monachorum et monacharum* (*On the Origin, Founders and Rules of Monks and Nuns*) was probably written at the Bohemian monastery of Brno, originally a tenth-century foundation.[54] Like Uthred of Boldon's *De substantialibus regule monachalis*, an examination of monastic Rules, this work addresses the link between contemporary monasticism and the Old Testament prophets.[55] Monks in England and Bohemia in the late fourteenth century may have been led to these historical interests in looking for ways to refute the attacks on monasticism by John Wyclif and Jan Hus and their followers. But an anonymous French treatise on monastic origins from the 1360s, written for the abbot of Tournus in Burgundy, indicates similar interests without the same external context.[56] Characteristic of all these works is the notion that although Benedict composed his Rule at a particular moment in history, Benedictine monasticism existed in some symbolic but 'real' fashion in the way of life of Old Testament precursors. Uthred of Bolden's treatise *De prima institutione monachorum* traced the origins of monasticism back to Elijah, Elisha and the sons of prophets, following the familiar path laid out by John Cassian in the fifth century and taken up again, for example, by the *Exordium magnum* of the Cistercians in the early thirteenth century. Uthred traces monastic history through early Christian authors and exemplars: Philo of Alexandria (*c.* 20 BC–AD 50); the

Ecclesiastical History of Sozomen, with its accounts of eremitical wanderings in Syria and Palestine; Pachomius's foundation at Tabennesi; the monks of the Thebaid; Anthony, Hilarion and Egyptian monks familiar from the *Apophthegmata Patrum* and Cassian: the two Macarii, John, Aurelius, Serapion, Dioscorus; Basil of Caesarea.[57] A profound interest in the Egyptian monks is also a feature of the French treatise *A quo tempore et a quibus patribus monachi duxerunt originem*.[58]

The desire to trace monastic roots demonstrates a concern for the idea of coherence in the monastic profession. In a sense we may take this as a sign that the institutional reforms since 1215 had not been fruitless. Although provincial chapters of Benedictines, Augustinians, Premonstratensians and others may not have delivered consistent reform in observances, they seem at least to have instilled a sense of monasticism as an Order of religious life within the Church. Interests in the origins of monasticism as a profession naturally took later medieval Latin monks back to the eastern Mediterranean. In a sense, this was far from new. As we have seen, the impetus behind the monastic reform of the eleventh and twelfth centuries was at least in part the rereading and copying of texts from the fourth to seventh centuries describing the way of life of the 'first monks'. By the mid-fourteenth century, however, ancient monasteries in the eastern Mediterranean such as St Sabas, and especially Mount Sinai, had become known to western pilgrims. It was now possible to witness the lives of the desert monks at first hand, through their direct descendants.

LATER BYZANTINE MONASTICISM

Two years prior to the Fourth Lateran, Pope Innocent III wrote a letter to the governing monastic council of Mount Athos. Praising the fertility of their monastic life, he apologised for the destruction of the property of some of the Athonite monasteries by Latins, but reassured them that Mount Athos was now to be placed under the spiritual protection of the holy see.[59] Over the following two centuries, popes would write in flattering terms to the Athonite monks but at the same time deploring their refusal to accept the primacy of the Roman pope.[60] Latin Europeans had always regarded Orthodox monks and monasticism with respect, tinged with suspicion. A telling example of this attitude is the episode in Odo of Deuil's account of the journey of the French king, Louis VII, to the East on the Second Crusade in 1147–8. Odo, a monk of St Denis, acknowledges how impressed he was by the celebration of the liturgy of St Dionysius that he heard at Hagia Sophia in Constantinople. Yet only a few pages earlier in his text, he had observed that it was common knowledge in the West that the Byzantines were schismatics and heretics.[61]

During the thirteenth and fourteenth centuries, parts of the Greek Orthodox world were ruled by Latins. Following the Fourth Crusade, Constantinople itself, Greece and the Greek islands came under the control of Frankish dynasties or the Republic of Venice, while Cyprus was ruled from 1192 by the Lusignans. Southern Italy and Sicily, where there was still a large Greek-rite population, were wholly ruled by western dynasties, first Norman, subsequently German and Spanish. Parts of the Holy Land and Syria remained under Latin rule until 1291. Although a Byzantine dynasty, the Palaeologi, retook control of Constantinople and much of Greece and Thrace in 1261, the Peloponnese remained under the rule of French families, and the islands, including Crete, remained Venetian until the seventeenth century, while Cyprus exchanged French rule for Venetian in the fifteenth century. Throughout the periods of Latin political domination, Greek-rite monasteries continued to function, albeit in straitened circumstances in certain regions.

Conquest or reconquest by non-Christian regimes, such as for example in the eastern Mediterranean during the thirteenth century, did not invariably spell the end of monasticism, but gradual decline set in because of the underlying political turmoil that brought to an end the period of Latin rule. Under the Mamluk regime in the Holy Land and Syria from the 1250s onwards, monasteries became prey to this political instability. For example, the Georgian monastery of Holy Cross near Jerusalem was raided and turned into a Sufi convent in the 1260s, the *hegoumen* being killed during the raid. But in 1305 the monastery was given back to the monks, and western pilgrims regularly visited it in the fourteenth century.[62] The monasteries of the Judaean desert and the Jericho plain suffered different fates in the fourteenth and fifteenth centuries, though in all cases the story seems to have been one of decline. St Sabas, the most celebrated and enduring of the monasteries, survived Mamluk raids in

1269, but by 1389 the Russian pilgrim Ignatios of Smolensk reports a drastic reduction in numbers of monks. The monastery of Chariton, a sixth-century *lavra*, was still functioning for part of the thirteenth century but seems to have been abandoned before 1300; St Mary Choziba, between Jerusalem and Jericho, was uninhabited by 1335; St Theodosius, near Bethlehem, was still active in *c.* 1360 but in ruins by 1400. Numbers of monks at St John Prodromos, by the river Jordan, had dwindled by 1384. In the same year St Gerasimos, also by the Jordan, was found by Italian pilgrims to be uninhabited. The monastic community at the monastery of the Temptation at Jebel Quruntul, which seems to have been thriving in 1289, had dwindled by 1384 to just a single monk.[63] In some cases these monasteries probably declined because of falling recruitment at a time of increasing instability, as had been the case in the early Arab period. In others, such as St Theodosius near Bethlehem, the end was probably sudden and violent. Monasteries' treasures were sometimes looted: a manuscript belonging to the monastery of Chariton since the eleventh century has a colophon bearing testimony to its having being part of the plunder taken at the fall of Acre in 1291, and later redeemed by a pious monk.[64] To set against this story of apparent decline, however, there is also an example – the exception that proves the rule, perhaps – of a new, very small foundation in Jerusalem, the monastery of Gerasimos, founded by a monk from Trebizond with connections to the Trapezuntine imperial dynasty.[65] As the visit of Fabri to St Sabas in the 1480s shows, monastic life continued in some centres throughout the fifteenth century; in the case of St Sabas, Mount Sinai and a few others, after the Ottoman conquest of the sixteenth century. Mount Athos, likewise, continued to be a centre for monasticism after the Ottoman conquest of Constantinople in 1453. Some Athonite monasteries, notably Vatopedi, were also centres of classical learning: the pilgrim Cyriacus of Ancona remarked on seeing a manuscript of Ovid with a Greek translation in the monastery.[66] Gennadios Scholarios, a celebrated scholar who became patriarch of Constantinople immediately after the Ottoman conquest of the city, abdicated his post in 1456 and withdrew to Athos to live as a scholar-monk.[67]

Monastic life across the Near East was also threatened by the arrival of the Mongols and their struggle against the Mamluks for territorial dominance in the region. Monasteries in exposed locations in Syria were depopulated as monks fled to safer locales such as Mount Sinai. But the Mongol advance affected monasteries across the Slavic lands north of the Caucasus as well. The Monastery of the Caves, originally founded as an Athonite *lavra* near Kyiv in the 1050s but which became a cenobitic monastery following the Studite Rule in the 1060s, was destroyed by the Mongols in the thirteenth century, along with other monasteries in urban or suburban locales that suffered alongside the fates of sacked cities. As a result, monasteries in Slavic territories tended to be refounded in more remote locations such as the vast forests of Russia.

After the return of a Byzantine dynasty, the Palaeologi, to rule in Constantinople, the Empire saw a revival of monastic life and traditions. The new Byzantine state, however, was perennially short of funds while beset by external threats, and Patriarch Athanasios I (1289–93 and 1303–9) made enemies of the monastic leadership by his attitude to endowed property, which he considered it legitimate for Emperor Andronikos II to impound in order to pay for armies. Athanasios issued a Rule that he intended to engender uniform monastic observance throughout the Empire, and although this was a failure in the sense that he had wanted, it is symptomatic of a period of what has been called 'patriarchal activism' in Byzantine monasticism.[68] In general, typika in the later Byzantine period tended to be written by patriarchs, emperors or members of the imperial family, rather than by 'working monks'. Thus, Emperors Andronikos II (1282–1328) and Manuel II (1391–1425) both wrote typika for new foundations, while the princess Theodora Synadene and her daughter Euphrosyne Palaiologina wrote another. Patriarch Athanasios's typikon (1303–5) was based firmly on the Evergetian tradition of the eleventh century. The rules on ownership of private property, dining together, care of the sick and cutting off relations with the monk's family all follow these cenobitic norms. But the stipulation that senior monks had a responsibility to inform the patriarch if the Rule was not being observed hints at the wider agenda behind Athanasios's typikon. As Timothy Miller has observed, the typikon departed from tradition not so much in its individual measures as in the assumption that it could work as an instrument to impose reforms on all monks and nuns in the Orthodox world: it was, in his words, 'the quintessential public sector challenge to the empire's private benefactors'.[69] One of the striking features of this period of monastic foundation was the attempt by patriarchs such as Isaias (1323–32) and John XIV Kalekas (1334–47) to curb the economic rights of founders or patrons in monasteries – and, conversely, the insistence of some founders, such as Emperor Michael VIII's niece Theodora Synadene, on retaining those rights. Emperors sometimes had a tendency to see monastic estates as a resource of the imperial fisc. In 1367, Emperor John V tried to follow Andronikos II in settling soldiers on monastic estates. This provoked a reasoned defence of independent monasteries' lands by the monk Nicholas Kabasilas, based on Roman property laws.[70]

Most typika of this later Byzantine period show some reliance on earlier Rules, though as John Thomas has observed, not always with an exact knowledge of the sources at their command. Although a connection can be seen to the practices of the Evergetian cenobitic reform of the eleventh century, founders such as Emperor Manuel II seem to have thought they were transmitting the ideals of a pre-Evergetian Athonite monasticism. According to Thomas, Palaeologan monasticism thought it was looking back to some 'original' form of monasticism in the distant past, when in fact many of the details of typika such as Manuel II's or that for Eleousa were actually Evergetian in origin. As we shall see, there are parallels here with some features of western monastic views, which likewise looked back to an idealised 'golden age' of monastic origins. A survey of later (i.e. post-1258) Byzantine foundations indicates some distinctive features held in common.[71] The monasteries founded in this period tended to be larger than previous private foundations. They were overwhelmingly cenobitic in character, though, with the exception of the convent founded by Theodora Synadene, they show little interest in manual labour. Liturgically, the model of St Sabas had become normative. Comparatively little attention was paid to philanthropy or charity. In terms of governance, founders tended to favour collaborative rather than autocratic forms, placing reliance on groups of experienced senior monks or nuns to make decisions. External authority was distrusted, though the actual extent of autonomy may have been less than in previous generations. In contrast to this centralising cenobitic tendency, some monasteries on Mount Athos developed a much looser type of community life. A return to the *lavra* model may have inspired the communities that elected superiors to supervise monastic 'families', but in which there was no observance of a Rule. Monks in these communities kept their own property and lived in their own cells. They might undertake individual manual labour, but study and contemplation were equally acceptable.

Attempts at centralised reform of monasteries with a view to undermining their autonomous control over private property took place against a backdrop of the continuing shrinking of the Byzantine state. As early as the 1370s, the advance of Ottoman forces had forced some monasteries on Mount Athos to build fortifications, and in 1372/3 the monastic peninsula was only narrowly saved from occupation by the intervention of a naval force. In this climate, some monasteries negotiated individually with the Ottomans: St John the Forerunner in Thrace, for example, obtained a promise of protection from Sultan Murad I even before the Ottoman conquest of the region in 1383. The unexpected defeat of the Ottoman Sultan Bayezid by Tamurlane in 1402 allowed the Empire to re-establish control over Athos and the Chalkidike in the early fifteenth century, and this was the background against which Emperor Manuel II issued his typikon of 1406. But by 1430, the Athonite commonwealth had submitted to the sultan and agreed to pay tribute in return for being left unmolested.

Monasteries in and near Constantinople continued to remain active at least until 1453, and sometimes played significant roles in religious life. But the Ottoman siege of the city between 1394 and 1402 ruined the endowments of monasteries, making academic the question of control over private property. Despite the growing Ottoman threat, monasticism continued to play a central role in the Empire. Monks were influential in the discussions over union with the Roman Church, culminating in the refusal of monastic opinion to accept the decrees of the Council of Florence (1439) and Ferrara (1444). The Ottoman conquest, if anything, advanced a process of centralisation of monasticism under patriarchal authority. Although episcopal appointments were subject to confirmation by the sultan, only the patriarch of Constantinople could appoint or depose a bishop. Clergy and monks were subject to the jurisdiction of the patriarchal court.

FRUIT IN ITS SEASON

HESYCHASM

The most important development in late Byzantine monasticism concerned the inner life of monks, yet it came to have a profound effect on the institution as well. Hesychasm was a method of prayer and contemplation with the purpose of 'facilitating ascent to a transformative communion with God'.[72] The practice is attested in the earliest monastic practice through what is known as the 'Jesus prayer', a short verse that in its simplest form comprises the words 'Lord Jesus Christ, Son of God, have mercy on me', repeated constantly, but it seems to have become a central feature of the personal spirituality of monks of Mount Sinai, and a chapter of John Klimakos's *Heavenly Ladder* was devoted to *hesychia*. Symeon the New Theologian approved the practice as a means of monastic prayer. In the thirteenth-century anonymous *Three Methods of Prayer*, the practice is described in precise terms:

> Once the hesychast has put himself under unquestioning obedience to a spiritual father, he is to sit on a stool with his head bowed and his gaze focused on his abdomen or navel. He is to control his breathing for the purpose of drawing his intellect down into his heart. There in the heart he will encounter his inner being flooded with light, filled with divine grace.[73]

Although hesychasm was a purely interior spiritual experience, it came to have a serious effect on ecclesiastical life and even imperial politics in the fourteenth century, especially during the civil war of 1341–47. Hesychasm had been revived on Mount Athos through teaching of the monk Gregory of Sinai.[74] Gregory was a native of Asia Minor, born in *c.* 1275. Captured as a young man by Turkish pirates, he was fortunate to be bought at the slave market by a pious Christian couple who gave him his freedom. He went first to Cyprus to learn anchoritic traditions, then joined the monastery of Mount Sinai, where he lived under the monastic regime that has been described by western pilgrims as strict and observant. At some point between 1307 and 1310 he left Sinai to settle on Athos, but his journey took him by way of Crete, where he encountered a monk who practised hesychasm. Gregory adopted the practice himself on Athos, where it was already known through the teachings of the monk Nikodemos of Vatopedi. Gregory's practice of hesychasm attracted some followers among the monks at Magoula, but also some opposition. He left Athos in 1326, and settled at Paroria, near the Bulgarian frontier, where he founded a monastery at Mount Katakekryomene, and died in 1346. Gregory's writings on the practice of hesychasm are practical rather than speculative: he instructs his readers what postures they should adopt in prayer, how much time they should give to psalm singing compared to the Jesus prayer, and how they should regulate their diet in order to best achieve a life of constant prayer.

Gregory of Sinai's most prominent follower as a hesychast was Gregory Palamas, archbishop of Thessaloniki (1347–59), though it is not certain whether they ever met in person. Born in Constantinople in *c.* 1296 to an aristocratic family, Palamas became a monk at the monastery of Vatopedi on Mount Athos in 1316.[75] Vatopedi was one of the larger and the second oldest of the Athonite monasteries, but he moved from here first to the Great Lavra, then to a hermitage (*skete*), where he practised hesychasm. Unlike Gregory of Sinai, who was evidently a charismatic teacher, Palamas was an intellectual: a theologian who was convinced of the theological as well as personal spiritual value of hesychasm. This led him into a celebrated controversy with the Calabrian monk Barlaam. A contemporary of Palamas, Barlaam had been a monk at the celebrated monastery of St Elias at Galatro in Calabria, and came to Thessaloniki and then Constantinople in the 1320s to study. He was drawn into theological debate with the envoys of Pope John XXII, which established him as a member of the intellectual elite and brought him to the attention of Emperor Andronikos III and his successor John Kantakuzene. In 1339 he was sent by Andronikos to the court of Philip VI of France to plead for western military help against the Ottomans. Barlaam initially attacked the practice of hesychasm in 1336, in a treatise called *Against the Messalians*, which only survives in fragments in other writings. He encountered the practice through correspondence with Palamas about the usefulness of Aristotle in achieving the kind of understanding of God through the intellect that the hesychasts sought from interior contemplation. To Barlaam, hesychasm smacked of heresy, with its mystical and visionary experiences, and out-of-body sensations. A follower of Barlaam, Gregory Akindynos, argued that God could only be known by what he had created, and that this could be understood through the operation of the intellect. In contrast, Palamas thought that an insistence on the action of the intellect removed God from human experience. We may not, as humans, be able fully to comprehend God's essence, but we can experience the divine through what he called his 'energies', through wilful act of communion in transfigurative prayer. This, to the anti-hesychasts, verged on the heretical because it appeared to suggest another layer of God-ness within the Trinity. Despite the support for hesychasm at a council in 1347, new voices emerged. The Neoplatonist Nikephoros Gregoras insisted that only through the 'motionless movement' of the mind, rather than through the sensory impressions stimulated by hesychasm, could God be understood.

The dispute over whether hesychasm was heretical dominated a series of ecclesiastical councils during the reign of John VI Kantakuzene. But after Barlaam's initial accusation of heresy against Palamas in 1340, it is difficult to identify either of the sides in the wider struggle between John VI and his rival John V as 'Palamite' or 'Barlaamite', because both could be found in both camps. The extent to which what had started as a recondite debate over a practice of prayer came to affect ecclesiastical politics can be seen in the struggle that Palamas encountered when, appointed metropolitan of Thessaloniki in 1347, he was unable to enter his city because of the activity of anti-Kantakuzene zealots. Generally speaking, however, the anti-hesychasts comprised a small circle of humanists and a few bishops, and in 1351 hesychasm was declared an official teaching of the Church.

REFORM MOVEMENTS IN THE LATE MIDDLE AGES

The popularity of the friars and the grip that mendicant forms of religious life took on the life of the Church in the thirteenth and fourteenth centuries should not be seen as invariably signalling a decline in the importance of enclosed monasticism.[76] Many other new forms of expression in religious life emerged at the same time, with varying degrees of closeness to 'traditional' monasticism.[77] Some, like the Beguines, can be seen as gendered responses to spiritual and devotional needs that could not easily be met within prevailing structures. Women dedicated to a life of prayer and service, Beguines neither took vows nor became members of an enclosed convent, although they lived in communities. They might even marry, and live apart from the community, while still remaining members. This was a largely urban phenomenon, emerging in the towns of Flanders and the Netherlands in the thirteenth century. The first beguinage seems to have been that at Mechlin as early as 1207, and most Flemish towns had at least one, sometimes several, by the end of the century.[78] The loose association represented by the Beguines (and for that matter the Begards, a male version) was in some ways a logical extension of existing ideas. Monasticism was malleable and permeable, and had always accommodated different forms of institutional life. Fluidity between enclosure and openness, community and anachoresis, was a constant feature of reform and regeneration in monasticism. Moreover, the idea of a professed man or woman living apart from an institutional community but associated with its members in prayer, even dependent on it for a supply of food, was common in monasticism. For that matter, 'house ascetics' – men and women living contemplative lives within a household – were a feature of monasticism since its earliest times. Prominent women might make choices to live in the world as religious rather than entering the cloister. Elisabeth of Hungary (d. 1231), Landgravina of Thuringia, known for her piety during her husband Louis's lifetime, was asked to consider taking vows after her husband's death, but chose instead to remain *soror in seculo* ('a sister in the world'). She established a hospital for the poor and organised her household to conduct charitable works. As a member of the social elite, her example of practical devotion to others through good works was a powerful example of how the scriptural model of Martha could best be followed without recourse to enclosure and vows.[79] Monastic identities, moreover, were not so easily fixed. When Yvette of Huy (1158–1228) began to care for lepers, she remained a laywoman but wore a Cistercian tunic under her clothes. Although she never professed as a nun herself, her family maintained close associations with a number of Cistercian communities in the region, and both her father and her sons entered Cistercian monasteries.[80]

The tendency for men and more especially women to pursue lives of devotion outside the convent became increasingly marked from the thirteenth century onwards, at a time when urban growth was providing more opportunities for them to exercise economic and civic agency.[81] Contemporaries were not always sure how such people should be categorised. A fifteenth-century Dominican, Johannes Nider, described women such as beguines as 'laywomen who lived as religious in the secular world'.[82] As has recently been pointed out, much of the scholarship on such groups necessarily focuses on negative identities: they were neither nuns nor laypeople. But part of the uncertainty about their status may arise from the desire of contemporary religious to 'claim' such women for their own identities. Elisabeth of Thuringia was retrospectively adopted as a Franciscan tertiary, but they did not yet exist as a defined group when she died in 1231.[83] Women such as Elisabeth pursued communal lives of piety that were centred on the secular world, and in so doing they challenged the norms and expectations associated with religious lives.

Notwithstanding this general trend, we should beware of exaggerating the polarity between the cloister and the world. In many ways, what happened inside the monastery could not help but be reflective of what was happening outside. Strict enclosure may have been considered by some a necessity for women. Despite the attempts of Clare of Assisi to follow the example of Francis, the female Orders of mendicants were enclosed rather than allowed an active ministry in the world. Even within a system of strict enclosure, however, 'nunnery walls served communities as permeable membranes rather than watertight seals'.[84] The papal decree *Ut periculoso* (1290) appears to have been an attempt to make enclosure watertight by prohibiting female religious from leaving their convents. On the face of it, this looks like an 'official' response to the dangers posed by transgressive nuns. But there is another way of looking at it, as Erin Jordan has observed: as a positive development to be welcomed by communities such as Cistercian nuns who wished to emphasise precisely where they differed from other new groups such as the Beguines.[85]

The tendency to looser forms of devotional life in the later Middle Ages, especially in cities, did not mean that monasticism lost its appeal.

If one form of monastic expression in the later Middle Ages was the semi-monastic culture of the beguinage, a return to a different non-Benedictine version of enclosure was the inspiration for a remarkable revival of one form of monastic life across Europe. In 1348, a London citizen, Walter Manny, rented 13 acres north of the city walls to found a chapel and graveyard for plague victims. This became the focal point for the foundation of a new Carthusian monastery, when in 1361 the bishop of London persuaded Manny to convert the chapel into a foundation to rival the Paris Charterhouse. Although both Manny and Bishop Northburgh left bequests for the construction of the monastery, little seems to have been done before 1370, when John Luscote, prior of the Carthusian house at Hinton, arrived with the first monks. Luscote had to badger Manny for the promised money simply to build permanent cells for the monks. As a recent study of the early documentation of the monastery shows, it was thanks to Luscote's ability to mobilise funds from William Walworth, a prominent fishmonger and mayor of London, and through him other London merchants, such as another former mayor, John Lovekyn, and the wool merchant Adam Fraunceys, that the first cells were constructed. The Charterhouse was, from the start, a project reflecting merchant piety.[86]

New Carthusian monasteries were founded elsewhere: Mount Grace in North Yorkshire; Paris, Dijon, Villeneuve-lès-Avignon. Carthusian spirituality had always had the capacity to appeal to discontented or unfulfilled members of other Orders. Adam of Dryburgh, a Premonstratensian, was a celebrated twelfth-century convert to the Order, and in 1241 a group of monks of Christ Church Canterbury became Carthusians.[87] But the revival of Carthusian monasticism across western Europe in the fourteenth and fifteenth centuries is one of the more surprising aspects of late medieval monasticism. Between *c.* 1380 and *c.* 1520, some two hundred monasteries were founded in eighteen provinces. Notwithstanding the example of the London Charterhouse, many of their new patrons were aristocratic or royal. The Order was especially patronised and prized by the higher nobility.[88]

As we saw in a previous chapter, the Carthusian model was based on the smallest self-enclosed unit of contemplative life: the cell. Monasteries were originally restricted to twelve choir monks, each of whom occupied an individual cell. In so far as they were communities, they functioned as such only during the daily and nocturnal office: all the other 'hours' were said privately by the monks in their cells. The hallmark of the cenobitic life, shared eating in the refectory, was virtually absent: instead, the brothers received and ate their meals in their cells, where they also pursued crafts and studied. The term 'cell' is somewhat misleading, especially in the late medieval Carthusian monastery. The examples that can still be seen – for example, at Villeneuve-lès-Avignon, or in outline at Mount Grace – were substantial apartments, often on two storeys, with separate rooms for study and work, and a small garden for each. This is one reason why sponsors were sought to subsidise the construction of individual cells or groups of cells.[89] One strikingly obvious feature of the late medieval Carthusian house is the sheer extent of the property required. Although, unlike Benedictine monasteries, Carthusian houses typically did not own huge rural estates or farms, the footprint of surviving buildings and properties was very large considering the ceiling on the numbers of monks in any single establishment. The monks were supported by at least an equal number of lay brothers, and the ethic of self-sufficiency demanded sufficient property for a small home farm. In a small town such as Villeneuve, the Carthusian house dominated the built environment; even in London, the presence of the estate just to the north of the city wall made clear the property-owning power of contemplation.

The popularity of the Carthusians is symptomatic of the same devotional turn that gave rise to other expressions of religious life. Medieval societies in the second half of the fourteenth century were in a shattered state. Endemic wars in Italy, the ravages of the Hundred Years War in France, the lack of central authority in the Empire all contributed to widespread political instability. By about 1300–20, the European population had probably reached a peak that would be unsurpassed before the seventeenth century, but a gradual change in climate patterns resulted in a period of poor harvests and widespread food shortages.[90] The Black Death, a wave of epidemic plagues that spread across the whole of Europe and the Near East from the 1340s until the end of the century, resulted in a loss of population of between 30 and 40 per cent. The economic effects of this dramatic collapse were mixed – there were fewer people to produce food, but fewer mouths to feed, and the balance of power shifted towards such labour as was still available. Standards of living for the survivors may have improved, but the emotional effects of such a rate of mortality must have been profound. It is not surprising that one response to the vulnerability of human society to sudden death through rapidly spreading disease was a heightened sense of devotional need. The monumental art of the post-Black Death period reflects an intense preoccupation with death and the passage of time.[91] Charterhouses were sometimes chosen as mausolea by wealthy families. In the Champmol charterhouse at Dijon, which became the dynastic burial chamber of the ducal family of Burgundy, the tombs of Duke Philip the Bold and John the Fearless were located between the monks' stalls inside the church, so that 'the antiphony of prayer went through them back and forth, and away up over them'.[92] Revivals of forms of contemplative life focused on intense personal piety must be seen against this cultural background.

The Carthusians represented the revival of an older traditional form of monastic life — a form that might even be seen in origin as a link to an eastern Mediterranean type of 'communal solitude'. Other expressions of monastic reform took new forms. The Brigittines, founded in the 1370s through the example of St Brigit of Sweden (*c.* 1303–1373), expanded over a similar period to the Carthusians.[93] The Brigittine Order was in many ways a response to perceptions of the decline of sincere observance in traditional female houses. Born into an aristocratic Swedish family, and related on her mother's side to the ruling dynasty, Brigit married at the characteristically early age for girls of her social class and became known for works of charity on behalf of mothers throughout Östergötland: Brigit herself gave birth to eight children. In 1341 she and her husband made a pilgrimage to Santiago de Compostela, and when she was widowed in 1344, she initially became a Franciscan tertiary before founding the first house of her new Order of the Most Holy Saviour at Vadstena. Like the Gilbertines and other previous reforming experiments, the Brigittines were double houses for men and women in separated accommodation and with separate cloisters. The emphasis was on communal poverty, but study was encouraged. In 1350, however, Brigit abandoned Sweden for Rome. Ostensibly this was to seek papal confirmation for her Order, but given that at that time the seat of the holy see was Avignon, there was perhaps a hint of disingenuity in this. At any rate, Brigit remained in Rome with her daughter Catherine until her death in 1373, save only for a pilgrimage to Jerusalem. Brigit's personal spirituality was influenced by devotion focused on the sufferings of Christ, which she saw reflected in the condition of the poor in her own day. Brigittine houses tended to be urban or fairly close to cities, such as the one at Isleworth, about 10 miles along the Thames from London.

The Pauline Order, given papal approval in 1308, provides a further example of the regeneration of earlier monastic forms in the late Middle Ages.[94] Extensively patronised by the crown and nobility of Hungary, especially from the 1380s, the Paulines showed elements of traditional regulated monasticism alongside others clearly influenced by eremitism and the mendicant movement. By *c.* 1500, there were some seventy Pauline monasteries, mostly in the kingdom of Hungary although other houses were founded in Poland, Silesia, Dalmatia and Austria. Most of their monasteries were small, housing perhaps ten monks on average. The Pauline profession, as the name suggests, centred on devotion to the figure of Paul the Hermit, whose relics were purchased for the Order's main monastery of St Lawrence in Buda by King Louis I from Venice in 1380. These were added to by subsequent kings, Louis II acquiring the saint's skull for St Lawrence in 1523. The Paulines were not, on the whole, a learned Order, although some of its members – the former bishop of Csanád Johannes Szokoli, for example – were already noted for their learning when they entered it. Some original Paulines produced original works: notably, the sixteenth-century history of the Order, Gregorius Gyöngyösi's *Vitae fratrum*, and a group of ascetic works by Vincent Fekete.[95] On the whole, however, the spiritual impetus of the Order was directed towards contemplation and liturgical observance. The Order's income from property was small, evidently never sufficient to cover its expenses, so like the mendicants it accepted donations from patrons and enjoyed a mixed economy of patronage from the crown, including from the reign of Louis I the farm of a salt rental.

How the Church in the West organised itself was the subject of intense argument and debate from the later fourteenth century until around the middle of the fifteenth. For most of the fourteenth century the papal court and its operations were in residence at Avignon rather than Rome, and the contentious question of the papal return to Rome caused a split, known as the Great Schism, in 1378. For several years rival popes were recognised in different parts of the West, according to the political alignments of the day. In order to resolve the division, and to deal with dissent that had manifested itself in movements such as the Lollards in England and the Hussites in Bohemia, who were challenging the authority of the Church as an institution, a series of councils was held in the first half of the fifteenth century. The Councils of Constance and Basel dealt not only with heresy and hierarchy, but also – as part of a wider recognition of the need for the regeneration of religious life – with the reform of monastic communities.

This reform was achieved initially through the operation of a traditional mechanism, the provincial chapter. Although chapters had been held regularly in England during the thirteenth and fourteenth centuries, this was far from the case in much of Europe. In 1417, however, a large meeting of Benedictine abbots at Petershausen, near Constance, prompted a new reform initiative that continued over the course of the next century through regular provincial chapters of the Mainz-Bamberg province. Other German-speaking provinces, for example in Austria, likewise revived provincial chapters. The mechanism of the chapter had been a feature of Orders such as the Cistercians since the first half of the twelfth century, and Cistercian chapters and visitations consequent on them continued into the sixteenth century. The third session of the Council of Trent (1561–3) brought a fresh impetus to the reforms of the previous century, for example, in reaffirming older decrees such as *Periculoso*. In fact there had been some discussion in this session of dissolving regular life altogether, before the council fathers settled on rather traditional reforming decrees: besides enclosure, they also prescribed a common life, outlawed ownership of private property by monks and nuns, and fixed the length of the novitiate at a minimum of sixteen months.

Between 1572 and 1574, for instance, Nicolas Boucherat, abbot of Cîteaux, visited all 104 Cistercian houses in German-speaking territories. The difference in scale between them was sometimes considerable. Günsterstal, a few miles from Freiburg im Breisgau, had eight choir nuns and one novice; Königsbrück, in the Alsace, had twenty-one sisters.[96] As the visitation remarked, it was difficult for a small community to conduct regular observance properly.[97] One method of inculcating reform in such communities was to educate them in the Order's history. In 1583, the professor of theology at the University of Freiburg, Jodocus Lorichius (1540–1612), translated the *Exordium Cistercii* into German as part of a compendium for the Günterstal community that also included the statutes of the Order; he also gave the nuns books including a German translation of a treatise on monasticism attributed to Bernard of Clairvaux.[98]

At the monastery of Kastl in Bavaria, the eleventh-century customary of Cluny was adopted. With the support of Duke Albert V of Austria, a group of German monks at Subiaco went to the monastery of Melk in 1419 in order to promote the strict Benedictine observance already being practised there. This in turn led to reforms at the ancient Carolingian foundations of Hirsau and Fulda. In some cases the reform arose directly out of the conciliar movement. Bursfeld in Hanover was reformed during the Council of Constance (1431–7). Perhaps paradoxically, the reform was initiated through the *commendam* system, by John Dederoth, appointed as abbot by the duke of Brunswick. As at Melk, learning and intellectual pursuits were integral to the Bursfeld reform. Education, in fact, was one of the vehicles of reform. Reform might mean disruption, sometimes uncomfortably so. In 1481 the German convent of Lune chose reform by first ejecting the abbess, Bertha, and replacing her with a new superior. The collection of letters to and from the nuns of Lune shows how reform ideas spread through correspondence, in this case with the reformed male community of Ebstorf.[99]

Just as Dederoth was appointed by a layman, so the Benedictine reform in Italy began with a lay initiative. In 1408 Pope Gregory XII gave a Venetian nobleman, Ludovico Barbo, charge of the abbey of Santa Giustina in nearby Padua, where the community had collapsed. Barbo, an abbot *in commendam*, eventually took the Benedictine habit, and led the reform of the abbey and its daughter-houses.[100] Pope Eugenius IV (1431–47) later provided a constitution that emphasised the discipline of a congregation of houses in the reform rather than – as was more typical in the German reform – the autonomy of the individual house. In this way the Italian reform, often referred to as the Subiaco reform because of the role played by that ancient monastery in its spread, was more like the Cistercian ideal than the traditional Benedictine scheme.[101] In devotional terms, the Subiaco reform reflected prevailing tastes for private prayer and meditation. By the 1490s the reform had spread to Spain, where Valladolid and Montserrat also adopted strict observance.

The grip of the *commendam* system meant that reform came later to French monasteries than in much of the rest of Europe. Here the crucial figure was Louis de Blois (1506–1566), also known as Blosius. Louis entered the monastery of Liessies, in northeastern France, aged fourteen, but was abbot ten years later. Although there are distinguished precedents for elevation at such a young age – one immediately thinks of Peter the Venerable at Cluny in 1122 – Louis's rapid advancement may in itself be an indication of the low quality of monastic life in this period. Louis had initially to overcome the resistance of a community that did not want to be reformed, and probably as a result the regime that he developed at Liessies was adapted to contemporary social habits. Although he insisted on cenobitism rather than the habit of monks living in what would be called in the Byzantine world 'idiorrhythmic' fashion, generous concessions were allowed. Abstinence was lightly observed, to the point of openly permitting meat-eating. Liessies has been called 'the first abbey of the post-Renaissance cultured society of Europe', and in many ways the Blosian reform prefigured the French monastic revival of the nineteenth century at Maredsous and Solesmes.[102]

DISSOLUTION

About half of Europe's monasteries and convents disappeared or ceased to exist during the sixteenth century. In some parts of Europe, particularly German-speaking regions, war and social unrest were responsible for the destruction of many communities. Although there was no systematic programme of destruction, more than 400 German monasteries and convents were physically attacked during the Peasants' War (1524–6). In other parts of Europe, monasteries and convents suffered similar destructive fates as a result of external circumstances. Many Bohemian monasteries had already suffered during the wars sparked by the rebellion of Jan Hus and his followers in the early fifteenth century. Hungarian monasteries were prey to confiscations and loss of income after the Ottoman conquests of the 1520s. The situation in France was different. Although some monasteries were attacked during the Wars of Religion (1562–93), observant monasticism had in any case declined markedly during the sixteenth century as a result of the concordat between Pope Leo X and King Francis I in 1516, which perpetuated the *commendam* system by giving the crown extensive rights of appointment to abbacies. In ways that paralleled the abuses of the *charistike* system in the eleventh-century Byzantine world, many French monasteries were in the hands of bishops or aristocrats.

The most striking acts of disappearance occurred in the British Isles and Scandinavia, where the crown brought an end to monasticism as an act of policy. In England, over the four years between 1536 and 1540, all 850 religious houses, monasteries, convents and mendicant priories were closed down, regardless of their numbers or financial health.[103] The closures were made by government agents, often against the will of the communities themselves and in ways that tore apart the social fabric of towns, villages and countryside. The situation in England differed from other parts of Europe where monasteries were closed in similar fashion because of the scale of the operation. The whole of Scandinavia, where religious houses were closed during the Reformation, had less than a quarter of the number of monasteries that England had.

The closures were the final acts of a process that had begun in 1534 with the assumption by Henry VIII of the headship of the Church in England by statutory act. Heads of religious houses, along with bishops, were obliged to swear their assent to the Act of Supremacy. Most were content to do so, and until the executions of Henry's Lord Chancellor, Thomas More, and John Fisher, bishop of Rochester, many probably did not understand the implications of royal supremacy.[104] The executions of John Houghton, prior of the London Carthusians, and some of his monks in May 1535 concentrated minds towards the determination of the government to assert its authority over the Church. The *Valor Ecclesiasticus*, an enquiry commissioned to determine the financial viability of monasteries, set the agenda for the closure, from 1536, of those institutions with an income of less than £200 annually. This was followed by a very swift, necessarily cursory, visitation of monasteries by a team of canon lawyers handpicked by Thomas Cromwell. In March 1536 the monasteries deemed to fall below this threshold – about 400 in England and Wales – were dissolved by an Act of Parliament, and 'surrenders' were obtained over the following eighteen months. It was not until 1538 that the aims of the government turned towards total dissolution and the seizure of assets. By the end of March 1540, when the last surrender, that of Waltham Abbey, was received, around 7,000 monks, nuns and mendicants had been turned out of what had been their homes and livelihoods. Of these, perhaps 2,000 were able to purchase dispensations to become secular clergy from the pension awarded to them by the government as part of the surrender.

As James Clark has recently observed, the closure of monasteries by the crown in England was not unprecedented. During the Hundred Years War, some seventy religious houses that were dependent or daughter-houses of French monasteries were closed. Even in times of peace monasteries might be closed because they no longer fulfilled the same purpose as when they had been founded, or because it had become too difficult for them to maintain a community. The kinds of changing devotional priorities and tastes that made some new congregations and houses so attractive also deflected support and affection from some others. Thomas Wolsey, the papal legate closed some houses in order to re-allocate their resources towards his new foundations at Oxford – Cardinal College, the precursor of Christ Church – and in his home town of Ipswich. In 1528 he was given a papal faculty to close any house with fewer than six members in the community.[105] New types of religious institution, such as urban chantry chapels and collegiate churches, provided competition for the pious-minded, especially in towns.[106]

One way of trying to understand the scale of the Dissolution in England is to note that, despite a major rebellion against the closure, the Pilgrimage of Grace, it proved impossible to undo when a Catholic ascended the throne again in 1553. This might, of course, be taken as an indication of how weak monasteries really were in the 1530s. The traditional narrative of the Dissolution is that there were more monasteries, many of them financially too weak, than could be supported by a society that had developed other ways of expressing their piety. Such a view is indeed supported by certain kinds of evidence. Episcopal visitations in the early sixteenth century found plenty to correct, notably the lack of genuine community when monks and nuns did not say the offices together regularly. Examples abound of monasteries that could not afford to keep up the fabric of their buildings: the spire of Rievaulx collapsed into the transept, while at the Welsh Cistercian house of Strata Florida the refectory and dormitory were in a ruinous condition.[107] The *Valor Ecclesiasticus* found many monasteries in a desperate financial state.

Criticism of monasticism and of the way of life of monks and nuns was of course common, not only in England but throughout western Europe, and can be seen with some consistency from the later twelfth century onwards. Some of the late medieval satire of monastic life came from monks and nuns themselves, as the caricatures of monks carved into misericords in abbey churches bears witness.[108] It can be argued that satire of an institution or practice reflects the deep-seated place that it has in a society as much as a desire to overthrow it. Even laypeople who might resent the presence of a monastery or see it as no longer reflective of their devotional piety might cavil at the abolition of buildings and institutions that characterised the landscape in which they lived, that housed the tombs of their ancestors and that had shaped regional and local histories and traditions. Monasteries were a distinctive presence in towns and countryside alike. Especially in cathedral priories, which had communities of either Benedictines or Augustinian canons, and urban monasteries in towns without cathedrals such as Westminster or Shrewsbury, monks were a familiar sight in pulpits at certain times of year.

In one sense, the intensive intervention of the English crown in monasticism in the 1530s was hardly unexpected. It followed from the *Praemunire* statutes of the fourteenth century (originally the Statute of Carlisle of 1307, followed up in 1353), in which the crown sought to prevent moneys raised from English ecclesiastical properties from going to papal funds.[109] As such, it attempted to shield monastic institutions and their property from the oversight of 'foreign' interests. Monasteries that were members of congregations that extended beyond England might find this left them stranded. In 1490, Henry VII refused to allow the abbot of Cîteaux to conduct a visitation of Cistercian houses in England. This was a signal that the crown saw itself not only as the custodian but also in some sense the owner of English monastic assets. In light of what unfolded some forty years later, it might even be seen as a warning sign. Some English monasteries' congregations seem to have preferred this state of affairs. In 1513, the Premonstratensians secured the support of Henry VIII to conduct a visitation free from the interference of the Order's chapter-general.[110] This, of course, allowed the Tudor monarchy to present itself as the governor of the monastic establishment in England. In many ways this was a highly traditional position, echoing as it did the sentiment of the tenth-century *Regularis Concordia*. Monastic heads did not necessarily find the centralising tendencies of the Tudor monarchy alarming, even when traditional rights of exemption from episcopal oversight were overridden. As James Clark has pointed out, there was good reason for heads of English monasteries to suppose that Henry VIII was sympathetic to them. Many were themselves supporters of humanist education and the reforms that were being promoted by influential members of the episcopal hierarchy in the early sixteenth century: John Fisher, bishop of Rochester, who begged Erasmus to teach him Greek; John Longland, a conscientious pastoral bishop of Lincoln; Richard Fox (1476–1528), bishop of Winchester and translator of the *Rule of Benedict* for Benedictine nuns of his diocese.[111] Even Thomas Wolsey, usually associated with the material excesses of a prince of the Church, had reforming credentials, and was a supporter of the Charterhouse. In the 1520s his hand was noticeable in a number of abbatial appointments to Benedictine and Cistercian houses.[112] Henry, moreover, like many of his predecessors, relied on members of the monastic hierarchy to advise him. The abbot of St Albans, Thomas Ramidge (r. 1492–1521), Richard Kidderminster, abbot of Winchcombe (r. 1488–1533/4), and John Islip (r. 1500–32), abbot of Westminster, were regularly at his court.

To many in the monastic world in England in the 1530s, the Dissolution looked at the outset like a sweeping reform of institutions that were in many cases struggling financially. Had they been able to take the privileged bird's-eye view of the historian, they might even have seen analogies with attempts to resolve similar problems in tenth- and eleventh-century Byzantium. Such a view must have seemed consistent with the creation of new monasteries in summer 1537, after almost 200 had already been closed in the previous year.[113] The Dissolution, in fact, looked to contemporaries like a visitation on a grand scale, but one undertaken through the agency of the government rather than bishops. Yet by Easter 1540 – 'four years and five festivals' after the start of the closures – all 660 monasteries in England and Wales had been closed. In some cases this was done with the acquiescence of the communities themselves, and sometimes with an apparent degree of inevitability: in the autumn of 1535, even before the closures had started, eleven monks of Roche Abbey, a Cistercian community, asked either to become seculars or take benefices as canons or priests.[114] In more remote areas, local communities had little idea what was happening until it was over. According to a local tradition, the first that the inhabitants of the Lune Valley in north Lancashire heard of the closure of Cockersand, a Premonstratensian monastery on the coast south of Lancaster, on 29 January 1539, was when the usual weekly supplies of fish sold by the monks at the village of Caton failed to materialise.[115] A combination of factors meant that what started as a critical enquiry into the viability of monasteries to continue running became, over the space of four years, the total dissolution of regular monasticism in a single country. John Guy has summarised this confluence of forces including the Act of Supremacy itself, which definitively stated that monasteries could harbour no allegiance to mother-houses outside the realm, but also the generation of humanist reform in which monastic endowments and assets had been vocally criticised. These criticisms were made against a background of land hunger at a time when the population was rising again after the plague of the fourteenth century.[116] But a further factor, according to Guy, was the opposition to Henry VIII from regulars, which outstripped that from any other section of the population.[117]

If the ostensible purpose of the visitation of 1535 was to determine the value of monastic properties, the result of the closure of monasteries was to enrich the crown through seizure and, in most cases, sale of the assets. The 'largest confiscation and redistribution of wealth since the Norman Conquest' yielded about £1.3 million in total from 1536 to 1547, from both rents and resale of lands and assets seized.[118] But the cost in shattered communities that had depended on monasteries, on groups forced apart, in the buildings, art and material culture dismantled and broken, is impossible to evaluate. The Dissolution in England was an act of unparalleled social and cultural disruption, the psychological effects of which must have been felt for generations. Antiquarians of the reigns of Elizabeth I and James I were already looking back in sadness at the end of a social and religious ecology that had literally shaped the landscape. As John Oglander observed, 'tyme pulleth downe greate things and setth up poore things'.[119]

By the end of the sixteenth century, the religious alignment of Europe brought about by the Reformation had devastated the monastic landscape. This did not happen in the same way or at the same rate everywhere. Some houses in reformed areas of Germany were taken over by municipalities, whereas the normal pattern in regions that remained Catholic was for religious life to remain as it was. In practice this meant that northern Germany lost most of its monasteries, while the south emerged with many intact. In Sweden, monastic estates were confiscated gradually over the course of decades after their surrender to the crown. In the Low Countries, monasteries in Protestant areas were closed, but even in Catholic regions many lost their independence to newly formed bishoprics.

Reformed Europe's monasteries may have disappeared, but wherever religious allegiance was contested they suffered through disruption, violence and uncertainty. Monasteries' symbiotic relationship with lay society meant that any disruptions to the normal workings of life affected communities of religious. Likewise, the conquest of the Byzantine world by the Ottomans led to the closure of many communities and the concentration of monks in areas such as Mount Latmos, on the west coast of Asia Minor, and Mount Athos.

Naturally reformers celebrated the closure of monasteries as part of the 'end of popery'. Yet in purely religious terms, there is no ostensible reason why the Reformation in itself should have brought about the end of monasticism. It was quite possible in principle for monasteries and convents to exist in non-Catholic societies where religious life still revolved around liturgical celebration, even if the theological understanding and practice of liturgy was different. In the nineteenth century, this is what happened with the emergence of monastic communities among Lutherans and Anglicans. That it took centuries for it to happen is in part a testimony to the deep scars of the religious wars of the sixteenth century.

Epilogue

FOR ABOUT A THOUSAND years, monks must have been a common and recognisable sight. They could be seen processing with relics on patronal feast days through the streets of the town, or preaching from the market cross, or dispensing alms to the poor at the monastery gates. One might encounter them conducting the business of their monastery as a landowner; assembled to judge a case between tenants; as witnesses to the issue of a charter or deed. They could be heard as a disembodied presence chanting the offices behind the screen that separated the choir from the nave in their abbey church. Monks were a presence at royal and noble courts; equally, monasteries could provide suitable accommodation for royal households and parliaments. Monks were sometimes intimate advisors and counsellors of rulers. Enclosed nuns were less commonly encountered, both because they were fewer in number across Europe as a whole, and because their enclosure was more carefully maintained; nevertheless, in areas where a convent was an important landowner, the nuns would likewise have constituted a familiar presence in local society.

In contrast, few people today ever encounter monks or enclosed religious sisters. Monasteries and convents do not enjoy anything like the prominent role that they did in medieval Europe: there are no longer monks in the higher echelons of political society, and even as landowners they impinge far less on local economies than they once did. Of course, there are also far fewer monks and nuns than in medieval Europe. Numbers declined across western Europe during the eighteenth and nineteenth centuries, to the point where the thousand monasteries in existence in *c.* 1750 had declined to fewer than fifty by *c.* 1820. In 1880, celebrated as the fourteenth millennial of St Benedict, just under a hundred monasteries using the Benedictine Rule were found in working condition, with 2,080 professed choir monks and 570 lay brothers.

Numbers of professed monks and nuns, perhaps surprisingly, have grown worldwide since the start of the twentieth century. A slow but steady increase in the last quarter of the nineteenth century and early years of the twentieth meant that in 1910 that number had risen to 140 monasteries, with 4,100 monks and 1,600 lay brothers.[1] In 1960, this had risen to 12,131 monks in 257 monasteries. By 1990, the number of monasteries had increased to 359 but they had become smaller, with only 9,096 monks. There were, however, about twice as many women following the *Rule of Benedict*.[2] The quickest expansion in monasticism in the twentieth and twenty-first centuries, however, has been in the developing world. By 2000, there were 334 monasteries for men and 245 for women in Africa, Latin America, Asia and Oceania, most of them founded since 1960.[3]

In the late nineteenth century, the papacy took steps – as in 1215 – to impose some kind of central organisation on monasteries and convents following the *Rule of Benedict*. In 1893, Pope Leo XIII founded the Benedictine Confederation for male monasteries, headed by an abbot primate who was to be resident in Rome. Within this loose structure were a number of congregations, some but not all of which conformed to national boundaries. The Cassinese Congregation in Italy permitted the formation of a separate Subiaco Congregation in 1851, the main purpose of which was to reintroduce a primitive observance. From 1872 this became an independent Congregation with international provinces; similarly, the Solesmes Congregation, expelled from France in the early years of the twentieth century, established monasteries at Quarr (for men) and Ryde (for women) on the Isle of Wight, and subsequently at Farnborough.

Today, each congregation operates its own federated structures of governance, and functions as an autonomous Order with a presiding abbot, general chapter and constitutions. Instruments of governance differ across congregations: some operate a central national novitiate, while others permit monasteries to recruit and train their own novices; some become involved in parochial ministry, or run schools, while others prefer to remain purely enclosed and contemplative. In some congregations, abbacies are held for a finite period; in others, for life.[4] Some of the congregations have medieval origins: Vallombrosa and Camaldoli were both eleventh-century foundations, while the Cassinese Congregation comes out of the reformed Congregation of Santa Justina founded in 1408. Most of the congregations predate the Leonine reform of 1893. A number were created in the seventeenth century: the Swiss Congregation in 1602, the Austrian in 1625, the Hungarian, originally founded in 1514, was restored in 1639, and the Bavarian in 1684. The English Congregation, which can claim its original formation in the fourteenth century, was restored in 1619 but operated until the nineteenth century exclusively outside England. Reformed national Congregations were instrumental in the revival of monasticism in the nineteenth and twentieth centuries. Monasteries were established by the Bavarian and Swiss Congregations in America, and by the 1920s there were twenty abbeys, with eight hundred monks and four hundred lay brothers, in the United States.

The nineteenth-century revival of monasticism in Britain, following the Catholic Emancipation Act of 1829, also led to the creation of Anglican communities adopting the *Rule of Benedict*. The first Anglican convent opened in 1845, and houses for men and women were subsequently founded in all parts of the world where the Anglican communion is observed. Similar revivals of monasticism can be seen in the Orthodox world, notably on Mount Athos but also in the Middle East. The collapse of communism in Russia and the Balkans has led to a revival of monasticism among the Slavic Orthodox, and to the cross-fertilisation of Orthodox monasticism more generally, for example as Russians and Serbs have entered Greek monasteries in the Holy Land. In the twenty-first century, Orthodox monastic communities are likely to be highly international institutions.

As Thomas Merton, perhaps the most famous monk of the twentieth century, remarked, the call of the monastic life has been heard in modern times most clearly after periods of shared societal trauma such as war. When we think about monasteries at all in the contemporary world, we probably think of them as places of retreat from the world, and monastic life as the abnegation of the stresses engendered by contemporary living. Although numbers of vocations in the western world have dwindled in the past generation, paradoxically, monasteries and monastic life have attracted attention from tourists, visitors and retreat-seekers. To an extent, this has always been the case. As we have seen, there are plenty of medieval examples of monks – and, to a lesser degree, nuns – for whom the enclosed space of the monastery represented an escape from the pressures bearing on them.

In many ways, this represents a romanticised ideal of a monastery. But this is not necessarily how monks see themselves or their lives. As Peter Eghwrudjakpor, prior of the Benedictine monastery of Ewu in Nigeria, has said, the prayerful and contemplative life of a monastery is part of a symbiotic relationship with work: 'Work is a form of prayer and prayer is a form of work.' Many monasteries and convents are local producers of consumables such as food and drink, cosmetics and craftwork. In recent years, management experts have looked to monasteries as exemplars of localised economies and labour markets.[5] The principles of governorship and management as expressed in the *Rule of Benedict* have recently been interrogated as ways of realigning modern methods of work as part of a focus on well-being within professional life. As early as the 1980s, an anthropologist of labour suggested that the monastic economy could 'constitute a force of change within the economy by introducing alternative ways of living'.[6] As economists and management theorists continue to explore ideas such as basic living incomes, four-day working weeks and modes of balancing work and leisure, the organisational principles of monasteries have become visible on the contemporary horizon in new ways.[7] Likewise, Benedict's teachings on leadership and authority are seen as fruitful ways of developing meaningful and productive relationships in organisational settings.[8]

In other ways, too, monasticism has come full circle since the first men and women began to live in regulated Christian communities apart from the world. Monastic life in the twenty-first century is based, as in the fourth, on the shared vocalisation of Scripture within a liturgical framework that also includes spoken formulas, prayers and bodily enacted ritual. A contemporary monk's observation that a lifetime of singing the psalms 'provides a language by which even the most esoteric interior states can be grasped and expressed' would surely have been familiar to monks and nuns over the course of the past millennium and longer.[9] Likewise, monks over a long period have found that the contemplative life demands practice and patience in the overcoming of acedia, so that the language deployed by a twelfth-century Cistercian, Galand of Reigny, finds echoes in the thinking of a contemporary French monk.[10] This does not mean, of course, that monasticism as a construct of practices and ideals has remained constant and unchanging over the centuries. Every generation gets the monasticism it needs, because monasteries are and have always been communities of people who bring the attitudes, knowledge and experiences of the outside world into the enclosed space of the cloister, church and cell.

This book has been an attempt to explore and explain how and why monasteries emerged from the early Christian world in the heartlands of the new religion, how diverse forms of monasticism developed in different parts of the Christian world and how monasticism changed in response to societal needs. Throughout the book, the focus has been on monasteries and convents as functioning communities operating in relation to both tradition and external stimuli. We have examined different circumstances leading to the founding of monasteries, types and sizes of community, and explored the kinds of people who professed as monks or nuns in different periods, their expectations, aspirations and needs. Monasticism reflected and represented much of the thinking of the world of which it was part, but it also shaped that thinking and provided new directions. Monasteries could be places of reaction and tradition, or of experiment and instability. They were supported by the powerful and wealthy and in turn gave their complicity to established wealth. At the same time they suffered exploitation at the hands of the powerful, while sometimes acting as exploiters themselves. They provided practical earthly means of support for the vulnerable, and invoked and channelled the awesome power of the saints to protect themselves and local communities. Over the course of the medieval period, monasteries encapsulated the contradictions, failings and achievements of the societies that created and shaped them – and in the end, outgrew them. Above all, they gave witness to the conviction that speaking to God through constant prayer and patterned liturgical ritual was the means to secure for themselves and all of humanity safety in this world and salvation in the next.

Glossary of Terms

anchorite	a man or woman leading a solitary religious life, usually in a fixed location
cenobitism	the practice of communal monastic life
chapter	daily meeting of the whole monastic community presided over by the abbot or prior
chapter-general	annual meeting of abbots representing monasteries of a given Order
charistike	system introduced in the tenth-century Byzantine Empire to provide funding for impoverished monasteries through the appointment of wealthy patrons as executives
conversi	lay brothers in a Cistercian monastery
corrody	an arrangement whereby laypeople made over assets to a monastery in return for rights of permanent residence and maintenance
hegoumen	a monastic superior, in the Greek tradition
hours	*see* offices
lavra	a monastic community, usually found in the Holy Land or Syria, comprising a group of monks occupying individual or shared cells who live apart from each other but join for regular communal liturgical observances and some meals, and who follow the same Rule

GLOSSARY OF TERMS

oblate	a child placed in a monastery or convent by parents or family
offices	the regular daily liturgical observances in a monastery or convent
Rule	a formula for living adopted by a monastic community or group of monasteries, usually outlining how the community is to be organised and providing details of liturgical observances and living arrangements
typikon (founder's)	testamentary document written by the founder of a Greek monastery, often outlining circumstances of foundation and details of internal organisation
typikon (liturgical)	document detailing liturgical observance in a Greek monastery

Notes

ABBREVIATIONS

AASS	*Acta Sanctorum*, ed. Bollandist Fathers, 63 vols (Antwerp, Paris, Rome, Brussels, 1643–)
AP (Alp)	*Apophthegmata Patrum*, PG 65, cols 70–438
AP (Sys)	*Les Apophtegmes des Pères: Collection systématique*, ed. Jean-Claude Guy (Paris, 1993–2003)
BMFD	*Byzantine Monastic Foundation Documents*, ed. John Thomas and Angela Constantinides Hero, Dumbarton Oaks Studies XXXV, 5 vols (Washington DC, 2000)
CHMMLW	*Cambridge History of Medieval Monasticism in the Latin West*, ed. Alison I. Beach and Isabelle Cochelin, 2 vols (Cambridge, 2020)
DOP	*Dumbarton Oaks Papers*
EHD	*English Historical Documents*, vol. 1 *c.* 500–1042, ed. Dorothy Whitelock (London, 1979)
EHR	*English Historical Review*
JMH	*Journal of Medieval History*
Mansi	G.D. Mansi (ed.), *Sacrorum conciliorum nova et amplissima collectio*, 31 vols (Florence and Venice, 1559–98, repr. Graz, 1960)
MGH (SS)	Monumenta Germaniae Historica, Scriptores
NCMH	*New Cambridge Medieval History*
	Vol. 1 *c.* 500–*c.* 700, ed. Paul Fouracre (Cambridge, 2005)
	Vol. 2 *c.* 700–*c.* 900, ed. Rosamond McKitterick (Cambridge, 1995)
OV	Orderic Vitalis, *Ecclesiastical History*, ed. and trans. Marjorie Chibnall, 6 vols (Oxford, 1969–78)
PL	*Patrologiae cursus completus. Series Latina*, ed. J-P. Migne, 221 vols (Paris, 1844–64)
RB	*Revue Bénédictine*
REB	*Revue des Études Byzantines*
RHGF	Recueil des Historiens des Gaules et de la France, 24 vols (Paris, 1738)

SCH   Studies in Church History
SSCISSM Settimane di studio del Centro italiano di studi sull'alto medioevo

INTRODUCTION

1. Ralph Glaber, *Five Books of Histories*, ed. and trans. John France (Oxford, 1989), V, i, pp. 216–17.
2. James Clark, *The Dissolution of the Monasteries* (New Haven and London, 2021), p. 53.
3. Kit Dollard, Anthony Marett-Crosby and Timothy Wright, *Doing Business with Benedict: The Rule of St Benedict and Business Management, A Conversation* (London, 2003).
4. Michel Foucault, *Discipline and Punish: The Birth of the Prison*, trans. A. Sheridan (Harmondsworth, 1977), p. 150, describes monasteries as 'great technicians of rhythm and regular activities'.
5. Erik Varden, *The Shattering of Loneliness: On Christian Remembrance* (London, 2018).

CHAPTER 1: THE EMERGING TRADITION

1. *Sancti Eusebii Hieronymi Epistulae*, CXXVII, ed. Isidorus Hilberg (Vienna, 1918), p. 149.
2. David Brakke, *Athanasius and the Politics of Asceticism* (Oxford, 1995); David Gwynn, *Athanasius of Alexandria: Bishop, Theologian, Ascetic, Father* (Oxford, 2012).
3. Edwin Judge, 'The Earliest Use of Monachos for "Monk"' (*P. Coll. Youtie* 77) and the Origins of Monasticism', *Jahrbuch für Antike und Christentum* 20 (1977), 72–89.
4. Brakke, *Athanasius*, p. 80.
5. Judge, 'The Earliest Use of Monachos for "Monk"'.
6. For a valuable summary of the problems and scholarly currents, see Samuel Rubenson, 'Asceticism and Monasticism. I: Eastern', *Cambridge History of Christianity*, vol. 2: *Constantine to c. 600* (Cambridge, 2007), pp. 637–68, esp. 638–42.
7. Derwas Chitty, *The Desert a City: An Introduction to the Study of Egyptian and Palestinian Monasticism under the Christian Empire* (Oxford, 1966), pp. 6–7. For a brief discussion of alternative ideas, see Marilyn Dunn, *The Emergence of Monasticism: From the Desert Fathers to the Early Middle Ages* (Oxford, 2000), pp. 1–2.
8. W.H.C. Frend, *The Rise of Christianity* (London, 1984), pp. 574–5.
9. Richard M. Price, 'Introduction', in Theodoret of Cyrrhus, *A History of the Monks of Syria*, trans. Richard M. Price (Kalamazoo, MI, 1985), p. xxiv.
10. Price, 'Introduction', in Theodoret of Cyrrhus, *A History of the Monks of Syria*, pp. xx–xxii.
11. As discussed by J.C. O'Neill, 'The Origins of Monasticism', in *The Making of Orthodoxy: Essays in Honour of Henry Chadwick*, ed. Rowan Williams (Cambridge, 1989), pp. 270–87.
12. William Harmless, *Desert Christians: An Introduction to the Literature of Early Monasticism* (Oxford, 2004), pp. 57–84, for a valuable guide.
13. Harmless, *Desert Christians*, pp. 78–81, for Anthony's letters.
14. (Oratio 21.5), cited in Brakke, *Athanasius*.
15. G.J.M. Bartelink (ed.), *Athanase d'Alexandrie* (Paris, 1994), with French translation; for an English translation, see Robert C. Gregg (ed. and trans.), *Athanasius: The Life of Antony and the Letter to Marcellinus* (New York, 1980).

NOTES to pp. 23–31

16. P.R. Coleman-Norton, *Roman State and Christian Church* (London, 1966), I, pp. 322–3.
17. David Brakke, 'The Making of Monastic Demonology: Three Ascetic Teachers on Withdrawal and Resistance', *Church History* 70 (2001), 32–41.
18. James Goehring, 'The Encroaching Desert: Literary Production and Ascetic Space in Early Christian Egypt', *Journal of Early Christian Studies* 1 (1993), 281–96.
19. A.-J. Festugière (ed. and trans.), *Historia monachorum in Aegypto*, XXIX (Brussels, 1951); Norman Russell (trans.), *The Lives of the Desert Fathers: The 'Historia monachorum in Aegypto'* (Kalamazoo, MI, 1981). See now Georgia Frank, *The Memory of the Eyes: Pilgrims to Living Saints in Christian Late Antiquity* (Berkeley, CA, 2000).
20. *Historia monachorum*, XX, pp. 120–3, describes the founding of Nitria; Chitty, *Desert*, pp. 29–35, on Nitria, Kellia and Skete.
21. P. Miquel (ed.), *Déserts chrétiens d'Egypte* (Nice, 1993), summarises recent archaeological studies of the site.
22. Jean-Claude Guy (ed.), *Jean Cassien: institutions cénobitiques* [henceforth: Cassian, *Institutes*], III, 2 (Paris, 1965), pp. 92–5.
23. Cassian, *Institutes*, x, 7, pp. 396–8.
24. Cassian, *Institutes*, x, 23, pp. 422–3.
25. Cassian, *Institutes*, x, 24, pp. 423–5.
26. *Les Apophtegmes des Pères: Collection systématique* [henceforth: *AP (Sys)*], VII.26, ed. Jean-Claude Guy, 3 vols (Paris, 1993–2003). For a useful summary of the edited collections that make up the *AP (Sys)*, Harmless, *Desert Christians*, pp. 183–4.
27. *AP (Sys)* 37; *AP (Alp)* PG 65:216.
28. *AP (Sys)* John 11; *AP (Alp)* PG 65:208.
29. *AP (Sys)* 10; *AP (Alp)* PG 65:216.
30. John Moschus, *Pratum Spirituale* 55, PG 87:3, trans. John Wortley as *The Spiritual Meadow* (Kalamazoo, MI, 1992), pp. 43–4.
31. Harmless, *Desert Christians*, p. 116. For a full discussion of Pachomius's monastic enterprises and the sources, see Philip Rousseau, *Pachomius: The Making of a Community in Fourth-Century Egypt* (Berkeley, CA, 1999); also James Goehring, 'New Frontiers in Pachomian Studies', in *The Roots of Egyptian Christianity*, ed. Birger A. Pearson and James E. Goehring (Philadelphia, 1986), pp. 236–57.
32. *The Lausiac History of Palladius*, XXXIII, ed. Cuthbert Butler, 2 vols (Cambridge, 1898–1904), II, pp. 96–7.
33. Harmless, *Desert Christians*, pp. 124, 130–1, 148–9.
34. Rebecca Krawiec, *Shenoute and the Women of the White Monastery* (New York, 2002).
35. Armaud Veilleux's preface to David N. Bell (trans.), *Besa: The Life of Shenoute*, Cistercian Studies 73 (Kalamazoo, MI, 1983), p. v: 'authoritarian, harsh and violent'.
36. Harmless, *Desert Christians*, p. 447.
37. Harmless, *Desert Christians*, pp. 169–80; Graham Gould, 'A Note on the *Apophthegmata Patrum*', *Journal of Theological Studies* 37 (1986), 133–8; see also Lucien Regnault, *Les pères du désert à travers leur apophtegmes* (Sablé-sur-Sarthe, 1987).
38. Joan M. Petersen (ed. and trans.), *Handmaids of the Lord: Contemporary Descriptions of Feminine Asceticism in the First Six Christian Centuries* (Kalamazoo, MI, 1996); Susanna Elm, *'Virgins of God': The Making of Asceticism in Late Antiquity* (Oxford, 1994); Gillian Cloke, *This Female Man of God: Women and Spiritual Power in the Patristic Age AD 350–450* (New York, 1995).

39. Harmless, *Desert Christians*, pp. 183–6. For an excellent overall guide to the *Apophthegmata* and the world they evoke, Douglas Burton-Christie, *The Word in the Desert: Scripture and the Quest for Holiness in Early Christian Monasticism* (Oxford, 1993).
40. Columba Stewart, 'Radical Honesty about the Self: The Practice of the Desert Fathers', *Sobornost* 12 (1990), 25.
41. Philip Rousseau, *Ascetics, Authority and the Church in the Age of Jerome and Cassian* (Oxford, 1978), p. 59; but see now for a different view Graham Gould, *The Desert Fathers on Monastic Community* (Oxford, 1993), pp. 57, 69.
42. N343, *Les Sentences des Pères du Désert. Vol. 5. Série des Anonymes*, trans. Lucien Regnault (Solesmes, 1985), p. 118.
43. Discussed by Gould, *Desert Fathers*, p. 61.
44. Poemen 8, *Les Sentences des Pères du Désert. Vol. 4. Collection Alphabétique*, trans. Lucien Regnault (Solesmes, 1981), pp. 224–5; Gould, *Desert Fathers*, p. 77.
45. Moses 6, *Les Sentences. Vol. 4*, p. 190.
46. Two further examples are Poemen 64 ('When we cover the sins of our brother, God covers ours. In the hour in which we reveal those of our brother, God reveals ours'), and Macarius 36 ('If we keep remembering the wrongs which men have done us, we destroy the power of the remembrance of God').
47. *AP (Sys)* Arsenius V; *AP (Alp)* PG 65:88–9.
48. Steven D. Driver, *John Cassian and the Reading of Egyptian Monastic Culture* (New York, 2002), p. 22.
49. Antoine and Claire Guillaumont, 'Introduction', *Évagre le Pontique: traité pratique ou Le Moine*, 2 vols (Paris, 1971), I, pp. 21–125.
50. Harmless, *Desert Christians*, p. 317. I have borrowed his word 'gnomic'.
51. *Praktikos* 1. 'Physics' meant the study of the natural world.
52. Harmless, *Desert Christians*, p. 320.
53. *Praktikos* 29.
54. Cassian, *Institutes*, Eng. trans. Boniface Ramsey, *John Cassian: The Institutes* (New York, 2000); E. Pichery, *Jean Cassien: Conférences*, 3 vols (Paris, 1955–9), Eng. Trans. Boniface Ramsey, *John Cassian: The Conferences* (New York, 1997).
55. There is an extensive literature on John Cassian; see especially Columba Stewart, *Cassian the Monk* (New York, 1998); Owen Chadwick, *John Cassian: A Study in Primitive Monasticism*, 2nd edn (Cambridge, 1968); Jean-Claude Guy, *Jean Cassien: Vie et doctrine spirituelle* (Paris, 1961).
56. Guy, *Jean Cassien*, pp. 363–72.
57. Harmless, *Desert Christians*, p. 378.
58. Driver, *John Cassian*, p. 5.
59. Harmless, *Desert Christians*, pp. 285–8 for this characterisation of the *Lausiac History*.
60. *Conférences*, XVIII, pp. 10–36.
61. J.N.D. Kelly, *Jerome: His Life, Writings and Controversies* (London, 1975), is a valuable introduction.
62. Harmless, *Desert Christians*, pp. 284–9.
63. *Egeria's Travels*, trans. John Wilkinson (Warminster, 1999).
64. E.D. Hunt, *Holy Land Pilgrimage in the Later Roman Empire, AD 312–460* (Oxford, 1982), pp. 160–79.
65. Eusebius, *Historia Ecclesiastica*, VI, 9; Chitty, *Desert*, pp. 13–14.
66. *Vita Charitonis*, ed. G. Garitte, 'La vie prémétaphrastique de S. Chariton', *Bulletin de l'Institut historique Belge de Rome* 21 (1940), 16–42.

67. Evelyn Patlagean, *Pauvreté économique et pauvreté sociale à Byzance* (Paris, 1977), pp. 300–38, suggests that this economic model may have corresponded to that common to village life in Palestine.
68. Joseph Patrich, *Sabas, Leader of Palestinian Monasticism: A Comparative Study in Eastern Monasticism, Fourth to Seventh Centuries* (Washington DC, 1995), pp. 51–168; for a different monastic tradition in Palestine see now Michael W. Champion, *Dorotheus of Gaza and Ascetic Education* (Oxford, 2022).
69. Cyril of Scythopolis, *Vita Sancti Euthymii*, ed. E. Schwartz, *Kyrillos von Skythopolis* (Leipzig, 1939), pp. 3–84; Cyril of Scythopolis, *The Lives of the Monks of Palestine*, trans. Richard M. Price (Kalamazoo, MI, 1991), pp. 1–92.
70. *Vita Euthymii*, XIX, pp. 16–17; trans. Price, *Lives of the Monks of Palestine*, p. 12.
71. Cyril of Scythopolis, *Vita Sabae*, ed. Schwartz, *Kyrillos*, p. 91; trans. Price, *Lives of the Monks of Palestine*, p. 99.
72. *Vita Sabae*, XXIX, pp. 114–15; trans. Price, *Lives of the Monks of Palestine*, p. 123.
73. *Vita Sabae*, XXVIII, p. 113; trans. Price, *Lives of the Monks of Palestine*, p. 122.
74. Yizhar Hirschfeld, *The Early Byzantine Monastery at Khirbet ed-Deir in the Judean Desert: The Excavations in 1981–87* (Jerusalem, 1999).
75. The *Life of Mary of Egypt* was composed by Sophronius, patriarch of Jerusalem (*c*. 560–638), and was translated into Latin, PL73:671–90, *AASS* Apr. I, pp. 67–90; *The Life of St Mary of Egypt*, trans. D.P. Curtin (Philadelphia, 2019).
76. Peter Brown, *The Body and Society: Men, Women and Sexual Renunciation in Early Christianity* (London, 1988), p. 243.
77. Yizhar Hirschfeld, *The Judean Desert Monasteries in the Byzantine Period* (New Haven, 1992), pp. 205–12.
78. *Vita Sabae*, XXXVI, p. 123; trans. Price, *Lives of the Monks of Palestine*, p. 132.
79. *Vita Euthymii*, XXVII, pp. 41–4; trans. Price, *Lives of the Monks of Palestine*, pp. 37–41; *Vita Sabae*, L–LXI, pp. 139–46; trans. Price, *Lives of the Monks of Palestine*, pp. 149–62.
80. Brakke, *Athanasius*, p. 82.
81. Cyril of Scythopolis, *Lives of the Monks of Palestine*, xl–xliii.
82. *Vita Sabae*, I, p. 86; trans. Price, *Lives of the Monks of Palestine*, p. 93.
83. *Vita Sabae*, XII, pp. 104–5, XXIII, p. 107, XXXIII, pp. 118–19, XXXIV, pp. 119–20, XLIX, 49, pp. 138–39; trans. Price, *Lives of the Monks of Palestine*, pp. 104–5, 116, 127–8, 128–9, 148–9.
84. Susan Ashbrook Harvey, *Asceticism and Society in Crisis: John of Ephesus and The Lives of the Eastern Saints* (Berkeley, CA, 1990), p. 5.
85. Price, 'Introduction', pp. xx–xxii.
86. Arthur Vööbus, *History of Asceticism in the Syrian Orient: A Contribution to the History of Culture in the Near East*, 2 vols, Corpus Scriptorum Christianorum Orientalium, Subsidia 14 & 17 (Louvain, 1958–60), I, pp. 10–14.
87. Theodoret of Cyrrhus, *Histoire des Moines de Syrie*, XXVII, ed. and trans. Pierre Canivet and Alice Leroy-Molingen, 2 vols (Paris, 1977–9), II, pp. 216–19; trans. Price, *Lives of the Monks of Syria*, p. 177; see also Pierre Canivet, *Le monachisme syrien selon Théodoret de Cyr* (Paris, 1977), pp. 66–79.
88. *Vita Sabae*, VIII, p. 92; trans. Price, *Lives of the Monks of Palestine*, p. 100; Theodoret, *Histoire*, Prol., I, p. 126; trans. Price, *Lives of the Monks of Syria*, p. 4, where monks are compared favourably with Olympic pancratiasts.
89. Theodoret, *Histoire*, I–II, pp. 160–245; trans. Price, *Lives of the Monks of Syria*, pp. 12–36.

90. Theodoret, *Histoire*, III, pp. 254–5; trans. Price, *Lives of the Monks of Syria*, pp. 38–9.
91. John of Ephesus, *Lives of the Eastern Saints*, XXXV, ed. and trans. E.W. Brooks, *Patrologia Orientalis* 18 (Paris, 1924), col. 612.
92. Theodoret, *Histoire*, XXVI, pp. 158–215; trans. Price, *Lives of the Monks of Syria*, pp. 160–76.
93. Peter Brown, 'The Rise and Function of the Holy Man in Late Antiquity', *Journal of Roman Studies* 61 (1971), 80–101.
94. Harvey, *Asceticism and Society*, p. 66.
95. Harvey, *Asceticism and Society*, p. 56.
96. Harvey, *Asceticism and Society*, p. 17.
97. Theodoret, *Histoire*, I, pp. 116–17; trans. Price, *Lives of the Monks of Syria*, pp. 13–14.
98. Derek Krueger (ed.), *Symeon the Holy Fool: Leontius's Life and the Late Antique City* (Berkeley, CA, 1996).
99. John of Ephesus, *Lives of the Eastern Saints*, LII, PO 19, cols 164–79.
100. Krueger, *Symeon the Holy Fool*, p. 153.
101. Krueger, *Symeon the Holy Fool*, p. 134.
102. Theodoret, *Histoire*, I, pp. 162–3; trans. Price, *Lives of the Monks of Syria*, pp. 13–14.
103. Translation from Sozomen, *Historia Ecclesiastica* VI, 32 by John Wortley, '"Grazers" (βοσκοί) in the Judaean Desert', in *The Sabaite Heritage in the Orthodox Church from the Fifth Century to the Present*, ed. Joseph Patrich, Orientalia Lovaniensia Analecta 98 (Leuven, 2001), pp. 37–48 at p. 41.
104. John of Ephesus, *Lives*, 16, PO 17, cols 229–47.
105. Sarra 4, *Les Sentences. Vol. 4*, pp. 306–7.
106. Elm, *Virgins of God*, p. 267.
107. *Vita S. Macrinae virginis*, PG 46:959; Elm, *Virgins of God*, pp. 78–105.
108. *Regulae fusius tractatae* (Longer Rule), PG 31:889–1053 and *Regulae brevius tractatae* (Shorter Rule), PG 31:1080–306. For discussion, see Emanuel Amand de Mendieta, 'Le système cénobitique basilien comparé au système cénobitique pachômien', RHR 152 (1957), 31–80; Gustave Bardy, 'Basile (Règle de saint)', DDC 2 (1937), cols 218–24; Ferdinand Laun, 'Die beiden Regeln des Basilius, ihre Echtheit und Entstehung', ZKG 44 (1925), 1–61; Adalbert de Vogüé, 'The Greater Rules of Saint Basil: A Survey', *Word and Spirit: A Monastic Review* 1 (1979), 49–85.
109. Dunn, *Emergence of Monasticism*, p. 34.
110. Joseph Lienhard, *Paulinus of Nola and Early Western Monasticism* (Cologne–Bonn, 1977), p. 61.
111. Ambrose, *Exameron* III, v, 23, ed. K. Schenkl, *Sancti Ambrosii Opera*, CSEL, 32:1, pp. 74–5.
112. For a summary of some of these views, F. Homes Dudden, *The Life and Times of St Ambrose*, 2 vols (Oxford, 1935), vol. 1, pp. 144–9.
113. Orosius, *Seven Books of History against the Pagans*, VII, 33, trans. Andy T. Fear (Liverpool, 2010), p. 381.
114. Robert Markus, *The End of Ancient Christianity* (Cambridge, 1990), p. 66.
115. Karl Heussi, *Der Ursprung des Mönchtums* (Tübingen, 1936), p. 53.
116. Robin Lane Fox, *Augustine: Conversions and Confessions* (London, 2015), pp. 181–99.
117. Augustine, *De moribus ecclesiae catholicae et de moribus Manichaeorum* I.33,70; *PL* 32: 1339–40.

118. *S. Paulini Nolani carmina*, XXI, ed. William De Hartel, new edn (Vienna, 1999), pp. 158–86; Lienhard, *Paulinus of Nola*, pp. 137–8.
119. *S. Paulini Nolani epistulae*, XXIII, 6, ed. William De Hartel (Vienna, 1884), pp. 162–3; Eng. trans. by P.G. Walsh, *Letters of St Paulinus of Nola*, 2 vols (London, 1967), II, pp. 197–8; Lienhard, *Paulinus of Nola*, p. 80.
120. *S. Paulini epistulae*, XXII, 2, pp. 155–6; trans. Walsh, II, p. 197.
121. *S. Paulini epistulae*, XXII, 1, p. 155; trans. Walsh, II, p. 197.
122. Jerome Ep 22, 34 CSEL 54, pp. 196–7.
123. Dunn, *Emergence of Monasticism*, p. 86.
124. Ambrose, *Epistolae* 63, *PL* 16: 1239–72. Sozomen, *Historia Ecclesiastica* VI, 31,11 writing in the fifth century, attests to the bishop of Rhinocorura, in Egypt, having also organised his clergy into an ascetic community.
125. William Klingshirn, *Caesarius of Arles: The Making of a Christian Community in Late Antique Gaul* (Cambridge, 1994), p. 62.
126. Adalbert de Vogüé, *Les Règles monastiques anciennes (400–700)* (Turnhout, 1985), p. 14, for a 'family tree' of monastic Rules; Albrecht Diem and Philip Rousseau, 'Monastic Rules (Fourth to Ninth Century)', *CHMMLW*, vol. 1, pp. 162–94, esp. 176–9.
127. Klingshirn, *Caesarius*, p. 30.
128. Klingshirn, *Caesarius*, p. 31.
129. Klingshirn, *Caesarius*, pp. 91–3.
130. Klingshirn, *Caesarius*, pp. 118–19.
131. Klingshirn, *Caesarius*, pp. 119–20.
132. See also Brown, *The Body and Society*, pp. 263–4.
133. Klingshirn, *Caesarius*, pp. 122–3.
134. *Vita Sabae*, LVIII, p. 160; trans. Price, *Lives of the Monks of Palestine*, p. 169.
135. David Dumville et al., *Saint Patrick AD 493–1993*, Studies in Celtic History XIII (Woodbridge, 1993), pp. 16–17, 179–81.
136. *BMFD* 1, vol. 1, pp. 51–8.
137. *BMFD* 1, vol. 1, pp. 55–6.
138. Michel Kaplan, *Les propriétés de la Couronne et de l'Église dans l'empire Byzantin (Ve–Vie siècles)* (Paris, 1976).
139. Kate Cooper, 'Property, Power, and Conflict: Re-Thinking the Constantinian Revolution', in *Making Early Medieval Societies: Conflict and Belonging in the Latin West, 300–1200*, ed. Kate Cooper and Conrad Leyser (Cambridge, 2016), pp. 16–32.

CHAPTER 2: A SCHOOL FOR GOD'S SERVICE: EARLY MEDIEVAL MONASTICISM IN THE WEST

1. Bede, *Life of Cuthbert*, XVII, ed. and trans. Bertram Colgrave, *Two Lives of Saint Cuthbert* (Cambridge, 1940), pp. 214–17.
2. Gregory the Great, *Dialogues*, II, 3, ii, ed. Adalbert de Vogüé, 3 vols (Paris, 1979), vol. 2, pp. 140–1.
3. Dunn, *Emergence of Monasticism*, p. 132.
4. Bryan Ward-Perkis, *The Fall of Rome and the End of Civilization* (Oxford, 2005), for a concise and trenchant assessment.
5. A factor mentioned, though not supported, by Dunn, *Emergence of Monasticism*, p. 127.

6. As implied by Markus, *End of Ancient Christianity*, pp. 196–7.
7. *The Rule of Saint Benedict*, ed. and trans. Bruce Venarde, Dumbarton Oaks Medieval Library (Cambridge, MA, 2011).
8. *Rule of Benedict*, prologue, pp. 8–9.
9. *Rule of Benedict*, LIV, pp. 176–7; LXIX, pp. 220–1.
10. *Rule of Benedict*, LXXII, pp. 226–7.
11. 'The energy created by this kind of living produces effects within the individual member, within the community and to some extent within the world at large,' *The Rule of St Benedict*, trans. with an introduction and notes by Anthony C. Meisel and M.L. del Mastro (New York, 1975), p. 9.
12. *Rule of Benedict*, LXVI, pp. 214–15.
13. Thomas Merton, *Elected Silence: The Autobiography of Thomas Merton* (London, 1949), pp. 304–5.
14. *Rule of Benedict*, I, pp. 16–17.
15. *Rule of Benedict*, I, pp. 18–19. As Albrecht Diem has pointed out, this strategy of ignoring those he chose not to see as 'proper' monks was a way of delegitimising groups and individuals whom contemporaries might have seen as entirely legitimate.
16. Louis Halphen, 'La Vie de Saint-Maur: exposé d'une théorie de M. Auguste Molinier', *Revue historique* 88 (1905), 287–95.
17. Guy Ferrari, *Early Roman Monasteries: Notes for the History of the Monasteries and Convents at Rome from the V through the X Century* (Vatican City, 1957), pp. 379–407.
18. Francis Clark, *The 'Gregorian' Dialogues and the Origins of Benedictine Monasticism* (Leiden, 2003), argued for a seventh-century date for the work, but the arguments for Gregory as author were laid out by Paul Mayvaert, 'The Authentic *Dialogues* of Gregory the Great', *Sacris Erudiri* 43 (2004), 55–130.
19. Gregory, *Hom. 10 in Matt.* II, *PL* 76: 1113–14.
20. Marilyn Dunn, 'Mastering Benedict: Monastic Rules and Their Authors in the Early Medieval West', *EHR* 105 (1990), 567–94.
21. Bryan Ward-Perkins, *From Classical Antiquity to the Middle Ages: Urban Public Building in Northern and Central Italy ad 300–850* (Oxford, 1984).
22. Krijnie Ciggaar, *Western Travellers to Constantinople: The West and Byzantium 962–1204, Cultural and Political Relations* (Leiden, 1996), pp. 47–77.
23. Gregory of Tours, *History of the Franks*, IX, 39–43, ed. Bruno Kursch, MGH Scriptorum rerum Merovingicarum I.1 (Hannover, 1951), pp. 460–74.
24. Gregory of Tours, *Glory of the Confessors*, ch. 104, trans. Raymond van Dam (Liverpool, 2004), pp. 78–81.
25. Asser, *Life of Alfred*, XIV–XV, ed. W. Stevenson and Dorothy Whitelock (Oxford, 1959), pp. 12–14.
26. Dunn, *Emergence of Monasticism*, p. 163.
27. Gregory, *History*, IX, 39, p. 460.
28. *The Life of the Holy Radegund by Venantius Fortunatus*, VIII, ed. and trans. Jo Ann McNamara and John E. Halborg with E. Gordon Whatley, *Sainted Women of Dark Ages* (Durham and London, 1992) p. 74.
29. Gregory, *History*, VIII, 15, pp. 380–3.
30. For Columbanus, see Jonas of Bobbio, *Vita Columbani abbatis*, MGH Scriptorum rerum Merovingicarum IV, p. 160; Donald Bullough, 'The Career of Columbanus', in *Columbanus: Studies on the Latin Writings*, ed. Michael Lapidge (Woodbridge, 1997), pp. 1–28; and now *Columbanus and the Peoples of Post-Roman Europe*, ed. Alexander O'Hara (Oxford, 2018).

31. Bede, *Ecclesiastical History*, III, 19, ed. and trans. Bertram Colgrave and R.A.B. Mynors (Oxford, 1969), pp. 270–1.
32. Bede, *Life of Cuthbert*, IX, pp. 184–7.
33. Alexander O'Hara, *Jonas of Bobbio and the Legacy of Columbanus: Sanctity and Community in the Seventh Century* (Oxford, 2018).
34. *Sancti Columbani Opera*, ed. G.S.M. Walker, Scriptores Latini Hiberniae 2 (Dublin, 1957), pp. 122–80; electronic edition at https://celt.ucc.ie/published/L201052.html.
35. Albrecht Diem, *The Pursuit of Salvation: Community, Space and Discipline in Early Medieval Monasticism* (Turnhout, 2021), with critical edition at pp. 60–154. Diem, however, rejects the term 'Columbanian', pp. 20–5. See also Albrecht Diem, 'Inventing the Holy Rule: Some Observations on the History of Monastic Normative Observance in the Early Medieval West', in *Western Monasticism ante litteram: The Spaces of Monastic Observance in Late Antiquity and the Middle Ages*, ed. Hendrik Dey and Elizabeth Fentress (Turnhout, 2011), pp. 53–84.
36. Dunn, *Emergence of Monasticism*, p. 135.
37. Bede, *Ecclesiastical History*, III, 8, pp. 236–9.
38. Bede, *History of the Abbots of Wearmouth and Jarrow*, XI, ed. and trans. Christopher Grocock and I.N. Wood, *Abbots of Wearmouth and Jarrow* (Oxford, 2013), pp. 48–9.
39. Bede, *History of the Abbots*, V, pp. 32–3.
40. Bede, *Letter to Bishop Egbert*, XII, in *Abbots of Wearmouth and Jarrow*, ed. Grocock and Wood, pp. 146–7.
41. Bede, *History of the Abbots*, XI, pp. 46–51.
42. Bede, *History of the Abbots*, XI, pp. 48–9.
43. Dunn, *Emergence of Monasticism*, pp. 199–200.
44. Alan Thacker, 'England in the Seventh Century', in *NCMH*, I *c.* 500–*c.* 700, ed. Paul Fouracre (Cambridge, 2005), p. 481.
45. Bede, *Life of Cuthbert*, III, pp. 162–3.
46. Eddius Stephanus, *Life of Bishop Wilfrid*, X, ed. and trans. Bertram Colgrave (Cambridge, 1927), pp. 20–3.
47. Eddius Stephanus, *Life of Wilfrid*, XLVII, pp. 94–6.
48. Symeon of Durham, *Historia Dunelmensis Ecclesiae*, II, 7, ed. T. Arnold, Rolls Series (London, 1882), I, pp. 58–9.
49. Asser, *Life of Alfred*, III, p. 5.
50. Thacker, 'England in the Seventh Century', p. 488.
51. Sarah Foot, *Veiled Women, I: The Disappearance of Nuns from Anglo-Saxon England* (Aldershot, 2001), p. 105.
52. Bede, *Life of Cuthbert*, XVI, pp. 206–9.
53. *Minsters and Local Churches: The Local Church in Transition 950–1250*, ed. John Blair (Oxford, 1988); *Pastoral Care Before the Parish*, ed. John Blair and Richard Sharpe (Leicester, 1992).
54. VIII Aethelred 5.1 (1014), in *EHD* I, p. 449.
55. Eric Cambridge and David Rollason, 'The Pastoral Organization of the Anglo-Saxon Church: A Review of the "Minster Hypothesis"', *Early Medieval Europe* 4 (1995), 87–104.
56. Cambridge and Rollason, 'Debate', p. 97.
57. H. Löwe (ed.), *Die Iren und Europa im früheren Mittelalter* (Stuttgart, 1982). The classic work, now largely superseded but still valuable, is John Ryan, *Irish Monasticism: Origins and Early Development* (Dublin, 1931).

58. These are [i] the 'Salamanca codex', now Brussels Royal Library MS 7672–4, ed. W.W. Heist, *Vitae sanctorum Hiberniae* (Brussels, 1965); [ii] the pair of Dublin manuscripts: Dublin Marsh Library V.3.4 and Dublin Trinity College E.3.11, ed. Charles Plummer, *Bethada Náem nErren*, 2 vols (Oxford, 1922); [iii] Oxford Bodleian Library Rawlinson B.485 and 505, ed. Charles Plummer, *Vitae sanctorum Hiberniae*, 2 vols (Oxford, 1910); see also *Lives of the Saints from the Book of Lismore*, ed. Whitley Stokes (Oxford, 1890).
59. Lisa M. Bitel, *Isle of the Saints: Monastic Settlement and Christian Community in Early Ireland* (Ithaca, NY, 1990), p. 43.
60. Bitel, *Isle of the Saints*, pp. 58–9.
61. Bitel, *Isle of the Saints*, pp. 60–1; see also the remarks of Charles Doherty, 'Monastic Towns in Early Medieval Ireland', in *The Comparative History of Urban Origins in Non-Roman Europe* (Oxford, 1984), ed. H.B. Clarke and A. Simms, pp. 45–9.
62. Plummer, *Bethada Náem nErren*, vol. 2, p. 179.
63. Michael Herity, 'The Buildings and Layout of Early Irish Monasteries before the Year 1000', *Monastic Studies* 14 (1983), 270–7.
64. Bitel, *Isle of the Saints*, p. 126.
65. Mac Eclaise, 'The Rule of St Carthage', *Irish Ecclesiastical Record* 27 (1910), 495–517 at p. 510.
66. Bitel, *Isle of the Saints*, p. 133.
67. Ludwig Bieler, *The Irish Penitentials* (Dublin, 1963), pp. 160–3.
68. Any kind of processing of food is a sign of weakness: Cóemgen turns cheeses given to monks while they are working in fields by locals into stone [PBNE 1.166].
69. 'The Life of Saint Monenna by Conchubranus', III, *Seanchas Ard Mhacha* 10 (1982), 426–53 at pp. 448–9.
70. Bitel, *Isle of the Saints*, p. 94.
71. Kathleen Hughes, 'The Church in Irish Society, 400–800', in *A New History of Ireland. Vol 1. Prehistoric and Early Ireland*, ed. Dáibhí ó Cróinín (Oxford, 2005), pp. 301–30.
72. Lisa Bitel, 'Women's Monastic Enclosures in Early Ireland: A Study of Female Spirituality and Male Monastic Mentalities', *JMH* 12 (1986), 15–37 at p. 21.
73. Bitel, 'Women's Monastic Enclosures', pp. 30–3.
74. Brown, 'Rise and Function of the Holy Man'.
75. Bitel, *Isle of Saints*, p. 149.
76. *The Annals of Clonmacnoise: Being Annals of Ireland from the Earliest Period to AD 1408*, ed. Denis Murphy (Felinfach, 1993), p. 173.
77. Francis J. Byrne, *Irish Kings and High Kings* (London, 1973), pp. 244–74.
78. J.G. O'Keeffe (ed.), *Buile Suibhne* (London, 1910).
79. Discussed at length in Mayke De Jong, *In Samuel's Image: Child Oblation in the Early Medieval West* (Leiden, 1996), pp. 73–96, on which I have relied heavily in my account.
80. *Rule of Benedict*, LIX, pp. 192–3.
81. Hrabanus Maur, *Liber de oblatione puerorum*, PL 107, cols 419–40.
82. De Jong, *In Samuel's Image*, p. 80.
83. *De oblatione puerorum* PL 107, cols 427–8.
84. De Jong, *In Samuel's Image*, p. 86.
85. *Die Klostergemeinschaft von Fulda im früheren Mittelalter*, ed. Karl Schmid et al, 3/ 5 vols (Munich, 1978), vol 3, pp. 211–15. Entries on the necrology roll of Fulda in 825/6 show that there were 600 monks in total in the monastery, St Riquier 300 + 100 boys.

86. Giles Constable, *Monastic Tithes: From Their Origins to the Twelfth Century* (Cambridge, 1964), p. 161.
87. De Jong, *In Samuel's Image*, p. 81.
88. John Boswell, *The Kindness of Strangers: The Abandonment of Children in Western Europe from Late Antiquity to the Renaissance* (London, 1988), pp. 228–55, esp. at 238–9: 'Oblation was in many ways the most humane form of abandonment ever devised in the West.'
89. Peter Brown, *The Rise of Western Christendom: Triumph and Diversity, AD 200–1000* (Oxford, 2013), p. 224.
90. Hans Haefele, 'Wolo cecidit. Zur Deutung einer Ekkeherd-Erzählung', *Deutsches Archiv* 35 (1979), 17–32.
91. *Smaragdi abbatis Expositio in regulam S. Benedicti*, LIX, ed. Alfred Spannagel and Pius Engelbert, Corpus Consuetudinum Monasticarum VIII (Siegburg, 1974), pp. 299–302. De Jong, *In Samuel's Image*, p. 103, points out that the text was also found in Italian usage into the eleventh century.
92. Paschasius Radbertus, *Expositio in psalmum XLIV*, III, ed. Beda Paulus, CCCM 94 (Turnhout, 1991), p. 104: in a phrase that looks startling to our eyes he describes them as 'a holocaust to the Lord'.
93. For insightful discussion of this point in a contemporary monastic setting, see Michael Casey, *Coenobium: Reflections on Monastic Community*, pp. 86–7.
94. Ekkehard IV of St Gall, *Casus Sancti Galli*, XXXV, ed. Hans Haefele (Darmstadt, 1980), pp. 80–2; De Jong, *In Samuel's Image*, p. 128.
95. De Jong, *In Samuel's Image*, pp. 86–7.
96. Hrabanus Maur, *Epistolae*, XLII, ed. Ernst Dümmler, MGH Epp V, p. 481.
97. De Jong, *In Samuel's Image*, p. 88.
98. Mayke De Jong, 'Carolingian Monasticism: The Power of Prayer', *NCMH*, 2, p. 628.
99. Martin Claussen, *The Reform of the Frankish Church: Chrodegang of Metz and the 'Regula canonicorum' in the Eighth Century* (Cambridge, 2004); Julia Barrow, 'Chrodegang, His Rule and Its Successors', *Early Medieval Europe* 14 (2006), 201–12.
100. MGH *Diplomatum Karolinum*, I, 141–2; repr. in McClendon, *The Imperial Abbey of Farfa* (New Haven, 1987), pp. 128–9.
101. McClendon, *Farfa*, pp. 6–7.
102. Scott Bruce, 'Sources for the History of Monasticism in the Central Middle Ages', *CHMMLW*, I, pp. 387–8.
103. Einhard, *Life of Charlemagne*, XXVI, trans. Lewis Thorpe (Harmondsworth, 1979), p. 80; De Jong, 'Carolingian Monasticism', p. 630; but see John Contreni, 'The Carolingian Renaissance: Education and Literary Culture', *NCMH*, 2, pp. 709–57, at pp. 711–12, for careful nuancing of the term.
104. De Jong, *In Samuel's Image*, p. 139.
105. Smaragdus, *Expositio in regulam Sancti Benedicti*, ed. F. Schmitt (Sieberg, 1974); Hildemar of Corbie and Civate, *Expositio Regulae Sancti Benedicti*, ed. R. Mittermüller (Regensburg, 1880); De Jong, 'Carolingian Monasticism', pp. 637–40.
106. Walter Horn, *Das Modell eines karolingischen Idealklosters nach dem Plan von St Gallen*. The inch measurement used in the Carolingian Empire was on a scale of one-sixteenth rather than one-twelfth. See now Giles Constable, 'Carolingian Monasticism as Seen in the Plan of St Gall', in *Le monde carolingien. Bilan, perspectives, champs de recherches*, ed. Wojciech Falkowski and Yves Sassier, Culture et Société 18 (Turnhout, 2009), pp. 199–217.

107. Casey, *Coenobium*, p. 96–7.
108. De Jong, 'Carolingian Monasticism', p. 635.
109. Nicholas I, *Epistolae* CXXXII, ed. Ernst Perels, MGH (Epp), vol. 6, pp. 652–4; cited in De Jong, *In Samuel's Image*, pp. 91–2.
110. De Jong, *In Samuel's Image*, p. 130: 'The population of religious institutions in those days had all the hallmarks of a conscript army.'

CHAPTER 3: PARALLEL PATHS: MONASTICISM IN THE NINTH AND TENTH CENTURIES

1. For a very brief introduction to imperial iconoclastic policy, see Marie-France Auzépy, 'State of Emergency' (700–850), in *The Cambridge History of the Byzantine Empire c. 500–1492*, ed. Jonathan Shepard (Cambridge, 2009), pp. 251–91, at pp. 279–91; Marie-France Auzépy, 'Les Enjeux d'Iconoclasme', in *Cristianità d'Occidente e cristianità d'Oriente (secoli VI–XI)* (Spoleto, 2004), pp. 127–69; Lesley Brubaker and John Haldon, *Byzantium in the Iconoclast Era, c. 680–850: A History* (Cambridge, 2011).
2. Hans-Georg Beck, *Kirche und theologische Literatur im Byzantinischen Reich* (Munich, 1959), pp. 207–27, lists 160 monasteries known from the literary record from the end of the sixth century. Peter Charanis, 'The Monk as an Element of Byzantine Society', *DOP* 25 (1971), 61–84, at p. 63, revised this to 241, but later gives the figure as over 700 (p. 65). Between 780 and 1200 we know of 159 monasteries in Constantinople, 75 of which had been founded by the ninth century, then 75 in the ninth century, 73 in the tenth, 87 in the eleventh and 78 in the twelfth century. For a list of monasteries in Constantinople up to 850, Peter Hatlie, *The Monks and Monasteries of Constantinople, ca. 350–850* (Cambridge, 2007), pp. 457–72.
3. Charanis, 'Monk', pp. 69–72.
4. Kaplan, *Les propriétés*.
5. *Regulae fusius tractatae*, PG 31:889–1053 and *Regulae brevius tractatae*, PG 31:1080–306; valuable studies include: Mendieta, 'Le système cénobitique basilien', 31–80; Bardy, 'Basile (Règle de saint)', cols 218–24; Laun, 'Die beiden Regeln', 1–61; Vogüé, 'The Greater Rules of Saint Basil', 49–85, and his *Ascetic Treatises*, which are often copied in Greek monastic MSS.
6. Valuable pioneering work on typika was done by Paul Gauthier, e.g. 'Diataxis for the Monastery of Christ Panoiktirmon', *REB* 39 (1981), 17–129; 'Hypotyposis for the Monastery of Theotokos Evergetis', *REB* 40 (1982), 15–95; 'Typikon for the Monastery of Theotokos Kecharitomene', *REB* 43 (1985), 5–165. An important general guide is Catia Galatariotou, 'Byzantine ktetorika typika: A Comparative Study', *REB* 45 (1987), 77–138. A comprehensive set of typika with detailed discussion was published by Harvard University's Byzantine Studies Institute, Dumbarton Oaks: *Byzantine Monastic Foundation Documents: A Complete Translation of the Surviving Founders' Typika and Testaments*, ed. John P. Thomas and Angela Hero, 5 vols (Washington DC, 2000) [henceforth: *BMFD*].
7. *BMFD*, I, p. 60. Curiously, the typikon survives only in a Church Slavonic translation, which suggests it may have been the model for a subsequent community in the Balkans. Vera von Falkenhausen, 'Il monachesimo greco in Sicilia', in *La Sicilia rupestre nel contesto delle civiltà mediterranee: Atti del sesto Convegno Internazionale di studio sulla civiltà rupestre medioevale nel Mezzogiorno d'Italia (Catania-Pantalica-Ispica, 7–12 settembre 1981)* (Galatina, 1986), pp. 135–74, esp. 152–7, noted Pachomian influences in the importance given to daily manual labour.

NOTES to pp. 122–130

8. *Theodore Studites: Testament of Theodore the Studite for the Monastery of St John Stoudios in Constantinople*, trans. Timothy Miller, *BMFD* I, p. 76.
9. Rosemary Morris, *Monks and Laymen in Byzantium 843–1118* (Cambridge, 1995), p. 15.
10. Charles Frazee, 'St Theodore of Studios and Ninth Century Monasticism in Constantinople', *Studia Monastica* 23 (1981), 27–58.
11. *Stoudios: Rule of the Monastery of St John Stoudios in Constantinople*, trans. Timothy Miller, *BMFD* I, pp. 108, 112.
12. *Stoudios*, *BMFD* I, p. 107; Alice Gardner, *Theodore of Studium: His Life and Times* (London, 1905), p. 75. Cf. the twelfth-century abbot of St John Patmos, who apparently banged the heads of monks whom he caught dozing in the offices against the nearest pillar to wake them.
13. *Stoudios*, *BMFD*, I, pp. 109–10.
14. *Stoudios*, *BMFD*, I, pp. 108, 114–15.
15. *The Life of Leontios, Patriarch of Jerusalem*, XVIII, ed. and trans. Dimitris Tsougarakis, The Medieval Mediterranean 2 (Leiden, 1993), pp. 52–5.
16. Morris, *Monks and Laymen*, p. 76.
17. *Vita S. Ioannicci a. S. Saba monacho*, *AASS* Nov. II, pp. 333–83.
18. Rosemary Morris, 'The Origins of Athos', in *Mount Athos and Byzantine Monasticism*, ed. Anthony Bryer et al. (Aldershot, 1996), pp. 37–46.
19. Peter Burridge, 'The Architectural Development of the Athonite Monastery', in *Mount Athos and Byzantine Monasticism*, ed. Bryer et al., pp. 171–88.
20. *Life of Athanasios the Athonite*, III, in *Holy Men of Mount Athos*, ed. and trans. Richard P. Greenfield and Alice-Mary Talbot (Cambridge MA, 2016), pp. 134–5.
21. *Life of Athanasios*, VI, pp. 140–1.
22. *Life of Athanasios*, IX, pp. 152–3.
23. *Life of Athanasios*, X, pp. 152–5.
24. *Life of Athanasios*, XIII, pp. 162–3.
25. *Life of Athanasios*, XV, pp. 166–7, XVII, pp. 172–3.
26. *Life of Athanasios*, XXII, pp. 186–7, XXIII, pp. 190–1.
27. *Life of Athanasios*, XXV, pp. 196–7, 198–9.
28. *Life of Athanasios*, XXVII, pp. 206–7.
29. *Life of Athanasios*, XXVI, pp. 202–5, XXIX, pp. 212–15.
30. *Life of Athanasios*, LXV–LXVI, pp. 330–5.
31. Julian Leroy, 'La conversion de saint Athanase l'Athonite à l'idéal cénobitique et l'influence studite', *Le millénaire du Mont Athos 963–1963* I (Chevetogne, 1963), pp. 101–20.
32. *Vitae duae antiquae Sancti Athanasii Athonitae, Vita A*, CLVVVIV, ed. J. Noret (Louvain, 1982), p. 13; see also *Life of Athanasios*, LXV, pp. 326–7, where specific comparisons are made to Pachomios and Sabas; also Kallistos Ware, 'Athanasius the Athonite: Traditionalist or Innovator?', in *Mount Athos and Byzantine Monasticism*, ed. Bryer et al., pp. 3–16.
33. J. Leroy, 'S. Athanase l'Athonite et la règle de S. Benoît', *Revue d'ascétique et de mystique* 29 (1953), pp. 108–22; but see also Paul Lemerle's scepticism in 'Introduction', *Actes de Lavra, Archives d'Athos*, IV, ed. P. Lemerle, N. Svoronos, A. Guillou and D. Papchryssanthou (Paris, 1970), p. 41.
34. *Ath. Testament: Testament of Athanasios the Athonite for the Lavra Monastery*, trans. George Dennis, *BMFD*, I, pp. 274.
35. *Ath. Testament*, *BMFD*, I, pp. 275–7.

36. Taxiarchis G. Kolias, *Nikephoros II. Phokas (963–969): Der Feldherr und Kaiser und seine Reformtätigkeit* (Athens, 1993).
37. Morris, *Monks and Laymen*, p. 234.
38. *Christodoulos: Rule, Testament and Codicil of Christodoulos for the Monastery of St John the Theologian on Patmos*, trans. Patricia Karlin-Hayter, *BMFD*, II, pp. 578–601.
39. *Life of Euthymios the Younger*, II–VII, in *Holy Men of Mount Athos*, ed. and trans. Patricia Karlin-Hayter and Richard P. Greenfield (Cambridge, MA, 2016), pp. 10–25.
40. *Life of Euthymios*, VIII–X, pp. 26–9.
41. Basil, *Shorter Responses*, 117, in *The Asketikon of St Basil the Great*, trans. A.M. Silwas (Oxford, 2005), p. 337.
42. *Narratio de monacho Palestinensis*, ed. Hippolyte Delehaye, 'Saints de Chypre', *Analecta Bollandiana* 26 (1907), 162–75.
43. Cyril of Scythopolis, *Vita Iohannis Hesychastes*, V, ed. Schwartz, *Kyrillos*, p. 205; trans. Price, *Lives of the Monks of Palestine*, p. 224.
44. Bruno of Querfort, *Vita S. Adalberti*, XIV, MHG (SS), IV, p. 602.
45. *Miracula Sancti Gorgonii*, XXVI, MGH (SS) IV, 246.
46. *Testamentary Rule of Neophytos the Recluse*, IV, ed. and trans. Nicholas Coureas, *The Foundation Rules of Medieval Cypriot Monasteries: Makhairas and St Neophytos*, Cyprus Research Centre Texts and Studies in the History of Cyprus XLVI (Nicosia, 2003), p. 135.
47. *Life of Euthymios*, XI, pp. 34–5.
48. *Life of Euthymios*, XII, pp. 36–7.
49. *Life of Euthymios*, XXII, pp. 66–7.
50. *The Life of Lazaros of Mt Galesion*, XVIII, XXXV, ed. and trans. Richard P. Greenfield (Washington DC, 2000), pp. 99, 122. Lazaros, as superior at Mount Galesion, refused to permit beds even for sick monks, CLXII, pp. 253–4; Tom Licence (ed.), 'The "Life and Miracles" of Godric of Throkenholt', *Analecta Bollandiana* 124 (2006), 15–43, at pp. 25–8.
51. Brakke, *Athanasius*, p. 87.
52. Cuthbert Butler, *Benedictine Monachism: Studies in Benedictine Life and Rule*, 2nd edn (Cambridge, 1924), pp. 280, 284.
53. www.sleepfoundation.org/shift-work-disorder/symptoms, accessed 02/04/2024.
54. *Life of Euthymios*, XVII, pp. 50–3.
55. *Life of Euthymios*, XVIII, pp. 54–5.
56. For full discussion, see Wortley, '"Grazers"', pp. 37–48.
57. F. Nau (ed.), 'Histoires des solitaires égyptiens', *Revue de l'Orient Chrétien*, 12–13 (1907–8), 181.
58. *Vita Sabae*, XLIX, pp. 138–9, trans. Price, *Lives of the Monks of Palestine*, pp. 148–9.
59. *Vita Euthymii*, XIII, p. 23; trans. Price, *Lives of the Monks of Palestine*, pp. 18–19.
60. *Life of Euthymios*, XXII, pp. 64–5.
61. Eunape de Sardes, *Vies de philosophes et de sophistes*, VI, 112–13, ed. and trans. Richard Goulet, 2 vols (Paris, 2020), vol. 2, pp. 40–1.
62. John Climacos, *Scala Paradisi*, PG 88:957.
63. Sergey Ivanov, *Holy Fools in Byzantium and Beyond* (Oxford, 2006), p. 90.
64. Ivanov, *Holy Fools*, pp. 140–1.
65. Theodore the Studite, *Great Catechesis*, LXXXII, ed. Costa-Luzza, *Nova partum bibliotheca* X (Rome, 1905), p. 25; *Un grand mystique byzantin: Vie de Syméon le Nouveau Théologien*, CX, ed. Irénée Hausherr (Rome, 1928), p. 210.

66. *Vita S. Nicolae Peregrini*, *AASS* Jun. I, pp. 231–46; Paul Oldfield, 'St Nicholas the Pilgrim and the City of Trani between Greeks and Normans, *c*. 1090–*c*. 1140' *Anglo-Norman Studies* 30 (2008), 168–81.
67. Gregory, *History*, VIII, 15, pp. 380–3.
68. *Life of Lazaros*, p. 25.
69. John Phokas, *Ekphrasis*, PG 133:952–3; for Gabriel, Bernard Hamilton and Andrew Jotischky, *Latin and Greek Monasticism in the Crusader States* (Cambridge, 2020), pp. 426–7.
70. Hamilton and Jotischky, *Latin and Greek Monasticism*, p. 366.
71. Alice-Mary Talbot, 'Women and Mt Athos', in *Mount Athos and Byzantine Monasticism*, ed. Bryer et al., pp. 67–79, points out that the ban on women is implied, though not actually stated, in different documents from Athos, such as the *Typikon* of Athanasios. The *Tragos* banned eunuchs and men without beards.
72. *Christodoulos*, *BMFD*, II, p. 584.
73. Agostino Pertusi, 'La spiritualité gréco-byzantine en Italie méridionale', in Agostino Pertusi, *Scritti sulla Calabria greca medievale* (Soveria Mannelli, 1994), pp. 99–116.
74. Cited by Talbot, 'Women and Mt Athos', p. 77.
75. *Holy Women of Byzantium: Ten Saints' Lives in Translation*, Byzantine Saints Lives in Translation 1, ed. and trans Alice-Mary Talbot (Washington DC, 1996), pp. 110–16, 143, 168.
76. Among the very wide scholarship, see Silvano Borsari, *Il monachesimo bizantino nella Sicilia e nell'Italia meridionale prenormanne* (Naples, 1963); Enrico Morini, 'Eremo e cenobio nel monachesimo greco dell'Italia meridionale nei secoli IX e X', *Rivista di storia della Chiesa in Italia* 31 (1977), 354–90; Agostino Pertusi, 'Rapporti tra il monachesimo italo-greco ed il monachesimo bizantino nell'alto medioevo', in *La chiesa greca in Italia dall' VIII al XVI secolo*, 2 vols (Padua, 1973), 2, pp. 473–520; Vera von Falkenhausen, 'I monasteri greci dell'Italia meridionale e della Sicilia dopo l'avvenuto dei normanni: continuità e mutamenti', in *Il Passaggio dal domino bizantino allo stato normanno nell'Italia meridionale* (Taranto, 1997), 197–229; Graham Loud, *The Latin Church in Norman Italy* (Cambridge, 2007), pp. 430–520; Paul Oldfield, *Sanctity and Pilgrimage in Medieval Southern Italy* (Cambridge, 2014); James Morton, *Byzantine Religious Law in Medieval Italy* (Oxford, 2021).
77. Saskia Sassen, *Territory, Authority, Rights: From Medieval to Global Assemblages* (Princeton, NJ, 2006), pp. 32–3.
78. *Vita di sant'Elia il giovane*, ed. M. Taibi (Palermo, 1962); M.V. Strattezeri, 'Una traduzione dal Greco ad uso dei normanni: la vita latina di sant'Elia lo Speleota', *Archivio storico per la Calabria e la Lucania* 59 (1992), 1–108, with edition at pp. 42–86.
79. Agostino Pertusi, 'Aspetti organizzativi e culturali dell'ambiente monacale greco dell'Italia meridionale', in *L'eremitismo in Occidente nei secoli XI e XII* (Milan, 1965), pp. 382–426, at p. 392; see also Pertusi, 'Rapporti'; Gregorio Penco, 'L'eremitismo irregolare in Italia nei secoli XI–XII', *Benedictinia* 32 (1985): 201–21.
80. OV, III, pp. 158–61; for fuller discussion of the text and the circumstances of its translation into Latin, see Andrew Jotischky, 'Monks and the Muslim Enemy: Conversion, Polemic and Resistance in Monastic Hagiography in the Age of the Crusades, *c*. 1000–1250', *Transactions of the Royal Historical Society*, 7th series, 1 (2023), 5–22 at pp. 17–18.
81. Annick Peters-Custot, *Les grecs de l'Italie méridionale post-byzantine (IXe–XIVe siècle). Une acculturation en douceur* (Rome, 2009), p. 177.

82. *Vita sancti Vitalis Siculi, AASS* Mar. II, cols 26–34.
83. *Life of Athanasios*, XLIII, 264–5.
84. *Life of Euthymios*, XXVIII–XXIX, pp. 84–9.
85. G. Da Costa-Louillet, 'Saints de Sicile et d'Italie méridionale aux VIIIe, IXe et Xe siècles', *Byzantion*, 29–30 (1959–60), 89–95; Peters-Custot, *Les grecs de l'Italie*, p. 179.
86. Gregory, *Dialogues*, III, 4, vol. 2, pp. 270–3; Peter Dinzelbacher, 'Der Kampf der Heiligen mit den Damonen', in *Santi e demoni nell'Alto Medioevo occidentale (secoli V–XI)*, SSCISSM XXXVI, 2 vols (Spoleto, 1989), II, p. 657.
87. Falkenhausen, 'I monasteri', pp. 197–229, at 221–2, for the diffusion of texts in southern Italy. The false accusation of theft against Elias in Patras also recalls the biblical parallel of Joseph and Benjamin (Genesis 44.33).
88. On Sabas, see Paul Oldfield, *Sanctity and Pilgrimage in Medieval Southern Italy, 1000–1200* (Cambridge, 2014), pp. 41–6.
89. *Vita Vitale Siculi*, I.5–6, *AASS* Mar. II, p. 27.
90. Peters-Custot, *Les grecs de l'Italie*, p. 210.
91. Leoluca: *AASS* Mar. I, p. 99; Gregory of Cassano: MGH (SS) XV, 1185–7; in general, Francesco Russo, 'La "peregrinatio" dei santi italo-greci nelle tombe degli Apostoli Pietro e Paolo a Roma, *Bollettino della Badia Greca di Grottaferrata*, n.s. 22 (1968), 89–99.
92. Bernard Hamilton, 'The Monastic Revival in Tenth-Century Rome', *Studia Monastica* 4 (1962), 35–68; Bernard Hamilton, 'The Monastery of S. Alessio and the Religious and Intellectual Renaissance in Tenth-Century Rome', *Studies in Medieval and Renaissance History* 2 (1965), 265–310; Bernard Hamilton, 'The House of Theophylact and the Promotion of Religious Life among Women in Tenth-Century Rome', *Studia Monastica* 12 (1970), 195–217.
93. E. Follieri, *Vita di San Fantino il Giovane*, XXVI (Brussels, 1993), p. 430.
94. Jean Heuclin, *Aux origines monastiques de la Gaule du Nord: Ermites et Reclus du Ve au XIe siècle* (Lille, 1988).
95. Paulette L'Hermite-Leclercq, 'Anchoritism in Medieval France', in Elizabeth McEvoy (ed.), *Anchoritic Traditions of Medieval Europe* (Woodbridge, 2010), p. 117.
96. Consuelo Aherne (ed.), *Valerio of Bierzo: An Ascetic of the Late Visigothic Period* (Washington DC, 1949); see now G. Cavero Domínguez, 'Anchorites in the Spanish Tradition', in McEvoy (ed.), *Anchoritic Traditions*, p. 93.
97. Suzanne J. Wemple, 'Late Ninth-Century Saints: Hathmudo and Liutberga', in *The Joy of Learning and the Love of God*, ed. E. Rozanne Elder (Kalamazoo, MI, 1995), pp. 33–47.
98. *Vitae sanctae Wiboradae. Die älteste Lebensbeschreibung der heiligen Wiborada. Einleitung, kritische Edition und Übersetztung*, ed. Walter Berschin (St Gallen, 1983).
99. *Grimlaici presbyteri regula solitarium*, PL 103: 574–664; *Grimlaicus, Rule for Solitaries*, trans. Andrew Thornton (Collegeville, MN, 2011). For discussion of the date, see Phyllis Jestice, *Wayward Monks and the Religious Revolution of the Eleventh Century* (Leiden, 1997), p. 92n, and K.S. Frank, 'Grimlaicus, "Regula solitariorum"', in *Vita religiosa im Mittelalter: Festschrift für Kaspar Elm*, ed. F.J. Felten and N. Jaspert (Berlin, 1999), pp. 21–35.
100. Ruotger, *Vita Brunonis archiepiscopi Coloniensis*, MGH (SRG) X (n.s.) ed. I. Ott (Weimar, 1951), p. 34.
101. *AASS* Sept. IV, pp. 41–4.
102. *AASS* Jun. V, pp. 387–93.

103. *AASS* Feb. III, p. 694. In general see Jestice, *Wayward Monks*, pp. 23–43; for recent discussion of Lambert, and other hermits of this period, see Ian Schwab, 'Undomesticated Faith: Outlying Ascetics *c.* 900–*c.* 1200', unpublished PhD thesis, Aberdeen University, 2020.
104. Jestice, *Wayward Monks*, p. 145.
105. *Grimlaici regula*, PL 103: 593–4.
106. Ivanov, *Holy Fools*, pp. 130–1.
107. *Life of Euthymios*, XXIV–XXV, pp. 76–7.
108. Pertusi, 'La spiritualité gréco-byzantine en Italie méridionale'.
109. *Vita sancti Vitalis Siculi*, *AASS* Mar. II, cols 26–34.
110. *La prise de Jérusalem par les Perses en 615*, VIII–X, ed. G. Garitte, Corpus Scriptorum Christianorum Orientalium, Scriptores Iberici 12 (1960); F.C. Conybeare, 'Antiochus Strategios' Account of the Sack of Jerusalem in AD 614,' *EHR* 25 (1910), 502–17; Bradley Bowman, *Christian Monastic Life in Early Islam* (Edinburgh, 2021), pp. 72–3; but see now Daniel Reynolds, 'Monasticism in Early Islamic Palestine: Contours of Debate', in *The Late Antique World of Early Islam: Muslims among Christians and Jews in the East Mediterranean*, ed. Robert Hoyland and M. Legendre (London, 2015), pp. 339–91.
111. Robert Schick, *The Christian Communities of Palestine from Byzantine to Islamic Rule* (Princeton, NJ, 1995).
112. Bowman, *Christian Monastic Life*, pp. 126–7.
113. *Passio SS XX martyrum S. Sabae*, ed. A. Papadopoulos-Kerameos, *Pravoslavnii Palestinski Sbornik* 57 (1907), 1–41 [Greek text]; *AASS* Mar. III, pp. 165–79 [Latin translation]; *Theophanis Chronographia*, ed. C. de Boor, 2 vols (Hildesheim, 1963), vol. 1, pp. 484, 499, *The Chronicle of Theophanes*, ed. and trans. C. Mango and R. Scott (Oxford, 1997), pp. 665, 693.
114. Jessica A. Coope, *The Martyrs of Córdoba: Community and Family Conflict in an Age of Mass Conversion* (Lincoln, NE, 1995).
115. Desiderius of Monte Cassino, *Dialogi de miraculis sancti Benedicti*, I, ed. G. Schwartz and A. Hofmeister, MGH (SS), XXX, pp. 1118–19.
116. Claude Carozzi, 'La vie de saint Bobon: un modèle clunisien de sainteté laïque', in *Guerriers et moines: Conversion et sainteté aristocratiques dans l'occident médiéval (IXe–XIIe siècle)*, ed. Michel Lauwers (Antibes, 2002), pp. 467–91.
117. Scott G. Bruce, *Cluny and the Muslims of La Garde-Freinet* (Ithaca, NY, 2015), provides an indispensable guide to these events and the retellings of the episode, and this paragraph is extensively a summary of his discussion on pp. 32–62.
118. Syrus, *Vita sancti Maioli*, III.5, ed. Dominique Iogna-Prat, *Agni Immaculati: Recherches sur les sources hagiographiques relatives à Saint Maieul de Cluny (954–994)* (Paris, 1988), pp. 163–285, at p. 253.
119. Bruce, *Cluny*, p. 54.
120. Sidney H. Griffith, 'Michael, the Martyr and Monk of Mar Sabas Monastery, at the Court of the Caliph 'Abd al-Malik: Christian Apologetics and Martyrology in the Early Islamic Period', *Aram* 6 (1994), 115–48.
121. Sidney H. Griffith, 'The Monk in the Emir's *Majlis*: Reflections on a Popular Genre of Christian Literary Apologetics in Arabic in the Early Islamic Period', in *The Majlis: Interreligious Encounters in Medieval Islam*, ed. H.L. Yafeh et al. (Wiesbaden, 1998), pp. 13–65.
122. On St Gellert in history and later tradition, see Andrew Jotischky, 'Gerard of Csanád and the Carmelites: Apocryphal Sidelights on the First Crusade', in

NOTES to pp. 153–161

Autour de la première croisade: Actes du colloque de la Society for the Study of the Crusades and the Latin East 1995, ed. Michel Balard, Byzantina Sorboniensa 14 (Paris, 1996), pp. 143–55.
123. *Vitae sanctae Wiboradae*, p. 84; Heuclin, *Aux origins monastiques*, pp. 227–34.
124. English translation by Robin Flower, *The Irish Tradition* (Oxford, 1947), p. 38.
125. Dáibhí Ó Cróinín, *Early Medieval Ireland 400–1200*, 2nd edn (London, 2017), pp. 253–4.
126. *Annals of Saint Bertin*, ed. Georg Waitz, MGH (SRG), vol. 5, pp. 50–1.
127. For an exact description of the robbing of Peterborough Abbey in an eleventh-century Viking raid, *The Anglo-Saxon Chronicle: A Collaborative Edition*, gen. eds David Dumville and Simon Keynes, 8 vols (Cambridge, 2004), vol. 7: MS E, ed. Susan Irvine, pp. 88–9; Eng. trans. *The Anglo-Saxon Chronicle*, ed. and trans. Dorothy Whitelock (London, 1961), pp. 150–2.
128. *Capitularia Regum Francorum*, II, MGH p. 115.
129. Pierre Riché, 'Conséquences des invasions normandes sur la culture monastique dans l'Occident franc', *Settimane* 16 (1969), 705–21.
130. Ralph Glaber, *Histories*, III, 18, pp. 124–5.
131. Ernst Sackur, *Die Cluniacenser in ihrer kirchlichen und allgemeingeschichtlichen Wirksamkeit bis zur Mitte des elften Jahrhunderts* (Halle, 1892–4). For a comprehensive survey of the first century of scholarship on Cluny, see Barbara Rosenwein, *Rhinoceros Bound: Cluny in the Tenth Century* (Philadelphia, 1982), pp. 3–29.
132. *Consuetudines Cluniacensium antiquiores cum redacionibus derivatis*, ed. Kassius Hallinger, CCCM VII.2 (Siegburg, 1983); *From Dead of Night to End of Day: The Medieval Customs of Cluny*, ed. Susan Boynton and Isabelle Cochelin, Studia Monastica 3 (Turnhout, 2005); *Synopse der cluniacensichen, Necrologien*, ed. Joachim Wollasch et al., Münstersche Mittelalter-Schriften 39.1 (Munich, 1982).
133. Rosenwein, *Rhinoceros Bound*; Giles Constable, 'Cluny in the Monastic World of the Tenth Century', in *Il secolo di ferro: Mito e realtà del secolo X (Spoleto, 19–25 aprile 1990)*, SSCISSM 38 (Spoleto, 1991), pp. 391–437.
134. *Recueil des Chartes de l'Abbaye de Cluny*, CXII, ed. Auguste Bernard and Alexandre Bruel, 6 vols (Paris, 1876–1903), vol. 1, pp. 124–8. In what follows, I refer for the sake of convenience to the charter as though William were the author, but it is of course likely that the author of the wording, if not the sentiments, was Berno.
135. *Chartes de l'abbaye de Cluny*, CXII, vol. 1, p. 125.
136. *Odon de Cluny, Vita sancti Geraldi Auriliacensis*, ed. Anne-Marie Bultot-Verleysen (Brussels, 2009).
137. *Chartes de l'abbaye de Cluny*, CXII, vol. 1, p. 126.
138. *Chartes de l'Abbaye de Cluny*, I, no. 379, p. 359; Giles Constable, 'Baume and Cluny in the Twelfth Century', in *Tradition and Change: Essays in Honour of Marjorie Chibnall*, ed. Diana Greenaway, Christopher Holdsworth and Jane Sayers (Cambridge, 1985), pp. 35–61, esp. 36–9.
139. Sackur, *Die Cluniacenser*, I, pp. 359–63, remains the seminal discussion of John and the composition of the *Life*. The *Life* was edited, along with other early Cluniac hagiographical material, by Dominque Iogna-Prat, and the discussion in his *Études clunisiennes* (Paris, 2002), pp. 35–73, is fundamental.
140. *Odon de Cluny, Vita sancti Geraldi*, II. 16, pp. 216–17. On early Cluniac spirituality, see Kassius Hallinger, 'The Spiritual Life of Cluny in the Early Days', in *Cluniac Monasticism in the Central Middle Ages*, ed. Noreen Hunt (London, 1971), pp. 29–55;

on Gerald of Aurillac, Mathew Kuefler, *The Making and Unmaking of a Saint: Hagiography and Memory in the Cult of Gerald of Aurillac* (Philadelphia, 2014).
141. Odon de Cluny, *Vita sancti Geraldi*, II. 8, pp. 206–9.
142. Scott G. Bruce, *Silence and Sign Language in Medieval Monasticism: The Cluniac Tradition, c. 900–1200* (Cambridge, 2007).
143. John of Salerno, *Vita Odonis*, II.12, *PL* 133: 67.
144. John of Salerno, *Vita Odonis*, I.32, *PL* 133: 57.
145. Hallinger, 'Spiritual Life', pp. 45–6, summarising Odo's *Collationes*, II, 28 and *Vita Geraldi*, II, 9, 16, 26.
146. John of Salerno, *Vita Odonis*, I.
147. *Chartes de l'abbaye de Cluny*, MIXMLVII, vol. 3, pp. 176–7; Jacques Hourlier, 'St Odilo's monastery', in *Cluniac Monasticism*, ed. Hunt, pp. 56–76 at pp. 70–2. The 64 may not represent the total number of monks since others would have been visiting dependent cells.
148. There is a wealth of scholarly research on Majolus, among which the most important works are: *Agni Immaculati*, ed. Iogna-Prat; Dominique Iogna-Prat and Barbara Rosenwein (eds), *Saint-Maïeul, Cluny et la Provence: Expansion d'une abbaye à l'aube du Moyen-Âge* (Mane, Haute-Provence, 1994); *Saint Mayeul et son temps: Actes du congrès international de Valensole 2–14 mai 1994* (Dignes-les-Bains, 1997); *San Maiolo e le influenze Cluniacensi nell'Italia del Nord: Atti del Convegno Internationale nel Millenario di San Maiolo (994–1994)*, ed. Ettore Cau and Aldo Settia (Como, 1998).
149. McClendon, *Farfa*, p. 10.
150. John of Salerno, *Vita Odonis*, I, 14.
151. Barbara Rosenwein, *To Be the Neighbor of Saint Peter: The Social Meaning of Cluny's Property, 909–1049* (Ithaca, NY, 1989), p. 38, summarising Georg Schreiber, 'Kirchliches Abgabwesen an französischen Eigenkirchen aus Anlass von Ordalien, in *Gemeinschaften des Mittelalters: Recht und Verfassung, Kult und Frömmigkeit* (Münster, 1948), pp. 162–82.
152. The following discussion is based on the analysis in Rosenwein, *To Be the Neighbor*.
153. Rosenwein, *To Be the Neighbor*, p. 41.
154. Rosenwein, *To Be the Neighbor*, p. 202.
155. Rosenwein, *To Be the Neighbor*, p. 145, from *Chartes de l'abbaye de Cluny*, I, p. 708, no. 751, II, pp. 299–30, no. 1139; II, p. 24, no. 911.
156. Rosenwein, *To Be the Neighbor*, passim, but see esp. pp. 202–7; see also De Jong, *In Samuel's Image*, p. 273.
157. Annette B. Weiner, *Inalienable Possessions: The Paradox of Keeping-While-Giving* (Berkeley, CA, 1992), p. 43.
158. Rosenwein, *To Be the Neighbor*, pp. 195–6.
159. Helen Waddell, *The Wandering Scholars* (London, 1926), p. 70. The characterisation of the tenth century as an 'age of iron' was coined in the seventeenth century by Cardinal Baronius, *Annales Ecclesiastici*, ed. A. Theiner, 37 vols (Bar-le-Duc, 1864–83), vol. 15, p. 467.
160. Giulia Barone, 'Jean de Gorze, moine bénédictine', in *L'Abbaye de Gorze au Xe siècle*, ed. M. Parisse and Otto Gerhard Oexle (Nancy, 1993), pp. 141–58. The contemporary life is *Vita Johannis abbatis Gorziensis* ed. G. Pertz, MGH SS IV, pp. 337–77.
161. *Vita Johannis*, p. 338; Dennis K. McDaniel, 'John of Gorze: A Figure in Tenth-Century Management', *Indiana Social Studies Quarterly* 31 (1978), 66–74.

162. Widukind of Corvey, *Deeds of the Saxons*, III, 13, trans. Bernard and David Bachrach (Washington DC, 1014), p. 106.
163. Asser, *Life of King Alfred*, ed. W. Stevenson (London 1904), pp. 79–85.
164. *Regularis Concordia*, ed. Thomas Symons (London, 1953), X, p. 7.
165. Douglas Dales, *Dunstan: Saint and Statesman* (Cambridge, 1988), pp. 25–9.
166. Aelfric, *Life of Aethelwold*, VII, in *Three Lives of English Saints*, ed. and trans. Michael Winterbottom (Toronto, 1972), pp. 19–20; Wulfstan of Winchester, *The Life of St Aethelwold*, X, ed. and trans. Michael Lapidge and Michael Winterbottom (Oxford, 1991), pp. 18–19.
167. Eric John, 'The King and the Monks in the Tenth-Century Reformation', in Eric John, *Orbis Britanniae* (Leicester, 1966), p. 159.
168. On Aethlwold's reputation, see Barbara Yorke, *Bishop Aethelwold: His Career and Influence* (Woodbridge, 1988).
169. Eadmar, 'The Life of St Oswald', trans. Andrew J. Turner and Edward J. Muir (Oxford, 2006), p. 251.
170. *Cartularium Saxonicum*, ed. W. de Gray Birch, 3 vols (London, 1885–93), vol. 3, Oswaldslow Charter no. 1135, pp. 377–82. The same alternative was offered to the canons at Ramsey: John, 'King and Monks', p. 164.
171. John of Salerno, *Vita Odonis*, PL 133: 81.
172. John, 'King and Monks', p. 176.
173. *Regularis Concordia* X, p. 7, XVIII, pp. 13–14.
174. John, 'King and Monks,' p. 159.
175. *Regularis Concordia*, I–III, pp. 1–2.
176. Steven Vanderputten, *Dark Age Nunneries: The Ambiguous Identity of Female Monasticism, 800–1050* (Ithaca, NY, 2018).
177. Bruce Venarde, *Women's Monasticism and Medieval Society* (Ithaca, NY, 1997), p. 9.
178. *Liber Eliensis*, ed. E.O. Blake (London, 1962), 55. The Fécamp story is a familiar trope found in many parallel situations, e.g. the nuns of Bethany under threat from Saladin's army in 1187.
179. Véronique Gazeau, *Normannia Monastica. II. Prosopographie des abbés bénédictins (Xe–XIIe siècles)* (Caen, 2007), pp. 101–5; *Monumenta Vizeliacansia*, ed. R.B.C Huygens (Turnhout, 1976), p. 261.
180. *Anglo-Saxon Chronicle*, ed. and trans. Whitelock, p. 109.
181. *Anglo-Saxon Wills*, ed. Dorothy Whitelock, new edn (Cambridge, 2011), pp. 6–9, 103–8. Shaftesbury was further endowed by Athelstan in 935; he referred to it in this charter as a 'monastic army', *Anglo-Saxon Charters: An Annotated List and Bibliography*, ed. Peter Sawyer (London, 1968), p. 438.
182. Karl Leyser, *Rule and Conflict in an Early Medieval Society: Ottonian Saxony* (London, 1979), p. 44.
183. *Les origines de l'Abbaye de Bouxières-aux-Dames au diocèse de Toul: Reconstitution du chartrier et édition critique des chartes antérieures à 1200*, ed. Robert-Henri Bautier (Nancy, 1987), pp. 11–50; Venarde, *Women's Monasticism*, pp. 29–30.
184. Vanderputten, *Dark Age Nunneries*, p. 146.
185. Denise Cassio-Rivière, 'Les origines de l'abbaye de la Trinité de Poitiers', *Bulletin de la société des antiquaries de l'Ouest*, ser. 3, 4 (1955), 59–72.
186. Elisabeth Magnou-Nortier, 'Formes féminines de vie consacrée dans les pays du Midi jusqu'au début du XIIe siècle', *Cahiers de Fanjeaux* 25 (1988), 192–216, makes a powerful argument for the importance of such communities in the south. Venarde, *Women's Monasticism*, p. 47, points out that the laws of Aethelred (1008)

distinguished nuns from 'women devoted to God', implying two distinct methods of religious life for women.
187. *Cartulary and Charters of Notre-Dame of Homblières*, ed. Theodore Evergates and Giles Constable (Cambridge, MA, 1990), pp. 37–9.

CHAPTER 4: 'THERE ARE ANGELS EVERYWHERE': REFORM IN THE ELEVENTH AND TWELFTH CENTURIES

1. P. Gautier (ed.), 'Requisitoire du Patriarche Jean d'Antioche contre le charistikarioi', *REB* 33 (1975), 77–131.
2. Mansi, *Concilia* XIX, cols 1025–8; *PL* 137: 932; *PL* 141: 1135. Most monasteries in practice needed bishops for certain duties such as ordaining monks as priests, but at Cluny in the eleventh and twelfth centuries there were often former bishops among the community who could perform this episcopal function.
3. *Evergetis: Typikon of Timothy for the Monastery of the Mother of God Evergetis*, trans. Robert Jordan, *BMFD*, II, pp. 454–506.
4. *Evergetis*, *BMFD*, II, p. 482.
5. These were probably from Constantine IX Monomachos (r. 1042–54), Michael VI (r. 1056–7) and Constantine X Doukas (r. 1059–67).
6. *Die Briefe des Petrus Damiani*, C, ed. V. Reindel, 4 vols, MGH (Ep), 3, pp. 101–15.
7. See the essays collected in *From Dead of Night*, ed. Boynton and Cochelin, especially Isabelle Cochelin, 'Customaries as Inspirational Sources', pp. 27–69; Noreen Hunt, *Cluny under Saint Hugh* (London, 1967), is still a valuable reference for daily life at the monastery in the second half of the eleventh century. More generally, Joan Evans, *Monastic Life at Cluny 911–1157* (London, 1931), provides a readable if now rather outdated overview.
8. Kassius Hallinger, 'Das Phänomen der liturgischen Steigerungen Klunys (10./11. Jh)', in *Studia historico-ecclesiastica: Festgabe für Prof. Luchesius G. Spätling OFM*, ed. Isaac Vásquez (Rome, 1977), pp. 183–236.
9. See the discussion in Hunt, *Cluny under Saint Hugh*, pp. 103–5.
10. Frederick S. Paxton, 'Death by Customary at Eleventh-Century Cluny', in *From Dead of Night*, ed. Boynton and Cochelin, pp. 297–318.
11. Eadmer, *Vita Sancti Anselmi*, V (London, 1962), ed. R.W. Southern, p. 9.
12. Peter of Blois, *Epistolae*, XLVII, *PL* 207: 137–41.
13. *Evergetis*, *BMFD*, II, p. 493: 'For prayer is indeed a fine thing, a very fine thing, bringing us into contact with God and raising us from earth to heaven, but love is of course greater and much more important.'
14. Bruce, *Silence*, pp. 13–52.
15. *Evergetis*, *BMFD*, II, p. 472.
16. Ulrich of Zell, *Consuetudines Cluniacensis*, III, 7, *PL* 149: 741; on *circatores* see Scott G. Bruce, 'Lurking with Spiritual Intent: A Note on the Origin and Functions of the Monastic Roundsman (*Circator*)', *RB* 109 (1999), 75–89.
17. See above ch. 2; Ekkehard, *Casus sancti Galli* XXXV, pp. 80–2.
18. Evans, *Monastic Life*, pp. 87–8, suggests that this was far from a daily occurrence but that light work in the garden such as weeding might be prescribed by the abbot on particular days.
19. Giles Constable, *The Reformation of the Twelfth Century* (Cambridge, 1996), pp. 210–15.
20. *The Coucher Book of Furness Abbey*, ed. J.C. Atkinson, Chetham Society IX (Manchester, 1886), p. 122.

21. *Evergetis*, *BMFD*, II, p. 492.
22. *Black Mountain: Regulations of Nikon of the Black Mountain*, trans. Robert Allison, *BMFD*, I, pp. 377–424.
23. Basil, *Longer Responses*, XLI,1, in *Asketikon*, pp. 251–2.
24. *Black Mountain*, *BMFD*, I, p. 408.
25. Carlo De Clercq, *Les textes juridiques dans les Pandectes de Nicon de la Montagne Noir* (Venice, 1942), XLII, p. 53.
26. On issues of dating and interdependence, and as a general introduction to these works, see Isabelle Cochelin, 'Évolution des coutumiers monastiques dessinée à partir de l'étude de Bernard', in *From Dead of Night*, ed. Boynton and Cochelin, pp. 29–66, and in the same volume, Gert Melville, 'Action, Text and Validity: On Re-Examining Cluny's *Consuetudines* and Statutes', pp. 67–83.
27. Summarising the argument of Anselme Davril, 'Coutumiers directifs et coutumiers descriptifs: d'Ulrich à Bernard de Cluny', in *From Dead of Night*, ed. Boynton and Cochelin, pp. 23–8.
28. Hourlier, 'St Odilo's Monastery', pp. 57–63, for the description of Cluny preserved in the Farfa customary.
29. *Evergetis*, *BMFD*, II, p. 468.
30. Irenée Doens, 'Nicon de la Montagne Noire', *Byzantion* 24 (1954), 131–40.
31. *Black Mountain*, *BMFD*, I, pp. 379–80.
32. Ralph Glaber, *Life of William of Volpiano*, VIII, ed. N. Bulot, in Glaber, *Histories*, pp. 272–3.
33. William of Malmesbury, *Gesta Regum Anglorum*, IV, 334, ed. and trans. R.A.B Mynors, R.M. Thomson and M. Winterbottom, 2 vols (Oxford, 1998), vol. 1, pp. 578–9.
34. *Evergetis*, *BMFD*, II, p. 483.
35. *Evergetis*, *BMFD*, II, pp. 483–4.
36. *Evergetis*, *BMFD*, II, pp. 485–6.
37. *Life of Lazaros*, p. 25, n.136, p. 27.
38. *Rule of Neophytos*, XV, p. 148.
39. John P. Thomas, *Private Religious Foundations in the Byzantine Empire* (Washington DC, 1987), p. 157.
40. Thomas, *Private Religious Foundations*, pp. 157–63.
41. Thomas, *Private Religious Foundations*, pp. 179–85.
42. Thomas, *Private Religious Foundations*, pp. 189–90.
43. *Christodoulos*, *BMFD*, II, p. 572. The provision for a *charistikarios* may have been introduced in the early 1090s at a time when Christodoulos had reason to fear for the safety of Patmos and to flee the island.
44. *Christodoulos*, *BMFD*, II, pp. 583, 584–5.
45. *Black Mountain*, *BMFD*, I, p. 410; *Rule of Neilos*, CXV, in *Foundation Rules*, trans. Coureas, p. 109.
46. *Pakourianos: Typikon of Gregory Pakourianos for the Monastery of the Mother of God Petritzonitissa in Backovo*, trans. Robert Jordan, *BMFD*, II, pp. 527–9.
47. *Pakourianos*, *BMFD*, II, p. 493; *Rule of Neilos*, XV, CIX–CX, pp. 70, 107.
48. Colin Phipps, 'Romuald – Model Hermit: Eremitical Theory in Saint Peter Damian's *Vita Beati Romualdi*, chapters 16–27', in William Sheils (ed.), *Monks, Hermits and the Ascetic Tradition*, SCH 22 (Oxford, 1985), pp. 65–78 at p. 66; see also Jean Leclercq, *Saint Pierre Damien, ermite et homme de l'Eglise* (Rome, 1960).

49. Giovanni Tabacco, 'Romualdo di Ravenna e gli inizi dell' eremitismo Camaldolese', in *L'eremitismo*, pp. 73–121; O. Capitani, 'San Pier Damiani e l'istituto eremitico', in *L'eremitismo*, pp. 122–63.
50. Jean Leclercq, 'La crise du monachisme aux XIe et XIIe siècles', *Bullettino dell'Istituto storico Italiano per il medio evo* 70 (1958), 19–41; Jestice, *Wayward Monks*, pp. 141–50.
51. Henrietta Leyser, *Hermits and the New Monasticism: A Study of Religious Communities in Western Europe, 1000–1150* (New York, 1984).
52. Constable, *Reformation*, pp. 153–61.
53. *De Gallica profectione*, PL 145: 874; for Hugh's career see Armin Kohnle, *Abt Hugo von Cluny (1049–1109)* (Sigmaringen, 1993).
54. Leyser, *Hermits and the New Monasticism*, pp. 32–3.
55. *The Letter Collection of Peter Abelard and Heloise*, VI, ed. and trans. David Luscombe (Oxford, 2013), pp. 218–59; on the development of the Paraclete, pp. xxxiv–xxxvii, and for list of early documents, pp. 552–3.
56. Guibert of Nogent, *Monodiae*, I, 11, ed. and trans. (French) Edmond-René Labande (Paris 1981), pp. 62–3; Eng. trans. John F. Benton, *Self and Society in Medieval France* (Toronto, 1984), p. 58.
57. William of Malmesbury, *Gesta Regum*, IV, 334, pp. 578–9.
58. Thomas, *Private Religious Foundations*, p. 220.
59. Conrad of Eberbach, *Exordium Magnum Cisterciense*, Dist. I, 2–3, ed. B. Griesser, Corpus Christianorum Continuatio Medievalis (CCCM) 138 (Turnhout, 1994), 7–9.
60. William of Saint-Thierry, *Vita prima sancti Bernardi*, I, vii, 34, *PL* 185, col. 247.
61. *Vita Bartholomaei Anachoretae*, VIII–IX, in Symeon of Durham, *Historia Dunelmensis*, Appendix II, pp. 295–325, at pp. 300–2; Cassian, *Institutes*, pp. 43–51; Tom Licence, *Hermits and Recluses in English Society 950–1200* (Oxford, 2011), pp. 139–40, 192–3.
62. A. Wilmart, 'Le couvent et la bibliothèque de Cluny vers le milieu du XIe siècle', *Revue Mabillon* 11 (1921), 110.
63. Jean Gribomont, *Histoire du texte des ascétiques de S. Basile* (Louvain, 1953), pp. 44–52.
64. Ferdinando Ughelli, *Italia Sacra Sive De Episcopis Italiae et Insularum Adiacentium*, 9 vols (Rome, 1644–62, repr. 1970), II, pp. 355–9.
65. *Chronica Monasterii Casinensis*, II, 30–31, ed. H. Hoffman, MGH (SS) XXIV (Hannover, 1980), pp. 646–7. This was not the first time a western monk had acted likewise as a result of Greek influence: in 933 John of Gorze introduced manual labour after seeing Greek monks at work at Monte Gargano in Italy, *Miracula s. Gorgonii: Studien und Texte zur Gorgonius-Verehrung im 10. Jahrhundert*, XXVI, ed. and trans. P.C. Jacobsen (Hannover, 2009), pp. 139, 163.
66. See Kathryn L. Jasper, 'Peter Damian and the Communication of Local Reform', *Catholic Historical Review* 104 (2018), 197–222, on the importance of social and personal networks as vehicles for reform practices.
67. Jean Leclercq, 'Les relations entre le monachisme oriental et le monachisme occidental dans le haut Moyen Âge', *Le Millénaire du Mont Athos*, II, pp. 49–80, at p. 55.
68. *The Life of Saint Neilos of Rossano*, ed. and trans. F.L. Capra et al. (Washington DC, 2018).
69. *Vita S. Adalberti* XV, MGH (SS) IV, p. 587; *Oriens Christianus* V (1905), 60–71 for edition of the hymn.
70. *Life of Neilos*, LXXII–LXXVIII, pp. 220–37.
71. *Vita de S. Johanne Matherensi*, *AASS* Jun. V, pp. 36–50.

72. *Vita S. Adalberti*, p. 602.
73. *Miracula Sancti Gorgoni*, LXXVII, ed. Georg Pertz, MGH (SS) IV, p. 358.
74. Leyser, *Hermits and the New Monasticism*, p. 33.
75. *Chronicon monasterii Cassinensis*, II, 28–9, ed. H. Hoffmann, MGH (SS) XXXIV, pp. 217–20; Loud, *Latin Church*, p. 56.
76. The best guide to these, and to Dominic's career, is John Howe, *Church Reform and Social Change in Eleventh-Century Italy: Dominic of Sora and His Patrons* (Philadelphia, 1997).
77. Howe, *Church Reform*, p. 87.
78. Howe, *Church Reform*, pp. 80–1.
79. *Lettres des premiers chartreux*, vol. 1: *S. Bruno, Guiges, S. Anthelme*, ed. Un Chartreux (Paris, 1962), pp. 68–9, no 1.
80. Francisco Trinchera, *Syllabus Graecarum Membranarum* (Naples, 1865), nos 59 (Sept. 1094), pp. 76–7; 60 (Feb. 1097), pp. 77–8; 69 (June 1101), pp. 86–7; Annick Peters-Custot, *Bruno en Calabre: Histoire d'une fondation monastique dans l'Italie normande*, Collection de l'École Française de Rome 489 (Rome, 2014), p. 143.
81. *Lettres des premiers chartreux*, p. 68, no. 1.
82. Peters-Custot, *Bruno en Calabre*, p. 148.
83. OV, V.16, p. 158.
84. *Fragala: Testaments of Gregory for the Monastery of St Philip of Fragala in Sicily*, trans. Patricia Karlin-Hayter and Timothy Miller, *BMFD* II, pp. 621–36. San Filippo di Argira, a sixth-century Sicilian foundation in disuse, was restored by Roger I but in 1126 ceded to the Benedictine monastery of St Mary Latin in Jerusalem. Lynn White Jr, *Latin Monasticism in Norman Sicily* (Cambridge, MA, 1938), pp. 105–17, 184–8.
85. *Luke of Messina: Typikon of Luke for the Monastery of Christ Savior (San Salvatore) in Messina*, trans. Timothy Miller, *BMFD* II, pp. 637–48 at p. 645.
86. For a recent biography, see André Ravier, *Saint Bruno: The Carthusian* (Leominster, 2017).
87. Guibert, *Monodiae*, I, 11, pp. 66–70.
88. *The Letters of Peter the Venerable*, ed. Giles Constable, 2 vols (Cambridge, MA, 1967), I, pp. 45–7.
89. *Vita Stephani Obazinensis*, I, 26, ed. M. Aubrun (Clermont-Ferrand, 1970), p. 82.
90. Eadmer, *Historia Novorum*, I, 27, ed. and trans. Geoffrey Bosanquet (London, 1964), p. 28.
91. Eadmer, *Vita Sancti Anselmi*, I, 7, p. 11.
92. Baudri of Dol, *First Life of Robert Arbrissel* [hereafter: *Robert of Arbrissel, First Life*], XVI, in *Robert of Arbrissel: A Medieval Religious Life*, trans. Bruce L. Venarde (Washington DC, 2003), pp. 14–15.
93. David Postles, '*Defensores astabimus:* Garendon Abbey and its Early Benefactors', in *Monasteries and Society in Medieval Britain: Proceedings of the 1994 Harlaxton Symposium*, ed. Benjamin Thompson (Stamford, 1999), pp. 97–116.
94. For Obazine, see *Vita Stephani Obazinensis*, and discussion in Leyser, *Hermits and the New Monasticism*, esp. pp. 18–28, 38–51.
95. Coureas, *Foundation Rules*, pp. 26–7; Janet Burton, *Monastic and Religious Orders in Britain, 1000–1300* (Cambridge, 1994), p. 57.
96. *Vita prima S. Bernardi*, I, VII, 35, ed. Paul Verdeyen, trans. Pauline Matarasso, *The Cistercian World: Monastic Writings of the Twelfth Century* (Harmondsworth, 1993), p. 31.

97. Glaber, *Histories*, III.13, pp. 116–17.
98. Burton, *Monastic and Religious Orders*, p. 32.
99. *Vita Stephani Obazinensis*, I, 7, pp. 54–5.
100. *Rule of Neophytos*, VI, IX, pp. 139–40.
101. Guibert, *Monodiae*, I.11, pp. 72–3, trans. Benton, p. 62.
102. Guibert, *Monodiae*, I.11, pp. 72–3, trans. Benton, p. 63.
103. Guibert, *Monodiae*, I.11, pp. 74–5, trans. Benton, p. 63.
104. Guibert, *Monodiae*, 1.8, pp. 50–1, trans. Benton, p. 54.
105. OV, VIII, 26, vol. 4, pp. 312–14.
106. The standard treatment of the subject is still Constable, *Monastic Tithes*.
107. OV, VIII, 26, vol. 4, pp. 312–14.
108. OV, VIII, 26, vol. 4, pp. 314–15.
109. OV, VIII, 26, vol. 4, pp. 320–1.
110. Benedicta Ward, 'The Desert Myth: Reflections on the Desert Ideal in Early Cistercian Monasticism', in *One Yet Two: Monastic Tradition East and West*, ed. M. Basil Pennington (Kalamazoo, MI, 1976), pp. 183–99.
111. *Exordium parvum*, IV–VI, in *Narrative and Legislative Text from Early Cîteaux*, ed. Chryosogonus Waddell, Commentarii cisterciennes studio et documenta XI (Nuits-Saint-Georges, 1999), pp. 240–1, 422–5.
112. *Narrative and Legislative Texts*, pp. 246, 428–9.
113. H.E.J. Cowdrey, 'Stephen Harding,' *ODNB*, www.oxforddnb.com, accessed 14/04/2024.
114. For a survey of the early history, see Emilia Jamroziak, *The Cistercian Order in Medieval Europe 1090–1500* (Abingdon, 2013), pp. 43–92.
115. Jean-Baptiste Van Damme, *The Three Founders of Cîteaux: Robert of Molesme, Alberic, Stephen Harding*, trans. Nicholas Groves and Christian Carr, arranged by Bede Lackner (Kalamazoo, MI, 1998), pp. 41–2.
116. Compare for example Jamroziak, *Cistercian Order*, p. 14, with Constance Berman, *The Cistercian Evolution: The Invention of a Religious Order in Twelfth-Century Europe* (Philadelphia, 2000), passim (pp. 93–5 for pithy statement of the argument).
117. Bede K. Lackner, 'The Liturgy of Early Cîteaux', in *Studies in Medieval Cistercian History Presented to Jeremiah F. O'Sullivan* (Shannon, 1971), pp. 6–8; Martha Newman, 'Stephen Harding and the Creation of the Cistercian Community', *RB* 107 (1997), 307–29.
118. William of Malmesbury, *Gesta Regum*, IV, 334, pp. 578–9.
119. For example, C.H. Lawrence, *Medieval Monasticism: Forms of Religious Life in Western Europe in the Middle Ages*, 2nd edn (London, 1989), pp. 174–6; for critique of the traditional problems over dating these documents, Berman, *Cistercian Evolution*, pp. 46–92.
120. Lawrence, *Medieval Monasticism*, pp. 186–7; Jean-Berthold Mahn, *L'ordre cistercien et son gouvernement 1098–1265* (Paris, 1946), p. 1: 'One of the unique features of the Cistercian Order is that it represented at the very start of the twelfth century a self-willed and self-conscious organization.'
121. For example, at KISH185.jpg (443×403), www.templarsnow.com/p/cistercian.html, accessed 18/07/2024.
122. Berman, *Cistercian Evolution*, p. 52.
123. *The Coucher Book of Furness Abbey*, IX, 122.
124. Andrew Jotischky, *The Perfection of Solitude: Hermits and Monks in the Crusader States* (University Park, PA, 1995), pp. 32–3; on Palmaria, Benjamin Z. Kedar, 'Palmarée, abbaye clunisienne du XIIe siècle en Galilée', *RB* 93 (1983), 260–9.

125. *Vita Stephani Obazinensis*, I, 7–9, II, 9, pp. 54–9, 108–9.
126. *Vita Stephani Obazinensis*, II, 13, p. 114.
127. Pierre-Roger Gaussin, 'Les communautés féminines dans l'espace languedocien de la fin du XIe à al fin du XIVe siècle', in *La femme dans la vie religieuse du Languedoc (XIIIe–XIVe siècle)*, Cahiers de Fanjeaux 23 (Toulouse, 1988), pp. 299–332; Constance H. Berman, 'Men's Houses, Women's Houses: The Relationship between the Sexes in Twelfth-Century Monasticism', in *The Medieval Monastery*, ed. Andrew MacLeish (Minneapolis, MN, 1988), pp. 43–52.
128. *The Book of St Gilbert*, XIII, ed. Raymonde Foreville and Gillian Keir (Oxford, 1987), pp. 41–3; see now Brian Golding, *Gilbert of Sempringham and the Gilbertine Order c. 1130–1300* (Oxford, 1995), pp. 40–2.
129. *Instituta Generalis Capituli*, IX, in *Narrative and Legislative Texts*, p. 460.
130. The following is based on Constable, *Monastic Tithes*, pp. 190–1.
131. Constable, *Monastic Tithes*, p. 152; idem, 'Cluniac Tithes and the Controversy between Gigny and Le Miroir', *RB* 70 (1960), 591–624.
132. Conrad Greenia, 'The Laybrother Vocation in the Eleventh and Twelfth Centuries', *Cistercian Studies* 16 (1981), 38–45; Bernadette Barrière, 'Les patrimonies cisterciennes en France', in *L'espace cistercienne*, ed. Léon Pressouyre (Paris, 1994), p. 66 n. 10. A charter from Obazine lists a baker, a smith, two weavers, a pelterer, a miller, a shoemaker and a master herdsman as *conversi*, *Le cartulaire de l'abbaye cistercienne d'Obazine (XIIe–XIIIe siècle)*, ed. Bernadette Barrière (Clermont-Ferrand, 1989), nos 202, 498, 759 and 1085.
133. *Cistercian Lay Brothers: Twelfth-Century Usages with Related Texts*, ed. and trans. Chrysogonus Waddell (Cîteaux, 2000).
134. *Twelfth-Century Statutes from the Cistercian General Chapter*, I.C.1188, ed. Chrysogonus Waddell, Commentarii Cistercienses Studia et Documenta XII (Cîteaux, 2002), p. 151; *Dictionnaire des auteurs cisterciens*, ed. E. Brouette, A. Dimier and E. Manning (Rochefort, 1975–), p. 486. And see Constance Berman, 'Distinguishing between the Humble Peasant and Lay Brother and Sister, and the Converted Knight in Medieval Southern France', in *Religious and Laity in Western Europe, 1000–1400*, ed. Emilia Jamroziak and Janet Burton (Turnhout, 2006), pp. 263–83, at pp. 265–7, arguing that before the 1170s many *conversi* were recruited from the knighthood and closer to the choir monks than later became the case.
135. David Williams, *The Cistercians in the Early Middle Ages* (Leominster, 1988), p. 81.
136. Megan Cassidy-Welch, 'Non conversi sed perversi: The Use and Marginalisation of the Cistercian Lay Brother', in *Deviance and Textual Control: New Perspectives in Medieval Studies*, ed. Megan Cassidy-Welch et al. (Melbourne, 1997), 34–55.
137. Walter Map, *De Nugis Curialium: Courtiers' Trifles*, I, 25, ed. and trans. M.R. James, C.N.L. Brooke and R.A.B. Mynors (Oxford, 1983), pp. 96–9; and see below, ch. 5.
138. Brian Noell, 'Expectation and Unrest among Cistercian Lay Brothers in the Twelfth and Thirteenth Centuries', *JMH* 32 (2006), 253–74, explores the stereotype of the disobedient *conversus* in Cistercian sources; James Donnelly, *The Decline of the Medieval Cistercian Laybrotherhood* (New York, 1949).
139. *Exordium magnum* V, 10, ed. Griesser, pp. 327–34.
140. Thomas de Burton, *Chronica monasterii de Melsa*, I, ed. Edward Bond, 3 vols (London, 1866–8), vol. 1, p. 432.
141. *Cistercians and Cluniacs: The Case for Cîteaux by Idungus of Prüfening*, trans. Jeremiah O'Sullivan, Joseph Leahey and Grace Perrigo (Kalamazoo, MI, 1977).

142. *Libellus de diversis ordinibus et professionibus qui sunt in aecclesia*, ed. and trans. G. Constable and B. Smith (Oxford, 1972).
143. Constable, *Reformation*, pp. 174–6.
144. *Vita prima S. Bernardi*, I, 38, p. 62; trans. Matarasso, p. 30.
145. The historiography on Bernard is vast. A good starting point is Gillian Evans, *Bernard of Clairvaux* (New York, 2000); on the historiographical tradition, see Adriaan Bredero, *Bernard of Clairvaux: Between Cult and History* (Edinburgh, 1996); also *Bernard of Clairvaux: Studies Presented to Dom Jean Leclercq*, Cistercian Studies 23 (Washington DC, 1973).
146. The standard edition of Bernard's works is *Sancti Bernardi Opera*, ed. Jean Leclercq, Henri Rochais and C.H. Talbot, 9 vols (Rome, 1957–77). English translations have been made of many of his major works, including *An Apologia to Abbot William*, in *The Works of Bernard of Clairvaux. Volume I. Treatises I*, Cistercian Fathers Series 1 (Shannon, 1970).
147. *Apologia ad Guillelmum Abbatem*, in *Sancti Bernardi Opera*, vol. 3, pp. 97–8; *Apologia to Abbot William*, pp. 55–6. Similar sentiments are expressed in his letter to Robert, a relative who had left Clairvaux for Cluny, *Epistolae*, I, *Sancti Bernardi Opera*, vol. 7, pp. 9–10.
148. See Bredero, *Bernard of Clairvaux*, pp. 227–47; Gillian Knight, *The Correspondence between Peter the Venerable and Bernard of Clairvaux: A Semantic and Structural Analysis* (Aldershot, 2002).
149. See for example David Knowles, 'Cistercians & Cluniacs: The Controversy between St Bernard and Peter the Venerable', in David Knowles, *The Historian and Character and Other Essays* (Cambridge, 1963), pp. 50–75; but now Constable, *Reformation*, pp. 128–35 for a more nuanced view.
150. *Sancti Bernardi Opera*, vol. 3, pp. 297–378, 381–493; Bernard of Clairvaux, *Five Books on Consideration: Advice to a Pope*, trans. John Anderson and Elizabeth Kennan (Collegeville, MN, 1976); Bernard of Clairvaux, *The Life and Death of Saint Malachy the Irishman*, trans. Robert T. Meyer, Cistercian Fathers Series 10 (Kalamazoo, MI, 1978).
151. *The Letters of Saint Bernard of Clairvaux*, trans. Bruno Scott James, with Introduction by Beverley Mayne Kienzle (London, 1953), p. xxi.
152. The episode is analysed extensively by Michael Casey, 'Bernard and the Crisis at Morimond: Did the Order Exist in 1124?', *Cistercian Studies Quarterly* 38 (2003), 119–75.
153. Hamilton and Jotischky, *Latin and Greek Monasticism*, pp. 150–1, 247.
154. *Epistolae*, IV, *Sancti Bernardi Opera*, vol. 7, pp. 24–7; Eng. trans. *Letters of St Bernard*, pp. 19–22, at p. 21, no. 4; see now Jean Leclercq, 'Lettres de saint Bernard: histoire ou littérature?', *Recueil d'études sur saint Bernard et ses écrits* IV, Storia e Letteratura 167 (Rome, 1987), pp. 125–225, at pp. 183–99.
155. *The Templars: Selected Sources*, ed. and trans. Malcolm Barber and Keith Bate (Manchester, 2002), pp. 25–30, for compilation of earliest accounts.
156. *Epistolae*, VII, *Sancti Bernardi Opera*, vol. 7, pp. 31–46; *Letters of St Bernard*, pp. 26–38, no. 8.
157. Casey, 'Bernard and the Crisis'. For a different chronology of events, see Christopher Holdsworth, 'The Early Writings of Bernard of Clairvaux', *Cîteaux* 45 (1994), 21–6.
158. Bredero, *Bernard of Clairvaux*, p. 283.

159. *Epistolae*, CCCLIX, *Sancti Bernardi Opera*, vol. 8, pp. 304–5; *Letters of St Bernard*, pp. 22–4, no. 5.
160. For an English translation of the *Vita prima*, *The First Life of Bernard of Clairvaux*, trans. Hilary Costello (Collegeville, MN, 2015).
161. Peter Abelard, *History of My Misfortunes*, trans. Betty Radice in *The Letters of Abelard and Heloise* (Harmondsworth, 1976), pp. 59–60; Constant J. Mews, 'William of Champeaux, the Foundation of Saint-Victor (Easter, 1111), and the Evolution of Abelard's Early Career', in *Arts du langage et théologie aux confins des XIe et XIIe siècles: Textes, maîtres, débats*, ed. Irène Rosier-Catach, Studia Artistarum: Études sur la faculté des arts dans les universités médiévales 26 (Turnhout, 2011), pp. 83–104.
162. *The Book of the Foundation of St Bartholomew's Church in London*, ed. Norman Moore, Early English Text Society 163 (1923), pp. 1–2, 33.
163. Patrick Greene, *Norton Priory: The Archaeology of a Medieval Religious House* (Cambridge, 1989), pp. 1–5. For a recent study of a highly influential French Augustinian house, see Yannick Veyrenche, *Chanoines réguliers et sociétés méridionales: L'abbaye de Saint-Ruf et ses prieurés dans le sud-est de la France (XIe–XIVe siècle)* (Turnhout, 2018).
164. The composition and dating of the Rule are discussed by Luc Verheijen, *Nouvelle Approche de la Règle de Saint Augustin* (Bégrolles-en-Mauges, 1980), pp. 58–74, and the manuscript tradition in Luc Verheijen (ed.), *La règle de S. Augustin*, 2 vols (Paris, 1967); Patricia Ranft, 'The Rule of St Augustine in Medieval Monasticism', in *Proceedings of the PMR Conference* 11, ed. Phillip Pulsiano (Villanova, PA, 1986), pp. 143–50.
165. Jean Châtillon, *Le mouvement canonial au moyen âge* (Paris, 1992), pp. 151–62.
166. https://liturgies.net/saints/augustine/rule.htm, accessed 18/07/2024.
167. Robert of Bridlington, *The Bridlington Dialogue*, trans. A Religious of CSMV (London, 1960), p. 126; see also David Jones, *An Early Witness to the Nature of the Canonical Order in the Twelfth Century: A Study in the Life and Writings of Adam Scot* (Salzburg, 1999).
168. Gerald of Wales, *Journey through Wales*, I.3, trans. Lewis Thorpe (London, 1984), p. 107.
169. Gerald of Wales, *Journey through Wales*, I.3, p. 101.
170. Bredero, *Bernard of Clairvaux*, pp. 222–3.
171. *Medieval Religious Houses, Scotland*, ed. Ian Cowan and David Easson, 2nd edn (London, 1976), pp. 66, 68–9, 72, 74–7, 88–93.
172. Christopher Brooke, 'Monk and Canon: Some Patterns in the Religious Life of the Twelfth Century', in *Monks, Hermits*, ed. Sheils, pp. 109–29, at p. 114.
173. Avrom Saltman, *Theobald, Archbishop of Canterbury* (London, 1955), pp. 8, 75–9.
174. William Dugdale, *Monasticon Anglicanum*, ed. John Caley, 6 vols (London, 1817–30), vol. 4, pp. 538–9.
175. W.M. Grauwen, *Norbertus, Aartsbisschop van Maagdenburg (1126–1134)* (Brussels, 1978). Early documents of the order are compiled in *Monasticon Praemonstratense*, ed. N. Backmund, 3 vols (Staubing, 1945–56).
176. *Abbayes, prieurés et monastères de l'ordre de Prémontré en France des origines à nos jours: dictionnaire historique et bibliographique*, ed. Bernard Ardura (Nancy, 1993), pp. 92–8.
177. Hamilton and Jotischky, *Latin and Greek Monasticism*, pp. 150–3, 153–5.

178. J. Kloczowski, 'Die Zisterzienser in Klein-Polen und das Problem ihrer Tätigkeit als Missionare und Seelsorger', in *Die Zisterzienser: Ordensleben zwischen Ideal und Wirklichkeit, 2. Ergänzungsband*, ed. Kaspar Elm and P. Joerissen (Cologne, 1982), pp. 71–8; Jamroziak, *Cistercian Order*, pp. 43–91.
179. Matthew Paris, *Chronica Maiora*, ed. Henry Luard, 7 vols (London, 1868–80), vol. 4, pp. 270–7.
180. An example studied by Jean Leclercq is John of Fécamp. Jean Leclercq, *Un maître de la vie spirituelle au XIe siècle: Jean de Fécamp* (Paris, 1946), e.g. p. 195.
181. John van Engen, 'The "Crisis of Cenobitism" Reconsidered: Benedictine Monasticism in the Years 1050–1150', *Speculum* 61 (1986), 269–304, responding to, amongst many such works: Leclercq, 'La crise du monachisme'; Norman F. Cantor, 'The Crisis of Western Monasticism 1050–1130', *American Historical Review* 66 (1960), 47–67; see also the acceptance of these views by Knowles, 'Cistercians & Cluniacs'.
182. William of Malmesbury, *Gesta Regum*, IV, 334, pp. 578–9; Guibert, *Monodiae*, 1.8, pp. 50–1, trans. Benton p. 54.
183. Steven Vanderputten, *Monastic Reform as Process: Realities and Representations in Medieval Flanders, 900–1100* (Ithaca, NY, 2013).
184. *Vita prima*, I, 35, pp. 60–1.
185. *Vita beati Romualdi*, LXIV, LXVII, ed. G. Tabacco (Rome, 1957), pp. 104–5, 109.
186. Ward, 'Desert Myth'.
187. Venarde, *Women's Monasticism*, pp. 13–14, but see also pp. 53–4.
188. Peter of Poitiers, *Privilegia pro ordine et congregatione Fontis Ebraldi*, I, PL 162, col. 1090.
189. Venarde, *Women's Monasticism*, pp. 60–4.
190. Venarde, *Robert of Arbrissel*, p. xxi.
191. Venarde, *Women's Monasticism*, p. 9.
192. Venarde, *Women's Monasticism*, p. 53, citing as an example Janet L. Nelson, 'Society, Theodicy and the Origins of Medieval Heresy', SCH 9 (1972), 74.
193. Venarde, *Women's Monasticism*, p. 54.
194. Venarde, *Women's Monasticism*, p. 54, n. 8.
195. This paragraph is largely based on the essays in *Christina of Markyate: A Twelfth-Century Holy Woman*, ed. Samuel Fanous and Henrietta Leyser (London, 2005); for the story of her life, see the contemporary *Life of Christina of Markyate: A Twelfth Century Recluse*, ed. C.H. Talbot, revised by Samuel Fanous and Henrietta Layser (London, 2009).
196. James G. Clark, 'Geoffrey de Gorham [Gorron]', *ODNB*, www.oxforddnb.com, accessed 20/12/2022.
197. *Gesta Abbatum monasterii sancti Albani*, I, ed. Henry Riley, Rolls Series (London, 1867–9), p. 73; *The Deeds of the Abbots of St Albans*, ed. and trans. David Preest and James Clark (Woodbridge, 2019), pp. 158–97, at p. 159.
198. Christine Walsh, *The Cult of St Katherine of Alexandria in Early Medieval Europe* (Aldershot, 2007), refers to this devotion as 'the thread that runs through his whole life', p. 146.
199. Andrew Jotischky, 'Saints' Cults and Devotions on the Norman Edge: The Case of St Katherine of Alexandria', in *The Normans and the 'Norman Edge': People, Polities and Identities on the Frontiers of Medieval Europe*, ed. Keith J. Stringer and Andrew Jotischky (London, 2019), pp. 191–218, esp. 217–18.

200. Constant Mews, *Abelard and Heloise* (Oxford, 2004), provides a good guide to the events.
201. *Letter Collection of Peter Abelard and Heloise*, VI, pp. 218–59.
202. Felicitas Corrigan, *Benedictine Tapestry* (London, 1991), p. 67.
203. *Letters of Peter the Venerable*, vol 1, pp. 303–6.
204. *Wulfric of Haselbury by John, Abbot of Ford*, ed. M. Bell, Somerset Record Society 47 (London, 1933); Henry Mayr-Harting, 'Functions of a Twelfth-Century Recluse', *History* 60 (1975), 337–52.
205. *Vita Anastasii*, PL 149: 425–32; Reginald of Durham, *The Life and Miracles of Saint Godric, Hermit of Finchale*, ed. and trans. Margaret Coombe (Oxford, 2022). Other eleventh-century examples from England include Wulfrig, Basing and Aelfwin, monks of Evesham who lived as anchorites by permission of the prior, who happened to be Wulfrig's brother. Thomas of Marlborough, *History of the Abbey of Evesham*, ed. and trans. Jane Sayers and L. Watkiss (Oxford, 2003), pp. 83, 322. Similarly, eleventh-century monks of Worcester Priory lived as hermits near Malvern.
206. Licence, *Hermits and Recluses*, pp. 150–72.

CHAPTER 5: THE MILL AND THE GRINDSTONE: MONASTERIES AND THE WORLD, c. 1100–1300

1. Eadmer, *Vita Sancti Anselmi*, XI, pp. 75–6.
2. The authoritative study is Susan Wood, *The Proprietary Church in the Medieval West* (Oxford, 2006).
3. Bernard, *Epistolae*, vol. 8, pp. 113–14, no. 237; Eugenius's reply appears to agree, Eugenius III, *Epistolae*, PL 180: 1015; see Andrew Jotischky, 'Introduction', in *Eugenius III, the First Cistercian Pope*, ed. Iben Fonnesberg-Schmidt and Andrew Jotischky (Amsterdam, 2018), pp. 17–20.
4. Roger of Wendover, *Flores Historiarum*, ed. Henry Coxe (London, 1841), p. 347.
5. M. Horn, *Studien zur Geschichte Papst Eugens III (1145–1153)*, Europäische Hochschulschriften, Reihe 3: Geschichte und ihre Hilfswissenschaften (Frankfurt am Main, 1992), p. 508.
6. Roberta Gilchrist, *Gender and Material Culture: The Archaeology of Religious Women* (London, 1994), p. 63.
7. Roger of Howden, *Chronica*, ed. William Stubbs, 4 vols (London, 1857–70), vol. 3, p. 72.
8. William of Tyre, *Chronicon*, XV, 21, 23, ed. R.B.C. Huygens, CCCM 62 (Turnhout, 1986), pp. 702–3, 705–6.
9. William of Tyre, *Chronicon*, XVIII, 24–5, pp. 846–9.
10. Roger of Howden, *Chronica*, vol. 3, p. xc.
11. *Annals of Roger de Hoveden*, trans. H.T. Riley (London, 1857), p. 12.
12. Roger of Howden, *Chronica*, vol. 3, p. 198.
13. Odo of Deuil, *De profectione Ludovici in orientem*, ed. Virginia Berry (New York, 1948).
14. James G. Clark, *A Monastic Renaissance at St Albans: Thomas Walsingham and his Circle c. 1350–1440* (Oxford, 2004), p. 10.
15. William of Malmesbury, *Gesta Regum*, pp. 6–9.
16. Procopius, *De Aedificiis* V, 8, ed. and trans. H.B. Dewing (London, 1940), pp. 354–6; George Manginis, *Mount Sinai: A History of Travellers and Pilgrims* (London, 2016), pp. 49–76.

17. See above, pp. 130–1; also Thomas, *Private Religious Foundations*, pp. 44–6.
18. Hamilton and Jotischky, *Latin and Greek Monasticism*, pp. 340–1.
19. *Life of Leontios*, 30, pp. 66–7; 61, p. 102.
20. *Kecharitomene: Typikon of Empress Irene Doukaina Komnene for the Convent of the Mother of God Kecharitomene in Constantinople*, trans. Robert Jordan, *BMFD*, II, pp. 649–724.
21. Beatrix Romhányi, 'The Role of the Cistercians in Medieval Hungary: Political Activity or Internal Colonization?', *Annual of Medieval Studies at Central European University* 1 (1994), 180–204; Ilona Valter, 'Die Ausgrabungen in der ehemaligen Zisterzienserabtei Cikádor', *Analecta Cisterciensia* 52 (1996), 251–64.
22. *Fragala*, *BMFD*, II, pp. 621–36.
23. For discussion of Louis IX's thoughts on monasticism and the crown, see William Chester Jordan, 'The Representation of Monastic-Lay Relations in the Canonization Records for Louis IX', in *Religious and Laity in Western Europe*, ed. Jamroziak and Burton, pp. 225–39.
24. John Phokas, *Ekphrasis*, PG 133:956, trans. in John Wilkinson, *Jerusalem Pilgrimage 1099–1185* (London, 1988), p. 332.
25. Johannes Pahlitzsch, 'Athanasios II, a Greek Orthodox Patriarch of Jerusalem', in *Autour de la première croisade*, ed. Balard, pp. 465–74, at pp. 459–71; Hamilton and Jotischky, *Latin and Greek Monasticism*, p. 363.
26. Robert Ousterhout, 'Rebuilding the Temple: Constantine Monomachus and the Holy Sepulchre', *Journal of the Society of Architectural Historians* 48 (1989), 66–78.
27. Andrew Jotischky, 'Christianity during the Crusades', in *Handbook of Christianity in the Middle East*, ed. M. Raheb and M.A. Lamport (Lanham, MD, 2021), pp. 66–76.
28. Patrick Healy, *The Chronicle of Hugh of Flavigny: Reform and the Investiture Contest in the Late Eleventh Century* (Aldershot, 2006), pp. 51–62.
29. Beata Kitsiki Panagopoulos, *Cistercian and Mendicant Monasteries in Medieval Greece* (Chicago, 1979), pp. 25–63.
30. Jamroziak, *Cistercian Order*, pp. 69–81.
31. Tore Nyberg, *Monasticism in North-Western Europe, 800–1200* (Aldershot, 2000), pp. 232–8.
32. A summary of Burton, *Monastic and Religious Orders*, pp. 22–3.
33. *Gesta Abbatum*, 14, xlv; *Deeds of the Abbots*, pp. 133–4.
34. Susan Ridyard, *The Royal Saints of Anglo-Saxon England: A Study of West Saxon and East Anglian Cults* (Cambridge, 1988).
35. John Gillingham, 'The Introduction of Knight Service into England', *Proceedings of the Battle Conference on Anglo-Norman Studies* 4 (1981), 53–64, 181–7; Marjorie Chibnall, *Anglo-Norman England*, pp. 28–30 (Oxford, 1987); Burton, *Monastic and Religious Orders*, pp. 27–8.
36. Hans E. Mayer (ed.), *Diplomata regum latinorum Hierosolimitanorum*, 4 vols (Hannover, 2010), no. 138–9, vol. 1, pp. 315–23; Hamilton and Jotischky, *Latin and Greek Monasticism*, pp. 72–4.
37. *Regularis Concordia*, I–III, pp. 1–2.
38. Jocelin of Brakelond, *Chronicle*, ed. and trans. H.E. Butler (London, 1949), p. 3.
39. Jocelin, *Chronicle*, p. 23.
40. Clark, *Monastic Renaissance*, p. 36–7, citing *Gesta Abbatum* III, pp. 149, 476.
41. *Vita Anselmi*, XXXI, pp. 54–5.
42. *Vita Anselmi*, XXXI, p. 56.
43. Richard W. Southern, *Saint Anselm: A Portrait in a Landscape* (Cambridge, 1990), p. 159.

44. *Liber Anselmi de humanis moribus* 84, in *Memorials of St Anselm*, ed. R.W. Southern and F.S. Schmitt (Oxford, 1969), pp. 73–4.
45. Southern, *Saint Anselm*, p. 164.
46. Southern, *Saint Anselm*, p. 165.
47. See for example David D'Avray, *Medieval Marriage: Symbolism and Society* (Oxford, 2005), esp. pp. 20–73.
48. *Vita Anselmi*, XXXI, p. 56.
49. *Lettres d'Adam de Perseigne*, XV, ed. and trans. (French) Jean Bouvet and Placide Deseille, 3 vols (Paris, 1960–2015), vol. 1, pp. 237–49; Aurélie Reinbold, 'Les cercles de l'amitié dans la correspondance d'Adam de Perseigne (1188–1221)', in *Les cisterciens dans le Maine et dans l'Ouest au Moyen Âge*, ed. Ghislain Baury, Vincent Corriol, Emmanuel Johans and Laurent Maillet, *Annales de Bretagne et des Pays de l'Ouest* 120 (2013), 87–98.
50. George Duby, *The Knight, the Lady and the Priest: The Making of Modern Marriage in Medieval France* (Harmondsworth, 1985).
51. *Epistolae*, CCCLIV, *Sancti Bernardi Opera*, vol. 8, pp. 297–8; *Letters of St Bernard*, no. 273, p. 346.
52. *Epistolae*, CCLXXXIX, *Sancti Bernardi Opera*, vol. 8, pp. 205–6; *Letters of St Bernard*, no. 274, pp. 347–8.
53. See above, ch. 4.
54. OV, III, vol. 2, pp. 64–5; the whole episode is at pp. 61–5.
55. For detailed valuable discussion of monasteries, litigation and mediation, see Stephen White, 'Garsinde v. Sainte Foy: Argument, Threat and Vengeance in Eleventh-Century Monastic Litigation', in *Religious and Laity in Western Europe*, ed. Burton and Jamroziak, pp. 169–81; and idem, *Feuding and Peace-making in Eleventh-Century France*, Variorum Collected Studies, 817 (Aldershot, 2005).
56. Geoffrey of Burton, *Life and Miracles of St Modwenna*, ed. and trans. Robert Bartlett (Oxford 2002), pp. li–lv.
57. *Chronicon Monasterii de Abingdon*, ed. Joseph Stevenson, 2 vols (London, 1858), vol. 2, p. 20.
58. *The Monastic Constitutions of Lanfranc*, ed. and trans. David Knowles and Christopher Brooke (Oxford, 2002), p. 21.
59. *Cartulaire general de l'Ordre des Hospitaliers de S. Jean de Jérusalem*, no. 443, ed. J. Delaville le Roulx, 4 vols (Paris, 1894), vol. 1, pp. 306–8. See the discussion by Christopher MacEvitt, *The Crusades and the Christian World of the Latin East: Rough Tolerance* (Philadelphia, 2008), pp. 112–14.
60. *Life and Miracles of St Modwenna*, XLIII, pp. 182–3.
61. *Life and Miracles of St Modwenna*, XLVII, pp. 190–1.
62. *Life and Miracles of St Modwenna*, XLVII, pp. 192–4; see also Robert Bartlett, *Why Can the Dead Do Such Great Things? Saints and Worshippers from the Martyrs to the Reformation* (Princeton, NJ, 2013), p. 111 for similar examples.
63. *Life and Miracles of St Modwenna*, XLIX, pp. 206–7.
64. Lactantius, *Divine Institutes*, VI, 12, trans. Anthony Bowen and Peter Garnsey, Translated Texts for Historians 40 (Liverpool, 2003), pp. 355–6.
65. *Rule of Benedict*, ch. 53.
66. See below, pp. 257, 262.
67. *Vita Iohannis Hesychastes*, V–VI, pp. 205–6.
68. Patrich, *Sabas*, pp. 180–2. At St Sabas, the guest master was also responsible for selling on the open market the baskets woven by the monks as their manual labour.

69. *Roidion* A3, *BMFD*, I, pp. 430–1.
70. *Regularis Concordia*, X, 63 p. 624.
71. Constable, *Monastic Tithes*, pp. 205–6.
72. *Observances in Use at the Augustinian Priory of St Giles and St Andrew at Barnwell*, XLI, ed. and trans. John Willis Clark (Cambridge, 1897), pp. 192–3.
73. *Life and Miracles of St Modwenna*, XLVIII, p. 198; William of Malmesbury, *Gesta Pontificum Anglorum* 3.134, ed. and trans. M. Winterbottom and R.M. Thomson, 2 vols (Oxford, 2007), p. 427.
74. *Chronicon Abbatiae de Evesham*, ed. William Dunn Macray, Rolls Series (London, 1863), pp. 91–3; Jocelin, *Chronicle*, p. 39.
75. TNA PRO SC 8/160/7968.
76. John Doran, 'Authority and Care: The Significance of Rome in Twelfth-Century Chester', in *Roma Felix: Formations and Reflections of Medieval Rome*, ed. Éamonn Ó Carragáin and Carol Neuman de Vegvar (Abingdon, 2007). In 1331 Edward, Prince of Wales told the royal justices that Chester, Combermere and Vale Royal had complained of the excessive burden of hospitality they were required to give to local dignitaries.
77. Anne E. Lester, 'Cares Beyond the Walls: Cistercian Nuns and the Care of Lepers in Twelfth- and Thirteenth-Century Northern France', in *Religious and Laity in Western Europe*, ed. Jamroziak and Burton, pp. 198–224; see also Sally Thompson, *Women Religious: The Founding of English Nunneries after the Norman Conquest* (Oxford, 1991), pp. 38–53 for English examples.
78. Lester, 'Cares Beyond the Walls', p. 211, citing deeds of 1242, 1253 and 1256.
79. William C. Jordan, 'The Cistercian Nunnery of La Cour Notre-Dame de Michery: A House that Failed', *RB* 95 (1985), 311–20.
80. *Book of Ste Foy* I.9, trans. Pamela Sheingorn (Philadelphia, 1995), pp. 68–9.
81. *Book of Ste Foy* II.12, pp. 137–8.
82. William of Malmesbury, *Gesta Pontificum*, 3.134, 1, p. 418; cf. *Historia translationum sancti Cuthberti*, Bibliographica Hagiographica Latina 2029, after 1122, trans. C.F. Battiscombe, *The Relics of St Cuthbert* (Oxford, 1956), pp. 99–107.
83. Suger, *De consecratione S. Dionysii* 2, ed. A. Lecoy de la Marche, *Oeuvres Complètes* (Paris, 1867), pp. 216–17. Relics were sometimes also taken on 'tours' in order to collect funds for their shrine churches: see Christine Oakland, 'Relic Tours in England and France, ca. 1050–1350', unpublished PhD thesis, University of Kent, 2019.
84. James Clark, *The Benedictines in the Middle Ages* (Woodbridge, 2011), p. 136.
85. S. Raban, *Mortmain Legislation and the English Church, 1279–1500* (Cambridge, 1982).
86. See for example *La ville de Cluny et ses maisons, XIe–XVe siècles*, ed. P. Garrigou Grandchamp (Paris, 1997); or, for an English example, P. Clery, *The Wealth and Estates of Glastonbury Abbey at the Dissolution in 1539* (Sutton Bridge, 2003).
87. T.R. Slater, 'Benedictine Town Planning in Medieval England: Evidence from St Albans', in *The Church in the Medieval Town*, ed. T.R. Slater and G. Rosser (Aldershot, 1988), pp. 155–76. See also Giles Constable, 'The Abbot and Townsmen of Cluny in the Twelfth Century', in *Church and City, 1000–1500: Essays in Honour of Christopher Brooke*, ed. David Abulafia, Michael Franklin and Miri Rubin (Cambridge, 1992), pp. 151–71.
88. James Clark, *Monastic Renaissance*, p. 76.
89. Jocelin, *Chronicle*, pp. 59–60.

90. *Statutes of 1134*, I, 14; Williams, *Cistercians*, p. 332.
91. *Gesta Abbatum*, I, pp. 410–11; *Deeds of the Abbots*, p. 513.
92. *Gesta Abbatum*, II, pp. 155–83; *Deeds of the Abbots*, pp. 646–60.
93. Jocelin, *Chronicle*, pp. 45–6.
94. Jocelin, *Chronicle*, p. 55. Although, as it turned out, he was unable to prevent them from ruining his sleep with their carousing and even breaking down the gates.
95. R.S. Gottfried, *Bury St Edmunds and the Urban Crisis, 1290–1539* (Princeton, NJ, 1982).
96. Jocelin, *Chronicle*, pp. 39–40.
97. *Life of Leontios*, 39, pp. 76–7. Of necessity, the monastery also owned a ship, on which they petitioned for exemption of tolls to Emperor Andronikos Komnenos in 1183.
98. An increased interest on the part of landowners in estate management is attested through the proliferation of texts such as Walter of Henley's on husbandry, *Walter of Henley and Other Treatises on Estate Management and Accounting*, ed. D. Oschinsky (Oxford, 1971).
99. Edmund King, *Peterborough Abbey 1086–1310: A Study in the Land Market* (Cambridge, 1973), pp. 161–2.
100. *Cartario dell'abbazia di Staffarda*, ed. F. Gabotto et al. (Pinerolo, 1900–2), I, pp. 70–1.
101. S. Raban, *The Estates of Thorney and Crowland* (Cambridge, 1977); Emmanuel Le Roy Ladurie, *The Peasants of Languedoc* (Urbana, IL, 1974), esp. pp. 36–7; J.S. Loengard, 'Lords' Rights and Neighbors' Nuisances: Mills and Medieval English Law', in *Wind and Water in the Middle Ages*, ed. S.A. Walton (Tempe, AZ, 2006), pp. 129–52.
102. Clairvaux, for example, had 37,000 acres of woodland, which dwarfed Cîteaux's 8,000. In England, most forest was in royal ownership, but Dore owned 1,000 acres and Netley 300. Williams, *Cistercians*, pp. 315–16.
103. M. Aston, *Medieval Fish, Fisheries and Fishponds in England*, 2 vols (Oxford, 1988). The monastery of Fécamp exploited fishing rights in Sussex ports. Cassandra Potts, *Monastic Revival and Regional Identity in Normandy* (Woodbridge, 1997), p. 129.
104. Williams, *Cistercians*, p. 321.
105. Miranda Threlfall-Holmes, *Monks and Markets: Durham Cathedral Priory 1460–1520* (Oxford, 2005), pp. 85–6; H.P.R. Finberg, *Tavistock Abbey: A Study in the Social and Economic History of Devon* (Cambridge, 1951), pp. 167–91.
106. Williams, *Cistercians*, p. 331.
107. R. Roehl, 'Plan and Reality in a Medieval Monastic Economy', *Studies in Medieval and Renaissance History* 9 (1972), 94.
108. Gerald of Wales, *Journey through Wales*, p. 106.
109. There is a huge literature on Cistercian grange economy: see for example Constance Berman, *Medieval Agriculture, the Southern French Countryside, and the Early Cistercians* (Philadelphia, 1986); R.A. Donkin, 'The Cistercian Grange in England in the Twelfth and Thirteenth Centuries, with Special Reference to Yorkshire', *Studia Monastica* 6 (1964), 95–144.
110. Williams, *Cistercians*, p. 278.
111. Gerald of Wales, *Journey through Wales*, IV, p. 206; *Chronica de Mailros*, ed. J. Stevenson (Edinburgh, 1835), p. 76; *Memorials of the Abbey of St Mary of Fountains*, ed. J.R. Walbran, J. Raine and J.T. Fowler, Surtees Society 42, 67 and

130 (Durham, 1863–1918), vol. 1, p. 124; *Fundacio abbathie de Kyrkestall*, Thoresby Society IV, pp. 169–70.
112. G. Coulton, *Medieval Village, Manor and Monastery* (New York, 1960), p. 156.
113. R.A. Donkin, *The Cistercians: Studies in the Geography of Medieval England and Wales* (Toronto, 1978), p. 49.
114. Williams, *Cistercians*, p. 278.
115. Coulton, *Medieval Village*, p. 224n.
116. Berman, *Cistercian Evolution*, pp. 93–160.
117. Lawrence McCrank, 'The Economic Administration of a Monastic Domain by the Cistercians of Poblet, 1150–1276', in *Studies in Medieval Cistercian History* II (Kalamazoo, MI, 1976), pp. 146–7; J. Wardrop, *Fountain Abbey and its Benefactors* (Kalamazoo, MI, 1987), p. 87.
118. *Statuta capitulorum generalium ordinis Cisterciensis, 1116–1786*, ed. J.-M. Canivez, 2 vols (Louvain, 1933–41), I, 251, 309–10, 346, 517.
119. For example, at Fontevraud, *Robert of Arbrissel, First Life*, XVII, p. 15, and at Obazine, *Vita Stephani Obazinensis*, I, 7–9, pp. 54–9: 'Everything that was harmful or useless they cut down, and in that place they built their house according to the plan of a monastery – in other words, a chapel, a dormitory, refectory, kitchen and, in the middle, a cloister. The whole place was just about bigger than the area of a big house.'
120. Noell, 'Expectation and Unrest', p. 269.
121. Walter Daniel, *Life of Ailred*, XXX, ed. and trans. F.M. Powicke (London, 1950), p. 38; Jamroziak, *Cistercian Order*, p. 65, for the German numbers.
122. The important guides here are M. Kaplan, 'Les moines et leurs biens fonciers à Byzance du VIIIe au Xe siècles: Acquisition, conservation et mise en valeur', *RB* 103 (1993), 209–23; idem, 'The Evergetis *Hypotasis* and the Management of Monastic Estates in the Eleventh Century', in *The Theotokos Evergetis*, ed. Margaret Mullett and Anthony Kirby (eds), *The Theotokos Evergetis and Eleventh-Century Monasticism* (Belfast, 1994), pp. 103–23; Konstantinos Smyrlis, 'The Management of Monastic Estates: The Evidence of the Typika', *DOP* 56 (2002), 245–61.
123. Smyrlis, 'Management', p. 246.
124. *Christodoulos*, *BMFD*, II, pp. 584–5. The total numbers of workers amounted to about 400 by 1270. Patricia Karlin-Hayter, 'Notes sur les archives de Patmos comme source pour la démographie et l'économie de l'île', *Byzantinische Forschungen* 5 (1977), 189–215.
125. *Pantokrator: Typikon of Emperor John II Komnenos for the Monastery of Christ 725 Pantokrator in Constantinople*, trans. Robert Jordan, *BMFD*, pp. 725–81.
126. *Rule of Neophytos*, X, p. 142. Nikon, however, prohibited the acquisition of new land for the Roidion monastery, *Roidion*, *BMFD*, I, p. 436.
127. *Cartulaire du chapitre du Saint-Sépulcre*, no. 133, ed. Geneviève Bresc-Bautier, pp. 259–60.
128. *Pakourianos*, *BMFD*, II, pp. 507–63.
129. *Papsturkunden für Kirchen im Heiligen Lande, Vorarbeiten zum Oriens Pontificius III*, ed. R. Hiestand, Abhandlungen der Akademie der Wissenschaften in Göttingen. Phil.-hist. Klasse, Dritte Folge, 136 (Göttingen, 1985) [henceforth: OP], p. 186, no. 60; *Chartes de Terre Sainte provenant de l'abbaye de Notre-Dame de Josaphat*, ed. H.-F. Delaborde, Bibliothèque des Écoles françaises d'Athènes et de Rome, 19 (Paris, 1880), pp. 35–6, no. 9.

130. As demonstrated by the extensive possessions recorded in the cartulary; see also Ch. Kohler, 'Chartes de l'abbaye de Notre-Dame de la vallée de Josaphat en Terre-Sainte', *Revue de l'Orient Latin*, 7 (1899), 108–222.
131. William of Tyre, *Chronicon*, X.15, p. 472.
132. OP III, pp. 181–2, no. 59. The original grant was from Bernard, bishop of Nazareth in 1116. For fuller discussion of this incident, see Andrew Jotischky, 'Eugenius III and the Church in the Crusader States', in *Eugenius III*, ed. Fonnesberg-Schmidt and Jotischky, pp. 348–65.
133. OP III, pp. 183–7, no. 60.
134. Delaborde, *Chartes de Terre Sainte*, pp. 56–8, no. 24; 58–9, no. 25; 64, no. 26; 82–3, no. 35.
135. Bernard Hamilton, *The Latin Church in the Crusader States: The Secular Church* (London, 1980), pp. 98–9, citing Delaborde, *Chartes de Terre Sainte*, pp. 72–8, no. 31.
136. OP III, p. 186, no. 60.
137. Kohler, 'Chartes de l'abbaye de Notre-Dame', pp. 87–8, no. 2.
138. Delaborde, *Chartes de Terre Sainte*, pp. 87–8, no. 40; Hamilton, *Latin Church*, p. 100.
139. Charles Spornick, 'The Life and Reign of Pope Eugene III (1145–1153)', unpublished PhD dissertation, University of Notre Dame (1988), p. 291, n. 9.
140. *Letters of Peter the Venerable*, vol. 2, p. 218.
141. John of Salisbury, *Historia Pontificalis*, I, ed. and trans. Marjorie Chibnall (London, 1956), pp. 4–6.
142. Rose Graham, *An Abbot of Vézelay: Pons de Montboissier* (London, 1918), pp. 84–6. H.E.J. Cowdrey, *The Cluniacs and the Gregorian Reform* (Oxford, 1970), pp. 86–7, shows that Bishop Henry's argument was specious, since Vézelay could seek ordinations and consecration from any bishop, not only their own diocesan.
143. *Monumenta Vizeliacensia: textes relatifs à l'histoire de Vézelay*, ed. R.B.C. Huygens, CCCM 42 (Turnhout, 1976), pp. 314–15, no. 28.
144. *Letters of Peter the Venerable*, vol. 2, p. 244, reports the end of the affair under Pope Anastasius IV, with the capitulation of Count William; *Monumenta Vizeliacensia*, p. 353, no. 49.
145. *Rule of Neilos*, XVI–XVIII, p. 71, and see also p. 21.
146. *Rule of Neophytos*, VI, p. 139.
147. Catia Galatariotou, 'The Bishop and the Hermit: Church Patronage in Action in Twelfth-Century Cyprus', *Epeteris Kentrou Epistemonikon Ereunon* 18 (1991), 85–103.
148. *Life of Lazaros*, LIII, pp. 139–42; see in general Morris, *Monks and Laymen*, pp. 148–9.
149. *Fragala*, *BMFD*, II, p. 623.
150. Loud, *Latin Church*, pp. 496–500.
151. Chrysovalantis Kyriacou, *Orthodox Cyprus under the Latins, 1191–1571: Society, Spirituality, and Identities* (Lanham, MD, 2018).
152. *Chronicon abbatiae de Evesham*, ed. William Dunn Macray, Rolls Series 29 (London, 1863) [hereafter: *Chron. Evesham*], pp. 109–10, and see below, pp. 280–1.
153. Christopher Cheney, *Episcopal Visitation of Monasteries in the Thirteenth Century*, 2nd edn (Manchester, 1983), pp. 17–25.
154. Cheney, *Episcopal Visitation*, p. xvi; Robert Brentano, 'The Bishops' Books of Città di Castello', *Traditio* 16 (1960), 241–54.
155. *Registrum visitationum Odonis Rigaudi archiepiscopi Rotomagensis*, *The Register of Eudes of Rouen*, trans. Sydney M. Brown (New York, 1964). For some other survivals of

visitations see Norwich (ed. Jessup Camden Society XLIII, 1818), *Visites pastorales et ordinations des évêques de Grenoble* (1874).
156. Peter of Blois, *Epistolae*, LXVIII, *PL* 207: 213.
157. Hugh of Poitiers, *The Vézelay Chronicle*, IV, trans. John Scott and John O. Ward (Binghamton, NY, 1992), pp. 134–6.
158. Andreas of Fontevraud, *Second Life of Robert Arbrissel* [hereafter: *Robert of Arbrissel, Second Life*], LXII, in Venarde, *Robert of Arbrissel*, p. 61.
159. Cheney, *Episcopal Visitation*, pp. 60–2.
160. *Register of Eudes*, pp. 595–6.
161. Penelope Johnson, *Equal in Monastic Profession: Religious Women in Medieval France* (Chicago, 1991), p. 71, from *Register of Eudes*, pp. 114, 353, 430, 687.
162. Johnson, *Equal in Monastic Profession*, p. 68.
163. Paul Le Cacheux, *L'Exemption de Montivilliers* (Caen, 1929), p. 12.
164. *Register of Eudes Rigaud*, pp. 401, 434–5.
165. Johnson, *Equal in Monastic Profession*, p. 70.
166. Matthew Paris, *Chronica Maiora*, p. 152.
167. William of Malmesbury, *Gesta Regum*, V, 409, pp. 738–9, praises the munificence of his building at Malmesbury, however; see also David Knowles, *The Monastic Order in England: A History of Its Development from the Times of St Dunstan to the Fourth Lateran Council, 940–1216* (Cambridge, 1963), pp. 131–2, 581, for other examples.
168. *Chronicon de Abingdon*, vol. 2, p. 287; *Life of Anselm*, XI, p. 74.
169. *Monastic Constitutions of Lanfranc*, II, ed. and trans. David Knowles (London, 1951), p. 73, indicate that the abbot will sleep in the dormitory.
170. *Documents Illustrating the Activities of the General and Provincial Chapters of the English Black Monks, 1215–1540*, ed. W.A. Pantin, Camden Society ser. 3, 45, 47, 54, 3 vols (London, 1931–7), I, pp. 8–9.
171. Thus Knowles, *Monastic Order*, p. 405.
172. *Gesta Abbatum*, II, pp. 183–5; for the full account of his abbacy, *Deeds of the Abbots*, pp. 661–723; Martin Heale, *The Abbots and Priors of Late Medieval and Reformation England* (Oxford, 2016), pp. 57–8.
173. Kedar, 'Palmarée', 260–9; Jotischky, *Perfection of Solitude*, pp. 30–3.
174. Jocelin, *Chronicle*; Robert Brentano, 'Samson of Bury Revisited', in *Vita religiosa*, ed. Felten and Jaspert, pp. 79–85.
175. *Waltham Chronicle*, 15, pp. 28–30. For discussion of how endowments were allotted to obedientiaries at Peterborough, see King, *Peterborough Abbey*, pp. 88–98.
176. Jocelin, *Chronicle*, p. 79. Anslem, as abbot of Bec, had understood that the offices of sacristan and cellarer were often difficult to maintain because of shortages. *Life of Anselm*, I, 28, p. 47.
177. Jocelin, *Chronicle*, p. 38.
178. Jocelin, *Chronicle*, p. 119.
179. *Gesta Abbatum*, II, pp. 132–42; *Deeds of the Abbots*, pp. 637–43; H.P. Palmer, 'William Somerton, Prior of Bynham', in H.P. Palmer, *The Bad Abbot of Evesham and Other Medieval Studies* (Oxford, 1932), pp. 63–77.
180. Jane E. Sayers, 'Roger Norreis [Norris]', *ODNB*, www.oxforddnb.com, accessed 07/07/2023.
181. *Chron. Evesham*, pp. 109–255 for the episode and its long drawn-out repercussions. The most recent study of the episode is Jane Sayers, 'English Benedictine Monks at the Papal Court in the Thirteenth Century: The Experience of Thomas of Marlborough', *Journal of Medieval Monastic Studies* 2 (2013), 109–30.

182. *Chron. Evesham*, pp. 200–1.
183. *Robert of Arbrissel, First Life*, XXI, p. 18.
184. *Robert of Arbrissel, Second Life*, V, p. 9.
185. Penelope Johnson, *Equal in Monastic Profession*, p. 170.
186. Jocelin, *Chronicle*, pp. 11–14.
187. *Rule of Benedict*, LXIV.
188. OV XI, 14, vol. 6, pp. 72–4.
189. Guibert, *Monodiae*, I. 19, p. 85.
190. Jocelin, *Chronicle*, p. 126.
191. Jocelin, *Chronicle*, pp. 20–4.
192. The involvement of the English crown in abbatial elections derived from the *Regularis Concordia*, IX, p. 6, which stipulated that elections were to be carried out 'with the consent and advice of the king'.
193. *Gesta Abbatum*, I, pp. 306–11; *Deeds of the Abbots*, pp. 433–43.
194. Basil of Caesarea, *Regulae brevis tractatae*, PG 31:1105–6; see also Philip Rousseau, *Basil of Caesarea* (Berkeley, CA, 1994), p. 211.
195. *Theodore Studites*, *BMFD*, I, p. 79; *Evergetis*, *BMFD*, II, pp. 483–6, 487, 488–9.
196. *Christodoulos*, *BMFD*, II, p. 595. Patricia Karlin-Hayter, commenting on the *Testament*, suggested that his authoritarianism may have led to defections from among the community, p. 573.
197. *Christodoulos*, *BMFD*, II, p. 595.
198. De Clercq, *Les textes juridiques* IX, pp. 29–30; Hamilton and Jotischky, *Latin and Greek Monasticism*, p. 383.
199. Hamilton and Jotischky, *Latin and Greek Monasticism*, p. 387.
200. *Life of Lazaros*, pp. 25, 27.
201. *Rule of Neophytos*, XV, p. 148.
202. *Rule of Neilos*, LIV, CXXII, p. 85, p. 111.
203. *Kecharitomene*, *BMFD*, II, pp. 674–7.
204. *Anglo-Saxon Chronicle*, ed. and trans. Whitelock, p. 160; among other witnesses: *Annales Monastici de Waverleia*, ed. Henry Luard, *Annales Monastici*, 5 vols (London 1864–9), vol. 2, p. 33; OV II, p. 226. In general, see Jane Sayers, 'Violence in the Medieval Cloister', *Journal of Ecclesiastical History* 41 (1990), 533–42.
205. Gervase of Canterbury, *Chronicle of the Reigns of Stephen, Henry II and Richard I*, ed. William Stubbs, 2 vols (London, 1879–8), vol. 1, p. 405; also recounted by Peter of Blois, *The Later Letters of Peter of Blois*, X, ed. Elizabeth Revell (Oxford, 1993), pp. 52–62.
206. Joachim Wollasch, 'Das Schisma des Abtes Pontius von Cluny', *Francia* 23 (1996), 31–52; Pietro Zerbi, 'Ancora intorno a Ponzio e allo "scisma" cluniacense: La "svolta" del 1124–25', in *Società, istituzioni, spiritualità: Studi in onore di Cinzio Violante*, ed. Girolamo Arnaldi, 2 vols (Spoleto, 1994), II, pp. 1081–91; Adrian Bredero, 'A propos de l'autorité abbatiale de Pons de Melgueil et de Pierre le Vénérable dans l'ordre de Cluny', in *Etudes de Civilisation Médiévale: Mélanges offerts à Edmond-René Labande* (Poitiers, 1974), pp. 63–75.
207. Peter Abelard, *History of My Misfortunes*, pp. 94–6.
208. Gervase of Canterbury, *Historical Works*, ed. William Stubbs, 2 vols (London, 1870–80), vol. 1, p. 504.
209. Rose Graham, 'The History of the Alien Priory of Wenlock', *Journal of the British Archaeological Association* 4 (1939), 117–40.
210. *Gesta Abbatum*, II, pp. 132–42; *Deeds of the Abbots*, pp. 637–43.

211. Jocelin, *Chronicle*, pp. 4, 49.
212. Matthew Paris, *Chronica Maiora*, Additamenta, pp. 152, 175.
213. Jocelin, *Chronicle*, p. 73.
214. Glaber, *Histories*, III, 11, pp. 112–13.
215. Hugh of Poitiers, *The Vézelay Chronicle*, p. 74.
216. *The Annals of Dunstable Priory*, trans. David Preest (Woodbridge, 2018), pp. 78–82.
217. *Acta Archiepiscoprum Rothomagensium*, ed. J. Mabillon, *Vetera Analecta*, pp. 224–6; A. Duchesne (ed.), *Hist. Normann. Script Antiq.*, pp. 1017–18.
218. Matthew Paris, *Chronica Maiora*, vol. 5, pp. 121–3.
219. *Liber miraculorum sanctae Fidis*, ed. Luca Robertini (Spoleto, 1994), I, 26; *Book of Ste Foy*, pp. 93–4.
220. Jocelin, *Chronicle*, p. 55.
221. See above, ch. 3.
222. Katherine Allen Smith, *War and the Making of Medieval Monastic Culture* (Woodbridge, 2011), esp. pp. 39–70.
223. Lawrence Duggan, *Armsbearing and the Clergy in the History and Canon Law of Western Christianity* (Woodbridge, 2013), pp. 22–5.
224. Eadmer, *Vita Sancti Anselmi*, II, xxl, p. 94; 2 Tim 2.4; *Rule of Benedict*, prol.
225. For extensive discussion, see Mette Birkedal Bruun, *Parables: Bernard of Clairvaux's Mapping of Spiritual Topography* (Leiden, 2006).
226. As testified by Godfrey of Viterbo in a letter to another abbot, *Goffridi abbatis Vindocinensis Epistolae*, IV, 21, *PL* 157: 162.
227. James Brundage, 'St Anselm, Ivo of Chartres and the Ideology of the First Crusade', in *Les mutations socio-culturelles au tournant des XIe–XIIe siècles, Colloques internationaux de CNRS, Le Bec-Hellouin, juillet 1982* (Paris, 1984), pp. 175–87; for the history of ecclesiastical prohibitions on clerical violence, see Duggan, *Armsbearing*, pp. 194–6.
228. Guibert of Nogent, *Dei Gesta per Francos*, ed. R.B.C. Huygens, CCCM 127A (Turnhout, 1996), p. 330; for other examples, see William Purkis, '"Zealous Imitation": The Materiality of the Crusader's Marked Body', *Material Religion: The Journal of Objects, Art, and Belief* 14 (2018), 438–53.
229. Alan Murray, *The Crusader Kingdom of Jerusalem: A Dynastic History, 1099–1125* (Oxford, 2000), pp. 50–1.
230. See for example Jay Rubenstein, *Armies of Heaven: The First Crusade and the Quest for Apocalypse* (New York, 2011).
231. Albert of Aachen, *Historia Ierosolimitana*, II, 37, ed. and trans. Susan Edgington (Oxford, 2007), pp. 126–8; *Robert the Monk's History of the First Crusade: Historia Iherosolimitana*, VII, 72, trans. Carol Sweetenham (London, 2016), p. 167, mentions monks at the siege of Antioch in 1097–8.
232. Conor Kostick, *The Social Structure of the First Crusade* (Leiden, 2008), pp. 107, 109.
233. *Vita S. Romualdi* XV, *PL* 144: 968–9; Nikolas Jaspert, 'Eleventh-Century Pilgrimage from Catalonia to Jerusalem: New Sources on the Foundations of the First Crusade', *Crusades* 14 (2015), 1–47 at p. 32. On this topic generally, see Giles Constable, 'Monachisme et pèlerinage au Moyen Age', *Revue Historique* 258 (1977), 3–27; reprinted in Giles Constable, *Religious Life and Thought (11th–12th Centuries)*, Variorum Collected Studies 89 (London, 1979).
234. *Vita S. Romualdi*, p. 38.

235. Gertrude Robinson, *The History and Cartulary of the Greek Monastery of St Elias and St Anastasius of Carbone*, Orientalia christiana XV (Rome, 1929), no. 56, pp. 166–70.
236. *Vita S. Hugonis IV*, *AASS* Apr. III, p. 768.
237. Marcus Bull, *Knightly Piety and the Lay Response to the First Crusade: The Limousin and Gascony, c.970–1130* (Oxford, 1993).
238. R.N. Sauvage, *L'abbaye de Saint-Martin de Troarn au diocèse de Bayeux* (Caen, 1911), pp. 357, 367.
239. Adso, abbot of Montier-en-Der (Haute-Marne), died on a pilgrimage to Jerusalem in 992. *Vita S. Bercharii*, II, 2 n.14, *AASS* Oct. VII, p. 1022; for Vitalis and Guesseran of Saint-Victor, Marseilles, *Cartulaire de l'abbaye de Saint-Victor de Marseille*, I (Paris, 1857), pp. 230, 287.
240. *Synodum Helenense*, RHGF XI, p. 514.
241. *Ex chronico Virdunensi* RHGF VIII, p. 291; Ademar of Chabannes, *Chronique*, III, ed. and trans. Yves Chauvin and Georges Pon (Turnhout, 2003), p. 24. Gerard, the founding abbot of Sauve-Majeure, in the Gironde, brought back gold vases and perfumes from his pilgrimage, *AASS* Apr. I, pp. 418–19, 425.
242. Raoul, abbot of Mont St-Michel and Thierry, abbot of S. Evroult, also died on pilgrimage, *Chron S. Michaelis in periculo maris* RHGF XI, p. 256; OV, VI, p. 10.
243. E. Martène and U. Durand (eds), *Veterum Scriptorum et Monumentorum amplissima Collectio*, 9 vols (Paris, 1724–33), V, pp. 1111, 1116, 1130.
244. *AASS* Apr. III, pp. 336, 338.
245. *AASS* Aug. IV, p. 853.
246. *Letters of Peter the Venerable*, LXXX, vol. 1, pp. 214–17.
247. Timothy Reuter, 'The "Non-Crusade" of 1149–50', in *The Second Crusade: Scope and Consequences*, ed. Jonathan Phillips and Martin Hoch (Manchester, 2001), pp. 150–63.
248. Odo of Deuil, *De profectione Ludovici*.
249. William of Newburgh, *Historia Rerum Anglicarum*, II.35, ed. Richard Howlett (London, 1884–9), vol. 1, p. 142.
250. Angeliki Laiou, 'The Just War of Eastern Christians and the Holy War of the Crusaders', in *The Ethics of War*, ed. Richard Sorabji and David Rodin (Aldershot, 2007), pp. 30–43.
251. Sini Kangas, *War and Violence in the Western Sources for the First Crusade* (Leiden, 2024), pp. 322–4.

CHAPTER 6: FRUIT IN ITS SEASON: LATE MEDIEVAL MONASTICISM

1. Felix Fabri, *Evagatorium in Terrae Sanctae, Arabiae et Egypti peregrinationem*, ed. Konrad Dieterich Hassler, 3 vols, Bibliothek des Litterarischen Vereins in Stuttgart 2–4 (Stuttgart, 1843–9), vol. 2, p. 149.
2. Richard W. Southern, *Western Society and the Church in the Middle Ages* (London, 1970), pp. 239–40.
3. See the summary of older and more recent views of the 'receding tide' of monasticism by Bert Roest, 'A Crisis of Late Medieval Monasticism?', *CHMMLW*, vol. 2, pp. 1171–90.
4. Frances Andrews, *The Early Humiliati* (Cambridge, 1999), pp. 39–40.
5. In England this meant in principle separate chapters for the provinces of Canterbury and York before 1340, when Pope Benedict XII united the provinces for the purposes of holding chapters.

6. David Knowles, *The Religious Orders in England, Vol. 1: The Thirteenth Century* (Cambridge, 1948), p. 29.
7. *Chapters of the Black Monks*, I, pp. 65–7.
8. *Les Statuts de Prémontré réformés sur les ordres de Grégoire IX et d'Innocent IV au XIIIe siècle*, II, 13, ed. E. Lefevre (Louvain, 1946), pp. 56–8.
9. Knowles, *Religious Orders*, p. 16.
10. Matthew Paris, *Chronica Maiora*, vol. 3, pp. 432–3.
11. *Chapters of the Black Monks*, I, pp. 34–5, Matthew Paris, *Chronica Maiora*, Additamenta, vol. 6, pp. 235–6.
12. *Chapters of the Black Monks*, I, p. 74.
13. Elizabeth Makowski, *Canon Law and Cloistered Women: Periculoso and Its Commentators, 1298–1545* (Washington DC, 1997).
14. Frances Andrews, *The Other Friars: Carmelite, Augustinian, Sack and Pied Friars in the Middle Ages* (Woodbridge, 2006).
15. Erin Jordan, 'Roving Nuns and Cistercian Realities: The Cloistering of Religious Women in the Thirteenth Century', *Journal of Medieval and Early Modern Studies* 42 (2012), 597–612.
16. Edmund Wareham, 'The Openness of the Enclosed Convent: The Evidence from the Lüne Letter Collection', in *Openness in Medieval Europe*, ed. Manuele Gragnolati and Almut Suerbaum, *Cultural Inquiry*, 23 (2022), 271–88.
17. Kathrynne Beebe, 'Imagined Pilgrimage', in *A Companion to Medieval Pilgrimage*, ed. Andrew Jotischky and William Purkis (forthcoming, Kalamazoo, MI, 2024).
18. Marie-Luise Ehrenschwendtner, 'Virtual Pilgrimages? Enclosure and the Practice of Piety at St Katherine's Convent, Augsburg', *Journal of Ecclesiastical History* 60:1 (2009), 45–73.
19. Kathryn M. Rudy, *Virtual Pilgrimages in the Convent: Imagining Jerusalem in the Late Middle Ages* (Turnhout, 2011).
20. Desiderius, *Dialogi*, I, MGH (SS) XXX(2), pp. 1124–5.
21. Robert of Arbrissel, *Praecepta recte vivendi*, PL 162: 1083–5.
22. *Letters of Peter the Venerable*, I, pp. 388–9.
23. Johnson, *Equal in Monastic Profession*, p. 147.
24. *Register of Eudes Rigaud*, p. 424.
25. Barbara Harvey, *Living and Dying in England, 1100–1540: The Monastic Experience* (Oxford, 1993), pp. 41–69, especially pp. 51–9 on meat-eating.
26. Harvey, *Living and Dying*, pp. 41–2.
27. *Registrum Malmesburiense*, ed. J.S. Brewer, 2 vols (London, 1879–80), vol. 2, p. 38; Knowles, *Religious Orders*, pp. 281–3 for other examples; Harvey, *Living and Dying*, pp. 41–2 for the relationship between misericord and refectory at Westminster.
28. See for example Paul Freedman, *Out of the East: Spices and the Medieval Imagination* (New Haven and London, 2008), pp. 1–18.
29. The following paragraph draws extensively from Irene Bueno, *Pope Benedict XII (1334–1342): The Guardian of Orthodoxy* (Amsterdam, 2018).
30. *Chapters of the Black Monks*, II, pp. 5–12.
31. David Carpenter, 'Richard of Ware', *ODNB*, www.oxforddnb.com, accessed 10/05/2024; N.E. Stacey, 'John of Taunton', *ODNB*, www.oxforddnb.com, accessed 10/05/2024; Clark, *Monastic Renaissance*, pp. 10–40, 89; Knowles, *Religious Orders*, p. 13; David Sullivan, *The Westminster Circle* (London, 2006), pp. 224–40; A.J. Piper, 'The Monks of Durham and the Study of Scripture', in *The Culture of Medieval English Monasticism*, ed. James G. Clark (Woodbridge, 2007), pp. 86–103.

NOTES to pp. 314–319

32. Boso, later abbot of Bec (r. 1124–36), became a monk out of the desire to study with Anselm, *Life of Anselm* I, 24, pp. 60–1; see also the example of Abbot Herluin.
33. Lawrence of Durham, the celebrated poet and author, was a native of Waltham: *Dialogi*, III, ed. James Raine, Surtees Society 70 (Durham, 1880), pp. xxviii, 92.
34. Lanfranc sent Bec monks to study with Gilbert, formerly a Bec monk himself, at Westminster, *The Letters of Lanfranc, Archbishop of Canterbury*, ed. and trans. Helen V. Clover and Margaret Gibson (Oxford, 1979), XX, p. 100.
35. Knight, *Correspondence*.
36. *The Letters of Peter of Celle*, ed. Julian Haseldine (Oxford, 2001).
37. *Gesta Abbatum*, I, pp. 230–2; *Deeds of the Abbots*, pp. 334–5.
38. Jocelin, *Chronicle*, p. 128.
39. Gerald of Wales, *Gemma Ecclesiastica*, ed. J.S. Brewer, Rolls Series 21 (London, 1862), p. lxiv.
40. Jean-Loup Lemaître, 'La visite des monastères limousins par Simon de Beaulieu en 1285', *RB* 114.1 (2004), 158–78; Fabrice Délivré, 'La visite du primat d'Aquitaine Simon de Beaulieu, archevêque de Bourges, dans la province ecclésiastique de Bordeaux (1284)', *Revue Mabillon*, 13 (2002), 133–60.
41. *Register of Eudes Rigaud*, p. 571.
42. Matthew Paris, *Chronica Maiora*, vol. 5, p. 79.
43. Thomas Sullivan, 'Monastic Values and Echoes of the Rule of Benedict in the Statutes of 1365 for the Cluniac College at Paris', *American Benedictine Review*, 63 (2012), 331–53.
44. *Chapters of the Black Monks*, I, pp. 27–8.
45. Knowles, *Religious Orders*, pp. 25–7.
46. Jocelin, *Chronicle*, p. 40; see also p. 36.
47. James G. Clark and Kate E. Bush, 'Monastic Preaching, c. 1350–1545', *CHMMLW*, vol. 3, pp. 1125–39.
48. Clark, *Monastic Renaissance*, passim.
49. Clark, *Monastic Renaissance*, pp. 148–9.
50. Clark, *Monastic Renaissance*, pp. 155–8.
51. John Taylor, 'Thomas Walsingham', *ODNB*, www.oxforddnb.com; for fuller discussion, see Clark, *Monastic Renaissance*, pp. 166–76.
52. On Dominicans and Carmelites see Andrew Jotischky, *The Carmelites and Antiquity: Mendicants and their Pasts in the Middle Ages* (Oxford, 2002), pp. 166–83; Kaspar Elm, '"Augustinus canonicus – Augustinus eremita": A Quattrocento cause célèbre', in *Christianity and the Renaissance: Image and Religious Imagination in the Quattrocento*, ed. Timothy Verdon and John Henderson (Syracuse, NY, 1990), pp. 84–107.
53. W.A. Pantin, 'Some Medieval English Treatises on the Origins of Monasticism', in *Medieval Studies Presented to Rose Graham*, ed. V. Ruffer and A.J. Taylor (Oxford, 1950), pp. 189–215.
54. *De origine, fundatoribus et regulis monachorum et monacharum*, Vienna, Nat. Bib. MS 341; Jotischky, *The Carmelites and Antiquity*, p. 303.
55. W.A. Pantin, 'Two Treatises of Uthred of Boldon on the Monastic Life', in *Studies in Medieval History Presented to Frederick Maurice Powicke*, ed. R.W. Hunt, W.A. Pantin and R.W. Southern (Oxford, 1948), pp. 368–85.
56. Pantin, 'Some Medieval English Treatises,' pp. 190–4.
57. Pantin, 'Two Treatises', pp. 369–70.
58. Pantin, 'Some Medieval English Treatises', pp. 190–4.

59. *Innocenti III Registrum*, no. 168, *PL* 216, cols 956–8; G. Hofmann, *Rom und Athosklöster* (Rome, 1926), p. 8; Zachary Chitwood, 'Elective Affinities: Papal and Regal Privileges for Mount Athos and the Holy Mountain's Relationship with the Medieval West', *Endowment Studies* 7.1 (Spring 2023), 44–69.
60. *Regesti Honorii papae tertii*, ed. P. Pressutti (Rome, 1895), 126, no. 4305: a letter of 22 April 1227; Hofman, *Rom und Athosklöster*, 9, 10, for letters of Clement VI (1343) and Pius II (1459) combining praise for Athonite monastic spirituality tempered by disapproval for Greek monastic attitudes to union.
61. Odo of Deuil, *De profectione Ludovici*, pp. 56–7; cf. Azenarius, abbot of St Martin, Massay, who in the eleventh century witnessed the Pentecost liturgy at Santa Sophia, Jordan of Limoges, *Acta Concilii Lemovicensis*, II, *PL* 142: 1356.
62. Pahlitzsch. 'Athanasios II', pp. 465–74, at pp. 469–71.
63. Hamilton and Jotischky, *Latin and Greek Monasticism*, pp. 309, 312, 313–16, 318.
64. Andrew Jotischky, 'Fortunes of War', *Crusades* 8 (2009), 173–4.
65. Andrew Jotischky, 'Meditating on Death: Greek Orthodox Monasticism in the Holy Land in the Mamluk Period', in *Identities, Boundaries and Connectivities in the Late Byzantine and Post-Byzantine Mediterranean: Reception and Reality*, ed. Charalambos Dendrinos and Chrysovolantis Kyriacou (Leiden, forthcoming).
66. E. Lamberz, Ἡ βιβλιοθήκη καὶ τὰ χειρόγραφά της, in *Ἱερὰ Μεγίστη Μονὴ Βατοπαιδίου. Παράδοση – Ἱστορία – Τέχνη* (Mt Athos, 1996), p. 570.
67. Christos Livanos, *Greek Tradition and Latin Influence in the Work of George Scholarios*, Perspectives on Philosophy and Religious Thought 12 (Piscataway, NJ, 2013).
68. John Thomas, 'Independent and Self-Governing Monasteries of the Fourteenth and Fifteenth Centuries', *BMFD*, IV, p. 1490.
69. *Athanasios I: Rule of Patriarch Athanasios I*, trans. Timothy Miller, *BMFD*, IV, pp. 1495–1504, at p. 1496.
70. Thomas, 'Independent and Self-Governing Monasteries', p. 1492.
71. Thomas, 'Independent and Self-Governing Monasteries', pp. 1483–94.
72. Norman Russell, *Gregory Palamas and the Making of Palamism in the Modern Age* (Oxford, 2019), p. 10; in general, see John Meyendorff, *Byzantine Hesychasm: Historical, Theological and Social Problems* (London, 1974).
73. Rikus Fick, Theodore Sabo and Dan Lioy, 'A Hesychasm before Hesychasm', *Journal of Early Christian History* 4 (2014), 88–96; *Three Methods of Prayer*, trans. Norman Russell (1995), p. 67.
74. The following draws on Kallistos Ware, 'The Hesychasts: Gregory of Sinai, Gregory Palamas, Nicolas Cabasilas', in *The Study of Spirituality*, ed. Cheslyn Jones, Geoffrey Wainwright and Edward Yarnold (London, 1986), pp. 242–55; Ioannis D. Polemis, 'The Hesychast Controversy: Events, Personalities, Texts and Trends', in *A Companion to the Intellectual Life of the Palaeologan Period*, ed. Sofia Kotzabassi, Brill's Companions to the Byzantine World, 12 (Leiden, 2023), pp. 345–98.
75. For a summary of Palamas's career, see Russell, *Gregory Palamas*.
76. Roest, 'A Crisis of Late Medieval Monasticism?', p. 1171.
77. Alison More and Anneke B. Mulder-Bakker, 'Striving for Religious Perfection in the Lay World of Northern Europe', *CHMMLW*, vol. 3, pp. 1057–74, gives an excellent introduction to some of these. See also Alison More, *Fictive Orders and Feminine Religious Identities, 1200–1600* (Oxford, 2018).
78. Walter Simons, *Cities of Ladies: Beguine Communities in the Medieval Low Countries, 1200–1565* (Philadelphia, 2003).

79. Uwe John and Helge Wittmann (eds), *Elisabeth von Thüringen: Eine europäische Heilige*, 2 vols (Petersburg, 2007).
80. Hugues de Floreffe, *Vita B. Juettae reclusae*, *AASS* Jan. II, pp. 145–69, and English translation as *The Life of Yvette of Huy by Hugh of Floreffe*, trans. Jo Ann McNamara (Toronto, 2000). There is a substantial scholarly literature on Yvette, among which see Anneke Mulder-Bakker, 'Ivetta of Huy: *Mater et magistra*', in *Sanctity and Motherhood: Essays on Holy Mothers in the Middle Ages*, ed. Anneke Mulder-Bakker (New York, 1995), pp. 225–58; Isabelle Cochelin, 'Sainteté laïque: l'exemple de Juette de Huy (1158–1228)', *Le Moyen-Age: Revue d'histoire et de philologie* 95 (1989), 397–417.
81. John van Engen, *Sisters and Brothers of the Common Life: The Devotio Moderna and the World of the Later Middle Ages* (Philadelphia, 2008).
82. John van Engen, 'Friar Johannes Nyder on Laypeople Living as Religious in the World', in *Vita Religiosa im Mittelalter: Festschrift für Kaspar Elm zum 70. Geburtstag* (Berlin, 1999), pp. 583–5.
83. More, *Fictive Orders*, pp. 7–8.
84. Johnson, *Equal in Monastic Profession*, p. 152.
85. Jordan, 'Roving Nuns', 597–614.
86. Andrew Wines, 'The Founders of the London Charterhouse', in *Studies in Carthusian Monasticism in the Late Middle Ages*, ed. Julian Luxford (Turnhout, 2008), pp. 61–72.
87. James Bulloch, *Adam of Dryburgh* (London, 1958); Matthew Paris, *Chronica Maiora*, vol. 4, p. 105.
88. Dennis D. Martin, 'Carthusians during the Reformation Era: *Cartusia nunquam deformata, reformari resistens*', *Catholic Historical Review* 81 (1995), 41–66.
89. Wines, 'Founders of the London Charterhouse', pp. 64–8, identifies the separate sponsorship of cells at the London Charterhouse by Walworth, Lovekyn and Fraunceys.
90. William C. Jordan, *The Great Famine: Northern Europe in the Early Fourteenth Century* (Princeton, NJ, 1998), pp. 10–12.
91. Paul Binski, *Medieval Death: Ritual and Representation* (London, 1996).
92. Wolfgang Braunfels, *Monasteries of Western Europe: The Architecture of the Orders* (London, 1972) p. 118.
93. Tore Nyberg, *Birgittinische Klostergründungen des Mittelalters* (Lund, 1965).
94. Beatrix Romhányi, 'Life in the Pauline Monasteries of Late Medieval Hungary', *Periodica Polytechnica* 43 (2012), 53–6.
95. Gregorius Gyöngyösi, *Vitae fratrum Eremitarum Ordinis Sancti Pauli Primi Eremitae*, ed. L. Hervay (Budapest, 1988).
96. Wolfgang Seibrich, *Gegenreformation als Restauration: Die restaurativen Bemühungen der alten Orden im Deutschen Reich von 1580 bis 1648*, Beiträge zur Geschichte des alten Mönchtums und des Benediktinertums, 38 (Münster, 1991), pp. 25–6.
97. Ernst Dreher, *Günterstal: Seine Geschichte von den Anfängen bis zur Klosterauflösung im Jahre 1806. Die Gemeinde Günterstal zwischen 1806 und 1830* (Lahr, 2001), pp. 68–70.
98. Edmund Wareham, '"Wann Du Fromm Lebst, So Wirst Du nimmer Trawrig": Professor Jodochus Lorichius and the Cistercian Nuns of Günsterstal', *Oxford German Studies* 43 (2014), 362–79.
99. Wareham, 'The Openness of the Enclosed Convent', 271–88.
100. Luigi Pesce, *Ludovico Barbo, vescovo di Treviso (1437–1443): Cura pastorale, riforma della Chiesa, spiritualità*, 2 vols (Padua, 1969).

101. Uwe Israel, 'Reform durch Mönche aus der Ferne: Das Beispiel der Benediktinerabtei Subiaco', in *Vita communis und ethnische Vielfalt: Multinational zusammengesetzte Klöster im Mittelalter. Akten des internationalen Studientags von 26. Januar 2005 im Deutschen Historischen Institut in Rom*, ed. Uwe Israel, Vita Regularis, 29 (Münster, 2006), pp. 157–78.
102. David Knowles, *Christian Monasticism* (London, 1969), pp. 139–41; Dieter Scheler, 'Zur Ästhetik der Devotio moderna: Louis de Blois in Liessies', in *Die Devotio Moderna, II: Sozialer und kultureller Transfer (1350–1580). Die räumliche und geistige Ausstrahlung der Devotio Moderna – Zur Dynamik ihres Gedankengutes*, ed. Iris Kwiatkowski and Jörg Engelbrecht (Münster, 2013), pp. 13–27.
103. Clark, *Dissolution*, p. 3. The following discussion relies heavily on this authoritative recent study.
104. John Guy, *Tudor England* (Oxford, 1990), p. 138.
105. Clark, *Dissolution*, pp. 4–6.
106. Clive Burgess, *The Right Ordering of Souls: The Parish of All Saints' Bristol on the Eve of the Reformation* (Woodbridge, 2018).
107. Clark *Dissolution*, pp. 82, 90–1.
108. Clark, *Dissolution*, p. 52.
109. The classic treatment is W.T. Waugh, 'The Great Statute of *Praemunire*', EHR 37 (1922), 173–205.
110. Clark, *Dissolution*, p. 162.
111. *Humanism, Reform and the Reformation: The Career of Bishop John Fisher*, ed. Brendan Bradshaw and Eamon Duffy (Cambridge, 1989); Richard Rex, *The Theology of John Fisher* (Cambridge, 1991); Margaret Bowker, *The Henrician Reformation: The Diocese of Lincoln under John Longland (1521–1547)* (Cambridge, 1982); C.S.L. Davies, 'Fox (Foxe), Richard' www.oxforddnb.com, accessed 10/05/2024.
112. Clark, *Dissolution*, pp. 183–4.
113. Clark, *Dissolution*, p. 25.
114. Clark, *Dissolution*, p. 320.
115. For the history of Cockersand, *Victoria County History: Lancaster II*, at www.british-history.ac.uk/vch/lancs/vol2, accessed 10/05/2024; for the tradition of the 'fish stones' at Caton, Julian Hight, *Britain's Tree Story* (London, 2011), p. 26.
116. Guy, *Tudor England*, p. 143.
117. Guy, *Tudor England*, p. 143.
118. Guy, *Tudor England*, p. 145.
119. *The Oglander Memoirs: Extracts from the MSS of Sir J. Oglander, Kt*, ed. W.H. Long (London, 1888), p. 202, cited in Clark, *Dissolution*, p. 537.

EPILOGUE

1. Butler, *Benedictine Monachism*, pp. 366–7.
2. *A Benedictine Century: The Story of St Benedict's Disciples in the Twentieth Century*, Pluscarden Pamphlets IV (2000), p. 3. These numbers do not include Cistercians of the Strict Observance, who by the mid-twentieth century numbered about 4,000 monks worldwide.
3. *Benedictine Century*, p. 3.
4. AIM – A History of Benedictine Congregations, aimintl.org.
5. Günter Müller-Stevens, Markus Muff and Thomas Eberle, 'Management von Klöstern: Ein Erfahrungsbericht', *Zeitschrift Führung und Organisation*, 83 (2014), 184–9.

6. R.H. Winthrop, 'Leadership and Tradition in the Regulation of Catholic Monasticism', *Anthropological Quarterly* 58 (1985).
7. Studia Anselmiana, *Monasticism and Economy: Rediscovering an Approach to Work and Poverty*, Acts of the Fourth International Symposium held at Rome, 7–10 June 2016.
8. Notker Wolf and Erica Rosanna, *The Art of Leadership* (Collegeville, MN, 2013); see also Benjamin Chaminade, 'Fidélisation versus retention', www.focusrh.com/article.php3?id_article=107, accessed 02/01/2024.
9. Casey, *Coenobium*, p. 32.
10. Galand de Reigny, *Parables*, XVI, 7, cited alongside Jean-Charles Nault, 'Acedia: Enemy of Spiritual Joy', *Communio* 31 (2004), 240, by Casey, *Coenobium*, p. 190.

Select Bibliography

This is in no way an attempt to produce a comprehensive bibliography for medieval monasticism, since such a thing would in any case be impossible. Even to produce a list of primary sources indispensable for the subject would add the equivalent of another chapter to an already long book. I have therefore limited this list of secondary sources to the works I have found most valuable. Full references to primary sources can be found in the endnotes. I have not listed every chapter of the monumental *Cambridge History of Medieval Monasticism in the Latin West* (2021), although most of the essays might have found a place here.

Berman, Constance Hoffman. *The Cistercian Evolution: The Invention of a Religious Order in Twelfth-Century Europe* (Philadelphia, 2000)

Berman, Constance Hoffman. *Medieval Agriculture, The Southern French Countryside, and the Early Cistercians* (Philadelphia, 1986)

Berman, Constance Hoffman. 'Men's Houses, Women's Houses: The Relationship between the Sexes in Twelfth-Century Monasticism', in *The Medieval Monastery*, ed. Andrew MacLeish (Minneapolis, MN, 1988), pp. 43–52

Bernard of Clairvaux: Studies Presented to Dom Jean Leclercq. Cistercian Studies 23 (Washington DC, 1973)

Binns, John. *Ascetics and Ambassadors of Christ: The Monasteries of Palestine, 314–631* (Oxford, 1994)

Bitel, Lisa. *Isle of the Saints: Monastic Settlement and Christian Community in Early Ireland* (Ithaca, NY, 1990)

Bitel, Lisa. 'Women's Monastic Enclosures in Early Ireland: A Study of Female Spirituality and Male Monastic Mentalities', *JMH* 12 (1986), 15–37

Blair, John (ed.). *Minsters and Parish Churches: The Local Church in Transition 950–1250* (Oxford, 1988)

Bloch, Herbert. 'Monte Cassino, Byzantium and the West in the Earlier Middle Ages', *DOP* 3 (1946), 163–224

Borsari, Silvano, *Il monachesimo bizantino nella Sicilia e nell'Italia meridionale prenormanne* (Naples, 1963)

SELECT BIBLIOGRAPHY

Bouchard, Constance Brittain. *Holy Entrepreneurs: Cistercians, Knights and Economic Exchange in Twelfth-Century Burgundy* (Ithaca, NY, 1991)

Bowman, Bradley. *Christian Monastic Life in Early Islam* (Edinburgh, 2021)

Boynton, Susan, and Isabelle Cochelin (eds). *From Dead of Night to End of Day: The Medieval Customs of Cluny*, Studia Monastica 3 (Turnhout, 2005)

Brakke, David. *Athanasius and the Politics of Asceticism* (Oxford, 1995)

Braunfels, Wolfgang. *Monasteries of Western Europe: The Architecture of the Orders* (London, 1972)

Bredero, Adriaan. *Bernard of Clairvaux Between Cult and History* (Edinburgh, 1996)

Brooke, Christopher. 'Monk and Canon: Some Patterns in the Religious Life of the Twelfth Century', in *Monks, Hermits and the Ascetic Tradition*, ed. W.J. Sheils (Oxford, 1985), pp. 109–29

Brown, Peter R.L. 'The Rise and Function of the Holy Man in Late Antiquity', *Journal of Roman Studies* 61 (1971), 80–101

Bruce, Scott. *Silence and Sign Language in Medieval Monasticism: The Cluniac Tradition, c. 900–1200* (Cambridge, 2007)

Bryer, Anthony, and Mary Cunningham (eds). *Mount Athos and Byzantine Monasticism* (Aldershot, 1996)

Bueno, Irene. *Pope Benedict XII (1334–1342): The Guardian of Orthodoxy* (Amsterdam, 2018)

Burton, Janet. *Monastic and Religious Orders in Britain, 1000–1300* (Cambridge, 1994)

Burton-Christie, Douglas. *The Word in the Desert: Scripture and the Quest for Holiness in Early Christian Monasticism* (Oxford, 1993)

Butler, Cuthbert. *Benedictine Monachism: Studies in Benedictine Life and Rule*, 2nd edn (Cambridge, 1924)

Cambridge, Eric, and David Rollason. 'The Pastoral Organization of the Anglo-Saxon Church: A Review of the "Minster Hypothesis"', *Early Medieval Europe* 4 (1995), 87–104

Caner, Daniel. *Wandering, Begging Monks: Spiritual Authority and the Promotion of Monasticism in Late Antiquity*, Transformation of the Classical Heritage 33 (Berkeley, CA, 2002)

Canivet, Pierre. *Le monachisme syrien selon Théodoret de Cyr* (Paris, 1977)

Casey, Michael. 'Bernard and the Crisis at Morimond: Did the Order Exist in 1124?', *Cistercian Studies Quarterly* 38 (2003), 119–75

Casey, Michael. *Coenobium: Reflections on Monastic Community* (Kalamazoo, MI, 2021)

Charanis, Peter. 'The Monastic Properties and the State in the Byzantine Empire', *DOP* 4 (1948), 51–118

Châtillon, Jean. *Le mouvement canonial au moyen âge* (Paris, 1992)

Cheney, Christopher. *Episcopal Visitation of Monasteries in the Thirteenth Century*, rev. edn (Manchester, 1983)

Chitty, Derwas. *The Desert a City: An Introduction to the Study of Egyptian and Palestinian Monasticism under the Christian Empire* (Oxford, 1966)

Clark, Francis. *The 'Gregorian' Dialogues and the Origins of Benedictine Monasticism* (Leiden, 2003)

Clark, H.B., and M. Brennan (eds). *Columbanus and Merovingian Monasticism* (Oxford, 1981)

Clark, James G. *A Monastic Renaissance at St Albans: Thomas Walsingham and His Circle c. 1350–1440* (Oxford, 2004)

Clark, James G. *The Benedictines in the Middle Ages* (Woodbridge, 2011)

SELECT BIBLIOGRAPHY

Clark, James G. *The Dissolution of the Monasteries* (New Haven and London, 2021)

Claussen, Martin. *The Reform of the Frankish Church: Chrodegang of Metz and the 'Regula canonicorum' in the Eighth Century* (Cambridge, 2004)

Cloke, Gillian. *This Female Man of God: Women and Spiritual Power in the Patristic Age ad 350–450* (New York, 1995)

Constable, Giles. *Medieval Monasticism*, Variorum Collected Studies (Abingdon, 2017)

Constable, Giles. *Monastic Tithes: From their Origins to the Twelfth Century* (Cambridge, 1964)

Constable, Giles. *The Reformation of the Twelfth Century* (Cambridge, 1996)

Constable, Giles. *Religious Life and Thought (11th–12th Centuries)*, Variorum Collected Studies 89 (London, 1979)

Corsi, Pasquale, 'Studi recenti sul monachesimo italo-greco', *Quaderni medievali* 8 (1979), 244–61

Cowdrey, H.E.J. *The Age of Abbot Desiderius: Montecassino, the Papacy and the Normans in the Eleventh and Early Twelfth Centuries* (Oxford, 1983)

Cowdrey, H.E.J. *The Cluniacs and the Gregorian Reform* (Oxford, 1970)

Dales, Douglas. *Dunstan: Saint and Statesman* (Cambridge, 1988)

Dembinski, M. 'Diet: A Comparison of Food Consumption between Some Eastern and Western Monasteries, Fourth to Twelfth Centuries', *Byzantion* 55 (1985), 431–62

Dickinson, John. *The Origins of the Austin Canons and Their Introduction into England* (London, 1950)

Diem, Albrecht. *The Pursuit of Salvation: Community, Space, and Discipline in Early Medieval Monasticism* (Turnhout, 2021)

Diem, Albrecht, and Philip Rousseau, 'Monastic Rules (Fourth to Ninth Century)', *CHMMLW*, vol. 1, pp. 162–94

Dietz, Maribel. *Wandering Monks, Virgins and Pilgrims: Ascetic Travellers in the Mediterranean World, AD 300–800* (University Park, PA, 2005)

Doens, Irenée. 'Nicon de la Montagne Noir', *Byzantion* 24 (1954), 131–40

Donkin, R.A. 'The Cistercian Grange in England in the Twelfth and Thirteenth Centuries, with Special Reference to Yorkshire', *Studia Monastica* 6 (1964), 95–144

Donkin, R.A. *The Cistercians: Studies in the Geography of Medieval England and Wales* (Toronto, 1978)

Donnelly, James. *The Decline of the Medieval Cistercian Laybrotherhood* (New York, 1949)

Driver, Steven. *John Cassian and the Reading of Egyptian Monastic Culture* (New York, 2002)

Duckett, Eleanor. *Saint Dunstan of Canterbury* (London, 1955)

Dumville, David et al. *Saint Patrick AD 493–1993*, Studies in Celtic History XIII (Woodbridge, 1993)

Dunn, Marilyn. *The Emergence of Monasticism: From the Desert Fathers to the Early Middle Ages* (Oxford, 2000)

Dunn, Marilyn. 'Mastering Benedict: Monastic Rules and Their Authors in the Early Medieval West', *EHR* 105 (1990), 567–94

Edwards, Jennifer. *Superior Women: Medieval Female Authority in Poitiers' Abbey of Sainte-Croix* (Oxford, 2019)

Elm, Kaspar. 'Die Bedeutung historischer Legitimation für Entstehung, Funktion und Bestand des mittelalterlichen Ordenswesens', in *Herkunft und Ursprung: Historische und mythische Formen der Legitimation*, ed. Peter Wunderli (Sigmaringen, 1994), 71–90

Elm, Susanna. *'Virgins of God': The Making of Asceticism in Late Antiquity* (Oxford, 1994)

Evans, Joan. *Monastic Life at Cluny, 910–1157* (Oxford, 1931)

SELECT BIBLIOGRAPHY

Fanous, Samuel, and Henrietta Leyser (eds). *Christina of Markyate: A Twelfth-Century Holy Woman* (London, 2005)

Farmer, Sharon, and Barbara Rosenwein (eds). *Monks and Nuns, Saints and Outcasts: Religion in Medieval Society. Essays in Honor of Lester K. Little* (Ithaca, NY, 2000)

Flusin, Bernard. *Miracle et histoire dans l'oeuvre de Cyrille de Scythopolis* (Paris, 1983)

Follieri, Enrica. 'Il culto dei santi nell'Italia greca', *La chiesa greca in Italia dall'VIII al XVI secolo*, vol. 2 (Padua, 1969), 553–7

Foot, Sarah. 'Parochial Ministry in Early Anglo-Saxon England: The Role of Monastic Communities', SCH 26 (1989), 43–5

Frazee, Charles. 'St Theodore of Studios and Ninth Century Monasticism in Constantinople', *Studia Monastica* 23 (1981), 27–58

Galatariotou, Catia. 'Byzantine Ktetorika Typika: A Comparative Study', *Revue des Études Byzantines* 45 (1987), 77–138

Galatariotou, Catia. *The Making of a Saint: The Life, Times and Sanctification of Neophytos the Recluse* (Cambridge, 1991)

Gardner, Alice. *Theodore of Studium: His Life and Times* (London, 1905)

Gilchrist, Roberta. *Gender and Material Culture: The Archaeology of Religious Women* (London, 1994)

Golding, Brian. *Gilbert of Sempringham and the Gilbertine Order c. 1130–1300* (Oxford, 1995)

Grauwen, W.M. *Norbertus, Aartsbisschop van Maagdenburg (1126–1134)* (Brussels, 1978)

Greenfield, Richard. 'Drawn to the Blazing Beacon: Visitors and Pilgrims to the Living Holy Man and the Case of Lazaros of Mount Galesion', *DOP* 56 (2002), 213–41

Griffith, Sidney H. *Arabic Christianity in the Monasteries of Ninth-Century Palestine* (London, 1992)

Griffith, Sidney H. 'Michael, the Martyr and Monk of Mar Sabas Monastery, at the Court of the Caliph 'Abd al-Malik: Christian Apologetics and Martyrology in the Early Islamic Period', *Aram* 6 (1994), 115–48

Guy, Jean-Claude. *Jean Cassien: Vie et doctrine spirituelle* (Paris, 1961)

Hamilton, Bernard. 'The Cistercians in the Crusader States', in *One Yet Two: Monastic Tradition East and West*, ed. M. Basil Pennington (Kalamazoo, MI, 1976), pp. 405–22

Hamilton, Bernard. 'The Monastic Revival in Tenth-Century Rome', *Studia Monastica* 4 (1962), 35–68

Hamilton, Bernard. 'S. Pierre Damien et les mouvements monastiques de son temps', *Studi Gregoriani* 10 (1975), 175–202

Hamilton, Bernard, and Andrew Jotischky. *Latin and Greek Monasticism in the Crusader States* (Cambridge, 2020)

Hamilton, Bernard, with P.A. McNulty. '*Orientale lumen et magistra latinitatis*: Greek Influences on Western Monasticism (900–1100)', in *Le millénaire du Mont Athos, 963–1963. Etudes et Mélanges*, vol. 1 (Chevetogne, 1963), pp. 181–216

Harmless, William. *Desert Christians: An Introduction to the Literature of Early Monasticism* (Oxford, 2004)

Harvey, Barbara. *Living and Dying in England, 1100–1540: The Monastic Experience* (Oxford, 1993)

Harvey, Susan Ashbrook. *Asceticism and Society in Crisis: John of Ephesus and the Lives of the Eastern Saints* (Berkeley, CA, 1990)

Hatlie, Peter. *The Monks and Monasteries of Constantinople, ca. 350–850* (Cambridge, 2007)

SELECT BIBLIOGRAPHY

Heale, Martin. *The Abbots and Priors of Late Medieval and Reformation England* (Oxford, 2016)

Heuclin, Jean. *Aux origins monastiques de la Gaule du Nord: Ermites et reclus du Ve au XIe siècle* (Lille, 1988)

Heussi, Karl. *Der Ursprung des Mönchtums* (Tübingen, 1936)

Hirschfeld, Yizhar. *The Judaean Desert Monasteries in the Byzantine Period* (New Haven, 1992)

Howe, John. *Church Reform and Social Change in Eleventh-Century Italy: Dominic of Sora and His Patrons* (Philadelphia, 1997)

Hughes, Kathleen. *The Church in Early Irish Society* (London, 1966)

Hunt, Noreen (ed.). *Cluniac Monasticism in the Central Middle Ages* (London, 1971)

Hunt, Noreen. *Cluny under Saint Hugh 1049–1109* (London, 1967)

Hutchison, C.A. *The Hermit Monks of Grandmont* (Kalamazoo, MI, 1989)

Ivanov, Sergey. *Holy Fools in Byzantium and Beyond* (Oxford, 2006)

Jamroziak, Emilia. *The Cistercian Order in Medieval Europe, 1090–1500* (Abingdon, 2013)

Jasper, Kathryn, and John Howe. 'Hermitism in the Eleventh and Twelfth Centuries', *CHMMLW*, vol. 2, pp. 684–96

Jestice, Phyllis G. *Wayward Monks and the Religious Revolution of the Eleventh Century* (Leiden, 1997)

John, Eric. *Orbis Britanniae and Other Studies* (Leicester, 1966)

Johnson, Penelope. *Equal in Monastic Profession: Religious Women in Medieval France* (Chicago, 1991)

Johnson, Penelope. 'Pious Legends and Historical Realities: The Foundations of La Trinité Vendôme, Bonport and Holyrood', *RB* 91 (1981), 184–93

Jones, David. *An Early Witness to the Nature of the Canonical Order in the Twelfth Century: A Study in the Life and Writings of Adam Scot* (Salzburg, 1999)

Jong, Mayke de. 'Growing Up in a Carolingian Monastery: Magister Hildemar and His Oblates', *JMH* 9 (1983), 99–128

Jong, Mayke de. *In Samuel's Image: Child Oblation in the Early Medieval West* (Leiden, 1996)

Jordan, Erin. 'Roving Nuns and Cistercian Realities: The Cloistering of Religious Women in the Thirteenth Century', *Journal of Medieval and Early Modern Studies* 42 (2012), 597–612

Jotischky, Andrew. 'Greek Orthodox and Latin Monasticism around Mar Saba under Crusader Rule', in *The Sabaite Heritage*, ed. Joseph Patrich (Leuven, 2001), pp. 85–96

Jotischky, Andrew. *The Perfection of Solitude: Hermits and Monks in the Crusader States* (University Park, PA, 1995)

Jotischky, Andrew. 'St Sabas and the Palestinian Monastic Network under Crusader Rule', in *International Religious Networks*, ed. Jeremy Gregory and Hugh McCleod, Studies in Church History Subsidia (Woodbridge, 2012), pp. 9–19

Kaplan, Michel. 'Les moines et leurs biens fonciers à Byzance du VIIIe au Xe siècles: Acquisition, conservation et mise en valeur', *RB* 103 (1993), 209–23

Kazhdan, Alexander. 'Hermitic, Cenobitic and Secular Ideals in Byzantine Hagiography of the Ninth to Twelfth Centuries', *Greek Orthodox Theological Review* 30 (1985), 473–87

Kedar, Benjamin Z. 'Gerard of Nazareth, a Neglected Twelfth-Century Writer in the Latin East: A Contribution to the Intellectual History of the Crusader States', *DOP* 37 (1983), 55–77

SELECT BIBLIOGRAPHY

Kedar, Benjamin Z. 'The Latin Hermits of the Frankish Levant Revisited', in *'Come l'orco della fiaba': Studi per Franco Cardini*, ed. M. Montesano (Florence, 2010), pp. 185–202

Kelly, J.N.D. *Jerome: His Life, Writings and Controversies* (London, 1975)

Klingshirn, W. *Caesarius of Arles: The Making of a Christian Community in Late Antique Gaul* (Cambridge, 1994)

Knowles, David. *Christian Monasticism* (London, 1969)

Knowles, David. *The Monastic Order in England: A History of Its Development from the Times of St Dunstan to the Fourth Lateran Council, 940–1216* (Cambridge, 1963)

Knowles, David. *The Religious Orders in England*, vol. 1 (Cambridge, 1948)

Kyriacou, Chrysovalantis, *Orthodox Cyprus under the Latins, 1191–1571: Society, Spirituality, and Identities* (Lanham, MD, 2018)

Lawrence, C.H. *Medieval Monasticism: Forms of Religious Life in Western Europe in the Middle Ages*, 2nd edn (London, 1989)

Leclercq, Jean, 'La crise du monachisme aux XIe et XIIe siècles', *Bullettino dell'Istituto storico Italiano per il medio evo* 70 (1958), 19–41

Leclercq, Jean. *Un maître de la vie spirituelle au XIe siècle: Jean de Fécamp* (Paris, 1946)

Leclercq, Jean. 'Les relations entre le monachisme oriental et le monachisme occidental dans le haut Moyen Âge', in *Le Millénaire du Mont Athos, 963–1963: Etudes et mélanges*, 2 vols (Chevetogne, 1963–4), vol. 2, pp. 49–80

Leclercq, Jean. *Saint Pierre Damien, ermite et homme de l'Eglise* (Rome, 1960)

Lekai, Louis. *The Cistercians: Ideals and Reality* (Kent, OH, 1977)

Leroy, Julien. 'S. Athanase l'Athonite et la règle de S. Benoît', *Revue d'ascétique et de mystique* 29 (1953), 108–21

Lester, Anne E. *Creating Cistercian Nuns: The Women's Religious Movement and Its Reform in Thirteenth-Century Champagne* (Ithaca, NY, 2011)

Leyser, Henrietta. *Hermits and the New Monasticism: A Study of Religious Communities in Western Europe, 1000–1150* (New York, 1984)

Licence, Tom. *Hermits and Recluses in English Society, 950–1200* (Oxford, 2011)

Lienhard, J.T. *Paulinus of Nola and Early Western Monasticism* (Cologne/Bonn, 1977)

Little, Lester K. *Benedictine Maledictions: Liturgical Cursing in Romanesque France* (Ithaca, NY, 1993)

Loud, Graham. *The Latin Church in Norman Italy* (Cambridge, 2007)

Luxford, Julian. *Studies in Carthusian Monasticism in the Late Middle Ages* (Turnhout, 2008)

McClendon, Charles. *The Imperial Abbey of Farfa: Architectural Currents of the Early Middle Ages* (New Haven, 1987)

McEvoy, Liz (ed.). *Anchoritic Traditions of Medieval Europe* (Woodbridge, 2010)

McLaughlin, T.P. 'Abelard's Rule for Religious Women', *Mediaeval Studies* 18 (1956), 241–92

Makowski, Elizabeth. *Canon Law and Cloistered Women: Periculoso and Its Commentators, 1298–1545* (Washington DC, 1997)

Mango, Cyril, and Ernest Hawkins. 'The Hermitage of St Neophytos and Its Wall Paintings', *DOP* 20 (1966), 63–94

Melville, Gert. 'Knowledge of the Origins: Constructing Identity and Ordering Monastic Life in the Middle Ages', in *Knowledge, Discipline and Power in the Middle Ages: Essays in Honour of David Luscombe*, ed. Joseph Canning, Edmund King and Martial Staub (Leiden, 2011)

Melville, Gert, and J. Mixon. 'The Institutionalization of Religious Orders (Twelfth and Thirteenth Centuries)', *CHMMLW*, vol. 2, pp. 783–802

SELECT BIBLIOGRAPHY

Melville, Gert, and Anne Müller (eds). *Mittelalterliche Orden und Klöster im Vergleich: Methodische Ansätze und Perspektiven* (Berlin, 2007)

Meyendorff, John. *Byzantine Hesychasm: Historical, Theological and Social Problems* (London, 1974)

More, Alison. *Fictive Orders and Feminine Religious Identities 1200–1600* (Oxford, 2018)

Morris, Rosemary. *Monks and Laymen in Byzantium, 843–1118* (Cambridge, 1995)

Morris, Rosemary. 'The Origins of Athos', in *Mount Athos and Byzantine Monasticism*, ed. Anthony Bryer et al. (Aldershot, 1996), pp. 37–46

Mullett, Margaret (ed.). *Founders and Refounders of Byzantine Monasteries*, Belfast Byzantine Texts and Translations 6.3 (2007)

Mullett, Margaret, and Anthony Kirby (eds). *The Theotokos Evergetis and Eleventh-Century Monasticism* (Belfast, 1994)

Newman, Martha. 'Stephen Harding and the Creation of the Cistercian Community', *RB* 107 (1997), 307–29

Nightingale, John. *Monasteries and Patrons in the Gorze Reform: Lotharingia c. 850–1000* (Oxford, 2001)

Nyberg, Tore. *Monasticism in North-Western Europe, 800–1200* (Aldershot, 2000)

O'Hara, Alexander. *Jonas of Bobbio and the Legacy of Columbanus: Sanctity and Community in the Seventh Century* (Oxford, 2018)

Oikonomides, Nikolas. 'The Monastery of Patmos and Its Economic Functions (11th–12th Centuries)', in *Social and Economic Life in Byzantium*, ed. Nikolas Oikonomides and Elizabeth A. Zachariadou, Variorum Collected Studies Series 799 (Aldershot, 2004), pp. VII:1–17.

Oldfield, Paul. *Sanctity and Pilgrimage in Medieval Southern Italy, 1000–1200* (Cambridge, 2014)

Palmer, Andrew. *Monk and Mason on the Tigris Frontier: The Early History of Tur ʿAbdin* (Cambridge, 1991)

Pantin, W.A. 'Some Medieval English Treatises on the Origins of Monasticism', in *Medieval Studies Presented to Rose Graham*, ed. V. Ruffer and A.J. Taylor (Oxford, 1950), pp. 189–215

Papachryssanthou, D. 'La vie monastique dans les campagnes byzantines du VIIIe au XIe siècles', *Byzantion* 43 (1973), 166–73

Patrich, Joseph. *Sabas, Leader of Palestinian Monasticism: A Comparative Study in Eastern Monasticism, Fourth to Seventh Centuries* (Washington DC, 1995)

Patrich, Joseph. *The Sabaite Heritage in the Orthodox Church from the Fifth Century to the Present*, Orientalia Lovaniensia Analecta 93 (Leuven, 2001)

Patzold, Steffen. 'Hraban, Gottschalk und der Traktat *De oblatione puerorum*', in *Raban Maur et son temps*, ed. Philippe Depreux, Stéphane Lebecq, Michel J.-L. Perrin and Olivier Szerwiniack, Haut Moyen Age 9 (Turnhout, 2010), pp. 105–18

Perrone, Lorenzo. 'Monasticism as a Factor of Religious Interaction in the Holy Land during the Byzantine Period', in *Sharing the Sacred: Religious Contacts and Conflicts in the Holy Land, 1st to 15th centuries*, ed. A. Kofsky and G. Strousma (Jerusalem, 1998), pp. 67–95

Pertusi, Agostino. 'Aspetti organizzativi e culturali dell'ambiente monacale greco dell'Italia meridionale', in *L'eremitismo in Occidente nei secoli XI e XII*, ed. Jean Leclercq, Leopold Genicot et al. (Milan, 1965), pp. 382–426

Pertusi, Agostino. 'Rapporti tra il monachesimo italo-greco ed il monachesimo bizantino nell'alto medioevo', in *La chiesa greca in Italia dall' VIII al XVI secolo*, 2 vols (Padua, 1973), vol. 2, pp. 473–520

SELECT BIBLIOGRAPHY

Peters-Custot, Annick. *Bruno en Calabre: Histoire d'une fondation monastique dans l'Italie normande*, Collection de l'École Française de Rome 489 (Rome, 2014)

Peters-Custot, Annick. *Les grecs de l'Italie méridionale post-byzantine (IXe–XIVe siècle). Une acculturation en douceur* (Rome, 2009)

Purkis, William. *Crusading Spirituality in the Holy Land and Iberia, c. 1095–c. 1187* (Woodbridge, 2008)

Reynolds, Daniel. 'Monasticism in Early Islamic Palestine: Contours of Debate', in *The Late Antique World of Early Islam: Muslims among Christians and Jews in the East Mediterranean*, ed. Robert Hoyland (London, 2015), pp. 339–91

Roest, Bert. 'A Crisis of Late Medieval Monasticism?', *CHMMLW*, vol. 2, pp. 1171–90

Rosenwein, Barbara. *Rhinoceros Bound: Cluny in the Tenth Century* (Philadelphia, 1982)

Rosenwein, Barbara. *To Be the Neighbor of Saint Peter: The Social Meaning of Cluny's Property, 909–1049* (Ithaca, NY, 1989)

Rousseau, Philip. *Ascetics, Authority and the Church in the Age of Jerome and Cassian* (Oxford, 1978)

Rousseau, Philip. *Basil of Caesarea* (Berkeley, CA, 1994)

Rudy, Kathryn M. *Virtual Pilgrimages in the Convent: Imagining Jerusalem in the Late Middle Ages* (Turnhout, 2011)

Russell, Norman. *Gregory Palamas and the Making of Palamism in the Modern Age* (Oxford, 2019)

Ryan, John. *Irish Monasticism: Origins and Early Development* (Dublin, 1931)

Schwab, Ian. 'Undomesticated Faith: Outlying Ascetics c. 900–c. 1200', unpublished PhD thesis, Aberdeen University, 2020

Sheils, William J. (ed.). *Monks, Hermits and the Ascetic Tradition*, SCH 22 (Oxford, 1985)

Simons, Walter. *Cities of Ladies: Beguine Communities in the Medieval Low Countries, 1200–1565* (Philadelphia, 2003)

Smith, Katherine Allen. *War and the Making of Medieval Monastic Culture* (Woodbridge, 2011)

Smyrlis, Konstantinos. 'The Management of Monastic Estates: The Evidence of the Typika', *DOP* 56 (2002), 245–61

Southern, Richard. *Saint Anselm: A Portrait in a Landscape* (Cambridge, 1990)

Stancliffe, Claire. *St Martin and His Hagiographer: History and Miracle in Sulpicius Severus* (Oxford, 1983)

Stewart, Columba. *Cassian the Monk* (New York, 1998)

Stöber, Karen, and Janet Burton. *Women in the Medieval Monastic World* (Turnhout, 2015)

Stöber, Karen, and Emilia Jamroziak (eds). *Monasteries on the Borders of Medieval Europe: Conflict and Cultural Interaction* (Turnhout, 2014)

Talbot, Alice-Mary. *Varieties of Monastic Experience in Byzantium, 800–1453* (Notre Dame, IN, 2019)

Thomas, John P. *Private Religious Foundations in the Byzantine Empire* (Washington DC, 1987)

Thompson, Sally. *Women Religious: The Founding of English Nunneries after the Norman Conquest* (Oxford, 1991)

Turner, H. *St Symeon: The New Theologian and Spiritual Fatherhood* (Leiden, 1990)

Vanderputten, Steven. *Dark Age Nunneries: The Ambiguous Identity of Female Monasticism, 800–1050* (Ithaca, NY, 2018)

Vanderputten, Steven. *Imagining Religious Leadership in the Middle Ages: Richard of Saint-Vanne and the Politics of Reform* (Ithaca, NY, 2015)

SELECT BIBLIOGRAPHY

Vanderputten, Steven. *Monastic Reform as Process: Realities and Representations in Medieval Flanders, 900–1100* (Ithaca, NY, 2013)

Vanderputten, Steven, 'Monastic Reform from the Tenth to the Early Twelfth Century', *CHMMLW*, vol. 2, pp. 599–617

Van Engen, John. 'The "Crisis of Cenobitism" Reconsidered: Benedictine Monasticism in the Years 1050–1150', *Speculum* 61 (1986), 269–304

Van Engen, John. *Rupert of Deutz* (Berkeley, CA, 1983)

Venarde, Bruce L. *Women's Monasticism and Medieval Society: Nunneries in France and England, 890–1215* (Ithaca, NY, 1997)

Vogüé, Adalbert de. 'The Greater Rules of Basil: A Survey', *Word and Spirit* 1 (1979), 49–85

Von Falkenhausen, Vera. 'Il monachesimo greco in Sicilia', in *La Sicilia rupestre nel contesto delle civiltà mediterranee: Atti del sesto Convegno Internazionale di studio sulla civiltà rupestre medioevale nel Mezzogiorno d'Italia (Catania-Pantalica-Ispica, 7–12 settembre 1981)* (Galatina, 1986), pp. 135–74

Vööbus, Arthur. *History of Asceticism in the Syrian Orient*, Corpus Scriptorum Christianorum Orientalium, Subsidia (Louvain, 1960)

Ward, Benedicta. 'The Desert Myth: Reflections on the Desert Ideal in Early Cistercian Monasticism', in *One Yet Two: Monastic Tradition East and West*, ed. M. Basil Pennington (Kalamazoo, MI, 1976), pp. 183–99

Ware, Kallistos. 'Athanasius the Athonite: Traditionalist or Innovator?', in *Mount Athos and Byzantine Monasticism*, ed. Anthony Bryer et al. (Aldershot, 1996), pp. 3–16

Wareham, Edmund. 'The Openness of the Enclosed Convent: The Evidence from the Lüne Letter Collection', in *Openness in Medieval Europe*, ed. Manuele Gragnolati and Almut Suerbaum, *Cultural Inquiry* 23 (2022), 271–88

White, Lynn T., Jr. *Latin Monasticism in Norman Sicily* (Cambridge, MA, 1938)

White, Stephen. *Feuding and Peace-making in Eleventh-Century France*, Variorum Collected Studies 817 (Aldershot, 2005)

Williams, David. *The Cistercians in the Early Middle Ages* (Leominster, 1988)

Wood, Susan. *The Proprietary Church in the Medieval West* (Oxford, 2006)

Wortley, John. '"Grazers" (βοσκοι) in the Judaean Desert', in *The Sabaite Heritage*, ed. Joseph Patrich (Leuven, 2001), pp. 37–49

Index

abbots 112–13, 278–88
   elections 282–6, 287–8
   households 278–9
   lay abbacies 113–14
   as pilgrims 299
Abelard, Peter 219, 223, 234, 290
Abingdon Abbey 254
Act of Supremacy 337
Adalbert of Prague 134, 197
Adam of Dryburgh 330
Adam of Perseigne, Cistercian abbot 251
Aelfric, homilist 170
Aelwin, prior of Durham 194–5
Aethelwold, bishop of Winchester 169
agriculture 74, 182, 262–9, 268–9
   see also granges
Albert of Aachen 297
Alcuin 113
Aldhelm 86, 92
alms-giving 257
Ambrose, bishop of Milan 55, 61
Amida 50
animals, and monks 136–7
   see also lions
Annals of Ulster 154
Anselm, archbishop of Canterbury 180, 236–7, 249–50, 295, 296
Anthony, first monk 20–3
apotaktikoi 17

Apophthegmata Patrum 19, 30–3, 52
Arles, convent at 63–4
arms, monks bearing 294–5, 296
   see also Crusades
Arnold, abbot of Morimond 220–2
Asser 79, 168
Athanasios, bishop of Alexandria 13–14, 15, 20–2, 45
   Life of Anthony 17, 19–23
Athanasios the Athonite 127–30
Augustine, bishop of Hippo 56–7
   Rule of Augustine 57
Avignon 244

Baldwin of Forde, archbishop of Canterbury 289
Barking Abbey 89, 173
Barlaam, Calabrian monk 326–7
Barnwell Observances 257
Basil of Caesarea 53–4
Battle Abbey 243, 247
Bede 69–70, 88–90, 93
beguines 327–8
Benedict XII, pope 312–13
Benedict of Aniane 110
Benedict of Nursia 70–2
Bernard of Clairvaux 215–23, 239, 251–2, 300
   Apologia 217–18

INDEX

Letter to Robert 216
Vita prima 222–3
Berno, abbot of Cluny 156–7, 160
Binham Priory 291
Biscop, Benedict 86–9
bishops, and monasteries 269–77
    episcopal visitations 274–8
Black Mountain, monastery of 185
Bobbio 77, 84
Boniface, archbishop of Canterbury 293
Brigit of Sweden 332–3
Bruno, archbishop of Cologne 147, 198–9
Bury St Edmunds 249, 250–2, 280, 283

Caesarius of Arles 61–4
    'Rule for Virgins' 63, 81
Carthusians 199–200, 329–32
    see also Bruno, archbishop of Cologne
    see also Chartreuse
Cassian, John 25–6, 31, 35–8, 195
    Conferences 37–8
    Institutes 36–7
Cassiodorus 64
cell, monastic 33, 331
chapters, monastic 306–8
charistike 188–90
Chariton 38–9
Chartreuse 199
Christ Church Canterbury 276, 289
Christina of Markyate 232–3
Christodoulos of Patmos 132, 140, 189, 268, 285–6
Chrodegang, bishop of Metz 108
Cistercians 206–15, 246, 261, 334–5
    Carta Caritatis (*Charter of Love*) 208
    Exordium Cistercii 209, 222
    Exordium Magnum 205–6, 208
    Exordium Parvum 208
    Llad management 265–7
    nuns and care of sick 258
    Usus conversorum 213
Cîteaux 206–7
cloister 111
clothing 307
Clonmacnoise 66, 95
    Annals of Clonmacnoise 100
Cluny 156–66, 177–8, 184, 310
    Customary of Ulrich 179, 181, 184, 335
    Foundation Charter 157–9

Cockersand Abbey 201, 341
Coldingham 92
Columbanus 66, 83–5
commendam 313, 335–6
confraternities 111, 254
Constantine, Emperor 14, 18
Constantine V, Emperor 117
Conrad of Eberbach 266
    see also Cistercians: *Exordium magnum*
conversi 213–14, 265–7
Council of Chalcedon 60
Crusades 296–7, 300
Cuthbert 69–70, 93
Cyril of Scythopolis 42–6, 52, 137
    Lives of the the Monks of Palestine 42, 47, 195
Cyprus, monasteries in 274

David I, king of Scotland 226
demons 22–3
diet 123
diplomacy, by monks 240–1
Dissolution, of monasteries 336–42
Dominic of Sora 197–8
double houses 92
Dover Priory 290
Dunstan, archbishop of Canterbury 168–9
Durham 258–9

Easter, dating of 85
Edgar, king of England 168, 171
Eadburh, english queen 79
Eadmer, monk of Canterbury 169, 200, 236, 249–50
Egeria 39
Egypt 13–14, 18–19, 39, 205
Einhard 113
Elias of Enna 143, 145, 150
Elias of Palmaria 279
Elias Speleota 142–3, 145, 150
    Life of Elias Speleota 143
Elizabeth of Thuringia 328–9
Ely 172
enclosure 308–9
    of nuns 63, 308–9, 329
Eugenius III, pope 219, 239, 271
Eudes Rigaud, archbishop of Rouen 275–7, 311

INDEX

Eunapius, sophist 138
Euthymios 'the Great' 39, 41–3, 45, 137
Euthymios the Younger 125, 132–6, 140
   Life of Euthymios the Younger 132–3–4, 137, 144, 150
Evagrius of Pontus 26, 31, 33–4, 39
Evergetis, monastery of 178, 180–1, 184–5, 285
Evesham Abbey 274, 280–1

Fabri, Felix 302
Farfa 109, 115, 155, 162–3, 184, 239, 246
Fécamp 172
finances, monastic 279–81
Fonte Avellana 177, 193
Fontevraud 231–2, 275
foraging, by monks 52, 136–7
Fourth Lateran Council 304, 306
Francis of Assisi 305
friendship, in monasteries 74, 250
Fulda 93, 101–3
Furness Abbey 210

Gabriel, Georgian monk 133, 140, 286
Geoffrey of Gorron, abbot of St Albans 232–4
Gerard, bishop of Csanád 153
Gerald of Aurillac 159, 294
Gerard of Brogne 167
Gerald of Wales 225–6, 264–5, 315
gifts, to monasteries 163–6
Gilbert of Sempringham 212, 226
Glaber, Ralph 1, 192, 201, 298
Glastonbury 288
Gottschalk 101–3, 106–7, 146
granges 265–6
   see also agriculture
Gregory of Sinai 325–6
Gregory of Tours 79, 81–2
Gregory Palamas 326–7
Gregory the Great, Pope 70, 76, 85
   Dialogues 70–1, 76–7, 89, 144, 290
Grimlaic 147, 148
Gualbert, John 193
Guibert, abbot of Nogent 194, 199, 202–3, 283
Guiges du Pin, prior of Chartreuse 199
gyrovagues 75, 107

Harding, Stephen 194, 206, 208
Heimerad, hermit 147–8
Héloïse 193, 234–5
Henry II, Emperor 172
Henry II, king of England 284–5
Henry VIII, king of England 340
hesychasm 325–7
Hilda, abbess of Whitby 89, 91
Hildemar of Corbie 111
History of the Monks of Egypt 24–5
Holy Cross, Jerusalem 320
Holy Cross, Poitiers 78–80
holy fools 138
hospitality 97, 256–7
Hrabanus Maur 101–3, 107
Hugh the Great, abbot of Cluny 180, 193
Humiliati 304–5
Hungary, monasteries in 243, 333

iconoclasm 118
Idungus of Prüfenung 215
   Dialogue of a Cistercian and a Cluniac 215, 226
imperial patronage 323–4
Ireland 65–66, 94–101
   nuns 99–100
Irene, Empress 124, 287
irrigation 263
Italo-Greek asceticism 142–5
Italy, south 142–5, 198–9

Jacob of Nisibis 38, 49, 51
Jarrow 87, 88, 202
Jerome 13, 38, 55, 59
Jerusalem, early monasticism and 44–5
   Kingdom of Jerusalem, monasteries 244–5
Jocelyn of Brakelond 261–2, 279–80, 282, 283
   see also Samson, abbot of Bury St Edmunds
John the Oxite, patriarch of Antioch 176–7, 189
John, king of England 240, 266
John of Gorze 134, 167, 197, 372
John Moschos 39
   Spiritual Meadow 27
John of Ephesus 49–50
   Lives of the Eastern Saints 51

INDEX

John of Matera 196
John the Hesychast 133
John Tzimiskes, Emperor 126, 130
Jonas of Bobbio 83–4. 85
Judean Desert 40, 320–1
Julian Saba 49

Kellia 25
Komnenos dynasty, as founders 242–4

Lambert, hermit 148
Lanfranc of Bec 247
latin, as spoken language 106, 315
lavra 40–5
Lazaros of Mt Galesion 135, 140, 187, 286
learning, in monasteries 195, 313–19
Leo XIII, pope 344
Lérins 61–2
letter-writing 220, 250
Lindisfarne 69–70, 90, 153, 155
lions 47, 137
liturgy, reforms to 110–11, 161, 179–80, 308
Liutberg, anchoress 146
Louis de Blois 336

Macarius, of Skete 43
Macrina 38, 52
Magyars, raids by 153
Majolus, abbot of Cluny 151–2, 162, 164
Makhairas, Cypriot monastery 190, 273, 287
manual labour 26–7, 28, 88, 97, 110, 121, 182–3, 196–7, 204, 308
and *conversi* 214, 267
Manuel Komnenos, Emperor 273
see also Komnenos dynasty
Marcigny 172
Martin of Tours 38, 54–5, 61
Marcigny 172
Mary the Egyptian 44
Matthew Paris, monk of St Albans 241, 277, 293
Mauger, bishop of Worcester 274
see also Evesham Abbey
meat-eating 262, 310–12
Melania the Elder 38, 39, 40
Melisende, queen of Jerusalem 251–2
Melrose 90

mendicants 305–6
Merton, Thomas 75, 345
Michael Atteliates 188
mining 263
minsters 93–4
Modwenna, *Life and Miracles* 255
Molesmes 192, 194, 203, 206
monarchy, and monasteries 168, 171, 239–49, 339–41
Monastery of the Caves 322
Monkwearmouth 87, 88, 202
Monte Cassino 72, 155
   Cassinese Congregation 344–5
   Chronicle of 195–6
Mount Athos 126–31, 319, 321, 324
   Great Lavra 128–9
Mount Latros 126
Mount Sinai 119
murder, in monasteries 290

Neophytos the Recluse 125, 134, 187, 202, 268–9, 273, 287
   Enkleistra 273
Nicholas the Pilgrim 139
Nikephoros Phokas, Emperor 118, 128, 130–1, 187, 300
Nikon, of the Black Mountain 183–4, 185, 189
Nilos of Rossano 196
Nitria 25
Noirmoutier 155
Norbert of Xanten 227–8
   see also Premonstratensians
Norries, Roger, abbot of Evesham 280–1
Notre-Dame de Josaphat, Jerusalem 269–71

Obazine 201, 211–12
obedience 73
oblation 102–6, 213
Odo, abbot of Cluny 161–2, 171
Odo of Deuil, monk of St Denis 319–20
Orderic Vitalis 76, 194, 203–5, 253, 295
ordination, of monks 115
Orosius 55–6
Oswald, bishop of Worcester 169–70
Ottomans, and Byzantine monasticism 324

408

INDEX

Pachomius 27–9
Palladius 28, 31, 38–9
   Lausiac History 31
Palmaria, Cluniac abbey 210–11
Pantelleria, monastery of 120–1
Paschasius Radbertus 105
Patrick, monastic founder 65–6
Paul the Deacon 109
Paula 39–40
Pauline Order 333
Paulinus of Nola 57–8, 61
Pbow 28
Pepin III, Frankish king 107–8
Persians, conquest of Jerusalem, 614 150
Peter Damian 177–8, 190–1, 230
Peter of Blois 180, 275
Peter the Venerable, abbot of Cluny 218, 300, 310
Peterborough Abbey 263
Petronilla, abbess of Fontevraud 282
Phoibammon, monastery in Egypt 67
pilgrimage
   to monasteries 258–9
   by monks/nuns 297–8, 309
Pons, abbot of Cluny 289
Post-medieval monasticism 343–7
preaching 316–17
Premonstratensians 227–8, 307, 340

Radegund of Poitiers 78–9, 81
refectory 190, 278, 310–12
reforms, later medieval 334–6
Regularis Concordia 168–9, 171, 173, 182, 257
Reichenau 110, 112
Reinfrid 202
Robert of Arbrissel 200, 231
   see also Fontevraud
Robert of Bridlington 225
Robert of Molesmes 194, 206
Roger II, king of Sicily 273
Roidion, monastery of 256
Romuald 191, 193, 196, 230
Rufinus, of Aquileia 20, 25, 38
Rules, monastic
   Rule of Augustine 224–5, 310
   Rule of Benedict 70–8, 98, 108–9, 119, 169–70, 282
      hospitality in 256
      eating in 311

Rule of St Basil 54, 98, 120
Rule of the Master 77
Rules of the Fathers 59, 62

Sabas 39, 41–3, 45, 47
Sabas of Collesano 144–5
St Albans 247, 249, 261
St Augustine's Canterbury 289
St Bartholomew's Priory, London 292
St Denis 241, 259
St Euthymios, monastery 133
St Foy, Conques 258
St Gall 115–16, 153
   Plan of 112–13
St John Patmos 132, 268
St John Stoudios 121–2
St Martin's, Dover 226–7
St Ouen, Rouen 292
St Sabas, lavra of 151, 256, 269, 302, 320–1
   see also Sabas
St Vanne, Verdun 246
St Victor, Paris 223, 314
Samson, abbot of Bury St Edmunds 193, 261–2, 279–80, 283–4, 291
   see also Jocelin of Brakelond
Scandinavia 337
Shaftesbury Abbey 172, 369
Shenoute of Atripe 29
Sicily 149–50, 243
silence 161
Skete 24–6
sleep 135
Smaragdus of Saint-Mihiel 105
Sozomen 136
Sqillace 198
Stephen of Obazine 200, 202, 211–12
Suger, abbot of St Denis 234, 241,
stylites 140
Sulpicius Severus 59
Symeon of Durham 92
Symeon the Holy Fool 51, 138
   Life of Symeon the Holy Fool 136
Symeon the New Theologian 139, 289, 290, 325
Symeon the Stylite 49–50

Tabennesi 27–8
Temple, Augustinian abbey in Jerusalem 248

409

INDEX

Theodore of Stoudios 121–4, 285
  see also St John Stoudios
Theodore of Tarsus 86, 89
Theodoret, bishop of Cyrrhus 48–9
  History of the Monks of Syria 48
Theoktistos 42
Thomas of Marlborough 281
Timothy of Evergetis 178, 181, 183, 186
tithes 203–5, 212–13, 270
towns, relations with monasteries 260–2, 292, 330
Troarn, Norman monastery 298
typika 118, 120, 131–2, 185, 268–9, 322

universities, and monasteries 315–16

Valerius of El Bierzo 146
Vallombrosa 193
Valor Ecclesiasticus 337, 339
Vézelay 172, 272, 275
violence, in monasteries 288–92

Vikings, attacks on monasteries 153–5
Vitalis of Castronuovo 143–5, 150
Vitalis of Mortain 210

Walsingham, Thomas 317–18
watermills 264
Westminster 249, 311
Whitby, synod of 90
Wiborad, anchoress 147, 153
William, abbot of Saint-Thierry 194, 201, 215
William, duke of Aquitaine 156–7
William of Malmesbury 194, 242
William of Volpiano 167, 172, 185, 192
Wilfrid, bishop of Hexham 86–8, 91
Wolsey, Thomas 338, 340
Wulfilaicus, stylite 82, 139

xenodochium 43, 256–7
  see also hospitality

Yvette of Huy 328